Days to mat.	.01% equiv.	Days to mat	.01% equiv.	Days to mat.	.01% equiv.	Days to mat.	.01% equiv.	Days to mat.	.01% equiv.	Days to mat.	.01% equiv.
181	$50.28	212	$58.89	243	$67.50	274	$76.11	305	$84.72	336	$93.33
182	50.56	213	59.17	244	67.78	275	76.39	306	85.00	337	93.61
183	50.83	214	59.44	245	68.06	276	76.67	307	85.28	338	93.89
184	51.11	215	59.72	246	68.33	277	76.94	308	85.56	339	94.17
185	51.39	216	60.00	247	68.61	278	77.22	309	85.83	340	94.44
186	51.67	217	60.28	248	68.89	279	77.50	310	86.11	341	94.72
187	51.94	218	60.56	249	69.17	280	77.78	311	86.39	342	95.00
188	52.22	219	60.83	250	69.44	281	78.06	312	86.67	343	95.28
189	52.50	220	61.11	251	69.72	282	78.33	313	86.94	344	95.56
190	52.78	221	61.39	252	70.00	283	78.61	314	87.22	345	95.83
191	53.06	222	61.67	253	70.28	284	78.89	315	87.50	346	96.11
192	53.33	223	61.94	254	70.56	285	79.17	316	87.78	347	96.39
193	53.61	224	62.22	255	70.83	286	79.44	317	88.06	348	96.67
194	53.89	225	62.50	256	71.11	287	79.72	318	88.33	349	96.94
195	54.17	226	62.78	257	71.39	288	80.00	319	88.61	350	97.22
196	54.44	227	63.06	258	71.67	289	80.28	320	88.89	351	97.50
197	54.72	228	63.33	259	71.94	290	80.56	321	89.17	352	97.78
198	55.00	229	63.61	260	72.22	291	80.83	322	89.44	353	98.06
199	55.28	230	63.89	261	72.50	292	81.11	323	89.72	354	98.33
200	55.56	231	64.17	262	72.78	293	81.39	324	90.00	355	98.61
201	55.83	232	64.44	263	73.06	294	81.67	325	90.28	356	98.89
202	56.11	233	64.72	264	73.33	295	81.94	326	90.56	357	99.17
203	56.39	234	65.00	265	73.61	296	82.22	327	90.83	358	99.44
204	56.67	235	65.28	266	73.89	297	82.50	328	91.11	359	99.72
205	56.94	236	65.56	267	74.17	298	82.78	329	91.39	360	100.00
206	57.22	237	65.83	268	74.44	299	83.06	330	91.67	361	100.28
207	57.50	238	66.11	269	74.72	300	83.33	331	91.94	362	100.56
208	57.78	239	66.39	270	75.00	301	83.61	332	92.22	363	100.83
209	58.06	240	66.67	271	75.28	302	83.89	333	92.50	364	101.11
210	58.33	241	66.94	272	75.56	303	84.17	334	92.78	365	101.39
211	58.61	242	67.22	273	75.83	304	84.44	335	93.06	366	101.67

Value of an 01 per $1 million = $\left(\dfrac{.01\% \times t}{360}\right)$ $1 million

Where t = Days to maturity

THE MONEY MARKET
myth, reality, and practice

THE MONEY MARKET
myth, reality, and practice

MARCIA STIGUM
Appendix by JOHN FRIEL

DOW JONES-IRWIN
Homewood, Illinois 60430

ISBN 0-87094-167-4
Library of Congress Catalog Card No. 78–059224

Printed in the United States of America

3 4 5 6 7 8 9 0 K 5 4 3 2 1 0 9

*To the many market participants
who gave, with grace and enthusiasm, their time
that I might write this story.*

Preface

THIS BOOK IS a comprehensive guide to the U.S. money market. It is intended for managers of short-term, fixed-income portfolios; for other corporate financial officers; for personnel in banks, dealerships, and other financial institutions; for people operating in the Eurodollar market, all of whom need to know about the U.S. money market; and for all others who have an interest in the market.

The book describes in detail the operations of money market banks and of money market dealers and brokers. It also describes the principles according to which a liquidity portfolio should be run and contrasts them with the way in which most such portfolios are in fact managed. With this background established, the book turns to the individual markets that comprise the money market. It describes for each such market the instrument traded, the risks, liquidity and return offered, and how the market is made by dealers, brokers, and investors.

The book presents an extensive description of the operation of the Eurodollar market. This market is really an extension of and thus an integral part of the U.S. money market. Therefore a description of the U.S. market would be incomplete without a thorough consideration of the Euro market and of the interconnections between the two. Also the Euro market offers interesting and inadequately understood opportunities to managers of short-term portfolios.

It is expected that many of the readers of this book will be relatively new to the money market. Part I provides all of the background needed by such readers to understand the rest of the book. It describes in simple terms what the instruments traded in the money market are, how yields on them are calculated, and how banks under the control of the Federal Reserve System create our money supply.

Much of the material in this book has never appeared in print before because surprisingly little has been written on the money market in recent times; and most of what has been written was incomplete to begin with and is currently out of date due to the rapidity with which change occurs in this innovative and fast-growing market.

In every area of life, people develop special terms or give common terms special meanings in order to describe and to communicate with each other about their particular interests and activities; hence *jargon*. The money market is no exception, and this book uses money market jargon extensively. To aid the reader, each piece of jargon used is carefully defined the first time it appears in the text. Also there is a Glossary at the end of the book in which a wide range of money market and bond market terms are defined.

A number of examples of simple money market calculations—such as determining equivalent bond yield on discount securities, "figuring the tail," and calculating profit on an arbitrage—are included in this book. Readers who have need for descriptions of all key money market formulas and examples of how they can be used should refer to my other book, *The Money Market, Calculations: Yields, Swaps, and Break-Even Prices,* also published by Dow Jones-Irwin.

The pronoun *he* is used frequently throughout this book. It is my opinion that *he* has for years been used to mean *person* and that any attempt to avoid this use of the term leads to nothing but bad and awkward English.

In conclusion I would like to thank the many typists who have labored on this manuscript and in particular Mike Nagle who hunted up numbers and drew the diagrams. I would also like to thank Loyola University of Chicago and Northwestern University for the support they gave me while I was researching and writing this book.

One final note: Effective August 24, 1978, the reserve requirements under Regs D and M on net Eurodollar borrowings by domestic banks were reduced by the Federal Reserve Board from 4 percent to zero percent. At the same time, the 1 percent reserve requirement on loans by foreign branches of U.S. banks to domestic borrowers was also eliminated.

August 1978   **Marcia Stigum**

Acknowledgments

THERE WAS ONLY ONE WAY that research for this book could be conducted. That was by interviewing at length participants in *every* area of the market: in New York, London, Chicago, and elsewhere. During the months I spent studying the market, everywhere I went I received incredible cooperation. People freely gave me hours of time, discussed their operations frankly and articulately, and then sent me on to others elsewhere in the market.

To all of these people, I would like to express a very heartfelt thanks for the patient and thoughtful answers they proffered to my many questions. A particular thank you goes to those who volunteered to read and criticize those chapters that covered their area of specialty. Needless to say, the author bears full responsibility for any remaining errors of fact, of which I hope there are few.

Some organizations have a policy that precludes acknowledging the assistance of company personnel; therefore, the acknowledgments that follow are incomplete. Of the over 200 people I interviewed, those whom I can publicly thank are:

THE UNITED STATES

Richard Adams
Robert P. Anczarki
J. Joseph Anderson
James T. Anderson
Timothy H. Anderson
Irving M. Auerbach
Edward G. Austin
David J. Barry
Kevin D. Barry
Robert Bartell
John F. Baumann
Sandra D. Beckner
Paul M. Belica
William Berkowitz
Robert H. Bethke
Paul J. Bielat
Irving V. Boberski
Frank Boswell
Chuck Bradburn
Milton Brafman
Rene O. Branch, Jr.

Donald G. Brodie
Joseph G. Brown
Ernst W. Brutsche
Neil J. Call
Bronislaw Chrobok
Allen B. Clark
Thomas Coleman
George E. Collins, Jr.
Wayne Cook
Michael J. Corey
Leonard F. Crescenzo
Edward T. Daly
James J. DeCantillon
Nicholas J. De Leonardis
Lawrence Deschere
Stanley Diller
Jay E. Dittus
William Donoghue
William J. Duffy
A. Fraser Dunnett
John F. Eckstein III

Burtt R. Ehrlich
Richard P. Eide, Jr.
Richard L. Falk
Emanuel J. Falzon
Hilliard Farber
Edward C. Fecht
Chester B. Feldberg
Richard C. Fieldhouse
Alvin Flamenbaum
Dennis G. Flynn
Peter E. Gall
Thomas E. Gardner
William P. Garry
Leonard Gay
Yoshiyasu Genma
Kenneth L. Gestal
Ronald B. Gray
Peter L. Greene
Eric A. Gronningsater
P. Jordan Hamel
Alan Hanley
Gabriel Hauge
Ralph T. Helfrich
Paul Henderson
Bill Hick
Russell G. Hiller
George R. Hinman
Neil Hirsch
Alan R. Holmes
Richard A. Hottinger
Mary Joy Hudecz
Howard G. Hudson
James E. Jack
Dale H. Jenkins
Colin Johnson
Glen Johnson
William J. Jordan
Arthur Kaley
Michael M. Karnes
George P. Kegler
Richard F. Kezer
Yukyo Kida
William M. Kidder
James R. Killeen
Dennis S. Kite
Aline Krala
Morton Lane
Curt J. Landtroop

David N. Lawrence
Ralph F. Leach
James F. Leary
Robert M. Lynch
James G. McCormick
John D. McElhinney
James E. McKee
Robert McKnew
Robert Mackin
William T. Maher, Jr.
John Mann
Karin L. Maupin
Donald R. A. Marshall
Michael F. Martin
Bruce B. Maxwell
Stan Meheffey
James W. Meighen
Robert L. Meyers
Ellen Michelson
Michael Mickett
J. Allen Minteer
Angelo Monteverde
James C. Morton
Edward J. Murphy
John J. Murray
Tsunehiro Nakayama
Hans U. Neukomm
Talat M. Othman
Bernard Pace
Michael J. Paciorek
Edward L. Palmer
Oscar J. Pearl, Jr.
Frank Pedrick
John H. Perkins
Ralph F. Peters
William H. Pike
Joseph P. Porino
Donald Reid
Robert Rice
Donald B. Riefler
David L. Roscoe, III
Paul J. Rozewicz
Alfred C. Ryan, Jr.
Lawrence J. Saffer
Richard Sandor
Irwin D. Sandberg
R. Duane Saunders
Edward Shannon

Nancy F. Shaw
Donald P. Sheahan
Richard Sheldon
Robert L. Siebel
Vance W. Siler
Ronald S. Simpson
Richard Singer
Frank P. Smeal
Brian E. Smith
Philip Smith
Thomas S. Smith
John S. Spencer
John A. Staley, IV
Werner A. Strange
John William Stanger
James Stanko
Peter D. Sternlight
Robert W. Stone
Thomas Sullivan
David G. Taylor
Myron R. Taylor

Edward M. Thomas
John Tritz
Sheila Tschinkel
Stephen A. Tyler
George M. Van Cleave
John A. Vernazza
Edward M. Voelker
James R. Wartinbee
Henry S. Wattson
Dennis Weatherstone
Jerry D. Wetterling
Gary F. Whitman
H. David Willey
Gary V. Williamson
Bryan Wilson
John R. Windeler
Thomas R. York
C. Richard Youngdahl
Edward F. Zimmerman, Jr.
Gene R. Zmuda

THE UNITED KINGDOM

A. T. Bell
William C. Bigelow
Brian G. Brown
John M. Bowcott
Trevor N. Cass
Peter Clayton
John E. Clinch
John A. Cummingham
David O. S. Dobell
James E. Geiger
James L. M. Gill
Kirk R. Hagan
Kenneth Haith
J. G. Hill
E. G. Holloway
Maurice Jacques
David B. Johnson
Colin I. Jones
Peter Lee
R. C. Lewis

Allen C. Marple
Richard J. Moreland
Peter Nash
Peter V. Nash
Alan D. Orsich
Geoffrey Osmint
Francesco Redi
John Robertson
Kenneth G. Robinson
Fabian P. Samengo-Turner
Tim Summerfield
Thomas Franklin Smith
Harrison F. Tempest
Rodney M. Thomas
C. C. Tucker
John Thorne
Robert A. Utting
Lord Wakehurst
Jerald M. Wigdortz

LUXEMBOURG

Roland Scharff

M.S.

Contents

PART II: THE MAJOR PLAYERS

Abbreviations

THIS BOOK is replete with quotations, many of which contain "street" abbreviations of the names of various institutions. The most common are:

Bankers Trust Co.	Bankers
Bank of America	B of A
Chase Manhattan Bank	Chase
Citibank	Citi
Merrill Lynch	Merrill
Manufacturers Hanover Trust Co.	Manny Hanny
Morgan Guaranty Trust Co.	Morgan
Salomon Brothers	Sali

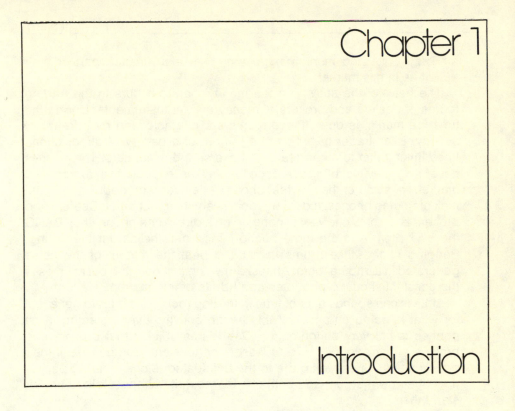

Chapter 1

Introduction

THE U.S. MONEY MARKET is a huge and significant part of the nation's financial system in which banks and other participants trade hundreds of billions of dollars every working day. Where those billions go and the prices at which they are traded affect how the U.S. government finances its debt, how business finances its expansion, and how consumers choose to spend or save. Yet we read and hear little about this market. The conspiratorially minded might consider its existence intentionally obscured. The reason most people are unaware of the money market is that it is a market that few businessmen encounter in their daily activities and in which the general public rarely invests.

The money market is a wholesale market for low-risk, highly-liquid, short-term IOUs. It is a market for various sorts of debt securities rather than equities. The stock in trade of the market includes a large chunk of the U.S. Treasury's debt and billions of dollars worth of Federal agency securities, negotiable bank certificates of deposit, bankers' acceptances, municipal notes, and commercial paper. Within the confines of the money market each day, banks, both domestic and foreign, actively trade in multimillion-dollar blocks billions of dollars of Federal funds and Eurodollars, and banks and nonbank dealers are each day the recipients of billions of dollars of secured loans through what is called the "repo

1

market." State and municipal governments also finance part of their activities in this market.

The heart of the activity in the money market occurs in the trading rooms of dealers and brokers of money market instruments. During the time the market is open, these rooms are characterized by a frenzy of activity. Each trader or broker sits in front of a battery of direct phone lines linking him to other dealers, brokers, and customers. The phones never ring, they just blink at a pace that makes, especially in the brokers market, for some of the shortest phone calls ever recorded. Despite the lack of ringing phones, a dealing room is anything but quiet. Dealers and brokers know only one way to hang up on a direct-line phone; they BANG the off button. And the more hectic things get, the harder they bang. Banging phones like drums in a band beat the rhythm of the noise generated in a trading room. Almost drowning that banging out at times is the constant shouting of quotes and tidbits of information.

Unless one spends a lot of time in trading rooms, it's hard to get a feel for what is going on amid all this hectic activity. Even listening in on phones is not very enlightening. One learns quickly that dealers and brokers swear a lot (it's said to lessen the tension), but the rest of their conversations is unintelligible to the uninitiated. Money market people have their own jargon, and until one learns it, it is impossible to understand them.

Once adjusted to their jargon and the speed at which traders converse, one observes that they are making huge trades—$5, $20, $150 million—at the snap of a finger. Moreover nobody seems to be particularly awed or even impressed by the size of the figures. A Fed funds broker asked to obtain $100 million in overnight money for a bank might reply contemptuously about the size of the trade, "The buck's yours from the B of A," slam down the phone, and take another call. Fed funds brokers earn only $1 per $1 million on overnight funds, so it takes a lot of trades to pay the overhead and let everyone in the shop make some money.

Despite its frenzied and incoherent appearance to the outsider, the money market efficiently accomplishes vital functions everyday. One is shifting vast sums of money between banks. This shifting is required because the major money market banks, with the exception of the Bank of America, all need a lot more funds than they obtain in deposits, while many smaller banks have more money deposited with them than they can profitably use internally.

The money market also provides a means by which the surplus funds of cash-rich corporations and other institutions can be funneled to banks, corporations, and other institutions that need short-term money. In addition, in the money market the U.S. Treasury can fund huge quantities of debt with ease. And the market provides the Fed with an arena in which to carry out open-market operations destined to influence interest rates and the growth of the money supply. The varied activities of money market participants also determine the structure of short-term interest rates, for example, what the yields on Treasury bills of different maturities are and how much commercial paper issuers have to pay to borrow. The latter rate is an important cost to many corporations, and it influences in particular the interest rate that a consumer who buys a car on time will have to pay on the loan. Finally, one might mention that the U.S. money market is becoming increasingly an international short-term capital market. In it the oil imports of the nationalized French electric company, Electricité de France, as well as the oil imports of Japan and a lot of other non–U.S. trade are financed.

Anyone who observes the money market soon picks out a number of salient features. First and most obvious, it is not one market but a collection of markets for several distinct and different instruments. What makes it possible to talk about *the* money market is the close interrelationships that link all these markets. A second salient feature is the numerous and varied cast of participants. Borrowers in the market include foreign and domestic banks, the Treasury, corporations of all types, the Federal Home Loan Banks and other federal agencies, dealers in money market instruments, and many states and municipalities. The lenders include almost all of the above plus insurance companies, pension funds—public and private, and various other financial institutions. And often standing between borrower and lender is one or more of a varied collection of brokers and dealers.

Another key characteristic of the money market is that it is a wholesale market. Trades are big and the people who make them are almost always dealing for the account of some substantial institution. Because of the sums involved, skill is of the utmost importance and money market participants are skilled at what they do. In effect the market is made by extremely talented specialists in very narrow professional areas. A bill trader extraordinaire may have only vague notions as to what the Euromarket is all about, and the Euro specialist may be equally vague on other sectors of the market.

Another principal characteristic of the money market is honor. Every day traders, brokers, investors, and borrowers do hundreds of billions of dollars of business over the phone and, however a trade may appear in retrospect, people do not renege. The motto of the money market is: *My word is my bond*. Of course, because of the pace of the market, mistakes do occur but no one ever assumes that they are intentional, and mistakes are always ironed out in what seems the fairest way for all concerned.

The most appealing characteristic of the money market is innovation. Compared with our other financial markets, the money market is very unregulated. If someone wants to launch a new instrument or to try brokering or dealing in a new way in existing instruments, he does it. And when the idea is good, which it often is, a new facet of the market is born

The focus of this book is threefold. First, attention is paid to the major players—who are they, why are they in the market, and what are they attempting to do? A second point of attention is on the individual markets—who is in each market, how and why do they participate in that market, what is the role of brokers and dealers in that market, and how are prices there determined? The final focus is on the relationships that exist between the different sectors of the market, for example, the relationship of Euro rates to U.S. rates, of Treasury bill rates to the Fed funds rate, and of certificate of deposit rates to bill rates.

This book is organized in a manner to enable readers with different backgrounds to read about and understand the money market. Part I contains introductory material for readers who know relatively little about the market. It is preface and prologue to Parts II and III, which are the real heart of the book. Thus readers may skim or skip Part I depending on their background and interests. They are, however, warned that they do so at their own peril, since an understanding of its contents is essential for grasping subtleties presented later in the book.

Part I

Some
Fundamentals

Chapter 2

Funds flows, banks, and money creation

AS PREFACE TO A DISCUSSION of the money market, a few words should be said about the U.S. capital market, how banks create money, and the Fed's role in controlling money creation.

THE MONEY MARKET

Roughly defined, the U.S. capital market is composed of three major parts: *the stock market*, *the bond market*, and *the money market*. The money market, as opposed to the bond market, is a wholesale market for high-quality, *short-term debt instruments*, or IOUs. Short term is a vague expression; the most one can say is that the bulk of money market activity is concentrated in the *one year and under range*, but some market participants stretch the definition of money market activity out to 5 years; certainly after that one enters the realm of the bond market.

The instruments of the money market consist of a wide range of securities: short-term government securities, short-term federal agency securities, state and local notes, repurchase agreements (essentially secured loans collateralized by money market instruments), bankers' acceptances, commercial paper, bank certificates of deposits, and Eurodollar deposits.[1] The major investors in the market are commercial banks, savings and loan associations, other financial corporations, large nonfinancial corporations, federal agencies, and—at times when interest rates are high—individual investors.

In a book about the money market, it would be appropriate to begin with a set of statistics on what securities are outstanding in the market, who uses them to borrow, and who invests in them. Unfortunately that cannot be done in other than a fragmentary way because the Federal Reserve—in the multitude of statistics that it collects on funds flows and on the financial assets and liabilities held by different sectors—mixes together so many different kinds of instruments, in particular long-term and short-term IOUs, that it is impossible to glean from them much information on the money market per se. What can be gleaned we present in later chapters.

Here it seems appropriate to concentrate on the overall pattern of flows in the U.S. capital market and on the key role played by various financial institutions in it.

FUNDS FLOWS IN THE U.S. CAPITAL MARKET

Every spending unit in the economy—business firm, household, or government body—is constantly receiving and using funds. In particular, a business firm receives funds from the sale of output and uses funds to cover its costs of production (excluding depreciation) and its current investment in plant, equipment, and inventory. For most firms *gross saving* from current operations (i.e., *retained earnings plus depreciation allowances*) falls far short of covering current capital expenditures; that is, net funds obtained from current operations are inadequate to pay capital expenditures. As a result, each year most nonfinancial business firms and the nonfinancial business sector as a whole run a large *funds deficit*.

The actual figures rung up by nonfinancial business firms in 1977 are given in column (2) of Table 2–1. They show that during this year business firms retained earnings of $21.0 billion and their capital consumption allowances totaled $159.5 billion, giving them a grand total of $180.5 billion of gross saving with which to finance capital expenditures. The latter, however, totaled $209.7 billion, so the business sector as a whole incurred a $29.2 billion funds deficit.

Running a large funds deficit is a chronic condition for the business sector. It is, moreover, to be expected, since every year the business sector receives a relatively small portion (9–13 percent) of total national income but has to finance a major share of national capital expenditures.

---

[1] All these instruments are defined in the next chapter.

Table 2-1
Funds flows in the U.S. capital market by sector, 1977 annualized rate ($ billions)

Transaction categories	Sectors					
	(1) House-holds	(2) Non-financial business	(3) State and local* governments	(4) U.S.* government	(5) Financial† business	(6) Rest of the world
1. Savings (net)	135.2	21.0	15.7	−56.4	8.4	19.1
2. Depreciation	164.8	159.5	0	0	5.4	0
3. Gross savings (1) + (2)	300.0	180.5	15.7	−56.4	13.8	19.1
4. Capital expenditures	259.9	209.7	0	−2.5	6.6	0
5. Funds surplus or deficit (3) − (4)	40.1	−29.2	15.7	−53.9	7.5	19.1
6. Net financial assets acquired	193.0	84.1	34.0	7.4	319.3	50.5
7. Net financial liabilities incurred	135.6	122.8	25.9	65.5	305.9	29.0
8. Net financial investment (6) − (7)	57.4	−38.7	8.1	−58.1	13.4	21.5
9. Sector discrepancy (5) − (8)	−17.3	9.5	7.6	4.2	−5.9	−2.4

* Capital expenditures are included with current expenditures in U.S. and state and local government spending accounts.
† The large size of the entries in lines 6 and 7 for this sector reflects the intersectoral and intrasectoral funds flows that are funneled through financial institutions.
Source: Board of Governors, Federal Reserve System.

Moreover, because of the depressed condition of the stock market in recent years, business firms have been able to obtain very little financing there. Thus the bulk of the funds they have obtained to cover their deficits has come through the sale of bonds and money market instruments.

In contrast to the business sector the consumer sector presents a quite different picture. As Table 2-1 shows, households in 1977 had gross savings of $300.0 billion and made capital expenditures of only $259.9 billion, leaving the sector with a *funds surplus* of $40.1 billion. This funds surplus is, moreover, a persistent phenomenon. Every year consumers as a group save more than they invest in housing and other capital goods.

Most of the consumer sector's funds surplus is absorbed each year by making loans to and equity investments in business firms that must seek outside funds to cover their funds deficits. This flow of funds from the consumer to the business sector is no cause for surprise. In any developed economy in which the bulk of investing is carried on outside the government sector, a substantial amount of funds flow year in and year out from consumers, who are the major income recipients, to business firms, who are the major investors.

Consumers and nonfinancial business firms do not, of course, make up the whole economy. Two other sectors of major importance are the U.S. government and state and local governments. In neither of these sectors are capital expenditures separated out from current expenditures. Thus for each sector the recorded funds deficit or funds surplus incurred over the year equals total revenue minus total expenditures, or *net saving*. Both sectors have run funds deficits most of the time in recent years, with the result that they compete with the business sector for the surplus funds generated in the consumer sector. This is what possible "crowding out" of business borrowers by government borrowing is all about.

For completeness still another domestic sector has to be added to the picture, *financial* business firms—banks, savings and loan associations, life insurance companies, and others. Most of the funds that these firms lend out to funds-deficit units are not funds of which they are the *ultimate* source. Instead, they are funds that these institutions have "borrowed" from funds-surplus units. If financial institutions only funneled funds from surplus to deficit units, we could safely omit them from our summary table. However, such activity is profitable, and every year financial firms accumulate some gross savings; these savings, moreover, normally exceed their modest capital expenditures, so the sector tends to be net a *small* supplier of funds.

The final sector in Table 2-1 is the rest of the world. Domestic firms cover some portion of the funds deficits they incur by borrowing abroad, and domestic funds-surplus units occasionally invest abroad. Thus to get a complete picture of who supplies and demands funds, we must include the rest of the world in our summary table. Also, when the exchange value of the dollar is weak, the central banks of Germany, Japan, and other countries become big buyers of dollars; they typically invest these dollars in U.S. government securities, thereby becoming financers of the U.S. government debt.

Every funds deficit has to be covered by the receipt of debt or equity capital from outside sources, and every funds surplus must be absorbed by supplying such capital. Thus if the funds surpluses and deficits incurred by all sectors are totaled, their sum should be zero. Actually, the figures on line 5 of Table 2–1 don't sum horizontally to zero because of inevitable statistical errors. In 1977 recorded sector deficits exceeded recorded sector surpluses by $0.7 billion, indicating that some sectors' surpluses had been overestimated and other sectors' deficits underestimated. The net discrepancy was, however, small relative to the surplus and deficit figures calculated for the major sectors, so the table gives a good overall picture of the direction and magnitude of intersectoral funds flows within the economy.

Net financial investment by sector

Funds flows between sectors leave a residue of *newly created* financial assets and liabilities. In particular, spending units that borrow incur claims against themselves, which appear on their balance sheets as liabilities, while spending units that supply capital acquire financial assets in the form of stocks, bonds, and other securities.

This suggests that since the consumer sector ran a $40.1 billion funds surplus in 1977, the sector's holdings of financial assets should have increased by a like amount over that year. Things, however, are not so simple. While the consumer sector as a whole ran a funds surplus, many spending units within the sector ran funds deficits. Thus the appropriate figure to look at is the sector's *net financial investment,* i.e., financial assets acquired minus liabilities incurred. For the household sector, this figure (see line 8, Table 2–1) was $57.4 billion in 1977, a number of the right sign and magnitude but larger than the sector's funds surplus; the difference between the two figures is due to the statistical errors that inevitably creep into such estimates.

The big funds deficit that the nonfinancial business sector ran up during 1977 indicates that the net rise in its financial liabilities outstanding over the year must have been substantial. The estimated figure ($38.7 billion) confirms this, but again a substantial discrepancy has crept into the picture.

Similar but smaller discrepancies exist between the funds surpluses or deficits run up by the other sectors in Table 2–1 and their net financial investments.

FINANCIAL INTERMEDIARIES

As noted, every year large numbers of business firms and other spending units in the economy incur funds deficits, which they cover by obtaining funds from spending units running funds surpluses. Some of this *external financing* involves what is called *direct finance*. In the case of direct finance, the *ultimate funds-deficit unit* (business firm, government body, or other spending unit) either borrows directly from *ultimate funds-surplus units* or sells equity claims against itself directly to such spending units. An example of direct finance would be when a corporation covers a funds deficit by issuing new bonds, some of which are sold directly to consumers or nonfinancial business firms that are running funds surpluses.

While examples of direct finance are easy to find, external financing more typically involves *indirect finance.* In that case the funds flow from the surplus to the deficit unit via a *financial intermediary.* Banks, savings and loan associations, life insurance companies, pension funds, and mutual funds are all examples of financial intermediaries. As this list makes clear, financial intermediaries differ widely in character. Nevertheless they all perform basically the same function. Every financial intermediary solicits and obtains funds from funds-surplus units by offering in exchange for funds "deposited" with it claims against itself. The latter, which take many forms, including demand deposits, time deposits, mutual funds shares, and the cash value of life insurance policies, are known as *indirect securities.* The funds that financial intermediaries receive in exchange for the indirect securities they issue are used by them to invest in stocks, bonds, and other securities issued by ultimate funds-deficit units, that is, in *primary securities*.

All this sounds a touch bloodless, so let's look at a simple example of financial intermediation. Jones, a consumer, runs a $20,000 funds surplus, which he receives in the form of cash. He promptly deposits that cash in a demand deposit at a bank. Simultaneously some other spending unit, say, the Alpha Co., runs a temporary funds deficit. Jones's bank trades the funds Jones has deposited with it for a loan note (IOU) issued by the Alpha Co. In doing this—accepting Jones's deposit and acquiring the note—the bank is of course funneling funds from Jones, an ultimate funds-surplus unit, to the Alpha Co., an ultimate funds-deficit unit; in other words, it is acting as a financial intermediary between Jones and this company.

Federal Reserve statistics that list the assets and liabilities of different sectors in the economy show the importance of financial intermediation. In particular at the beginning of 1978 consumers, who are the major suppliers of external financing, held $2,920.6 billion of financial assets. Of this total, $1,184.4 billion represented consumers' deposits at commercial banks and other thrift institutions, $180.8 billion the cash value of their life insurance policies, and $477.7 billion the reserve funds backing pensions eventually due them. The other $1,077.7 billion represented consumers' holdings of primary securities: corporate stock, U.S. government bonds, state and local bonds, corporate and foreign bonds, and assorted other IOUs. Thus in 1977 more than 60 percent of the funds that had flowed out of households running funds surpluses were channeled to other spending units through financial intermediation.

Financial intermediaries are a varied group. To give some idea of the relative importance of different intermediaries, Table 2–2 lists the assets

Table 2–2
Total assets of major financial institutions,
beginning of 1978 ($ billions)

Institutions	Assets
Commercial banks	1068.2
Savings and loan associations	459.2
Life insurance companies	337.6
Private pension funds	189.4
Mutual savings banks	146.7
Federal Reserve banks	142.9
State and local government retirement funds	132.2
Finance companies	124.8
Federally sponsored credit agencies	175.1
Other insurance companies	100.1
Open-end investment companies	42.8
Credit unions	51.5
Real estate investment trusts	7.6
Money market funds	3.5
Securities brokers and dealers	28.5

Source: Board of Governors, Federal Reserve System.

of all the major intermediaries at the end of 1977. As one might expect, commercial banks are by far the most important intermediaries. Following them at a considerable distance are savings and loan associations (S&Ls), life insurance companies, and the fast-growing private pension funds.

The reasons for intermediation

The main reason for all of the intermediation that occurs in our economy is that the mix of primary securities offered by funds-deficit units is not particularly attractive to many funds-surplus units. With the exception of corporate stocks, the minimum denominations on many primary securities are high relative to the size of the funds surpluses that most spending units are likely to run during any short-term period. Also, the amount of debt securities that deficit units want to borrow long term far exceeds the amount that surplus units—consumers and corporations that often desire high liquidity—choose to lend long term. Finally, some risk is attached to many primary securities, more than most surplus units would like to bear.

The indirect securities offered to savers by financial intermediaries are quite attractive in contrast to primary securities. Many such instruments, e.g., time deposits, have low to zero minimum denominations, are highly liquid, and expose the investor to negligible risk. Financial intermediaries are able to offer such attractive securities for several reasons. First, they pool the funds of many investors in a highly diversified portfolio, thereby reducing risk and overcoming the minimum denominations problem. Second, because one saver's withdrawal is likely to be met by another's deposit, intermediaries such as banks and S&Ls can with reasonable safety borrow short term from depositors and lend long term to borrowers. A final reason for intermediation is the tax advantages that some forms of intermediation, e.g., participation in a pension plan, offer individuals.

BANKS, A SPECIAL INTERMEDIARY

Banks in our economy are an intermediary of special importance for several reasons. First, they are by far the largest intermediary; they receive huge quantities of *demand deposits* (i.e., checking account money) and time deposits, which they use to make loans to consumers, corporations, and others. Second, in the course of their lending activity, *banks create money*. The reason is that demand deposits, which are a bank liability, count as part of the money supply—no matter how one defines that supply. And today, thanks to the growing attention paid to the monetarists who argue that the money supply is immensely important in determining economic activity, all eyes tend to focus on growth of the money supply.

Just how banks create money takes a little explaining. We have to introduce a simple device known as a *T-account,* which shows, as the account below illustrates, the changes that occur in the assets and liabilities of a spending unit—consumer, firm, or financial institution—as the result of a specific economic transaction.

**T-Account for a
Spending Unit**

Changes in assets	Changes in liabilities

Consider again Jones, who takes $20,000 in cash he has received and deposits that money in the First National Bank. This transaction will result in the following changes in the balance sheets of Jones and his bank:

Jones		First National Bank	
Cash −20,000 Demand deposits +20,000		Reserves (cash) +20,000	Demand deposits to Jones +20,000

Clearly Jones's deposit results in $20,000 of cash being *withdrawn from circulation* and put into bank (cash) reserves, but simultaneously $20,000 of new demand deposits are created. Since every definition of the money supply includes both demand deposits and currency *in circulation,* this deposit has no net effect on the size of the money supply; instead it simply alters the composition of the money supply.

Now enter the Alpha Co., a funds-deficit unit, which borrows, say, $15,000 from the First National Bank. If the bank makes the loan by crediting $15,000 to Alpha's account, changes will again occur in its balance sheet and in that of the borrower, too.

Alpha Co.		First National Bank	
Bank loan +15,000	Demand deposits +15,000	Loan to Alpha Co. +15,000	Demand de- posits to Alpha Co. +15,000

As the T-accounts show, the immediate effect of the loan is to *increase* total demand deposits by $15,000, but no offsetting decrease has occurred in the amount of currency in circulation. Thus by making the loan, the First National Bank has *created* $15,000 of new money (Table 2–3).

Table 2–3
Money supply

Step 1: Jones holds $20,000 in cash.
      Money supply equals:
      $20,000 in cash.

Step 2: Jones deposits his $20,000 of cash at the First National Bank.
      Money supply equals:
      $20,000 of demand deposits held by Jones.

Step 3: The First National Bank lends $15,000 to the Alpha Co.
      Money supply equals:
        $20,000 of demand deposits held by Jones.
      + $15,000 of demand deposits held by Alpha Co.

        $35,000 total money supply.

The Alpha Co., of course, presumably borrows money in order to make a payment. That, however, in no way alters the money creation aspect of the bank loan. To illustrate, suppose the Alpha Co. makes a payment for $15,000 to the Beta Co. by drawing a check against its new balance and depositing it in another bank, the Second National Bank. Then the following changes will occur in the balance sheets of the two banks in our example.

The Second National Bank		The First National Bank	
Reserves (cash) +15,000	Demand deposits to Beta Co. +15,000	Reserves (cash) −15,000	Demand deposits to the Alpha Co. −15,000

The assumed payment merely switches $15,000 of demand deposits and reserves from one bank to another bank. The payment therefore does not alter the size of the money supply.

Bearing this in mind, let's now examine how the Fed regulates the volume of bank intermediation and what effect its actions have on the money supply and interest rates.

THE FEDERAL RESERVE'S ROLE

The Fed's life has been one of continuing evolution, first in determining what its goals should be and second in learning how to use the tools available to it to promote these goals. When Congress set up the Fed in 1913, it was intended to perform several functions of varying importance. For one thing, the Fed was charged with creating an elastic supply of currency, that is, one that could be expanded and contracted in step with changes in the quantity of currency (as opposed to bank deposits) that the public desired to hold. Creating an elastic currency supply was viewed as important because, under the then-existing banking system, when a prominent bank failed and nervous depositors at other banks began demanding currency for deposits, the banks were frequently unable to meet these demands. Consequently on a number of occasions, the panic of 1907 being a case in point, currency runs on solvent banks forced these banks to temporarily suspend the conversion of deposits into cash. Such suspensions, during which currency traded at a premium relative to bank deposits, caused inconvenience to depositors and disruption to the economy.

The Fed was to solve this problem by standing ready during panics to extend to the banks at the discount window loans whose proceeds could be paid out in Federal Reserve notes. To the extent that the Fed fulfilled this function, it was acting as a lender of last resort, satiating the public's appetite for cash by monetizing bank assets. Today, acting as a lender of last resort remains an important Fed responsibility, but the Fed fulfills it in a different way.[2]

Congress also intended that the Fed carry out a second and more important function, namely, regulating the overall supply of money and bank credit so that changes in them would promote economic activity rather than disrupt it. This function too was to be accomplished at the discount window. According to the prevailing doctrine, changes in money supply and bank credit would be beneficial if they matched in direction and magnitude changes in the level of productive activity in the economy. Such beneficial changes in money and bank credit would, it was envisioned, occur in a semi-automatic way with the Fed in operation. When business activity expanded, so too would the demand for bank loans; and as growth of the latter put pressure on bank reserves, the banks would obtain additional reserves by rediscounting at the Fed (i.e., borrowing against) *eligible paper*—notes, drafts, and bills of exchange arising out of actual commercial transactions. Conversely, when economic activity slackened, bank borrowing at the discount window, bank loans, and the money supply would contract in step.

Events never quite followed this smooth pattern, which in retrospect is not to be regretted. As theorists now realize, expanding money and bank credit without limit during an upswing and permitting them to contract without limit during a downswing, far from encouraging stable growth, tend to amplify fluctuations in income and output. In particular, unlimited money creation during a boom inevitably fuels any inflationary fires and other excesses that develop.

Today the Fed sees its major policy job as pursuing a *countercyclical monetary policy*. Specifically it attempts to promote full employment and price stability by limiting the growth of bank intermediation when the economy expands at a too vigorous pace and by encouraging it when the economy slips into recession.

Controlling the level of bank intermediation

The Fed controls the level of bank intermediation—the amount of bank lending and money creating—through several tools. One key tool is *reserve requirements*. Since the 1930s the Fed has been responsible for setting the limits on the percentage of reserves that member banks are required to hold against deposits made with them. Each member bank must place all of its reserves, except vault cash, on deposit in a non–interest-bearing account at one of the 12 regional Federal Reserve banks. All nationally chartered banks must join the Federal Reserve System. The same requirement does not hold for state-chartered banks, many of which have opted to not join the system because of the high cost

---

[2] See Chapter 8, particularly the discussion of the discount window.

of tying up some of the money deposited with them in a non–interest-bearing reserve account at the Fed.[3] Thus each district Federal Reserve Bank acts in effect as a banker to commercial banks in its district, holding what amounts to checking accounts for them.

The existence at Federal Reserve banks of member bank reserve accounts explains, by the way, how the Fed can clear checks drawn against one bank and deposited with another so easily. It does so simply by debiting the reserve account of the bank against which the check is drawn and crediting by an equal amount the reserve account of the bank at which the check is deposited.

The member banks' checking accounts also make it easy for the Fed to circulate currency in the form of Federal Reserve notes (a non–interest-bearing *indirect security* issued by the Fed). Currency runs on banks are a thing of the past, but the Fed must still constantly increase the amount of currency in circulation because, as the economy expands, more currency is needed by the public for ordinary transactions. Whenever people demand more currency, they demand it from their commercial banks, which in turn get it from the Fed by trading reserve deposits for currency. Since the Fed, as noted below, creates bank reserves by buying government securities, the currency component of our money supply is in effect created by the Fed through *monetization* of a portion of the federal debt. All of this correctly suggests that the Fed, despite its lofty position at the pinnacle of the financial system, is none other than one more type of financial intermediary.

The second key tool of the Fed is *open-market operations,* that is, purchases and sales of government securities, through which it creates and destroys member bank reserves. Whenever the Fed, operating through the trading desk of the New York district bank, buys government securities, its purchases inevitably increase member bank reserves by an amount equal to the cost of the securities purchased. When the source of the securities purchased is a member bank, this result is obvious. Specifically, a purchase of $10 million of government securities would lead to the following changes in the balance sheets of the Fed and of a member bank.

The Fed		A Member Bank	
Government securities +10 million	Member bank reserves +10 million	Reserves +10 million Government securities −10 million	

[3] In 1978 the Fed and Congress showed renewed and vigorous interest in having the Fed pay interest on the reserve deposits held with it by member banks in order to make Fed membership more attractive to banks. One logical concommittant change would be for the Fed to charge member banks for services which it now provides free. Another would be to permit banks to pay interest on demand deposits and to charge their customers for services which they now give away in exchange for the receipt of demand deposits.

Even if the source of the government securities purchased by the Fed is a nonbank spending unit, the result will be essentially the same, since the money received by the seller, say, a nonbank dealer, will inevitably be deposited in a commercial bank, leading to the following balance sheet changes.

The Fed		A Member Bank	
Government securities +10 million	Member bank reserves +10 million	Reserves +10 million	Deposits to nonbank seller +10 million

A Nonbank Seller	
Government securities −10 million Demand deposits +10 million	

In the case of sales of government securities by the Fed, the process described above operates in exactly reverse fashion and member bank reserves are destroyed.

With the exception of loans extended by the Fed at the discount window (discussed below), the *only* way member bank reserves can be created is through Fed purchases of government securities, and the only way they can be destroyed is through bill sales by the Fed of such securities.[4] Thus the Fed is in a position to control directly and precisely the quantity of reserves available to the banking system.

The lid on bank intermediation

Taken together, reserve requirements and the Fed's ability to control the level of bank reserves permit the Fed to set a tight limit on the level of intermediation in which banks may engage. Let's use a simple illustration. Suppose the Fed were to require member banks to hold reserves equal to 10 percent of total deposits. If the Fed were then to create, say, $90 billion of bank reserves, the maximum deposits the banks could create through intermediation would be $900 billion (10 percent of $900 billion being $90 billion).

Naturally if the Fed were to increase bank reserves through open-

---

[4] There are some minor exceptions: In particular, movements of Treasury deposit balances between commercial banks and Fed banks affect member bank reserves, but the Fed tracks these movements daily and offsets them through purchases and sales of government securities. Seasonal and long-term changes in the public's demand for currency also affect bank reserves, but these changes too can be and are offset by the Fed through appropriate open-market operations. Finally, under the current system of "dirty" currency floats, U.S. and foreign central bank operations in the foreign exchange market may have some effect on domestic bank deposits and reserves.

market purchases of government securities, that would increase the quantity of deposits banks could create, whereas open-market sales by the Fed would have the reverse effect. For example, with a 10 percent reserve ratio, every $1 billion of government securities purchases by the Fed would permit a $10 billion increase in bank assets and liabilities, whereas $1 billion of sales would do the opposite.

Our example, which points up the potency of *open-market operations* (purchases and sales by the Fed of government securities) as a tool for controlling the level of bank intermediation, is of course oversimplified. For one thing, the percentage of reserves that must be held by a bank against its deposits varies depending on the type of deposit and the size of the bank accepting the deposit. Currently, required reserve ratios range from a high of 16.25 percent against demand deposits at large banks to a low of 1 percent against time deposits maturing in 4 years or more. Thus the actual amount of deposits (demand plus time) that a given quantity of reserves will support depends partly on the mix of deposits demanded by the public and partly on the size of the banks receiving those deposits.

This, together with the fact that banks may choose to not fully utilize the reserves available to them, means that there exists some slack in the Fed's control over deposit creation. Nevertheless open-market operations are a powerful tool for controlling the level of bank activity, and they are used daily by the Fed to do so.

The discount window

As noted earlier, the founders of the Fed viewed discounting as its *key* tool. In practice things have worked out differently. The main reason is that over time the Fed switched from controlling bank reserves through discounting to controlling them through open-market operations. This switch makes sense for several reasons. First, it puts the Fed in the position of being able to take the initiative. Second, the size and liquidity of the market for government securities mean that the Fed can make substantial purchases and sales there without disrupting the market or causing more than negligible price changes. The latter is important since in order for the Fed to fine tune bank reserves, it is constantly in the market buying and selling such securities. Part of this activity results from what is called the Fed's *defensive* operations, open-market purchases and sales designed to counter the effect on bank reserves of outside forces, such as changes in the amount of currency in circulation and movements of Treasury balances between member banks and the Fed. In addition, of course, the Fed undertakes open-market operations to effect whatever overall changes in bank reserves are called for by the current stance of monetary policy.

The discount window does still exist and banks do borrow there. This activity creates some slack in the Fed's control over member bank reserves, so the Fed has to limit bank borrowing at the window. One way it could do this would be charge a high penalty rate on discounts, one that would discourage banks from borrowing except in cases of real and temporary need. The Fed, however, has not followed this course. Instead it typically sets the discount rate at a level in step with other money market rates, with the result that the banks can at times profit by borrowing at the discount window and relending elsewhere. To limit such arbitrage and to maintain control over bank reserves, the Fed has made it a policy that borrowing at the discount window is a privilege that a bank may use only sparingly and on a temporary basis.

Today borrowing at the discount window represents a small but highly variable element in the total reserves available to member banks. In recent years monthly figures on such borrowings have ranged from a few million to over $3 billion. The high numbers all occurred in years of tight money, but even in such periods member bank borrowings represented no more than 10 percent of total bank reserves.

MONEY SUPPLY AND THE FED FUNDS RATE

The Fed has for a good portion of its life been concerned with the level of interest rates. As explained later, banks borrow and lend excess reserves to each other in the *Fed funds market*. The rate at which this lending and borrowing occurs is called the *Fed funds rate*.

When the Fed cuts back on the growth of bank reserves, this tightens the supply of excess reserves in the banking system and tends to drive up the Fed funds rate, which in turn drives up other short-term interest rates. These developments curb the growth of bank lending and the expansion of economic activity.

All this would be well and good if the Fed always wanted to force up the Fed funds rate and other short-term rates when it wanted to cut back on bank lending and vice versa, that is, if a given move would have the desired effect on both variables. In fact, as noted in later chapters, that is not always the case. At times the Fed would be content to force up interest rates without sharply curbing the growth of the money supply and vice versa.

Moreover, to make matters worse, the Fed currently calculates five measures of money supply (Table 2–4). These five measures of the money supply reflect the fact that money's crucial characteristic is that it is the most liquid of all financial assets. Obviously demand deposits and cash have 100 percent liquidity, but many other near monies such as savings deposits have almost as much liquidity and are as good as money for many transactions purposes.

Table 2–4
The Fed's measures of money stock

M1:   Currency in circulation plus private demand deposits.
M2:   M1 plus bank time and savings deposits other than large negotiable
        certificates of deposit.
M3:   M2 plus deposits at mutual savings banks, savings and loan associations,
        and credit unions.
M4:   M2 plus large negotiable certificates of deposit.
M5:   M3 plus large negotiable certificates of deposit.

To keep matters simple, the Fed centers most of its attention on the M1, M2, and M3 measures of the money supply, but even these three measures have an annoying habit of growing at different rates over time. Thus the Fed, which has one major string to its bow—the ability to alter the level of bank reserves (or to change the level of required reserves, which has the same effect), is left rather in the position of William Tell, who is asked to hit four apples that are not all in the same place with *one* arrow.

More about that later. The purpose of this chapter has been to introduce a few fundamentals as a base for later discussion. The next two chapters, which present more fundamentals, describe money market instruments in simple terms: what they are, how yields on them are calculated, and the way their prices fluctuate as the general level of interest rates changes in the economy.

Chapter 3

The instruments in brief

HERE'S A QUICK RUNDOWN of the major money market instruments. Don't look for subtleties; just enough is said to lay the groundwork for the chapters that follow.

DEALERS AND BROKERS

The markets for all money market instruments are made in part by brokers and dealers. *Brokers* bring buyers and sellers together for a commission. By definition, brokers never position securities. Their function is to provide a communications network that links market participants who are often numerous and geographically dispersed. Most brokering in the money market occurs between banks that are buying funds from or selling funds to each other and between dealers in money market instruments.

Dealers make markets in money market instruments by quoting bid and asked prices to each other, to issuers, and to investors. Dealers buy and sell for their own accounts, so assuming a position is an essential part of a dealer's operation. If dealers buy and hold securities, they are said to have a *long* position; if they sell securities they do not own, they have a *short* position.

U.S. TREASURY SECURITIES

To finance the huge U.S. national debt, the Treasury issues several types of securities. Some are nonnegotiable, for example, series E and H savings bonds sold to consumers and special issues sold to government trust funds such as the Social Security Trust Fund. The bulk of the securities sold by the U.S. Treasury are, however, negotiable.

What form these securities take depends on their maturity. Those with a maturity at issue of a year or less are known as *Treasury bills,* or for short, *T bills* or just plain *bills.* T bills do not bear interest. An investor in bills earns a positive return because bills are issued at a discount from face value and redeemed by the Treasury at maturity for the full face value. The amount of the discount at which investors buy bills and the length of time bills have to be held before they mature together imply some specific yield that the bill will return if held to maturity. How that yield is calculated is explained in Chapter 4.

T bills are currently issued in 3-month, 6-month, and 1-year maturities. In issuing bills the Treasury does not set the amount of the discount. Instead the Federal Reserve auctions off each new bill issue to investors and dealers in government securities, with the bills going to those bidders offering the highest price, i.e., the lowest interest cost to the Treasury. By using the auction technique, the Treasury lets currently prevailing market conditions establish the yield at which each new bill issue is sold.

The Treasury also issues interest-bearing *notes*. These securities are issued at or very near face value and redeemed at face value. Notes have an *original maturity* (maturity at issue) of 1 to 10 years. Currently the Treasury issues 2- and 4-year-notes on a regular cycle. Notes of other maturities are issued periodically depending on the Treasury's needs. Interest is paid on Treasury notes semiannually. Notes like bills are typically sold through auctions held by the Federal Reserve. In these auctions bidders bid yields, and the securities offered are sold to those dealers and investors who bid the lowest yields, that is, the lowest interest cost to the Treasury. Thus the coupon rate on new Treasury notes, like the yield on bills, is normally determined by the market. The only exceptions are occasional subscription and price auction issues on which the Treasury sets the coupon (see Chapter 7).

In addition to notes, the Treasury also issues interest-bearing negotiable *bonds* that have a maturity at issue of 10 years or longer. The only difference between Treasury notes and bonds is that bonds are issued in longer maturities. In recent years the volume of bonds offered by the Treasury has been relatively small. The reason is that Congress has established a 4.25 percent ceiling on the rate the Treasury can pay on bonds. Since this rate has for years been far below prevailing market rates, the Treasury is able to sell bonds only to the extent that Congress authorizes it to issue bonds exempt from the ceiling, something that Congress does only sparingly. Currently Treasury bonds, like notes, are normally issued through yield auctions.

Banks, other financial institutions, insurance companies, pension funds, and corporations are all important investors in U.S. Treasury securities. So too are some foreign central banks and other foreign institutions. The market for government securities is largely a wholesale market and, especially at the short end of the market, multimillion-dollar transactions are common. However, when interest rates get extremely high, as they did in 1974, individuals with relatively small amounts to invest are drawn into the market for government securities.

Because of the high volume of Treasury debt outstanding, the market for bills and short-term government securities is the most active and most carefully watched sector of the money market. At the heart of this market stands a varied collection of *dealers* who make the market for *governments* (market jargon for government securities) by standing ready to buy and sell huge volumes of these securities. These dealers trade actively not only with retail accounts but also with each other. Most trades of the latter sort are carried out through brokers, who form an efficient communications network linking traders at different dealer shops.

Governments offer investors several advantages. First, because they are constantly traded in the *secondary* (resale) *market* in large volume and at narrow spreads between the bid and asked prices, they are highly *liquid*.[1] A second advantage is that governments are considered to be free from credit risk because it is inconceivable that the government would ever default on these securities short of destruction of the country. Third, interest income on governments is exempt from state taxation. Because of these advantages, governments normally trade at yields below those of other money market instruments. Municipal securities are an exception because they offer a still more attractive tax advantage.

Generally yields on governments are higher the longer their *current maturity*, that is, time currently left to run to maturity.[2] The reason, explained in Chapter 4, is that the longer the current maturity of a debt security, the more its price will fluctuate in response to changes in interest rates and therefore the greater the *price risk* to which it exposes the investor.

---

[1] An asset is said to be *liquid* if it can be turned into cash rapidly without substantial loss in value.

[2] A 5-year note has an *original maturity* at issue of 5 years. One year after issue it has a *current maturity* of 4 years.

T BILL FUTURES MARKET

In talking about the market for governments, we have focused on what is called the *cash market,* that is, the market in which existing securities are traded for cash. In addition, there are markets in which Treasury bills and bonds are traded for future delivery. In these markets contracts are actively traded for the future delivery of 3-month bills having a face value of $1 million at maturity and of government bonds having a par value of $100,000. Both futures markets are relatively new and still small, but growing in importance.

The T bill futures market offers institutions that know they are going to borrow or lend short term in the future a way to hedge that future position, that is, to lock in a reasonably fixed borrowing or lending rate. It also provides speculators with a way to bet money on interest rate movements that is easier and cheaper than going short or long in cash bills.

The mechanics and uses of the bill futures market, a complicated subject, are of little concern in the next few chapters. We leave their description to Chapter 14.

FEDERAL AGENCY SECURITIES

From time to time Congress becomes concerned about the volume of credit that is available to various sectors of the economy and the terms at which that credit is available. Its usual response is to set up a federal agency to provide credit to that sector. Thus, for example, there is the Federal Home Loan Bank System which lends to the nation's savings and loan associations as well as regulates them, the Government National Mortgage Association which funnels money into the mortgage market, the Banks for Cooperatives which make seasonal and term loans to farm cooperatives, the Federal Land Banks which give mortgages on farm properties, the Federal Intermediate Credit Banks which provide short-term financing for producers of crops and livestock, and a host of other agencies.

Initially all the federal agencies financed their activities by selling their own securities in the open market. Today all except the largest borrow from the Treasury through an institution called the Federal Financing Bank. Those agencies still borrowing in the open market, basically the ones named above, do so primarily by issuing notes and bonds. These securities (known in the market as *agencies*) bear interest, and they are issued and redeemed at face value. Instead of using the auction technique for issuing their securities, federal agencies look to the market to determine the best yield at which they can sell a new issue, put that yield on the issue, and then sell it through a syndicate of dealers.

Some agencies also sell short-term discount paper that resembles commercial paper, an instrument discussed later in this chapter.

Normally agencies yield slightly more than Treasury securities of the same maturity. There are several reasons for this. Agency issues are smaller than Treasury issues and are therefore less liquid. Also, while all agency issues have *de facto* backing from the federal government (it's inconceivable that the government would let one of them default on its obligations), the securities of only a few agencies are explicitly backed by the full faith and credit of the U.S. government. Thus investors view some agency securities as carrying a small but perceptible credit risk. A third disadvantage of some agency issues is that interest income from them is not exempt from state taxation.

The agency market, while smaller than that for governments, has in recent years become an extremely active and important sector of the money market. Agencies are generally traded by the same dealers who trade governments and in much the same way. Trades in agencies between dealers are, like those in governments, often brokered.

The specific functions of the key federal credit agencies and the securities they issue are described in Chapter 7.

FEDERAL FUNDS

As noted in Chapter 2, all banks that are members of the Federal Reserve System are required to keep reserves on deposit at their district Federal Reserve Bank. A commercial bank's reserve account is much like a consumer's checking account; the bank makes deposits into it and can transfer funds out of it. The main difference is that whereas a consumer can run the balance in his checking account down to zero, each member bank is required to maintain some minimum average balance over the week in its reserve account. How large that minimum balance is depends on the size and composition of the bank's deposits over the previous two weeks.

Funds on deposit in a bank's reserve account are referred to as *Federal funds,* or *Fed funds.* Any deposits a bank receives add to its supply of Fed funds, while loans made and securities purchased by it reduce that supply. Thus the basic amount of money any bank can lend out and otherwise invest equals the amount of funds it has received from depositors minus the reserves it is required to maintain.

For some banks this supply of available funds roughly equals the amount of money they choose to invest in securities plus that demanded from them by borrowers. But for most banks it does not. Specifically, because the nation's largest corporations tend to concentrate their borrowing in big money market banks in New York and other financial centers, the loans and investments these banks have to fund are much greater than the deposits they receive. Many smaller banks, in contrast, receive more money from local deposits than they can lend locally or choose to otherwise invest. Because large banks have to meet their reserve requirements regardless of what loan demand they face and because excess reserves yield no return to smaller banks, it was natural for larger banks to begin borrowing the excess funds held by smaller banks.

This borrowing is done in the *Federal funds market.* Most Fed funds loans are overnight transactions. There are, as explained in later chapters, several reasons why most Fed funds transactions are done on an overnight basis. One is that the amount of excess funds a given lending bank holds varies daily and unpredictably. Some transactions in Fed funds are made directly, others through New York brokers. Once a bank has agreed to lend another bank money that it holds in its reserve account, it wires the Fed requesting that the money be transferred from its account to the reserve account of the borrowing bank. The next day the borrowing bank reverses the process by requesting the Fed to return the funds it has borrowed plus interest due to the lending bank.

Despite the fact that transactions of this sort are all loans, the lending of Fed funds is referred to as a *sale* and the borrowing of Fed funds as a *purchase*.

While overnight transactions dominate the Fed funds market, there are also some lending and borrowing for longer periods of time. Fed funds traded for periods other than overnight are referred to as *term* Fed funds.

The rate of interest paid on overnight loans of Federal funds, which is called the *Fed funds rate,* is *the* main interest rate in the money market, and all other short-term rates key off it. The level of the Fed funds rate is pegged by Federal Reserve activity, as explained in Chapter 8.

EURODOLLARS

Many foreign banks will accept deposits of dollars and grant the depositor an account denominated in dollars. So too will the foreign branches of U.S. banks. The practice of accepting dollar deposits outside of the United States began in Europe, so such deposits came to be known as *Eurodollars.* The practice of accepting dollar deposits later spread to Hong Kong, Singapore, the Middle East, and other centers around the globe. Consequently today a *Eurodollar deposit is simply dollars deposited in a bank outside the United States,* and the term *Eurodollar* has become a misnomer.

Most Eurodollar deposits are for large sums. They are made by big corporations—foreign, multinational, and domestic; foreign central banks and other official institutions; U.S. domestic banks; and wealthy individuals. With the exception of call money,[3] all Euro deposits have some fixed term, which can range from overnight to 5 years. The bulk of Euro transactions are in the range of 6 months and under. Banks receiving Euro deposits use these dollars to make loans denominated in dollars to foreign and domestic corporations, foreign governments and government agencies, domestic U.S. banks, and other large borrowers. As the above suggests, the Euromarket today is a huge and growing capital market.

For reasons explained in Chapter 6, banks participating in the Eurodollar market actively borrow and lend Euros among themselves just as domestic banks borrow and lend in the market for Fed funds. The major difference between the two markets is that, in the market for Fed funds, most transactions are on an overnight basis while in the Euromarket interbank placements (deposits) of funds for longer periods are common.

Since hundreds of banks all over the world participate in the Euromarket, it would be difficult for a bank wanting to borrow Eurodollars to call around and find the bank willing to lend at the lowest rate. Thus most interbank dealing in Euros is done through brokers who are linked via vast communications networks to major banks around the world.

For a domestic U.S. bank with a reserve deficiency, borrowing Eurodollars is an alternative to purchasing Fed funds. Also, for a domestic bank with excess funds, a Euro *placement* (i.e., a deposit of dollars in the Euromarket) is an alternative to the sale of Fed funds. Consequently the rate on overnight Euros tends to track closely the Fed funds rate. It is also true, for reasons explained in Chapter 17, that as one goes out on the maturity scale, Euro rates continue to track U.S. rates, though not always so closely as they do in the overnight market.

CERTIFICATES OF DEPOSIT

The maximum rate banks can pay on savings deposits and time deposits (a time deposit is savings-type deposit with a fixed maturity) is set by the Fed through *Regulation Q.* Essentially what Reg Q does is to make it impossible for banks to compete with each other or with other savings institutions for small deposits by offering depositors higher interest rates. On large deposits, $100,000 or more, banks can currently pay any rate they choose so long as the deposit has a minimum maturity of 30 days.

There are, of course, many corporations and other large investors that have hundreds of thousands, even millions of dollars they could invest in

---

[3] Call money is money deposited in an interest-bearing account that can be called (withdrawn) by the depositor on a day's notice.

a bank time deposit. Few do so, however, because they lose liquidity by making a time deposit with a fixed maturity. Liquidity is important to most investors for two reasons. Money invested may for some unexpected reason be needed before anticipated. Also, as conditions change, more attractive investment alternatives might appear to the investors, one of which they would like to take immediate advantage.

The lack of liquidity of time deposits and their consequent lack of appeal to investors led the banks to invent the *negotiable certificate of deposit, or CD* for short. Banks also issue nonnegotiable certificates of deposit but they are not a money market instrument, so the money market refers to negotiable CDs simply as CDs.

CDs are normally sold in $1 million pieces. They are issued at face value and typically pay interest at maturity. CDs can have any maturity longer than 30 days, and some 5- and even 7-year CDs have been sold (these pay interest semiannually). Most CDs, however, have an *original maturity* of 1 to 3 months.

The quantity of CDs that banks have outstanding depends largely on the strength of loan demand. When demand rises, banks issue more CDs to help fund the additional loans they are making. The rates banks offer on CDs depend on their maturity, how badly the banks want to write new CDs, and the general level of short-term interest rates.

The bulk of bank CDs are sold directly by the banks to investors. Some, however, are issued through dealers, often for a small commission. These same dealers also make an active secondary market in CDs.

Yields on CDs exceed those on bills of similiar maturities by varying spreads. One reason for the bigger yield is that buying a bank CD exposes the investor to some credit risk—would he be paid off if the issuing bank failed? A second reason CDs yield more than bills is that they are less liquid.

EURODOLLAR CERTIFICATES OF DEPOSIT

A Eurodollar time deposit, like a domestic time deposit, is an illiquid asset. Since some investors in Eurodollars wanted liquidity, banks accepting such deposits in London began to issue Eurodollar CDs. A *Eurodollar CD* resembles a domestic CD except that instead of being the liability of a domestic bank, it is the liability of the London branch of a domestic bank or of a British bank or of some other foreign bank with a branch in London.

Many of the Eurodollar CDs issued in London are purchased by other banks operating in the Euromarket. A large proportion of the remainder are sold to U.S. corporations and other domestic institutional investors. Many Euro CDs are issued through dealers and brokers who also maintain an active secondary market in these securities.

The Euro CD market is younger and much smaller than the market for domestic CDs, but it has grown rapidly since its inception. For the investor, a key advantage of buying Euro CDs is that they offer a higher return than domestic CDs. The offsetting disadvantages are that they are less liquid than domestic CDs and they expose the investor to some extra risk because they are issued outside of the United States.

COMMERCIAL PAPER

While there are some cash-rich industrial and manufacturing firms that participate in the bond and money markets only as lenders, there are many more who must at times borrow to finance either current operations or expenditures on plant and equipment. Spending of the latter sort is most appropriately financed by issuing bonds, and corporations each year issue huge quantities of long-term bonds to finance capital spending.

Current operations, however, can be and are financed with short-term debt, which offers several advantages. It is normally cheaper than long-term debt, and it can be varied in amount to meet seasonal and other fluctuations in a firm's borrowing needs.

One source of short-term funds available to a corporation is bank loans, and corporations do borrow extensively from banks. Large firms with good credit ratings have, however, an alternative source of funds that is normally significantly cheaper than a bank loan, namely, the sale of commercial paper.

Commercial paper is an unsecured promissory note issued for a specific amount and maturing on a specific day. All commercial paper is negotiable, but most paper sold to investors is held by them to maturity. Commercial paper is issued not only by industrial and manufacturing firms but also by finance companies, such as Ford Credit and Household Finance, which use the money obtained to fund loans, credit sales, and other transactions. Finance companies normally sell their paper directly to investors. Industrial firms, in contrast, typically issue their commercial paper through dealers. Commercial paper transactions are usually for large amounts, and the purchasers are institutions such as corporations, insurance companies, pension funds, and bank trust departments.

The maximum maturity for which commercial paper can be sold is 270 days, since paper with a longer maturity would have to be registered with the Securities and Exchange Commission, a time-consuming and costly procedure. In practice, very little 270-day paper is sold. Most paper sold is in the range of 30 days and under.

Since commercial paper has such short maturities, the issuer typically will not have sufficient funds coming in before the paper matures to pay off his borrowing. Instead he expects to *roll* his paper, that is, sell new paper to obtain funds to pay off the maturing paper. Naturally the possibility exists that some sudden change in market conditions, such as when the Penn Central went "belly up" (bankrupt) might make it difficult or impossible for him to sell paper for some time. To guard against this risk, commercial paper issuers back all or a large proportion of their outstanding paper with lines of credit from banks. A *line of credit* is simply an agreement on the part of a bank to lend any amount up to some specified limit to the issuer should he need funds. Bank lines are paid for with compensating balances and/or fees.

The rate offered on commercial paper depends on its maturity, on how much the issuer wants to borrow, on the general level of money market rates, and on the credit rating of the issuer. Almost all commercial paper is rated with respect to credit risk by one or more of several rating services: Moody's Investors Service, Standard & Poor's Corporation, and Fitch Investors Service. While only top-grade credits can get ratings good enough to sell paper these days, there is still the slight risk that an issuer might go bankrupt with paper outstanding, as the Penn Central did in another era. Because of this risk, yields on commercial paper are higher than those on Treasury obligations of similar maturity.

BANKERS' ACCEPTANCES

Bankers' acceptances (*BAs*) are an unknown instrument outside the confines of the money market. Moreover, explaining them isn't easy because they arise in a variety of ways out of a variety of transactions. The best approach is to use an example.

Suppose a U.S. importer wants to buy shoes in Brazil and pay for them 4 months later, after he has had time to sell them in the United States. One approach would be for the importer to simply borrow from his bank; however, short-term rates may be lower in the open market. If they are, and if the importer is too small to go into the open market on his own, then he can go the bankers' acceptance route.

In that case he has his bank write a letter of credit for the amount of the sale and then sends this letter to the Brazilian exporter. Upon export of the shoes, the Brazilian firm, using this letter of credit, draws a time draft on the importer's U.S. bank and discounts this draft at its local bank, thereby obtaining immediate payment for its goods. The Brazilian bank in turn sends the time draft to the importer's U.S. bank, which then stamps "accepted" on the draft (that is, the bank guarantees payment on the draft and thereby creates an *acceptance*). Once this is done, the draft becomes an irrevocable primary obligation of the accepting bank. At this point, if the Brazilian bank did not want cash immediately, the U.S. bank would return the draft to that bank, which would hold it as an investment and then present it to the U.S. bank for payment at maturity. If, on the other hand, the Brazilian bank wanted cash immediately, the U.S. bank would pay it and then either hold the acceptance itself or sell it to an investor. Whoever ended up holding the acceptance, it would be the importer's responsibility to provide its U.S. bank with sufficient funds to pay off the acceptance at maturity. If the importer should fail for any reason, his bank would still be responsible for making payment at maturity.

Our example illustrates how an acceptance can arise out of a U.S. import transaction. Acceptances also arise in connection with U.S. export sales, trade between third countries (e.g., Japanese imports of oil from the Middle East), the domestic shipment of goods, and domestic or foreign storage of readily marketable staples. Currently most BAs arise out of foreign trade; the latter may be in manufactured goods but more typically it is in bulk commodities, such as cocoa, cotton, coffee, or crude oil, to name a few. Because of the complex nature of acceptance operations, only large banks that have well-staffed foreign departments act as accepting banks.

Bankers' acceptances closely resemble commercial paper in form. They are short-term, noninterest-bearing notes sold at a discount and redeemed by the accepting bank at maturity for full face value. The major difference between BAs and commercial paper is that payment on commercial paper is guaranteed by only the issuing company. In contrast, bankers' acceptances, in addition to carrying the issuer's pledge to pay, are backed by the underlying goods being financed and also carry the guarantee of the accepting bank. Consequently bankers' acceptances are less risky than commercial paper, and thus sell at slightly lower yields than commercial paper.

The big banks through which bankers' acceptances originate generally keep some portion of the acceptances they create as investments. The rest are sold to investors through dealers or directly by the bank itself. Major investors in BAs are other banks, foreign central banks, corporations, and other domestic and foreign institutional investors. BAs have liquidity because dealers in these securities make an active secondary market in them. Interdealer trades in BAs began to be brokered in 1977.

REPURCHASES AND REVERSES

A variety of bank and nonbank dealers act as market makers in governments, agencies, CDs, and BAs. Because dealers by definition buy and sell for their own accounts, active dealers will inevitably end up holding some securities. They will, moreover, buy and hold substantial positions in various money market instruments if they believe that interest rates are likely to fall and that the value of these securities is therefore likely to rise. Speculation and risk taking are an inherent and important part of being a dealer.

While dealers have large amounts of capital, the positions they take are often several hundred times that amount. As a result, dealers have to borrow to finance their positions. Dealers, using the securities they own as collateral, can and do borrow from banks at the dealer loan rate. For the bulk of their financing, however, they resort to a cheaper alternative, entering into *repurchase* (*RP or repo for short*) *agreements* with investors.

Much of the RP financing done by dealers is on an overnight basis. In brief, it works as follows. The dealer finds a corporation or other investor who has funds to invest overnight. He sells this investor, say, $10 million of securities for roughly $10 million, which is paid in Federal funds to his bank by the investor's bank against delivery of the securities sold. At the same time the dealer sells the securities, he agrees to repurchase them the next day at a slightly higher price. Thus the buyer of the securities is in effect making the dealer a one-day loan secured by the obligations sold to him. The difference between the purchase and sale prices on the RP transaction is the interest the investor earns on his loan. Alternatively, the purchase and sale prices in an RP transaction may be identical; in that case the dealer pays the investor some explicit rate of interest.

Often a dealer will take a speculative position that he intends to hold for some time. In that case he might do an RP for 30 days or longer. Such agreements are known as *term* RPs.

From the point of view of the investors, overnight loans in the RP market offer several attractive features. First, by rolling overnight RPs, investors can keep surplus funds invested without losing any liquidity or incurring any price risk. Second, because RP transactions are secured by governments or other top-quality paper, investors expose themselves to little or no credit risk.

The overnight RP rate generally lies below the Fed funds rate. The reason is that the many nonbank investors who have funds to invest overnight or very short term and who do not want to incur any price risk have nowhere to go but the RP market, because they cannot (with the exception of S&Ls) participate directly in the Fed funds market. Also, lending money through an RP transaction is safer than selling Fed funds because a sale of Fed funds is an unsecured loan.

On term as opposed to overnight RP transactions, investors still have the advantage of their loans being secured but they do lose some liquidity. To compensate for that, the rate on an RP transaction is generally higher the longer the term for which funds are lent.

Banks making dealer loans fund them by buying Fed funds, and the lending rate they charge—which is adjusted each day—is the prevailing

Fed funds rate plus a one-eighth or one-quarter markup. Because the overnight RP rate is lower than the Fed funds rate, dealers can, as noted, finance their positions more cheaply by doing RP than by borrowing from the banks.

Since the overnight RP rate is one of the lowest rates in the money market, the borrowing rate a dealer has to pay to finance securities in his position is typically much lower than the return yielded by these securities. The resulting *positive carry* is a source of profit to dealers and thus one more factor encouraging them to position securities.

A dealer who is bullish on the market will, as noted, position large amounts of securities.[1] If he's bearish because he expects interest rates to rise, he will *short* the market, that is, sell securities he does not own. Since the dealer has to deliver any securities he sells whether he owns them or not, a dealer who shorts has to borrow securities one way or another. The most common technique these days for borrowing securities is to do what is called a *reverse RP* or simply a *reverse*. To obtain securities through a reverse, a dealer finds an investor holding the required securities; he then buys these securities from the investor under an agreement that he will resell these same securities to the investor at a fixed price on some future date. In this transaction the dealer, besides obtaining securities, is extending a loan to the investor for which he is paid some rate of interest.

As you probably noted, an RP and a reverse are identical transactions. What a given transaction is called depends on who initiates it: typically if a dealer hunting money does, it's an RP; if a dealer hunting securities does, it's a reverse.

The market in RPs and reverses is huge and rapidly growing. It is also one of the most innovative and exciting sectors of the money market.

A final note: The Fed uses reverses and RPs with dealers in government securities to make adjustments in bank reserves. We come to that in Chapters 8 and 11.

MUNICIPAL NOTES

Debt securities issued by state and local governments and their agencies are referred to as *municipal securities.* Such securities can be divided into two broad categories: bonds issued to finance capital projects and short-term notes sold in anticipation of the receipt of other funds, such as taxes or proceeds from a bond issue. Municipal bonds are not traded in the money market, but *muni notes* are an important money market instrument.

---

[1] A person who is *bearish* on the market expects securities prices to fall, one who is *bullish* expects them to rise. In the money market, rising interest rates depress the prices of money market instruments; falling interest rates do the opposite.

Municipal notes are issued with maturities ranging from a month to a year. They bear interest and minimum denominations are highly variable, ranging anywhere from $5,000 to $5 million.

Most muni notes are general obligation securities; that is, payment of principal and interest is secured by the issuer's pledge of its full faith, credit, and taxing power. This sounds impressive, but as the spectacle of New York City tottering on the brink of bankruptcy brought home to all, it is possible that a municipality might default on its securities. Thus the investor who buys muni notes assumes some credit risk. To aid investors in evaluating this risk, publicly offered muni notes are rated by Moody's just as commercial paper is. The one exception is project notes, which are issued by local housing authorities to finance federally sponsored programs, and which are backed by the full faith and credit of the federal government.

The major attraction of municipal notes to an investor is that interest income on them is exempt from federal taxation and usually also from any income taxes levied within the state where they are issued. The value of this tax exemption is greater the higher the investor's tax bracket, and the muni market thus tends to attract only highly taxed investors—commercial banks, cash-rich corporations, and wealthy individuals.

Large muni note issues are sold to investors by dealers who obtain the securities either through negotiation with the issuer or through competitive bidding. These same dealers also make a secondary market in muni notes, so the instrument has good liquidity.

The yield a municipality has to pay to issue notes depends on its credit rating, the length of time for which it borrows, and the general level of short-term rates. Normally a good credit can borrow at a rate well below the yield on T bills of equivalent maturity. The reason for this is the value to the investor of the tax exemption on the municipal security. A corporation that has its profits taxed at a 50 percent marginal rate would, for example, receive the same after-tax return from a muni note yielding 3 percent that it would from a T bill yielding 6 percent.

Chapter 4

Discount and interest-bearing securities

THE MONEY MARKET deals in essentially two types of securities, *interest-bearing securities* and *discount paper*. Yields on these two types of instruments are calculated and quoted in quite different ways. Thus any discussion of the money market has to be prefaced by some simple math which shows how yields on these different instruments are calculated and how they can be made comparable. We start with discount securities.

TREASURY BILLS

To illustrate how a discount security works, we assume that an investor who participates in an auction of new Treasury *year bills* picks up $1 million of them at 6 percent. What this means is that the Treasury sells the investor $1 million of bills maturing in 1 year at a price approximately but not precisely 6 percent below their face value. The "approximately but not precisely" qualifier takes a little explaining. Offhand one would expect the amount of the discount to be the face value of the securities purchased times the rate of discount times the *fraction of the year* the securities will be outstanding. In our example the discount calculated this way would equal $1 million times 6 percent times 1 full year, which

37

amounts to $60,000. That figure, however, is incorrect for two reasons. First, the year bill is outstanding not for a year but for 52 weeks, which is 364 days. Second, the Treasury calculates the discount as if a year had only 360 days. So the fraction of the year for which the security is outstanding is 364/360, and the true discount on the security is:

$$\text{Discount on \$1 million of year bills issued at 6\%} = \$1,000,000 \times 0.06 \times \frac{364}{360} = \$60,666.67$$

Because the Treasury calculates the discount as if the year had 360 days, our investor gets his bills at a discount that exceeds $60,000 even though he invests for only 364 days. The price he pays for his bills equals *face value minus the discount,* i.e.,

$$\text{Price paid for \$1 million of year bills bought at 6\%} = \$1,000,000 - \$60,666.67 = \$939,333.33$$

Generalizing from this example, we can construct formulas for calculating both the discount from face value and the price at which T bills will sell, depending on their current maturity and the discount at which they are quoted. Let

D = Discount from face value
F = Face value
d = Rate of discount
t = Days to maturity
P = Price

Then

$$D = F \left(\frac{d \times t}{360} \right)$$

and

$$P = F - D = F \left(1 - \frac{d \times t}{360} \right)$$

EQUIVALENT BOND YIELD

If an investor lent $1 million for one 365-day year and received at the end of the year $60,000 of interest plus the $1 million of principal invested, we would—calculating yield on a *simple interest basis*—say that he had earned 6 percent.[1] Using the same approach—return earned divided by principal invested—to calculate the return earned by our investor who bought a 6 percent year bill, we find that, on a

---

[1] By *simple interest* we mean interest is paid once a year at the end of the year. There is no compounding as, for example, on a savings account.

simple interest basis, he earned significantly *more than* 6 percent. Specifically,

$$\text{Return on a simple interest basis on} \atop \text{\$1 million 6\% year bills held to maturity} = \frac{\$60,666.67}{\$939,333.33} \div \frac{364}{365} = 6.48\%$$

In this calculation, because the bill matures in 364 days, it is necessary to divide by the fraction of the year for which the bill is outstanding to annualize the rate earned.

Treasury notes and bonds, which—unlike bills—are *interest bearing*, pay the holder interest equal to the face value times the interest (i.e., *coupon*) rate at which they are issued. Thus an investor who bought $1 million of Treasury notes carrying a 6 percent coupon would receive $60,000 of interest during each year the securities were outstanding.

The way yields on notes and bonds are quoted, 6 percent notes selling at *par* (i.e., face value) would be quoted as offering a 6 percent yield. An investor who bought these notes would, however, have the opportunity to earn more than 6 percent simple interest. The reason is that interest on notes and bonds is paid in semiannual installments, which means that the investor can invest during the second 6 months of each year the first semiannual interest installment.

To illustrate the effect of this on return, consider an investor who buys at issue $1 million of 6 percent Treasury notes. Six months later he receives $30,000 of interest, which we assume he reinvests at 6 percent. Then at the end of the year he receives another $30,000 of interest plus interest on the interest he has invested; the latter amounts to $30,000 times 6 percent times the one-half year he earns that interest. Thus his total dollar return over the year is:

$$\$30,000 + (0.06)(\$30,000)(0.5) + \$30,000 = \$60,900$$

and the percentage return that he earns, expressed in terms of simple interest, is

$$\frac{\$60,900}{\$1,000,000} = 6.09\%$$

Note that what is at work here is *compound interest;* any quoted rate of interest yields more dollars of return and is thus equivalent to a higher simple interest rate the more frequently interest is paid and the more compounding that can thus occur.

Because return can mean different things depending on the way it is quoted and paid, an investor can compare meaningfully the returns offered by different securities only if these returns are stated on a comparable basis. With respect to *discount* and *coupon* securities, the way yields are made comparable in the money market is by restating yields quoted on a *discount basis*—the basis on which T bills are quoted—in terms of *equivalent bond yield*—the basis on which yields on notes and bonds are quoted.

We calculated above that an investor in a year bill would, on a simple interest basis, earn 6.48 percent. This is slightly higher than the rate he would earn measured on an equivalent bond yield basis. The reason is that equivalent bond yield understates, as noted, the true return on a simple interest basis that the investor in a coupon security would earn if he reinvested interest. When adjustment is made for this understatement, the equivalent bond yield offered by a 6 percent year bill turns out to be something less than 6.48 percent. Specifically, it is 6.38 percent.

The formula for converting yield on a bank discount basis to equivalent bond yield is complicated for discount securities that have a current maturity of longer than 6 months, but that is no problem for investors and other money market participants because bills yields are always restated on dealers' quote sheets in terms of equivalent bond yield (Table 4–1) at the *asked* rate.

Table 4–1
Selected quotes on U.S. Treasury bills, January 6, 1978

Billions outstanding	1978 maturity	Bid	Asked	Equivalent bond yield
5.7	Jan. 12	6.00	5.10	5.17
5.7	Jan. 19	6.00	5.20	5.28
2.2	Feb. 16	6.00	5.70	5.81
5.8	Mar. 16	6.10	5.90	6.05
3.4	Apr. 13	6.35	6.15	6.34
3.3	May 18	6.45	6.25	6.48
3.3	June 22	6.50	6.30	6.58
3.0	Aug. 22	6.55	6.35	6.66
3.1	Oct. 17	6.60	6.40	6.75
3.4	Dec. 12	6.60	6.40	6.80

On bills with a current maturity of 6 months or less, the problem of compounding does not arise, and yield on a discount basis can be converted to equivalent bond yield by a simple formula: Let

$$r = \text{equivalent bond yield}$$

Then on a security quoted at the discount rate d, equivalent bond yield is given by

$$r = \frac{365 \times d}{360 - (d \times t)}$$

For example, on a 3-month bill purchased at 5 percent, equivalent bond yield is

$$r = \frac{365 \times 0.05}{360 - (0.05 \times 91)} = 5.13\%$$

From the examples we have considered, it is clear that the yield on a discount security is *significantly less* when measured on a discount basis than when measured in terms of equivalent bond yield. The absolute divergence between these two measures of yield is, moreover, not constant but varies depending on both the discount security's absolute yield and its maturity. As Table 4–2 shows, the

Table 4–2
Comparisons, at different rates and maturities, of rates of discount and equivalent bond yields

Yields on a discount basis (%)	Equivalent bond yields (%)		
	30-day maturity	182-day maturity	364-day maturity
4	4.07	4.14	4.18
5	5.09	5.20	5.27
6	6.11	6.27	6.38
7	7.14	7.36	7.50
8	8.17	8.45	8.63
9	9.20	9.56	9.79

greater the yield and the longer the maturity of the security, the greater the divergence.[2]

FLUCTUATIONS IN A BILL'S PRICE

Normally the price at which a bill sells will rise as the bill approaches maturity. For example, to yield 9 percent on a discount basis, a 6-month bill must be priced at $95.45 per $100 of face value. For the same bill 3 months later (3 months closer to maturity) to yield 9 percent, it must have risen in price to $97.72. The moral is clear: If a bill always sold at the same yield throughout its life, its price would rise steadily toward face value as it approached maturity.

A bill's yield, however, is unlikely to be constant over time; instead it will fluctuate for two reasons: (1) changes may occur in the general level of short-term interest rates, and (2) the bill will move along *the yield curve.* Let's look at each of these factors.

Short-term interest rates

T bills are issued through auctions in which discounted prices (yields) are bid. The rate of discount determined at auction on a new bill issue depends on the level of short-term interest rates prevailing at the

[2] For a more complete conversion table, see back end papers.

moment of the auction. The reason is straightforward. Investors who want to buy bills at the time of a Treasury auction have two alternatives—to buy new bills or to buy existing bills from dealers. This being the case, investors will not bid for new bills a rate of discount lower than that available on existing bills; if they did, they would be offering to buy new bills at a price higher than that at which they could buy existing bills. Also, investors will not bid substantially higher rates of discount (lower prices) than those prevailing on existing bills, because if they did, they would not obtain bills, since they would surely be underbid by others trying to get just a slightly better return than that available on existing securities. Thus, the prevailing level of short-term rates determines within a narrow range the discount established on new bills at issue.

However, the going level of short-term rates is not constant over time. It rises and falls in response to changes in economic activity, the demand for credit, investors' expectations, and monetary policy as set by the Federal Reserve System. Figure 4–1, which plots yields on 6-month T bills for the period 1970–78, portrays vividly the volatility of short-term interest rates. It shows both the sharp ups and downs that occurred in these rates as the Fed successively eased and tightened and the myriad of smaller fluctuations over the period in response to short-lived changes in other determinants of these rates.

Figure 4–1
Market yields on 6-month Treasury bills (average monthly quotes, 1970–1978)

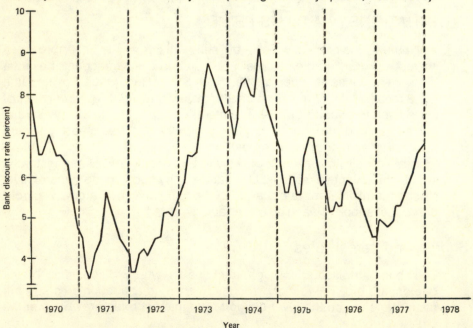

If the going level of short-term rates (which establishes the yield at which a bill is initially sold) falls after a bill is issued, then this bill—as long as its price doesn't change—will yield more than new bills. Therefore, buyers will compete for this bill, and in doing so they will drive up its price and thereby force down its yield until the bill sells at a rate of discount equal to the new lower going interest rate. Conversely, if short-term rates rise after a bill is issued, the unwillingness of buyers to purchase any bill at a discount less than that available on new issues will drive down its price and thereby force up its yield.

The yield curve

Even if the going level of short-term interest rates does not change while investors holds bills, it would be normal for the rate at which they could sell their bills to change. The reason lies in the *yield curve*.

Price risk. In choosing among alternative securities, an investor considers three things: risk, liquidity, and return. Purchase of a money market instrument exposes an investor to two sorts of risk: (1) *a credit risk:* will the issuer pay off at maturity? and (2) *a price risk:* if the investor later sold the security, might he have to do so at a loss because interest rates had subsequently risen? Most money market investors are risk averse, which means that they will accept lower yield to obtain lower risk.

The price risk to which bills and other money market instruments expose the investor is *larger* the *longer* their current maturity. To see why, suppose that short-term interest rates rise a full percentage point across the board; then the prices of all bill issues will drop, *but the price drop will be greater, the longer an issue's current maturity*. For example, a 1 percentage point rise in market rates would cause a 3-month bill to fall only $0.25 in price per $100 of face value, whereas the corresponding price drop on a 9-month bill would be $0.76 per $100 of face value.

The slope of the yield curve. Because a 3-month bill exposes the investor to less price risk than a 9-month bill, it will normally yield less than a 9-month bill. In other words, the bill market yield curve, which shows the relationship between yield and current maturity, normally slopes upward, indicating that the longer the time to maturity, the higher the yield. We say "normally" because other factors, such as the expectation that interest rates are going to fall, may, as explained below, alter this general relationship.

To illustrate the concept of the yield curve, we have used the bid quotes in Table 4–1 to plot a yield curve in Figure 4–2; each dot is one quote. Our results show a normal upward-sloping yield curve. Lest you try doing the same and be disappointed, we should admit that we cheated a bit in putting together our demonstration yield curve. On Jan-

Figure 4–2
Yield curve for Treasury bills, January 6, 1978

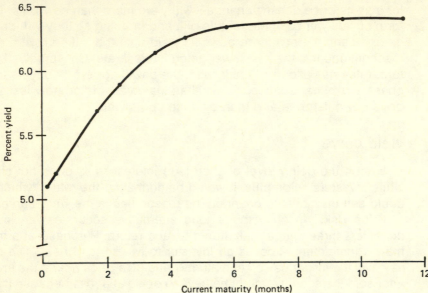

uary 6, 1978, there were many more bill issues outstanding than those quoted in Table 4–1. Had we plotted yields on all of these in Figure 4–2, we would have found that yield did not rise quite so consistently with maturity; the points plotted for some bill issues would have been some-what off a smooth yield curve. Yields may be out of line for various reasons. For example, a bill issue maturing around a tax date might be highly desired by investors who had big tax payments to make, and for this reason it might be bid to a yield that was relatively low compared with yields on surrounding issues.

While the yield curve for short maturities normally slopes upward, its shape and slope vary over time. Thus, it is difficult to pinpoint a "normal" spread between, say, 1-month and 6-month bills. Yield spreads between different securities are always measured in terms of basis points. *A basis point is 1/100 of 1 percentage point.* Thus, if 5-month bills are quoted at 5.25 and 6-month bills at 5.35, the spread between the two is said to be 10 basis points. A yield spread between two securities of 100 basis points would indicate a full 1 percent difference in their yields.

Yield realized on sales before maturity

If an investor buys 1-year bills at 6 percent and holds them to maturity, he will earn on a bank discount basis precisely 6 percent over the holding period. If alternatively he sells the bills before maturity, he will earn 6 percent over the holding period only if he sells at 6 percent, a relatively unlikely outcome. If he sells at a lower rate, he will get a higher price for his bills than he would have if he had sold them at 6 percent, and he will therefore earn more than 6 percent. If, on the other hand, he sells at a rate higher than 6 percent, he will earn something less than 6 percent.

The equivalent bond yield that an investor earns on bills purchased at one rate and subsequently sold at another can, assuming the holding period is less than 6 months, be calculated by using the formula

$$r = \frac{\text{Sales price} - \text{Purchase price}}{\text{Purchase price}} \div \frac{t}{365}$$

where t equals the number of days held. To illustrate, assume that an investor buys $1 million of 1-year bills at 6.00 percent and sells them 3 months later at 6.25 percent. His return over the period would be

$$r = \frac{\$952,604 - \$939,333}{\$939,333} \div \frac{91}{365} = 5.67\%$$

Bankers' acceptances and commercial paper

In talking about discount securities, we have focused on bills since they are the most important discount security traded in the money market. Everything we have said about yields on bills is, however, equally applicable to yields on BAs and commercial paper, both of which are sold on a discount basis with the discount being calculated on the basis of a 360-day year.

INTEREST-BEARING SECURITIES

The stock in trade of the money market includes, besides discount securities, a variety of *interest-bearing* instruments—Treasury and federal agency notes and bonds, municipal notes and bonds, and bank certificates of deposit. Notes, bonds, and other interest-bearing debt securities are all issued with a fixed *face value;* they mature at some specified date, and all carry a *coupon rate* which is the annual rate of interest that the issuer promises to pay the holder on the security's face value so long as the security is outstanding.

Some notes and bonds are issued in *registered* form; that is, the issuer keeps track of who owns its outstanding IOUs just as a corporation keeps track of who owns its common stock. Most notes and bonds, however, are issued in *bearer* form. To prove ownership of a bearer security, the owner must produce or bear it. An issuer with $50 million of bearer bonds outstanding does not know where to send interest when a payment date comes along. Consequently, such securities carry *coupons,* one for each interest date. When that date arrives, the investor or his bank clips the appropriate coupon from the security and sends it to the issuer's paying agent, who in turn makes the required payment.[3] Generally interest payments are made semiannually on coupon securities. Because notes and bonds carry coupons, the return paid on face value is called the *coupon rate,* or simply the *coupon.*

Notes and bonds with a short current maturity are referred to as *short coupons,* those with an intermediate current maturity (2–7 years) as *intermediate coupons,* and those with a still longer current maturity as *long coupons.*

CALL AND REFUNDING PROVISIONS

Once a bond issue is sold, the issuer might choose to redeem it early. For example, if interest rates fell, the borrower could reduce his interest costs by refunding his loan, that is, by paying off outstanding high-coupon bonds and issuing new lower-coupon bonds.

For the investor, early repayment on a bond is almost always disadvantageous because a bond issuer will rarely be tempted to repay early when interest rates are rising, a time when it would be to the bondholder's advantage to move funds out of the issuer's bonds into new higher-yielding bonds. On the other hand, early payment looks attractive to the issuer when interest rates are falling, a time when it is to the investor's advantage to keep funds invested in the issuer's high-coupon securities.

To protect investors making long-term commitments against frequent refundings by borrowers out to minimize interest costs, most bonds contain call and refunding provisions. A bond issue is said to be *callable* when the issuer has the option to repay part or all of the issue early by paying some specified redemption price to bondholders. Most bonds offer some call protection to the investor. Some are noncallable for life, others for some number of years after issue.

Besides call protection, many bonds offer refunding protection. Typically, long-term industrial bonds are immediately callable *but* offer 10 years of protection against calls for refunding. Such a bond is referred to as *callable except for refunding purposes.* If a bond offered refunding protection through 1985, that would be indicated on a dealer's quote sheet by the symbol NR85.

Call provisions usually specify that the issuer who calls a bond must pay the bondholder a price above face value. The *call premium* frequently equals the coupon rate on early calls and then diminishes to zero as the bond approaches maturity.

---

[3] The procedure is different on Treasury and agency securities, which are now being issued in book-entry form. See Chapter 13.

Price quotes

Note and bond prices are quoted in slightly different ways depending on whether they are selling in the new issue or the secondary market. When federal agency and municipal notes and bonds are first issued, the price at which they are offered to investors is normally quoted as a *percentage* of face value. To illustrate, the federal agency issues announced in Figure 4–3 were offered at a price of 100 percent, which means that the investor had to pay $100 for each $100 of face value. This

Figure 4–3
Pricing announcement for two federal agency issues

The Twelve Federal Land Banks

$925,000,000 7.50% Consolidated Bonds

| Series-H 1979 | CUSIP No. 901178 CE 1 |
| Dated January 23, 1978 | Due July 23, 1979 |

Interest payable July 23, 1978 and semi-annually thereafter

$449,800,000 8.20% Consolidated Bonds

| Series-A 1990 | CUSIP No. 901178 CF 8 |
| Dated January 23, 1978 | Due January 22, 1990 |

Interest payable July 22, 1978 and semi-annually thereafter

The Bonds are the secured joint and several obligations of The Twelve Federal Land Banks established in 1916 and are issued under the authority of the Farm Credit Act of 1971.

The Bonds are eligible for investment by National banks, State member banks of the Federal Reserve System, Federal credit unions, and Federal savings and loan associations. Under the laws of various States, including New York and Massachusetts, the Bonds are also legal investments for savings banks, trust companies and trust funds.

Price 100%

This offering is made by The Twelve Federal Land Banks through their Fiscal Agency, with the assistance of a nationwide Selling Group of recognized dealers in securities.

Fiscal Agency of the Federal Land Banks
90 William Street, New York, N.Y. 10038

Aubrey K. Johnson
Fiscal Agent

Gerald F. Kierce
Deputy Fiscal Agent

percentage price is often called the bond's *dollar price*. The first security described in Figure 4–3 carries a 7.50 percent coupon and was offered at par, so the actual yield it offered equaled the coupon rate. This is typical for agency new issues but not for municipal new issues.

Once a note or bond issue is distributed and trading in it moves to the secondary market, prices are also quoted on a percentage basis but always, depending on the security, in 32nds, 8ths, 4ths, or halves. Table 4–3 reproduces by way of illustration a few quotes on Treasury notes

Table 4–3
Quotations for selected U.S. Treasury notes, January 6, 1978

Amount outstanding ($ billions)	Coupon	Maturity	Bid	Asked	Yield to maturity	Yield value, $^1/_{32}$
2.5	6⅜	Jan. 31, 1978	99–31	100– 1	5.72	0.5250
2.9	5⅞	Jan. 31, 1979	98–24	98–28	6.99	0.0313
4.5	6½	Feb. 15, 1980	98–14	98–18	7.25	0.0164
2.7	5⅞	Dec. 31, 1980	96– 2	96– 8	7.32	0.0122
2.9	8⅛	Aug. 15, 1982	102– 0	102– 4	7.57	0.0081
2.0	7⅝	Nov. 15, 1987	98–18	98–22	7.82	0.0046

posted by a dealer on January 6, 1978. The first bid is 99–31, which means that this dealer was willing to pay 99^{31}/_{32}$, which equals $99.9687, per $100 of face value for that issue. The advantage of dollar pricing of notes and bonds is that it makes securities with different denominations directly comparable in price.

Treatment of interest in pricing

There's another wrinkle with respect to note and bond pricing. Typically interest on notes and bonds is paid semiannually to the holder on the coupon dates. This means that the value of a coupon security rises by the amount of interest accrued as a payment date approaches and falls thereafter by the amount of the payment made. Since notes and bonds are issued on every business day and consequently have coupon dates all over the calendar, the effect of accrued interest on the value of coupon securities would, if incorporated into the prices quoted by dealers, make meaningful price comparisons between different issues difficult. To get around this problem, the actual prices paid in the new issue and in secondary markets are always the quoted dollar price *plus* any accrued interest. For example, if an investor—3 months before a coupon date—bought $100,000 of 6 percent Treasury notes quoted at 100, he would pay $100,000 plus $1,500 of accrued interest:

$$\$100,000 + 0.5 \left[\frac{(0.06)(\$100,000)}{2} \right]$$

where (0.06)($100,000)/2 represents the $3,000 semiannual interest due on the notes.

FLUCTUATIONS IN A COUPON SECURITY'S PRICE

When a new note or bond issue comes to market, the coupon rate on it is, with certain exceptions, set so that it equals the yield prevailing in the market on securities of comparable maturity and risk. This permits the new security to be sold at a price equal or very nearly equal to par.

The price at which the security later trades in the secondary market will, like that of a discount security, fluctuate in response to changes in the general level of interest rates.

Yield to maturity

To illustrate, let's work through a simple example. Suppose a new 6-year note with an 8 percent coupon is issued at par. Six months later the Fed tightens, and the yield on comparable securities rises to 8.5 percent. Now what is this 8 percent security worth? Since the investor who pays a price equal to par for this "seasoned issue" is going to get only an 8 percent return, while 8.5 percent is available elsewhere, it is clear that the security must now sell at *less* than par.

To determine how much less, we have to introduce a new concept—*effective yield*. When an investor buys a coupon security at a *discount* and holds it to maturity, he receives a two-part return: the promised interest payment *plus* a capital gain. The capital gain arises because the security that the investor bought at a price below par is redeemed at maturity for full face value. The investor who buys a coupon issue at a *premium* and holds it to maturity also receives a two-part return: interest payments due plus a capital *loss* equal to the premium paid.

For dollars invested in a coupon issue that sells at a discount or premium, it is possible to calculate the overall or effective rate of return received, which is the rate that the investor earns on his dollars when both interest received *and* capital gains (or losses) are taken into account. Naturally, an investor choosing between securities of similar risk and maturity will do so, not on the basis of coupon rate, but on the basis of effective yield, referred to in the financial community as *yield to maturity*.

To get back to our example, it is clear that once rates rise to 8.5 percent in the open market, the security with an 8 percent coupon has to be priced at a discount sufficiently great so that its yield to maturity equals 8.5 percent. Figuring out how many dollars of discount this requires involves complicated calculations. Dealers used to use bond tables, but most have now switched to computers. Using either tool, one can determine in a few seconds that, with interest rates at 8.5 percent, a

$1,000 note with an 8 percent coupon and a 3½-year current maturity has to sell at $985.13 (a discount of $14.87) in order to yield 8.5 percent to maturity.

Current maturity and price volatility

A capital gain of $14.87, which is what the investor in our discounted 8 percent note would realize if he held it to maturity, will raise effective yield more, the faster this gain is realized (the shorter the current maturity of the security). Conversely, this capital gain will raise effective yield less, the more slowly it is realized (the longer the current maturity of the security).[1]

But if this is so, then a one-half percentage point rise in the yield on comparable securities will cause a much larger fall in price for a security with a long current maturity than for one with a short current maturity. In other words, the discount required to raise a coupon security's yield to maturity by one-half percentage point is *greater,* the *longer* the security's maturity.

By reversing the argument presented above, it is easy to see that, if 6 months after the 6-year 8 percent note in our example were issued, the yield on comparable securities *fell* to 7.5 percent, the value of this note would be driven to a *premium,* i.e., it would sell at a price above par. Note also that a one-half percentage point *fall* in the yield on comparable securities would force an outstanding higher-coupon security to a *greater* premium, the *longer* its current maturity was.

As these observations suggest, when prevailing interest rates change, prices of long coupons respond more dramatically than prices of short coupons. Figure 4–4 shows this sharp contrast. It pictures for a $1,000 note carrying an 8 percent coupon, the relationship between *current* maturity and the discount that would prevail if the yield on comparable securities rose to 8.5 percent or to 10 percent. It also plots the premium to which a $1,000 note with an 8 percent coupon would, depending on its current maturity, be driven if the yield on comparable securities fell to 6 percent.

Coupon and price volatility

The volatility of a note or bond's price in the face of changing interest rates also depends on its coupon; the *lower* the coupon, the *greater* the

---

[1] If you don't see this, just think—somewhat imprecisely—of the capital gain as a certain number of dollars of extra interest paid out in yearly installments to the investor as his security matures. Clearly the shorter the security's current maturity, the higher these extra annual interest installments will be, and consequently the higher the overall yield to the investor.

Figure 4–4
Premiums and discounts at which a $1,000 note with an
8 percent coupon would sell, depending on current
maturity, if market yields on comparable securities
were 6 percent, 8.5 percent, and 10 percent

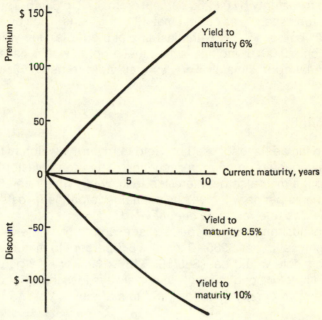

percentage change in price that will occur when rates rise or fall. To
illustrate, consider two notes with 4-year current maturities. Note A has
an 8 percent coupon and note B a 6 percent coupon. Both are priced to
yield 8 percent. Suppose now that interest rates on comparable securities rise to 10 percent (the big credit crunch arrives). Note A will fall in
price by $6.46; since it was initially priced at $100, that works out to a
6.46 percent fall in value. Note B's dollar price drops from $93.27 to
$87.07—a $6.20 fall, which equals a 6.64 percent loss of value. The
reason for the greater percentage fall in the price of the low-coupon note
is that capital appreciation represents a greater proportion of promised
income (capital appreciation plus coupon interest) on the low coupon
than on the high coupon. Therefore, for the low-coupon note's yield to
maturity to rise two percentage points, its price has to fall relatively *more*
than that of the high-coupon note.

Prices of government and federal agency securities are quoted in
32nds. The greater the change in yield to maturity that results from a
price change of $1/32$, the less volatile the issue's price will be in the face
of changing interest rates. As a result, dealers include on their quote

sheets for such securities a column titled *Yield value* of $1/32$. Looking back at Table 4–3, we see that the yield value of $1/32$ on Treasury notes maturing on January 31, 1978, was 0.5250, which means that a fall in the asked price on this security from 100– 1 to 100 (a $1/32$ fall) would have raised yield to maturity by 0.5250 percent, from 5.72 to 6.245. The yield value of $1/32$ drops sharply as current maturity lengthens. Thus on notes maturing on November 15, 1987 (the last line of the table), the yield value of $1/32$ was only 0.0046, indicating that these notes would have had to fall in value by approximately $114/32$ for their yield to rise 0.5250 percent.

Current yield

So far we have focused on yield to maturity, which is the yield figure always quoted on coupon securities. When the investor buys a note or bond, he may also be interested in knowing what rate of return interest payments per se will give him on the principal he invests. This measure of yield is referred to as *current yield*.

To illustrate, consider our earlier example of a note with an 8 percent coupon selling at $985.13 to yield 8.5 percent to maturity. Current yield on this note would be: ($80/$985.13) × 100, or 8.12 percent. On a discount note or bond, current yield is always less than yield to maturity; on a premium bond it exceeds yield to maturity.

THE YIELD CURVE

From the examples we have worked through, it is clear that investors in notes and bonds expose themselves, like buyers of discount securities, to a *price risk*. Moreover, even though longer-term rates fluctuate less violently than short-term rates (Figure 4–5), the price risk associated with holding debt securities tends to be greater the longer their current maturity. Thus one would expect the yield curve to slope upward over the full maturity spectrum. And most of the times it does.

Price risk, however, is not the only factor affecting the shape of the yield curve. Borrowers' and investors' *expectations* with respect to future interest rates are also an important—at times dominant—factor.

If the general expectation is that interest rates are going to rise, investors will seek to keep their money in short coupons to avoid getting locked into low-yield long coupons. Borrowers, on the other hand, will try to lengthen the maturity of their outstanding debt in order to lock in prevailing low rates for as long as possible. Both responses tend to force short-term rates down and long-term rates up, thereby accentuating the

Figure 4–5
Short-term rates are more volatile than long-term rates

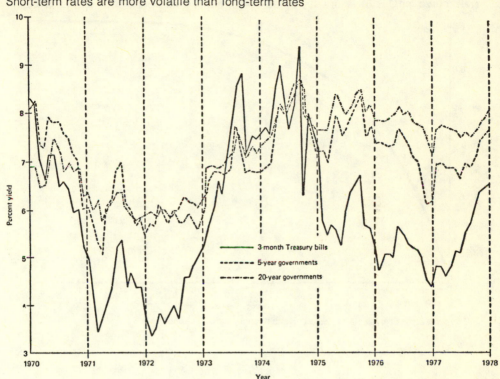

upward slope of the yield curve. The expectation that interest rates would rise was widespread in August 1975, the time of the yield curve pictured in Figure 4–6; this expectation explains in part why the yield curve sloped so steeply upward.

People, of course, may expect interest rates to fall. When this is the case, investors respond by buying long coupons in the hope of locking in a high yield. In contrast, borrowers are willing to pay extremely high short-term rates while they wait for long rates to fall so that they can borrow long-term more cheaply. The net result of both responses is that, when interest rates are expected to fall, the normal yield curve (or at least some part of it) may be *inverted,* with short-term rates above long-term rates. Figure 4–7 pictures the yield curve in the late summer of 1974, when people anticipated a fall in rates. Note that after a current maturity of 5 months, the slope of this curve becomes sharply negative.

If, inspired by our yield curves, you start pouring over dealer quote

Figure 4–6
Yield curve for U.S. Treasury securities—bills, notes, and bonds (August 19, 1975)

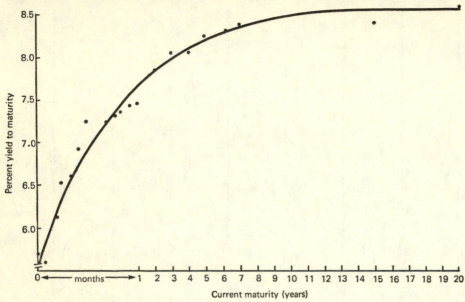

Dots represent observed yields; yield curve is fitted to them.

sheets on governments, you are bound to discover some out-of-line yields. The reasons are varied.[5] For one thing sale of a large new issue may cause a temporary upward bulge in the yield curve in the maturity range of the new issue. Also a security with an out-of-line yield may have some special characteristic. Some government bonds (*flower bonds* to the street) are acceptable at par in payment of federal estate taxes when owned by the decedent at the time of death. These bonds, which all currently sell at substantial discounts, have yields to maturity much lower than those on straight government bonds.

In calculating the yield on discount securities, we found that a considerable discrepancy exists between yield measured on a bank discount basis and equivalent bond yield. There are also numerous discrepancies—albeit smaller ones—between the ways that interest is measured and quoted on different interest-bearing securities. For example, interest on Treasury notes is calculated for actual days on the basis of a 365-day year, while interest on CDs is calculated for actual days on

[5] One trivial reason may be a mistake in the quote sheet. These are typically compiled daily in great haste with the result that errors creep in. For this reason, such sheets often carry a footnote stating that the quotes are believed to be reliable but are not "guaranteed."

Figure 4–7
Yield curve for U.S. Treasury securities—bills, notes, and bonds (August 30, 1974)

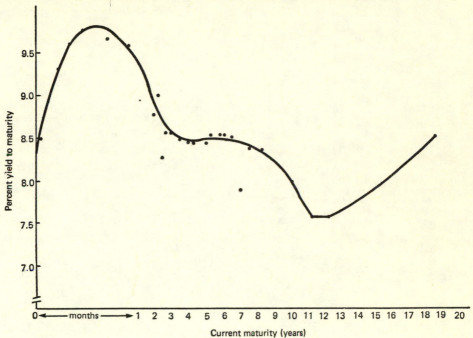

the basis of a 360-day year. Thus a 1-year CD issued at 6 percent would yield a higher return than a 6 percent year note selling at par. Partially offsetting this advantage, however, is the fact that a 1-year CD would pay interest only at maturity, while the year note would pay it semiannually. This disadvantage disappears, however, on CDs with a maturity longer than 1 year, since such CDs pay interest semiannually.

Another discrepancy: When government notes and bonds are sold, accrued interest is calculated between coupon dates on the basis of actual days passed since a coupon date, while on agency securities it accrues as if every month had 30 days. Thus agency securities accrue, for example, no interest on October 31, but they do accrue interest on February 30!

These and the many other minor discrepancies that exist among yields on interest-bearing securities have little importance for understanding the workings of the money market, but they are important to the portfolio manager out to maximize return.[6]

[6] For a discussion of how yields on different money market instruments can be restated on a comparable basis, see the Appendix at the end of the book.

Part II

The major players

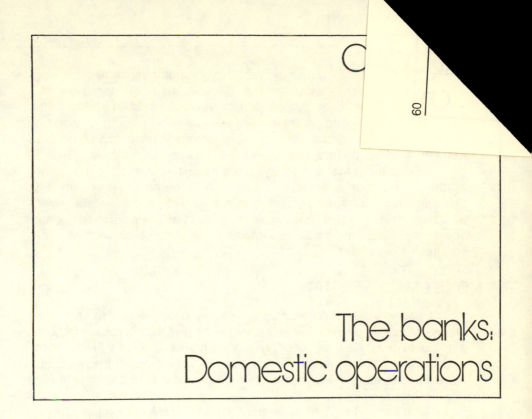

The banks:
Domestic operations

THERE ARE VARIOUS PEOPLE, including bankers, who have an image problem. The first "crime" bankers are widely charged with is creating a situation in which interest rates range from high to damnably high. Their second alleged "crime" is that they periodically threaten the whole economy by acting so irresponsibly that some of them end up having problems or, worse still, failing.

Both charges reflect the following serious misconceptions entertained by much of the public and more than a few politicians. First, low interest rates are always good for the economy. Second, it is bankers, not the Fed, that set the general level of short-term interest rates. Third, banking is riskless or, alternatively, riskless banking is what the country needs. Fourth, the Fed would permit or might not be able to avoid the failure of one or more major banks, which would indeed wreak economic havoc. None of these misconceptions is easy to correct; hence, bankers' rather intractable image problem. To be a banker is to be neither widely understood nor loved. It is not, however, to be unimportant. In the money market, in particular, bankers are players of such major importance that any serious discussion of the various markets that comprise the money market has to be prefaced with a careful look at banking.

59

In the United States, unlike in most foreign countries, bank branching has always been severely restricted. Because bank charters were initially granted only by the states, banks have never been permitted to branch interstate, and in most states—California being a notable exception—even intrastate branching is severely restricted or prohibited. As a result there are in the United States currently over 14,000 banks. Comparing the largest and the smallest, one might almost conclude that the most they have in common is the name *bank*. Actually that's extreme; all institutions called banks accept deposits, make loans, and have at least a few government securities on their balance sheets. There, however, the similarity between the largest banks and their smaller sisters ends.

A MONEY MARKET BANK

The nation's largest banks, true giants, are often referred to as *money market* or *money center banks*. The term *money market bank* is apropos, since activity in every sector of the money market is strongly influenced and in some cases even dominated by the operations of these institutions. Thus to understand the money market, one has to begin by studying the great banks.

While it's easy to talk about a money market bank, it is not so easy to list just which banks are included in this category. The property of being a money market bank is like liquidity, something measured in degrees. Certainly all of the nation's top ten banks are important money market banks. As one goes further down the list of U.S. banks ranked by size, one continues to find banks that are active in some if not all sectors of the money market, but the smaller a bank's size and the narrower its range of activities, the smaller the likely impact of those activities. At some point as bank size diminishes, one encounters what is clearly a regional bank of secondary importance as opposed to a money market bank of primary importance. The Wachovia Bank and Trust Company, the 30th largest bank in the country, is big and important; it's also clearly not in the same class as the Chase Manhattan, the third largest bank.

The activities of a money market bank encompass several separate but related businesses. All money market banks engage in traditional banking operations: lending, managing an investment portfolio, and running a trust department. In addition, a number act as dealers in government securities and as dealers in and underwriters of municipal securities, and several have extensive operations for clearing money market trades for nonbank dealers. A final important activity in which major banks engage is foreign operations. Banks operate abroad in two ways. They participate as lenders and borrowers in the broad international capital market known as the *Euromarket;* also they operate within the confines of other national capital markets, accepting deposits and making loans in local currency.

Of the various banking activities we have described, two—trust operations and clearing operations per se as opposed to granting dealer loans—could be described as largely off-balance-sheet profit centers. Both require capital in the form of space and equipment but do not require substantial funding from the bank. The trust department invests other people's money and the clearing operation provides a service. In contrast, the banks' three other primary domestic activities—lending, running a portfolio, and dealing in securities—have to be funded, since each involves acquiring substantial assets.

To finance its operations, a money market bank draws funds from various sources. It starts with a fairly stable base of money—bank capital and the demand, savings, and small-denomination time deposits it receives in the normal course of its commercial banking activities. The total of these is typically far below the value of the assets the bank wants to finance, so there is a funding gap that the bank fills by buying money in the Federal funds market, the CD market, the RP market, and at times the Euromarket.[1]

As the above suggests, managing a money market bank involves a host of decisions concerning what assets to hold and what liabilities to incur. Before we say more about these, two comments are in order. First, one cannot separate a bank's domestic operations from its foreign operations. But we are going to try—treating domestic operations in this chapter and Euro operations in the next. The reason for this is that the Euromarket is a fascinating and complex story that deserves a full chapter. Second, money market banks are, as indicated by Table 5–1, a disparate collection of animals. Some of their differences reflect differences in circumstances: the Bank of America (B of A) with more than 1,000 domestic branches is deposit rich; the Morgan with four domestic branches is, like most money market banks, deposit poor. Other differences reflect variations in historical patterns of development, areas of specialization, and management philosophy.

Profit and risk

However heterogeneous the nation's largest banks may be, there still are strong similarities in the way that top management in these banks view and attack the problem of managing a large bank. First, their objective is, like that of management in any industrial, manufacturing, or other business concern, to earn *profits*. Second, banks, like nonbank firms, operate under uncertainty and thus face *risk*. Risk in banking arises from

---

[1] See Chapter 3 for an introduction to these markets and the instruments traded in them.

Table 5-1
The top ten U.S. banks, beginning of 1978

	Total deposits		Capital funds ($ millions)	Net income ($ millions)	Total loans ($ millions)	Securities holdings ($ millions)
Bank	$ millions	% foreign				
1. Bank of America	67,242	44.0	3,231	402.5	41,619	10,169
2. Citibank	56,455	66.1	3,291	371.7	43,886	5,259
3. Chase Manhattan Bank	43,829	52.3	2,465	154.7	35,021	3,832
4. Manufacturers Hanover						
Trust Company	29,502	34.6	1,445	138.4	18,314	2,106
5. Morgan Guaranty Trust Company......	23,841	51.1	1,724	211.0	15,684	3,011
6. Chemical Bank	23,215	43.8	1,509	108.5	15,539	4,732
7. Continental Illinois National						
Bank and Trust Company	18,430	45.2	1,102	139.4	14,627	2,737
8. First National Bank of Chicago	17,075	44.1	937	108.4	12,299	2,790
9. Bankers Trust Company.............	16,685	44.1	955	58.4	11,860	1,130
10. Security Pacific National Bank.......	14,890	20.8	848	101.7	11,704	1,903

Source: Bank: Data through 12/31/77, A. G. Becker & Co., Incorporated.

several sources. On every loan a bank makes there is a *credit risk,* that is, the risk that the borrower won't pay back the money lent. On loans made at a fixed rate for some period of time, *fixed-rate term loans,* there is also the risk that the cost of funding might escalate during the term of the loan; that could be called a *rate risk.* The banker also faces a substantial *price risk* as a result of his portfolio and dealer operations. Finally, there is the *liquidity risk,* which is really the risk of illiquidity. Every money market bank is to some extent borrowing short and lending long. The liquidity risk is the danger that the availability of the short-dated (short-term) funds the bank is continually buying might be sharply curtailed.

Because any attempt by a banker to make profits involves risks, his objective inevitably becomes *to maximize profits subject to the constraint that perceived risks be held to some acceptable level.* Also since bank analysts, investors, and bank depositors all focus strongly on current income, bankers have a strong predilection for an earnings pattern that displays steady growth over time.

MANAGING A MONEY MARKET BANK

Economists' favorite term, *decision variable,* denotes something having a value that is the result of a conscious decision. *Exogenous variables,* in contrast, are things having a value that is more or less thrust on the decision maker by the outside world. On a bank's balance sheet, in the short run at least, there are both sorts of variables. Let's start with the exogenous ones.

Every bank establishes credit standards to limit credit risk. Once it has done this, a bank will normally do everything possible to meet the legitimate loan demands of any customer who meets these standards. Loans are a key source of bank profits, and loan customers normally provide a bank with deposits and other business as well. The quantity of loans demanded from a bank depends largely on the state of the economy and on what funds are available to would-be borrowers from other sources. These factors are beyond the control of the banks, so their loan volume is very much an exogenous variable. Bankers can wish they had more loans but they can't decide to have them if demand for bank loans is weak.

In the short run, bank capital is also an exogenous variable, having a value that depends on past decisions. A third variable that is largely exogenous in the short run is the sum of demand deposits, savings deposits, and small-denomination time deposits received by the bank. Over time a bank will have built up a customer base that supplies it with a fairly stable amount of such deposits. To significantly enlarge that base would take time and effort. A final important exogenous variable from the point of view of a bank is the reserves against deposits that it must keep with the Fed.

From a bank's viewpoint, the decision variables it faces in the short run are the size and composition of its investment portfolio, the dealer position it assumes, and the quantities and maturities of the monies it buys in the Fed funds market, the RP market, the CD market, and at times the Euromarket.

In assigning values to these decision variables, the bank is determining in part what asset portfolio it will hold and how it will fund that portfolio. In other words, it is choosing a balance sheet that meets its goal of maximizing return subject to the constraint that perceived risks be held at an acceptable level.

Several facts of life are of crucial importance for the bank in making these balance sheet choices. One is that buying money is going to be a continuing way of life for a money market bank. Capital plus what we called *exogenous deposits* minus whatever reserves have to be held against such deposits are available to a bank for funding loans. However, since money market banks as a group tend to be deposit poor, it is not unusual for these sources of funds to be insufficient to cover loans, not to speak of funding a securities portfolio and a dealer position.

Thus a second crucial fact of life for a money market bank is that it must have the preservation of liquidity as a concern of overriding importance. Here, by liquidity we mean the bank's ability to acquire money whenever it is needed in huge and highly variable sums. Since the principal, in fact almost the only, source of liquidity a money market bank has is its ability to buy money, maintaining access to its markets for bought money—RP to CD—becomes the *sine qua non* for the continued operation of such a bank.

A third fact of life facing a bank is the yield curve. As noted in Chapter 4, money market and bond yields are normally higher the longer the maturity of an instrument except when a downturn in interest rates is anticipated. This means, as any banker knows, that one path to profits and prosperity, at least 90 + percent of the time, is acquiring assets with maturities that are longer than those of the liabilities used to fund them—*borrowing short and lending long.* A Euro banker would call this running a *mis-matched* or *short book*. It contrasts with running a *matched book*—that is, funding every asset acquired with a liability of identical maturity.

Asset and funding choices

The facts of life we have just discussed influence in a profound way the asset and funding choices bankers make. Let's look first at loans. When loan demand increases, the shape of the yield curve tempts bankers to fund those extra loans by buying the shortest-dated money they can. Yet bankers rarely do so except for short periods of time when they are waiting to see if the increase in loans is going to be sustained. One reason is that regulators would frown on such a policy. A second and more important consideration is that funding loans with overnight money on a large scale would conflict with the bank's need for continued liquidity. As banker after banker will note: "If we tried to finance a big increase in loans by suddenly buying a lot more overnight money, that would be immediately visible in the market and later visible in our published statements. People, particularly suppliers of funds, would begin to question why we were getting out of line with 'safe practices' [roughly the average of what other banks are doing] and our ability to continue to buy money might be impaired. That is something we could not allow to happen." The upshot of all this concern is that bankers tend to fund loan increases largely through the purchase of additional CD money, 30 days and longer.

A bank's securities portfolio is a very different breed of animal from its loan portfolio with respect to conditions of both acquisition and funding. On the funding side, the principal difference is that under present Fed regulations a bank can finance its holdings of governments and agencies in the RP market (by selling them under an agreement to repurchase on an overnight or longer basis) without incurring any reserve requirement.

Money market banks acquire portfolios of government securities for various reasons. First, there is a cosmetic motive. Traditionally *all* banks held governments for liquidity; as a result even today a money market bank that had no governments on its balance sheet would raise eyebrows. Second, some money market banks that are dealers in government securities seem to feel that it would be awkward for them to sell governments if they did not themselves maintain large holdings of such securities. Third and most important, money market banks hold governments, sometimes *very* large amounts, for profit. When economic growth slackens and interest rates are low or falling, money market banks tend to increase their holdings of governments because at such times governments can be financed at an attractive positive spread in the RP market.[2] The trick of course in a hold-bonds-for-profit strategy is not to be holding too many when interest rates start their next cyclical upswing and bond prices begin to fall as financing costs rise.

Bankers feel quite comfortable financing a large proportion of their government portfolios on an overnight basis because government securities, unlike loans, are highly liquid and the banks can and sometimes

---

[2] The *financing spread* is said to be *positive* if the cost of the funds borrowed is less than the yield on the securities financed.

do sell off large amounts of such securities over short periods. Consequently long-term funding of the portfolio, besides being expensive, is neither needed nor necessarily appropriate.

To the extent possible, banks use the RP market rather than the Fed funds market for funding their portfolios. Generally overnight RP money is cheaper than overnight Fed funds. Also the RP market, unlike the Fed funds market, is an anonymous market in the sense that no other banks or brokers are tracking how much a given bank borrows there. Thus a bank can make substantial use of the RP market without impairing its liquidity.

Money market banks, like other banks, also hold portfolios of municipal securities. The principal advantage of such securities is that interest income on them is tax exempt. How large a portfolio of *munis* a given bank holds is thus largely a function of its effective tax rate. The disadvantage of municipals are that they can't be *RPed* (financed in the RP market) but instead have to be financed with Fed funds or other monies.

Many money market banks act as dealers in government and municipal securities. Since a dealer by definition acts as a principal in all transactions, buying and selling for its own account, a bank running a dealer operation inevitably assumes both long and short securities positions. Bank dealerships also acquire securities holdings, at times quite large ones, because they are positioning for profit. Banks finance their dealer positions in governments and munis in the same way they finance their investment portfolios.

Mismatching the book

Earlier we said that banks have to be concerned with rate risk and liquidity risk. Matching asset and liability maturities to the extent possible would appear to be a way for a bank to limit both risks. However, it's impossible to find a banker who professes to follow this strategy. One reason is that it would be difficult if not impossible for a bank to do so. Few, if any, assets on a bank's balance sheet have a definite maturity. A 10-year bond or a 2-year note in the bank's portfolio might be sold tomorrow. Term loans are often prepaid, and 3-month loans are frequently rolled (renewed). Also, the latter are often made at a floating rate so that funding 3-month loans with 3-month money would not lock in a specific spread between the bank's borrowing and lending rates; instead of eliminating rate risk, it would create it. On the liability side of the balance sheet, many items have specific maturities—RPs, CDs, Fed funds purchased—but a question arises as to how to view demand deposits. Technically, demand deposits can be withdrawn at any time, but in practice demand deposits in the aggregate provide a bank with a quite stable source of funds. Besides being impractical, any attempt to match asset and liability maturities would be expensive to a bank because lending long and borrowing short is a potential source of bank profits.

All bankers profess to follow the *pool* concept of funding; instead of matching specific assets against specific liabilities, they think of all the funds raised by the bank as a pool that in the aggregate finances the bank's assets. In the next breath, of course, the same bankers will say that they RP their governments and meet increases in loans with the sale of CDs. What is really going on?

The bank typically sets up some sort of high-level committee, which, besides making general decisions about what sorts of assets the bank should acquire, attempts to measure in some fashion, however arbitrary, the average maturity of the bank's assets and liabilities, and thereby the implicit mismatch in the bank's overall position. The committee's objective is to profit from this maturity mismatch while also monitoring its size so that the mismatch never grows so large as to endanger the bank's liquidity or expose it to an undue rate risk. Under an approach of this sort, big increases in loans inevitably end up calling for the bank to write more CDs, while an increase in Treasury bill holdings can comfortably be accommodated by increased borrowings of overnight money.

To this rough generalization several comments should be added. First, banks don't just react to current conditions. Management is constantly attempting to predict what the future will bring and to position itself so as to maximize future earnings. In particular, banks are constantly forecasting loan demand, deposits, and interest rates. On the basis of such forecasts, a bank might, for example, decide to issue more CDs than normally because it expects interest rates and loan demand to rise sharply. Or it might decide to rely more heavily on Fed funds purchased than normally because it expects loan demand and interest rates to fall. Interest rate forecasts also strongly influence the bank's decision about the size and maturity distribution of the portfolio and dealer positions it will carry.

The brief picture we have just presented of management of a big bank leaves a lot unsaid. The rest of the chapter attempts to fill in some of the missing subtleties. Also, banks are active in every market we describe, so they will be with us throughout the rest of the book.

BANK LENDING

Money market banks, like other banks, extend credit to consumers and make home mortgage and other real estate loans. However, the largest proportion of their domestic lending is to commercial and industrial (C&I) customers. C&I loans are granted by banks at the prime rate to top credits and at prime plus some markup to weaker credits. Borrowers are normally required to keep a percentage of loan proceeds, anywhere from 10 to 20 percent, on deposit as a *compensating balance* with the lending bank. Customers who choose not to hold compensating balances are charged a higher rate. The C&I sector of bank lending is of special importance to a discussion of the money market because bank C&I loans are highly volatile, and whether the volume of them is up or down is a crucial factor in determining the stance banks take in the money market.

Over the last 40 years the environment in which banks operate has been subject to constant, sometimes dramatic change. One result is that banks have had to continually alter their lending practices, searching for areas in which they have a real and potentially profitable role to play in supplying credit.

Before World War II much bank commercial lending was short term. Firms in wholesale trade and commodities needed financing, often on a seasonal basis, to fill their warehouses; and their bank supplied it. The normal arrangement was that the bank would look over the customer's books once a year and decide how large a line of credit it was willing to grant this firm. The firm could then borrow during the year any sum up to that amount, provided no material change occurred in its circumstances after the line was granted. The customer paid for its line with compensating balances, borrowed as necessary on the basis of 90-day notes, and was expected to give the bank a *clean up* (pay off all its borrowings) at some time during the year.

When World War II came along, the situation changed. Defense contractors had to invest huge sums of money in new plant and equipment. They could have financed these investments through the sale of long-term bonds, the traditional approach, but that seemed inappropriate. First, they didn't expect the war to continue forever. Second, they believed they could pay for their new plant and equipment rapidly because they had a customer, Uncle Sam, who was sure to pay and because they could depreciate their plant and equipment at an accelerated rate. So they asked the banks for term loans. The banks provided such credits with amortization built in, and while criticized at the time for doing so, they ended up successfully entering the area of medium-term commercial lending.

After the war, borrowers who had become accustomed to 5-year credits decided to try for more flexibility. On a term loan they didn't always want to have to take down all the money right away; also they wanted the right to prepay some or all of their loan if their cash flow improved seasonally or permanently. So bankers said, "Alright that's a revolving credit. You can have it, but at some point, you'll have to give us a clean up." The final step in this evolutionary trend came when the customer said to his bank: "I am not sure I will ever need to borrow from you, but I want to know that I can if I need to, not just now but for some number of years." In response bankers developed a *revolving line of credit;* the customer paid balances *plus a commitment fee;* in exchange for the latter, the bank promised to honor the line for the life of the agreement. A customer could turn such a *revolver* into a term loan simply by borrowing.

Rate risk

From the beginning of World War II until 1951, the Fed pegged yields on government bonds, and interest rates did not move much. Then in 1951, after considerable infighting, the Treasury agreed that the Fed should be permitted to pursue an independent monetary policy.[3] This Treasury-Fed accord spelled the end of rate pegging, and interest rates began a secular climb punctuated with periodic ups and downs. The pace of this climb was, however, slow. As a result bankers rarely changed the prime rate that they charged their best customers and they felt safe lending at a fixed rate not only on 90-day notes but also on term loans; the rate risk in both sorts of lending seemed small. Then, as Figure 5–1 shows, things changed. Inflation became a problem, and to fight it, the Fed pushed up interest rates sharply and rapidly on a number of occasions starting in the mid-1960s.

The banks felt the impact of the initial credit crunch largely in terms of opportunity cost. At that point they were not buying huge amounts of money, so tight money did not dramatically increase their cost of funding. It did mean, however, that funds locked up in old low-interest term loans could not be lent out at the higher rates currently prevailing. Later, as the banks began to rely more and more on bought money, tight money did significantly increase their cost of funding; and the rate risk implied in fixed-rate lending became more pronounced.

To minimize this risk, banks changed their lending practices. They began adjusting the prime rate more frequently, and they started altering the rate on existing as well as on new short-term loans whenever the prime rate changed. They also made it a rule to put term loans on a floating-rate basis. The rule, of course, was not and is not always followed. As one executive noted: "We bankers are not as smart as we could be. When rates get near the peak and we ought to be making fixed-rate term loans, we shy away from doing so. Then when loan demand and lending rates decline and we are out scrambling for loans, we are tempted to make fixed-rate term loans at just the time when we shouldn't." Actually even fixed-rate term loans made during periods of high interest rates are not always as advantageous to banks as one might suppose. Once rates decline, the borrower of such money is likely

---

[3] See page 182.

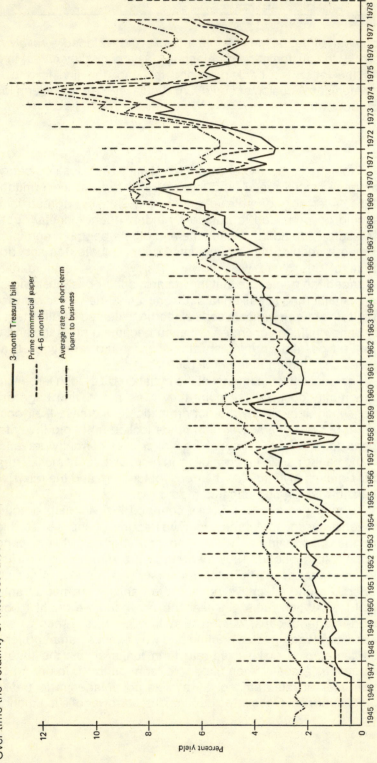

Figure 5-1
Over time the volatility of interest rates has increased

to say to his banker, "You're my banker and you know that the best thing for me would be to refinance this loan in the bond market or on other terms," and typically the banker lets the borrower do so without a penalty, regardless of whether the loan agreement calls for one. On variable-rate term loans, the rate charged generally goes to an increasing spread above the prime rate during the latter years of the loan. This maturity spread is supposed to compensate the banker for his long-term commitment, but he rarely earns it because of prepayment or renegotiation.

To some extent bankers tend to think of their special niche in commercial and industrial lending today as being providers of flexible medium-term financing. Also the money they provide is "warm" money in the sense that the lending arrangement is not only open to negotiation initially but also subject to renegotiation should the borrower's position change.

While banks have done much to increase the attractiveness of bank loans, it is also true that by moving to floating-rate loans, they have shifted much of the rate risk involved in lending from their own shoulders to those of the borrower. This may, depending on borrowers' risk preferences and rate views, make bank loans appear less attractive and thereby slow the growth of bank lending.

The prime rate, although viewed by some as a collusive price-fixing device, has always been responsive to open-market conditions. A fall in open-market rates attracts bank customers to the open market and to other nonbank financing sources, and thus puts pressure on the banks to lower the prime, whereas a rise in open-market rates increases the cost of bank funding and the demand for bank loans, and so tends to do the opposite.

When the Fed tightens credit, the resulting increases in the prime rate, particularly if they are frequent and sharp, make bankers unpopular with politicians and the public. So gradually bankers have moved away from what appeared to be an arbitrarily set prime to one that is based on money market rates and fluctuates up and down with them. Citibank began the trend in 1971 by linking its prime to the 90-day commercial paper rate. Specifically Citi said that henceforth it would set its prime at the 90-day paper rate plus a spread, which has fluctuated from as little as 1/8 to as much as 1½ percentage points.

While pricing loans at a flexible prime was supposed to eliminate a bank's rate risk on loans by tying its lending rate to its cost of funds, banks still encounter difficulties during periods of very tight money. In the United States, as in many other countries, the prime rate has been so politicized that at times it becomes impossible for the banks to raise it further. This happened, for example, in 1974. During such periods banks can and have found themselves forced to make new loans at rates *below* their marginal cost of funds, that is, at rates below the cost of the extra money they had to buy to fund these loans.

Competition from commercial paper

For the commercial or industrial firm in need of short-term financing, the sale of commercial paper has always been an alternative to and competitive with short-term bank loans. In recent years, however, the volume of such paper outstanding has risen so rapidly that it seems to throw into question the banks' traditional role as suppliers of short-term finance, at least to all but their smaller and less creditworthy customers. One reason is that, except in times when political pressures hold the prime rate artificially low, commercial paper rates are consistently lower than bank lending rates (see Figure 5–1). Another factor is that in recent years the commercial paper market has matured; distribution facilities have improved and a growing number of investors have been attracted to the market—all of which makes it possible for more firms to borrow there and for them to borrow larger amounts.

Ironically the banks fostered the development of the commercial paper market by granting issuers backup lines of credit for their paper. Specifically the banks promised in exchange for balances and/or fees to provide commercial paper issuers with money should they encounter difficulties in rolling their paper.[4] This commitment gave the issuers the liquidity required to make their paper salable.

At this point there seems to be little the banks can do to recapture the business that has moved to the commercial paper market. Reserve requirements, by forcing the banks to buy more funds than they can lend, impose what amounts to a substantial tax on banking. Because of this tax, banks would be hard put to meet commercial paper rates even if they were willing to buy money and lend it out on a break-even basis. Another problem banks face is that most commercial paper has a maturity at issue of 30 days or less. The banks' prime rate in contrast is keyed off normally higher 90-day money market rates. To really compete with commercial paper, banks would have to institute a range of primes: the one-week prime, the two-week prime, etc. They could do this, but they have not so far. One reason is the difficulty this would cause because of the huge number of loans outstanding that have been priced in terms of "prime" without specifying which maturity prime was meant. Another reason banks have not instituted multiple prime rates is the fear that doing so would decrease their revenue from loans without adding significantly to loan volume.

In 1977 the Morgan Bank initiated a program under which it offered to

---

[4] To *roll* paper means to repay maturing paper by selling new paper.

lend funds to commercial paper issuers who had purchased backup lines from it for very short periods at a cost only marginally above the Fed funds rate. A bank can make loans of this sort without incurring much of a rate risk, but if it made a large volume of them, it would impair its capital ratios to earn a small profit. Thus lending of this sort is unlikely to displace much borrowing in the commercial paper market. It may, however, give a bank offering such loans a competitive edge in selling other bank services to paper issuers. Since the Morgan began its program, several other banks have followed its lead and also started to offer commercial paper issuers special adjustment facilities.

Bankers' acceptances

The closest banks come to competing directly with the commercial paper market is by issuing loans in the form of bankers' acceptances. On certain types of transactions—financing exports, imports, and the storage and shipment of goods at home and abroad—the bank can take the borrower's note, accept it (guarantee payment at maturity), and then sell it in the open market without incurring a reserve requirement. The interest rate charged the borrower is determined by rates prevailing in the bankers' acceptance market. These are normally less than commercial paper rates, but the banks' standard acceptance fee is 1.5 percent, so the *all-in cost* to the BA borrower exceeds rates on commercial paper.[5] When loan demand is high, bankers normally sell the BAs they originate and take their spread, but when loan demand is slack, they may hold them as earning assets.

The real dilemma

While periods when loan demand is slack leave bankers feeling less than prosperous, some of the most difficult problems with respect to bank lending arises when money is tight. By accepting deposits from a firm and by building a customer relationship with it, a bank makes an often unwritten but nevertheless real commitment to lend to that firm when the latter needs funds. The bank, however, does not know when that need will occur or how large it will be. It can only be sure that the tighter money gets, the more loan seekers it will have on its doorstep. To compound this problem, the one time that commercial paper issuers are likely to want to come or be forced to the banks for money is when money is tight. Thus a question arises as to whether banks will be able to honor all their written and unwritten commitments to lend when money

---

[5] As noted in Chapter 18, there is in practice a lot of variation in the acceptance fees charged by banks.

tightens. Also, if they do honor them, will they be thwarting Fed policy by raising their lending at a time when the Fed is trying to contain overall bank lending?

Leasing

Banks and bank holding companies entered the leasing business in the early 1960s. It was a natural adjunct to their normal lending activities since a financial lease is the functional equivalent of a loan; under it the lessee is obligated to make a stream of payments to the lessor, the amount of which equals or exceeds the price of the asset leased.

Leasing has attractions to a bank. First, because a bank can take advantage of the investment tax credit and of accelerated depreciation on equipment it leases, leasing provides a tax shelter that permits the bank to *defer* taxes on current income. Second, leasing gives a bank protection against inflation; presumably the higher the rate of inflation, the greater the scrap value of the items leased will be at the end of the lease period.

Because many lease agreements entered into by banks run for years, sometimes even several decades, a natural question is how banks control the rate risk that would seem to be inherent in making such indirect long-term loans. The answer varies with the segment of the market considered.

The leasing of small-ticket, short-lived items—autos, postage meters, and others—is normally not tax-shelter oriented, and the rates charged are high, 10–15 percent. Even if allowance is made for the fact that some part of these high rates is compensation for the credit risks assumed, the rates are still sufficiently high, history suggests, to protect a bank's spread between its lending and borrowing rates.

In leasing big-ticket items, tax considerations are often of paramount importance. There are firms, not necessarily weak credits, that have such tremendous capital needs that they exhaust the tax benefits available to them under the investment tax credit and through accelerated depreciation before they make all the investments they require. If a bank that has taxable income leases equipment to such a firm, it can take advantage of tax benefits that the firm itself could not take on investment in the leased equipment.

Maturities on big-ticket, tax-oriented leases may run from 7 years on a computer to 25 years on a utility plant or oil loading dock. Such lease agreements always contain a clause that requires the lessees to pay a substantial penalty if they break the lease. Surprisingly a bank has little funding exposure on very long-term leases. The reason is that most leases are *leveraged leases*. The bank puts up 20 percent or more of the money required, enough to get the total tax benefits available; it then borrows the remaining funds required on a long-term basis from, say, an insurance company that has long-term funds available but, because of its low marginal tax rate, would not get the same tax benefits as a bank does from having the leased asset on its books. On a leveraged lease the bank's funding exposure lasts only 3 to 5 years. After that the rentals collected are used to repay the money borrowed and to build up a fund from which the taxes that the lease arrangement defers are eventually paid.

Balance sheet figures are very misleading with respect to the importance of leasing to a bank or bank holding company. Only the lessor's equity in the item leased shows up as an asset, and in the case of leveraged leases, this equity drops to zero in a few years. However, the assets are still there; and even if the impact of leasing on the balance sheet is minimal, it may have a substantial effect on the bank's tax situation and on the return earned by the bank's stockholders.

THE BANK'S PORTFOLIO

It used to be standard practice for a bank to invest some fraction of the funds deposited with it in government securities that could be sold off to meet increases in loan demand or depositor withdrawals. In other words, the bank's portfolio provided liquidity and some earnings on the side.

For the nation's largest banks, with the possible exception of the deposit-rich B of A, this began to change in the early 1960s. At that time many large banks, particularly those in New York, found that the secular uptrend in bank loans had eaten away most of the excess liquidity (bloated bond portfolios) with which they had emerged from World War II. At the same time, corporate treasurers began to manage their cash more actively, taking idle deposit balances out of the banks and investing them in commercial paper and other money market instruments. This too created liquidity problems. To solve them, the banks turned to the newly invented negotiable CD and other methods for buying money. Liability management was born and the big banks' liquidity became their ability to buy money.

A second factor that discouraged banks from holding a bond portfolio primarily to provide liquidity was the ever-widening fluctuations that occurred in interest rates as a result of cyclical swings in economic activity and changes in Fed policy. What the banks found was that as loan demand slackened, interest rates would fall sharply, and as loan demand picked up, they would rise sharply. In this environment, using bonds as a source of liquidity meant buying bonds at high prices and selling them at low prices. Thus a bank that viewed its bond portfolio as a source of liquidity found it to be an automatic money loser; over time it provided some interest income and a lot of capital losses.

Today since a large bank's government portfolio is financed in the RP market, it is more a *use* of liquidity than a *source*. Also, if such a bank sells securities, the RP borrowings used to finance them have to be repaid, so portfolio sales produce no money to fund loans or meet other cash needs.

Maturity choice

Because the yield curve normally slopes upward, the yield on a 2-year note typically exceeds the overnight RP rate by more than does the yield on a 90-day bill. Thus a bank will get a better spread between the yield on its portfolio and its financing cost the longer it extends in buying governments along the maturity scale. This tempts a bank that is building up its portfolio to buy at least some governments and agencies with 2-year, 4-year, or even longer maturities, but doing so poses a risk.

An upturn in rates would cause not only a rise in financing costs but also a fall in the value of the securities held, and the longer the maturity of these securities, the more dramatic that fall would be. Thus a bank with governments extending out on the maturity scale might end up in a position where rising financing costs tell it to sell governments at a time when it can do so only at a substantial loss.

To avoid getting into such a bind, banks use several strategies. One is to minimize the damage that rising interest rates can do by holding securities with short current maturities. Another is to match the maturity of the securities purchased with the time span over which interest rates are expected to be down—a policy that will result in a runoff of the portfolio as rates start up again. A third strategy is to count on being smart enough to know when to buy and when to sell. Both of the latter strategies will be successful only to the extent that the bank succeeds in predicting interest rate trends. That, however, is a difficult trick. Thus, it's not surprising that most large bank portfolios could have been managed better with hindsight than they were with foresight.

Portfolio management

Active portfolio management by a bank—a willingness to make judgments about interest rates trends and adjust maturities accordingly, to ride the yield curve, and to pursue other potentially profitable strategies—can significantly increase the return earned by the bank on its portfolio. Nevertheless, some large banks and many smaller banks do not engage in such management.

Under federal tax laws, net capital gains earned by a bank on its portfolio used to be taxed at the capital gains rate, while net capital losses were deductible from ordinary income. This created an incentive for banks to bunch capital gains into one tax year and capital losses into another. Managing a bank's portfolio thus boiled down to deciding whether the current year was a gain or a loss year, which wasn't difficult. If the market was up, it was a gain year; if it was down, it was a loss year. During a loss year a bank might find it had paper losses on securities it did not want to sell. That difficulty could be gotten around by selling these securities, taking the loss, and buying other securities that were similar but not so similar that the IRS would view the transaction as a wash sale.

At the end of 1969 tax laws were changed: all bank capital gains on portfolio transactions are now treated as ordinary income and all capital losses as deductions from ordinary income. This tax change created for the first time a real profit incentive for banks to actively manage their portfolios.

One reason many still do not has to do with bank accounting practices. Table 5–2 presents in bare-bones style the format of a bank in-

Table 5–2
Typical format for a bank income statement

+ Interest income
  (including interest income on securities held)
− Interest expenses
+ Other operating income
  (including trading account profits)
− Noninterest operating expenses
  (including taxes other than those on capital gains)

Income before securities gains (losses)
+ Securities gains (losses) net of tax effect

Net income

come statement. Note that *two* profit figures are given, *Income before securities gains (losses)* and *Net income.* The first figure excludes capital gains and losses; the second reflects them as well as their effect on taxes due.

The special place given to securities gains and losses on a bank's income statement highlights them as an extraordinary item, and bank stockholders and stock analysts thus focus much attention on *Income before securities gains or losses*. Since interest income on securities is included in this figure but capital gains and losses on securities trades are not, bankers prefer interest income from their portfolio to capital gains. In addition, because stockholders and analysts like to see sustained earnings growth, bankers want this number to grow steadily on a year-to-year basis.

That desire can at times discourage a bank from managing its portfolio. To illustrate, consider a bank that buys 3-year notes in a high-rate period such as 1974. Two years later, interest rates have fallen substantially, and the 3-year notes, which have moved down the yield curve, are trading at a yield to maturity well below their coupon. At this point the bank might feel that in order to maximize profits over time, it should sell these notes and buy new ones that have a longer current maturity and therefore sell at a higher yield. The logic of such an *extension swap* is that the capital gains earned immediately on the sale of the old notes plus the interest earned on the new notes would over time amount to more income than the interest that would have been earned by holding the old notes to maturity and then reinvesting. The swap, however, creates a capital gain in the current year and lowers interest income in the following year. To the banker who wants *Income before securities gains or losses* to rise steadily, such a redistribution of income often seems too great a price to pay for maximizing profits over time; so he doesn't do the swap.

A concern with steady earnings may also lead a bank to hold more governments or governments of longer maturity than caution would dictate. Conditions may suggest that loan demand is about to pick up, that interest rates are about to rise, and that the bank should therefore reduce its holdings of governments or the maturity of those holdings. Doing so in anticipation of the event would, however, mean a temporary earnings dip, something a bank may be unwilling to accept.

A bank can put some of its portfolio into a *trading account*. The advantage in doing so is that capital gains realized in the trading account are included in the top-line income figure. The disadvantage is that securities in this account have to be valued on the bank's balance sheet at the lower of market value or cost, whereas other securities in the bank's portfolio do not. At many banks one finds an anomalous situation. The bank works hard to earn profits on the 10–30 percent of its portfolio that is in a trading account, while the rest of its portfolio is largely unmanaged.

Municipal portfolio

State and local securities (*municipals* for short) offer banks the advantage that interest income on them is not subject to federal taxation. It is also often exempt from state and local taxation if the securities held are issued by or within the state in which the bank is located. However, some states and localities (New York and New York City, in particular) impose a franchise tax on bank income that is based on total earnings, including tax exempt income. Municipal securities, unlike governments, carry a real credit risk. Thus credit analysis plays a large role in a bank's decision about what municipal securities to buy.

While a bank's main objective in buying municipals is to obtain tax-exempt income, other motives may influence this decision. Banks receive large deposits from state and local governments, and these have to be collateralized. Sometimes the collateral used is governments, more often it is municipals. Also, a bank may invest in municipals because the issuer is a valued depositer.

The securities held in a bank's municipal portfolio typically range in maturity from short-term notes to bonds with a 10- or 15-year maturity. A bank often perceives its holdings of short-term muni notes as a true source of liquidity since their sale will in fact free funds for other uses.

A bank's incentive for buying long-term munis is to obtain a higher yield by taking advantage of the upward slope of the yield curve. Long-term munis, however, expose the holder to a substantial price risk. In investing in municipal securities, many banks seek to compromise between price risk and yield by *laddering* the maturity of their portfolios out to 10 or 15 years (i.e., by buying something in every maturity range). However, in munis as opposed to governments, the investor is paid to extend maturity virtually to the end of the maturity spectrum. As a result some banks are willing to hold munis of very long maturity. In doing so they follow what's called a *barbell* strategy, buying muni notes for liquidity and investing, when they like the market, in long-term munis for yield. This sounds risky but practitioners argue that the supply of funds going into the far end of the market from fire and casualty insurance companies and from individuals is stable, whereas in the 10- to 15-year range dominated by the banks, it is highly cyclical; as a result, yields on medium-term munis go through large gyrations, and the medium-term investor who misplays his hand can be hurt as badly as the investor in long bonds.

Generally banks do not actively trade their muni portfolios. One reason for this is tax considerations. A bank that buys tax-exempt issues when interest rates are high and later sells them at a capital gain when interest rates are lower is trading future nontaxable interest payments for current taxable capital gains, an operation that is normally unattractive when evaluated in terms of its effect on after-tax income.

DEALER OPERATIONS

Most money market banks have extensive dealer operations. The biggest part of their activity is in Treasury and federal agency securities, but banks also deal heavily in and are underwriters of state and local general obligation securities. In addition some banks deal in the CDs of other banks and in bankers' acceptances. Banks used to underwrite corporate issues, but since passage of the Glass-Steagall Act in 1936, they have been forbidden to do so.

Running a dealer operation makes sense for a large bank. Smaller banks often look to money market banks with whom they have a correspondent relationship to buy securities both for their own portfolio and for their customers. Also large corporations, which are prime customers of money market banks and often have millions of dollars of short-term funds to invest, are ready customers for securities traded by bank dealerships. In this respect it should be noted that, while the Glass-Steagall Act forbids banks from underwriting and dealing in corporate securities, banks can and do sell commercial paper issued by corporations. The big direct issuers of commercial paper post rates with the banks, which in turn quote these rates to customers; if a customer wants $1 million of General Motors Acceptance Corporation (GMAC) paper, the bank carries out the transaction between the customer and GMAC and safekeeps the paper for the customer until it matures.

Besides being a profit center, a bank's dealer department also provides it with useful, up-to-the-minute information on developments in the money and bond markets. There's much to be said about how a dealer operation, bank or nonbank, runs. We turn to that topic in Chapter 9.

DEMAND DEPOSITS

Demand deposits have traditionally been a key source of bank funding, and as such they are an important and valuable raw material to banks. Yet in the United States, unlike in many foreign countries, banks are not permitted to pay interest on demand deposits. So long as interest rates were low, forbidding the payment of interest on demand deposits caused bankers no problems; despite the fact that deposit balances offered a zero return, bank customers were willing to hold substantial amounts because the *opportunity cost* (foregone earnings opportunity) of doing so was negligible.

During the 1950s, however, things started to change. Interest rates began a secular climb, which, coupled with the periodic forays the economy made into the world of very tight money and very high interest rates in the 1960s, drove home to corporate treasurers, state and local financial officials, and other holders of large short-term balances a new fact of life: the cost of holding idle balances was high and growing. The response of these depositors was to trim their demand balances to the minimum level possible and invest excess short-term funds in interest-bearing instruments.

Because demand deposits are valuable to banks and because holders of such deposits incur a substantial opportunity cost, an elaborate system of barter has developed in which banks trade services to customers in exchange for deposits. On small accounts the barter does not involve very precise calculations. It amounts to the bank giving free checking services to all customers or to those with some minimum balance.

On large accounts the barter is more scientific, banks provide many services to corporate and other big customers: accepting deposits, clearing checks, wire transfers, safekeeping securities, and others. In providing these services, banks incur costs that they could recover by charging fees. Instead they ask customers to "pay" by holding demand deposits.

To determine the amount of deposits appropriate for each customer, the bank first costs out each type of service it provides. It then sets up an activity analysis statement for each account, showing the types and volume of services provided and the costs incurred. Some of the demand deposits customers leave with a bank go to meet reserve requirements; the rest can be invested. Taking reserve requirements and current investment yields into account, the bank estimates the rate of return it earns on demand deposits. Finally, using that rate it determines what dollar balances each account must hold so that the bank's earnings on the account cover the costs incurred in servicing it.

Banks also charge for credit lines by requiring compensating deposit balances, the standard formula being 10 percent of the unused portion of the line and 20 percent of any funds actually taken down.

As might be expected in a barter situation, the compensation arrangements worked out between banks and customers are subject to much negotiation and vary not only from bank to bank but often from customer to customer at a given bank. Many customers obtain lines at less than the usual 10–20 formula, and good customers may be able to get their banks to double-count balances for some purposes.

A bank that requires compensating balances on lines and loans is getting at zero interest deposits on which it can earn a return. An alternative way it could earn the same return would be to charge a fee for lines and higher rates on loans. Some customers prefer the latter approach, and in recent years it has become more common for banks to grant fee lines and to quote two loan rates, a standard rate for loans with balances and a higher rate for loans without. For some public utility customers this approach is mandatory since regulators will not permit them to hold large idle balances.

To the extent that banks obtain demand deposits either from retail customers by establishing expensive branch networks or from large depositors by exchanging services or reducing lending rates, they are paying some implicit rate of interest on such deposits even though the nominal rate is zero. The *all-in* cost, moreover, of demand deposits is still higher than this implicit rate because, a Table 5–3 shows, the reserve requirement on demand deposits is 16¼ percent for a large bank,

Table 5-3
Reserve requirements for banks that are members of the Federal Reserve System

Type of deposit and deposit interval ($ millions)	Requirements in effect Jan. 31, 1978		Previous requirements	
	Percent	Effective date	Percent	Effective date
Net demand*				
0–2	7	12/30/76	7½	2/13/75
2–10	9½	12/30/76	10	2/13/75
10–100	11¾	12/30/76	12	2/13/75
100–400	12¾	12/30/76	13	2/13/75
Over 400	16¼	12/30/76	16½	2/13/75
Time*†				
Savings	3	3/16/67	3½	3/2/67
Other time				
0–5, maturing in				
30–179 days	3	3/16/67	3½	3/2/67
180 days to 4 years	2½‡	1/8/76	3	3/16/67
4 years or more	1‡	10/30/75	3	3/16/67
Over 5, maturing in				
30–179 days	6	12/12/74	5	10/1/70
180 days to 4 years	2½‡	1/8/76	3	12/12/74
4 years or more	1‡	10/30/75	3	12/12/74

* (a) Requirement schedules are graduated, and each deposit interval applies to that part of the deposits of each bank. Demand deposits subject to reserve requirements are gross demand deposits minus cash items in process of collection and demand balances due from domestic banks.

(b) The Board's Regulation M requires a 4 percent reserve against net balances due to domestic banks from their foreign branches. Effective Dec. 1, 1977, a 1 percent reserve is required against deposits that foreign branches of U.S. banks use for lending to U.S. residents. Loans aggregating $100,000 or less to any U.S. resident are excluded from computations, as are total loans of a bank to U.S. residents if not exceeding $1 million. Regulation D imposes a 4 percent reserve on net borrowings from foreign banks by domestic offices of a member bank.

† Negotiable orders of withdrawal (NOW) accounts and time deposits such as Christmas and vacation club accounts are subject to the same requirements as savings deposits.

‡ The average of reserves on savings and other time deposits must be at least 3 percent, the minimum specified by law.

Note: Required reserves must be held in the form of deposits with Federal Reserve banks or vault cash.

Source: *Federal Reserve Bulletin.*

which means that such a bank can invest only $83.75 of every $100 it takes in. Also, a bank has to pay the Federal Deposit Insurance Corporation (FDIC) a premium of ½ of 1 percent on all deposits it accepts.

However high the all-in cost of demand deposits may be, banks are eager to obtain all the demand deposits they can. One reason is that the quantity of such funds supplied to a bank is quite stable over time, and a bank can thus count on these deposits being there regardless of what happens to economic conditions or interest rates. Banks also attach importance to demand and time deposits for other reasons: regulators like to see a lot of deposits as opposed to bought money on a bank's balance sheet; banks are typically ranked by deposit size rather than asset size; and bank analysts attach what is probably undue importance to the share of deposits in a bank's total liabilities.

While exchanging services for deposits has enabled banks to hold onto substantial amounts of demand deposits, banks have no way to bid for additional funds from this source. The demand deposits they get are limited to the amounts consumers choose to leave with them plus the amounts needed to cover the services large customers choose to buy from them. This contrasts sharply with the situation in the Euromarket where banks bid actively for deposits of all maturities, including call and overnight money (see Chapter 6).

SMALL-DENOMINATION TIME DEPOSITS

The major competitors of banks in accepting time and savings deposits are savings and loan associations. When money becomes tight and interest rates soar, S&Ls are at a competitive disadvantage relative to banks. Because banks have many short-term and variable-rate assets on their books, they are in a position to capture rapidly rising interest rates on the asset side of their balance sheets. In contrast the asset portfolios of S&Ls consist largely of fixed-rate, long-term mortgages. It thus takes considerable time for S&Ls to translate rising interest rates into rising revenues, and when money tightens, banks are therefore in a stronger position than S&Ls to bid for savings and time deposits by raising deposit rates.

To protect S&Ls from bank competition, the Fed imposes under *Regulation Q* lids on the rates that banks may pay on small-denomination savings and time deposits. These lids, which are periodically adjusted as economic conditions change, become higher as the maturity of the deposit lengthens (Table 5–4). The Federal Home Loan Bank Board, which regulates S&Ls, also establishes lids on the deposit rates S&Ls may pay; typically these are set 0.25 percent above the rates banks can pay on the theory that if S&Ls did not enjoy a rate advantage, consumers would for convenience opt to hold their savings accounts at commercial banks where they hold their checking accounts. Other nonbank savings institutions enjoy the same rate advantage over banks that S&Ls do.

However justified or unjustified Reg Q may be economically, it does exist, and because of it banks cannot bid actively for small savings and time deposits. Banks get what retail customers give them. For some money market banks with a lot of retail business the amount received is large, for other wholesale banks it is minuscule.

The Fed initially applied Reg Q lids to deposits of all sizes, but since 1973 it has exempted all deposits of $100,000 or more. Thus banks are currently free to bid whatever rate they choose for large time deposits, a freedom S&Ls also enjoy.

On June 1, 1978, the Fed authorized banks to pay on 6-month certifi-

Table 5–4
Maximum interest rates payable by banks on time and savings deposits

Type and maturity of deposit	In effect June 1, 1978		Previous maximum	
	Percent	Effective date	Percent	Effective date
Savings	5	7/1/73	4½	1/21/70
Negotiable order of withdrawal (NOW) accounts	5	1/1/74		
Time (multiple- and single-maturity unless otherwise indicated)				
30–89 days				
Multiple-maturity ....}	5	7/1/73	{4½	1/21/70
Single-maturity ....}			{5	9/26/66
90 days to 1 year				
Multiple-maturity ....}	5½	7/1/73	5	{7/20/66
Single-maturity ....}				{9/26/66
1–2 years.....................................}	6	7/1/73	{5½	1/21/70
2–2½ years ....}			{5¾	1/21/70
2½–4 years	6½	7/1/73	5¾	1/21/70
4–6 years*	7¼	11/1/73		
6 years*	7½	12/23/74	7¼	11/1/73
8 years or more*.............................	7¾	6/1/78		
Government units (all maturities)†	8	6/1/78	7¾	12/23/74
Individual retirement accounts and Keogh (H.R. 10) plans‡	8	6/1/78	7¾	7/6/77

 * $1,000 minimum except for deposits representing funds contributed to an Individual Retirement Account (IRA) or a Keogh Plan.
 † Government units are state, local, and federal agencies. They may receive the highest rate any depository institution may pay, which is always the highest rate a *nonbank* savings institution such as an S&L is permitted to pay.
 ‡ 3-year minimum maturity.
 Source: *Federal Reserve Bulletin.*

cates with a minimum denomination of $10,000 the average return on T bills of the same maturity. S&Ls and savings banks were authorized to pay ¼ more on similar certificates. The purpose of the new savings certificate was to cushion the savings and loan industry from an outflow of funds into the money market and thereby protect the supply of funds flowing into home mortgages.

The all-in cost of time deposit money to a bank depends in part on the reserves the bank must hold against these deposits. As Table 5–3 shows, reserve requirements are much lower on savings and time deposits than on demand deposits; and on time deposits they are lower the longer the maturity of the deposit.

FEDERAL FUNDS

Smaller banks typically receive more deposits than they need to fund loans, whereas large banks are in precisely the opposite position. The

logical solution to this situation, in which small banks have excess reserves and large banks suffer reserve deficiencies, would be for large
banks to accept the excess reserves of smaller correspondent banks as
deposits and pay interest on them, a practice that used to be common
before banks were forbidden to pay interest on demand deposits.

To get around this prohibition, the Federal funds market, somno-
lent since the 1920s, was revived during the 1950s. In this market banks
buy Fed funds (reserve dollars) from and sell Fed funds to each other.
Since purchases of Fed funds are technically borrowings instead of
deposits, banks buying Fed funds are permitted to pay interest on these
funds. The all-in cost of Fed funds to the purchasing bank is the rate paid
plus any brokerage incurred. Because Fed funds purchased are not
deposits, there is no FDIC tax on them. They are also not subject to
reserve requirements, since the reserve requirement has been met by
the bank that accepted as a deposit the funds sold.

Most sales of Fed funds are made on an overnight basis, but some are
for longer periods. Overnight transactions in Fed funds provide the purchasing bank with a cheap source of money and a convenient way to
make sizable day-to-day adjustments in its reserves. For the selling
bank, Fed funds sold provide a convenient form of liquidity. Small banks,
unlike large money center banks, cannot count on being able to buy
funds whenever they need them. Therefore they have to keep their liquidity resident in assets, and because overnight sales of Fed funds can
be varied in amount from day to day, they give such banks flexibility to
adjust to the daily swings that occur in their reserve positions.

Since the difficulties of the Franklin National were brought to light,
banks have become acutely aware that, in selling Fed funds, they are
making unsecured loans to other banks, and moreover they are doing so
at one of the lowest rates prevailing in the money market.[6] This being the
case, banks carefully monitor the credit risks they assume by selling Fed

---

[6] In the spring of 1974 the Franklin National Bank, then the 20th largest bank in the U.S.,
disclosed that it had sustained a $46 million loss through unauthorized speculation by
traders in its foreign exchange department. The Fed, realizing the serious consequences
that failure of the Franklin might have, particularly under the then prevailing tight conditions in the money and bond markets, promised immediately and publicly to support the
Franklin by lending to it at the discount window whatever sums were necessary. Fed loans
to the Franklin eventually reached an unprecedented $1.75 billion.

Had the Franklin's troubles been simply a temporary loss of confidence due to a single
misstep, the Fed's actions combined with some minimal assistance from the FDIC might
have sufficed to permit the Franklin to recover. Unfortunately as a result of chronically weak
management, the Franklin also suffered from excessive leverage at unfavorable rates, an
overloaded and badly depressed bond portfolio, and low-quality business loans. Thus, it
was insolvent not only in the technical sense of having liabilities greater than assets but
also in a second and more serious sense—it was no longer able to operate profitably. As a
result, by fall the FDIC felt compelled to force the Franklin to merge with another large and
profitable bank, the European American Bank and Trust Co. In that merger the Franklin's
depositors were fully protected.

funds. They will sell Fed funds only to banks to which they have established lines of credit, and they will sell to these banks only up to the amount of the lines granted. In establishing a line to another bank, the selling bank will consider the other bank's reputation in the market, its size, its capital structure, and any other factors that affect its creditworthiness. The selling bank may also consider whether the buying bank is at times also a seller of funds. A bank that is always a buyer is viewed less favorably than one that operates both ways in the market. Selling funds is also important for a would-be buyer because the Fed funds market is one into which some banks have to buy their way. They do this by selling funds to a bank for a time and then saying to that bank, "We sell funds to you, why don't you extend a line to us?"

REPOS

The reemergence of the Fed funds market gave banks a backdoor way to pay interest on demand deposits received from other banks. Corporations, state and local governments, and other big nonbank investors that have funds to invest for less than 30 days can't, however, sell that money directly in the Fed funds market because they are not banks. Partly to meet the needs of such investors, the RP market has developed into one of the largest and most active sectors of the money market. In it, banks and nonbank dealers create each day billions of dollars worth of what resembles interest-bearing demand deposits. In fact an investor that does an RP transaction with a bank is making a loan secured by U.S. Treasury or other securities; investing in RPs thus exposes the investor to less credit risk than depositing funds directly in the bank would.

A large percentage of all RPs done by banks are on an overnight basis, but term RPs are also common. Since the yield curve typically slopes upward, the rate on term RPs normally exceeds the overnight rate, with the spread being larger the longer the maturity of the term RP. Thus, from a cost point of view, an overnight RP tends to be more attractive. However, excessive reliance on overnight RPs and purchases of Fed funds may create a shorter book (a greater mismatch between asset and liability maturities) than a bank wants to run. If so, the bank can use term RPs to snug up its book.

Since the RP money a bank buys is not deposits, it does not have to pay FDIC premiums on such funds. It also does not incur any reserve requirements on money purchased in the RP market provided that the collateral used is government or federal agency securities. However, on RPs done with other collateral, there is a reserve requirement. RP transactions always involve some paper work, and if the buyer of the securities wants them safekept by another bank, there is a clearing charge. Banks doing a lot of RPs carefully track these costs, because they can raise significantly the all-in cost of RP money, especially if it is bought on an overnight basis. To avoid clearing charges, banks prefer to do RPs with customers that will safekeep with them the securities "purchased."

The overnight RP rate is normally lower than the overnight Fed funds rate for two reasons. First, lenders in this market do not have direct access to the Fed funds market. Second, doing RP does not expose the lender to the same credit risk that selling Fed funds would. The banks' main alternative to buying funds in the term RP market is buying term Fed funds. The decision between the two is likely to be made strictly on the basis of which sells at the lower all-in cost. Normally this will be term RP, which tends to trade below term Fed funds for the same reasons that overnight RP money is normally cheaper than overnight Fed funds.

Because RP money is cheap and because a money market bank buys lots of it, such banks carefully search out and cultivate big investors in RP. They make it a point to know the needs of their big customers—whether they can buy commercial paper, repo, or what—and they call these customers everyday to get a feel for what monies they have available. The banks also keep track of who is issuing bonds and who is therefore going to get big money. For example, if New York State floats a $2 or $3 billion bond issue to obtain funds that it intends to pay out to school districts 2 months hence, every money market bank will know that the state has money to invest in RP, and they will all be calling the state to get some of it.

Doing RP with customers is the way banks get most of the RP money they buy. However, banks that are primary dealers in government securities also frequently do RP transactions with the Fed and reverses as well. As explained in Chapter 8, the Fed relies heavily on repos and reverses with dealers in governments to make short-term adjustments in bank reserves.

NEGOTIABLE CDS

In the early 1960s the demand for funds at New York money market banks began to outstrip their traditional sources of funds. These banks had, moreover, no way to bid for funds outside their own geographic area, for example, to pull time deposits in from the West Coast. To solve this problem, Citibank introduced the negotiable CD, an innovation that became an instant success and was widely copied. Today CDs are a key funding instrument for every major bank.

The CD became important to domestic banks not only because it allowed them to tap the national market for funds, but also because it provided them with a means, really the only one available, to bid for longer-term funds in volume. In the domestic market, unlike in the Euromarket, the supply of large-denomination time deposits offered by investors is thin at best. Large corporations don't want to hear about time deposits; they want liquidity. State and local governments used to give large time deposits to banks, but they too have become increasingly interested in liquidity. Also, time deposits held by state and local governments have the disadvantage from the point of view of the accepting bank that they have to be collateralized by Treasury or municipal securities.

In buying longer-maturity funds, the only alternatives a bank has to issuing CDs are to do term RP, or buy term Fed funds. Term RP is a limited alternative, because if a bank RPs any asset other than governments and agencies (banks have attempted to RP everything including loans), it incurs a reserve requirement. Purchases of term Fed funds are a viable alternative to the sale of CDs, but the market for such funds has nowhere near the breadth of the CD market.

The all-in cost to an issuing bank of CD money is the rate paid on the CD plus FDIC insurance plus the reserve cost plus the commission paid to the issuing dealer if one is used. At times this all-in cost exceeds that of term Fed funds of comparable maturity. When it does, a bank will lean in the direction of buying term Fed funds, but within limits. All banks are conscious of their statements; term Fed funds are classified for statement purposes as borrowed funds, CDs as deposits. Thus cosmetic considerations guarantee that a bank will buy in the CD market some multiple of the funds it buys in the term Fed funds market.

The major choice a bank faces in issuing CDs is what maturity money to take. If a bank thinks its book is running too short or that interest rates and loan demand are likely to rise sharply, it will be tempted to buy longer-dated funds, say, 6-month rather than 3-month money. Because of availability and risk considerations, however, most of the money banks buy in the CD market is purchased at the short end of the maturity spectrum.

When a bank opts to issue longer-term (say, 6-month) CDs, it is typically gambling that interest rates will rise. With a normal upward-sloping yield curve, this is an expensive bet because in buying 6-month money a bank forgoes the normally cheaper alternative of buying two consecutive batches of 3-month money. Thus interest rates have to rise sharply for a purchase of long-term money in anticipation of rising interest rates to pay off; banks therefore buy 6-month money in volume only if they believe strongly that the Fed is going to raise interest rates or if the yield curve is relatively flat.

When a bank buys long-term money, it gambles not only that rates will rise, but also that it will have some use for the expensive money it is acquiring. Should loan demand be less than anticipated, a bank that had bought 6-month money would find itself holding high-cost funds for which it had no high-yield use.

Availability is also a consideration in a bank's choice of CD maturities. The real depth in the CD market is in the 1- to 3-month range. There is a market for 6-month paper but it is thin, and the market for 1-year paper is still thinner. Thus banks have little choice but to buy the bulk of their money in short maturities.

This, moreover, becomes increasingly true during periods of tight money. When interest rates are rising and a bank expects them to continue to rise, it will be tempted to increase the average maturity of the CDs it sells. It is selling its CDs, however, to sophisticated investors who are likely to share its view on rates and who therefore want—just when the bank is trying to increase maturities—to decrease the maturity of the CDs they buy. Generally the investors get their way because banks can only sell paper that the market will accept. Thus tight money and rising interest rates tend to force *down* the average maturity of CDs sold.

Effect of reserve requirements on the cost of CD money

To the above it should be added that at times the structure of rates may be such that 6-month money becomes attractive to banks on a cost basis, and they will then buy relatively large amounts of it. As Table 5–3 shows, the Fed imposes on large banks (those holding more than $500 million in time deposits) a 6 percent reserve requirement on CDs with a maturity of less than 6 months; this is substantially greater than the 2.5 percent reserve requirement it imposes on CDs of longer maturity. The disparity between the two reserve ratios has the effect of decreasing or even reversing the sign of the difference in the *all-in* cost to a large bank of buying 3-month versus 6-month money. For example; if 3-month CD money were available to a bank at 4.25 percent and 6-month money at 4.50 percent, the respective all-in costs of 3- and 6-month money would, when required reserves were taken into account, be 4.52 and 4.62 percent, respectively; and the true difference in cost between 3-month and 6-month money would equal not the 25 basis points difference in quoted rates but instead only 10 basis points.

If, moreover, interest rates were to rise 4 percentage points with *no* change in yield spreads, that is, if 3-month CDs were trading at 8.25 percent and 6-month CDs at 8.50 percent, the all-in cost would— because of the difference in reserve costs—actually be lower for 6-month than for 3-month money: 8.78 percent on 3-month money versus 8.72 percent on 6-month money.

Issuing CDs

In issuing CDs banks generally prefer to get these securities into the hands of investors who are likely to hold them at least for a substantial period, if not to maturity. That banks should attempt to sell an instrument, whose appeal by design is liquidity, to buyers who will rarely if ever trade it seems incongruous to the outside observer, but not to bankers. A banker doesn't mind an investor selling a CD because of an unexpected cash need, but sales by trading accounts are something else. As the banker sees it, paper bought by trading accounts and subsequestly dumped on the street could provide unwanted competition for any new paper his bank might later choose to write.

In their search for "warm nosed" money, most banks prefer to sell as many of the CDs they issue as possible through their own sales forces to their own customers. However, as noted in Chapter 15, a good portion of CDs are issued through dealers.

In the CD market, as in other sectors of the money market, a bank cannot buy unlimited quantities of funds. The reason is that not all investors in the money market are free to buy bank CDs, because of either regulation or self-imposed investment parameters. And those that are free limit their purchases of paper to specific names and specific amounts for each name. Thus at any time there is some maximum amount of its paper that a bank can push into the market. That limit is one that most banks have never approached and all banks attempt not to approach.

Several major banks have, however, breached this limit with unfortunate consequences. They suddenly found they could sell only small amounts of new paper to the market. Also the excess supply of their paper on the street drove down its price, which in turn soured investors who were holding that paper and threw questions on the bank's name. Once a bank gets itself into such a situation, it takes time to remedy. The bank may for awhile have to cut back sharply on the CDs it issues and attempt to selectively place these CDs, perhaps at a premium rate, with investors who will hold rather than trade them.

EURODOLLARS

A final source of funding to which a bank may turn is the Euromarket, where it can bid for deposits (*take* money) of essentially any maturity from overnight on out. A bank can also invest (*place*) money it has raised in the domestic market in Euro time deposits. The reserve requirement on Euros is established under *Regulations M* and *D*, which currently require a domestic bank to hold reserves equal to 4 percent of any *net* borrowings (borrowings minus placements) of Euros that it makes for its domestic book over a 28-day averaging period.[7] Because of Regs *M* and *D*, a bank that takes Euros of one maturity will often place Euros of some

---

[7] See footnote (b), Table 5–3, p. 82.

other maturity during the averaging period so that its reserve cost on the money borrowed is zero.

The head offices of money market banks are very active in the Euromarket for several reasons. First, as described in Chapter 17, they engage in continuing *technical arbitrages* between Euros and Fed funds, that is, arbitrages that arise due to technicalities in the way required reserves are calculated and the way Euros are cleared.[8] Second, they are constantly alert to the opportunities for arbitrage between the domestic and the Euromarkets that arise because of transitory rate discrepancies. For example, if 6-month Euros are selling at 7.75 percent and 6-month money can be purchased at 6 percent in the domestic CD market, a bank will take domestic 6-month money and place it in the Euromarket through its London or Nassau branch. Doing so, besides locking in a spread for the bank, permits the bank to bring back short-dated Euros at no reserve cost. Such intrabank arbitrages play an important role in holding Euro and U.S. rates in line.

BANK CAPITAL ADEQUACY

In talking about bank capital adequacy, the first thing to note is that the essence of banking is to raise the return earned by the bank on its capital base through leverage. To illustrate leverage at work, let's use a simple example. Suppose an investor has $1,000 of capital to invest. He can borrow additional funds at 4 percent and he can invest at 5 percent. If he invests only his $1,000 of capital, he will earn $50 for a return of 5 percent on that capital. If alternatively he borrows $5,000 and invests a total of $6,000, he will have an investment income of $300, interest costs of $200, and profits of $100, which amount to a 10 percent return on his $1,000 of capital (Table 5–5). By borrowing funds at a low rate and investing them along with his capital at a higher rate, our investor has levered up the return on his capital.

In an uncertain world, leverage of course can work against as well as for the investor. If, for example, our investor, who anticipated earning 5 percent on his investment, earned only 3 percent, then his profit would be −$20, for a rate of return on capital of −2 percent (Case III, Table 5–5).

Because bankers operate with borrowed funds that amount in total to a substantial multiple of their capital, they engage in leverage on a grand scale. Moreover, because assuming both a credit risk by lending and a rate risk by running a short book are fundamental elements of banking, the banker can never be sure either what average return he will earn on his assets or what his cost of funds will be. The purpose of bank

---

[8] Strictly defined, to arbitrage means buying something where it is cheap and selling it where it is dear.

Table 5–5
Leverage at work: Investor has $1,000 of capital

Case I: No borrowed funds used; investment returns 5%:

Investment income = 5% × $1,000 = $50
−Interest cost = 4% × 0   =   0
Profit   = $50

$$\text{Rate of return on capital} = \frac{\$50}{\$1,000} = 5\%$$

Case II: $5,000 of borrowed funds costing 4% used; investment returns 5%:

Investment income = 5% × $6,000 = $300
−Interest cost = 4% × $5,000   = $200
Profit   = $100

$$\text{Rate of return on capital} = \frac{\$100}{\$1,000} = 10\%$$

Case III: $5,000 of borrowed funds costing 4% used; investment returns 3%:

Investment income = 3% × $6,000 = $180
−Interest cost = 4% × $5,000   =   200
Loss   = −$20

$$\text{Rate of return on capital} = \frac{-\$20}{\$1,000} = -2\%$$

capital is to cushion bank depositors and other suppliers of debt capital to banks against any losses the bank might incur due to unfavorable leverage—borrowing costs higher than return earned.

While it's easy to see that a bank needs capital, the question of how much money is difficult and perhaps unanswerable. In attempting to measure bank capital adequacy, the yardstick used to be the ratio of a bank's deposits to its loans, its major risk assets. Then as banks became active buyers of money, focus shifted to the ratio of equity to assets. However well or poorly this ratio may measure bank capital adequacy, it in no way solves the question of what minimum value it should have. For every $1 of capital, should a bank borrow at most $10, $20, or what? Any intelligent answer to this question should probably be based on a bank's earning power as measured by certain historical indexes and modified to allow for the bank's bad-debt experience. Such numbers, however, vary from bank to bank, suggesting that no absolute industry-wide standard can or should be set.

As a practical matter, the capital ratios currently prevailing in banking in no way reflect reasoned decisions by either bankers or regulators as to what these ratios should be. Quite to the contrary, what they are at any point reflects historical evolution and prevailing economic conditions. In particular during the post–World War II period, as loan demand surged and banks strove for continued earnings growth, bank capital ratios declined substantially. It is, moreover, not clear that an end to this downward trend is in sight.

The attitude of bankers toward the capital adequacy question is well illustrated by the words of one bank president: "Back in the credit crunch of 1974, because of inflation and an insatiable demand for credit, we got to the point where equity was about 4 percent of assets, so we had leverage of 25 to 1. At the peak we and a lot of bankers asked how far can this go, and we decided we had better slow down and tighten up. So we set a leverage maximum of 25 to 1." In the next breath the same banker added: "We of course have to forget all about that standard when we deal with foreign banks. The leading Israeli banks have about 1 percent capital ratios and in Japan the figure is 1 or 2 percent." In effect this banker and other U.S. bankers as well measure capital adequacy in domestic and foreign banks by differing standards, a practice that suggests they have no absolute notion of what capital ratios should be.

Since the whole question of capital adequacy boils down to asking how much capital a bank needs to assure its survival under unknown future conditions, it is no surprise that neither bankers nor regulators have come up with a definitive answer to this question. The typical banker's motto in determining what minimum capital ratio his bank should maintain seems to be: *Stay with the herd*. Banking tends to be a homogeneous industry and as such is characterized by pattern thinking. A banker judges his leverage ratio to be high or low in terms of where he is vis à vis his peers. If the pack lets their capital ratios fall, he is comfortable to follow, but he does not want to be in the lead. This attitude makes sense for several reasons. First, the Fed tends to judge banks against the pattern of what their competitors are doing. Second, bank customers who watch leverage carefully will penalize a bank that gets out of line.

Bank regulation

Banking in America is often referred to as a "dual" system because some banks operate under federal charters obtained from the Comptroller of the Currency, while others are chartered by the states. Banks operating under a federal charter are required to join the Federal Reserve System; state-chartered banks are not. As Table 5–6 shows, state banks are more numerous than national banks and the majority of them have not joined the Federal Reserve System, primarily because reserve requirements make Fed membership expensive. National banks are larger than state banks on the average, and as a result banks that are members of the Fed, while fewer in number, accept over 70 percent of the deposits received by domestic banks. Almost all banks in the country have opted to have their deposits insured by the Federal Deposit Insurance Corporation.

Table 5–6
U.S. commercial banks, June 1977

	Number of banks		Total deposits	
Category	Number	Percent	Amount ($ millions)	Percent
All commercial banks	14,718	100	862,031	100
National banks	4,701	32	476,381	55
State banks	10,017	68	385,650	45
Fed member banks	5,720	39	628,854	73
Nonmember banks...............	8,998	61	233,177	27
FDIC-insured banks..............	14,425	98	847,373	98
Noninsured banks	293	2	14,658	2

Source: *Federal Reserve Bulletin.*

Bank regulation in the United States comes in layers. State banks are regulated by state banking authorities, national banks by the Comptroller. In addition, banks that are members of the Fed are regulated by the Fed, and the FDIC regulates insured banks. The obvious overlap in bank regulation has led to periodic calls for a single unified system of bank regulation. Movement in this direction seems, however, unlikely because state banks, which are numerous and have considerable clout in Congress, are anxious to preserve a system in which the primary responsibility for regulating them lies with the local state banking authority; these banks fear being forced into a single national banking system.

Fortunately the regulatory overlap is less than appears on paper. Often the state regulators will focus on checking the accuracy of the bank's audited statements, whereas examiners from the Fed will be more concerned with whether the bank is being properly run.

The regulations under which U.S. banks, as opposed to British banks (see Chapter 6), operate are numerous, detailed, and complex; and they become more so all the time. Perhaps one reason is the checkered history of the U.S. banking system, which periodically experienced waves of failures and suspensions of payments right up into the 1930s. A second reason is that flexible regulation may be impractical in a country where there are 14,000 different banks, a situation unparalleled in any other major country.

Many people, particularly members of Congress, feel that if the regulators were doing their job, no bank would have problems, and that the existence of problem banks indicates the need for more and/or better regulation. Yet, as one regulator noted, the same member of Congress who says there should never be problem banks is also quick to complain, when wheat prices are low and there is a big overhang in the wheat market, that Nebraska farmers are having trouble getting bank credit

The nature of banking is taking risks by lending and by doing some maturity arbitrage. Good regulators see their job as trying to keep these risks prudent. They also recognize that the regulatory structure should not be such that no bank ever fails. If it were, banking as a creative force would be stifled.

When a bank experiences such severe problems that it ceases to be a viable institution, the regulators will normally arrange some sort of merger between that bank and another strong bank. This salvage operation may involve, as it did in the case of Franklin National, first substantial loans from the Fed to the ailing bank and later cash injections by the FDIC in exchange for some of the bank's less desirable assets.

The merger, if it occurs, is typically forced by events, not by the regulators. As one regulator noted: "When a bank has problems, we try to save it so long as it's a viable institution. We will make suggestions to management but it is their responsibility to right the situation. A bank ceases to be viable when public confidence in the bank weakens, usually due to some easily identifiable event. Before that occurs, we may look in the wings for potential marriage partners—act if you will as marriage brokers—but there is *no* shotgun for the marriage until public confidence is lost."

The fact that the Fed and the FDIC have not in recent decades permitted a major bank to fail with losses to depositors raises an interesting question: Would they ever? The answer, most observers believe (including some inside the Fed), is no. The reason is that the economic consequences of permitting a major bank to fail with losses to depositors would be enormously more costly than acting to protect depositors. Still there is what might be called the *political risk,* that is, the possibility that a large bank might through its actions so arouse the public's ire that the Fed and the FDIC would not be permitted to save it.

BANK HOLDING COMPANIES

Almost all large banks and many smaller banks in the United States are owned by holding companies. Prior to the 1960s bank holding companies were used primarily to surmount restrictions on intrastate branching by bringing under a single organization a number of separately chartered banks. Formation of multibank holding companies was brought under regulation by the Bank Holding Company Act in 1956. The purpose of this act, which is administered by the Federal Reserve Board, was twofold: to prevent the creation of monopoly power in banks and to prevent banks from entering via their holding company what were traditionally nonbank lines of activity.

In the late 1960s many of the nation's largest banks formed one-bank holding companies, which were not subject to the provisions of the 1956 act. One of their objectives in doing so was to create a vehicle through which they could enter indirectly activities they could not carry out directly. The banks' ability to achieve such diversification was, however, severely limited by the Bank Holding Company Act of 1970. This act brought one-bank holding companies under regulation by the Federal Reserve Board, which is responsible for restricting their activities to those "which are so closely related to banking as to be a proper incident thereto."

A second reason banks formed one-bank holding companies was to achieve greater flexibility in liability management. During the late 1960s open-market rates rose on several occasions above the Reg Q ceiling, and banks had difficulty selling CDs. To solve the resulting funding problem, the banks segregated certain loans on their books, put them in the holding company, and issued commercial paper, which was not subject to Regulation Q, to fund these loans. The Fed's response to this end run around Reg Q was to impose a reserve requirement on any paper sold to fund such loans. This reserve requirement does not apply to other assets sold by a bank to its holding company.

Today bank holding companies enter the story of the money market primarily as issuers of commercial paper. They use the proceeds to fund various assets on their own books and on those of their nonbank subsidiaries (known as *subs*). These include bank credit card receivables purchased from the bank, assets leased, and loans extended through a nonbank sub of the holding company.

EDGE ACT CORPORATIONS

A 1919 amendment to the Federal Reserve Act permits national banks and state banks that are members of the Federal Reserve System to establish international banking corporations, known familiarly as Edge Act corporations.

The operations of *Edge Act corporations* within the United States are restricted to activities that are incidental to the parent bank's international business—holding demand and time deposits received from foreign sources, issuing letters of credit, financing foreign trade, and creating bankers' acceptances. Edge Act corporations are also permitted to engage in overseas operations, to provide certain types of specialized financing such as loan syndication, and to make equity investments in foreign financial institutions.

Today all major U.S. banks have established one or more Edge Act corporations. The principal function for which these subs are used is to carry out international banking business for the parent within the United States. The ability to set up an Edge Act sub, which because of its federal charter is exempt from state corporation and banking laws, gives banks a means to engage in interstate banking, albeit for limited purposes. This is particularly important to non-New York banks that use New York-based Edge Act subs to operate the equivalent of an international department in New York, the major domestic center for international banking. Edge Act corporations are also used by New York banks to participate in the regional markets for international banking that have developed in San Francisco, Chicago, Miami, and other commercial centers. For banks in high-tax states, Edge Act corporations offer an additional benefit—the ability to earn and book some income in lower-tax states.

With respect to the money market, Edge Act corporations are most prominent in the BA market. Currently a substantial fraction of all BAs outstanding are Edge Act corporation paper.

Domestic banks carry out the bulk of their foreign activities not through Edge Act corporations, but through foreign branches. The extensive activities of these foreign branches in the Eurodollar market are the topic of the next chapter.

Chapter 6

The banks: Euro operations

ACCORDING TO PROPAGANDISTS on both sides of the Iron Curtain, communists and capitalists are implacable enemies. It thus comes as surprise to find that communist central banks bear as much responsibility as anyone for giving birth to one of the fastest growing, most vital and important capitalist institutions—namely, the international capital market known as the *Eurodollar market*. But then neither communist nor capitalist bankers had much idea of the long-run implications of what they were doing when the Euromarket was born.

EURO TRANSACTIONS IN T-ACCOUNTS

The best way to start a discussion of the Euromarket is by explaining the mechanics of Euro deposits and loans, about which there is much confusion. First, a definition: *Eurodollars are simply dollars held on deposit in a bank or bank branch located outside the United States*. If a U.S. investor shifts $1 million of deposits from a New York bank to the London branch of a U.S. bank, to Barclays London, or to the London branch of any French, German, or other foreign bank and receives in exchange a deposit denominated in dollars, he has made a *Eurodollar deposit*. Such deposits came to be known as *Eurodollars* because initially banks in Europe were most

99

active in seeking and accepting such deposits. Today, however, banks all over the globe are active in the Eurodollar market and the term *Eurdodollar* is a misnomer.[1]

The first important point to make about Eurodollars is that regardless of where they are deposited—London, Singapore, Tokyo, or Bahrain—they never leave the United States. Also, they never leave the U.S. regardless of where they are lent—to a multinational firm, to an underdeveloped country, or to an East European government. Let's work that out with T-accounts. As noted in Chapter 2, a T-account shows *changes in assets and liabilities* that result from a given financial transaction, as shown below.

T-Account

Change in assets	Change in liabilities

Suppose, to get our example going, Exxon moves $10 million from its account at Morgan in New York to the London branch of Citibank. (You can think of Exxon as writing a check against Morgan New York and depositing it in Citi London, but the transaction is done by wire or Telex.) Clearing of this transaction, which normally occurs on the day after it is initiated, will result in several balance sheet changes, as shown in Table 6–1.

Before we look at these changes, two preliminary remarks are in order. First, Citi's London branch is an integral part of Citibank; and when the bank publishes statements, it consolidates the assets and liabilities of the head office and all foreign branches. However, on a day-to-day operating basis, Citi New York, Citi London, and Citi's other foreign branches all keep separate books. Second, Citibank has just one account at the Fed, that held by Citi New York, the head office.

Now let's look at Table 6–1. It shows that as a result of the transaction, Exxon exchanges one asset, $10 million of demand deposits at Morgan New York, for another, $10 million of Euro deposits at Citi London. To make this exchange, Exxon withdrew funds from Morgan and deposited them at Citi. This means of course that when the transaction clears, Morgan has to pay Citi the funds Exxon has transferred from one bank to the other. Morgan does this in effect by transferring money from its reserve (checking) account at the Fed to Citi's reserve account at the Fed. Thus the transaction causes Morgan to lose reserves and Citi New York

---

[1] There is today a growing tendency to refer to dollar deposits accepted in Singapore and other Far East centers as *Asian dollars*. The natural extension of this practice would be to refer to dollar deposits accepted in Bahrain as Middle East dollars and dollar deposits accepted in Nassau as Caribbean dollars, that is, to use a multitude of terms to describe the same thing, an offshore deposit of dollars. The logical alternative to the term Eurodollar is *international dollar,* an anything but catchy phrase that has never caught on.

Table 6–1
A Euro deposit is made and cleared

Exxon

	Demand deposits, Morgan N.Y. −10 million (Euro) time deposits, Citi London +10 million

Citi N.Y.

Reserves +10 million	London office dollar account (a "due to" item, Citi N.Y. to Citi London) +10 million

Citi London

New York office dollar account (a "due from" item, Citi London to Citi N.Y.) +10 million	(Euro) time deposits +10 million

Morgan N.Y.

Reserves −10 million	Demand deposits, Exxon −10 million

New York Fed

	Reserves, Morgan −10 million Reserves, Citi +10 million

to gain them. At Morgan the loss of reserves is offset by a decrease in deposit liabilities.

At Citibank the situation is more complicated, as Table 6–1 shows. Citi London has received the deposit but Citi New York has received the extra reserves. So Citi New York in effect owes Citi London money. This is accounted for by adjusting the *New York office dollar account,* which can be thought of simply as a checking account that Citi London holds with Citi New York. To Citi London, as long as this account is in surplus, which it normally would be, the account is a *due from* item and it shows up on Citi London's balance sheet as an asset. On Citi New York's balance sheet the same account is a *due to* item, and consequently it shows up on Citi New York's balance sheet as any other deposit would. With this accounting framework in mind, it's easy to follow what happens on Citibank's books as a result of Exxon's deposit. Citi London gets a new $10 million liability in the form of a time deposit, which is offset by an equal credit to its account with home office. Meanwhile, home office gets $10 million of extra reserves, which are offset by a like increase in its liability to its London branch.

Note several things about this example. First, the changes that occurred on every institution's balance sheet were offsetting; i.e., net worth

never changes. This is *always* the case in any transaction the consequences of which can be illustrated with T-accounts.

A second and more important point is that, while Exxon now thinks of
itself as holding dollars in London, the dollars actually never left the
United States. In effect the whole transaction simply caused $10 million
of reserves to be moved from Morgan's reserve account at the New York
Fed to Citi's account there (see Table 6–1). This, by the way, would have
been the case in any Euro deposit example we might have used. Regardless of who makes the deposit, who receives it, and where in the world it
is made, the ultimate dollars never leave the United States.

A Euro loan

In our example we left Citi London with a new time deposit on which it
has to pay interest. To profit from that deposit, Citi London is naturally
going to lend those dollars out. Suppose, for the sake of illustration, that
Citi London lends the dollars to Electricité de France (EDF). Initially this
loan results in EDF's being credited with an extra $10 million in deposits
at Citi London, as Table 6–2 shows. EDF of course has borrowed the
money, so the $10 million will not sit idly in its account.

Table 6–2
A Euro loan is granted to EDF

Citi London		EDF	
Loan, EDF +10 million	(Euro) deposits, EDF +10 million	(Euro) deposits, Citi London +10 million	Loan, Citi London +10 million

Let's assume that EDF uses the dollars it has borrowed to pay for oil
purchased from an Arab seller who banks at Chase London. Table 6–3,
which should be self-explanatory to anyone who has followed Table 6–1,
shows the balance sheet changes that will result from this transaction.
Note in particular that when EDF pulls $10 million out of Citi London, the
latter, since it has no real dollars other than a deposit balance with Citi
New York, must in effect ask Citi New York to pay out this money with
dollars that Citi New York has in its reserve account at the Fed. As this is
done, offsetting changes naturally occur in the New York and London
office dollar accounts at Citibank. Meanwhile opposite but similar
changes are occurring on the books of Chase London and Chase New
York.

It is important to note that in this Euro loan transaction, just as in the
Eurodollar deposit transaction we worked through above, the dollars
never leave New York. The transaction simply results in a movement of

Table 6–3
EDF uses its borrowed dollars to pay for oil

EDF		Arab Oil Seller	
(Euro) deposits −10 million	Accounts payable −10 million	Accounts receivable −10 million (Euro) deposits, Chase London +10 million	

Citi London		Chase London	
New York office dollar account −10 million	(Euro) deposits, EDF −10 million	New York office dollar account +10 million	Time deposits, Arab oil seller +10 million

Citi N.Y.		Chase N.Y.	
Reserves −10 million	London office dollar account −10 million	Reserves +10 million	London office dollar account +10 million

New York Fed	
	Reserves, Citibank −10 million Reserves, Chase +10 million

$10 million from Citi's reserve account at the New York Fed to that of the Chase. One might, of course, argue that we have not yet gone far enough—that the Arab oil seller is going to spend the dollars he has received and that they might then leave the United States. But that is not so. Whoever gets the dollars the Arab spends will have to deposit them somewhere, and thus the spending by the Arab of his dollars will simply shift them from one bank's reserve account to another's. In this respect it might be useful to recall a point made in Chapter 2. The only way reserves at the Fed can be increased or decreased in the aggregate is through open-market operations initiated by the Fed itself. The one exception to this statement is withdrawals of cash from the banking system. If the Arab oil seller were to withdraw $10 million in cash from Chase London and lock it up in a safe there or elsewhere, the dollars would in effect have actually left the United States. However, no big depositor is going to do that because of opportunity cost; Euro deposits yield interest, whereas cash in a vault would not.

A Euro placement with a foreign bank

In the Euromarket it's very common for banks to lend dollars to other banks by making deposits with them and to borrow dollars from other banks by taking deposits from them. People in the Euromarket and people in New York with international experience always refer to the depositing of Eurodollars with another bank as a *placement* of funds and to the receipt of Eurodollar deposits from another bank as a *taking* of funds. Other people in the U.S. money market are likely to use the jargon of the Fed funds market, referring to placements of Euros as sales of funds and to takings of Euros as purchases of funds.

To illustrate what happens when a foreign bank ends up holding a Eurodollar deposit, let's work through the mechanics of a placement of Eurodollars with such a bank. Assume that Chase London places a $20 million deposit in the London Branch of Crédit Lyonnais.

The special feature of this example is that Crédit Lyonnais, unlike an American bank, is not a member of the Federal Reserve System and consequently does not have a reserve account at the Fed. Thus it has to keep its dollars on deposit in a U.S. bank. Suppose that in this case the dollars are deposited in a Crédit Lyonnais account at Morgan New York. Then, as Table 6–4 shows, the net effect of the transaction will be that Crédit Lyonnais ends up with dollars on deposit in New York, and reserves

Table 6–4
A Eurodollar interbank placement

Chase London		Crédit Lyonnais, London	
(Euro) time deposit, Crédit Lyonnais, London +20 million New York office dollar account −20 million		Deposit, Morgan N.Y. +20 million	Time deposit, Chase London +20 million

Chase N.Y.		Morgan N.Y.	
Reserves −20 million	London office dollar account −20 million	Reserves +20 million	Deposits, Crédit Lyonnais, London +20 million

New York Fed	
	Reserves, Chase −20 million Reserves, Morgan +20 million

move from Chase's account at the Fed to Morgan's account. Note again that the dollars remain in New York, even though they are now held by the London branch of a French bank.

In constructing our example, we tried to keep things simple to follow, and so ignored an important complication, namely, how Euro transactions are cleared. In the United States it is customary for banks to make payments between each other in Federal funds, that is, by transferring funds on deposit at the Fed over the Fed wire; also all large payments in the money and bond markets are made in Fed funds. In contrast, in the Euromarket money transfers are made in *clearing house funds:* these become Fed funds only on the day after receipt. The distinction between clearing house funds and Fed funds is something we will cover in the discussion of the Euro time deposit market in Chapter 16. It's a distinction of crucial importance because it creates a basis for certain interbank arbitrages that occur on a large scale between Fed funds and Euro dollars.

HISTORY OF THE MARKET

Anyone following Tables 6–1 through 6–4 is likely to wonder what the rationale is for carrying on outside the United States huge volumes of dollar deposit and loan transactions in what seems to be a rather complicated fashion. The best way to answer is to describe briefly the stimuli that gave birth to the Euromarket.

Long before World War II it was not uncommon for banks outside the United States to accept deposits denominated in dollars. The volume of such deposits, however, was small and the market for them had little economic significance. During the 1950s things began to change. One reason was the activities of the communist central banks. Since Russia and other communist countries imported certain goods that had to be paid for in dollars and exported others that could be sold for dollars, the central banks of these countries ended up holding dollar balances. Initially these balances were held on deposit in New York, but as the cold war tensions heightened, this practice became less attractive to the communists, who feared that at some point the United States might block their New York balances. As a result they transferred these balances to banks in London and other European centers. The value of the dollar goods the communist countries wanted to import often exceeded the amount of dollars they were earning on exports, so these countries became not only important lenders to the Eurodollar market but also important borrowers in this market.

While the cold war may have kicked off the Euromarket, there were other factors that stimulated its development. Historically the pound sterling played a key role in world trade. A great deal of trade not only within the British Commonwealth but also between Commonwealth nations and the rest of the world and between third countries was denominated in British currency, the pound sterling, and financed in London through borrowings of sterling. After World War II this began to change. Britain ran big balance of payments deficits (that is, spent more abroad than it earned), and as a result devaluation of the British pound—a decrease in the amount of foreign exchange for which a pound could be traded—was a constant threat and in fact actually occurred several times during the period of pegged exchange rates. The chronic weakness of the pound made it a less attractive currency to earn and to hold, which in turn stimulated the trend for more and more international trade to be denominated in dollars. It also caused the British to impose restrictions on the use of sterling for financing international trade. Specifically in 1957 the British government restricted the use of sterling in financing trade between non-sterling-area countries, and in 1976 it restricted the use of sterling in financing trade between Commonwealth countries and non-sterling-area countries. Because of the increased use of dollars as the availability of sterling financing decreased, importers began borrowing Eurodollars to finance trade, and the Euromarket emerged first as a nascent and then as a fast-growing and important international capital market.

A third factor that stimulated the growth of the Euromarket was the operation of Regulation Q during the tight money years of 1968 and 1969. At that time U.S. money market rates rose above the rates that banks were permitted to pay under Reg Q on domestic large-denomination CDs. In order to finance loans, U.S. banks were forced to borrow money in the Euromarket. All this resulted in a sort of merry-go-round operation. A depositor who normally would have put his money in, say, a Chase New York CD gave his money (perhaps via a Canadian bank because of U.S. controls on the export of capital) to Chase London, which then lent the money back to Chase New York. In effect Reg Q forced a portion of the supply of bought money that money market banks were coming to rely on in funding to move through London and other Euro centers. The operation of Regulation Q also encouraged foreign holders of dollars who would have deposited them in New York to put their dollars in London. Thus, for example, surplus German dollars borrowed by Italians ended up passing through London instead of New York.

Another important stimulus to the Euromarket was the various capital controls that were instituted during the 1960s to improve the U.S. balance of payments, which was in deficit. The first of these, the Interest Equalization Tax passed in 1964, was designed to discourage the issuance by foreign borrowers of debt obligations in the U.S. market. This measure was followed in 1965 by the Foreign Credit Restraint Program, which limited the amount of credit U.S. banks could extend to foreign borrowers. Finally in 1968 the government passed the Foreign Investment Program, which restricted the amount of domestic dollars U.S. corporations could use to finance foreign investments. Whatever the wisdom and effectiveness of these programs (they were eliminated in 1974), there is no doubt that they substantially increased the demand for dollar financing outside the United States, that is, for Eurodollar loans.

The persistent balance of payments deficits in the United States have often been given substantial credit for the development of the Euromarket; by spending more abroad than it earned, the United States in effect put dollars into the hands of foreigners and thus created a natural supply of dollars for the Euromarket. There is some truth to this, but it should be noted that U.S. balance of payments deficits are neither a necessary nor a sufficient condition for a thriving and growing Euromarket. After all, foreigners can deposit dollars in New York *and* domestic holders of dollars can place them in London. Where dollars are held need not be a function of who owns them. It is quite often a function of the relative attractiveness of the domestic and the Euromarkets to depositors. What has made the Euromarket attractive to depositors and given it much of its vitality is the freedom from restrictions under which this market operates and in particular the absence of the implicit tax that exists on U.S. domestic banking activities because of the reserve requirements imposed by the Fed.

A final important stimulus was given to the Euromarket by the hike in the price of oil that occurred in 1974. Due to that price rise, the Organization of Petroleum Exporting Countries (OPEC) suddenly found member nations holding massive balances of dollars, which they deposited in the Euromarket. Meanwhile many countries that were importers of oil experienced severe balance of payments difficulties and were forced to borrow dollars in the Euromarket to pay for their oil imports.

Just as dollars can be deposited in banks and bank branches outside the United States to create Eurodollars, the currencies of European countries can also be deposited outside their country of origin and thereby give rise to other types of *Eurocurrency deposits.* For example, German marks deposited in London in exchange for a mark balance are *Euromarks.* The major currencies other than dollars in which Eurocurrency deposits are held are German marks, the British pound, and Swiss francs (*Swissy* to the irreverent). There is also a limited market in Dutch guilders and rather difficult markets in other currencies. While the Euromarket is still primarily a dollar market, Euro deposits of other currencies are an important and growing part of the total market.

THE MARKET TODAY

From the inception of the Eurodollar market, London has been its biggest and most important center. That this role fell to London is hardly surprising. London has a long history as a world center for a host of financial activities: international lending, trade financing, commodities trading, stock trading, foreign exchange trading, insurance, and others. In truth, that square mile of London known as *the City of London,* or more often as just *the City,* is and has been since the 19th century the financial capital of the world.

Some of the many factors that contributed to London's development as an international financial center were the freedom and flexibility with which financial institutions were permitted to operate there. That freedom and flexibility still prevail, and because they do, London—with its huge concentration of financial expertise—was the logical place for the nascent Euromarket to develop and flourish. Throughout London's history as a Euro center, foreign banks have been permitted to open London branches and subsidiaries with ease and operate these branches and subsidiaries with a minimum of regulation. The Bank of England has imposed no specific capital requirements on the London branches of foreign banks and it has imposed no reserve requirements on the Eurocurrency deposits they accept. Britain taxes the profits earned by foreign banks' branches and subsidiaries but has imposed no withholding taxes on the interest banks pay to nonresident depositors.

While London has remained the preeminent center of the Euromarket, other centers have over time also developed. The Euromarket is, after all, a worldwide market. In the Far East in particular, Singapore and Hong Kong have both become important centers for Asian trading in Eurodollars. These centers suffer the disadvantage, however, that the natural sources of dollar supply and demand arising from trade and other activities in the Far East are not as great as those that focus on London, so their role remains a secondary one.

From the banks' point of view one growing disadvantage of basing Euro operations in London is the high taxes that must be paid on profits earned there. Largely to avoid these taxes, *booking centers* have developed in several localities offering favorable tax treatment of profits—Bahrain in the Mideast, Nassau, and the Cayman Islands, to name the most important. Banks that operate branches in these centers book there loans negotiated and made in London, New York, or elsewhere. They fund these loans either by having their branch buy money in its own name in the Eurodollar market or by funding the operation with dollars purchased in the name of their London branch. Nassau and the Cayman Islands offer one important advantage over Bahrain; they are in the same time zone as New York and only one hour ahead of

Table 6-5
Eurocurrency market, based on foreign-currency liabilities of banks in major European countries, the Bahamas, Bahrain, Cayman Islands, Panama, Canada, Japan, Hong Kong, and Singapore ($ billions)

	1970 Dec.	1971 Dec.	1972 Dec.	1973 Dec.	1974 Dec.	1975 Dec.	1976 Dec.	1977 Jun.	1977 Sep.	1977 Dec.*	1978 Mar.*
Estimated size											
Gross	110	145	200	305	370	455	560	590	615	660	670
Net	65	85	110	160	215	250	310	340	360	380	390
Eurodollars as percent of all Euro-currencies—gross	81	76	78	73	77	78	79	79	79	78	n.a.†

* Preliminary.
† n.a. = not available.
Source: Morgan Guaranty Bank, *World Financial Markets*, April 1978.

Chicago. Thus it is easy for management in U.S. money market banks to direct their operations in these centers during normal working hours.

Next to London the second most important center of the Euromarket is New York. Banks operating there naturally cannot accept Euro deposits, but New York is still an important center in Euro trading for several reasons. First, the New York banks are active takers of Euros in the names of their Nassau and Cayman branches. There are also several foreign bank branches in New York that are active takers of Euros for the same reason. A second reason New York is an important trading center for Euros is that New York and other banks engage very actively in arbitrage between Euro and "domestic" dollars (see Chapter 17). A final reason for the prominence of New York as a Euro center is that many of the nation's largest banks direct their worldwide Euro operations from New York.

In addition to the major centers of the Euromarket we have described, there are numerous centers of lesser but growing importance, for example, Paris, Frankfurt, and Luxembourg in Europe. Many financial centers that would seem logical candidates to become Euro trading centers have in fact not done so. Generally, the reasons have to do with local exchange controls, bank regulations, taxation, or other inhibiting factors. The Japanese banks, for example, are important participants in the Eurodollar market but Tokyo has never become an important center of this market, in part because foreign depositors are excluded.

From rather meager beginnings the Euromarket has developed into a truly huge market. Unfortunately, it is impossible to say just how huge because there is no worldwide system for collecting data on the Eurocurrency market. The best figures available are probably the estimates made by the Morgan Guaranty Bank. Its figures (Table 6–5) cover Euro deposits in all significant Euro centers. The *gross* number in Table 6–5 include sizable amounts of interbank placements. Using estimates, Morgan eliminates these placements to get figures on the *net* amounts of Eurodollars and other Eurocurrencies that nonbank depositors have placed with banks in the reporting countries. From these net figures it is evident that both Eurodollars and other Eurocurrency deposits have grown phenomenally over the last decade.

OVERVIEW OF BANK EURO OPERATIONS

In a very real sense the Eurodollar market is a true international market without location, which means in effect that it is not really a domestic market for any bank. Thus every bank active in the market tends to compartmentalize its activities there, to think in terms of what Eurodollar assets and liabilities it has acquired. In the jargon of the market, every Euro banker is running a *Eurodollar book.* In the case of foreign banks the reason is obvious; they are dealing in a foreign currency, the dollar, which has limited availability to them at best. In the case of U.S. banks, the distinction between domestic and Euro operations arises from a less fundamental but still important consideration, namely, the fact that Fed reserve requirements and other factors create a real distinction between Eurodollars and domestic dollars, one that is of varying importance depending on economic conditions and on the maturities of the domestic and Eurodollar assets and liabilities compared.

Banking ground rules in the Euromarket are quite different from those that prevail on the U.S. banking scene, with the result that the character of U.S. bank operations in the Euromarket differs from that of their operations in the domestic money market. Thus we will present a quick overview of bank Euro operations before we talk in detail about their deposit accepting and lending activities in this market.

The first important distinction between U.S. banks' domestic and Euro operations is in the character of their Euro liabilities. In the Euromarket all deposits, with the exception of call money, have a fixed maturity (*tenor* in British jargon) which may range anywhere from 1 day to 5 years. Also, interest is paid on all deposits, the rate being a function of prevailing economic conditions and the maturity of the deposit. While most bank Euro liabilities are straight time deposits, banks operating in the London market also issue Eurodollar CDs. Like domestic CDs, these instruments carry a fixed rate of interest, are issued for a fixed time span, and are negotiable.

A second important distinction between banks' domestic and Euro operations is that no reserve requirements are imposed against banks' Eurocurrency deposits. Thus every dollar of deposits accepted can be invested.

Banks accepting Eurodollar deposits use these dollars to make two sorts of investments, loans and interbank placements. All such placements, like other Euro deposits, have fixed maturities and bear interest. The market for Eurodollar deposits, nonbank and interbank, is highly competitive and the rates paid on deposits of different maturities are determined by market supply and demand. Since the Euromarket operates outside the control of any central bank, there are no Reg Q or other controls limiting or setting the rates that Eurodollars can command. As one might expect, Euro rates are volatile, rising when money is tight and falling when it is easy.

The rate at which banks in London offer Eurodollars in the placement market is referred to as the *London interbank offered rate,* or *LIBOR* for short. In pricing Euro loans, LIBOR is of crucial importance.

In the Euromarket, unlike the domestic market, all loans have fixed maturities, which can range anywhere from a few days to 5 years or longer. The general practice is to price all loans at *LIBOR plus a spread.*

On some term loans the lending rate is fixed for the life of the loan. By far the more usual practice, however, is to price term loans on a *rollover basis*. This means that every 3 or 6 months the loan is repriced at the then-prevailing LIBOR for 3- or 6-month money plus the fixed, agreed-upon spread. For example, a 1-year loan might be rolled after 6 months, which means that the first 6-month segment would be priced at the agreed-upon spread plus the 6-month LIBOR rate prevailing at the time the loan was granted, while the second 6-month segment would be priced at the same spread plus the 6-month LIBOR rate prevailing 6 months later. On Euro loans banks never require the borrower to hold compensating balances.

The job of running a bank's Eurodollar book boils down to much the same thing as running a domestic banking operation. The Euro banker has to decide which assets to hold and what liabilities to use to fund them. In making these decisions, the Euro banker faces the same *risks* that a domestic banker does—a credit risk, a liquidity risk, and a rate risk. And his objective, like that of the domestic banker, is to maximize profits subject to the constraint that risks are held to an acceptable level.

In a bank's Euro book, credit risk exists both on ordinary loans and on interbank placements, which—like sales of Fed funds—are unsecured loans. To control risk on ordinary loans, banks impose credit standards on borrowers as well as limits on the amount they will lend to any one borrower. On placements with other banks, credit risk is controlled, as in the case of Fed funds sales, by setting up lines of credit that limit the amount the bank will lend to any other banking institution. As noted below, banks also use lines to limit what is called *country risk*.

Because most of a Euro banker's assets and liabilities have fixed maturities, it would be possible for a Euro banker, unlike a domestic banker, to run a *matched book,* that is, to fund every 3-month asset with 3-month money, every 6-month asset with 6-month money, and so on. If he did so, moreover, he would reduce his rate risk to zero because every asset would be financed for its duration at a locked-in positive spread. He would also minimize his liquidity risk; but he would not eliminate it, since on rollover loans he would still have to return periodically to the market to obtain new funding.

While running a matched book would reduce risk, it would also limit the bank's opportunity to earn profits in an important and traditional way—by lending long and borrowing short. Euro bankers are conscious of the profit opportunities that a mismatched book offers, and to varying degrees they all create a conscious mismatch in their Eurodollar books—one that is carefully monitored to prevent unacceptable risks. How great a maturity mismatch a given bank will permit in its Euro book depends on various factors: the shape of the yield curve, its view on interest rates, and its perception of its own particular liquidity risk.

THE INTERBANK PLACEMENT MARKET

The pool of funds that forms the basis for the Eurodollar market is provided by a varied cast of depositors: large corporations (domestic, foreign, and multinational), central banks and other government bodies, supranational institutions such as the BIS, and wealthy individuals. Most of these funds come in the form of time deposits with fixed maturities. The banks, however, also receive substantial amounts of *call money,* which can be withdrawn by the depositor on a day's notice. Banks normally offer a fixed rate for call money, which they adjust periodically as market conditions change. The major attraction of a call money deposit to the holder is liquidity. Time deposits pay more, but a penalty is incurred if such a deposit is withdrawn before maturity. From the point of view of the banks, call money is attractive because it is cheap. Also, despite its short-term nature, call money turns out to be a fairly stable source of funds, so much so that a big bank might, in running its Euro book, feel comfortable viewing half of its call money deposits as essentially long-term funds.

Banks receiving Euro deposits frequently choose for reasons discussed below to place some portion of the deposits given to them with other banks, often while simultaneously taking deposits of other maturities. As a result of all this buying and selling, a very active, high-volume market in interbank placements has developed. This market is worldwide. It also has a huge number of participants, which reflects two facts. First, banks from countries all over the world participate in the market. Second, every one of a bank's foreign branches (and many U.S., European, and Japanese banks have large numbers of them) participates in this market as a separate entity. This means, for example, that Citibank's foreign branches in London, Singapore, Bahrain, Nassau, and elsewhere all take and place Eurodollars in their own name.

Because there are so many players in the Eurodollar market and because they are scattered all over the globe, it would be difficult and extremely costly for all of them to communicate their bids and offers for deposits directly to each other. To fill the gap, a number of firms have gone into the business of brokering Euro time deposits.

While the proportion of total Euro placements that is brokered is significant, not all such placements pass through the brokers' market. In particular a fair amount of money is sold by continental banks to big London bidders on a direct basis, with the London bidder quoting rates based on those prevailing in the brokers market. Also, a bank branch normally won't trade with another branch of the same bank through brokers, since the two are in direct communication with each other.

A bank placing funds in the interbank market faces two risks. First, there is the *credit risk,* which banks seek to control through the use of credit lines. In establishing lines to foreign banks, a U.S. bank will look at the normal criteria of creditworthiness such as size, capitalization, profitability, and reputation. In addition, a bank will be concerned about *country* or *sovereign risk.* Specifically, it will consider various factors about the bank's country of origin that might influence either the bank's viability or its ability to meet commitments denominated in a foreign currency. Of particular interest would be factors such as whether the country of origin was politically stable, whether nationalization on terms unfavorable to foreign depositors was a possibility, and whether the country's balance of payments was reasonably strong.

There's also a second aspect of sovereign risk that banks placing Eurocurrency deposits with other banks worry about. A bank selling Euros to, say, the London branch of the Bank of Tokyo must be concerned not only about the creditworthiness of that bank and the Japanese country risk but also about the economic and political climate in London: Is it conceivable that by nationalizing foreign bank branches, freezing their assets, or some other action the British might render it impossible for these branches to honor their commitment to repay borrowed dollars? Questions of this sort are less of a concern with respect to London than with respect to smaller and newer Euro centers such as Bahrain and Nassau. Banks seek to limit the sovereign risk to which they are exposed by imposing country limits on their lendings and interbank placements.

The administration of these limits requires much painstaking work for several reasons. First, two sets of limits apply, country limits and limits to individual banks. Second, for Bank A to keep track of how much credit in the form of Eurodollar placements it has granted to Bank B, it has to track the Euro sales of *all* its branches to *all* Bank B's branches. Third, at the same time that Bank A is selling Euros to Bank B, it will also be granting credit to Bank B in other ways, for example, through the sale of Fed funds or via letters of credit.

Granting lines to buyers of Eurodollars used to be more casual and less cautious than it is now. In 1974 the Bankhaus I D Herstatt, a medium-sized German bank, failed under conditions that left several banks standing in line along with other creditors to get funds due them. This event, along with the difficulties experienced during the same year by the Franklin National Bank, sent shock waves through the Euromarket and caused banks to review with an air of increased caution the lines they had granted to other banks. The upshot was that many smaller banks lost the lines they had enjoyed and they experienced difficulty buying Euros; some were even forced out of the market. *Tiering* also developed in market rates, with banks that were judged poorer credit risks being forced to pay up. In particular, the Japanese banks that are consistently big net takers of Euros had to pay up 1–2 percent and so did the Italian banks because of unfavorable economic and political developments within Italy. Several years have now passed since the Herstatt crisis; the Euromarket has regained much of the confidence it lost in 1974 and lines have again been enlarged. Tiering, however, has remained a phenomenon in the market, being more pronounced the tighter money gets and the higher rates rise.

Most banks, because of their size, nationality, and customer base, tend to be natural net sellers or buyers of Euros. However, it's important for a bank that wants to buy Euros to also sell them some of the time, since one way a bank gets lines from other banks is by placing deposits with them. In the Euromarket, as in the Fed funds market, some banks have to buy their way in.

There is much more to be said about how Euros are quoted and traded in the brokers market and about the arbitrages between Eurodollars and domestic dollars. These topics are covered in Chapters 16 and 17.

EURO CERTIFICATES OF DEPOSIT

Because Eurodollar time deposits, with the exception of call money, have fixed maturities, from the point of view of many investors they have one serious disadvantage, namely, illiquidity. To satisfy investors who needed liquidity, Citbank began issuing *Eurodollar certificates of deposit* in London. Its example was quickly followed by other U.S. and foreign banks with London branches.

Because of the liquidity of Euro CDs, banks issuing them are able to sell them at rates slightly below those offered on time deposits of equivalent maturity, ¼ to ⅛ percent less when the market is quiet. While Euro CDs were originally designed for corporations and other investors who wanted real liquidity, following the Herstatt incident an interesting development occurred in the Euro CD market. Many smaller banks and foreign banks as well felt the need for the appearance of greater liquidity in their Eurodollar books. To get it, they bought Euro CDs from other banks with the understanding that the bank buying the CD would never trade that CD and that it would moreover permit the selling bank to safekeep the CD to ensure that this understanding was honored. CDs sold on these terms, known as *lock-up CDs,* are very close to a time deposit from the point of view of the issuing bank, and normally the rate paid on them is very close to the time deposit rate. While no figures are available, it is estimated by some that as much as 50 percent of all Euro CDs sold are lock-up CDs; others put the figure much lower. Some of the remaining Euro CDs sold are purchased by Swiss banks for investors whose funds they manage; these CDs too are rarely traded. Most of the rest of the Euro CDs issued in London are sold to investors in the United States: corporations, domestic banks, and others.

Since the major advantage to the issuing bank of writing Euro CDs is that CD money is cheaper than time deposit money, banks issuing such CDs carefully hold down the volume they write so that the spread between the rates at which they can buy CD money and time deposit money is preserved. To issue CDs, the banks normally post daily rates, the attractiveness of which reflects both their eagerness to write and the maturities in which they want to take money. Occasionally when the banks are anxious to write, they will also issue through either London CD brokers or the various U.S. money market dealers who have set up shop in London. These brokers and dealers also make a secondary market for Euro CDs, without which these instruments would have liquidity in name only.

The Euro CD market is smaller than the domestic CD market, and Euro CDs are less liquid than domestic CDs. More about that and the mechanics of Euro CD trading is given in Chapter 15.

EURO LENDING

Today the Eurodollar market is *the* international capital market of the world, which is very much reflected in the mix of borrowers that come to this market for loans. Their ranks include U.S. corporations funding foreign operations, foreign corporations funding foreign or domestic operations, foreign government agencies funding investment projects, and foreign governments funding development projects or general balance of payments deficits.

Lending terms

All Euro loans are, as we have said, priced at LIBOR plus a spread. Since different banks may be offering Eurodollars at not quite identical rates, the LIBOR rate used in pricing a loan is usually the average of the 11:00 A.M. offering rates of three to five reference banks, the latter always being top banks in the market.

How great a spread over LIBOR a borrower is charged is a function of risk and market conditions. In a period of slack loan demand, a top borrower might be able to get funds at LIBOR plus as little as ½ percent. In contrast, a second-class credit shopping for a loan when money was tight might have to pay as much as LIBOR plus 2½ percent.

On rollover loans, which most Euro loans are today, the bank normally allows the borrower to choose whether to take 3-month or 6-month money each time a rollover date comes up. Banks will also grant a 1-year rollover option to good customers but try to discourage the inclusion of this option in loan agreements because match funding maturities beyond 6 months can sometimes be difficult due to the thinness of the market in longer-term deposits. What choice of maturity the borrower makes on a rollover date depends on whether he expects interest rates to rise or fall.

The bank may at the borrower's request also include in a rollover loan agreement a *multicurrency clause* that permits the borrower to switch from one currency to another—say, from dollars to German marks—on a rollover date. Multi-currency clauses usually stipulate that nondollar funds will be made available to the borrower conditional upon "availability." This clause protects a bank from exchange control regulations and other factors which might dry up the market and prohibit the bank from acquiring the desired funds, even in the foreign exchange market.

While fixed-rate, fixed-term loans do occur in the Euromarket, they are uncommon. Banks are generally unwilling to make them unless they match fund, a policy that makes such loans so expensive that the borrower is likely to conclude that his funding cost over the life of the loan would be less with a rollover loan. Also a prime borrower willing to pay up to lock in a fixed borrowing rate may find a Eurobond issue cheaper than a fixed-rate term loan.

The maximum maturity that Euro bankers will grant on term loans generally is around 7 years, although some banks are willing to go to 10. In judging what maturity it will grant on a specific loan, a bank will consider the borrower's underlying need (what is he financing?), his ability to repay, and—if the loan is to be shared by several banks—what the market will accept. Typically the slacker the loan demand, the longer the maturity that is acceptable.

Often term loans extended to finance capital projects have an availability *period* during which the borrower receives funds according to some prearranged schedule based on his anticipated needs. The availability period may be followed by a grace period during which no repayment of principal is required. After that the normal procedure is for the loan to be amortized over its remaining life. Some *bullet loans* with no amortization are granted, but they are the exception not the rule.

On Euro loans the standard practice has been not to permit prepayment, but some agreements do permit it on rollover dates with or sometimes without payment of a penalty. To gain greater flexibility the borrower can negotiate a *revolving facility,* which permits him during the life of the loan agreement to take down funds, repay them, and take them down again if he so chooses.

The fact that Euro loans are made to borrowers all over the world could create considerable legal complications for lenders, especially in the case of default. To minimize these, Euro loan agreements generally specify that the loan is subject to either U.S. or British law.

Many Euro loans granted to U.S. corporations by U.S. banks are negotiated at the bank's head office in the United States. This is particularly likely to be the case if the loan is granted to a foreign subsidiary that is kept financially anemic because it is operating in a weak-currency country or if management of the overall firm is strongly centralized. If, on the other hand, the sub is financially strong and its management is largely autonomous, the negotiation for a Euro loan will occur abroad, frequently in London because the expertise is there.

Loan syndication

Over time syndication of Euro loans has become increasingly common. There are various reasons a bank might choose to syndicate a loan. On corporate loans for big projects (e.g., development of North Sea oil) the amount required might exceed a bank's legal lending limit, or the bank might not choose to go to that limit in the interests of diversification of risk. On country loans the basic chip can be $1 billion or more, and there is no bank that could write that sort of business alone. Country loans often are for such huge amounts these days because certain borrowers, especially underdeveloped countries, are financing big development projects. Other countries with substantial borrowing needs are financing balance of payments deficits that they have incurred in part because the prices of oil and other raw material imports have risen sharply.

Big Euro loan syndication agreements are negotiated in London. Often the lead bank is a top U.S. bank, but in recent years German banks have become more aggressive in this area. While many of the banks that participate in a typical Euro syndication are based in London, it is not uncommon for continental banks and even domestic U.S. banks with no London branch to take a piece of such loans. Doing so may provide them with both a good rate and a chance to diversity their assets.

Loan syndication normally starts with the borrower accepting the loan terms proposed by a bank and giving that bank a mandate to put together a credit for it. Most such agreements are on a *fully underwritten basis,* which means that the lead bank guarantees the borrower that he will get all of the money stipulated in the loan proposal.

Since the amount guaranteed is more than the lead bank could come up with alone, it selects *comanagers* that help it underwrite the loan. Once the lead bank and the comanagers have split up the loan into shares, they have about two weeks to sell off whatever portion of their underwriting share they do not want to take into portfolio. At the end of this selling period, the lead bank advises the borrower as to what banks have participated in the syndication. Then the borrower and these banks attend a closing at which the final loan agreement is signed. Two days later the borrower gets his money. From the point of view of the lender, participation in a syndicated loan carries a commitment to lend for the life of the loan, since such participations are rarely sold by one bank to another.

A number of different fees are charged on a loan syndication. First there is the management fee, which may run from as low as ⅜ percent up to 1 percent or more, depending on market conditions and the borrower's name. Normally the lead bank shares some portion of this front-end fee with the banks that take significant portions of the total loan into portfolio.

A second fee the borrower pays is a spread over LIBOR on whatever funds he takes down. The borrower also pays a commitment fee, generally around ½ percent, on any monies committed but not drawn. Finally, there is an agency fee that goes to the bank responsible for interfacing between the lending banks and the borrower, that is, for the receipt and disbursement of loan proceeds and for general supervision of the operation of the credit agreement.

Merchant banks.   Loan syndication can be done directly by a bank. It has, however, become increasingly common for large U.S. banks to set up separate merchant banking subsidiaries with the principal function of syndicating loans. Loans are also syndicated by consortium banks, that is, by banks set up and jointly owned by several banks, frequently of different nationalities.

A British bank can engage in a much wider range of activities than a U.S. bank can. There has, however, tended to be some degree of specialization between different British banks. In particular the so-called merchant banks have specialized primarily in providing not loans of their own funds, but various financial services to their customers. These include accepting bills arising out of trade, underwriting new stock and bond issues, and advising corporate customers on acquisitions, mergers, foreign expansion, and portfolio management.

One reason why several top U.S. banks have opened merchant banking arms in London is that these subs can engage in activities, such as bond underwriting, that the branch itself could not because of the Glass-Steagall Act. Another reason is that some U.S. banks feel that merchant banking activities, including loan syndication, are a different sort of business from commercial banking—one that requires deals-oriented money raisers and more continuity of personnel than is found in commercial banking. As one banker put it: "Merchant banking is using other people's assets and getting paid a fee for it; the other people in this case may include anyone in the market, including the parent bank. In loan syndications where we add value is by taking a view on price, terms, conditions, and amounts that can be done for a borrower and by then assembling the group which will manage and sell the issue."

Most U.S. banks' merchant banking subs do not keep substantial amounts of the loans they syndicate on their own books. Their objective is to provide the parent bank with the portion of the loan it wants and sell the rest to the market. One reason for this approach is that the parent bank has a comparative advantage over the sub in funding. It has a stronger name in which to buy funds, and it has experienced dealers and other funding personnel that the merchant bank could duplicate only at considerable expense, if at all.

Consortium banks. A number of U.S. banks, in addition to or instead of setting up a merchant banking subsidiary, have joined with other banks to form consortium banks. These can and do carry out much the same activities as their merchant banking subs do. The objectives of U.S. banks in joining such groups have been mixed, depending on the size and experience of the bank. Some smaller banks joined in order to be able to participate in medium-term Euro financing. Other banks joined to gain experience in international financial markets in general, in specific geographic markets, or in new lines of business. Consortia formed by large banks obviously provide a large standing capability for syndicating loans, and these institutions are active in this area.

Euro lines

In addition to granting straight loans, Euro bankers grant lines of credit to a varied group of borrowers, including both domestic and foreign firms issuing commercial paper in the U.S. market.

Euro lines, unlike U.S. lines, are granted on a strict fee basis; no compensating balances are required. Many Euro lines are revolvers that legally commit the bank to provide the line holder with funds if he requests them. Euro bankers, however, have also granted Eurodollar and multicurrency lines on a more or less no-change-in-material-circumstances basis.

Generally speaking, the Euromarket is more transactions oriented than the customer-oriented U.S. market. One result of this is that when money is easy, Euro lines are often cheaper than lines of credit in the United States. In contrast, when money tightens, Euro lines tend either to dry up in terms of availability or to rise dramatically in price.

In the Euromarket and in foreign banking in general, some of the most important lines granted by banks are not lines to customers but lines to other banks. A French bank operating a dollar book in the London or New York market is running a book in a foreign currency, and so in a U.S. bank running a French franc book in Paris or a sterling book in London.

All these banks worry with good reason about liquidity, that is, about their ability to fund on a continuing basis in a foreign currency the various assets they have acquired that are denominated in that currency.

To reduce the risks in running books denominated in foreign currencies, many of the major banks of the world have set up reciprocal line agreements. Under such an agreement a big French bank that naturally is going to have better access than a U.S. bank to the domestic French franc market would agree to provide a U.S. bank with francs in a time of crisis. In exchange the U.S. bank would extend to the French bank a promise to supply it with dollars should its access to dollar funding be threatened.

Another way foreign banks operating in the Euromarket enhance their dollar liquidity is by purchasing for a fee backup lines from U.S. banks. The attractiveness of such lines depends in part on the shape of the yield curve. Assume, for example, that such a line cost 0.5 percent. If the foreign bank could take 1-year dollars at 6 percent and lend them day to day at 5.75 percent, borrowing long and lending short in the placement market would be a cheaper way to acquire liquidity than taking out a line, and it might also do more for the foreign bank's balance sheet. If, on the other hand, the yield curve were steep, buying lines would be the more attractive alternative.

Euro loans for domestic purposes

While the bulk of Euro lending is to foreign borrowers or to U.S. corporations that are funding foreign operations, a growing number of U.S. corporations have been borrowing money in the Euromarket for domestic purposes. Their major incentive for doing so is to reduce their borrowing costs. Frequently the rate quoted on a Euro loan by a bank's London branch will be cheaper than the *all-in* cost (prime plus compensating balances) quoted by the same bank on a domestic loan, a situation that one top U.S. bank executive described as "sillier than hell."

There are several reasons for this price discrepancy. First, reserve requirements, which prevail in domestic banking but not in Euro banking, constitute in effect a tax on domestic banking that tends to force domestic lending rates above Euro rates. Second, U.S. banks have only a single prime based on 90-day money market rates. With an upward-sloping yield curve from 1 day out to 90, this arrangement naturally penalizes borrowers who want very short-term money. In the Euromarket there is no such penalty. A 1-month loan is priced at LIBOR for 1-month money plus a spread, an all-in rate that may be significantly less than LIBOR on 3-month money plus the same spread. In effect Euro bankers charge *money market rates* on loans, while domestic bankers do not.

The potential advantages of borrowing in the Euromarket have led some large U.S. corporations to exert pressure on their banks to grant them *either-or facilities,* that is, to permit them to borrow from their bank's head office or a foreign branch as they desire. Generally the banks have resisted, citing the importance of customer relationships, loyalty, and other factors. They have two reason for doing so. First, their profit margin is likely to be larger on a domestic loan than on a Euro loan. Second, they know they can't be competitive in the market for Euro loans. When a U.S. bank lends Eurodollars to a domestic borrower for domestic purposes, it incurs under Reg M a 1 percent reserve requirement, which forces it to raise the Euro rate it quotes to a domestic borrower a slight fraction above the rate it quotes to foreign borrowers. Foreign banks lending into the United States incur no such reserve requirement and thus are in a position to consistently underprice U.S. banks on such loans.

So far relatively few of the U.S. corporations that might at times benefit by borrowing in the Euromarket have seriously attempted to do so. Part of the reason is ignorance and inertia. It is also true that a domestic corporation borrowing from a foreign bank may find that the foreign bank understands its position less well than its domestic bank does, that there are communications problems, and that in general some of the important elements of the customer relationship it has built up with its domestic bank are hard to establish with a foreign bank.

RUNNING A EURO BOOK

In running their Eurodollar books, the big U.S. banks have taken almost two decades to develop strategies that are sophisticated and with which they feel comfortable. One reason is that the top executives of money market banks were and by and large still are people with little experience in international business. Also during the early years of the Euromarket, no one really understood the market or knew where it was going. Gradually, of course, some market expertise developed in London but that spread only slowly across the Atlantic. Thus when the London branches of the big U.S. banks began running dollar books, the edict went out from home office that asset and liability maturities were to be matched in order to minimize rate and liquidity risks.

The emphasis on matching continued for some time. In fact, it has only been in the last 5 years that U.S. banks have become willing to mismatch their Euro books in an aggressive way in order to increase profits. Oddly enough the Herstatt crisis probably contributed to their willingness to do so. As it blew over, bankers concluded that if the Euromarket had survived Herstatt, it was mature enough to survive anything.

Today all the major U.S. banks have several foreign branches running Euro books, so their overall exposure to risk in the Euromarket is the sum of the risks associated with several separate branch books. So far as liability management is concerned, management's main concern is with the rate and liquidity risks that are created through the mismatch of the bank's consolidated Euro position. To control those risks, management sets up guidelines within which each branch is supposed to operate.

Obviously there is no precise way to compare the risk associated with funding, say, a 3-month loan with overnight money versus lending 6-month money and funding the first 4 months with 4-month money. So head office guidelines take arbitrary and quite different forms. The purpose, however, is always the same—to limit the degree of mismatch the branch can practice.

Euro bankers often refer to the practice of lending long and borrowing short as running an *open book.* Head office might, for example, control the mismatch on a branch's book by setting limits on the open positions that the branch could assume beyond 2 months, 4 months, and 6 months. An alternative approach is to apply different weights to the mismatches in different maturity ranges (larger weights, the longer the maturity range) and then require that the weighted sum of all mismatches be less than some maximum dollar figure.

The job of operating the branch's book under these guidelines falls to local funding officers. In the London branch of a large U.S. bank there will be several senior people responsible for making overall policy decisions and a number of dealers under them who actually buy and sell money. Much of the work of the senior people involves formulating a view on what is likely to happen to interest rates and then deciding, in light of that view and current market conditions, what strategies should be followed in taking and placing deposits.

In making decisions of this sort, the Euro liability manager is in a position quite different from that of his domestic counterpart. As a London Euro banker who moved to the New York head office put it: "In the United States a bank doesn't have to work very hard on liability management; if the cost of money goes up, the bank puts the prime up. Thus buying long money involves taking a view that the bank doesn't really have to,[1] and the typical practice is for the bank to fund the bulk of its domestic loans with short or very short money. In the Euromarket, in contrast, the only assets the bank can take on are fixed-rate, fixed-maturity assets. Thus, the Euro banker who mismatches incurs a very real rate risk, and the existence of this risk forces him to constantly make interest rate predictions and to structure his asset and liability maturities accordingly."

---

[1] *Taking a view* is a London expression for forming an opinion as to where interest rates are going and acting on it.

If a Euro banker expects interest rates to stay steady or fall, he will tend to lend long and borrow short, i.e., run a *short* book, assuming a normally shaped yield curve. How short depends in part on the slope of the yield curve. As one banker noted: "There's no incentive to take money at call and put it out for 3 or 6 months for a ¼ or ⅜ spread. With a flat yield curve like that, you are taking a tremendous risk for little reward; if rates back up, you are left with a negative carry. But when the yield curve is steep, say, a 1 percent spread between call and 1-year rates, there is a real incentive to overlend and take the spread."

The dealers

Once a decision about the maturity structure of the branch's assets and liabilities is made, the responsibility for implementing this decision falls on the chief dealer and his assistants. The London dealing room of a large bank is a fascinating and busy place, populated during trading hours by a bevy of time deposit and foreign exchange traders engaged in rapid-fire, nonstop conversations with brokers and large customers.

The "book" that is thrust into the chief dealer's care is a sheet of data giving the current amounts and maturities of all the bank's assets and liabilities. The salient features of this book are something a good dealer keeps in his head—the mismatch in different maturities, the amounts of funds he is likely to have to buy or sell in coming days, and when and in what maturity ranges rate pressures might develop from big rollovers. On the basis of this information, the overall guidelines established for the branch, and the strategies set by local funding officers, the dealer's job is to do the necessary buying and placing of funds as profitably as possible for the bank. This may sound simple, but it leaves much room for the exercise of strategy and judgment.

On every Eurodollar loan a bank makes and funds, it has three potential sources of profit. First, there is the spread the bank gets over LIBOR, which compensates it for operating expenses and the credit risk it is assuming. Second, there is the extra $1/16$ or $1/8$ percent that the bank may be able to make if its dealers can pick up the needed funds a little below LIBOR, for example, through astute timing of the purchase. A third way a bank can profit from a loan is through mismatching its book.

While major decisions about mismatch are made by senior funding officers, the dealer has and needs some leeway in implementing them. When a big syndicated loan rolls over and a lot of banks are in the market trying to "match fund" their participation in the loan, a good dealer may find that he is forced to mismatch—buy funds in anticipation of need or pick them up later—if he does not want to overpay for his money.

In this respect it's worth noting that when the Eurodollar market was younger, a big rollover could cause a perceptible if temporary upward bulge in Euro rates. This is considerably less true today because of banks' increasing willingness to mismatch and because of the market's increasing depth. In fact, today a $1 billion loan rollover can occur with no real impact on market rates.

Euro bankers take time deposits from two sources, bank customers and the bank placement market. A major bank branch in London will have several people whose job is to contact major depositors, such as big corporate customers (e.g., the oil companies), certain central banks, and other big depositors. Unlike the time deposit dealers, these customer representatives have time to chat with depositors about market conditions and rates. The banks like to pick up money this way since it saves them brokerage costs. Also at times such money may be cheaper than what they could pick up in the interbank market. That depends on the sophistication of the depositor.

Banks that are large takers of funds also try to cultivate direct relationships with other banks. Banks, unlike corporations, can go into the brokers market to place Eurodollars. Thus a bank attempting to pick up money direct from other banks in order to save brokerage normally tries to be very fair about the bid rates it posts for different maturities, and to suggest indirectly at least that sellers go elsewhere on days that it is posting noncompetitive rates because it does not need money. In this respect it's interesting to note that a major bank that posts noncompetitive rates may still pick up some deposits either because the lender has lines to only a few banks or because his lines to other banks are full.

While large banks prefer to get money direct in order to save brokerage costs, brokers are extremely useful to them. For one thing, although brokers have to be paid, they save the banks money on both communications and personnel. A funding officer of one of the largest U.S. banks estimated offhand that without the brokers, he would need 200 telephone lines and 50 dealers to run the London dealing room. The brokers are also useful to a bank that suddenly discovers it has an hour to raise $200 million of short-dated funds, an amount that might take some time to dig out directly. A third advantage the brokers offer is the cloak of anonymity. As a funding officer at the London branch of one of the largest U.S. banks put it: "Suppose I want to sell $50 million and I call a bank direct, one who would have been prepared to do that transaction in the brokers market. He sees that it is my bank on the other side and he gets nervous and wonders—what are they trying to do, $50 million or $200 million? So he does a $10 million deal and now not only have I not done the transaction, but also I have disclosed the amount I am trying to do." Anonymity in this respect is useful for all the top banks. They are a bit like bulls in a barnyard; whenever they move, their smaller companions get nervous.

Euro placements

One of the curious things about the Euromarket, at least to the uninitiated, is that many participants in the market are busily taking deposits
with the right hand and placing them with the left. In the beginning,
interbank placements may have been made partly out of a concern for
balance sheet cosmetics. In domestic operations, it's not considered
proper for a bank to loan out all the funds it takes in, the idea being that
this would leave the bank with no bonds to sell and thus with a potential
liquidity problem. For a money market bank, this notion makes little
sense, but no U.S. bank, big or small, is going to get caught with no
securities on its balance sheet. In their Euro operations banks don't pick
up any salable securities unless they run a Euro CD portfolio. Thus,
especially in the early days of the Euromarket when matched funding
was the rule, a book in which all assets were loans would have been
logical and would have posed no great liquidity threat. It would, however, have looked bad according to the traditional criteria of bank management. Placements, which are not classed as loans but can be just as
illiquid, do not present this difficulty. Thus cosmetic considerations were
one incentive for Euro placements. Once banks became willing to mismatch, *profits* became another incentive.

A domestic bank that has a strong view on where interest rates are
going is hard put to place a big bet based on that view. If it expects
interest rates to fall, there is no interbank market in which it can sell
long-dated money in volume; and since a savvy corporate treasurer is
likely to have the same interest rate view that the bank does, his bank is
not going to get him to take out a fixed-rate term loan at such a time. If
alternatively a domestic banker expects rates to rise, he will want to buy
long-dated money but he has no place where he can do this in volume.
Whatever his expectations, his options for structuring maturities are
limited.

In the Euromarket things are different. A bank can't, of course, order
its customers to take fixed-rate term loans whenever it would like them to.
But in the placement market a bank can buy and sell funds in reasonable
volume over a wide range of maturities. There are several reasons for the
contrast in maturity options between the U.S. market and the Euromarket.
First, the Euromarket is traditionally more accustomed to dealing in longer
dates. On the deposit side in particular there have always been some
suppliers of funds who were concerned primarily with preservation and
safety of principal as opposed to maximizing return and were willing for a
spread to supply long-dated funds to creditworthy banks. The ranks of such
depositors have been joined in recent years by the Arabs, who are willing to
offer top banks deposits with maturities as long as 5 years in order to
stockpile oil income earmarked to finance planned investments.

The contrast in maturity options between the U.S. market and Euromarket also reflects differences in the positions of banks operating there. The natural customer base of a foreign bank, for example, will include firms that don't have the same access to dollar financing that U.S. firms have in the domestic capital market, and that therefore may choose to borrow on terms different from those on which a large U.S. corporation would. Also because the dollar is not their domestic currency, foreign banks are and should be more anxious to match fund than U.S. banks are. Smaller regional U.S. banks are in a somewhat similar position to foreign banks; they do not have the assurance that, say, Citi or Morgan has that they will be able to buy whatever money they need whenever they need it. Liquidity considerations are a final reason that a foreign bank might want to buy long-dated funds when a top U.S. bank would not. Especially since the Herstatt crisis, foreign banks operating in the Euromarket have been concerned with liquidity, and one way they can get it is by buying, say, 1-year money and lending it out short term.

Placements are generally not as profitable as loans because they don't offer the built-in spread over LIBOR. But because of the maturity options in the placement market, they offer at times attractive possibilities for speculating on interest rate changes. Assuming a normally shaped yield curve, such speculation is more attractive when interest rates are expected to fall than when they are expected to rise. A bank that expects interest rates to fall will lend long and borrow short. In doing so it gets paid for taking a view (the spread between the long lending rate and the lower short borrowing rate) *and,* if the bank is right, it earns something extra as the borrowing rate falls.

Alternatively, if a bank expects rates to rise, the natural strategy is for it to lend short and borrow long. Doing so will, however, cost the bank money, so it will come out ahead only if it is right and rates do rise sharply. Some banks, when they expect rates to rise will, instead of borrowing long and lending short, continue the pattern of lending long and funding short. Or they will fund in a barbell fashion, taking both very short and very long (six months and over) deposits. The success of this strategy depends on the speed and extent of the rate rise. A number of studies have shown that, during a period of rising rates, the barbell strategy provides funds at the cheapest cost because frequently rates do not rise quickly or sharply enough to offset the advantages of the cheap short-dated funds used.

While there is a lot of variability, it would not be unusual to find the London branch of a large U.S. bank holding 50 percent of its Euro assets in placements and 50 percent in loans.

Mismatch strategies

Because of rollovers most assets that a bank in the Euromarket is financing have original maturities of 3 or 6 months, although some may go longer. In financing these, a bank can mismatch in various ways. The most extreme approach would be to rely on overnight money. Doing so would normally create the greatest positive spread from mismatch, but it would also expose the bank to the greatest rate risk. An alternative approach would be to fund a new asset for part of its life. For example, a bank might fund a 6-month asset with 4-month money (*buy 4's against 6's* in the jargon of the trade) and then fund the remaining 2 months with overnight money or a purchase of 2-month Euros. One consideration in plotting this sort of strategy is the maturities that are most actively traded in the Euromarket. Funding a 6-month asset with, say, 1-month money would leave the bank, which planned to match fund the tail of the asset, in need of 5-month money, a maturity in which the market is thin.

If a bank buys 4's against 6's or pursues some similar strategy, it creates an open position in its book and thereby assumes a rate risk. One way it can seek to eliminate that risk while simultaneously locking in a profit from mismatch is by entering into a *forward forward* contract, that is, *buying money of a fixed maturity for future delivery*. In the example above, the appropriate forward forward contract would be for 2-month money to be delivered 4 months hence. In the Euromarket there is a certain amount of trading in forward forwards but the market is relatively thin.

The seller of a forward forward assumes a rate risk because he cannot be sure how much it will cost him to fund that commitment. Therefore he will not enter into such a contract unless he is compensated for his risk. In our example, the seller of 2-month money 4 months hence is going to want to get something more than the rate he expects to prevail on 2-month money 4 months hence. For his part, if the borrower is locking up a profit on his mismatch, he might well be willing to pay some premium on the forward forward contract. Another reason a buyer and seller might strike a forward forward deal is that they entertain diverse opinions with respect to where interest rates are headed.

In an interesting book on Euro banks, Steven Davis, a Euro banker, tested statistically the results over time of several arbitrary strategies for mismatching. His conclusion was that, while mismatching is common in the Euromarket, it is not profitable over the long run.[2] This conclusion tends to surprise funding officers who have long experience in the Euromarket. Most of them claim that over time they can and have made money thru mismatching. Perhaps one reason is that they follow more flexible strategies than those tested by Davis.

Another factor worth mentioning in this respect is that in the game of mismatching the big U.S. banks have a considerable advantage over their competitors in forecasting Euro rates. One reason is that Euro rates tend, as shown in Chapter 17, to track U.S. rates very closely, with U.S.

---

[2] Steven I. Davis, *The Euro-Bank; Its Origins, Managements and Outlooks* (London: The Macmillan Press Ltd., 1976).

rates generally doing the leading and Euro rates the following. This means that banks that are active in the U.S. money market and have a close feel for developments there, i.e., domestic banks, have an edge over their foreign brethren in predicting Euro rates.

Also the bigger the bank, the better the input it is likely to get from head office and the more intimate the contact between London and head office is likely to be. As the chief dealer in the London branch of a top U.S. bank put it: "We get tremendous input from New York. I speak to people there 2 hours every afternoon on the phone. Also the foreign exchange desk next to mine has a direct line open to New York at all times, and we have direct telex, too. All that information permits us to quickly build up a feel for conditions in the U.S. market. There's no way a smaller bank or a foreign bank can get access to the same information. They can read it tomorrow in the paper, we get it right away. That's important because in this market half an hour sometimes makes a big difference."

The information flow between London and New York is, of course, not only one way. At times London sees things New York does not, and the two have differing rate views. For example, at a time when New York anticipated continued ease, a London dealer looking at his book might conclude that both Euro and domestic rates in a certain maturity range were likely to firm up temporarily at least due to a confluence of scheduled Euro rollovers. Alternatively, if New York foresaw an upturn in rates because domestic loan demand was beginning to revive, London might temper that view by arguing that no parallel increase in loan demand was occurring outside the United States.

Role of Euro CDs

In talking about bank funding in the Euromarket, we have relegated the issuance of Euro CDs to the end of our discussion. The reason is that CD money is much less important to a Euro banker than to a domestic banker. In the United States large investors are not in the habit of making time deposits, and the market for term Fed funds is extremely thin. Thus the domestic banker who wants to take 3-, 6-, or 9-month money is more or less forced to go to the CD market to get it. In the Euromarket, in contrast, a banker can obtain time deposits of any maturity either directly from nonbank depositors or in the interbank market.

Because of the availability of time deposit money, a Euro bank will issue CDs only if there is a distinct rate advantage in doing so. Also, because the overall market for such CDs is thin and the market for any one bank's CDs is thinner still, a Euro banker is very cautious about the quantity of CDs he writes, particularly if the CDs issued are likely to turn out to be *trading paper* as opposed to lock-up CDs. The danger of overwriting is not only that the bank will lose its rate advantage in the CD market but also that it may block actions that it wants to take in the future. For example, if a bank writes a lot of 9-month CDs and then 3 months later wants to take 6-month money, it may find that it can't do so unless it pays up because there is so much of the old 9-month paper, which now has a 6-month current maturity, in the hands of dealers. A similar fear may also inhibit a Euro banker from writing very short-maturity CDs. He reasons that writing a 1-month CD is not going to save his bank enough money to compensate for the fact that the presence of such securities in the market might during their life block his bank from seizing an attractive opportunity to write longer-term CDs. Investors after all are going to be willing to hold only so much of any one bank's paper in their portfolios.

Most Euro CDs have a maturity at issue of 1 year or less, but it is much more common for CDs with longer maturities—2, 3, or even 5 years—to be issued in the Euromarket than in the domestic market. While a bank will normally take any short-dated CD money offered to it by a nonbank customer, it is likely to be unwilling to issue longer-term CDs unless it has a specific use for such funds, for example to match fund a longer-term asset coming onto its book.

Particularly in the aftermath of Herstatt, buyers of Euro CDs have become highly selective. As a result only major U.S. banks can today raise money in real volume in this market. Other banks, U.S. and foreign, do issue CDs to their customers, sometimes at the same rates a Citi or Morgan would pay. But were they to try to really write in volume, they would be forced to pay up, how much depending on the name, nationality, and size of the bank. As noted in Chapter 15, tiering is quite pronounced in the secondary market for Euro CDs.

Arab dollars

In the Euromarket the top U.S. banks, because of their size, reputation, and customer base, have always tended to be the recipients of extremely large deposits from nonbank depositors. Both because they could earn profits by laying off such deposits in the interbank market and because the maturity structure of the deposits they received was not necessarily what they desired for their Euro book, these banks naturally became big sellers as well as takers of funds. In effect they acted as dealers in Eurodollar deposits.

After the OPEC nations dramatically increased the price of oil in 1974, the dealer banks rapidly became recipients of huge short-term deposits from Arab oil sellers. As they assumed this new responsibility of recycling petro dollars, their balance sheets changed dramatically, with placements becoming much more important than previously relative to loans.

Their new role as recyclers of petro dollars created problems for the big banks. One concerned liquidity. In taking a lot of short-term money from the Arabs, these banks were violating two basic rules of liability management: (1) a bank should not take a significant portion of its deposits from a single depositor or group of depositors, and (2) a bank should not accept big deposits of volatile short-term (*hot*) money. The one comfort that the big banks could take in this matter was that, regardless of what the Arabs did with their dollars, these dollars could not disappear altogether from the system. Thus, if the Arabs pulled a lot of money out of one bank, that bank could almost certainly buy back the lost dollars in the interbank market from the bank or banks in which the Arabs subsequently redeposited their dollars.

A second problem created by big Arab deposits was credit risk. By taking in huge amounts of Arab money and redepositing it with other banks, the dealer banks were forced to assume a credit risk that they thought properly belonged to the original depositor. To compensate for this risk, the dealer banks attempted to buy Arab money as cheaply as possible, a policy the Arabs seem to have understood. A final problem for a bank receiving big Arab deposits was that the resulting $2 or $3 billion increase in deposits and redeposits on its balance sheet tended to perceptibly erode the bank's capital ratios. Such erosion was something that a big bank might willingly have accepted to increase bread-and-butter loan business but not to earn a minuscule margin in the placement market. To cope with these problems, a few big banks attempted to limit the size of their Eurodollar book, a policy that offered the side benefit of enabling them to buy money more cheaply than other banks could.

Over time the problems created by Arab dollars have eased somewhat, partly because the Arabs gradually became more willing to place funds with the bottom end of the triple-A banks and the top end of the double-A banks. Whereas 5 years ago 10 or 15 banks were receiving the bulk of Arab deposits, the list has now expanded to 50 or 60 banks and it includes more non–U.S. names. In addition to expanding the number of banks with which they were willing to place money, the Arabs also became much more willing to give top banks longer-term deposits, out to as long as 5 years. Thus the price advantage to the top banks of buying Arab money has tended to slip from the shorter to the longer end of the maturity spectrum. This occurred, however, at a time when bank borrowers were loath to take down long-term, fixed-rate loans, so the development was of less immediate advantage to the big banks than might otherwise have been the case.

The problems created by the huge flows of Arab money, while less acute than they once seemed, have not vanished. For one thing the total volume of such funds keeps growing. Also, the pattern of oil royalty payments creates a sharp periodicity in such deposits.

One fact that seems to surprise many people is that, as the Arabs acquired so many dollars, the Middle East did not expand into a major center for the Euromarket. Bahrain, after all, is primarily a booking center funded to a significant degree out of London. Part of the explanation is that the Middle East has always been viewed as an area of political instability, so people there prefer to keep their funds elsewhere. Also the Arabs have displayed little talent for the sort of cooperation that would be required to develop a major Middle East Euro center. In addition, unlike, say, the Chinese of Singapore, the Arabs have never displayed much interest in or aptitude for banking and finance.

Worldwide funding

As noted, the major U.S. and foreign banks participating in the Euromarket all have branches running their own separate Eurodollar books in each of the major centers of the market and in other newer peripheral centers as well. This proliferation of Euro activity naturally raises a question as to how centralized a bank's overall Euro activities should be.

In the past it was typical for a bank's branches in different dealing centers to act in a highly independent way, each creating its own dollar book under guidelines set by home office. Some banks now see benefits in greater coordination of the Euro activities of their different branches and are attempting to achieve it. Others, however, prefer to stick to decentralization. In this respect, Citibank and Chase are probably at extreme opposite poles; Citi having a reputation for decentralization and Chase for increasing coordination.

One argument for giving branches a high degree of autonomy is that funding at each is headed by senior and experienced officers who expect to accept responsibility and need it to develop. Also, if funding officers in some branches are bullish while others are bearish, letting each put his money where his mouth is has a pro side as well as a con. While it does mean that the bank will not make as much money as it would have if every branch had acted on a *correct* rate view promulgated by head office, it also means the bank won't lose as much money as it would have if every branch had acted on an incorrect view. Another argument for branch autonomy is that in a huge worldwide organization, coordination of what everyone is doing is infeasible or, alternatively, if feasible, would be costly and might take so long that the bank would be handicapped in taking advantage of constantly changing opportunities.

One advantage of coordinating the activities of a bank's individual branches and thereby creating a global Euro book for the bank is that doing so permits the bank to take its maximum open position in the most advantageous tax areas, for example, to run a very short book in Nassau and compensate by snugging up its London book. To the extent that the yield curve is upward sloping, this policy has the advantage of shifting the most expensive funding to the highest-tax areas. A second argument for coordination is that a bank may feel so confident in its rate predictions that it wants to make all its bets in the same direction.

Another question with respect to the funding of a bank's worldwide Euro operations is the extent to which each branch should be expected to finance its operations by buying funds in its own name. This question arises for two reasons. First, the "natural" (local) supply of and demand for Eurodollars is not balanced in different Euro centers; Singapore, Bahrain, and the Caribbean centers, for example, all tend to be big net buyers of funds. Second, lenders of dollars perceive the country risks associated with net buying centers outside London as being somewhat greater than those associated with London, and they are therefore not willing to lend as much to banks in these centers. Together these two factors create a situation in which a bank's branches outside London may have to pay more for funds than the same bank's London branch would. For example, where the London branch might be able to buy in the middle of the market or at the bid side, the non-London branch might have to buy at the offered side of the market.

While this price differential does not amount to much, $1/16$ to $1/8$ percent typically, to the extent that it exists, there is naturally a temptation for a bank to have its London branch buy extra funds in its name and then relend them to its branches in other centers. The only real cost to this operation is that the British Inland Revenue requires that the London branch make some small taxable profit on such transactions. Currently the minimum acceptable markup is $5/64$. Since this is a modest figure, many banks do fund—sometimes to a significant degree—the operations of their branches in other centers with funds purchased in London.

There are, however, banks that think every branch should stand on its own feet and do its own funding. One argument for this position is that centers outside London will never be built up as meaningful entities in the global Euromarket unless they are seen to perform in the marketplace in their own names. A second argument is that "sourcing" in London huge quantities of funds that are destined to be used in other centers makes London appear to be a much bigger buyer of Euros than it really is, and may thereby impinge on London's sovereign value.

Earlier we said that there was a lot of dealing in New York and elsewhere in the United States in Euros for funding the assets of bank branches located in the Caribbean. This funding is all done in the name of the branch, since if a New York bank bought Euros in the name of head office, these dollars would become "domestic" dollars and as such would be subject to a reserve requirement. The fact that the funding and lending operations of the Caribbean branches of U.S. banks are carried out mainly by personnel at head office naturally raises the question of whether the profits of such branches should be treated as domestic income subject to domestic taxation or as foreign income subject to taxation at lower foreign rates. The most authoritative view seems to be that neither the United States nor New York State has a strong enough case to tell Nassau that U.S. bank Euro operations there are really domestic U.S. operations.

Eurocurrency swaps

As noted earlier, the bulk of the Eurocurrency market consists of Eurodollar deposits, but it also includes Euro deposits of German marks, sterling, Swiss francs, Dutch guilders, Belgian francs, French francs, and other currencies. The uninitiated might think of a bank accepting deposits in all of these currencies as ending up with a mixed bag of different kinds of money. Not so the Euro banker; he knows that he can turn one currency into another through the simple device of a *swap.* To him money is money whatever its country or origin.

In the foreign exchange market, currencies are traded for each other on two bases, *spot* and *forward.* In a spot transaction, say, deutsche marks (DM) for dollars, the currencies exchanged are normally delivered two days after the trade is made. In a forward transaction the exchange occurs at some specified date further in the future, perhaps months later. *A swap is a pair of spot and forward transactions in which the forward transaction offsets or unwinds the spot transaction.* For example, if a holder of marks traded them for dollars in the spot market and simultaneously entered into a forward contract to sell these dollars for marks 3 months hence, he would have engaged in a swap. Note that the effect of this transaction is to permit the holder of marks to go into dollars for 3 months without assuming any *foreign exchange risk.* Specifically, by locking in a selling rate for the dollars he acquires, the swapper eliminates any risk that he might suffer a loss due to a fall in the exchange value of the dollar against the mark during the period when he holds dollars.

Most large banks act as dealers in foreign exchange. The individuals who run this part of the bank's operations naturally take speculative positions long and short in various currencies as part of their normal dealing activities—making markets and servicing customers' buy and sell orders. In addition, based on their expectations of probable changes in exchange rates, they will assume speculative positions in foreign exchange designed to earn profits for the bank. Such activities expose the bank to foreign exchange risk. This risk, however, is one that the bank is prepared to assume within limits because the individuals running the foreign exchange department are experts in this area.

Funding officers, in contrast, have their greatest expertise in areas other than foreign exchange. As a result, banks in their Euro operations confine their speculation in foreign exchange to the foreign exchange department and require that funding officers match their Euro book in terms of currencies (e.g., use dollar liabilities to fund dollars assets). Thus, when a Euro banker receives a deposit of a currency other than the dollar, he will either sell that deposit in the interbank market or swap it for dollars. Also if he is asked to extend a loan denominated in a currency other than the dollar, he will fund that loan either by buying a deposit of that currency or by swapping dollars into that currency.

Most of the time the spot and forward rates at which any currency trades against the dollar will *not* be identical. In particular the dollar price that a foreign currency commands in the forward market will be higher than the spot rate if this currency can be borrowed more cheaply than the dollar and/or if it is expected to appreciate in value relative to the dollar. The opposite conditions will, of course, cause the currency to sell at a discount in the forward market.

If a currency is selling at a premium in the forward market, a swap out of the dollar into that currency will yield some gain, while a swap out of that currency into the dollar will produce some loss. If, alternatively, a currency is selling at a discount in the forward market, the result will be the reverse. The gain or loss inherent in any swap, the amount of which can be calculated at the time the transaction is arranged, can be expressed as an annualized percentage rate of gain or loss through the use of a simple formula.[3] This rate of gain or loss is a crucial element in a bank's decisions about what rates to charge on nondollar loans and pay on nondollar deposits.

For example, suppose that a corporation offers a bank a 3-month DM deposit and that the mark is selling at a premium in the forward market. If the bank accepts the deposit, it will swap these marks into dollars and in doing so it will incur some loss. It will, however, also earn the going 3-month LIBOR rate on the dollars it obtains from the swap. Thus the rate that the bank offers the depositor will equal roughly 3-month LIBOR minus the annualized rate of loss on the swap. In costing a nondollar loan, the bank follows a similar approach.

Note that on such swap transactions, interest payments generate a residual foreign exchange exposure. For example, if a bank takes in a 3-month DM deposit and swaps it into dollars, the bank assumes a foreign exchange risk because it is committed to pay interest in DM on the DM deposit at maturity, while it will earn interest at maturity in dollars

---

[3] For a numerical example of a swap, see Chapter 16.

on the dollars it has placed or loaned. If the bank chooses to avoid this risk, it can lock in a fixed spread on the overall swap transaction by buying DM (selling dollars) *forward* in an amount equal to the interest to be paid in DM.

Several very large banks that receive many deposits of Euromarks and Swiss francs and also receive many requests for loans denominated in those currencies have departed somewhat from the swap-everything-into-dollars approach we have just described. Specifically they have begun to run books in each of these currencies, matching off deposits in these currencies against loans and placements in the same currencies. Doing so eliminates certain transactions costs associated with swaps into and out of dollars—the foreign exchange dealers' spreads between bid and asked in the spot and forward markets and some bookkeeping and ticket costs. Banks running books in Euromarks and Euro Swissy feel that this reduction in costs permits them to offer depositors and borrowers of these currencies slightly better rates than they could if they consistently swapped all the *natural* DM and Swiss franc business they received into dollar assets and liabilities.

We have talked about banks using swaps to match their Euro books (in terms of currencies held and lent). Banks also use swaps extensively in another way, to minimize funding costs. Suppose, for example, that a bank wants to fund a 6-month dollar loan. To any funding officer, every Eurocurrency deposit is nothing but a Eurodollar deposit with a swap transaction tagged on. Thus, in shopping for 6-month money, a bank dealer will price out not only 6-month dollar deposits, but also 6-month dollars obtained by swapping deposits of other currencies into dollars. If 6-month dollars can be obtained more cheaply by buying 6-month Euromarks and swapping them into dollars than by buying straight dollars, the dealer will go the swap route.

Because all the banks in the Euromarket seize every opportunity available to reduce their borrowing costs through swaps, the all-in cost of dollars obtained by swapping any actively traded Eurocurrency into dollars tracks very closely the yield on straight dollar deposits of the same tenor. Thus the rate savings that a bank can obtain by using a swap to obtain dollars usually amounts to no more than a very narrow spread. However, when the foreign exchange market starts moving dramatically, short-lived opportunities for saving ⅛ or ¼ percent through a swap do occur.

BANK OF ENGLAND REGULATION

Since London is the preeminent center of the Euromarket, it is important to ask who regulates what goes on in the London market, how they do it, and how well they do it.

The first important point to make is that regulation of domestic banking has always been much less formal in Britain than in the United States or on the Continent. Unlike many U.S. bank regulators, the Bank of England proceeds on the assumption that bankers are prudent, honest people who know as much if not more about banking than regulators do. Thus their approach has not been to impose regulations and ratios on the banks; instead they ask for periodic reports from the banks. On the basis of these, they discuss in an informal way with each bank's top management the quality of the bank's loans, their liquidity, any features of the bank's condition that the Bank of England views as unusual or out of line, and any suggestions that the Bank of England might make with respect to the bank's operations.

When foreign banks come to London, they are treated in much the same way as domestic British banks. If the Bank of England recognizes a bank as reputable in its home country, it will permit that bank to open a London branch with a minimum of red tape. The bank does not have to put in any capital; all it has to do to open an office is to agree to comply with certain regulations, and it is granted the same right to engage in banking that any other bank in the United Kingdom has. Foreign banks establishing independent entities, merchant banking subs or banking consortia, do have to put in capital but again if the parentage is reputable, the red tape is minimal. As an executive of a large U.S. bank noted: "When we went to the Bank of England for permission to open a merchant banking arm, they said: 'You need a foreign exchange trader, someone who knows British exchange control regulations, some capital, and since you are asking to be recognized as a bank, at least a window where you could take deposits whether you do or not. Oh, and one other thing. We'd like you to locate in the City of London. The rents are high which keeps out the riffraff.' "

In justification of the Bank of England's rather casual regulation of foreign banks, it might be added that the bank operates on the quite logical assumption that foreign bank branches are an inextricable part of the parent, which implies two things. First, it is difficult if not impossible to regulate these branches as independent entities. Second, it is also natural to assume that these branches are being regulated indirectly by banking authorities in the parent country, which regulates the activities of the parent bank as a whole.

The ease with which foreign banks can enter the London market and the minimal regulations imposed on their activities there have encouraged the entry of several hundred foreign banks into London. It has also permitted the rapid *growth* and constant *innovation* that have been characteristic of the Euromarket.

To a U.S. regulator the British approach to bank regulation might seem like a time bomb guaranteed to create monumental difficulties at some time. Yet the record shows that the British approach to bank regulation has been at least as successful, if not more so, than the U.S. approach. One reason is that there is a lot of mutual respect between banks operating in Britain and the Bank of England. Because of this and because of the real powers the Bank of England possesses, banks don't fight "The Old Lady (of Threadneedle Street)"; instead they take her suggestions seriously. Another reason the Bank of England approach has been so successful is that it is responsible for overseeing the operations of only a limited number of banks, about 100 domestic and 200 foreign banks. In contrast, U.S. regulators have to cope with over 14,000 banks. As one Bank of England official noted, the limited number of banks in Britain has permitted the Bank of England to know on an almost personal basis the managers of these institutions and thus whether they do or do not need closer supervision.

Naturally with the entry of so many foreign banks into London, it is becoming more and more difficult for the Bank of England to pursue this sort of personal regulation. As a result, in recent years the Bank of England has asked the banks to report to it with increasing frequency and it has visited them more often.

SOVEREIGN RISK

Investors, both bank and nonbank, depositing dollars in a bank or bank branch located in a foreign country are always concerned with *sovereign* or *country risk.* In the case of U.S. investors in particular, at least those with little experience in international business, there is very real concern over the sovereign risk associated with making dollar deposits in London. As these investors see it, the periodic crises through which the pound sterling passes and the chronic weakness of the British economy both suggest that at some time the British might be tempted to block payment on the dollar liabilities of London banks. While it is impossible to say that this could never happen, there is only one conclusion that anyone who has studied the London market carefully can reach, namely, that the sovereign risk attached to dollar deposits in London is very close to zero.

One practical reason is that Britain would gain nothing from blocking payment of the Eurodollar liabilities of London banks during a sterling crisis. Since the end of World War II, the pound sterling has been a weak currency; and to prop up its value, the British have maintained tight controls on the use of sterling by domestic holders. Because of these controls the Euromarket in London, which would in any case have been largely a market in offshore funds, is strictly a market in offshore funds. With the few exceptions permitted by the British exchange control authorities, all the Eurodollars that flow into London are owned by foreign depositors and all the Eurodollars that flow out go to foreign borrowers. In effect London acts largely as a conduit through which dollars flow from foreigners to foreigners. Thus inflows of Eurodollars to London do not add to British foreign exchange reserves and outflows do not subtract from them, which means in turn that blocking payment on the Eurodollar liabilities of London banks would do nothing to stem the loss by Britain of foreign reserves during a sterling crisis.

Currently the financial activities centered in the City of London, including Eurodollar transactions, earn Britain considerable amounts of foreign exchange, provide thousands of jobs, and add vitality to the whole economy. A second practical reason Britain would not block payment on Eurodollar deposits is that, if it did, it would lose all these advantages. As a Bank of England official noted: "If the British interfered with the payout of Eurodollars, nationalized foreign branches, or whatever, that would kill more than the Euromarket, it would kill London. Any action taken against Euro operations in London would immediately spread to London as a banking center; and if London is not a banking center, then it isn't a commodity market, it isn't an international insurance center, it isn't a stock or investment market generally. In London these things dovetail very closely, so if you damage one, you damage the lot. The game would not be worth the candle."

To the above it should perhaps be added that Britain could, of course, attempt to improve its reserve position by a two-pronged ploy: blocking payment on Eurodollar deposits in London banks *and* simultaneously seizing the dollar assets of these banks. However, this course of action, in addition to posing the difficult question of how Britain could as a practical matter seize the offshore assets of foreign banks, would be even more inconceivable than a mere blocking of Eurodollar deposits, since its long-run consequences would if anything be still more disastrous for the British economy.

Were Britain during a sterling crisis willing to do something dramatic and potentially dangerous to its economy, the logical step would be to block the large sterling balances held by Commonwealth nations. That would directly act to stem the loss by Britain of foreign exchange reserves by preventing conversion of these balances into foreign exchange. Blocking sterling balances is, it should be noted, a course of action that has been open to Britain during every sterling crisis. Yet the British have never taken it, presumably in part because of the effect doing so would have on London's role as a world financial center.

LENDER OF LAST RESORT

Another question that troubles some Euromarket watchers is: Who is to act as lender of last resort if some event much more shaking than the failure of the Herstatt hits it? This question really involves two separate questions: Who lends if the supply of Eurodollars dries up? Who lends if the solvency of a major bank or group of banks in the Euromarket is threatened through bad loans or other losses?

As noted, dollars can't disappear, but they can move from place to place. Thus it's conceivable, though highly unlikely, that the supply of dollars in the Euromarket could dry up because holders of dollars for some reason decided to move their deposits from banks in Euro centers to banks in New York or elsewhere in the United States. Such an eventuality would not cause U.S. banks severe liquidity problems with respect to their Euro operations; they could always buy back in the U.S. market the dollars they had lost in the Euromarket and use them to fund their Euro assets. The major inconvenience to them in doing so is that they would incur a reserve cost on domestic dollars funneled to the Euromarket. To some extent foreign banks could do the same thing, buy more dollars in New York and funnel them abroad. They would incur no reserve cost in doing so but they would face a more crucial problem, namely, that most of them would be able to buy in the U.S. market only a small fraction of the dollars they were accustomed to buying in the Euromarket. Thus, in the unlikely event of dollars drying up in the Euromarket, foreign banks could face a real liquidity problem.

Central banks have discussed at length, in meetings in Basel, Switzerland, the question of lender of last resort to the Euromarket and have reached the conclusion that each one looks after his own. Thus the Fed is the appropriate lender of last resort to a U.S. bank whether its troubles arise from its operations in New York or London, and the Bank of England stands behind the operations of its domestic banks both at home and abroad. The logical thrust of this philosophy is that if foreign banks experienced liquidity problems with respect to their dollar operations, it would be up to their respective central banks to provide them with dollars, something that the central banks of major countries could certainly do either from their own reserves or by obtaining dollars through swaps from the Fed.

With respect to the second question concerning the possible failure by a major Euro bank or group of banks, the comment of a German banker is quite relevant. In speaking of the Herstatt failure, which sent shock waves through the Euromarket, he said: "The Bundesbank [German central bank] will never admit that they made a mistake, but in retrospect they know they did. They should not have permitted the Herstatt to fail; instead they should have merged it into one of the larger German banks. A bank failure on that scale will, I guarantee, never occur in Germany again."

The development of the Euromarket as an international capital market has made a significant contribution over the last several decades to the world economy by providing financing for a huge expansion in international trade and investment. The development of this market has also tied in ways hitherto unknown the economies, capital markets, and fortunes of many free-world countries, including all of the major ones. Thus to allow this market to falter or fail would create economic havoc on a world scale. Central bankers know this and the almost universal opinion among bankers is thus that no central bank in a major country will again let one of its key banks fail. Moreover, if a group of banks were threatened, say, by defaults on loans to underdeveloped countries, the central banks standing behind those banks would undoubtedly keep them afloat through individual or coordinated actions. As a top banker noted: "No central bank will ever commit itself publicly to keeping all domestic banks above size *x* afloat, but they know—and we know they know—that, should a major bank be threatened, the economic costs of inaction on their part would *far exceed* the cost of action. Therefore they would act."

The question of who is the lender of last resort in the Euromarket has particularly troubled the Bank of England because of the extensive Euro operations carried out in London by foreign banks. The understanding under which foreign banks are permitted to open branches in London has always been that the parent would stand behind the branch, whatever difficulties it might encounter. In the case of merchant banking subs and consortium banks, this understanding was implicit but perhaps less formal. During the nervous and anxious period that prevailed after the Herstatt failure, the Bank of England acted to formalize this commitment by asking for "comfort letters," stating that each parent of a merchant banking sub or consortium bank would provide support, if required, to that entity up to its share of ownership.

FOREIGN BANK OPERATIONS IN THE UNITED STATES

Foreign banks have used various organizational vehicles to enter the U.S. market. A few have set up wholly owned subsidiaries operated under a domestic banking charter. Of these a handful are long-standing operations like Barclays' extensive banking system in California. Others are of fairly recent origin.

Another form of organization commonly used by foreign banks to enter the U.S. market is the *agency bank*. An agency bank cannot accept deposits in its own name and it cannot hold loans on its own books. Instead it acts as a loan production office and funding agent for the parent bank. It arranges loans and then books them at some branch of the parent, for example, Nassau or head office. It also acts as an agent for the parent in the New York money market, buying and selling Fed funds and Euros for head office's account. There are several advantages to a foreign bank in setting up an agency bank instead of a U.S. branch. Agency banks are not subject to U.S. taxes on the loans they originate, and they are not subject to U.S. regulation. Also, in setting up an agency, a foreign bank avoids a lot of the overhead it would incur in setting up a branch with facilities for accepting deposits.

A third way a foreign bank can enter the U.S. market is by setting up a branch. The growth of such branches in recent years has been explosive. A single New York branch of one large foreign bank held assets in 1977 equal to almost the total assets held 5 years before by all foreign bank branches in New York. Foreign bank branches operate under state banking laws and are regulated by state banking authorities. Most are located in New York, California, and Illinois, which have specific enabling legislation permitting the establishment of branches by foreign banks. Generally such branches can engage in the full range of domestic banking activities.

Setting up a branch in the United States is expensive for a foreign bank not only in terms of overhead, but also in terms of taxation. Once a foreign bank establishes a U.S. branch, all of its income on loans into the United States becomes subject to U.S. taxation. Yet the U.S. market, and more particularly the New York market, act as a magnet drawing in more and more foreign bank branches.

Foreign banks setting up U.S. branches do so for several reasons. First, they are attempting to follow their customers to the United States just as U.S. banks followed their customers abroad; the growth of international banking is in part a response to the emergence of multinational firms. Foreign banks are also attempting to develop relationships with large U.S. corporations; most of these have foreign operations and a foreign bank can therefore provide them with special services and expertise. A third reason foreign banks have set up New York branches is to obtain access to the huge domestic reservoir of dollars. Finally, New York is a convenient place for foreign banks to run and fund a Nassau or Cayman Islands Eurodollar book.

Most foreign bank branches tend to be primarily wholesale operations servicing large as opposed to retail accounts. For example, the customers of one big foreign bank branch in New York include a large proportion of the Fortune 500, big European corporations, Japanese trading corporations, large firms trading in commodities, and foreign banks for which the branch acts as a clearing agent. Foreign bank branches fund themselves much as domestic money market banks do, by accepting deposits and by purchasing monies in the Fed funds, Eurodollar, and CD markets. There are, however, differences. One is that CDs issued by foreign bank branches still have only limited acceptance in the U.S. market. Another is that for a foreign bank branch there is no distinction between Eurodollars and "domestic" dollars, because foreign bank branches are not members of the Fed and therefore do not have to hold reserves against any of the funds they receive in deposit or purchase.

The position of a foreign bank operating in the New York market is much the same as the position of the London branch of the same bank in the Eurodollar market. It is acquiring assets and incurring liabilities in a foreign currency, the dollar, and it thinks of itself as running a dollar book. In running this book, moreover, the New York branch, like the London branch, is concerned about mismatch and is subject to guidelines from home office with respect to the degree of mismatch it can run. One difference, however, is that foreign bank branches in New York, like domestic U.S. banks, make a lot of variable-rate loans, so mismatch on their books can't be measured or controlled in quite the same way in New York as it is in London.

The United States is the home of the dollar, so having a U.S. branch provides a foreign bank with additional funding and liquidity for its over-all Eurodollar operation because the U.S. branch can tap directly the vast domestic market for dollars. Setting up a U.S. branch also permits a foreign bank to establish an entity to which other branches in the bank's international network can turn to make adjustments in their dollar books; for example, if the bank's Iranian branch were getting short-term dollar deposits but had to fund longer-term dollar loans, it might ask the New York branch to lay off its short-term deposits and buy it longer-term money.

Competition to U.S. banks

Because they are able to buy money without incurring a reserve re-quirement, foreign bank branches have a certain cost advantage over U.S. banks in making loans to domestic firms for domestic purposes. This cost advantage is partially offset by the fact that foreign bank branches have to pay up slightly for money they buy in the domestic market and by the fact that any Euros they buy are marginally more expensive than domestic money of the same tenor. In any case, foreign bank branches in major financial centers have been quoting loan rates to domestic corporations at LIBOR plus a spread, which works out to a rate below the U.S. prime plus balances. This practice has put pressure on domestic banks in these centers to make loans to prime customers at a rate below prime.

The growing competition provided by foreign banks adds one more reason to several existing ones for making a *major* change in U.S. bank-ing practices: namely, permitting the Fed to pay interest on member bank reserves and permitting banks to pay interest on demand deposits. Such a step would put domestic and foreign banks on a more equal footing. It would also remove the onerous implicit tax that reserve re-quirements now impose on member banks and thereby reverse the cur-rent trend for banks to leave the system. In addition, it would permit banks to unbundle their prices—to eliminate the barter involved in compensating balance requirements and to substitute explicit charges for the services they provide their customers. Finally, the change would make sense given the possible nationwide spread of negotiable order of withdrawal (NOW) accounts, which permit a depositor to write what are essentially checks on a savings account; NOW accounts are currently offered by commercial banks, S&Ls, and savings banks in six New England states.

In 1977 a Federal Reserve staff report suggested that the Fed be permitted to pay interest on bank reserves and that banks be permitted to pay interest on demand deposits. While this change should and may well come, there are two major obstacles to getting the necessary legislation through Congress. First, many small nonmember banks, who as a group have considerable influence in Washington, are opposed to paying interest on demand deposits. Second, since most of the profits earned by the Fed are paid out to the Treasury, having the Fed pay interest on member bank reserves might cut Fed payments to the Treasury by as much as $6 billion.

Regulation of foreign branch operations

State regulation of the operations of foreign bank branches in the United States is much stricter and more detailed than the regulation to which foreign bank branches are subject in London. In New York State, for example, foreign banks are subject to all the detailed provisions of the state's banking law. In addition they are required to hold qualifying assets equal to 108 percent of their total liabilities (intrabank deposits excepted); and of this 108 percent, 5 percent must be held in T bills or certain other instruments in a special account with a depository bank. Since the qualifying assets that a foreign bank branch may use to satisfy the 108 percent requirement include a wide range of instruments—loans on its New York book, CDs bought, deposits at other banks, Fed funds sold, bankers' acceptances held in its portfolio, and broker/dealer loans—this requirement does not impose the costs on foreign banks that reserve requirements impose on banks that are members of the Fed. On the other hand, the 108 percent requirement does mean that a foreign bank's branch has to net borrow funds from the rest of the system—funds that constitute in effect the branch's U.S. capital base. The New York State 108 percent rule is designed to ensure that a foreign bank branch will always have sufficient assets to meet its deposit and other liabilities. As such, it has been viewed abroad as a model for foreign bank branch regulation and has been widely copied.

In the eyes of some foreign bankers, however, the New York State regulation is anything but a model. One British bank commented: "It's far too complex and to some extent outdated. In these days when funds can be moved rapidly, a foreign bank in trouble could rape its New York branch before the regulators smelled trouble. The only regulation that makes sense and that is going to be effective over the long run is to grant branch licenses only to banks that are credit and trustworthy."

One advantage that foreign banks enjoy over domestic banks is that they can currently open branches in several different states, whereas domestic banks are not permitted to engage in interstate banking. Because of this and other issues as well, there has been considerable pressure in Congress to pass new foreign bank legislation in order to put foreign and domestic banks on an equal footing. With respect to this issue, there are several points worth making. One is that domestic banks themselves manage to engage in a fair amount of interstate banking through the use of Edge Act subs and loan offices. Second, because foreign banks are not well known in the United States, they must, as noted, pay marginally more to buy funds domestically than top domestic banks do. Finally, given that there is considerable pressure for changes in the regulations under which domestic banks operate, it could be argued that Congress should wait until it has decided what to do about domestic banking legislation before it writes additional foreign bank legislation.

Chapter 7

The Treasury and the federal agencies

THE SINGLE MOST IMPORTANT ISSUER of debt in the money market is the U.S. Treasury. It is closely followed in importance by federal agencies as a group.

U.S. GOVERNMENT SECURITIES

At the beginning of 1978, the U.S. government had $721.6 billion of debt outstanding. As Table 7–1 shows, about 11 percent of the Treasury's outstanding debt is represented by Series E and H bonds, which are *nonnegotiable savings bonds* sold to individuals.[1] The Treasury also issues substantial amounts of special *nonnegotiable* issues to (1) foreign central banks that have accumulated dollars through their foreign exchange operations, through the sale of oil for dollars, or in other ways, and (2) federal agencies and trust funds that have surplus funds to invest.

The remainder of the Treasury's outstanding debt is *negotiable* is-

---

[1] For a description of these securities, see the appendix at the end of this chapter.

Table 7–1
Gross U.S. public debt, January 1978
($ billions)

Bills	161.2
Notes	257.1
Bonds ....,........	48.5
Total marketable	466.8
Savings bonds	77.4
Special issues to U.S. government agencies and trust funds	136.4
Foreign issues	22.8
Other	18.2
Total gross debt	721.6

Table 7–2
Federal budget receipts and outlays, fiscal years 1960–1978 ($ millions)

Fiscal year	Receipts	Outlays	Surplus or deficit (−)
1960	92,492	92,223	269
1961	94,389	97,795	−3,406
1962	99,676	106,813	−7,137
1963	106,560	111,311	−4,751
1964	112,662	118,584	−5,922
1965	116,833	118,430	−1,596
1966	130,856	134,652	−3,796
1967	149,552	158,254	−8,702
1968	153,671	178,833	−25,161
1969	187,784	184,548	3,236
1970	193,743	196,588	−2,845
1971	188,392	211,425	−23,033
1972	208,649	232,021	−23,373
1973	232,225	247,074	−14,849
1974	264,932	269,620	−4,688
1975	280,997	326,092	−45,095
1976	299,197	365,643	−66,446
Transition quarter*	81,687	94,657	−12,970
1977	356,861	401,902	−45,040
1978†	400,387	462,234	−61,847
1979†	439,583	500,174	−60,586

*Under provisions of the Congressional Budget Act of 1974, the fiscal year for the federal government shifted beginning with fiscal year 1977. Through fiscal year 1976, the fiscal year ran from July 1 through June 30; starting in October 1976 (fiscal year 1977), the fiscal year ran from October 1 through September 30. The 3-month period from July 1, 1976, through September 30, 1976, is a separate fiscal period known as the *transition quarter*.

† Estimates.

Source: *Economic Report of the President,* January 1978.

sues, all of which are actively traded in the money and bond markets. Currently the Treasury issues three types of negotiable securities:[2]

1. Noninterest-bearing *bills* that have an original maturity of 1 year or less.
2. Interest-bearing *notes* that have an original maturity of 1 to 10 years.
3. Interest-bearing *bonds* that have an original maturity of more than 10 years.

Volume outstanding

A huge expansion has occurred in recent years in total Treasury debt outstanding, as Figure 7–1 shows. The principal cause of the increase is the enormous deficits that the federal government has consistently incurred since 1975 (see Table 7–2). A second factor contributing to the

Figure 7–1
Treasury debt outstanding

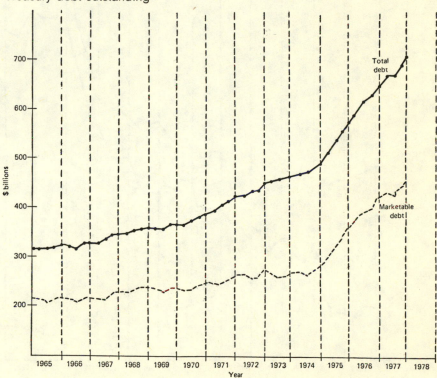

_____

[2] The Treasury used to issue interest-bearing *certificates* with an original maturity of 1 year or less. It has not done so since 1967.

Figure 7–2
Composition of the U.S. government's marketable debt

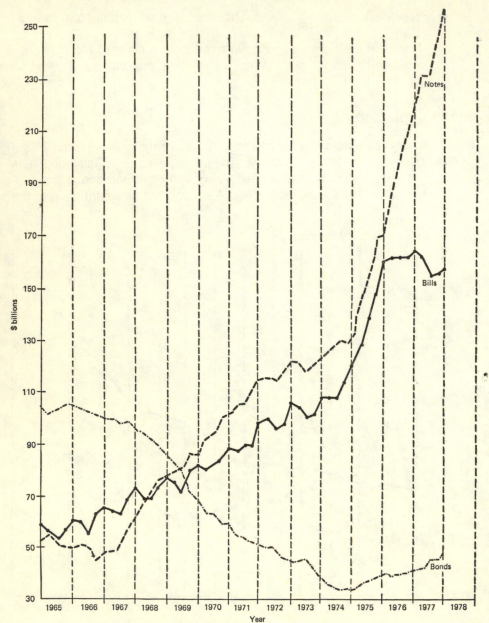

increase in Treasury debt outstanding is that the Treasury began in 197⁴ to borrow money in its own name to fund the lending activities of the Federal Financing Bank, discussed later in this chapter.

The recent sharp increase in Treasury debt has resulted in a very substantial rise in the amount of marketable Treasury securities outstanding (see Figure 7–2). Most of this rise has occurred though increases in the amounts of notes and bills outstanding. Negotiable bonds represent only a small fraction of the Treasury's total marketable debt (Figure 7–2).

TREASURY DEBT MANAGEMENT

Funding the federal debt is no small job for the Treasury. In the years 1970–77 the Treasury sold $2.7 trillion of securities. Most of this borrowing was to roll maturing debt; only 8 percent represented new money.

Academic economists have long argued that the Treasury in selling debt should structure the maturities it offers to the market so as to counter the business cycle. Specifically, it should shorten the maturity of the debt it issues when economic conditions are depressed and interest rates are falling in order to further reduce long-term interest rates and thereby stimulate investment spending; conversely, when the economy is overheated and interest rates are rising, it should lengthen the maturity of the debt it offers to push long-term interest rates higher and thereby discourage investment spending. Because such a countercyclical policy of debt management calls for the Treasury to issue long-term debt when interest rates are highest, it would maximize the cost to the Treasury of issuing debt. An alternative strategy is that the Treasury should issue long-term debt when interest rates are down and short-term debt when interest rates are high so as to minimize its borrowing costs.

In fact the Treasury, because of the sheer size of the debt it issues, has little latitude to pursue either policy. In issuing debt, the Treasury's key consideration is the debt's *structure*—maturity distribution. In recent years the average maturity of Treasury debt outstanding has fallen steadily, as Figure 7–3 shows. The short average maturity (less than 3 years) of the debt means that the Treasury must always be in the market borrowing huge sums just to roll maturing debt. When money is tight, it is difficult for the Treasury to constantly sell huge new issues and its doing so is disrupting to the market; therefore one of the key objectives of debt management currently is to increase the average maturity of the debt.

As a practical matter the best time for the Treasury to extend maturities is when interest rates are down. In such periods the sale by the Treasury of large long-term debt issues does not disrupt capital markets as it would when money is tight, and the Treasury has in recent years sold several large long-term note issues when the market was in a good position to absorb them.

Figure 7–3
Average maturity of Treasury debt outstanding

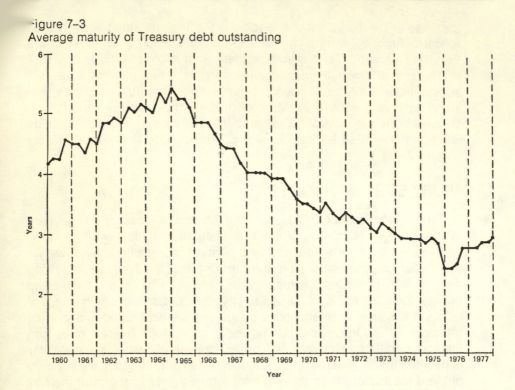

The Treasury, on the other hand, also makes it a policy to regularly issue long-term bonds at each quarterly financing. The rationale for this is that if portfolio managers know the Treasury is coming with a long bond issue once a quarter—as they know that the telephone company does—they will adjust their portfolios so that, when the new government bonds come to market, other bonds will have been swapped out to make room for them. This gives the Treasury a share of the market under all conditions—a share that the Treasury can and does increase when conditions are favorable and rates are down.

Another consideration for the Treasury is the preferences of the major buyers of its debt. Banks are by far the largest private investors in marketable governments. There is tremendous bank interest in the 3- to 7-year area, and the Treasury rarely goes beyond that in note issues except when it is reaching for nonbank investors and in particular for the general public.

Debt issuance in the mid-1960s

Over the last decade the Treasury has made substantial changes in the types of securities it offers to the market and in the way it sells these securities. These changes were made in response to two pressures: the Treasury's need to be able to market its debt in the face of increasingly variable interest rates and its need to be able to market rapidly growing amounts of debt.

In the mid-1960s the Treasury funded the debt as follows. It sold 3-month and 6-month bills at weekly auctions and 9-month and 1-year bills at monthly auctions. In addition, there was a quarterly financing in the middle of each quarter when the Treasury sold notes and bonds. The bills were sold as they are today through auctions, the notes and bonds through exchange and subscription offerings.

Bill auctions

In a bill auction, money market banks, dealers, and other institutional investors who buy large quantities of bills submit *competitive* bids, that is, for the bills they want to buy they bid a discounted price expressed on the basis of 100. For example, a dealer who wanted to buy $100 million of 3-month bills might bid a price of 98.375, which is equivalent to a yield of 6.429 on a discount basis.[3] The prices dealers and investors bid for bills depend both on the rates yielded by outstanding money market instruments and on what (if any) movement they think is occurring in short-term rates.

The less expert investor who is not prepared to work out a bid to three decimal points can put in a *noncompetitive* bid that states no price.

After the auction closes, bids are forwarded to the Treasury Department in Washington and tabulated for each issue. First, the volume of noncompetitive awards is subtracted from the total amount to be issued. Government and Federal Reserve Bank tenders, which are noncompetitive, are accepted in full. Noncompetitive tenders of private investors are accepted in full up to [the current limit on such tenders]. The remainder is allocated among competitive bidders beginning with those that bid the highest prices and ranging down in price until the total amount is issued. The lowest accepted price is called the *stop-out* price. Since a number of bids may have been entered at the stop-out price, the

---

[3] Rearranging the formula

$$D = F \left(\frac{d \times t}{360} \right)$$

which was given on page 38, we get

$$d = \frac{D \times 360}{F \times t}$$

In the above example D equals 1.625 per 100 of face value, and t equals 91 (13 weeks × 7 days per week). Thus

$$d = \frac{1.625 \times 360}{100 \times 91} = 6.429$$

Treasury may award each of the bidders at this price only a portion of the amount requested.

After the auction on Monday, the amount and price range of accepted bids are announced, and competitive bidders are advised of the acceptance or rejection of their tenders. Competitive bidders pay the price that they bid while noncompetitive entries pay the weighted average price to three decimals of accepted competitive bids.[4]

Exchange offerings

When the Treasury sold bonds through exchange offerings, it used two techniques. In a *straight exchange offer,* the Treasury sought to refund maturing securities by offering their holders new securities with the same par value. In an *advance refunding* or *pre-refunding,* the Treasury offered holders of an outstanding issue the opportunity to exchange their securities for new securities of the same par value in advance of maturity.

Holders of eligible securities who did not wish to invest in the new issue could sell their *right* to the new issue to other investors or turn in their maturing securities for cash. The purpose of straight exchange offerings was to encourage existing bondholders to roll their bonds, thereby permitting Treasury refundings to be carried out with minimal disruption to the market. In the case of pre-refundings, an additional objective was to reduce Treasury borrowing costs by taking advantage of the interest rate cycle; the Treasury would pre-refund when interest rates were expected to rise and pre-refunding looked cheap relative to refunding at maturity. Exchange offerings were usually made on generous terms so that issues for which exchange offerings were made tended to rise in value, reflecting the *rights* value they acquired through the exchange offering. The practice of exchange offerings also led to speculative demand for issues that were considered likely candidates for pre-refunding.

Subscription issues

In a subscription offering [which the Treasury has used to raise new cash], the Treasury announces the amount to be sold, the interest coupon on the issue, and the price of the issue. The Treasury reserves the right to change the amount sold and the allotment procedures after all subscriptions have been submitted. Additional amounts are issued to Federal Reserve and Government accounts after allotments to the public.

---

[4] Margaret Bedford, "Recent Developments in Treasury Financing Techniques," *Monthly Review,* Federal Reserve Bank of Kansas, July–August 1977, p. 17.

Investors enter subscriptions for the amount of securities they wish to purchase at the Treasury's given price and yield. Since investors may enter subscriptions totaling more than the amount offered by the Treasury, the allotment procedure becomes important for limiting the size of the issue. Allotments can be made by awarding a percentage of the amount of each tender or by setting a maximum dollar amount to be accepted for each tender.

The Treasury usually offers to accept some tenders in full on a preferred allotment basis. Preferred tenders are limited in size (up to $500,000 in recent offerings) and must be accompanied by a deposit of 20 percent of the face value of securities applied for.[5]

The rate lid on bonds

Congress permits the Treasury to pay whatever rate of return is necessary to sell bills and notes, but bars the Treasury from paying more than 4.25 percent on bonds. This rate lid created no problem when long-term rates were below 4.25 percent. But since the mid-1960s they have risen well above this level, making it impossible for the Treasury to sell new bonds, with one minor exemption.

In the early 1970s the Treasury was given permission to sell $10 billion of bonds exempt from this rate ceiling. The amount of this exemption was raised on several occasions and equaled $27 billion in early 1978, a small amount relative to the size of the Treasury's total marketable debt. The 4.25 percent rate lid, despite its popularity with members of Congress who favor low interest rates, does nothing to hold down interest rates. It does, however, bar the Treasury from competing directly with private corporations and municipal borrowers in the long-term market and from pulling funds directly out of the mortgage market, which explains some of the support for retaining the lid.

In this respect it is worth noting that the lid's indirect effect on the flow of funds is more difficult to gauge. Concentrating huge quantities of Treasury debt in short-term instruments tends to drive up short-term rates to levels higher than normal relative to long-term rates (it tends to flatten the normal yield curve), which in turn naturally pulls money out of long-term securities and into shorter-term securities. Also, high-coupon Treasury notes pull funds directly out of S&Ls and mutual savings banks, which in turn diminishes the flow of funds to the mortgage market.

Changing policies of debt issuance

The fact that after the mid-1960s the Treasury could not sell any long-term bonds left it in the position where the longest-maturity security it

[5] Ibid., p. 23.

could sell was a 5-year note. As a result, the average maturity of the debt began to decline at a disturbing rate (see Figure 7–3). To counter this trend, the Treasury sought and received from Congress in 1967 permission to raise the maximum maturity of notes from 5 to 7 years.

As interest rates became more volatile in the late 1960s, it became increasingly difficult for the Treasury to issue new debt through subscription issues on which both the price and the coupon were announced several days before the date on which investors tendered for the issue. In a 1970 refunding the Treasury experimented, using for the first time a *price auction* instead of the subscription technique to sell new notes and bonds to the general public.

Price auctions

In the price auction, the Treasury announces the amount to be sold to the public, and a few days prior to the auction sets a coupon rate and a minimum acceptable price. Competitive bidders state the price they are willing to pay on the basis of 100 to two decimals. These bids may be at par ($100 per $100 face), at a price below par (at a discount), or at a price above par (at a premium). The price bid would reflect the investor's judgment as to how attractive the coupon rate is compared to other market rates. The rate associated with a price of par is the coupon rate; paying a premium will result in a lower effective yield than the coupon rate; and buying at a discount will yield an effective return higher than the coupon rate. As in the Treasury bill market, the noncompetitive tenders are subtracted from the amount to be sold and the remainder is distributed by accepting the highest price bid on down until the amount of the issue is taken. Competitive bidders pay the price that they bid, and noncompetitive bids are accepted in full at the average price of competitive bids. However, since the competitive bids are not necessarily at par, the average price paid by noncompetitive bidders may be more or less than par and thus they will receive an effective yield somewhat different from the coupon rate.[6]

Switch to yield auctions

In 1973 the Treasury made further changes in its policies issuance. It again sought and received from Congress permi raise the maximum maturity on notes, this time from 7 to 10 ye because of its increasing cash needs, it discontinued excha ings with the February 1973 refunding and began to rely sol tion sales. The Treasury also began to issue 2-year notes cycle but later discontinued this cycle; it also disconti 9-month bills because of a lack of investor acceptance of

The year 1974, which was characterized by high and

---

[6] Ibid., p. 22.

Investors enter subscriptions for the amount of securities they wish to purchase at the Treasury's given price and yield. Since investors may enter subscriptions totaling more than the amount offered by the Treasury, the allotment procedure becomes important for limiting the size of the issue. Allotments can be made by awarding a percentage of the amount of each tender or by setting a maximum dollar amount to be accepted for each tender.

The Treasury usually offers to accept some tenders in full on a preferred allotment basis. Preferred tenders are limited in size (up to $500,000 in recent offerings) and must be accompanied by a deposit of 20 percent of the face value of securities applied for.[5]

The rate lid on bonds

Congress permits the Treasury to pay whatever rate of return is necessary to sell bills and notes, but bars the Treasury from paying more than 4.25 percent on bonds. This rate lid created no problem when long-term rates were below 4.25 percent. But since the mid-1960s they have risen well above this level, making it impossible for the Treasury to sell new bonds, with one minor exemption.

In the early 1970s the Treasury was given permission to sell $10 billion of bonds exempt from this rate ceiling. The amount of this exemption was raised on several occasions and equaled $27 billion in early 1978, a small amount relative to the size of the Treasury's total marketable debt. The 4.25 percent rate lid, despite its popularity with members of Congress who favor low interest rates, does nothing to hold down interest rates. It does, however, bar the Treasury from competing directly with private corporations and municipal borrowers in the long-term market and from pulling funds directly out of the mortgage market, which explains some of the support for retaining the lid.

In this respect it is worth noting that the lid's indirect effect on the flow of funds is more difficult to gauge. Concentrating huge quantities of Treasury debt in short-term instruments tends to drive up short-term rates to levels higher than normal relative to long-term rates (it tends to flatten the normal yield curve), which in turn naturally pulls money out of long-term securities and into shorter-term securities. Also, high-coupon Treasury notes pull funds directly out of S&Ls and mutual savings banks, which in turn diminishes the flow of funds to the mortgage market.

Changing policies of debt issuance

The fact that after the mid-1960s the Treasury could not sell any long-term bonds left it in the position where the longest-maturity security it

---

[5] Ibid., p. 23.

could sell was a 5-year note. As a result, the average maturity of the debt began to decline at a disturbing rate (see Figure 7–3). To counter this trend, the Treasury sought and received from Congress in 1967 permission to raise the maximum maturity of notes from 5 to 7 years.

As interest rates became more volatile in the late 1960s, it became increasingly difficult for the Treasury to issue new debt through subscription issues on which both the price and the coupon were announced several days before the date on which investors tendered for the issue. In a 1970 refunding the Treasury experimented, using for the first time a *price auction* instead of the subscription technique to sell new notes and bonds to the general public.

Price auctions

In the price auction, the Treasury announces the amount to be sold to the public, and a few days prior to the auction sets a coupon rate and a minimum acceptable price. Competitive bidders state the price they are willing to pay on the basis of 100 to two decimals. These bids may be at par ($100 per $100 face), at a price below par (at a discount), or at a price above par (at a premium). The price bid would reflect the investor's judgment as to how attractive the coupon rate is compared to other market rates. The rate associated with a price of par is the coupon rate; paying a premium will result in a lower effective yield than the coupon rate; and buying at a discount will yield an effective return higher than the coupon rate. As in the Treasury bill market, the noncompetitive tenders are subtracted from the amount to be sold and the remainder is distributed by accepting the highest price bid on down until the amount of the issue is taken. Competitive bidders pay the price that they bid, and noncompetitive bids are accepted in full at the average price of competitive bids. However, since the competitive bids are not necessarily at par, the average price paid by noncompetitive bidders may be more or less than par and thus they will receive an effective yield somewhat different from the coupon rate.[6]

Switch to yield auctions

In 1973 the Treasury made further changes in its policies of debt issuance. It again sought and received from Congress permission to raise the maximum maturity on notes, this time from 7 to 10 years. Also, because of its increasing cash needs, it discontinued exchange offerings with the February 1973 refunding and began to rely solely on auction sales. The Treasury also began to issue 2-year notes on a regular cycle but later discontinued this cycle; it also discontinued issuing 9-month bills because of a lack of investor acceptance of this maturity.

The year 1974, which was characterized by high and volatile interest

---

[6] Ibid., p. 22.

rates, was a difficult time for the Treasury to sell debt. To ease its problems, the Treasury increased the size of the noncompetitive bids that could be tendered for notes and bonds to $500,000 in order to broaden the appeal of its debt to a wider class of investors. It also began to issue on an occasional basis special longer-term bills issued for nonstandard periods when additional funds were needed.

The final and most important change the Treasury made in 1974 was to switch its auctions of notes and bonds from a price to a yield basis. Under the price auction system, at the time a new issue was announced, the Treasury set the coupon on the issue in line with market rates, so that the new issue's price, determined through auction, would be at or near par. If rates moved away from the levels prevailing on announcement day, the prices bid on auction day would move correspondingly away from par. For example, if rates fell between the announcement of an issue and the auction, bid prices would be above par, whereas a rise in rates would bring in bids below par. As interest rates became increasingly volatile, deviations of bid prices from par became more and more of a problem. In August 1974, for example, one Treasury issue was sold at 101 while another failed to sell out because the Treasury did not receive an adequate quantity of bids at or above the minimum price it would accept. The Treasury feared that above-par prices would discourage some bidders and that below-par prices would place purchasers in an unanticipated tax position (the amount of the discount at issue being taxable at maturity as ordinary income). Another problem with price auctions was that, when the Treasury set coupons, the market tended to move to them, so that price auctions were slightly disturbing to the market. To solve both problems and to ensure that its issues sold out, the Treasury moved in late 1974 to a new technique, in which would-be buyers bid *yields* instead of prices.

In a yield auction for notes and bonds, the Treasury announces the new issue a week or more before the auction date. At that time it tells the market what amount of securities it is going to issue, when they will mature, and what denominations will be available. *Competitive* bidders bid yields to two decimal points (e.g., 8.53) for specific quantities of the new issue. After bids are received, the Treasury determines the stop-out bid on the basis of both the bids received and the amount it wishes to borrow. It then sets the coupon on the security to the nearest ⅛ of 1 percent necessary to make the average price charged to successful bidders equal to 100.00 or less. Once the coupon on the issue is established, each successful bidder is charged a price (discount, par, or premium) for his securities; the price is determined so that the yield to maturity on the securities a bidder gets equals the yield he bid. *Noncompetitive* bidders pay the average price of the accepted competitive tenders.

TABs, strips, and cash management bills

In 1975, when the Treasury was faced with the problem of refunding huge quantities of maturing debt and financing a burgeoning federal debt as well, it made still further changes in its policies of debt issuance.

From time to time the Treasury finds it necessary to sell special bill issues to meet short-term borrowing needs. Prior to 1975 the Treasury used *tax anticipation bills* (TABs) and bill *strips* for this purpose.

Tax anticipation bills were issued to help the Treasury smooth out its tax receipts, and they could be submitted in payment of income taxes. Commercial banks were usually permitted to make payment for TABs by crediting Treasury tax and loan accounts and thus became underwriters for these issues. About 28 TAB offerings were made during the 1970–74 period, and they ranged in maturity from 23 to 273 days.

A bill strip is a reopening of a number of issues of outstanding bill series. Strips enabled the Treasury to raise a large amount of short-term funds at one time rather than spreading out receipts through additions to weekly bill auctions. In the 1970–74 period, nine strips of bills were issued ranging from additions to 5 series to additions to 15 series and averaging 22 days to 131 days in maturity.[7]

In 1975 the Treasury discontinued the use of TABs and strips and replaced them with *cash management bills*. Cash management bills are usually reopenings of an outstanding issue and often have quite short maturities. When they are auctioned, the minimum acceptable bid is $10 million and only competitive bids are accepted. Cash management bills are usually bought by banks and dealers at some spread to their cost of money and held to maturity.

Regularization of debt issuance

The most important innovation in debt management that the Treasury made in 1975 and the most important it made over the last decade was to adopt a program of *regularization of debt issuance.* Under this program, the Treasury began to issue 2-year, 4-year, and 5-year notes on a regular cycle. A 2-year note is issued at the end of each month, a 4-year note in the middle of the second month of each quarter, and a 5-year note in the middle of the first month of each quarter. The normal quarterly refunding, at which the Treasury offers a mix of notes and bonds to refund maturing issues and raise new cash, occurs at the middle of the second month of each quarter. Thus the Treasury now issues coupons on a regular schedule of six dates a quarter (Table 7–3).

The Treasury now appears committed to continuing a 2-year note cycle. It has also issued the 4-year note regularly since the inception of

---

[7] Ibid., p. 18.

Table 7–3
Quarterly schedule of Treasury coupon
offerings

Quarterly dates	Issue offered
First month	
Middle	5-year note
End	2-year note
Second month	
Middle	Quarterly refunding
End	2-year note
Third month	
Middle	4-year note
End	2-year note

that cycle. The 5-year note cycle was, however, interrupted in 1977 because the Treasury did not need to raise a lot of new cash on a date when a 5-year note was scheduled.

The Treasury moved to regularize its issuance of debt for several reasons. First, doing so was viewed as a means to improve the maturity structure of the debt, and in 1977 the average maturity of Treasury debt outstanding did in fact rise slightly for the first time in years (see Figure 7–3).

A second consideration was to avoid bunching too much Treasury debt in the quarterly financings. There is some limit as to how much debt the market can absorb and dealers can distribute at any one time; it was thought that if the Treasury continued to issue most of its coupon debt on four dates a year, that limit would be breached and the Treasury would be forced to pay higher rates than it would have had to if bunching were avoided. Under the current program the market has a chance to digest one issue before it girds up to take another.

A third important objective of the Treasury, when it regularized debt issuance and adopted yield auctions, was to facilitate the operation of monetary policy. Under the current system, Treasury issues do not disturb the money and bond markets as they did when the Treasury made frequent, large, and unanticipated offerings. Also the current system of debt issuance permits the Federal Reserve to make small moves in monetary policy without fear that these will disrupt Treasury financings.

Removing the rate lid on bonds

While the current program of debt regularization had done much to ease the Treasury's problems in funding the debt, there is another important step that should be taken, namely removing the 4.25 percent lid on the rate the Treasury can pay on bonds. The six possible maturity dates now available to the Treasury during each quarter are all being used. The market is not currently able, estimates one banker close to the market, to absorb more on average than $2 or $3 billion of coupons on each of these dates; and the amounts being offered by the Treasury are moving toward this limit.

The Treasury could attempt to avoid reaching the critical point at which it overloads possible maturity dates in a quarter by issuing notes and bonds 12 times a quarter, but the market is not prepared to absorb weekly coupon issues. The only other way for the Treasury to relieve the strain on maturity dates is by issuing more long-term debt, something the Treasury cannot do unless Congress removes the rate lid on bonds or vastly expands the exemption it has granted to the Treasury from this lid.

Exceptions to the general pattern

Currently the Treasury relies primarily on yield auctions to sell new coupon securities. It makes exceptions to this practice for several purposes. First, the Treasury sometimes *reopens* (sells more of) an already outstanding note or bond issue. In that case the coupon on the issue has already been determined in a previous auction; therefore the new securities offered must carry that coupon and must be sold through a *price* auction.

Second, on several occasions in 1976 the Treasury used subscription issues because it had such an enormous volume of new debt to place that it feared it would strain the underwriting and distribution capacity of the street if it used the normal auction procedure. Instead it issued notes carrying an attractive coupon at a fixed price through subscription offerings. This strategy enabled the Treasury to reach beyond its normal market directly to individual investors. A coupon of 8 percent is currently thought to be a magic number; whenever the Treasury puts an 8 percent or higher coupon on an issue, individuals—comparing that rate with what they can get on savings accounts and time deposits—rush out to buy it, and typically they then hold the issue to maturity.

More recently, as part of the February 1978 quarterly financing, the Treasury offered a 6-year note with an 8 percent coupon through a price auction. The Treasury's objective in fixing the coupon instead of using a yield auction was to sell a larger-sized issue by appealing to individual as well as institutional investors.

Too many issues

One question frequently raised on the street is whether the Treasury program of debt regularization is creating a situation in which Treasury issues are too numerous to be tradable. Opinions vary.

One dealer commented: "The Treasury should start reopening issues. Currently they have so many outstanding that it is impossible to keep track of them all. This puts a premium on active issues; people will buy and be active only in current on-the-run issues because to get off the run is to forgo so much liquidity as to be painful."

A second dealer argued: "Debt regularization is a necessity. You can't have the Treasury just popping in selling 5 billion of this or that and the market never knowing what is coming. It is not good for the market to know that the Treasury has a 15 billion financing job to do in a quarter and to have no idea of where [in the maturity spectrum] or when the issues will come. It would be easier for the traders to have fewer issues, but for the market and the Treasury—it is better to have debt regularization."

FEDERAL AGENCIES ISSUING SECURITIES

In Chapter 2 we talked about financial intermediaries, which are institutions that act as conduits through which funds are channeled from consumers, firms, and other spending units with funds surpluses to spending units (consumers, firms, and government bodies) running funds deficits. Most financial intermediaries in the United States are private (albeit government regulated) institutions: commercial banks, savings and loan associations, credit unions, life insurance companies, and private pension funds, to name a few.

In addition to these private institutions, there is also a large and growing number of government credit agencies that act as financial intermediaries. These agencies borrow funds and then use them to make various types of loans to specific classes of borrowers. The reason for all this government competition to private intermediation is that Congress has periodically taken the position that for some groups of borrowers, the available supply of credit was too limited, too variable, or too expensive. In each instance the remedy was for Congress to set up a federal agency charged with providing a dependable supply of credit at the lowest cost possible to these disadvantaged borrowers. Some federal agencies are owned and directed by the federal government, and their debt obligations are backed by the full faith and credit of the U.S. government. Others are federally sponsored but privately owned. The obligations of federally sponsored agencies presumably have *de facto* backing from the federal government.

The largest government credit agencies specialize in providing mortgage money for housing and agriculture, two favored children of policy makers. In addition, there are agencies that provide credit to small business firms, students, communities financing development projects, and so forth.

Most federal agencies are supposed to set their lending rates so that they at least cover their borrowing costs and perhaps even earn a modest profit. Since each agency's function is to supply funds to borrowers at minimum cost, the rational approach would have been to have the agencies borrow from the cheapest possible source. Because its securities carry zero risk of default, the Treasury can always borrow at lower rates than any other issuer, municipalities excepted. Thus, having the Treasury lend to the agencies funds that it had borrowed in the open market would have been the least-cost way to funnel money into the agencies.

This approach, however, was not taken. Instead, until 1974, almost all agencies issued their own securities, each carrying some degree of backing from the federal government. The main reason for taking this approach was that if the agencies had all borrowed from the Treasury, the Treasury's outstanding debt would have gone up commensurately. Today it would be $110.4 billion greater than the $721.6 billion figure quoted earlier in this chapter.

Such an increase in Treasury debt could have created problems for several reasons. First, Congress imposes a statutory limit on Treasury borrowing. This limit has no perceptible impact on government spending because Congress always pauses—between passing spending bills—to raise it. Nevertheless Congress has at times been stubborn and slow about raising the debt limit, with the result that in practice it might have been difficult for the Treasury to borrow sufficient funds to meet *all* the agencies' needs. Also there are voters who lose sleep over the size of the national debt. In this respect, it is important to note that agency and federal debts differ sharply with respect to both source and character. Most Treasury debt is the result of government deficits, a true national debt. In contrast, agency debt is incurred to make loans, largely to creditworthy borrowers.

THE FEDERAL FINANCING BANK

As federal agencies proliferated, their borrowings from the public caused several problems. One had to do with calendar scheduling. Each year federal agencies issue substantial quantities of new debt. Agency issues compete with each other and with Treasury issues for investors' funds, and an uneven flow of agency and Treasury issues to the market could result in rates being driven up one week and down the next. To avoid this, the Treasury schedules the timing and size of both its own and agency issues to ensure a reasonably smooth flow of federal issues to the market. In 1973 minor federal agencies made 75 separate offerings, so many that it made Treasury calendar scheduling of new issues difficult. Another problem resulting from the proliferation of federal agencies was that the new small agencies constantly being created by Congress were not well known to investors; and because of their small size, their issues were less liquid than Treasury issues. Consequently small agencies had to pay relatively high borrowing rates.

To deal with these problems, in 1973 Congress set up the *Federal Financing Bank* (FFB), a government instrument supervised by the Secretary of the Treasury. The FFB buys up the debt issues of the smaller agencies and its clientele currently includes about 20 separate agencies, essentially all federal agencies except for the seven major ones described below.

The FFB was supposed to obtain funds by issuing securities fully

Figure 7–4
Borrowings of the Federal Financing Bank from the U.S. Treasury

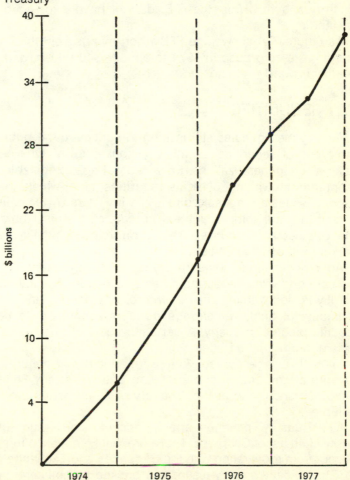

backed by the government in a fashion similar to the way the Treasury issues its securities. It tried this approach once with an offering of short-term bills. This offering was bid for by dealers and others at yields close to those prevailing on T bills, but the issue fell in price in the secondary market, which was discouraging to both dealers and the Treasury. Some dealers felt that if the FFB had continued to issue its securities, they would—after five or six issues—have been accepted by investors as equal to Treasury issues and would have sold at yields no higher than those on Treasury issues. The Treasury, however seems to have doubted this; one reason being that FFB offerings would have been small relative to Treasury offerings and consequently less liquid. In any case, the FFB discontinued its public offerings and now borrows from the Treasury. Today there are only seven major federal agencies still issuing new securities to the market. However, some of the smaller agencies, which now borrow from the FFB, do still have a few long-term issues outstanding.

As Figure 7–4 shows, the FFB's borrowings from the Treasury have risen from a zero base in 1974 to almost $40 billion, and the trend is steadily upward.

AGENCY SECURITIES

Among the agencies still issuing securities to the public, practices and types of securities issued vary considerably. One can, however, make a few generalizations. Each federal agency establishes a fiscal agent through which it offers its securities, all of which are negotiable. Agency issues are not sold directly to investors by these fiscal agents. Instead they are sold through a syndicate of dealers, who distribute the agency's securities to investors and participate in making a secondary market for these securities.

Agency securities come in varying forms: short-term notes sold at a discount and interest-bearing notes and bonds. Agency bonds are frequently issued with the title *debenture.* Any bond is an interest-bearing certificate of debt. A *mortgage bond* is secured by a lien on some specific piece of property. A debenture is a bond secured only by the general credit of the issuer.

Interest on agency securities and principal at maturity are usually payable at any branch of the issuing agency, at any Federal Reserve bank or branch, and at the Treasury. Agency bonds are typically not callable.

Like Treasury securities, agency securities are issued under the authority of an act of Congress. Therefore, unlike private offerings, they are exempt from registration with the Securities and Exchange Commission (SEC). Typically agency issues are backed by collateral in the form of cash, U.S. government securities, and the debt obligations that the issuing agency has acquired through its lending activities. A few agency issues are backed by the full faith and credit of the United States. A number of others are guaranteed by the Treasury or supported by the issuing agency's right to borrow funds from the Treasury up to some specified amount. Finally, there are agency securities with no direct or indirect federal backing.

HOUSING CREDIT AGENCIES

The major federal agencies still offering securities differ considerably in mission and method of operation, so we have organized our survey of them by function: first the mortgage-related agencies and then the farm credit agencies.

Federal Home Loan Banks

Behind the nation's commercial banks stands the Federal Reserve System, which regulates member banks, acts as a lender of last resort, and otherwise facilitates a smooth operation of the banking system. Behind the nation's S&Ls stands a somewhat similar institution, the *Federal Home Loan Bank* system. The FHLB, created in 1932, is composed of 12 regional banks and a central board in Washington.

S&Ls, savings banks, and insurance companies may all become members of the FHLB system; federally chartered S&Ls are required to do so. Currently about 4,100 S&Ls belong to the FHLB system; these S&Ls hold over 98 percent of the total assets of all S&Ls in the country.

The Federal Home Loan banks are owned by the private S&Ls that are members of the system, just as the 12 Federal Reserve banks are owned by their member banks. The private ownership is, however, only nominal since the FHLB, like the Fed, operates under federal charter and is charged by Congress with regulating member S&Ls and with formulating and carrying out certain aspects of government policy with respect to the savings and loan industry. Thus the Federal Home Loan banks are in fact an arm of the federal government.

In addition to overseeing member S&Ls, the FHLB also lends to member S&Ls just as the Fed lends to commercial banks. Here, however, the similarity ends. The Fed obtains money to lend to banks at the discount window by monetizing debt. The Federal Home Loan banks have to borrow the money they lend to member S&Ls. Most of the money S&Ls provide to home buyers comes from their depositors. The FHLB lends to member S&Ls primarily to augment this source of funds. In a nutshell, the FHLB borrows money in the open market, then relends it to S&Ls, which in turn relend it again to home buyers.

One purpose of this involved operation is to aid S&Ls with a temporary liquidity problem. A more important function is to channel money into the S&Ls when money is tight and rate lids cause a slowdown of the inflow of funds into S&Ls or even generate a net outflow of funds from such institutions. During such periods the FHLB has to pay more to borrow in the open market than S&Ls are paying depositors. For example, the FHLB issued 37-month bonds with a 9.5 percent coupon in September 1974, a time when the maximum rate S&Ls could pay on a 4- to 6-year time deposit was 7.5 percent. Since the rate S&Ls have to pay on FHLB loans is set sufficiently high to cover the FHLB's borrowing costs, such loans are not a cheap source of funds to S&Ls. Also the FHLB's borrowings in the open market create an interesting (disturbing to the FHLB) possiblity for disintermediation: S&L depositors, seeking a higher return on their funds, might take money out of S&Ls and buy FHLB securities. To preclude this short-circuiting of the S&Ls, the FHLB raised the minimum denomination on its bonds from $5,000 to $10,000 in 1970.

The main security issued by the FHLB is consolidated *bonds,* "consolidated" referring to the fact that the bonds are the joint obligation of all 12 Federal Home Loan banks. FHLB bonds have a maturity at issue of 1 year or more, pay interest semiannually, and are not callable. They are issued in bearer and book-entry form[8] and are now sold in denominations of $10,000, $25,000, $100,000, and $1 million. FHLB bonds often appear on dealers' quote sheets as *FHLB notes.* The FHLB used to issue short-term, interest-bearing notes, but it switched some time ago to the sale of discount notes to raise short-term money. These discount notes have a minimum denomination of $100,000.

FHLB securities are backed by qualified collateral in the form of secured advances to member S&Ls, government securities, insured mortgages, etc. FHLB securities are *not* guaranteed by the U.S. government. However, they are the obligation of the FHLB system, which plays a key federal role in regulating and assisting the S&L industry. Given this role and the importance of the S&L industry to the economy, it is inconceivable that the U.S. government would ever permit the FHLB to default on outstanding securities.

Interest income from FHLB securities is subject to full federal taxes but is specifically exempt from state and local taxation.

Federal National Mortgage Association

Most money market instruments are extremely liquid (commercial paper being the main exception). The reason is not simply that these

---

[8] Under the *book-entry* system, to which the Treasury and the major federal agencies are moving, securities are not represented by engraved pieces of paper but are maintained in computerized records at the Fed in the names of member banks that in turn keep computerized records of the securities they own as well as those they are holding for customers. The book-entry system is described in Chapter 13.

securities are stamped *negotiable* but more importantly that they have a broad and active secondary market. One of the major factors contributing to the existence of this secondary market is the homogeneity (one unit is just like another) of bills, bonds, and notes. Because mortgages lack homogeneity, a wide secondary market for mortgages has never developed in the United States. The lack of a secondary market for mortgages makes these instruments illiquid, which in turn tends to diminish the flow of funds into the mortgage market.

The *Federal National Mortgage Association* (FNMA), popularly known as "Fannie Mae," was set up in 1938 by Congress to create a secondary market in FHA mortgages (mortgages insured by the Federal Housing Administration). Initially Fannie Mae was wholly government owned and its funds came from the Treasury. Later in 1954, Fannie Mae was split into three separate divisions: secondary market operations, special assistance functions, and management and liquidating functions.

The secondary market division was supposed to attract money to the mortgage market by providing liquidity for government-insured mortgages. To do so, it bought and sold mortgages insured or guaranteed by the Federal Housing Administration, the Veterans Administration, and the Farm Home Administration. Institutions dealing as buyers or sellers in mortgages with Fannie Mae were required to buy small amounts of Fannie Mae stock, thereby permitting the secondary market division of Fannie Mae to be converted from government ownership to private ownership.

In 1968, Congress completed its partition of Fannie Mae by putting its special assistance and management and liquidating functions into a new government-owned corporation, the *Government National Mortgage Association.* The remaining secondary market division of Fannie Mae, which retained the title Federal National Mortgage Association, was converted into a privately owned corporation. The corporation's private ownership is, however, to some degree nominal since the government retains broad powers to direct and regulate the operations of Fannie Mae through the Secretary of Housing and Urban Development (HUD). In 1977 the question of just how much control HUD could exercise over Fannie Mae was actively disputed by both parties. HUD sought more control, suggested that Fannie Mae's profits were perhaps too high, and attempted to force the agency to funnel more funds into mortgages on inner-city housing.

Currently Fannie Mae's function is to buy government-insured or guaranteed mortgages (also conventional mortgages since 1970) when mortgage money is in short supply and to sell them when the demand for mortgage money slacks off. It does this through auctions at which it buys and sells some preannounced total of mortgages. For a fee Fannie Mae also extends advance commitments to buy mortgages. In the recent years of tight money and recurring shortages of mortgage funds, Fannie Mae has been more often a buyer than a seller of mortgages. Nevertheless, this agency and others created to serve the same purpose have made significant progress toward increasing the liquidity of mortgages and attracting into mortgages funds that would otherwise have flowed elsewhere.

To finance its mortgage purchases, Fannie Mae relies primarily on the sale of debentures and short-term discount notes. The latter, whose maturities range from 30 to 270 days, are available in bearer form only and the minimum purchase is $50,000. Fannie Mae adjusts periodically the rates it offers on its discount notes so that they are in line with T bill rates. Fannie Mae debentures, which are not callable (with one exception), are issued in bearer and book-entry form. They pay interest semiannually and the smallest denominations available are $10,000 and $25,000. Fannie Mae debentures are not backed by the federal government, but given the association's role as a government policy tool and its government supervision, it seems highly improbable that the government would permit a default on Fannie Mae obligations.

Interest income on Fannie Mae securities is subject to full federal taxation and is not exempt from state and local taxation. The large volume of Fannie Mae securities outstanding makes availability and marketability in the secondary market excellent.

Government National Mortgage Association

The 1968 partition of the old Federal National Mortgage Association spawned yet another financial lady, "Ginnie Mae," more formally known as the *Government National Mortgage Association* (GNMA). Ginnie Mae, a wholly government-owned corporation within the Department of Housing and Urban Development, took over the special assistance and the management and liquidating functions that had formerly been lodged in FNMA. These functions involve activities that could not be profitably carried out by a private firm. Ginnie Mae's mission is also to make real estate investment more attractive to institutional investors, which it has done by designing and issuing—partly in conjunction with private financial institutions—new mortgage-backed securities for which an active secondary market has developed.

Under its management and liquidating functions, Ginnie Mae sold mortgages—some inherited from FNMA's earlier operations as a three-division organization and some acquired in the mid-1960s from other government agencies. It did this by creating pools of mortgages and selling participations in these pools to private investors. Currently there are about 15 issues of GNMA participation certificates still outstanding (none has been issued since 1968). These were issued in bearer and registered form and have minimum denominations of $5,000 and $10,000, depending on the issue. All participation certificates are guaranteed by Ginnie Mae with respect to payment of both principal and interest; they also carry the full faith and credit backing of the U.S. government.

Under its special assistance function, Ginnie Mae provides financing for selected types of mortgages through mortgage purchases and commitments to purchase mortgages. Under one program, for example, Ginnie Mae provides funds for the rehabilitation of deteriorating housing, which is subsequently resold to low-income families. Ginnie Mae finances its special assistance operations partly with funds obtained from the Treasury. To limit its borrowings from this source, Ginnie Mae currently operates most special assistance projects under a tandem plan. As Ginnie Mae acquires mortgages or mortgage purchase commitments, it resells them at market prices to other investors. Typically, under its special assistance function, Ginnie Mae buys mortgages at prices above prevailing market levels. Thus, to resell under the tandem plan, it has to absorb some loss, making it in effect a source of subsidy for certain types of mortgages.

Under the pass-through approach, private mortgage lenders assemble pools of mortgages acquired through Ginnie Mae auctions or from other sources and then sell certificates backed by these mortgages to investors. These certificates are referred to as *pass-through securities* because payment of interest and principal on mortgages in the pool is passed on to the certificate holders after deduction of fees for servicing and guarantee. Pass-through certificates have stated maturities equal to those of the underlying mortgages. However, actual maturities tend to be much shorter because of prepayments, the average life on single-family mortgages being approximately 12 years. On pass-through securities, principal and interest are paid *monthly* to the investor. Because payments are made monthly and because the amount passed through varies from month to month due to mortgage prepayment, pass-throughs are issued in registered form only. Pass-through certificates have a minimum denomination of $25,000. They carry Ginnie Mae's guarantee of timely payment of both principal and interest and are backed in addition by the full faith and credit of the U.S. government.

Federal Home Loan Mortgage Corporation

The *Federal Home Loan Mortgage Corporation* (FHLMC) was created in July 1970 through enactment of Title III of the Emergency Home Finance Act of 1970. The organization's purpose is to promote the development of a nation-wide secondary market in conventional residential mortgages. To accomplish this, the FHLMC buys residential mortgages and then resells them via the sale of mortgage-related instruments. The FHLMC's operations are directed by the Federal Home Loan Bank system, which provided the new agency with its initial capital.

To some extent the FHLMC duplicates the activities of Fannie Mae. But it has a special feature; it may purchase mortgages only from financial institutions that have their deposits or accounts insured by agencies of the federal government. The requirement that it deal with only regulated institutions (whereas Fannie Mae also buys mortgages from mortgage bankers) permits the FHLMC to cut documentation and paper requirements on mortgage purchases and thereby operate at lower cost. Unlike Fannie Mae, which has borrowed over $30 billion to finance its mortgage holdings, the FHLMC has pursued a course similar to that of Ginnie Mae—namely, selling its interest in the mortgages it purchases through mortgage-backed, pass-through securities.

Specifically the FHLMC sells two types of pass-through securities, *mortgage participation certificates* (PCs) and *guaranteed mortgage certificates* (GMCs). PCs resemble Ginnie Mae pass-throughs. Each PC represents an undivided interest in a pool of conventional residential mortgages underwritten and previously purchased by the FHLMC. Each month the certificate holder receives a prorated share of the principal and interest payments made on the underlying pool. The FHLMC guarantees timely payment of interest on PCs and the full return of principal to the investor. While PCs technically have a maturity at issue of 30 years, their average weighted life is assumed to be 12 years or less.

Guaranteed mortgage certificates also represent an undivided interest in conventional residential mortgages underwritten and previously purchased by the FHLMC. These certificates pay interest semiannually and return principal once a year in guaranteed minimum amounts. The final payment date on GMCs is 30 years from the date of issue, but the expected average weighted life of these securities is around 10 years. Certificate holders may require the FHLMC to repurchase certificates at par 15 to 25 years (the put date varies with the issue) after they are issued.

Both PCs and GMCs are issued in registered form in initial principal amounts of $100,000, $500,000, and $1 million. Currently the FHLMC has approximately $8 billion of such securities outstanding.

In addition to selling pass-through securities, the FHLMC has also sold $1.7 billion of bonds guaranteed by Ginnie Mae and backed by FHA and VA mortgages.

All securities issued by and through the FHLMC are subject to full state and federal taxation on income.

FARM-CREDIT AGENCIES

The production and sale of agricultural commodities require large amounts of credit. So too does the acquisition by farmers of additional land and buildings. To assure an adequate supply of credit to meet these needs, the government has put together over time the Farm Credit Administration. This administration, which operates as an independent agency of the U.S. government, oversees the Farm Credit System, which operates in all states plus Puerto Rico. Under this system, the country is divided into 12 farm credit districts. In each of these, there is a Federal Land Bank, a Federal Intermediate Credit Bank, and a Bank for Cooperatives, each supplying specific types of credit to qualified borrowers in its district. To obtain funds, these 36 banks plus a Central Bank for Cooperatives all issue securities through a common fiscal agency in New York City.

Banks for Cooperatives

The 12 district *Banks for Cooperatives,* organized under the Farm Credit Act of 1933, make seasonal and term loans to cooperatives owned by farmers, engage in purchasing farm supplies, provide business services to farmers, and market farm output. These loans may provide working capital or finance investments in buildings and equipment. The Central Bank for Cooperatives participates in large loans made by individual district banks. Initially the Banks for Cooperatives were owned by the U.S. government. Since 1955, however, government capital has been replaced by private capital, and ownership is now private.

The major means by which the Banks for Cooperatives finance new loans is through the sale of Consolidated Collateral Trust Debentures (*Co-ops*). These debentures, which are not callable, are typically offered to investors once a month. They are issued in bearer and book-entry form, and the smallest denominations available are $5,000 and $10,000. Many recent issues have had an original maturity of 6 months and pay interest at maturity, but longer-term (2–5 years) Co-ops have also been issued.

All debentures issued by the Banks for Cooperatives must be secured by acceptable collateral in the form of cash, Treasury securities, and notes or other obligations of borrowers from the banks. Also, each bank is examined at least annually by the Farm Credit Administration. Obligations of these banks are not, however, guaranteed either directly or indirectly by the U.S. government. Nevertheless, given the semioffical status of the Banks for Cooperatives and the government's high degree of concern for agriculture, it seems unlikely, to say the least, that the government would permit these banks to default on their securities.

Interest income from debentures issued by the Banks for Cooperatives is subject to full federal taxation but is specifically exempt from state and local income taxes.

Federal Land Banks

The 12 *Federal Land Banks* were organized under the Federal Farm Loan Act of 1916. These banks extend first mortgage loans on farm properties and make other loans through local Federal Land Bank (FLB) associations, which now number 700. Mortgage loans must be made on the basis of appraisal reports and may not exceed 65 percent of the appraised value of the mortgaged property. Maturities on FLB loans may run from 5 to 40 years, but most have original maturities of around 20 years. Although the Federal Land Banks were set up under government auspices, all government capital in these banks has been replaced by private capital, and they are now owned by the FLB associations, which in turn are owned by the farmers who have obtained FLB loans through these associations.

The Federal Land Banks obtain funds to lend out primarily by issuing Consolidated Federal Farm Loan bonds and by occasional short-term borrowings between bond issues. Since 1963 all FLB bond issues have been noncallable. These securities range in maturity from a few years to 15 years. Most have an original maturity of longer than 1 year. Securities with a maturity of less than 5 years are issued in bearer and book-entry form. Those with a maturity of more than 5 years are also issued in registered form. Interest on FLB bonds is payable semiannually. The smallest denominations available are $1,000, $5,000, and $10,000.

S&Ls are placed in an uncomfortable position whenever interest rates rise because the nature of their business is to borrow short and lend long. Federal Land Banks are in a somewhat similar situation since maturities on the loans they extend tend to be longer than the original maturities of the bonds they issue. To avoid the danger inherent in this position, Federal Land Banks now write only *variable-rate* mortgages. This approach enables them to keep loan income in line with borrowing costs whether interest rates rise or fall.

FLB bonds must be backed with collateral in the form of cash, Treasury securities, or notes secured by first mortgages on farm properties. Federal Land Banks are examined at least annually by the Farm Credit Administration. Their securities are not guaranteed either directly or indirectly by the U.S. government. However, their semiofficial status makes it extremely unlikely that the government would ever permit default on their securities.

Income from FLB bonds is subject to full federal taxation but is exempt from state and local taxation.

Federal Intermediate Credit Banks

The 12 *Federal Intermediate Credit Banks* (FICB) were organized under the Agricultural Credit Act of 1923. Their job is to help provide short-term financing for the seasonal production and marketing of crops and livestock and for other farm-related credit purposes. These banks do not lend directly to farmers. Instead they make loans to and discount agricultural and livestock paper for various financial institutions that lend to farmers.[9] These institutions include commercial banks, production credit associations organized under the Farm Credit Act of 1933, agricultural credit corporations, and incorporated livestock loan companies. Originally, Federal Intermediate Credit Banks were government owned, but like the other farm credit banks discussed above, today their ownership is wholly private.

While FICBs are authorized to borrow from commercial banks and to rediscount agricultural paper with the Fed, the principal source of their funds is monthly sales of consolidated collateral trust debentures. These debentures are issued in bearer and book-entry form and come in denominations of $5,000 to $500,000. The Federal Intermediate Credit Banks are authorized to issue securities with a maturity of up to 5 years, but many of their obligations are issued with 9-month maturities with interest payable at maturity. Farmers may order and purchase FICB securities directly from the production credit associations of which they are members. Otherwise FICB securities are sold through dealers, as in the case of other agency securities.

FICB debentures are backed by collateral in the form of Treasury securities, other farm credit agency securities, cash, and the notes, discounted obligations, and loans that these banks acquire through their lending activities. Federal Intermediate Credit Banks are regularly examined by the Farm Credit Administration. Their securities are not guaranteed by the government, but as in the case of the institutions discussed above, their semiofficial status offers considerable assurance to the investor that the government would not permit default on FICB debentures.

Interest income on FICB debentures is subject to full federal taxation but exempt from state and local taxation.

FEDERAL AGENCY SECURITIES

Federal agency securities have not been around in significant volume for very long—only two decades—but during their brief existence, the outstanding volume of these securities has grown rapidly to an impressive total, as Figure 7–5 shows. In January 1978, marketable Treasury

---

[9] *Discounting agricultural paper* means buying up farmers' loan notes at a discount.

Figure 7–5
Outstanding volume of selected federal agency securities*

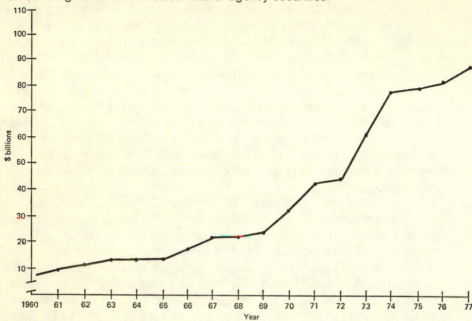

* Issuers covered: the Federal Home Loan Banks, the Federal Home Loan Mortgage Corporation, the Government National Mortgage Association, the Federal National Mortgage Association, the Federal Land Banks, the Federal Intermediate Credit Banks, and the Banks for Cooperatives. (Excludes pass-through securities: these instruments are not debts of the agencies through which they are marketed.)
Source: *Federal Reserve Bulletin*.

issues equaled $467 billion, while agency securities (excluding pass-throughs) totaled $97 billion.

Attraction to investors

Federal agency securities are attractive to a wide range of investors for a number of reasons. First, most agency issues are backed either *de jure* or *de facto* by the federal government, so the credit risk attached to them is zero or negligible. Second, many agency issues offer the tax advantage that interest income on them, like interest income on governments, is exempt from state and local taxation.

A third advantage of many agency issues is liquidity. Agency issues are smaller in size than Treasury issues so they do not have the same liquidity Treasury issues do, but relative to other money market instruments they are highly liquid.

Normally agencies trade at some spread to Treasuries of the same maturity. This spread varies considerably depending on supply conditions and the tightness of money. Over the last 4 years, agencies with a 2-year maturity have offered investors a yield advantage over governments that ranged from 3 to 87 basis points. For agencies with a 10-year maturity, the highs and lows of the yield advantage over governments were 134 and 7 basis points, respectively. The spread at which agencies trade in relation to governments appears to reflect differences in the liquidity of the two sorts of instruments, since capital-rich institutions like the Federal Home Loan banks have to pay to borrow at the same rates as more poorly capitalized federal agencies.

APPENDIX: SERIES E AND H SAVINGS BONDS

At the beginning of 1978, consumers' holdings of government savings bonds totaled $77.4 billion and represented over 66 percent of consumers' holdings of government securities. In recent years the growth of savings bonds outstanding has been sluggish because these instruments are not an attractive alternative to a time deposit at a savings institution, their closest competitor for the consumer's savings dollars.

Currently the federal government issues two sorts of savings bonds: Series E and Series H bonds. The main difference between the two is that E bonds are discount securities whereas H bonds pay interest semiannually. Both types of bonds currently yield 6 percent if held to maturity. Because of the secular upward trend in interest rates, the yield on government savings bonds has been raised by Congress several times in recent years, the latest revision being in December 1973. At that time the new higher rate was applied both to newly issued bonds and to outstanding bonds.

Series E bonds

Series E bonds may be purchased by all investors except commercial banks. They are registered in the name of the buyer and are nonnegotiable. They may, however, be cashed in at any time, provided that at least 2 months have passed since issue. They may also be exchanged for Series H bonds, and under certain conditions they may be transferred from one individual to another. E bonds have a maturity of 5 years but, if they are not cashed in, they will continue to yield the holder 6 percent for up to 10 more years. In such cases interest accruing on the mature but unredeemed bond is credited to its redemption value. Second and third 10-year extensions of maturity are also available. E bonds are noncallable and are available in denominations ranging from $25 to $1,000. The denomination is the face value paid at maturity. E bonds pay no interest; they yield a return to the investor by being sold at a 25 percent discount from face value and appreciating to full face value over a 5-year period.

Table 7A–1
Redemption value and yield on a $1,000 government E bond issued at $750 and
maturing in 5 years

Time elapsed after issue (years)	Redemption value (dollars)	Yield earned on purchase price from date of purchase to date of redemption (percent)	Yield to maturity on redemption value if bond is held to maturity (percent)
Less than ½	750.00	0.00	6.00
½ to 1	764.00	3.73	6.25
1 to 1½	784.00	4.54	6.37
1½ to 2	804.00	4.69	6.57
2 to 2½	824.00	4.76	6.83
2½ to 3	845.60	4.86	7.15
3 to 3½	868.40	4.95	7.59
3½ to 4	892.40	5.03	8.29
4 to 4½	918.80	5.14	9.48
4½ to 5	946.80	5.25	12.93
5	1,008.00	6.00	—

Table 7A–1 shows how this works for a $1,000 E bond. The bond is
initially purchased for $750. Thereafter its redemption value is raised
semiannually until after 5 years it has reached $1,008, which represents
a 6 percent return compounded semiannually on the $750 initially in-
vested.

The rate at which the redemption value of an E bond appreciates rises
as the bond approaches maturity. This is to discourage early redemptions by imposing a yield penalty on them. The third column in Table
7A–1 records the effects of this penalty on yield realized. The fourth
column shows the yield to maturity an individual would at any point in the
life of an E bond realize on its *current redemption value* if he held the
bond to maturity.

During a single year an individual may buy E bonds with a face value of
no more than $10,000. If he buys a large-denomination E bond and later
wants to free some of his capital, he can ask for a partial redemption of
his bond. In that case, a new lower-denomination bond will be issued to
him. Partial redemptions and reissues of E bonds are permitted in multiples of $25. E bonds may not be used as collateral for a loan.

Series H bonds

Series H bonds may be purchased by all investors except commercial banks. They are registered in the name of the purchaser. H bonds
have a 10-year maturity and yield 6 percent if held to maturity. H bonds
are not negotiable, but they can be cashed in for full face value at any

time. H bonds are noncallable, and 10-year extensions of maturity are permitted.

H bonds are available in denominations of $500 to $10,000. Like E bonds, there is an annual $10,000 limit on purchases by a single individual.

The major difference between H and E bonds is that H bonds provide regular income in the form of semiannual interest checks. The rate of interest paid under the latest rate schedule is 5.6 percent a year for the first 5 years and 6.5 percent for the remaining 5 years, which works out to be an average yield over 10 years of 6 percent. Because the rate paid on an H bond is less than 6 percent for the first 5 years it is held and more than 6 percent for the second 5 years, the actual yield realized over the period rises gradually and reaches 6 percent only at maturity.

Partial redemptions and reissues are permitted on H bonds as on E bonds, but only in multiples of $500.

Chapter 8

The most watched player:
The Fed

THE FEDERAL RESERVE SYSTEM, the nation's central bank, was established by act of Congress in 1913. The Federal Reserve Act divided the country into 12 districts and provided for the creation within each of a *district Federal Reserve bank.* Responsibility for coordinating the activities of the district banks lies with the Federal Reserve's *Board of Governors* in Washington, D.C. The board has seven members appointed by the President and confirmed by the Senate.

The main tools available to the Fed for implementing policy are: open-market operations, reserve requirements, and the discount rate. On paper authority for policy making at the Fed is widely diffused throughout the system. In practice, however, this authority has gradually been centered in the *Federal Reserve Open Market Committee* (FOMC), which was established to oversee the Fed's open-market operations. Members of the FOMC include all seven governors of the system, the president of the New York Fed, and the presidents of four of the other 11 district banks; the latter serve on a rotating basis. Every member of the FOMC has one vote, but it has become tradition that the chairman of the Board of Governors plays a decisive role in formulating policy and acts as chief spokesman for the system, which is why that position is viewed as one of power and importance.

179

In establishing policy, the Fed enjoys considerable independence on paper from both Congress and the executive branch. Members of the Board of Governors are appointed to 14-year terms so that a given President has limited control over who serves during his term of office. The chairman of the board, who is designated as such by the President, serves in that capacity for only 4 years but his term is not coincident with that of the President, so an incoming President may have to wait until well into his first term to appoint a new chairman.

Congress, like the President, has no lever by which it can directly influence Fed policy or the way it is implemented. In creating the Fed, Congress endowed this institution with wide powers and granted it considerable leeway to exercise discretion and judgment. Having said that, one must hasten to add that the autonomy enjoyed by the Fed is in reality much less than it appears. Presidents who are concerned that the Fed is forcing interest rates too high (Presidents *never* seem to be concerned over interest being too low) attack the Fed subtly and not so subtly from the White House. Also the Fed is well aware that Congress, should it become too distressed over high interest rates, might take away the autonomy granted by it to the Fed.

The perception that its independence is limited can and has influenced Fed policy. In particular during times when the Fed was tightening and it appeared that interest rates might reach unacceptable levels, the Fed has more than once attempted to force a contraction in bank lending while simultaneously preventing interest rates from rising to market-clearing levels. "It is not always politically feasible," commented one banker, "for the Fed, when it wants to curtail bank lending, to allow interest rates to go where they must to do so. The Fed would never admit or write this down, but they know they are a creature of Congress, and Congress would never let the prime go to 15 percent—one way or another it would remove in one fell swoop the so-called independence of the Fed. That is why the Fed forced the banks to institute a two-tier prime in 1971. We could raise the prime to big corporations but not on small loans. It was a terribly populist policy, but the Fed in instituting it was recognizing political reality." Politicalization of the prime rate has occurred not only in the United States but in Britain and other countries as well.

SOME HISTORY

The primary policy tool available to the Fed is open-market operations, the ability to create bank reserves in any desired quantity by monetizing some portion of the national debt.[1] The Fed could in theory

---

[1] See Chapter 2 for an explanation of debt monetization.

monetize anything—scrap metal to soybeans—but it has stuck largely to Treasury IOUs because there has never been any shortage of them in the market, and in addition they are highly liquid so the Fed can sell them with as much ease as it buys them. In formulating policy, the first question the Fed faces is what macroeconomic *targets* to pursue. There are various possibilities—full employment, price stability, or a stable exchange value for the dollar. The achievement of *all* of these targets is desirable. However, since the Fed has only *one* powerful string to its bow—the ability to control bank reserves and thereby money creation by the private banking system—it is often forced to make hard choices between targets, to choose for example to pursue policies that would promote price stability but might increase unemployment.

Once the Fed has chosen its policy targets, it faces a second difficult question: What policies should it use to achieve these targets? If it wants to pursue a tight money policy to curb inflation, does that mean it should force up interest rates, strictly control the growth of the money supply (if so, which money supply), or what?

Not surprisingly the Fed's answers to the questions of what targets it should pursue and of how it should do so have changed considerably over time. One reason is that external conditions—the state of the domestic and world economy—have been in constant flux. A second reason is that central banking is an art form that is not fully understood, and the Fed's behavior at any time is therefore partly a function of how far it has progressed along its learning curve.

Before we look at how the Fed operates today, a few words on history are appropriate. During World War II inflation was one extra disruption that the nation could well do without. Thus during the war the appropriate stance for monetary and financial policy would have been for the federal government to raise taxes to cover as much of the war expenditures as possible and for the Fed to pursue simultaneously a policy of restraint to discourage private spending. This, however, was not done. Taxes were held down so as to not discourage incentives, and rationing and price controls were used to contain private spending and control the price level. Meanwhile the Fed assumed responsibility for pegging interest rates at the low levels that prevailed when the country entered the war. The rationale was to encourage individuals and institutions to buy bonds by eliminating the price risk that would normally attach to holding such securities. The policy had the additional advantage of minimizing the cost to the Treasury of financing the burgeoning national debt.

In guaranteeing to buy whatever quantity of government securities was necessary to peg both long-term and short-term interest rates at low levels, the Fed lost all control over the money supply; and its policy permitted a big buildup of private liquidity. In retrospect this buildup was not totally undesirable because the liquid assets acquired by citizens during the war permitted them to finance at the war's end the purchase of cars and other goods that had been unavailable during the war. The resulting spending spree prevented a much-feared big postwar slump.

Inflation, however, did arrive on the scene. By 1948 the Fed was feeling uncomfortable about its obligation to peg bond prices, since that left it with no tool to fight inflation. The recession of 1949 provided some relief, but inflation again became a problem during 1950 when the Korean War broke out. Again, the Fed wanted to tighten but the Treasury resisted, arguing that higher interest rates would disrupt Treasury refundings, increase the cost of financing the national debt, and inflict capital losses on those patriotic individuals and institutions that had bought bonds during the war.

Finally the Fed threw the gauntlet down to the Treasury in September 1950 by raising the discount rate. The Treasury retaliated by announcing a 1-year financing based on the old discount rate of 1.25 percent. Rather than allowing the financing to fail or rescinding the rate increase, the Fed bought the Treasury's new issue, stuck to its higher discount rate, and then resold the issue to the market at a slightly higher rate. This started a 6-month battle with the Treasury, ending in the famous March 1951 *accord* between the Fed and the Treasury, which read:

The Treasury and the Federal Reserve System have reached full accord with respect to debt management and monetary policies to be pursued in furthering their common purpose to assure the successful financing of the Government's requirements and, at the same time, to minimize monetization of the public debt.

This statement, despite the fact that it appears to be a prime example of "governmentese" that says nothing, was in fact important. The reason is that the key phrase, "to minimize monetization of the public debt," gave the Fed the right to henceforth pursue an independent monetary policy. The following year the Fed, to protect its flank, adopted a second policy of *bills only;* in the future the Fed would confine its purchases of governments largely to bills. In adopting this policy, the Fed was saying to the market and the Treasury that henceforth the market would set the yield curve and in particular the yields on long-term Treasuries.

As a price for its accord with the Treasury, the Fed agreed to stabilize credit market conditions during Treasury financings. This policy, known as *even keeling* was pursued until recently. The reason such stabilization was required was that the Treasury used to fix both the coupon and the price at the time it announced a new issue on Wednesday. Thus if anything important had happened after the announcement of an issue but before it was sold the following week, that would have killed the auction; that is, the Treasury would have been unable to sell its securities—something that neither the Treasury nor the Fed could risk.

While even keeling prevailed, the Fed tried to plan major moves so that the market would have time to react to them before a Treasury financing. It also insisted, however, that Treasury financings had to meet the test of the market; the Treasury could not rely on direct support from the Fed.

In recent years even keeling has gradually died an untolled death. One reason is that the Treasury adopted the policy of selling almost all of its coupon issues through yield auctions. Also, the Treasury's new policy of issuing notes of different maturities on a regular cycle has created a situation in which the Treasury is in the market so often with new coupon issues that, if the Fed were to even keel, it would have almost no "windows" during which it could decisively shift policy.

Before the accord the Fed was forced to focus almost solely on interest rates. After the accord, the Fed's focus gradually shifted to *free reserves*—excess reserves minus borrowed reserves. The Fed reasoned that the stance of monetary policy would be sufficiently easy during a recession if free reserves were increased, thereby promoting additional bank lending and falling interest rates; and that during periods of excessive demand for output the stance of monetary policy would be appropriately tight if free reserves were decreased, thereby promoting a reduction in bank lending and a rise in interest rates.

This sounds reasonable, but it contained a fatal flaw. During a recession, interest rates are likely to fall by themselves as the demand for bank credit diminishes, so increases in free reserves may be consistent with a falling money supply and a tight monetary policy. In an overheated economy, in contrast, limiting free reserves to some small sum does not necessarily mean tight money. So long as the Fed continues to supply banks with reserves and the banks utilize them, a policy of holding free reserves to a low figure is consistent with a rapid expansion of the money supply.

After a decade of obsession with free reserves, in the early 1960s the Fed shifted the focus of its policy to interest rates. During this time the economy was recovering sluggishly from a severe recession, and it therefore seemed appropriate to stimulate investment spending, which meant in turn that long-term interest rates should be lowered. However, the United States was also experiencing a disturbing deficit in its balance of payments and the defense of the dollar therefore called for high short-term interest rates. In response to both needs, the Fed adopted *operation twist;* that is, it started buying long-term bonds instead of bills in an attempt to force up short-term interest rates while simultaneously lowering long-term interest rates.

Whether operation twist was successful in altering the slope of the yield curve, in stimulating investment, or in decreasing the balance of payments deficit has been much debated. In any case the policy died in

1965, a victim of the Vietnam War, which encouraged inflationary pressures in the economy and caused the Fed to turn the focus of its policy to curbing inflation. In 1966 the Fed introduced the first of several credit crunches that drove interest rates to historic highs.

As fighting inflation came to be a key target of Fed policy, another change was also occurring—a gradual shift in the focus of the Fed's attention away from interest rates and toward the growth of the money supply. One reason is that the level of interest rates does not necessarily indicate how tight or easy monetary policy is because interest rates respond not only to what the Fed is doing but also to general economic conditions. During a recession interest rates can fall, as occurred in early 1960, even though bank reserves and the money supply are shrinking. Similarly during an expansionary period, rising interest rates are compatible with rapidly increasing bank reserves, bank credit, and the money supply. A second reason for the increased attention given to monetary aggregates by the Fed was the increasing popularity of monetarism—a view that the rate of growth of the money supply plays a dominant role in determining various macroeconomic variables, in particular the rate of inflation.

In the decade following 1966, during which the Fed continued to be concerned much of the time with controlling inflation, it gradually put more and more stress on measuring monetary tightness and ease in relation to the rate of growth of the money supply and in doing so abandoned its old concern with free reserves. This switch in focus was encouraged by Congress, which in a 1975 joint resolution required that the Fed henceforth set and announce targets for monetary growth.

While the Fed now sets such targets at each meeting of the FOMC and attempts to keep the growth of the monetary aggregates at the targeted levels, the Fed has never fully bought the monetarist doctrine. It is not certain that money matters as much as Milton Friedman, the leading monetarist, argues; and in addition the Fed perceives that as a practical matter it cannot control the growth of the monetary aggregates, M1 to M5, with the precision envisioned in textbooks.[2]

MONETARY POLICY TODAY

The Fed's ultimate policy goals today are what they have always been: price stability, high employment, and a stable dollar. However, as

[2] Because it has difficulty controlling precisely—even gauging precisely—the size of the money supply by any measure, the Fed in 1972 adopted as an operating policy target bank *reserves available to support private deposits (RPDs)*. The idea was that, by controlling this aggregate, the Fed could control closely, albeit indirectly, the money supply available to the private nonbanking sector, that is, the total money supply minus Treasury balances at commercial banks and interbank deposits, both of which are excluded from Fed money supply figures. After several years of experimentation, the Fed gave up on RPDs as a target because RPDs proved as difficult to control and measure as the money supply itself.

economic conditions shift, so too does the focus of Fed policy. That was demonstrated by the jolt the Fed gave to the capital markets in early 1978 when it tightened, unexpectedly in the face of a sluggish economy, to defend the exchange value of the dollar.

Whatever its ultimate macroeconomic goals may be, the Fed currently states its immediate policy objectives in terms of (1) desired rates of growth over a 2-month period for the monetary aggregates M1 and M2 and (2) a target rate for Fed funds. If the monetary aggregates begin to grow too rapidly, the Fed raises its target rate for Fed funds; if they grow too slowly, it lowers that rate. Meanwhile, because the Fed has not become completely monetarist in its thinking and because of outside pressures from Congress and the President, it also seeks to maintain interest rates at levels that are consistent with achieving full employment. This sounds as if the Fed must at times be trying to do the impossible, which is true. When unemployment is high and the money supply starts growing at an out-of-bounds rate, there is no way the Fed can simultaneously control that rate of growth and maintain low interest rates. Thus the Fed on occasion is strongly criticized by Congress and the President, who tend to demand that it do both.

The FOMC directive

Approximately once a month the FOMC meets to review economic conditions, its macro goals, and the guidelines it has set with respect to open-market operations for achieving those goals. At the end of the meeting, it issues a directive to the manager of the system's open-market account in New York. The December 19, 1977, directive read as follows:

The information reviewed at this meeting suggests that real output of goods and services is growing in the current quarter at about the pace in the third quarter. The dollar value of total retail sales, which had increased sharply in October, rose considerably further in November. Industrial production continued to expand, and employment increased substantially. However, the unemployment rate, at 6.9 percent, remained in the narrow range prevailing since April. The wholesale price index for all commodities rose sharply in November for the second successive month, reflecting another large increase in average prices of farm products and foods. However, the rise in average prices of industrial commodities was less rapid than in the preceding 2 months. The index of average hourly earnings has advanced at a somewhat faster pace so far this year than it had on the average during 1976.

The dollar has been under considerable pressure in foreign exchange markets in recent weeks, and its trade-weighted value against major foreign currencies has declined more than 3 percent further since mid-November. In October the U.S. foreign trade deficit widened sharply, primarily as a result of the dock strike at many U.S. ports.

M-1—which had expanded substantially in October—declined slightly in November, and M-2 increased relatively little. The total of savings deposits and small-denomination time deposits at commercial banks declined somewhat, but growth in large-denomination time deposits accelerated sharply further as credit demands remained strong. Inflows to nonbank thrift institutions slowed further in November. Market interest rates have changed relatively little since mid-November.

In light of the foregoing developments, it is the policy of the Federal Open Market Committee to foster bank reserve and other financial conditions that will encourage continued economic expansion and help resist inflationary pressures, while contributing to a sustainable pattern of international transactions.

At its meeting on October 18, 1977, the Committee agreed that growth of M-1, M-2, and M-3 within ranges of 4 to 6½ percent, 6½ to 9 percent, and 8 to 10½ percent, respectively, from the third quarter of 1977 to the third quarter of 1978 appears to be consistent with these objectives. These ranges are subject to reconsideration at any time as conditions warrant.

At this time, the Committee seeks to maintain about the prevailing money market conditions during the period immediately ahead, provided that monetary aggregates appear to be growing at approximately the rates currently expected, which are believed to be on a path reasonably consistent with the longer-run ranges for monetary aggregates cited in the preceding paragraph. Specifically, the Committee seeks to maintain the weekly-average Federal funds rate at about the current level, so long as M-1 and M-2 appear to be growing over the December–January period at annual rates within ranges of 2½ to 8½ percent and 6 to 10 percent, respectively.

If, giving approximately equal weight to M-1 and M-2, it appears that growth rates over the 2-month period are approaching or moving beyond the limits of the indicated ranges, the operational objective for the weekly-average Federal funds rate shall be modified in an orderly fashion within a range of 6¼ to 6¾ percent. In the conduct of day-to-day operations, account shall be taken of emerging financial market conditions, including the unsettled conditions in foreign exchange markets.

If it appears during the period before the next meeting that the operating constraints specified above are proving to be significantly inconsistent, the Manager is promptly to notify the Chairman who will then decide whether the situation calls for supplementary instructions from the Committee.[3]

There are several things to note about this directive. First, target rates of growth are stated not for one monetary aggregate but for several; also they are stated in terms of *bands*. One reason is that, as economic conditions change, the public responds by altering the form in which it chooses to maintain its liquidity. As interest rates rise, people shift funds out of demand deposits into time deposits, which slows the growth of M1 but does not affect that of M2; when interest rates fall, people do the reverse, and the growth of M1 speeds up relative to that of M2. A second reason for stating monetary rates of growth in terms of bands is that seasonal factors, shifts in money balances between the Treasury and the public, and changes in the volume of trading in financial markets can

---

[3] *Federal Reserve Bulletin,* February 1978.

and do have dramatic short-term effects on the growth of the monetary aggregates. There is, moreover,

. . . no really good way [for the Fed] to detect when short-run deviations in monetary growth from longer run targets are truly temporary and when they reflect more fundamental developments. Judgment, and the concomitant risk of error, is unavoidable in these situations. To avoid overreacting to short-term developments, the Federal Reserve has in practice tended to "tolerate" short-run swings in monetary growth rates over fairly wide ranges. The limits to such "toleration" have usually been expressed as upper and lower limits on two-month average growth rates—known, obviously enough, as "tolerance ranges." These ranges are set at levels that reflect the Open Market Committee's estimates of the various short-run influences that may be impinging on the monetary aggregates at any given time. As a result, the short-term tolerance ranges for any particular two-month period may differ significantly from the underlying one-year target ranges. . . . Moreover, reflecting the highly unpredictable nature of short-term movements, the percentage point spreads embodied in the two-month tolerance ranges have normally been set wider than the spreads contained in the one-year target ranges.[4]

A second point to note about the FOMC's current directives to the manager of the open-market account is that they specify a narrow band within which Fed funds are to trade. As an official on the open-market desk in New York noted: "As the Fed paid more attention to the monetary aggregates, we have become increasingly concerned about controlling the funds rate. When we were working on a free-reserves target, we were much more relaxed about the funds rate. We had an idea of where it should be but if it moved 1/8, OK. As we moved to monetary aggregates, which had been thought to mean we would abandon pegging the Fed funds rate, the FOMC directed us to control it much more closely. Now when the funds rate moves 1/8 from where we want it, we are more likely to react than we would have been 10 years ago." Note this is not a necessary development but it is the sort of instructions the desk gets from the committee.

Day-to-day operations of the open-market desk

As noted, the FOMC gives the account manager in New York two sorts of directions, a set of targets for monetary growth and a target range for Fed funds.[5] The account manager operating within these guidelines is supposed to keep the Fed funds rate tightly controlled unless growth of

[4] Richard G. Davis, "Monetary Objectives and Monetary Policy," *Federal Reserve Bank of New York Quarterly Review* 2 (1977): 35–36.

[5] People at the Fed make a distinction between quarterly *targets* and *tolerance ranges* that are permissible within any month; the latter are wider because the shorter the period, the more difficult it is to tightly control the rate of monetary growth.

the monetary aggregates gets out of hand. In that case he is supposed to nudge the Fed funds rate up if monetary growth is too great and down if monetary growth is too slow.

Thus in the *very* short run it is fair to describe the Fed's open-market operations as being designed to *peg the Fed funds rate*. How this is done was described by a person on the desk as follows: "We have in mind a degree of reserve availability that we think is consistent with the desired Fed funds rate. If, for example, we want funds to trade in the range of 4⅝–¾, that permits us to build in our minds from a body of past experience a picture of what degree of reserve availability—essentially excess reserves less borrowing at the discount window—would be consistent with that rate. We might, for example, think that to get the funds rate we want—given that the discount rate is at 5¼—free reserves ought to be 150 million." Note free reserves have crept back into the picture, but the focus of policy is on pegging the level of the Fed funds rate *not* the level of free reserves.

The above description of how open-market operations are carried out makes them sound simpler than they are in practice. In deciding whether to inject or drain bank reserves, the Fed starts with one given, the average daily reserves the banks must maintain during the current reserve week; this is based on the deposits held by the banks during a reserve week 2 weeks earlier.[6] What daily reserves will actually be available to the banks over the reserve week or whatever remains of it is a number that the desk must estimate.

Treasury balances

One reason that the Fed has to estimate the amount of reserves is the Treasury balance problem. Because of tax collections and securities sales, the Treasury holds huge and highly variable deposit balances. It used to keep these balances primarily in commercial banks in what are called *Treasury tax and loan accounts*. When it did so, the Treasury as it needed to make disbursements, would transfer funds from its *TT&L* accounts into its account at the Fed and write checks against that.

Then in 1974 the Treasury adopted a new policy—it began to hold the bulk of its deposit balances at the Fed. Its primary reason for doing so was to increase Treasury revenue. By depositing huge sums in its account at the Fed (which drained bank reserves, see Table 8–1), the Treasury forced the Fed to expand its portfolio via additional open-market purchases, and the result was that the Fed earned more profit. All Fed profits in excess of a small amount are paid out to the Treasury. So by holding its balances at the Fed, the Treasury was able in effect to turn them into interest-bearing deposits.

After the Treasury began holding the bulk of its funds at the Fed,

---

[6] Just how the banks settle with the Fed is discussed in Chapter 11.

Table 8–1
When the Treasury transfers funds from an account at a commercial bank to its account at the Fed, this decreases bank reserves

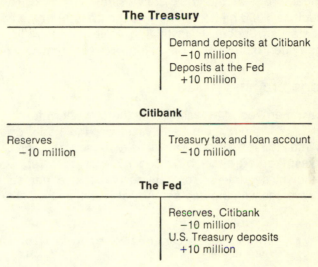

The Treasury

	Demand deposits at Citibank −10 million Deposits at the Fed +10 million

Citibank

Reserves −10 million	Treasury tax and loan account −10 million

The Fed

	Reserves, Citibank −10 million U.S. Treasury deposits +10 million

movements of funds into and out of its account there became both huge and at times difficult to predict. The sheer size of the shifts in Treasury balances created operational problems for the Fed, which found it difficult to offset smoothly these flows through normal open-market operations. To alleviate this problem, Congress—prodded by the Fed—acted to permit banks and other financial institutions to begin sometime in 1978 paying the Treasury interest on demand balances held with them. For its part the Treasury was to pay these institutions for banking services which were previously provided free to it in exchange for noninterest-bearing deposits.

Float

A second remaining problem for the Fed in estimating the size of the reserve balances available to the banks is the variations in float. Whenever a check is cleared through the Fed, the Fed first credits the reserve account of the bank that receives the check in deposit by the amount of the check and then debits the reserve account of the bank against which the check is drawn by a like amount. Sometimes the reserve credit is made before the reserve debit, which results in a temporary and artificial increase in bank reserves. This increase is referred to as the *float.* Since the size of the float can be affected by such factors as the weather (when planes can't fly, movement of checks and reserve debiting are slowed), float has been and remains a highly difficult variable to estimate.

Because of the unpredictable changes in the size of both Treasury balances and float, the Fed's daily estimates of bank reserves could be as much as $800 million off prior to the change in the handling of Treasury balances. Successful institution of that change will presumably make things better, but the Fed will still have to estimate.

Adding and draining

Having arrived at an estimate of the amount of funds that need to be injected or drained from bank reserves, the Fed's open-market desk goes into the market each day to make those additions or drains. To add reserves, the Fed either buys securities *or* does repos with dealers in government securities. To drain reserves, it either sells securities *or* does reverses with the dealers. As Table 8–2 shows, when the Fed does

Table 8–2
The Fed adds to bank reserves by doing a repo with a
bank dealer

The Fed

Bills bought under repurchase agreement +10 million	Reserves, Continental Bank +10 million

Continental Bank of Chicago

Reserves +10 million	Securities sold under agreement to repurchase +10 million

a repo with a bank dealer, this adds to bank reserves just as an outright purchase of bills would; a repo done with a nonbank dealer would have the same effect on bank reserves. Reverses done by the Fed are repos in reverse gear and they drain reserves.

The securities the Fed buys vary from day to day, and depend in part on the supply available in the market. Bills can usually be easily bought in big amounts, and the Fed holds a large proportion of its portfolio in bills (Table 8–3). Much of the rest is in notes, which, due to the changes in Treasury debt management noted in Chapter 7, represent a steadily growing portion of the Treasury's outstanding debt. Occasionally the Fed

Table 8–3
The Federal Reserve's portfolio, beginning of 1978
($ millions)

Loans	
Member bank borrowings	265
Acceptances	
Bought outright	0
Held under repurchase agreements	954
Federal agency obligations	
Bought outright	8,004
Held under repurchase agreements	457
U.S. government securities	
Bought outright	
Bills	41,561
Notes	50,509
Bonds	8,848
Total	100,918
Held under repurchase agreements	1,901
Total U.S. government securities	102,819
Total loans and securities	112,493

Source: *Federal Reserve Bulletin*.

will buy bonds because of supply conditions, but such amounts are small.

The Fed also buys federal agency securities, in part because it was directed to do so by Congress in 1971 to help support the market for these securities. The Fed imposes various guidelines on what agency issues it will buy. Currently it will buy only issues for which there is an active secondary market; guidelines in this respect are that an agency issue, in order to be eligible for purchase, must be at least $300 million in size if its maturity is less than 5 years and $250 million in size if its maturity is more than 5 years. Since the Fed created these guidelines, the agencies have been careful to ensure that their new issues comply. The Fed no longer buys securites issued by agencies that can obtain funding from the Federal Financing Bank. Thus the agencies whose securities it now buys are limited to the FHLB, the farm-credit agencies, and Fannie Mae. The Fed does not buy pass-throughs.

The Fed used to buy BAs in volume as part of its program to encourage the growth of the domestic BA market (see Chapter 18). However, now that the market has grown and matured, the Fed no longer purchases BAs for its own portfolio.

There are other considerations in the Fed's choice of what to buy. It seeks to maintain a reasonable mix in its portfolio. Also, it can buy bills for cash settlement and almost always does so; thus bill purchases have a quick impact on reserves. In buying agencies and coupons the Fed buys for regular settlement and sometimes for skip-day settlement, so such purchases are not as useful for meeting immediate needs for changes in reserves.[7]

When the Fed wants to reduce reserves by selling securities, it sells securities of short maturity. Said someone at the Fed: "I do not remember a time in the last 15 years that we have sold coupon issues longer than 2 years. The market would be shocked and bewildered if we did so; it is taken as a given fact that we do not, so—to do so—we would have to educate the market."

In carrying out open-market operations, the Fed constantly has two objectives in mind: (1) the need to offset short-term fluctuations in reserves due to changes in float and other variables, and (2) the need to gradually and secularly increase bank reserves so that the money supply and bank credit can expand in step with economic activity and national output. In making day-to-day short-term adjustments in reserves, the Fed relies primarily on repos and reverses, which it does against governments, agencies, and BAs (Table 8–4). Permanent injections of reserves are done through purchases of bills, notes, and other securities.

The line between Fed actions that are a reaction to short-term fluctuations in reserves and those designed to add permanent reserves is difficult to draw because the two operations often mesh. Also, because of uncertainty with respect to reserve availability, the Fed is often forced to switch gears. Here's a scenario of how things on the desk might go during reserve week: "Our research department does projections of available reserves and some are done in Washington at the board. We compare notes on these projections during our morning conference call with the board. Mostly we focus on our projections for the current week but, to give perspective to any action we might want to take, we give projections for the next five or six weeks. Then we build up a program for the day based on what we think the need is and on the information flowing in from the market.

"Say it is Thursday, we don't want funds to rise, and we figure we need $150 million of free reserves on average over the week.[8] Our projection shows a billion of net borrowed reserves. So we face a sizable job of adding. Say we also project $600 million of net borrowed reserves in the next week. So some of the need is temporary and some is permanent.

---

[7] A skip-day trade is settled two business days after the trade is made. A cash trade is settled on the same day it is made.

[8] As explained in Chapter 11, settlement by the banks is based on their average reserve balances over the settlement week. So the Fed's concern is with the average reserve balances available daily to the banks over the settlement week. Which banks get or lose reserves as a result of Fed open-market operations is of no concern to the Fed because banks with surpluses sell funds to banks with reserve deficits in the Fed funds market.

Say also that funds are trading up a bit. Then we have a consistent picture—everything gives us the same signal to add. Given the size of that need and its persistence, we might do a couple of things: buy some bills outright and do some repo over the weekend—say, buy $400 million of bills in the market and do a billion of repo over the weekend. A billion for four days would add about $550 million to the weekly average. Now we have got the expected reserve figure up to minus $200 million. Then Friday we would make a whole new projection. We might discover a considerable shortfall in reserves. We might discover that, due to unforeseen changes, reserves are $500 million short. Bills bought add to permanent reserves so—to not overdo for the following week—we might now do something with temporary impact, say another billion of repo for the weekend. If Fed funds are still trading in the range we want, that would be consistent with our doing more adding. Then maybe on Monday we might find that free reserves look as if they will be plus $200 million for the week due to more unforeseen changes, but funds are still trading where we want them. Then we might do nothing that day. And the next day we might find still greater reserves showing up, say, plus $300 million, but funds still at least as firm as we desired. Then we might still do nothing. Maybe, on the final day of the week, the excess would finally start to weaken the Fed funds rate; and, if that happened early enough, we might do some reverses. We are always working on the basis of our projection with respect of reserve needs and our perception of the market. The above week was simple. At other times things can be much more difficult."

Another Fed official added: "We think of a 3-week reserve need as permanent. In effect it turns out to be that way because a growing economy has a way of catching up with all the reserves that are in the system, and you see you need still more of them. If you get a temporary excess, you just do reverses."

As the quotes above suggest, the Fed is in part stumbling in the dark in carrying out open-market operations—operating on the basis of reserve availability estimates that can be far off. Because of this, it is extremely important for the desk to monitor the market, which it constantly does by calling firms that broker Fed funds, the dealers, and the money desks of major banks that are massive buyers and sellers of Fed funds.

While such calls are useful, information gleaned from bank money desks and the Fed funds rate as well have become less reliable barometers of reserve availability than they were 5 or 6 years ago. The reason is that the Fed now controls the Fed funds rate so tightly that it has reduced the ability of the market to reflect reserve availability. *Funds trade where the market thinks the Fed wants them to trade.* And the

Table 8-4
Federal Reserve open-market transactions ($ millions)

Type of transaction	1975	1976	1977	1977						
				June	July	Aug.	Sept.	Oct.	Nov.	Dec.
U.S. GOVT. SECURITIES										
Outright transactions (excl. matched sale-purchase transactions)										
Treasury bills:										
1 Gross purchases	11,562	14,343	13,738	2,696	118	812	2,005	....	436	3,109
2 Gross sales	5,599	8,462	7,241	1,154	753	176	303	1,877	300	311
3 Redemptions	26,431	25,017	2,136	600	500	....	317	....	....	....
Others within 1 year:[1]										
4 Gross purchases	3,886	472	3,017	89	....	....	2,616	....	....	99
5 Gross sales	....	....	....	....	....	....	....	....	....	....
6 Exchange, or maturity shift	-4	792	4,499	478	238	2,321	320	-45	1,352	623
7 Redemptions	3,549	....	2,500	....	....	....	....	2,500	....	....
1 to 5 years:										
8 Gross purchases	23,284	23,202	2,833	200	....	....	681	....	....	628
9 Gross sales	....	177	....	....	....	....	....	....	....	....
10 Exchange, or maturity shift	3,854	-2,588	-6,649	-478	-238	-1,664	-320	45	-1,267	-623
5 to 10 years:										
11 Gross purchases	1,510	1,048	758	68	....	....	96	....	....	166
12 Gross sales	....	....	....	....	....	....	....	....	....	....
13 Exchange, or maturity shift	-4,697	1,572	584	....	....	-782	....	....	-325	....
Over 10 years:										
14 Gross purchases	1,070	642	553	114	....	....	128	....	....	108
15 Gross sales	....	....	....	....	....	....	....	....	....	....
16 Exchange, or maturity shift	848	225	1,565	....	....	125	....	....	240	....

All maturities:[1]										
17 Gross purchases	[2] 21,313	219,707	20,898	3,167	118	812	5,526	....	....	4,110
18 Gross sales	5,599	8,639	7,241	1,154	753	176	303	1,877	436	311
19 Redemptions	[2] 9,980	[2] 5,017	4,636	600	500	....	317	2,500	300	....
Matched sale-purchase transactions										
20 Gross sales	151,205	196,078	425,214	36,258	27,947	45,831	39,552	48,204	56,899	32,320
21 Gross purchases	152,132	196,579	423,841	36,449	27,301	46,170	39,694	44,772	57,477	35,001
Repurchase agreements										
22 Gross purchases	140,311	232,891	178,683	14,748	13,973	4,397	16,700	9,578	6,472	18,071
23 Gross sales	139,538	230,355	180,535	11,506	15,719	5,648	15,469	11,889	4,433	18,208
24 Net change in U.S. Govt. securities	7,434	9,087	5,798	4,845	-3,528	-276	6,279	-10,118	1,880	6,342
FEDERAL AGENCY OBLIGATIONS										
Outright transactions:										
25 Gross purchases	1,616	891	1,433	380	....	....	....	....	....	707
26 Gross sales	....	....	....	....	....	....	....	....	....	....
27 Redemptions	246	169	223	33	....	-69	25	....	*	32
Repurchase agreements:										
28 Gross purchases	15,179	10,520	13,811	1,656	1,672	265	1,136	741	615	2,712
29 Gross sales	15,566	10,360	13,638	1,056	1,938	459	978	1,051	484	2,392
BANKERS ACCEPTANCES										
30 Outright transactions, net	163	-545	-196	-15	-24	-15	*	-4	....	....
31 Repurchase agreements, net	-35	410	159	528	-204	-247	351	-478	248	705
32 Net change in total System Account	8,539	9,833	7,143	6,305	-4,020	-801	6,764	-10,910	2,260	8,042

1 Both gross purchases and redemptions include special certificates created when the Treasury borrows directly from the Federal Reserve, as follows (millions of dollars): 1975, 3,549; 1976, none; Sept. 1977, 2,500.

2 In 1975, the System obtained $421 million of 2-year Treasury notes in exchange for maturing bills. In 1976 there was a similar transaction amounting to $189 million. Acquisition of these notes is treated as a purchase; the run-off of bills, as a redemption.

NOTE.—Sales, redemptions, and negative figures reduce holdings of the System Open Market Account; all other figures increase such holdings. Details may not add to totals because of rounding.

Source: *Federal Reserve Bulletin*.

moment they get out or threaten to get out of that range, phone buttons start blinking on the desk.

There is, as might be expected, a tendency for banks and government securities dealers to try to influence what the Fed does on a daily basis by calling the desk to paint dire pictures. The Fed's reaction tends to be: If you need to buy funds and you want us to do repo, you have to bid the funds rate up and you have to do it in size. That can be expensive, and it is one way the Fed tries to keep everyone honest.

Another problem the Fed faces is that the distribution of reserves within a week can be highly skewed, with a lot of reserves being available early or late in the week. Because most banks are currently unwilling to run reserve deficits or surpluses in size on a day-to-day basis, this creates artificial tightness or ease which the Fed feels compelled to offset and can do only with difficulty. Said one person at the Fed: "A major problem that is not widely recognized is the distribution of reserves within the week. If early in the week there is a shortage of reserves, even if we pump in reserves, the market may still be tighter than we like. Any by pumping in all those reserves, we may be creating a problem because we are putting in more reserves than we can take out at the end of the week. The market is often not capable of handling a large amount—either because on the repo side they do not have collateral or because on the reverse side we have exhausted the supply of banks that care to engage in that activity.

"Banks who do reverses with us are not as welcome at the discount window as they would be if they did not. So there is some reluctance on their part to do reverses because they fear the money market might tighten and they might have to come into the discount window. The rationale for this policy is that a bank should not borrow from us money that they have in fact lent us. The banks are discouraged from doing reverses and borrowing at the discount window even when they would be taking a loss on the *net* transaction, which at times they would be."

Another difficulty from the Fed's point of view of being forced to engage in massive open-market operations to offset shifts in Treasury balances is that at times the large injections or withdrawals of reserves required to do so may—depending on market conditions—be mistakenly interpreted by the market as a signal of a shift in Fed policy.

Problems of the sort just described are the reason the Fed lobbied to have the Treasury hold the bulk of its deposit balances in TT&L accounts at private banks.

Regardless of how well the Treasury's new deposit arrangements work out, the Treasury will still have to keep sizable balances at the Fed. Any time these balances run below $1 billion, the Treasury runs a risk, unless it puts more money in, of ending up *OD* (*overdrawn*) at the Fed.

When this occurs, the Treasury issues the Fed special certificates, which usually are on the Fed's books for no more than a day or two.

A GO-AROUND

The Fed goes into the market to do open-market operations after the morning conference call between the New York desk and the board in Washington. "Usually," commented one inside observer, "this is around 11:30 or 11:45. Occasionally, however, we will go in earlier if there is a very clear situation we want to address ourselves to—a big job obviously has to be done and funds are trading off from where we want, so we need to act fast. Maybe that is one of ten occasions. Also at times we know what we want to do but are waiting for confirmation from the market, so we sort of drag our feet. This irritates people in the market. They want to know why we act so late in the day. It is because we were waiting. We projected a reserve need, but funds were trading well at 4¾ and we just waited until they got to 4⅞.

"On rare occasions we will use an announcement of repo or reverses for the following day to influence where the market is trading. More often we make an announcement of what we want to do tomorrow because we know that there is an exceptionally large job to be done. In some weeks on Wednesday, knowing that we have a big job to do for the next week, we have informed the dealers that we would like to review propositions for repo or reverse the next morning."

When the Fed goes into the market to do normal daily open-market operations, the size is usually large. A typical bill operation for the open-market account currently varies from $300 to $600 million. In Treasury coupons and agencies, it will run from $300 to $500 million. Repos and reverses can run from $1 to $4 billion.

Once the Fed decides what it wants to do in the way of open-market operations, it does what is called a *go-around*. It calls all of the primary dealers in government securities and informs them that it wants to buy securities, sell securities, do repo, or do reverses and asks them for bids and offers, as the case may be.

On securities purchases and sales, the Fed compares dealers' bids and offers with current market quotes and determines on which issues yields are most attractive and on which of these issues it has gotten the best quotes. It then does business with those dealers who have given it the highest bids or lowest offers on those issues.

To get current market quotes on governments and agencies, the Fed asks on a rotating basis five of the primary dealers in governments to give it quotes for a wide range of securities on an hourly or more frequent basis. Providing such quotes is a nuisance for the dealers, which is why the Fed rotates the job.

The word that a go-around is being done is flashed out to all the dealers within 30 seconds. Thereafter the process slows. It takes the dealers time to get back to the Fed with their offerings or bids, and then it takes the Fed time to compare the dealers' propositions and select the most favorable. Particularly in agencies, the whole process can easily consume more than an hour. To cut this time, the Fed plans to move to a computer system that will permit the dealers' bids and offers to be directly transmitted to the Fed's computer, which may eventually be programmed to select the best bids or offers. Developing and installing such a system is, however, a large job and is unlikely to be done for some time.

In addition to its normal open-market transactions with the dealers, the Fed uses transactions with foreign central banks that hold dollars as a way to affect bank reserves. Such transactions are marginal on a long-term basis but can be significant in the day-to-day control of reserves. "Foreign accounts have buy and sell and repo orders every day," said one person on the desk. "We can choose to be on the other side of any one of those transactions, which gives us flexibility. Say that funds are trading where we want them to and there is a big excess of reserves in the market. If we try to drain reserves, the market may conclude we want an even higher funds rate. But if we do transactions internally with foreign accounts, no one sees them and no one is upset. Such transactions do what a market transaction would do without providing any signal." Foreign account transactions on an average day in 1977 amounted to $100 to $250 million on the buy side and the same amount on the sell side. The repo amounts ran from $800 million to $1.5 billion a day.

THE DISCOUNT WINDOW

When a bank borrows at the discount window, reserves are created just as they are when the Fed does repos in the course of open-market operations (Table 8–5). Back in the 1920s granting banks loans at the discount window was the Fed's main technique for creating bank reserves. Gradually this technique of reserve creation was replaced by open-market operations, and the primary function of the discount window today is to provide member banks, which encounter any one of a range of possible difficulties, with a means to adjust in the short run.

A bank's borrowings at the discount window have to be collateralized. According to the old commercial loan theory of banking, it was proper for banks to make only *short-term* loans because their liabilities were short-term in nature. Also bank loans were supposed to be *self-liquidating,* that is, to fund an activity that would automatically generate funds required to repay the loan. Finally, bank loans were to be *productive,* that

Table 8–5
When a bank borrows $50 million at the discount window it increases bank reserves by a like amount

The Fed

Member bank borrowing +50 million	Reserves of borrowing bank +50 million

The Borrowing Bank

Reserves +50 million	Borrowing from the Federal Reserve +50 million

is, to fund the production and marketing of goods not, for example, the carrying of securities. Influenced by this doctrine, the authors of the Federal Reserve Act stipulated that only notes arising from short-term, self-liquidating, productive loans were *eligible* as collateral at the discount window. Notes not meeting these conditions are deemed to be *ineligible* collateral. When a bank borrows against ineligible collateral, it has to pay a rate at least ½ of 1 percent above the posted discount rate.

Currently the Fed classifies (reflecting various congressional amendments to the Federal Reserve Act) as eligible collateral: Treasury securities, federal agency securities, municipal securities with less than 6 months to run, and commercial and industrial loans with 90 days or less to run. What banks use as collateral at the window has varied over time. There was a time when banks borrowed at the discount window almost exclusively against governments. Then large banks began to finance their government portfolios with repo money and turned to the use of customer promissory notes as collateral. Major banks make it a practice to try to always hold at the Fed adequate collateral against possible borrowings. However, when loan demand is slack, the banks scurry to find any type of collateral, including BAs, that would be eligible at the window; they may even hold ineligible paper at the Fed as collateral against possible borrowings, so as to avoid churning their custody department on a Wednesday settlement date to get the right collateral to the Fed.

Bank attitudes toward discounting

The Fed has always taken the position that access to the discount window is a privilege and that banks should borrow there only when they have a legitimate need and then only for reasonable amounts and periods. The discount rate is sometimes set at a penalty rate, but often it is set at a level such that it is cheaper for a bank to borrow at the discount window than to buy overnight Fed funds (Figure 8–1).[9] The discount rate,

Figure 8–1
Relationship of the discount rate to the Fed funds rate

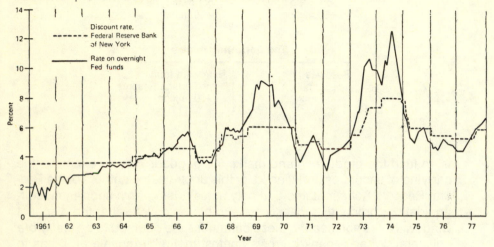

unlike the Fed funds rate, is not typically a major beacon pointing up the direction of Fed policy; it is normally adjusted up or down only after other short-term rates have moved (see Figure 8–1).

The Fed's guideline on use of the discount window is vague at best, and not surprisingly there is a wide range of views among bankers with respect to the window and its proper use.

At one extreme are some small banks that feel that a stigma is attached to use of the discount window. Other banks, which take a less extreme point of view, have very conservative senior management who regard it as a sign of weakness to borrow at the window; they are happy and proud to say that they have not found it necessary to borrow at the window in 5 years, or whatever. This attitude led one bank during the 1974 credit crunch to pay, on a settlement day when Fed funds were tight, 25 percent for overnight funds rather than going to the window.

---

[9] In 1971 the Fed switched from actually discounting paper at the window to making straight loans against collateral. As a result the discount rate is not quoted on a bank discount rate basis as Treasury bill rates are; instead the discount rate is an add-on rate that is directly comparable to the Fed funds rate, which is also an add-on rate. In making the 1971 switch in window practice, the Fed's major motive was to simplify lending at the window. The change also permitted the banks to borrow more dollars against a given amount of collateral.

Such behavior is dismaying to the Fed. It is also foolhardy because in paying an exorbitant rate for funds, a bank risks raising more questions in the mind of the public than it would ever do by borrowing at the window.

Still other banks, typically larger banks, regard the discount window as what it truly is—a lender-of-last-resort facility that they use occasionally because they experience, due to an unexpected occurrence, difficulty in settling on a Wednesday. Examples are: a clearing bank that gets hit by dealers loans late on a Wednesday when Fed funds are trading at a high rate, a bank that experiences large unanticipated withdrawals, and a bank that makes a mistake in tracking its reserve position and ends up short.

Finally there are banks that will borrow at the discount window whenever there is a rate advantage to doing so (the discount rate is below the Fed funds rate) as much as they feel they can without being criticized by the Fed. A bank that dips its ladle into the bucket every time there is a rate advantage will eventually get a call from the Fed to say that its borrowing pattern is exceeding the typical borrowing pattern for a bank with its characteristics. Once a bank gets such a call, it will withdraw for a time, clean up its record, and then perhaps come back into the window to test the Fed again.

The Fed's attitude toward discounting

Today the Fed uses open-market operations to make overall adjustments in reserves. The impact of such aggregate actions can differ for individual banks. The Fed views the discount window in part as a safety valve for those banks that are adversely affected by actions taken on the open-market desk. From the desk's point of view, it is valuable to know that the discount window is there because it allows the desk to take actions it otherwise might hesitate to because of the potential impact on individual banks.

Just what, in the Fed's view, is an appropriate use of the discount window varies depending on a bank's size and position. The Fed feels that big banks have a greater number of short-term borrowing alternatives open to them than smaller banks do, so their need for the discount window should be less frequent than that of smaller banks.

Settlement date is the most likely time for banks of any size to come to the discount window. On a Wednesday banks of any size can find their position much shorter than they anticipated, and rates can get out of hand in the Fed funds market on Wednesday afternoon. The reserve week ends on Wednesday so that is the day banks make final settlement with the Fed (see Chapter 11). The Fed takes the position that if the choice facing a bank on a Wednesday is between paying an "exorbitant" rate for funds and coming to the discount window, it should come into the window. This view, however, still leaves room for judgment. If the discount rate is 5¼ and Fed funds are at 6, is 6 a bandit rate? If not, what about a 1-point spread? Whether use of the discount window is legitimate on a Wednesday also depends on how late in the day it is, how much a bank needs, and the lines available to it in the Fed funds market.

A small bank has less access to the Fed funds market than a large bank; it does not have access to the Euromarket; and it may not have many repo possibilities. When such a bank experiences a sudden run-off in deposits (the school district withdraws balances) or increased local demand for loans, it may not be in a position to immediately react to that development. It may not have liquid assets to pay off deposits that are running off; it may not have short-term liquidity to fund a big increase in loan demand. In that type of situation, the Fed would view short-term use of the discount window by the bank as appropriate, and it would carry the bank for as long as it took to make the fundamental adjustment required in its asset and liability structure. Normally the Fed would expect this to take no longer than 3 months, but that is a flexible number.

"Informational" and other calls

Normally the first time a bank borrows from the Fed, the Fed will not call the bank to ask why it is borrowing. The Fed tries to encourage the notion that a loan at the discount window for a legitimate purpose is available on a no-questions-asked basis. If borrowing continues, the Fed—taking into consideration the amount of the borrowing, the bank's past borrowing record, its frequency of borrowing, and conditions affecting banks of its type at that time—may eventually conclude that the borrowing is getting out of range of the typical need.

Then it would make an *informational call*. This, from the Fed's point of view, has no stigma attached to it. The Fed is trying to get a fix on where the bank is and on how much longer it expects to rely on the Fed. The call lets the bank know that it has reached a point where the Fed is taking an interest in it, and it gives the bank an opportunity to tell the Fed what its problems are and what it is doing to cope with them. Normally this suffices, and within a few weeks the bank will have taken steps to cope with its problems—cut its loans or sought out new deposits.

But if an additional period goes by and no improvement occurs, the Fed will make a second *administrative counseling call*. The purpose of this call is to tell the bank that its borrowing pattern is becoming atypical or excessive and that it is time for the bank to terminate its borrowing. Normally such a call will end the borrowing. It is rare that the Fed has to make a final call to say that the bank must terminate its borrowing as of a certain date.

Reverses and loans at the window

The Fed has an administrative rule that a bank should not do reverses with the Fed if it expects at the time that it might borrow from the Fed during the settlement week. The rationale is to prevent banks from using the window to fund a profitable arbitrage. However, there are qualifications to this rule. If a bank thinks it is in good shape with respect to its reserve position and does reverses and then something changes in the interim—operational problems or whatever—the Fed would not object to the bank borrowing at the window. Also there is no problem in borrowing if a bank acts as a conduit for customer funds in doing reverses.

The Fed has an additional rule that a bank should not be a net seller of Fed funds during a period in which it borrows at the discount window. This again is to prevent borrowing at the discount window from being part of a for-profit arbitrage.

Emergency credit

In addition to granting loans at the window to faciliate short-term adjustments, the Fed will grant longer-term financing to banks encountering fundamental problems. There are two types of situations in which the Fed provides such emergency aid. One is when an act of God—flood, hurricane, or whatever—adversely affects a group of banks, their borrowers or their depositors. For example, a hailstorm wipes out a crop and causes farmers to withdraw deposits from local banks. Such a situation would call for prolonged loans to the affected banks and a program to restore them to financial health.

The Fed will also grant emergency long-term financing to a single bank if in its judgment the risks to the banking system as a whole of not doing so are sufficiently great to warrant providing credit to that bank while another solution is worked out. This is the primary reason the Fed got into the Franklin Bank loan and let it get up to $1.7 billion; the Penn Central and the Herstatt had already failed. Thus, failure of the Franklin at that time might have threatened the public's confidence in the whole banking system.

Even if a single bank's failure would not threaten to bring down the whole house of cards, the Fed feels a responsibility to help out a bank that gets into trouble if it is fact salvageable. In the Fed's view, a bank that is a member of the system has paid its dues, and help in time of need is one of the benefits that goes with membership.

The Fed also has limited statutory authority to grant emergency loans to individuals, partnerships, and corporations. This authority was used during the 1930s to grant about 125 loans totaling a mere $1 million; it has not been used since. However, questions have been raised as to whether the Fed could or should use this authority to bail out the Penn Central, Lockheed, and more recently New York State agencies and New York City. In the case of the latter, the Fed's response was that—if the federal government *broadly defined* were going to provide assistance to states, municipalities, and their agencies individually—it should do it directly by decision of Congress and the administration. Had the Fed gotten into the business of lending to New York City, it would have been faced with the question of also lending to Detroit and other troubled cities.

Seasonal credit

In 1973 the Fed instituted a program for providing seasonal credit to smaller banks that lack access to the national money market. The purpose of the program was to meet anticipated borrowing needs for banks in resort communities, agricultural centers, and other areas where local businesses need to borrow funds early in the seasonal cycle and make their profits later. Loans made under this program represent only a small proportion of the total credit granted by the Fed at the discount window.

Collateral

Banks make uncollateralized loans to their customers on the basis of their financial position. So it is natural to ask why the Fed, instead of demanding collateral at the discount window, should not make unsecured loans to member banks that it regulates and whose condition it knows well.

The answer is that the Fed would like to do away with collateral at the discount window because doing so would reduce record keeping, securities transfers, and other paper work associated with discounting, which in turn would make discounting cheaper and simpler both for it and for banks that borrow at the window. For the collateral requirement on loans at the discount window to be eliminated, however, Congress would have to amend the Federal Reserve Act. Passage of such an amendment appears politically impossible because many members of Congress would view such a change as subjecting the Fed to a risk of loss. That risk, however, is one to which the Fed is already exposed because of its recognized responsibility to provide emergency aid to troubled banks, which presumably might result in its lending against questionable collateral, as in the Franklin Bank situation.

WATCHING THE FED

While it has not always been the case in the past, the Fed today tightly controls the Fed funds rate. Said one dealer, "The Fed is not even abashed any more to admit that they set the funds rate. They are our own little Gosplan [Russian economic planning agency] pegging a key interest rate in the midst of a 'free-market' economy."

In the money market there is tremendous substitutability between instruments for both borrowers and lenders. Banks that need funds can go to the Fed funds market, the Euromarket, the repo market, and the CD market, or they can sell off BAs and other securities. Investors have in every maturity range a variety of instruments among which to choose, and, depending on their needs and their rate forecasts, instruments of different maturity can also be close substitutes for them. Because of all this substitutability, changes in the Fed funds rate are immediately transmitted to every other sector of the money market through a variety of channels.

Because a change in the Fed funds rate affects in a quite predictable way all other short-term rates, everyone in the money market has a tremendous stake in predicting the next move in the funds rate. Banks base the maturity structure of their liabilities in part on where they anticipate funds will trade, and dealers and portfolio managers position on the basis of where they think funds will trade. When either the banks or the dealers position on the basis of a correct prediction, the payoff can run into tens, even hundreds, of millions of dollars; and when they are wrong, the losses can be equally staggering. In early 1978, when the Fed tightened unexpectedly to defend the dollar, one large dealership that was long had to mark down its position $25 million in a single day.

Everyone on the street watches the Fed in much the same way. They read the minutes of FOMC meetings, which are released a month after each meeting, to learn the Fed's current targets for money supply growth and the Fed funds rate. Then they track what has actually been happening to money supply figures against the Fed's target rates of growth. If money supply growth is exceeding the Fed's targets, they anticipate a possible tightening, and if it has been sluggish, they anticipate a weakening of the funds rate.

"Watching the Fed is," said one dealer, "very easy if one can read. There are sunshine laws available. All one has to read is how they go about what they do—and get some experience in watching their little points of finesse such as how they handle customer repo. Watching the Fed is in fact getting all too easy. The dealers have become relatively more aggressive because the Fed has become more predictable than it used to be due largely to sunshine laws."

There is, of course, a 30-day lag between when the Fed sets targets and when the street can read what those targets are. But the street attempts to compensate for this by taking into account everything they know about economic trends and developments in the capital market when they surmise what, if any, changes in targets the FOMC might have made at its most recent meeting.

However easy some dealers may consider watching the Fed, it is still a tricky game. The Fed is looking closely at *two* money supply figures, M1 and M2, which don't always behave in the same way relative to the Fed's target rates of growth for them, as Figure 8–2 shows. Also (see again Figure 8–2) the Fed tends to respond with a *lag* to out-of-bounds growth rates in the money stock because it waits to see whether a given month's figures reflect a temporary aberration or a longer-term trend that must be counteracted.

Figure 8–2
FOMC ranges for short-run monetary growth and for the Federal funds rate, 1976

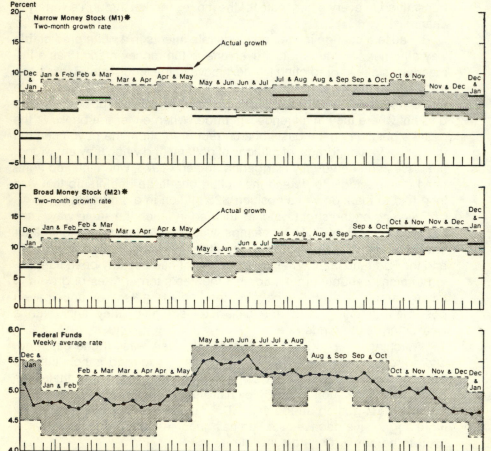

* Seasonally adjusted annual rates.
  Note: Shaded bands in the upper two charts are the FOMC's specified ranges for money supply growth over the 2-month periods indicated; in the bottom chart they are the specified ranges for Federal funds rate variation. Actual growth rates in the upper two charts are based on data available at the time of the second FOMC meeting after the end of each period.
  Source: *Federal Reserve Bank of New York Quarterly Review*, Spring 1977, p. 42.

Besides watching the Fed in what might be called the big-picture way—focusing on trends over time—the street also watches the Fed on a moment-to-moment basis, looking for some clue as to whether a change in policy might be underway. To do so, the resident Fed watchers at the banks and the dealers make their own estimates of shifts in Treasury balances, of changes in reserve availability, and of the adding or subtracting job the Fed must do. On the basis of these, the street interprets every open-market move the Fed makes. If the Fed is doing reverses, they want to know whether it is draining reserves to meet a temporary need or initiating a new tightening.

Even the minute—five minutes early or late—at which the Fed comes into the market is interpreted by some as a signal of Fed policy. The street's attempts to read a signal into even the Fed's smallest moves reminds one of a gypsy reading tea leaves. And when carried to extremes, these attempts probably have about the same level of reliability. A common comment on the desk is that the street constantly attributes motives and levels of sophistication to Fed actions that simply do not exist. This is not surprising, since the Fed itself is groping on a moment-to-moment basis to determine what, if anything, needs to be done in the *very* short run.

THE M1 GAME

Every week the Fed compiles and publishes on Thursday afternoon figures on the size of the money supply according to the M1 and M2 measures, which were defined in Chapter 2.[10] These weekly figures are at best estimates and are subject later to substantial revisions.

There are various reasons for the unreliability of weekly and monthly figures on the money supply. One quarter of all deposits are held by nonmember banks that report their deposits on only four call dates a year; the rest of the time the Fed has to estimate what deposits they hold. Also seasonal factors are important but so erratic that it is difficult to build up enough experience to tell what the seasonal adjustment factors should be. It is also hard to adjust for changes in float, Treasury balances, tabulating errors, and the like. The impact of the latter factors on money supply figures was described in a report to the Fed as follows:

Our analysis suggests that such day-to-day transitory variations alone can introduce a substantial, nonsystematic variability, or error, in reported growth rates. From month to month the transitory component in the annualized growth rate of M_1 is likely to exceed 2½ percentage points one-third of the time; from quarter to quarter, to exceed ½ percentage point one-third of the time. The comparable transitory component, or error, in M_2 will be about half as large. Users

---

[10] Figures on M3 are published only quarterly by the Fed.

should be aware of the dangers of placing too much emphasis on reported short-term variations in the monetary aggregates, especially on less than quarterly changes.[11]

However worthless figures on weekly changes in the money supply may be, they are taken very seriously by the street. The Fed claims that errors and random changes in weekly money supply figures are so great that it never bases its actions on one week's numbers; therefore it is absurd for the street to place great emphasis on them. But the street believes that one week's figures can make a difference. There is probably some justification for this view because, while just a week of high or low monetary growth won't stir the Fed to action, it is true that every now and then one week's numbers turn out to be the straw that broke the camel's back—that caused the Fed to conclude that a trend that must be counteracted was under way.

There is also another element to the street's attitude. The street needs a benchmark and it always picks one. In that selection it is not the least bit dogmatic. It used to look at free reserves, now it looks at money supply figures. Moreover, while the Fed says that it places equal weight on both the M1 and M2 figures, the street has made its *own* judgment that M1 counts more, and that is the number to which it reacts.

Because the street watches money supply figures so closely and has so much faith that they influence Fed policy, the reaction of the street to Thursday afternoon announcements of money supply figures is *violent*. If money supply growth is way down, a buying panic occurs, and if it is way up, a selling panic occurs.

Because the stakes are huge, every large bank and dealer on the street has someone tracking money supply figures and making in-house predictions of how the money supply will change over the week. The incentive, of course, is that real money can be made and losses avoided by basing short-term positions on correct predictions of money supply figures.

However, no matter how much information and manpower street firms put into their money supply projections, and some put in a considerable amount, these projections turn out to be quite poor. Said a top practitioner of the art: "I predict money supply figures every week but the traders in the shop treat my predictions with some reservation. I get lucky at times and at other times I am not. On the whole I do not know of anyone doing this sort of work whose record is good." This is hardly surprising given the many random elements and errors that affect the weekly money supply figures published by the Fed.

---

[11] Board of Governors of the Federal Reserve System, *Improving the Monetary Aggregates*, 1976, p. 5

Because money supply figures are considered to be so important by the street and because no one can predict them accurately, Thursday afternoon has come to be a giant crap game on the street. It is as if the Fed every Thursday afternoon threw dice and all the dealers and banks bet on the outcome. Commented one dealer with slight exaggeration: "It's crazy what goes on. The stakes are getting so large that it is coming to the point where we are inviting the mafia to come in and find out ahead of time what the M1 figure on Thursday will be."

The Fed would like to remedy this situation, but there seems to be no way it can. "We do not know," said one thoughtful observer at the Fed, "what to do about the Thursday afternoon crap game. The market looks at the numbers because we do. The market is not the least bit doctrinaire and will look at anything we look at. They do not care about the relationship of money supply to economic activity. We are the source of the problem. I do not know of any way out, and I think that the market would like to get out from this situation. We cannot publish the numbers less frequently, and the numbers are unlikely to get a lot better in the next few years. So unless we abandon the monetary aggregates as targets, we are never going to solve this problem."

WHEN AND WHAT TO ANNOUNCE

A question that is often raised in the money market and has even been raised in court is whether the Fed ought to be permitted to wait 30 days before publishing the minutes of the latest FOMC meeting. Many argue that the street and the public have a right to know what the Fed intends to do as soon as it makes its decision and that quicker publication of Fed decisions would cut down the uncertainty under which the market currently operates.

"There is," commented someone at the Fed, "a strong view that the Fed should publish the FOMC minutes as the decisions are made. I do not think so. It would create sharp swings in the market. The way things are, we are able to moderate the changes that have to occur—to provide some pace to these changes that is useful from the point of view of orderly markets and market resilience. I am sympathetic to reducing the amount of Fed watching that goes on, but how? We are not nearly as diabolical as most Fed watchers seem to assume nor as clever. It is interesting to sit in our seats and hear the rationalizations that are given for our actions; they are often much more clever than anything we had thought of."

Since the Fed, in fact, pegs the funds rate, it could also be argued that the Fed, when it decides to change the Fed funds rate, should announce that change rather than implementing it gradually. Commenting on that, one dealer said: "If you had an overnight announcement that the Fed was moving to a higher funds target, you would have massive selling, everyone trying to get through the door at the same time. And no matter how convinced people were that the market was overreacting, there would be no firm large enough to absorb the panic selling. Now there is uncertainty which creates differences of opinions, and differences of opinions are what create markets."

To the above it should be added that if the FOMC were to announce its decisions sooner or if the Fed were to announce rather than implement changes in the Fed funds rate, doing so would simply shift the locus of uncertainty, rather than reducing it.

FORECASTING INTEREST RATES

Every bank, dealer, and investor is busily predicting interest rates over various time spans. Money market participants base many of their decisions on relatively short time horizons, and they are most concerned with and have the most confidence in quite short-term predictions of interest rates. A good many of them would argue that interest rate levels can be predicted with better than 50 percent accuracy for short periods—a month or two or three—but that somewhere beyond that their predictability diminishes sharply.

In predicting short-term interest rates, Fed watching is a big input in everyone's calculations. There are, however, other inputs. Interest rate predictors are voracious readers of every bit of news on economic trends and the ups and downs of economic indicators. In addition, they estimate the funds that borrowers are likely to demand and lenders are likely to supply; more demand than supply means that rates are likely to be forced up. One important element in such estimates is the Treasury's projected borrowing needs. The Treasury estimates them, but there is a feeling on the street that the Treasury's figures are often unrealistic because of political considerations—the Treasury has to stick with the official projection of GNP in predicting its revenues and with the official projection of the inflation rate in predicting its expenditures. Other problems also crop up. The Defense Department, for example, may find that its expenditures figures run for months below projected levels due to unanticipated delays in procurement.

People on the street predicting interest rates also plug into their calculations the predictions of interest rates produced by the major economic models—the Wharton model and the models constructed by Data Resources, Chase Econometric Associates, and others. In addition, many banks, dealers, and even large investors have their own sophisticated computer models for making interest rate predictions. The time span of econometric projections of interest rates tends, however, to be longer than the time horizon on which money market participants base most of their decisions. So the economists and econometricians who are employed by banks and dealers—and they are legion—are by and large kept politely but firmly out of the trading room.

The yield curve as a predictor

Another predictor of interest rates that many people on the street look at is the yield curve. The argument for the yield curve as a predictor of interest rates is best illustrated with an example. In January 1978 the 3-month bill was trading at 6.30, the 6-month bill at 6.50, and the 9-month bill at 6.60 (see Figure 8–3). Presumably many people holding the

Figure 8–3
The yield curve in the bill market, January 1978

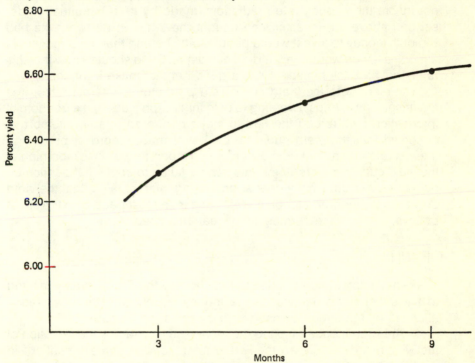

3-month bill had longer-term money to invest and could therefore have bought the 6-month bill, which was yielding 20 basis points more than the 3-month bill. For them not to have done so implies that they expected that the 3-month bill 3 months hence would yield 6.70, i.e., that by rolling the 3-month bill they could earn the same *average* return over 6 months as they could by buying the 6-month bill. Similarly, the fact that the 9-month bill yielded 6.60 implies that investors expected the 3-month bill 6 months hence to also trade at 6.70. This sort of argument can be applied to any stretch of the yield curve, so that throughout its length the shape of this curve reflects the street's expectations as to what future interest rates will be, and thus provides implicit consensus predictions of future rates.

How good these predictions are is a subject of debate. Presumably they have a bearish cast, because the farther the investor goes out along the maturity scale, the greater the price risk to which he is exposed. The amount of that bearish bias is impossible to measure but the normal assumption, for what it is worth, is that it works out in ordinary times to be 1 percent over the length of the yield curve.

Whether the yield curve is a good predictor of interest rates, as some would argue, or a useless one, as others would argue, the investor cannot ignore the implicit rate predictions made by it. In the situation described above, an investor who bought the 3-month bill when he had 6-month money to invest would be implicitly betting that the 3-month bill 3 months hence would be yielding at least 6.70. He should know that this is his bet and ask himself if it is a good bet, not make it randomly.

With respect to the yield curve as a predictor of interest rates, it is amusing and perhaps revealing to note that Ralph Nader, in a freedom of information suit, forced the Fed to make public an internal memo that observed that the yield curve had a better track record at predicting interest rates than the Fed's own model. Depending on one's opinion of the yield curve as a predictor, this can be taken to imply that econometric models are abysmally poor at predicting interest rates, that the yield curve is a better predictor of interest rates than most people on the street believe, or that interest rates simply can't be predicted!

M1 OR WHAT?

We have noted the importance attached by the Fed in policy making to the effect of its actions on the money supply and the importance attached by the street to changes in money supply figures.

All the prominence given to the money supply raises the question of just what money is. Clearly the Fed is not quite sure, since it mentions in the FOMC directive three measures of money—M1, M2, and M3—and it also calculates M4 and M5.

Economists are of no more help in providing a definitive answer as to what money is. Monetarists argue that money is whatever balances the public holds in order to make transactions. Such balances obviously include all demand deposits and should perhaps include savings deposits. They should not, however, include long-term time deposits (which are included in M2) because they are illiquid. But these balances should probably include large-denomination short-term CDs held by money market investors because they are highly liquid. *And* they should probably include all the various highly liquid short-term instruments (*near monies*), such as overnight RP, Euro call deposits, and short-term commercial paper, that corporations and other investors hold to fund anticipated payments for taxes, to suppliers, and to others. No definition of the money supply comes near to being that inclusive.

Economists who are not monetarists argue that money is demanded not only for transactions purposes, but also as a financial asset. This position certainly opens the door to a very inclusive measure of money supply. But it is not possible to say just what that measure should be because the attraction of money as a financial asset lies in its liquidity, and liquidity is a property that assets possess in degrees.

The facts that it is impossible to measure the money supply at any point in time and that what serves as money undoubtedly changes over time throw into question the validity of making the growth of the money supply a major policy target. In this respect the comment of one of the street's most astute Fed watchers is of interest: "There is no question but that the Fed responds to short-run gyrations in the money supply. But the Fed is eclectic. I think they align their 2-month growth targets to give them that policy which most closely follows the policy they want to implement based on the fundamentals of the economy—the unemployment rate, the inflation rate, and so forth. I think the Fed now realizes the unimportance of short-run changes in money supply and uses them as a basis to change policy merely as a front to insulate its policies from criticism by Congress."

Perhaps—an intriguing possibility—money supply isn't so important after all.

Chapter 9

The market makers:
Dealers and others

THE COLLECTION OF MARKETS described in this book is called *the* money market. This suggests that the market's participants trade in a single market where at any time one price reigns for any one instrument. This description is accurate, but that is startling. Money market instruments, with the exception of futures contracts, are traded not on organized exchanges but strictly over the counter. Moreover, money market participants, who vary in size from small to gargantuan, are scattered over the whole United States—*and* throughout Canada, Europe, and elsewhere on the globe. Thus one might expect some fragmentation of the market, with big New York participants dealing in a noticeably different market from their London or Wichita counterparts. However, money market lenders and borrowers can operate almost as well out of Dearborn, Michigan, Washington, or Singapore as they can from Wall Street. Wherever they are, their access to information, bids, and offers is (time zone problems excepted) essentially the same. That the money market is in fact a single market is due in large part to the activities of the dealers and brokers who weld the market's many participants into a unified whole, and to the modern techniques of communication that make this possible.

215

THE DEALERS

Money market dealers are, like bankers, a mixed bag. Some are tiny, others huge. Some specialize in certain instruments, others cover the waterfront. One is also tempted to say that some are immensely sharp and others not so sharp, but the not-so-sharp players lead short lives. Despite dealers' diversity, one can generalize about their operations.

Activities

The hallmark of a dealer is that he buys and sells for his own account, that is, trades with retail and other dealers off his own position. In addition, dealers engage in various activities that come close to brokering.

The prime example of the latter is commercial paper dealers. Each day they help their customers borrow hundreds of millions of dollars from other market participants. Commercial paper dealers' responsibilities are: (1) to advise their clients on market conditions, (2) to ensure that their clients post rates for different maturities that give them the lowest possible borrowing costs but are still high enough to get their paper sold, and (3) for a ⅛ commission, to show and sell that paper to retail. Positioning is part of a commercial paper dealer's operation but only marginally so. Paper dealers will position any of their clients' paper that is not sold, but only on a small scale. One reason is that they are careful to ensure that their clients post realistic rates. A second reason is that commercial paper dealers as a group feel that it is not in their best interests or in that of their clients for them to position large amounts of paper. Commercial paper dealers do, however, stand ready to bid for paper bought from them by retail and thus make a secondary market in paper. Such activity leads them at times to position paper, but the amounts are small because the secondary market in commercial paper is not active. Thus dealers in commercial paper act more like brokers than like true dealers.

Dealers also act at times like brokers in the CD market. A bank that wants to do a large program in one fast shot may call one or more dealers and offer them an 05 (5 basis points) on any CDs they can sell to retail. Finally, smaller dealers who are hesitant about the market or who are operating outside their normal market sector at times act more or less as brokers, giving a firm bid to retail only if they can cross the trade on the other side with an assured sale.

As noted, however, brokering is not what dealing is all about. The crucial role dealers play in the money market is as market makers, and in performing that role they trade off their own positions.

Part of the dealers' role as market makers involves underwriting new issues. Most large municipal note issues are bought up at issue by dealers who take them into position and sell them off to retail. In the market for governments there is also some underwriting, though of a less formal nature; frequently dealers buy large amounts of new government issues at auction and then distribute them to retail.

In the secondary market dealers act as market makers by constantly quoting bids and offers at which they are willing to buy and sell. Some of these quotes are to other dealers. In every sector of the money market, there is an *inside market* between dealers. In this market dealers quote price *runs* (bids and offers for securities of different maturities) to other dealers, often through brokers. Since every dealer will *hit* a bid he views as high or take an offering he views as low, trading in the inside market creates at any time for every security traded a prevailing price that represents the dealers' consensus feeling of what that security is worth.

Dealers also actively quote bids and offers to retail. In doing so they consistently seek to give their customers the best quotes possible because they value retail business and they know that other shops are competing actively with them for it. This competition between dealers ensures that dealers' quotes to retail will never be far removed from prices prevailing in the inside market. Thus, all the money market's geographically dispersed participants can always trade at close to identical bids and offers.

As the above suggests, through their trading activities, the dealers give the secondary market for money market instruments two important characteristics. First, they ensure that at any moment a single price level will prevail for any instrument traded in it. Second, by standing ready to quote firm bids and offers at which they will trade, they render money market instruments highly liquid.

Profit sources

Dealers profit from their activities in several ways. First, there are the 05s and ⅛s they earn selling CDs and commercial paper. Particularly for firms that are big commercial paper dealers, these commissions can mount up to a substantial sum, but in total they represent only a small part of dealers' profits.

A second source of dealers' profits is *carry*. As noted below, dealers finance the bulk of their long positions (muni notes excepted) in the repo market. Their RP borrowings are of shorter maturity than the securities they position. Thus their financing costs are normally less than the yields on the securities they finance, and they profit from *positive* carry.

Carry, however, is not a dependable source of profit because, when the yield curve inverts, carry turns negative.[1] As one dealer com-

---

[1] The yield curve is said to be *inverted* when short-term rates exceed long-term rates. For an example of an inverted yield curve, see Figure 4–7.

mented: "Back in 1974 when Fed funds were 10 to 14 percent, there was nothing you could position at a positive carry. You might position because you thought rates were going to fall, but not for carry. And you knew *ex ante* that, if you positioned and the market did not appreciate, you would lose money on two levels: carry and depreciation of values. This led to the phenomenon of the Friday night bill trader. At one point, to carry bills over the weekend cost 5 basis points. So traders would attempt on Friday to sell the 90-day bill for cash settlement and buy it back for regular settlement."

A third source of dealer profits is what might be called day-to-day trading profits, buying securities at one price and reselling them shortly at a slightly higher price, or shorting securities and covering in at a slightly lower price. How traders seek to earn 02s and 32nds from such trading is discussed later.

The sources of profit mentioned so far suffice to pay dealers' phone and light bills—to cover their overhead. Dealers earn really big money on position plays, that is, by taking into position huge amounts of securities when they anticipate that rates will fall and securities prices will rise or by shorting the market when they are bearish.

Being willing to position on a large scale is characteristic of all dealers, although the appetite of some shops for such *speculation* is stronger than that of others.[2] One might argue that positioning done specifically to speculate as opposed to the positioning that arises out of a dealer's daily trading activities with retail and other dealers is not an inherent part of being a market maker. But such speculation serves useful functions. It guarantees that market prices will react rapidly to any change in economic conditions in demand, supply, or rate expectations. Also and more important, the profits dealers can earn from correct position plays are the prime incentive they have for setting up the elaborate and expensive operations they use daily to trade with retail and each other. In effect position profits help to oil the machinery that dealers need to be effective market makers.

To the above it might be added that dealers possess no crystal balls enabling them to perfectly foresee the future. They position on the basis of carefully formulated expectations. When they are right, they make huge profits; when they are wrong, their losses can be staggering. Thus the successful shops and the ones that survive are those that are right on the market more often than wrong.

---

[2] The term *speculation* as used here and throughout the book is *not* meant to carry any pejorative connotation. *Speculation is taking an unhedged position, short or long.* A homeowner who buys a house financed with a mortgage is assuming a speculative, levered position in real estate. A dealer who buys governments with RP money is assuming a speculative, levered position in governments. The only difference between the two is that the dealer knows he's speculating, and the homeowner typically does not think of it that way.

DEALER FINANCING

The typical dealer is running a highly levered operation in which securities held in position may total 500 or 600 times capital. Some dealers rely heavily on dealer loans from New York banks for financing, but as one dealer commented: "The state of the art is that you don't have to." RP money is cheaper, and sharp dealers rely primarily on it to meet their financing needs. For such dealers the need to obtain RP money on a continuing basis and in large amounts is one additional reason for cultivating assiduously their retail customers. The corporations, state and local governments, and other investors that buy governments and other instruments from them are also big suppliers of RP money to the dealers.

A good bit of the borrowing dealers do in the RP market is done on an overnight basis. One reason is that the overnight rate is typically the lowest RP rate. A second is that securities "hung out" on RP for one night only are available for sale the next day. Nonbank dealers have to clear all their RP transactions through the clearing banks, which is expensive. As a result they also do a lot of *open repos* at rates slightly above the overnight rate. Open or demand repos have an indefinite term and either the borrower or the lender can each day choose to terminate the agreement.

Banks prefer to do overnight repos with customers who will permit them to safekeep the securities bought. This saves clearing costs and ensures that the bank will have the securities back at 9:00 A.M. the next day. On repos where the securities are transferred out of the bank, there is always the possibility that the securities will not be delivered back to the bank until 12:00 or 1:00 the next day, which might be too late for the bank to repo them or to make delivery if they had been sold. To make RP as convenient an investment as possible, some banks have minimum balance arrangements with customers, under which any excess deposit balances the customer holds with them are automatically invested in RP. In effect what such a bank is doing is getting around Reg Q and paying the customer interest on any demand deposits he holds in excess of the minimum compensating balance the bank requires him to maintain.

The financing needs that nonbank dealers do not cover in the RP market are met by borrowing from the banks at the dealer loan rate. Even dealers who look primarily to the RP market for financing will use bank loans to finance small pieces they hold in inventory. A typical nonbank dealer commented: "The smallest RP ticket I will write is 2 [million]. On a transaction of less than 2, writing the tickets and making deliveries is not worth the cost and trouble. I can combine small pieces but generally I let such junk just sit at the bank."

In financing, bank dealers have one advantage over nonbank

dealers—they can finance odd pieces they do not RP by directly buying Fed funds in their own name.

While much dealer financing is done using open or very short-term repos, dealers will sometimes finance speculative positions they anticipate holding for some time with term RP, taking in money for 30, 60, or even 90 days.

A DEALER'S BOOK

A dealer who positions in a big way is operating like a banker. He acquires assets of varying types and maturities and incurs liabilities of varying maturities to finance them. And, like a banker, he faces *risks:* credit risks, a rate risk, and a liquidity risk.

Because dealers confine themselves to buying very high-grade paper, as opposed to making loans to LDCs, dealers assume fewer and smaller credit risks than banks do. But, because they borrow so much short-term money and are so highly levered, the rate risk they assume is substantial. This is especially true because the classic way dealers make a bullish bet is not only to buy *more* securities, but also to *extend* to longer maturities where they get more bang for the buck from rate movements. With respect to rate risk, a dealer does have one advantage over a bank. A bank that makes a fixed-rate term loan can't readily sell off that asset in order to cut its losses if rates start to climb. In contrast, a dealer who positions the 8's of '86 has acquired a liquid asset that can always be sold at some price, no matter how bad the market gets.[3] Every dealer, because he is exposed to a large rate risk, is very conscious of the fact that he is running a large *unmatched book.* Moreover he seeks, like a bank, to profit from that mismatch while simultaneously monitoring it to ensure that it does not become so large that it exposes him to *an unacceptable level* of risk. As one dealer noted: "Any guy who can run a large dealer operation on leverage could run a bank, not the esoterica of loans to Zaire, but the nuts and bolts of asset and liability management."

While bankers talk about managing the mismatch in their book, dealers talk about *tail management,* by which they mean the same thing. Dealers also talk about *indices,* where an index is some average of asset and liability maturities that measures in a meaningful way the rate risk to which they are exposed.

One difference between dealers and banks is that there is much more pressure on the dealer to be right, and to be right in the short run. One reason is that dealers mark all of their assets to market on a daily basis and track daily their profit and loss record overall and by instrument. A

[3] The 8's of '86 are a popular and actively traded Treasury note issue that carries an 8 percent coupon and matures in 1986.

second reason is that dealers' annual compensation is tied very closely to performance through bonuses or other devices. As one dealer noted: "If we buy at the wrong moment, we cannot hold a 2-year note, let alone a 10-year bond, to maturity not only because of profit considerations, but also because of the emotional and psychological damage that holding that security and marking it to market would have on the work group. We have to be right on balance, and we don't have the luxury of being able to wait for the long run to prove us right." A bank, in contrast, while it marks its dealer and trading portfolios to market, may or may not track the performance of its investment portfolio daily, and it certainly does not attempt to mark its loans to market. Thus, in managing its overall position, a bank is confronted less frequently than a dealer with the consequences of its actions, and it can brush under the carpet the consequences of ill-conceived plays by lumping their impact on profit in with overall profits instead of isolating them.

INTEREST RATE PREDICTIONS

The key rate in the money market is the Fed funds rate. Because of the role of this rate in determining dealers' cost of carry (the RP rate is usually slightly below the funds rate), the 90-day bill rate settles close to the Fed funds rate, and other short-term rates key off this combination in a fairly predictable way. Thus when a dealer positions, he does so on the basis of a strongly held view with respect to where the Fed is going to peg the Fed funds rate; and *every long position he assumes is, in particular, based on a implicit prediction of how high Fed funds might trade* within the time frame of his investment. In formulating expectations about the funds rate, dealers engage in constant and careful Fed watching of the sort described in Chapter 8.

CONFIDENCE LEVEL IN POSITIONING

Positioning is a form of gambling, and the dealers most skilled in this art attempt first to express their expectations about what might occur in terms of probabilities of various outcomes and second to estimate the payoff or loss that a given strategy would yield if each of these outcomes were to occur. Then on the basis of these numbers, they decide whether to bet and how much to bet.

Probabilists who have theorized about gambling like to talk about a fair gamble or a *fair game*. A fair game is one that, if played repeatedly, will yield the player neither net gains nor losses. For example, suppose a person plays the following game: A coin is flipped; if it lands heads up, he wins $1; if it lands heads down, he loses $1. The probability that the coin will land heads up is ½. So half the time he bets our player will lose

$1; half the time he will win $1; and his *expected winnings* or *return,* if he plays the game repeatedly, is *zero.*

There is nothing in it for a dealer to make a fair bet. What he looks for is a situation in which expected return is *positive;* and the more positive it is, the more he will bet. For example, if a dealer believed: (1) that the probabilities that the Fed would ease and tighten were 60 percent and 40 percent, respectively, and (2) that a given long position would return him $2 if the Fed eased and would cause him to lose $1 if the Fed tightened, then his *expected* winnings would be

$$0.6 \times \$2 - 0.4 \times \$1 = \$0.80$$

In other words, the gamble is such that, if the dealer made it ten times, his expected winnings would be $8. That degree of favorableness in the bet might suffice to induce the dealer to position.

If the game were made still more favorable, for example by an improvement in the odds, then he would gamble still more. For example, if the dealer believed: (1) that the probabilities that the Fed would ease and tighten were 70 percent and 30 percent, respectively, and (2) that a given long position would again return him $2 if the Fed eased and lose him $1 if the Fed tightened, then his expected winnings would be

$$0.7 \times \$2 - 0.3 \times \$1 = \$1.10$$

In other words, the gamble is such that, if he made it ten times, his expected winnings would be $11. That's the sort of gamble that might cause the dealer to pull up the delivery trucks and position securities in size.

All this may sound a bit theoretical, but it is the way good dealers think, explicitly or intuitively; and such thinking disciplines them in positioning. As one dealer noted: "The alternative is a sloppy operation in which a dealer runs up his position because he sort of likes the market now or runs it down because he doesn't like the market."

Quantifying his thinking about the market also helps a dealer provide retail with useful suggestions. Most customers can find fair bets on their own. What they appreciate is a dealer who can suggest to them a favorable bet, that is, one on which the odds are out of synchronization with the payoff, and the expected return is therefore positive.[4]

---

[4] To keep things simple we assumed in our examples that only two interest rate outcome were possible. More might be, each with its own associated payoff. Let p_1 equal the probability of the first interest rate outcome and x_1 the associated payoff; p_2 the probability of the second interest rate outcome and x_2 the associated payoff; etc. Then the expected return or value (*EV*) on a bet in which it is assumed that the Fed might peg Fed funds at any one of three possible levels would be:

$$EV = p_1 x_1 + p_2 x_2 + p_3 x_3$$

Using this approach, one can easily generalize the technique to any number of possible outcomes.

In quantifying expectations and payoffs and acting on them, fleet-footedness is of the essence. Everyone on the street is playing the same game, and the market therefore frequently anticipates what the Fed is going to do. Thus the dealer who waits until the Fed is ready to move will probably be too late to make money, the market having already discounted much or all of that move.

THE MATURITY CHOICE

We suggested above that the more favorable the gamble a dealer is faced with, the more securities he's likely to position. And this is precisely the way dealers talk about what they do; specifically, dealers frequently comment: "The higher our *confidence level,* the more we will position." Translated into the jargon we've used, this means simply that the higher the probability associated with gain and the lower that associated with loss (that is, the higher the expected return), the more the dealer will bet.

There is, however, one more wrinkle to the dealer's positioning decision. As noted, a classic part of a bullish strategy is for a dealer to extend to longer maturities. The reason he is tempted to extend is that the longer the maturity of the securities he positions, the more price play he will get. To illustrate, suppose that a dealer believes that the probability that the Fed funds rate will fall by ¼ is 70 percent and the probability it will rise by ¼ is 30 percent. If the dealer positions the 90-day bill, which has a yield that is likely to move roughly as many basis points as the Fed funds rate does, he will be making a bet on which his potential gains and losses per $1 million of securities positioned are a little over $600. If alternatively—to make the example extreme—he invests in the 8's of '86, his potential gains and losses will be in the range of $2,000 per $1 million even if a ¼-point move in the Fed funds rate is assumed to move the yield on these securities only 4 basis points. Whether he positions 90-day bills or the 8's of '86, the dealer is making a favorable bet. However, positioning the 8's of '86 is a much *riskier* proposition than positioning the 90-day bill because, if rates rise, the dealer will lose much more owning the 8's of '86 than he will owning the 90-day bill.

Dealers are very conscious that extending to longer maturities exposes them to greater *price risk.* They also tend to think that extending to longer maturities exposes them to greater risk for another reason: namely, the predictability of long-term rates is less than that of short-term rates. Short rates relate directly to Fed policy; long rates do so to a much lesser extent because they are also strongly influenced by the *slope* of the yield curve. Thus the dealer who extends must be prepared not only to predict wiggles in Fed policy, something most money market specialists feel confident they can do correctly 50+ percent of the time, but also to predict shifts in the slope of the yield curve—an art that is separate from and, in the eyes of many dealers, more difficult than successful Fed watching.

To protect against the risks posed by extending maturity, some dealers confine their unhedged positions largely to securities of short current maturity. A dealer typical of this group noted: "We are accused of being an inch wide and a mile deep—the mile deep being in securities with a maturity of a year and under. There are various arts in this business: predicting spreads, predicting the yield curve, predicting the trend in interest rates. You go with the learning curve of the organization you have, and ours is very strong in predicting short-term spreads and yields."

Other dealers are more willing to extend maturity to reach for gains, but in doing so they seek to control carefully the price risk they assume. The guidelines used to control price risk—frequently they take the form of smaller position limits on longer maturities—vary considerably from shop to shop. One reason is that there is no objective way a dealer can compare the risk he assumes in holding 6-year notes to that he assumes in holding 6-month bills. Another is that in establishing position limits by instrument and maturity, a dealer is inevitably making subjective judgments about the ability of each of his traders.

Shorting

When money market dealers are bullish, they place their bets by positioning securities; when they are bearish, they do so by shorting. One might expect that the quantity of securities a dealer would short, if he believed that the probability of a fall in securities prices was 80 percent, would be as great as the quantity of securities he would position if he believed that the probability of a rise in securities prices was 80 percent. But in fact dealers will, at a given confidence level, short smaller amounts of securities than they would position. There are several reasons for this. First, the only instruments dealers can short are governments and agencies; other instruments such as commercial paper, BAs, and CDs are too heterogeneous with respect to name, maturity, and face amount to short. Second, shorting securities tends to be more cumbersome and expensive than going long because the short seller has to find not only a buyer, but also—since the shorted securities must be delivered—a source of these securities.

In recent years it has become increasingly common for dealers to *reverse in* securities shorted rather than to borrow them. One reason is that the reverse may be cheaper. When a dealer borrows securities, he gives up other securities as collateral and pays the lender a borrowing fee, which typically equals ½ of 1 percentage point but may be a bit more if many people want to go short at once. On a reverse the dealer obtains the securities shorted by buying them from an investor with an agreement to repurchase. In effect the dealer is extending a collateralized loan to the owner of these securities. The owner takes the loan because he needs cash or, more typically, because he can reinvest the loan proceeds at a higher rate, and the reverse thus becomes to him part of a profitable arbitrage.

Whether a dealer borrows securities or reverses them in, he has to make an *investment*—in the first case in collateral, in the second case in a loan to the institution on the other side of the reverse. To figure which investment would yield more, he compares the rate he could earn on the collateral *minus* the borrowing fee with the reverse rate. For example, suppose a dealer has some short-dated paper yielding 5.25 percent he could use as collateral. If he did so, he would own that paper at 5.25 percent minus the 0.5 percent borrowing fee, that is, at an effective rate of 4.75 percent. If the reverse rate were 4.90 percent, he would do better on the reverse.

A dealer's overall cost on a short is (1) the interest that accrues on the securities shorted (rise in value in the case of a discount security) over the period the short is outstanding, *minus* (2) the yield on the offsetting investment he makes. If the reverse rate exceeds the net rate he could earn on collateral backing a borrowing, reversing will be the cheaper way to support his short.

A dealer who borrows securities to support a short can never know with certainty how long he can have those securities because borrowed securities can be called by the lender on a day's notice. If, alternatively, a dealer reverses in securities for some fixed period, he knows he will have the securities for that time. Thus a dealer who anticipates maintaining a short for some time may choose to cover through a reverse rather than a borrowing not only because the reverse is cheaper, but also because it offers him certainty of availability.

In this respect it should be mentioned that a dealer can borrow securities from the Fed. He is supposed to do so only when he can't make delivery on securities he has sold because he has been *failed to;* that is, because the firm from which he bought the securities he has sold failed to deliver them to him. Dealers who experience difficulty covering a short sometimes stretch a point and borrow the securities shorted from the Fed. However, the Fed's borrowing rate, which increases sharply the longer the borrowing is maintained, is higher than anyone else's, so dealers view borrowing securities from the Fed as a last resort.

RP and reverse book

A large dealer who is known to the street can borrow more in the repo market and at better rates than can a small dealer or a corporate portfolio

manager. Thus a large dealer finds knocking at his doors not only customers who want to give him repo money, but also would-be borrowers
who want to reverse out securities to him because that is the cheapest
way they can borrow. In response to the latter demand, large dealers
have taken to doing repo and reverse not just to suit their own needs but
also as a profit-making service to customers. In providing that service,
the dealer takes in securities on one side at one rate and hangs them
out on the other side at a slightly more favorable (lower) rate; or to put it
the other way around, the dealer borrows money from his repo customers
at one rate and lends it to his reverse customers at a slightly higher rate.
In doing so, the dealer is of course acting like a bank. And dealers know
this well. As one noted: "This shop *is* a bank. We have customers lining
up every morning to give us money. Also we are in the business of
finding people who will give us securities at a little better rate than we
can push them out the repo door. So we are a bank taking out our little
spread, acting—if you will—as a financial intermediary."

A dealer who seeks to profit by borrowing in the repo market and
lending in the reverse market ends up in effect running a *book* in repo.
And, like a bank, he can mismatch that book to increase his profit, that is,
borrow short and lend long. A dealer who runs a short book in RP incurs
not only a rate risk, but other risks as well. What these risks are and how
different shops seek to control them is a topic left to Chapter 12, where
we examine the repo and reverse markets in detail.

STRATEGIES TO EARN POSITION PROFITS

We have said so far that a dealer will position if he is bullish, that he
will short securities if he is bearish, and that—when he is bullish—risk
will be a determining factor in his decision on how to allocate his overall
long position between securities of different maturities. There are some
important subtleties to be added. Let's turn first to *tails*.

Figuring the tail

As noted, dealers sometimes finance securities they position with
term RP, for example, finance with 30-day RP a security with 3 months to
run. Whenever they do so, they are creating a future security and betting
that they can sell it at a profit. In judging the attractiveness of this bet,
dealers always rely on an explicit prediction of where funds will trade
and what yields spreads will prevail at the time the term RP comes off.

The easiest way to explain what is involved is with an example. Assume a dealer is operating in an environment in which the 90-day bill is
trading at a rate ⅛ below the Fed funds rate. Assume also that Fed funds
are trading at 4⅞, the 90-day bill at 4¾, and 30-day term RP at 4½.

If in this environment the dealer were to buy a 90-day bill and finance it with 30-day term RP, he would earn over the 30-day holding period a positive carry equal to

$$4\tfrac{3}{4} - 4\tfrac{1}{2}$$

or a profit equal to ¼ over 30 days. He would also have created a *future* 60-day bill, namely, the unfinanced *tail* of the 90-day bill purchased.

If he thought, as dealers do, of the carry profit over the initial holding period as raising the yield at which he in effect buys the future security, then by purchasing the 90-day bill at 4¾ and RPing it for 30 days at 4½, he would have acquired a future 60-day bill at a yield of 4⅞.[5] The ¼ carry, which is earned for 30 days, adds only ⅛ to the yield at which the future security is effectively purchased because the latter has a maturity of 60 days, which is twice as long as the period over which positive carry is earned.

Faced with this opportunity the dealer would ask himself: How attractive is it to contract to buy a 60-day bill at 4⅞ for delivery 30 days hence? Note the dealer would precisely break even, clearing costs ignored, if he were able to sell that future bill at a rate of 4⅞. Thus, contracting to buy the future bill will be attractive if he believes he can sell the future bill at a rate lower than 4⅞.

The dealer's answer to the question he has posed might run as follows: Currently the yield curve is such that 60-day bills are trading ⅛ below the rate on 90-day bills. Therefore, if the 60-day bill were to trade at 4⅞ 1 month hence and if yield spreads did not change, that would imply that the 90-day bill was trading at 5 and Fed funds at 5⅛, that is, at a level ¼ above the present rate. I do not believe that the Fed will tighten or that yield spreads will change in an unfavorable way, therefore I will do the trade.

If the dealer were correct and the Fed did not tighten and yield spreads did not change, he would be able to sell 30 days hence the future 60-day bill he had created at 4⅝, which is the rate that would be the prevailing rate at that time on the 60-day bill, if his predictions with respect to yield and yields spread were correct.[6] In doing so, he would make a profit equal to ¼ (the purchase rate 4⅞ minus the sale rate 4⅝) on a 60-day security.

Of course, the dealer's predictions might prove to be too favorable. Note, however, he has some built-in margin of protection. Specifically, if he is able to sell his future bills at any rate above 4⅝ but still below 4⅞,

---

[5] Note that the *higher* the yield at which a discount security is purchased, the *lower* the purchase price. So buying the future security at 4⅞ is, from the dealer's point of view, better than buying it at 4¾.

[6] Recall the 60-day bill was assumed to be trading at a rate ⅛ below the rate on the 90-day bill, at 4¾ − ⅛ = 4⅝.

he will make some profit, albeit less than he would if he sold at 4⅝. If, on the other hand, rates or rate spreads move so unfavorably that he ends up selling his future 60-day bill at a rate above 4⅞, he will suffer a loss.

For the benefit of those who like to look at dollar numbers rather than yields, we have reworked the example just presented in dollars in Table 9–1. Recall the 60-day bill was assumed to be trading at a rate ⅛ below the rate on the 90-day bill, at 4¾ − ⅛ or 4⅝.

In deciding whether to buy securities and finance them for some period, dealers invariably "figure the tail," that is, determine the effective yield at which they are buying the future security created. Whether the security financed is a discount security or an interest-bearing one, this yield can be figured approximately but quite accurately as follows:

$$
\begin{pmatrix} \text{Effective yield} \\ \text{at which future} \\ \text{security is} \\ \text{purchased} \end{pmatrix} = \begin{pmatrix} \text{Yield at} \\ \text{which cash} \\ \text{security is} \\ \text{purchased} \end{pmatrix} \times \frac{\begin{pmatrix} \text{Rate of} \\ \text{profit} \\ \text{on carry} \end{pmatrix} \times \begin{pmatrix} \text{Days} \\ \text{carried} \end{pmatrix}}{\begin{pmatrix} \text{Days left to maturity} \\ \text{at end of carry period} \end{pmatrix}}
$$

Applying this formula to our example, we get:

$$
4¾ + \frac{¼ \times 30}{60} = 4¾ + ⅛ = 4⅞
$$

Risk. A dealer who engages in the sort of transaction we have just described incurs a rate risk. He might end up with a loss or a smaller profit than anticipated because the Fed tightened when he did not expect it to; because bill rates rose relative to the Fed funds rate due to, say, heavy bill sales by the Treasury; and/or because a shift in the yield curve narrowed the spread between 60- and 90-day bills. Thus whether a dealer who thinks such a transaction would be profitable actually decides to take the position and the size in which he takes it will depend both on the level of confidence he has in his rate and spread predictions and the magnitude of the risk to which he thinks it would expose him.

The same sort of transaction could also be done in other securities: BAs, commercial paper, or CDs. In each case the yield spreads that would have to be estimated would differ from those estimated in our T bill example. If the instrument purchased and financed were CDs, the risk would be perceptibly greater than if the instrument were bills, because supply is more difficult to predict in the CD market than in the bill market, and CDs back up faster than bills.

One way a dealer can and sometimes does reduce the risk associated with a future security he creates by putting a security he owns out on term RP is by selling bill futures as a hedge. How this works and how good the hedge is are topics we take up in Chapter 14.

Table 9–1
Figuring the tail: An example*

Step 1: The dealer buys $1 million of 90-day bills at a 4¾% rate of discount.

$$\text{Discount at which bills are purchased} = \frac{d \times t}{360} \times F = \frac{0.0475 \times 90}{360} \times \$1,000,000$$
$$= \$11,875$$

$$\text{Price at which bills are purchased} = F - D = \$1,000,000 - \$11,875$$
$$= \$988,125$$

The dealer finances the bills purchased for 30 days at 4½%.

$$\text{Financing cost}\dagger = \frac{0.045 \times 30}{360} \times \$1,000,000$$
$$= \$3,750$$

Step 2: At the end of 30 days the dealer owns the bills at a net cost figure. Determine what yield this cost figure implies on the future 60-day bills created.

$$\text{Net cost of future 60-day bills} = \text{Purchase price} + \text{Financing cost}$$
$$= \$988,125 + \$3,750$$
$$= \$991,875$$

$$\text{Net discount at which future 60-day bills are owned} = F - \text{Net cost}$$
$$= \$1,000,000 - \$991,875$$
$$= \$8,125$$

$$\text{Rate at which future 60-day bills are purchased}\ddagger = \frac{360 \times D}{t \times F} = \frac{360 \times \$8,125}{60 \times \$1,000,000}$$
$$= 0.04875$$
$$= 4\tfrac{7}{8}\%$$

Step 3: Future 60-day bills created are sold at a 4⅝% discount rate. Calculate dollar profit.

$$\text{Discount at which bills are sold} = \frac{d \times t}{360} = F$$
$$= \frac{0.04625 \times 60}{360} \times \$1,000,000$$
$$= \$7,708$$

$$\text{Profit} = \textit{Net} \text{ purchase discount} - \text{Discount at sale}$$
$$= \$8,125 - \$7,708$$
$$= \$417$$

Step 4: Figure the annualized yield on a bank discount basis that $417 represents on a 60-day security.

$$d = \frac{360 \times D}{t \times F} = \frac{360 \times \$417}{60 \times \$1,000,000}$$
$$= 0.0025$$
$$= \tfrac{1}{4}\%$$

---

* For explanation of formulas used, see pages 37–38.

† Actually less than $1 million has to be borrowed, so the dealer's approach to figuring the tail is only an approximation, but it is a close one.

‡ Solving the equation

$$D = F \left(\frac{d \times t}{360} \right)$$

for *d*, gives us

$$d = \frac{360 \times D}{t \times F}$$

Relative value

Every rational investor is interested in risk, liquidity, and return. Specifically he wants maximum return, maximum liquidity, and minimum risk. When he goes shopping for securities, however, he finds that the real world presents him with nothing but trade-offs between these properties. Securities offering higher rates of returns tend to be riskier and/or less liquid than securities offering lower rates of return. This is as true in the money market as elsewhere, and it is the reason money market dealers think first of relative value when they decide to position.

If the spread at which one security is trading relative to another is more than adequate to compensate for the fact that the higher-yield security is riskier and/or less liquid than the lower-yield security, the higher-yield security has greater relative value and should be positioned in preference to the lower-yield security. If alternatively the spread is inadequate, then the lower-yield security has greater relative value and should be positioned in preference to the higher-yield security. Clearly when dealers talk about relative value, they are really talking about credit risk management and liquidity management.

Just how relative value considerations affect a dealer's decisions as to what to position was illustrated rather nicely by one dealer: "When we are all bullish, my bill trader, my CD trader, and my BA trader all want to take on stuff and my reverse trader wants to take on 90-day collateral. At that point we have to sit down and get our heads together about relative value theory. Say we want to position $100 million in 6 months and under. Our most obvious options are CDs and bills. If, because of unusual supply conditions in the CD market, CDs are trading at a narrow spread—8 basis points—to bills, we are not going to buy CDs. Now picture a slightly different situation. Loans are not increasing at major New York banks and additionally CDs are trading in the 6-month area 35 basis points off bills. We expect market rates to fall, and we also expect the spread between CDs and bills to narrow. In this situation CDs have greater relative value, so we will buy some. *But* putting all our eggs in one basket might be terribly unwise because we can only make an intelligent guess about supply in the CD market. Morgan might do a large Euro loan and fund the first 6 months with domestic CDs. If so, bing, we get knocked out of the water. We do not get the price action we expected out of the CD market even though the market as a whole rallies. Because that's possible, we might go 60 percent CDs and 40 percent bills—hedge our bets by diversifying. That way we will not miss the entire flip. I have seen it happen on numerous occasions, when we have done half bills and half CDs, that bills rallied 15 basis points—a nice flip we had anticipated—and CDs just sat there like a rock."

Relative value considerations arise not only in choices between different instruments but also in choices between different maturity sectors of the same market. A dealer might ask whether he should position 6-month or 1-year bills. If the yield curve were unusually steep out to 1 year, and the dealer expected it to flatten, then the year bill would have more relative value than the 6-month bill.

Relative value analysis, besides guiding a dealer in his decisions about what securities to position or short, is also useful for generating business with customers, and dealers use it that way constantly. To take an example, suppose BAs and bills in a given maturity range are normally spread 5 basis points. The spread is now 20 basis points, which more than compensates for the extra risk and lesser liquidity of the BAs. Moreover the dealer anticipates that the spread at which BAs trade to bills will narrow. Then the BAs have greater relative value than the bills, and by pointing this out to retail customers holding bills, the dealer could probably induce some of them to *swap* for a yield pickup out of their bills into BAs (to sell their bills and buy BAs).

ARBITRAGES

Strictly defined, the term *arbitrage* means to buy at a low price in one market and simultaneously resell at a higher price in another market. Some arbitrages in this strict sense do occur in the money market. For example, when a Canadian agency bank accepts an overnight Eurodollar deposit from a U.S. corporation and resells the funds at ⅛ markup in the Fed funds market, it is (besides offering the corporation backdoor entry to the funds market) also engaging in arbitrage in the strict sense of the term. So too are U.S. and foreign banks that engage in weekend arbitrage between Fed funds and Euros.[7] Still another example of pure arbitrage would be a dealer who takes in collateral on a reverse for a fixed period and RPs it at a lower rate for precisely the same period, that is, a matched transaction in repo.

Money market participants use the term *arbitrage* to refer not only to such pure arbitrages, but also to various transactions in which they seek to profit by *exploiting anomalies* either in the yield curve or in the pattern of rates established between different instruments. Typically the anomaly is that the yield spread between two similar instruments is too wide or too narrow; that is, one instrument is priced too generously relative to the other. To exploit such an anomaly, the arbitrager *shorts* the expensive instrument and goes *long* in its underpriced cousin; in other words, he shorts the instrument that has an abnormally low yield relative to the yield on the instrument in which he goes long.

If the arbitrager is successful, he will be able to unwind his arbitrage at a profit because the abnormal yield spread will have narrowed in one

---

[7] Such arbitrage is described in Chapter 17.

of several ways: (1) the security shorted will have fallen in price and risen in yield, (2) the security purchased will have risen in price and fallen in yield, or (3) a combination of the two will have occurred.

In the money market, yield spread arbitrages are often done (1) between identical instruments of similar maturity (one government is priced too generously relative to another government of similar maturity) and (2) between different instruments of the same maturity (an agency issue is priced too generously relative to a government issue of the same maturity).

Note that in a strictly defined yield spread arbitrage (the long and the short positions in similar maturities), the arbitrager exposes himself to *no market risk.* If rates rise, the resulting loss on his long position will be offset by profits on his short position; if rates fall, the reverse will occur. Thus the arbitrager is not basing his position on a prediction of the direction of market rates, and he is concerned about a possible move up or down in interest rates only insofar as such a move might alter yields spreads in the money market.

An arbitrage in the purest sense of the term involves *no* risk of any sort since the sale and purchase are assumed to occur simultaneously or almost so. An arbitrage based on a yield spread anomaly involves, as noted, no market risk. But it does involve risk of another sort; the arbitrager is in effect speculating on yield spreads. If he bets that a given spread will narrow and it in fact widens, he will lose money. Thus, even a strictly defined yield spread arbitrage offers no locked-in profit.

Most money market dealers, with the exception of commercial paper and muni note dealers, are active players of the arbitrage game. They have stored in a computer all sorts of information on historical yield spreads and have programmed the computer to identify anomalies in prevailing spreads as they feed data on current yields into it. Dealers use the resulting "helpful hints to the arbitrager" both to set up arbitrages themselves and to advise clients of profitable arbitrage opportunities.

Generally in a dealer shop arbitrage is done in an account that is separate from the *naked trading* account. The reason is that arbitrage and naked trading are distinctly different lines of business. The trader who seeks to profit from a naked position long or short is a specialist in one narrow sector of the money market, and the positions he assumes are based on a prediction of interest rate trends and how they are likely to affect yields in his particular sector of the market. The arbitrager, in contrast, has to track yields in a number of market sectors, and if he engages in strictly defined yield spread arbitrage, he is not much concerned with whether rates are likely to rise or fall.

Anomalies in yield spreads that offer opportunities for profitable arbitrage arise due to various temporary aberrations in market demand or supply. For example, if the Treasury brings a big 4-year note issue to market, it might trade for a time at a higher rate than surrounding issues because investors were loath to take the capital gains or losses they would have to in order to swap into the new issue. In this case the cause of the out-of-line yield spread would be, for the time it persisted, that the new issue had not been fully distributed. Alternatively, an anomaly might be created by a particular issue being in extremely scarce supply.

Example of an arbitrage

Here's an example of an arbitrage *along the yield curve* based on supply conditions. The Treasury, as noted in Chapter 7, markets a new 2-year note at the end of each month. In contrast it offers 3-year notes only in connection with quarterly financings; thus a new 3-year note comes to market at most once a quarter.

In late January 1978, the yield curve in the 2- to 3-year area was relatively flat, partly because the Treasury had not offered a new 3-year note for 3 months. The market anticipated, however, that the Treasury would include a 3-year note in its February financing and that this new offering would widen yield spreads in the 2- to 3-year area. Thus buying the current 2-year note and shorting the current 3-year note appeared to be an attractive arbitrage.

Here's how one dealer did this arbitrage. On January 30, for settlement on January 31, he bought the current 2-year note, 7 1/2N 1/31/80, at a yield to maturity of 7:44. At the same time he shorted the current 3-year note, 7 1/8N 11/15/80, at a yield to maturity of 7.51.

The current 2-year note was trading at a dollar price of 100 − 3 +, and the yield value of $1/32$ on it was 0.0171.[8] The current 3-year note was trading at a dollar price of 99 − 1, and the yield value of $1/32$ on it was 0.0127. The smaller yield value of $1/32$ on the 3-year note meant that, for a given movement up or down in interest rates, the 3-year note would move 135 percent as far up or down in price as the 2-year note would.[9] This in turn meant that, if the arbitrage were established on a dollar-for-dollar basis, that is, if the amount of 3-year notes shorted equaled the amount of 2-year notes purchased, the arbitrage would expose the dealer to market risk. In particular, if rates should fall while the arbitrage was on, the dealer would lose more on his short position in the 3-year note than he would gain on his long position in the 2-year note. To minimize market risk, the dealer set the arbitrage in a *ratio* based upon the yield values of $1/32$ on the two securities. Note that this procedure insulated the arbitrage

---

[8] The + in the quote equals $1/64$.

[9] The calculation is

$$\frac{0.0171}{0.0127} = 135\%$$

against general movements up or down in yields but not against a relative movement between yields on the two securities.

Table 9–2 shows precisely how the arbitrage worked out. The dealer bought for January 31 settlement $1.35 million of the current 2-year note and financed these securities by RPing them at 6.65 percent. Simultaneously he reversed in $1 million of the 3-year note at the lower 6.20 reverse repo rate and sold them. Sixteen days later, when the Treasury was offering a new 3-year note in connection with its February financing, the dealer was able to unwind his arbitrage, which he put on at a *7-basis-point* spread, at a *9-basis-point* spread (Step 2, Table 9–2). The dealer's total return on the arbitrage was, as Step 3 in Table 9–2 shows, $375 per $1 million of securities arbitraged.

On an arbitrage of this sort, risk is limited to the spread relationship, so the size in which dealers do such arbitrages depends only upon their ability to finance the securities purchased and to borrow the securities shorted. In practice such arbitrages are commonly done for $50 or $100 million.

Risk: The unexpected occurs

When a strictly defined yield spread arbitrage fails to work out, the reason is usually that something unexpected has occurred. Here's an example. On several occasions in the spring of 1977, the old 7-year note and the current 7-year note, whose maturities were only 3 months apart, traded at a 10-basis-point spread. This made no sense since it implied that, at the 7-year level, the appropriate spread between securities differing by 1 year in maturity was 40 basis points—an impossible yield curve. One dealer successfully arbitraged this yield spread three times by shorting the high-yield current note and going long in the old note. On his fourth try the unexpected occurred. In his words: "We stuck our head in the wringer. We put on the 'arb' at 10 basis points and, while we had it on, the Treasury reopened the current 7-year note. That did not destroy the productive nature of the arbitrage but it did increase the time required before it will be possible to close it out at a profit. The costs of shorting the one issue and being long in the other (especially delivery costs on the short side) are high so at some point we will probably have to turn that arbitrage into a loss trade. Had the Treasury reopened some other issue, we would have made $20,000 bang. Instead we're looking at a $40,000 paper loss."

The arbitrage in this example comes close to being a strictly defined yield arbitrage. Many money market arbitrages do not. Dealers will often go long in an issue of one maturity and short another issue of quite different maturity. An arbitrage of this sort resembles a strictly defined yield spread arbitrage in that it is a speculation on a yield spread. But it

Table 9–2
An arbitrage along the yield curve

Step 1: Set up the arbitrage for settlement on January 31, 1978.

   A. *Buy* $1.35 million of the current 2-year note, 7½N 1/31/80, at 100-3 + (7.44 yield).

Principal	$1,351,476
Accrued interest	0
Total purchase price	$1,351,476

   Repo these securities at 6.65.

   B. Reverse in and *sell* $1 million of the current 3-year note, 7⅛N 11/15/80, at 99- 1 (7.51 yield).

Principal	$ 990,312
Accrued interest	15,155
Total sale price	$1,005,467

   Reverse rate 6.20.

Step 2: Unwind the arbitrage for settlement on February 16, 1978.

   A. Sell out the long position in the 2-year note at 99-28 (7.57 yield).

Principal	$1,348,312
Accrued interest	4,475
Total sale price	$1,352,787

   Pay financing cost at 6.65 repo rate for 16 days: $3,994.

   B. Cover the short position in the 3-year note at 98-22 (7.66 yield).

Principal	$ 986,875
Accrued interest	18,304
Total purchase price	$1,005,179

   Receive return on reverse at 6.20 for 16 days: $2,770.

Step 3: Calculate net return on arbitrage:

   Return on short position in the 3-year note:

Sale price	$1,005,467
Purchase price	−1,005,179
Income on reverse	2,770
Total return	$ 3,058

   Return on long position in the 2-year note:

Purchase price	$−1,351,476
Sale price	1,352,787
Cost of repo	− 3,994
Total return	$− 2,683

   Net return on overall arbitrage:

Return on short position	$3,058
Return on long position	−2,683
Net return on the arbitrage	$ 375

is more risky than such an arbitrage, because if interest rates move up or down, the price movement in the longer-maturity security will normally exceed that in the shorter-maturity security; thus the arbitrage exposes the investor who puts it on to a *price risk*.

Dealers are not unaware of this, and they attempt to offset the inherent price risk in an arbitrage involving securities of different maturities by adjusting the sizes of the two sides of the arbitrage, as in the arbitrage example above. If for instance the arbitrage involves shorting the 2-year note and buying the 7-year note, the arbitrager will short more notes than he buys. Such a strategy, however, cannot completely eliminate market risk; a movement in interest rates may be accompanied by a change in the slope of the yield curve, and the difference in the price movements the two issues would undergo if interest rates changed can therefore only be estimated.

Bull and *bear market arbitrages* are based on a view of where interest rates are going. A bull market arbitrager anticipates a fall in interest rates and a rise in securities prices. Thus he might, for example, short 2-year Treasuries and go long in 10-year Treasuries on a one-for-one basis, hoping to profit when rates fall from the long coupon appreciating more than the short coupon. If alternatively the arbitrager were bearish, he would do the reverse: short long governments and buy short ones.

An arbitrage can also be set up to profit from an anticipated change in the slope of the yield curve. For example, an arbitrager who anticipated a flattening of the yield curve might buy notes in the 7-year area for high yield and short notes in the 2-year area, not necessarily on a one-to-one basis. If the yield curve flattened with no change in average rate levels, the 7-year note would appreciate, the 2-year note would decline in price, and the arbitrage could be closed out at a profit.

One sort of arbitrage that has developed since the opening of the Treasury bill futures market is between bill futures and cash notes and bills. That's a topic we'll get to in Chapter 14.

Money market practitioners are wont to call any pair of long and short positions an arbitrage, but it is clear that as the maturities of the securities involved in the transaction get further and further apart, price risk increases, and at some point the "arbitrage" becomes in reality two separate speculative positions, one a naked long and the other a naked short.

Money market arbitragers normally put on both sides of an arbitrage simultaneously, but they rarely take them off simultaneously. As one dealer noted: "The compulsion to *lift a leg* [unwind one side of an arbitrage before the other] is overwhelming. Hardly anyone ever has the discipline to unwind both sides simultaneously. Instead they will first unwind the side that makes the most sense against the market. If, for example, the trader thinks the market is going to do better, he will lift a leg by covering the short."

Support personnel play an important part in any arbitrage operation. As one dealer noted: "The one thing in an arbitrage account that can force a paper loss to become a realized loss is if you lose control of your ability to support your short side. You don't want your traders worrying about when securities are due back, so you need someone else who assumes responsibility for making sure that people doing RP and reverse keep the needed supply of securities you have shorted on hand."

Money market dealers seek out promising arbitrage opportunities not only because they can profit from them in their own trading, but also because arbitrage suggestions passed on to customers are a source of customer business. As one dealer commented: "We're in a competitive business, and the customer looks for the guys with the best ideas and information. If we supply them, he trades with us."

One of the shops that has gone furthest in providing suggestions of and information on possible arbitrages is Carroll McEntee & McGinley. Its computer, into which current market prices are inputted several times a day, is programmed to seek out promising arbitrages, which are then transmitted on special pages of Telerate.[10] A subscriber to the service can request and get within two minutes a matrix of projections as to how any arbitrage he proposes would work out if interest rates levels and/or the shape of the yield curve were to change. The possibilities with respect to the kinds of information and analysis the system might provide are limitless, and it is constantly being expanded.

The persistence with which dealers and their customers arbitrage every out-of-line yield spread they find has an important impact on the money market; it ensures that spreads relationships never get far out of line or, to put it another way, that the differences in the yields on instruments of different types and maturities mirror quite consistently differences in the relative values of these instruments.

Given all the arbitrage on the street, the question arises: How can there be anything left to arbitrage? The answer seems to be that opportunities continue to exist partly because of the constantly increasing size of the market and partly because of the constant entry of new investors, not all of whom are sophisticated players. As would be expected, opportunities for arbitrage increase noticeably whenever the market becomes volatile.

Hedges

A dealer in long coupons exposes himself to a sizable price risk every time he goes long or short. Yet in the course of servicing customer buy and sell orders, he inevitably has to do so. Frequently if a trader in such securities has no particular view on where the market is going and does

---

[10] Telerate is a market information system described later in this chapter.

not want to take on any additional price risk, he will hedge any position put on his book by customer business. For example, if a customer sells him $1 million of thinly traded long bonds, he will short a nearby issue until he can unwind both his long and short positions at what he considers reasonable prices.

A trader wishing to hedge a security that he has in position must always be careful, in establishing his hedge, to use a security that is comparable in all respects. An example of what can happen when a noncomparable security is used was provided by a trader who bought flower bonds and sold Treasuries of comparable maturity against them. When the tax law was changed that exempted the capital gain earned on flower bonds used to pay estate taxes, this trader lost 6 points overnight on each "hedged" bond he owned.

RUNNING A DEALER OPERATION

We have talked a lot about how money market "dealers" operate, but a dealership, of course, consists of many people. At its heart are a manager, who is invariably a highly savvy street person, a group of specialized traders, and a sales force that contacts retail.

The manager (or managers—in large firms responsibility is layered) has various responsibilities. First, he has to establish guidelines to limit the total risk the firm assumes at any one time. Second, it is his responsibility to develop a forecast of short-term interest rates—using inputs from his resident Fed watcher, his traders, and retail. Then he must decide, based on the level of confidence he has in that forecast, whether his firm should make a market play, how big that play should be within the firm's position limits, and the instruments and maturity range in which it should be made.

In implementing such decisions the manager faces a delicate task. If he wants good traders, he has to give them some freedom, but he can't give them so much that he loses control over the size and composition of the firm's position. One manager described the problem well: "Every trader is entitled to trade his markets, to have a certain degree of free hand. Traders are big boys. Sometimes, however, I find, much to my dismay, that our bill futures trader is short, our bill trader long, our CD trader even to a little long, and our coupon trader short. Thanks to the grace of God, it often all works out because our traders know their markets and the technicals in them. But, when we are making a major position play, my allowance for each trader doing his own thing in his own market does not hold. If I were to let our traders run up the firm's position to the point where we were $500 million long in some instruments and equally short in others, the firm would be taking a lot of risk and running up expenses to earn nothing."

The traders

Because there are so many types of money market instruments, because they trade so differently, and because they vary so in maturity, money market dealers all have a bevy of traders, each trading a single *narrow* sector of the market such as short bills, 2–4-year notes, CDs, BAs, or short agencies.

Trading on an hour-to-hour, day-to-day basis is a fine art that those with the inherent knack pick up through on-the-firing-line training. A good trader bases every trade he makes on his feel about the levels at which every instrument he deals in ought to be trading. That feel will tell him, for example, that a 6 bid for one instrument is the same as a 13 bid for another, in other words, that he should be *indifferent* between selling one instrument at 6 and the other at 13; also if his market trades at a $2/32$ spread, he should be indifferent between buying the one instrument at 8 and the other at 15. So the trader will quote these two markets, 6–8 and 13–15. If someone hits his bid at 13 and takes his offer at 8, he will, if his indifference levels are correct, have earned $2/32$ and established a position (long in the one security and short in the other) that he can with patience unwind for another $2/32$. The unwinding is, of course, likely to occur one leg at a time. Retail might pick up the securities in which he is long, then he would have to buy something else to keep his *net* book even. And if such *chain trading* caused a maturity gap in his book, he would seek out other trades to close it—tell the sales force to look to buy this one or sell that one. The essence of successful trading is to be able to set correct indifference levels and then keep the position moving—buying here, selling there, and picking up 32nds along the way.

Of course, at times the firm may take a strong view with respect to where interest rates are going and want the trader to run a net long or short position in his book. To establish that position, he will have to be a net buyer or seller, but once he has established the position, trading again becomes calculating indifference levels and trading off them in a fashion that keeps his book where he wants it.

A trader is a highly paid professional whose life is his market. Most traders are young; they have to be since they operate under a lot of pressure, both because of the hectic pace of the market and because the results of what they do get thrown at them daily in the form of a profit and loss statement on their previous day's trades. Most traders are also highly competitive. As one dealer noted: "A trader is the archetype I-will-kill-you player of tennis, backgammon, and other games. He knows this is a killer business, and to him winning is everything—it's his mission in life, and when he wins, he won't even be nice about it."

A trader's job is to work, not to manage. He has to quote markets, write tickets, and make things happen, all the while interjecting his personality into what he is doing. Few traders have any academic training for what they are doing and, in seeking out potential traders, dealers more often eschew than seek out those with such training. Said one dealer of MBAs: "The universities send us a bunch of academically oriented capons who don't know what it is to bitch, sweat, live, and die with positions of hundreds of thousands of dollars. There are a lot of bright guys down here with degrees, and they construct models on the computer of future interest rates, but when Sali's trader says to them, 'The 6-month bill is 29–28, what do you want to do?' they face a whole different class of decision. There may be beneficial sorts of training that could be given them beforehand but there is no possible training for meeting that sort of situation well."

Sales force

There is a lot of variability from dealer to dealer in the size of the sales force and its function. At one extreme are houses that are big in commercial paper and put their sales force to work selling Amco Credit and have them do repo as an afterthought. At the other extreme are the position houses that look to their sales force first as sellers of repo, second as a source of information on how retail is behaving in and views the market, and third as an outlet to retail business when the firm wants it. A few such firms even reward their sale force according to the amount of repo they do, which is fairly unusual.

The level of sophistication among sales personnel varies considerably. It takes little expertise to sell commercial paper to the average corporate treasurer but a lot to deal with some of the sharper players in the market.

In most corporations, running the short-term portfolio is a rookie job, in a scant few it is done by highly paid professionals.[11] The dealers staff accordingly; rookies talk to and advise rookies, and pros talk to pros. Said one dealer: "It works fine hiring a rookie to talk to a rookie. They relate to each other and have a good time. I can't have a hot-shot trader of mine talking to the money trader for some average corporation. They're separated by an unbridgeable cultural gap."

Controls

The topic of personnel brings up a housekeeping detail—controls. There is no way a dealer can protect against fraud (a trader or salesman, for example, selling something to a customer and buying it back if it does not appreciate) except by bonding. He can, however, give his firm

---

[11] See Chapter 10.

protection against traders overstepping their trading authority by having traders confirm all trades on the phone *and* in writing, with the written confirms going at the end of the day to the confirmation or auditing department where they are balanced out. Such controls are standard practice. Still it does happen, albeit infrequently, that a trader oversteps his bounds, perhaps in collusion with someone in the cage, and loses large sums through unsuccessful and unauthorized trading.

THE CONTRAST IN SHOPS

We have noted throughout this chapter the variability that exists between the different money market dealers, a point that's hard to overemphasize. In terms of size, there are at one extreme Merrill Lynch and Salomon Brothers, both with enormous market-making capability and, particularly in the case of Merrill Lynch, with a superb distribution system. At the other extreme are some small highly specialized shops that deal in only a single instrument, BAs or muni notes.

Money market shops also vary tremendously in their attitude toward positioning. Salomon is known for its willingness to take risk, to assume huge positions, and to be prepared to take huge losses. Aubrey Lanston is another house with a reputation for positioning. One dean of the market described it as "a firm willing and able to engage in brilliant and massive speculation in governments when it likes the market and to disappear when it doesn't." Among the banks, there are also players willing to take on huge positions, Morgan in particular. At the opposite extreme, one encounters very customer-oriented firms like Carroll McEntee & McGinley, which was built to service retail (the small portfolio manager as well as the large) and is not a big position house.

Another difference between houses is the maturities that they trade and position. Some houses are equally active in all sectors of the government and corporate securities market. Others feel comfortable taking on positions only in securities of relatively short maturity. Said the manager of one such firm: "What is a long bond worth, 7.80 or 7.90? Who knows? Yet the price difference is enough to wipe you out."

As noted, some dealers are banks and others are nonbank firms. Either has its advantages and disadvantages. Bank dealers can carry municipal securities tax-free, nonbank dealers cannot; also banks have direct access to the Fed funds market for financing. Nonbank dealers, on the other hand, can deal in commercial paper, corporate bonds, and municipal revenue bonds, which banks are forbidden to do by the Glass-Steagall Act.

There are also other more subtle differences between bank and nonbank dealers. Banks are in the business of commercial banking and all else is collateral. Everything they do is designed to serve the customer rather than the bank, and their government bond trading operations are no exception. They were created to serve correspondent banks and the emerging corporate treasurer who was trying to utilize cash balances he had previously held idle. The trading operation in a bank was and is directed predominantly toward customer satisfaction, whereas the nonbank dealer is likely to feel some compulsion to profit on every transaction since he has no other function. Also, whether a bank would admit it or not, it makes better markets to its best banking customers than it does to strangers. There is, however, a counterpart to this among the nonbank dealers. A dealer that is also a big investment banking house is not going to hold at arms' length in its dealer operation a huge corporation that is one of its prime investment banking customers. Corporate finance is to investment banking firms what commercial banking is to a bank, only it is not as wide and deep.

Another difference between the bank and nonbank dealers lies in the quality and continuity of personnel. The industry standard in the nonbank dealer shops and even in the bank dealers is that personnel get some form of incentive pay. That pay, which can range at a nonbank dealer from $50,000 to well over $100,000 for a good trader, tends to create a situation in which aggressive, comparatively seasoned, and terribly smart people with a bent for the money market are drained out of the banks, which compensate less generously, and corporations unless they aspire to be a high bank or corporate executive. Big banks and corporations could, of course, afford to pay traders and portfolio managers the same salaries nonbank dealers pay them, but it is hard for them to defend paying somebody who is nowhere on the firm's organization chart the same salary an executive vice president is getting. Because of this, bank trading rooms tend to be a training ground for traders, from which many of the best entrants move on to nonbank shops in search of more money once they have mastered their skill. Some bright bank traders, of course, remain but for them a trading room position, whatever it is, tends to be an interim assignment. In a bank, as in a corporation, good people have to be given room to move up.

THE CLEARING BANKS

We have described at length the role of dealers as market makers in the money market. There are also other institutions that play a vital role in this process—the clearing banks and the brokers. The *clearing banks* clear trades for nonbank dealers in governments, agencies, and other money market instruments. The bank with by far the largest clearing operation is Manufacturers Hanover Trust (*Manny Hanny* or just *Manny* to all who know her). The next largest clearing bank is Irving Trust, followed in importance by Marine Midland. Other banks—Morgan, Chase, and Citi—have also become active in clearing in recent years.

In acting as a clearing agent, a clearing bank makes payments against securities delivered into a dealer's account and receives payments made to the dealer against securities delivered out of its account. It also safekeeps securities received by a dealer and makes payments into and out of the account that the dealer holds with the bank. Finally, a clearing bank provides dealers with any financing they require at its posted *dealer loan rate*.

Clearing, which sounds simple in theory, turns out in practice to be a huge and complex operation because of the tens of thousands of trades and RP transactions that occur daily in the New York market. The vast majority of money market instruments traded in the national money market are payable in New York regardless of where the issuer is located and are safekept in New York regardless of where the investor is located.

Large dealers have a computer-to-computer link-up with their clearing bank. Smaller houses deliver trading tickets by hand to their clearing bank, often the night before clearing if the trade is for regular settlement. As securities are delivered to a clearing bank, the bank matches them up with a dealer's purchase tickets, and payment is made against receipt. When securities go out, the procedure is reversed. Despite all the computerization that has been applied to securities clearing (all governments are delivered and paid for over the Fed wire), a clearing operation still involves a great deal of labor. Manny Hanny has 11 people on the desk handling the Merrill Lynch account alone, and the size of its clearing floor, which is jammed with computer terminals making and receiving messages, rivals that of a football field.

Extending dealer loans is an inherent and important part of a bank's clearing operations. When securities come into a clearing bank for a dealer's account, the banks pay for them whether or not the dealer has funds in its account, and it takes in any payments made to the dealer on security sales. Then at the end of the day, the bank net settles with each dealer. Since payments out of a dealer's account are made against the receipt of securities, and payments in are made against the delivery out of securities, if a dealer ends up net short on cash for the day, he will have bought more securities than he sold, and the bank will have collateral against which to lend to him. Dealer loans are always made on an overnight basis. The collateral is returned to the dealer's account the next morning, and his account is charged for the loan amount plus interest.

Because overnight repo is cheaper than dealer loans, most dealers use dealer loans only to finance odd pieces and securities they hold because they failed on a delivery. There are, however, some dealers who work the RP market less hard than most and use dealer loans regularly. The clearing banks are happy with the relatively small reliance dealers place on dealer loans for their financing; in fact, they tell the dealers not to think of them as a primary supplier of position financing except when they have an excess of cash and call the dealers to tell them they are looking for loans. The reason is that the size of dealer's positions is so huge that these positions could not be financed in toto by the clearing banks or even by the whole New York banking community. Despite the fact that dealers eschew bank financing, dealer loans can reach large proportions. A top clearing bank might lend as much as $400 million to a single dealer and have total dealer loans of as much as $1 billion outstanding overnight.

Normally clearing banks post their dealer loan rate at around 11:00 A.M. It runs ⅛ to ¼ above the Fed funds rate when money is easy and as much as 1 point above Fed funds when money is tight. This rate typically prevails for the rest of the day, but if the level at which Fed funds trade alters sharply, it will be changed on late transactions. This occurs most often on Wednesdays when the banks are settling with the Fed.

Clearing banks attempt to get estimates from the dealers of their anticipated borrowings as early as possible so that they can adjust their Fed funds positions accordingly. A dealer may end up needing much less financing than he anticipated, or significantly more. Thus a clearing bank does not know the full size of its loans to dealers until after the national money market has closed, the Fed wire has closed, and sometimes the bank itself has closed. This causes the major clearing banks no problem in settling with the Fed because they have automated their wire to the Fed and so know their reserve balance instantaneously even if they can't identify as quickly the sources and uses of funds that led to that balance.

If a clearing bank gets hit with big dealer loans late on a Wednesday and Fed funds are very expensive, it may go to the discount window for funds. This is something the Fed understands and the clearing banks probably go to the discount window more often than most banks their size. The clearing banks manage to accommodate the wide fluctuations that occur in their loans to dealers only because they are large banks with big reserve positions and the ability to buy huge and highly variable sums of money in the Fed funds market. A smaller bank without that ability could not function as a major clearing bank.

On dealer loans the clearing banks normally require collateral plus some margin, 2 percent on most short-term instruments and maybe 5 percent on a longer-term instrument, such as a Ginny Mae pass-through. If a dealer ends up with insufficient collateral, the clearing bank still makes all payments due out of his account and gives him an overdraft, for which it charges a rate higher than its normal dealer loan rate.

Clearing banks are not the only banks that provide dealers with overnight money. If other banks happen to find themselves with excess funds, perhaps because they have been hosed with money by correspondent banks that sell them Fed funds, they will call the dealers and offer them dealer loans at an attractive rate. Said one such banker: "We do not finance the dealers on an ongoing basis but, when we do it, we do it at a very nice rate. We are either all the way in or all the way out." For such a bank, making dealer loans is an attractive alternative to selling excess funds in the Fed funds market.

Clearing charges represent an important part of every dealer's costs. Clearing banks used to set their fees on the basis of the par value of the securities cleared. Then, as automation reduced their costs, they switched to a per-ticket pricing structure, and as they did, the net cost of clearing to dealers fell. Fees for clearing vary from one bank to another and also at a given clearing bank they may vary for different dealers. As one dealer noted: "We have a sweetheart relationship with our clearing bank, and whatever the banks may say, such relationships are common."

Fails and the fails game

If, on the settlement date of a trade, a seller does not make timely delivery of the securities purchased, delivers the wrong securities, or fails in some other way to deliver in proper form, the trade becomes a *fail*. In that case the buyer does not have to make payment until proper delivery is made, presumably the next day; *but* he owns the securities as of the initially agreed-upon settlement day. Thus, on a fail the security buyer (who is *failed to*) receives a one-day free loan equal to the amount of the purchase price, that is, one day's free financing. And if the fail persists, the free loan continues. Fails occur not only in connection with straight trades, but also in connection with repos; on a repo the lender has to make timely return of the collateral he is holding in order to unwind the transaction and get his money back.

Dealers often play some portion of their financing needs for a fail; that is, they estimate on the basis of past experience the dollar amount of the fails that will be made to them and reduce their RP borrowing accordingly. If their estimate proves high, more securities will end up in their box at the clearing bank than they had anticipated, and that bank will automatically grant them a box loan against that collateral. On such last-minute loans the clearing banks charge the dealer a rate that's a tiny margin above their posted dealer loan rate in order to encourage dealers to keep track of their positions and run an orderly shop. Note that a dealer who plays the *fails game* is in effect using his clearing bank as a lender of last resort.

THE BROKERS

A broker is a firm that brings buyers and sellers together for a com-mission. Unlike dealers, brokers by definition do not position. Brokers are everywhere in the money market. They are active in the *interdealer* markets in governments, agencies, CDs, bankers' acceptances, repo, and reverse, and in the *interbank* markets for Fed funds and Euro time deposits.

Volume and commissions

The volumes of funds and securities that are brokered each business day are staggering. Unfortunately, because statistics on brokered trades are not collected in most sectors of the market, it is impossible to put precise dollar figures on these amounts. It is possible, however, to give a few suggestive numbers. On an active day one of the top Fed funds brokers, who is in competition with nine other brokers of varying size, may broker over $6 billion of funds! Currently about 70 percent of inter-dealer trades in governments and agencies is done through brokers.

Brokers could not survive without a huge volume of trades because the commissions they receive per $1 million of funds or securities bro-kered are so small. In the bill market, brokerage on 90-day bills works out to $12.50 per $1 million; in the Fed funds market, on overnight trades it's only $0.50 per $1 million. In some sectors of the market (Fed funds and Euros) brokerage is paid by both the buyer and the seller; in others (governments and agencies) it is paid only by the dealer, who initiates a trade by either hitting a bid or taking an offer quoted by the broker.

The service sold

Much of what a broker is selling to his clients is a fast information service that tells the trader where the market is—what bids and offers are and how much they are good for. Speed of communication is thus crucial to a money market broker, and each one has before him a board of direct phone lines through which he can contact each important trader he services by merely punching a button. Over those lines brokers con-stantly collect bids and offers throughout the day. They pass these on to other traders either by direct phone calls or in some cases over display screens, referred to throughout the industry as *CRTs*—short for cathode ray tubes.

In many sectors of the market (governments, Euro time deposits) the broker gives runs: bids and offers for a number of issues or maturities. In others (the market for overnight Fed funds) just one bid and offer are quoted. In some sectors of the market, bids and offers are good until they are withdrawn; in others they are understood to be good for only a few minutes.

The pace at which brokering is done in all sectors of the money market is hectic most of the time and frantic at certain crucial moments—in the Fed funds market on Wednesday afternoon when the banks settle with the Fed in the government market on Thursday afternoon after the Fed announces money supply figures.

Brokerage operations vary a lot in size. Since shops dealing in CDs have a single CD trader, CDs can be brokered by just a couple of people sitting in a small room with a battery of direct phone lines. Brokering governments or Euros takes more personnel because there are many more traders to be covered and many more bids and offers to be quoted. Some brokerage outfits are large because they broker a number of different instruments. A Euro broker, for example, often brokers foreign exchange, and some firms that broker Fed funds also broker a potpourri of other instruments.

A broker has to be not only quick but also *careful,* because he is normally expected to substantiate any bid or offer he quotes. This means that if he quotes a market inaccurately to a trader, he will have to either (1) pay that trader an amount equal to the difference between the price he quoted and the price at which the trade can actually be got off or (2) buy securities from or sell securities to that trader at the quoted price and then cover, typically at a loss, his resulting long or short position.

The ethics of brokering are very strict in all sectors of the money market. In particular, a broker is not supposed to and never will give up the names of the dealers or banks that are bidding or offering through him. He simply quotes prices and size. However, in certain markets, once a bid is hit or an offer taken, names are given up. In the Fed funds market, for example, before the seller can agree to a trade, he must know to whom he is selling because he has to check that he has a line to the buyer and that it is not full. Also the buyer has to know who the seller is because the two institutions clear the transaction directly with each other over the Fed wire. In governments, in contrast, the seller knows who the buyer is and vice versa.

There are also certain rules of ethics that the brokers' clients are expected to observe. In particular, in markets in which names are given up, the customer is not supposed to then go around the broker and do the trade direct. Also, brokers feel it is unfair of a trader to use them as an information service and just do small trades through them. Traders who make a practice of this get to be known and ignored by brokers.

Usefulness of brokers

In recent years brokerage has been introduced to many sectors of the money market in which it previously did not exist; and in those market sectors where it did exist, the use of brokers has increased dramatically. One reason is that the number of dealers in all sectors of the market has expanded sharply; as a result, it has become increasingly difficult for a trader to know where other traders are quoting the market and to rapidly disseminate his own bids and offers other than through the communications network provided by the brokers. In the government market, there are over 35 primary dealers, and no bill trader can possibly keep in touch with his counterparts at other shops by talking to each of them directly.

Another important reason brokers are used is anonymity. A big bank or dealer may operate in such size that simply by bidding or offering, he will affect either market quotes or the size for which they are good. A trader who would be willing to buy $15 million in bills through a broker might, for example, be leery of buying the same amount at the same price from a big position house like Salomon Brothers for fear that Sali might have a lot more of these bills to sell.

A second reason anonymity is valued by traders is the "ego element." In the words of one dealer: "Anonymity is very important to those giant egos on Wall Street. When they make a bad trade, they just do not want the whole world to watch them unwind it at a loss."

Still another reason the brokers are used is because a lot of traders literally hate each other, usually because of some underlying ethical issue, real or perceived. As one trader noted: "There are guys I would not deal with personally, but if it happens through a broker, well OK. Money is green whatever the source."

A final reason brokers are used, particularly in the government market, is that the brokers' screens provide an arena in which a trader can paint pictures and play other trading games.

Personnel

Brokering is much more than quoting rates. As brokers are wont to note, it's a highly professional business. The broker is often required to make split-second decisions about difficult questions. If a trader offers at a price and the broker has x bids at that price on his pad, with which buyer does he cross the trade? Technically he attempts to decide who was there first, but the choice is often complicated by the fact that the offer is for one amount, the bids for others.

Also, in some sectors of the money market, a broker does more than quote rates. The buyer or seller may look to him for information on the tone of the market, and it's the broker's job to sense that tone and be able to communicate it—to say, for example, to a bidder: "The market's $5/16$–$3/8$, last trade at 5, but I think it could be worth $3/8$."

Being a broker is also part salesmanship, to get a buyer or seller who has done one trade to let the broker continue to work for him. This is especially the case in markets, such as those for Fed funds and Euros, where a dealer who does a trade is likely to have a lot more business to do in the same direction during the day. In one area of brokering, the reverse market, salesmanship is crucial. To get a bank or an S&L to reverse out securities, the broker almost always has to point out a profitable arbitrage and then sell the institution on doing that arbitrage.

Being a good broker requires a special mix of talents. As noted, salesmanship is one. In addition, a broker has to be able to listen with one ear on the phone and keep the other tuned to bids and offers coming in around him, to maintain a feel for his own market and for other related markets as well. A good broker also has to be able to think on his feet and often use his own personality to put trades together. As one broker noted: "Brightness is not enough; anyone can quote a market."

Many brokers are ex-traders, people who have the advantage when they come to brokering of knowing a market and how traders operate on it. One reason traders become brokers is the pressure under which traders operate. Another is their own inability to do what many good traders do, forget their position when they go home. Said one successful broker: "Trading is a problem. You track the things you think might impact the market, and then buy. All too often the unexpected—war in the Middle East—happens and you end up being right for the wrong reason, or vice versa. Once as a trader, I was down three-quarters of a million. I made 2 million the next month, but accepting the fact that I had done something stupid at one point in time was too much. It's part of the reason I became a broker."

COMMUNICATIONS

In a discussion of the makers of the money market, ignoring the phone company, Telexes, CRTs, computers, and other communications facilities would be a serious omission. Without Mother Bell and her foreign counterparts, the money market would be an utterly different place. That the money market is a single market that closely approaches the economist's assumption of perfect information is currently due in no small part to the fact that New York brokers and traders are one push of a direct-phone-line button away from the B of A and often only a four-digit extension from London, Singapore, and other distant spots. All this is extremely expensive. Banks are estimated to spend well in excess of $500 million on phone bills; and the nonbank dealers and brokers spend huge amounts in addition to that. To cut costs, the banking industry is currently considering setting up a private interbank phone network, which would be the most ambitious private phone network in the country.

The phone bill is one reason for the concentration of the money market in New York. The brokers in particular have to be there to minimize communications costs. It is cheaper to be in New York with one direct phone line to the B of A than to be in San Francisco with 30 direct lines to New York.

Phones, while ubiquitous, are not enough. Giving and receiving quotes over the phone takes more time than money market participants have, thus the growing role of CRTs.

Only a few years ago the only way money market participants could get current quotes was by calling brokers and dealers. Moreover, to get a range of quotes they had to make several calls because no quote system covered the whole market. In 1968 a new organization, *Telerate*, began to remedy this situation by quoting commercial paper rates on a two-page, cathode-ray-tube display system; it then had 50 subscribers. From this modest start, the system was quickly expanded because people wanted more information.

Today several hundred pages of information on credit market quotes and statistics are available to Telerate subscribers; the subscriber gets the page he wants by pressing a series of numbered buttons. Information on current quotes, offerings, and bids are inputted into the system through computers around the country; and the system is dynamically updated; that is, if GMAC changes its posted rate while a viewer is looking at the commercial paper quotes, the quotes change as GMAC inputs its new rates into the system. A wide range of institutions now use Telerate; its advent has not only eliminated a lot of phone calls, but also vastly improved communications within the money market. On the international scene, there is a similar *Reuters* system that flashes information on the Euromarket, the foreign exchange market, and other related markets into foreign countries and the United States.

Some brokers in the government and agency market have also replaced endless phone quotes with CRTs that they have placed before the traders at dealer shops. Today every trading room is literally strewn with CRTs.

While impressive, the present CRT systems are not the ultimate state of the art, and it's a common view that the money market is on the threshold of a communications revolution. One London dealer noted: "We are working on a system by which we will show our offerings and rates on a CRT. Say Ford in Dearborn, Michigan, hits our code. They will be able to type on a machine, like a Telex, a message that will come up on our CRT in London: 'Want to buy your 5 million Chases, Oct. 17th, bid you $5^7/_8$.' We are offering at $^{13}/_{16}$ and decide to take hit their bid. So we type in, 'OK, done.' Then they type in, 'Deliver to Morgan,' and the confirmations come out of the machine. We are going to put on the screen actual offerings; Cantor Fitzgerald already does that in governments but they do not trade off the machine."

Said another dealer, envisioning much the same sort of development: "The firms like us without branch offices will introduce machines to the world to undercut the branch office franchises of the Merrills and the Salis. It is clear that for firms which, like us, do not have branch offices, this is the cost-effective way to compete. We will trade off those machines; the black box is coming and, when it does, the market will go central marketplace."

Chapter 10

The investors:
Running a short-term portfolio

MONEY MARKET INVESTORS include a wide range of institutions: commercial banks, savings and loan associations, insurance companies of all sorts, mutual savings banks, other financial institutions, federal agencies, nonfinancial corporations, international financial institutions such as the World Bank, foreign central banks, and foreign firms—financial and nonfinancial. Also, when interest rates get sufficiently high, individual investors make forays into certain sectors of the money market.

One might expect most institutional portfolios to be managed with considerable sophistication, but "the startling thing you would find, if you were to wander around the country talking to short-term portfolio managers [bank and corporate], is the basic underutilization of the portfolio." These are the words of the sales manager of the government department in one of the nation's top banks. Another dealer described portfolio management practices similarly, but in slightly different terms: "Most portfolio managers would describe themselves as 'conservative,' by which they mean that the correct way to manage a portfolio is to look to your accounting risk and reduce that to zero. The opportunities thereby forgone are either ignored or more frequently not even perceived." Most short-term portfolios are poorly managed, many are not managed at all. Before we talk about that, let's look first at how a liquidity portfolio should be managed.

CONTRAST OF A PORTFOLIO MANAGER WITH A DEALER

In Chapter 9, we noted that dealers' biggest profits result over time from well-chosen position plays, and a crucial ingredient in a successful dealer operation is therefore the ability to manage well a highly levered portfolio.

Much of what we said in Chapter 9 about how a good dealer manages his portfolio applies to bank and corporate portfolio managers as well. There are, however, important differences in perspective between the two. First, a dealer is likely to be *much* less risk averse than the typical manager of a liquidity portfolio because it is the dealer's job to speculate on yields and yields spreads, whereas the portfolio manager's job is first to ensure that the funds he invests will be available whenever his firm needs them and only second to maximize the return he earns on these funds. A second difference in perspective is that, whereas the portfolio manager has free funds that he has to invest, the dealer has no such funds, and his decision to invest is therefore always based on a view of the market. A third difference in perspective is the time horizon. A dealer often buys securities on the expectation that he will be able to resell them at a higher price within a few hours or a few days. The portfolio manager, in contrast, is normally looking for instruments that he would be comfortable holding for some longer period of time—how long depends on the type of portfolio he is running.

THE PARAMETERS

A liquidity portfolio is always managed within certain investment *parameters* that establish limits with respect to: (1) the types of instruments the portfolio may buy; (2) the percentage of the portfolio that may be invested in any one of these instruments (in T bills the limit might be 100 percent, whereas in CDs, which are less liquid, it might be much lower); (3) the kind of exposure to names and credit risk the portfolio may assume (which banks' CDs and which issuers' commercial paper it may buy and how much of each name it may buy); (4) how far out on the maturity spectrum the portfolio may extend; and finally (5) whether the portfolio may short securities or repo securities.

The investment parameters within which every liquidity portfolio operates are set by top management. Because senior management delineates the portfolio manager's playing field and thereby the kinds of winnings—return on investment—that he can seek to earn through managing the portfolio, it is important that management take time to learn what the game is about before establishing such guidelines. Another input in this decision should be an evaluation of the kind of money that the firm is likely to have to invest short term: How big is it likely to be? How variable will it be? A third important input is the firm's management style. There are swinging corporations and there are very conservative corporations, and that difference should be reflected in their styles of portfolio management. A fourth factor is the caliber of the personnel the firm hires to manage its short-term portfolio. Investment parameters are meant to limit the portfolio manager's freedom of judgment, and inevitably they will at times prevent him from pursuing strategies that he correctly believes would increase return. For example, tight restrictions on the amount a portfolio manager could invest in BAs might prevent him, when BAs were trading at an attractive spread to bills, from making a profitable swap out of bills into BAs. The more qualified the personnel the firm anticipates hiring to run its liquidity portfolio, the wider guidelines should be set and the greater the latitude the portfolio manager should be given to exercise judgment.

MANAGING A LIQUIDITY PORTFOLIO

In large institutions a portfolio manager is often given several portfolios to manage—one for the firm itself, another for its financing sub, still others for self-insurance funds, and so forth. With respect to each portfolio, the manager has to ask: What are the size, variability, and predictability of the money I am investing? The answer obviously depends in part on the purpose for which the funds are held. For example, the short-term portfolio of a manufacturing firm that experiences big seasonal fluctuations in cash flows, as auto firms and food packers do, will be more variable and less predictable in size than a portfolio supporting a self-insurance fund. A second element in the portfolio manager's evaluation of the sort of money he is investing is the cash forecasts the firm gives him—their frequency, the periods for which they are available (these might be tomorrow, the next week, the next month, and the current quarter), and the confidence that historical experience suggests he can put in these forecasts. The portfolio manager's assessment of the sort of money he is investing tells him how long he is likely to be able to hold securities he buys and thus the planning horizon—30 days, 90 days, 1 year, or longer—upon which he should base investment decisions.

Relative value

Once he has determined his planning horizon, the portfolio manager asks, just as a dealer does: *Where is relative value?* The answer to this question requires knowledge, experience, and feel for the market.

On a purely technical level, the portfolio manager first has to face the problem that yields on money market instruments are not quoted on comparable bases. The problem is not just that yields on discount securities are quoted on a discount basis while yields on interest-bearing instruments are quoted on another basis. There are, in addition, all sorts of other anomalies with respect to how interest accrues, how often it is paid, whether the security is U.S. or Canadian (Canadian CDs trade on a 365-day-year basis, domestic CDs on a 360-day-year basis), whether it is a leap year, whether a security happens to mature on a holiday, and other factors. These anomalies are, moreover, *not* reflected in the yield to maturity figures on dealers' quote sheets.

A number of portfolio managers, who run such large sums of money that the cost is justified, have developed sophisticated computer programs that permit them to calculate yields on a wide range of securities on a comparable basis. One such portfolio manager noted: "I developed a program that incorporated a day algorithm which I got from a mathematician. I wanted the computer to know when a weekend occurs and to skip it in evaluating yield on a Friday trade I do for regular settlement. I also wanted the computer to recognize that in agencies July 31 is a nonday [in terms of interest accrued], that February 29 exists whether or not it actually does, and so too does February 30; there's an arbitrage from February 28 to March 1 in agencies, and I want the computer to recognize this. The computer also knows a Canadian security from a U.S. security."

In evaluating the relative value of different instruments, being able to calculate their yields on a comparable basis is just a starting point. In addition, the portfolio manager has to have a good feel for the *liquidity* of different instruments, under both prevailing market conditions and those he foresees might occur. This can involve subtle distinctions. The manager of a large portfolio commented: "I buy only direct issue [commercial] paper that I know I can sell to the dealers—GMAC but not Prulease. It's a question of liquidity, not quality. Also I buy paper from dealers only if they are ready to take it back."

To determine relative value among different instruments, the portfolio manager must also have a good feel for *yield spreads:* what they are, and how and why they change. This too involves subtleties. Here's an example given by one investor: "Lately the 6-month bill has been trading above Fed funds. I ask, 'Why?' The technical condition of the market has been excellent with little supply on the street [in dealers' hands]. So the 6-month bill should have done better, but it didn't. The reason is that we've got a pure dealer market. The retail buyer, who is scared and going short, is simply not there."

Finally, to determine where relative value lies among different *maturity* sectors of the market, the portfolio manager must explicitly predict interest rates *and* the slope of the yield curve over at least the time span of his planning horizon. Such predictions will, as noted in Chapter 8, be based on a wide range of factors, including a careful tracking of the Fed's stated objectives and whether it is currently achieving these objectives.

Relative value, in addition to depending on all the factors we have enumerated, may also be a function in part of the temperament of the portfolio manager—whether he has the psychology of a trader, as a number of top portfolio managers do, or is more inclined to make a reasoned bet and let it stand for some time, an attitude characteristic of other successful portfolio managers. As one investor noted, it makes a difference: "The 9-month bill will, except in very tight markets, trade at yield levels close to the corresponding long issue, which is the 1-year bill. So if you are looking for the most return for your dollar on a buy-and-hold strategy, you buy the 9-month bill and ride it for 3 months. If, however, you want to trade the portfolio—to buy something with the idea that it will go up $4/_{32}$'s—you are better off staying in the active issue, which would be the current year bill."

Credit risk

Most companies, when they have money and are trying to increase yield, will start reaching out on the credit spectrum—buying A-2 or P-2 paper.[1] A few do so in an intelligent and reasoned way, devoting considerable resources to searching out companies that are candidates for an upgrading of their credit rating to A-1 or P-1 and whose paper thus offers more relative value than that of A-1 and P-1 issuers.

The average firm would, however, probably be well advised not to take this route. As the sales manager of one bank dealership noted: "We tell a company doing this: 'It's the wrong thing for you to do because you do not know how to do it. You have no ability to track these companies. Also their financial statements are not worth very much and you of all people should know this because you know what you do to your own.' They sort of look at us with jaundiced eyes, and say, 'Oh, yes, I guess that's so.' "

The ablest portfolio managers tend as a group to steer clear of credit analysis. As one of the sharpest commented: "We are not interested in owning anything that does not have unimpeachable credit because, on an instrument that does not, credit will tend to dominate the performance of the instrument more than interest rates. Also, I am a one-man band, and I simply do not have time to evaluate credit risk."

---

[1] Commercial paper, as noted on page 32, is rated by several rating services. A-2 and P-2 paper are a grade off top-rated A-1 or P-1 paper.

Among large-portfolio managers, the exception to this attitude is most often found in those in insurance companies, which are a different breed. They are far more comfortable than most with credit exposure. This is an offshoot of their purchases of long corporate bonds. Because of these purchases, insurance companies are following many corporations and consequently they can and do knowledgeably buy a lot of lesser-grade commercial paper that other portfolios would not touch.

Maturity choice

While a good portfolio manager can, as many do, refuse to get into credit analysis, he *cannot* avoid making explicit interest rate predictions and basing his maturity choices upon them. As one portfolio manager pointed out: "The mistake many people make is to think that they do not have to make a forecast. But buying a 90-day bill and holding it to maturity *is* making a forecast. If you think that rates are going to move up sharply and soon, you should be sitting in overnight RP; and then when rates move up, you buy the 90-day bill."

Making rate predictions is important not only because an implicit rate prediction underlies every maturity choice a portfolio manager makes, but also because good portfolio managers feel as a group that the way yield on a large portfolio can most effectively be increased is by positioning correctly along the maturity spectrum—by recognizing which maturity sectors of the market are basically cheap (have relative value) and which are basically expensive, and buying or shifting accordingly.

An example

The best way to illustrate the kind of dividends yielded by maturity choices based on an explicit prediction of how interest rates might move is with a few concrete examples. Let's start by illustrating how a technique commonly used to raise return—namely, *riding the yield curve*—must be based on an explicit prediction of where Fed funds might trade. The idea of riding the yield curve is to increase return by buying a security out on the shoulder of the yield curve and holding that security until it can be sold at a gain because its current maturity has fallen and the yield at which it is currently trading has consequently decreased. Note that the main threat to the success of such a strategy is that short-term rates might rise across the board.

Riding the yield curve

Assume that an investor has funds to invest for 3 months. The 6-month (180-day) bill is trading at 5.41 and the 3-month (90-day) bill is trading at

5.21 (Figure 10–1). The alternatives the investor is choosing between are: (1) to buy the 90-day bill and mature it and (2) to buy the 6-month bill and sell it 3 months hence. To assess the relative merits of these two strategies, the investor does a *break-even analysis*.

Figure 10–1
Yield curve in an example of riding the yield curve

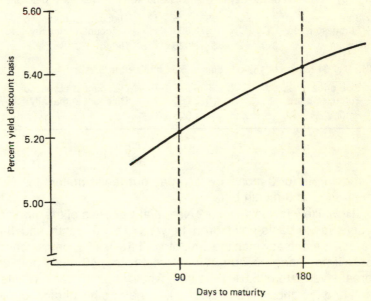

On $1 million of bills, a 90-day basis point (a basis point earned for 90 days) is worth $25.[2] If the investor bought the 6-month bill, he would earn 20 basis points more than if he bought the 3-month bill. Thus, he could sell out the 6-month bill after 3 months at a rate 20 basis points above the rate at which he bought it, that is, at 5.61, and still earn as many *dollars* on his investment as he would have if he had bought and matured the 3-month bill (Table 10–1). Therefore the rate on the 3-month bill 3 months hence would have to rise above 5.61 before holding the

---

[2] The formula used (see page 38) is:

$$D = \left(\frac{d \times t}{360}\right) \times \$1,000,000$$

The calculation is as follows:

$$\left(\frac{0.0001 \times 90}{360}\right) \times \$1,000,000 = \$25$$

Table 10–1
Dollar calculations of return in example of riding the yield curve

I. Buy $1 million of 90-day bills at 5.21 and hold to maturity.

Face value..............	$1,000,000		Discount at purchase	$13,025
– Purchase price	986,975		– Discount at maturity	0
Return	$ 13,025		Return	$13,025

II. Buy $1 million of 180-day bills at 5.41 and sell at break-even yield of 5.61.

Sale price	$985,975		Discount at purchase	$27,050
– Purchase price	972,950		–Discount at maturity	14,025
Return	$ 13,025		Return	$13,025

III. Buy $1 million of 180-day bills at 5.41 and sell at 5.21.

Sale price	$986,975		Discount at purchase	$27,050
– Purchase price	972,950		– Discount at maturity	13,025
Return	$ 14,025		Return	$14,025

6-month bill for 3 months would pay out fewer dollars than buying and maturing the 3-month bill.

How likely is this to occur? Note that because of the slope of the yield curve (a 20-basis-point drop between the 6-month and 3-month bill rates), the rate at which the 3-month bill trades 3 months hence would be 5.21 if no change occurred in interest rates, 40 basis points below the break-even rate of 5.61. Thus the investor has 40 basis points of protection and the question he has to ask in making his choice is: How likely is it that the Fed will tighten in the next 3 months so sharply that the 3-month bill will rise 40 basis points, from 5.21 to 5.61? If his answer is that it is highly unlikely, then he would buy the 6-month bill and ride the yield curve.

Note that if the investor buys the 3-month bill and matures it, he will earn $13,025 on each $1 million of bills he buys (see Table 10–1). If, alternatively, he opts to ride the yield curve and does so successfully (i.e., buys the 6-month bill and is able, because the Fed does not in fact tighten, to sell out at 5.21), he will earn $14,025, which exceeds $13,025 by $1,000. This $1,000 equals the extra 40 90-day basis points he earns: 20 because the 6-month bill is bought at a 20-basis-point spread to the 3-month bill and 20 because he is able to sell it 3 months later at a rate 20 basis points below the rate at which he bought it.

Actually the investor riding the yield curve in our example has more protection than we indicated. The reason is that, when he buys the 6-month bill, he invests fewer dollars than when he buys the 3-month bill. So on a *simple interest basis,* he would earn an annualized rate of return of 5.35 if he bought and matured the 3-month bill, whereas if he bought the 6-month bill at 5.41 and sold it as the break-even level of 5.61, he would earn an annualized return, again on a simple interest (365-day-year) basis, of 5.43, which is greater.[3] To earn an annualized return of only 5.35 on the funds invested in the 6-month bill, the investor would have to sell it out after 3 months at a discount of 5.68, which is 47 basis points above 5.21. The first break-even calculation we made on a dollar-return basis is intuitively easier to follow, but this second more refined calculation is the one the investor should make if he is interested in maximizing yield.

Another maturity decision

Here's a second example of how a conscious prediction of interest rates over the investor's time horizon can help an investor increase yield. When it appears that the Fed might tighten, the reaction of many portfolio managers is to retreat in panic to the base of the yield curve. Whether doing so is wise depends on the opportunities available and on how fast and how far the Fed is likely to tighten.

In April 1977, it was felt that the Fed was tightening. Funds were trading at 4¾ and no one was sure where that rate was going. It was the feeling of the market that a ¾ point move was needed and that 5½ would probably be the top side, but some in the market suggested 5¾. Just prior to this period, 6-month BAs had risen in yield from 5.20 to 5.85 because of a lack of demand on the part of investors; the yield on 3-month BAs was 5.45. At this point a portfolio manager with 3-month money to invest faced a choice. One alternative, assuming he was managing an S&L portfolio, would have been to adopt the bearish strategy of selling overnight Fed funds in anticipation of eventually getting a 5½ overnight rate.[4] Alternatively, he could have decided to buy 6-month BAs and sell them after 3 months.

Using the same sort of break-even analysis illustrated in the previous example, one investor facing this choice concluded that if he bought 6-month BAs at 5.85, he could after 90 days sell them at 6.30, and do as well as he would have if he had invested in overnight Fed funds and the Fed funds rate had in fact immediately moved to 5½.[5] In other words, he

---

[3] The formula is:

$$\text{Annualized return on a simple interest basis} = \left(\frac{\text{Dollar return}}{\text{Principal invested}}\right) \div \left(\frac{\text{Days held}}{365}\right)$$

[4] The alternative facing a corporate portfolio manager would have been to invest in overnight RP at a slightly lower rate.

[5] The calculation assumes that the same number of dollars would have been invested in both instruments. It also allows for the fact that the investor of large sums in Fed funds gets in effect daily compounding of interest. The Fed funds rate is quoted on a 360-day-year basis.

could sell 6-month BAs 3 months hence at 85 basis points above the rate at which 3-month BAs were then trading and still earn as many dollars as he would have by rolling funds overnight at 5½. That 85 basis points of protection seemed more than sufficient, so he bought the 6-month BAs. As things turned out, the Fed's target for funds was only 5¼–⅜, so the BAs turned out to be by far the better investment. An investor who did not use this analysis would, however, have probably missed this opportunity.

Asymmetric positions of the investor and the issuer

The two maturity-choice examples we worked through involved a choice between riding the yield curve and making an alternative invest-ment: in one case buying and maturing the 3-month bill, and in the other case rolling funds in the overnight market.

With respect to riding the yield curve, it should be noted that the bank liability manager issuing CDs or a firm issuing commercial paper is playing precisely the opposite ball game from the investor—one is trying to minimize interest costs, the other to maximize return earned. If the issuer of paper finds that, from a cost point of view, it makes sense to roll 3-month CDs, then the investor should be buying 6-month paper and riding it for 3 months rather than rolling 3-month paper.

Stability of return

As one good portfolio manager after another will note: "Real money is to be made by positioning correctly along the maturity spectrum—by making conscious market judgments and acting on them."

Such positioning does not, however, guarantee *steady* high return. One reason is that sometimes the portfolio manager will be wrong in his rate predictions. A second reason is well described by one manager: "If you can invest out to 2 years and you feel strongly that rates are going to fall, you might choose to have an average 9- or 12-month maturity—not everything out in the longer spectrum. If you are correct and the market rallies, the proper response is to shorten the portfolio—not just to sit there and hold this apparent book yield, but to recognize it. The reason you sell is that the market eventually gets to a point where you think it has reached a peak and might go lower. If after you sell you decide that you were wrong and believe—on the basis of a new rate forecast—that rates are likely to go still lower, you buy in again long term."

It's hard to produce a stable income pattern with that sort of portfolio management, and thus it would be criticized by some. But the basic assumption is that the firm is a going concern. Therefore, the portfolio manager's primary goal should be long-term profitability, not stability of income.

In this respect the track record of the World Bank's liquidity portfolio is interesting. The managers of this portfolio are constantly making maturity choices of the sort described above. In February 1977, their treasurer noted that over the previous 29 months, they had earned on their dollar portfolio a high average return, 9.32 percent, but their monthly annualized returns had fluctuated from a low of −0.67 percent in one month to a high of almost +32 percent in another.[6]

As that track record suggests, in evaluating the performance of a managed portfolio, monthly figures are meaningless. A portfolio manager needs to look at his average record for 6 months or longer to get a true feel for his performance.

Time horizon and maturity of securities purchased

In the example we gave of why the return on a managed portfolio is likely to fluctuate from month to month, the portfolio manager—believing that rates were likely to fall—might well have extended maturity into the 2-year area. In this respect it's important to note that such an extension does not imply that either the portfolio manager's planning horizon or his interest rate forecast extends anywhere near 2 years. It simply implies that he is confident that rates will fall during some much shorter time period and that he is willing to sell and realize his gain once this occurs.

Good managers of short-term portfolios, in which the maturity parameters are widely set, frequently buy Treasury notes and other longer-term instruments in the hope of realizing short-term gains. Said an ex-portfolio manager: "If I liked the market, I'd buy a 10-year bond even if I needed the money tomorrow." That's an extreme example, but this portfolio manager had the inborn instincts of a good trader, which he eventually became.

Changing relative value

The search for relative value is not a one-time affair. The money market is dynamic; changes in demand, supply, expectations, and external events—from announcements of the latest M1 figures to changes in tax laws—are constantly having an impact on it. And as they do, yield spreads and rates change. Thus relative value may reside in one sector today, in another tomorrow.

A good portfolio manager must reassess his position each day, asking not only whether his expectations with respect to interest rates have changed, but also whether transitory anomalies have arisen in spreads or distortions in rates from which he could profit.

One cause of transitory rate distortions is overreactions by investors. Said one portfolio manager: "When I saw that huge 5 billion M1 figure

---

[6] *The Money Manager*, February 14, 1977, p. 3.

last Thursday, I started buying, knowing that in a few days the market would come back. This sort of overreaction has been much more common since '74, in part because there are so many more players in the market today."

Here's an example of another transitory rate situation from which a corporate portfolio manager could benefit. Capital gains are taxed as ordinary income for banks, at the capital gains rate for corporations. Thus a longer-term municipal note selling at a discount from par offers a double-barreled tax advantage to a corporation but not to a bank.[7] Banks, however, are such big investors in this market that at times discount muni notes are priced to the bank market rather than to the corporate market. When they are, a corporation can earn a much higher after-tax return on such notes than it could from taxable securities of comparable maturity and risk.

Tracking changes in relative value takes time and effort but, as a portfolio manager gains experience, it becomes almost second nature. Also a portfolio manager can rely on the dealers for help. Once a portfolio manager recognizes that a change in relative value has occurred between instruments or maturity sectors, his response should be to *swap* or *arbitrage.*

As one portfolio manager with wide parameters observed: "Arbitrating a portfolio is one way to make money, whether it's a complete arbitrage or a swapping arbitrage between sectors of the market. Money market instruments oscillate in relative value for very good reasons; and as you get experienced, you can with not too much time keep asking why one sector of the market is out of line with where it should be—the latter judgment being more than an extrapolation of a historical average. Once you have convinced yourself that the reason is transitory, then not to own the instrument that is undervalued and be short in the other instrument that is out of line is foolhardy."

Extension swaps

We discussed various arbitrage strategies in Chapter 9. One very simple swap strategy many portfolio managers often use is to do *extension swaps.* They pick a maturity sector of the market they like, say 2- or 3-year governments, and then, for example, adopt the strategy of *extending* (lengthening maturity) a few months whenever they can pick up 5 basis points and of *backing up* (shortening maturity) a few months whenever that costs only 3 basis points. If market conditions are such that many such swaps can be done, a portfolio manager can pick up

---

[7] This assumes that the corporation is in a position to benefit from tax-exempt income. See page 512.

basis points this way. Note that, whereas a 90-day basis point is worth only $25 per $1 million, a 3-year basis point is worth $300.[8]

A similar practice used by some investors in bills to pick up basis points is to roll the current 3-month or 6-month bill each week when new bills are auctioned. If conditions are such that new bill issues, which the market has to absorb, are priced in the auction cheap relative to surrounding issues, then by rolling his bills the investor may be able to pick up each week two or three $25 or $50 basis points by doing this. A second advantage of this strategy is that it keeps the investor in current bills which are more liquid than off-the-run issues.

In swapping and trading generally, "it's important," as one portfolio manager noted, "to know what dealer will deal in what and who will make the best markets. Say a bank has a big writing program and uses the dealer community—Becker, Sali, and Goldman. The bank sells the dealers 70 million, and they resell them to retail. If I have some of that bank's CDs, I would not go to Goldman, since I know their customers are stocked up on those CDs. Instead, I would go to some fourth dealer whose customers are light in that bank's CDs."

Leverage

Like a dealer, a portfolio manager can repo securities he owns.[9] If the portfolio is that of a fair-sized bank, the portfolio manager will probably be able to repo securities directly with retail customers. If, alternatively, the portfolio is that of a corporation or other institution that does not have direct contact with suppliers of repo money, the portfolio manager can always RP his securities with the dealers, who will in turn hang them out on the other side (see Chapter 12).

The ability to repo securities can be used by a portfolio manager in various ways. If an unanticipated short-term need for cash arises at a time when the portfolio manager has established a position he wants to maintain, he can bridge that gap by borrowing RP money instead of selling securities. Said one corporate portfolio manager: "We never fund to dates. We fund to market expectancy—what we think is going to happen to interest rates. We can repo the portfolio so we never have problems raising money for short periods. If we have to raise money for a

---

[8] The calculation is:

$$3(0.0001 \times \$1,000,000) = \$300$$

[9] Jargon in this area is confusing. Dealers talk about "doing repos" when they are financing their position and about "doing reverses" when they are borrowing securities. Some portfolio managers who use repurchase agreements—just as dealers do—to lever, talk about doing repo, others talk about doing a reverse (i.e., reversing out securities). We have opted to use the word *repo* when the initiative comes from the side wanting to borrow money, and *reverse* when the initiative comes for the side wanting to borrow securities.

long period of time to meet a portfolio embarrassment [securities in the portfolio can only be sold at a loss], that means we made an error and had better face up to it."

Another way a portfolio manager with wide parameters can use the RP market imaginatively is to buy a security, finance the first part of its life with term RP, and thereby create an attractive future security. That is a technique of portfolio management, the rewards and risks of which we discussed in Chapter 9. A corporate manager can use it as well as a dealer, and some do.

Still another way a portfolio manager can use the RP market is to out and out lever his portfolio—buy securities at one rate, turn around and RP them at a lower rate, and then use the funds borrowed to buy more securities. Or the portfolio manager can simply buy securities for which he has no money by doing a repo against them at the time of purchase. A portfolio manager who uses this technique commented: "I repo the portfolio as an arbitrage technique everyday and probably run the biggest matched sale book in American industry. We RP anything we can, even corporates. In doing RP, I am either financing something I have or buying something I don't have any money for. We take the RPs off for quarter ends because they might comprise the aesthetics of our statement." Avoiding repos across quarter ends is common among those corporations that use repos, so it is impossible from looking at financial statements to determine whether a corporation uses repos to borrow.

To the corporate portfolio manager who can use repos, it is, in the words of one," the most flexible instrument in the money market. You can finance with repo, you can borrow using it, and you can ride the yield curve using it—buy a 2-month bill, put it out on repo for a month, and then sell it or do a 30-day repo again. And you can use repo to create instruments; put a 6-month bill out on a 2-month repo, and you have created a 4-month bill 2 months out."

Despite the many and reasonable ways in which the ability to borrow in the repo market can be used, it is rare for a corporate short-term portfolio manager to be able to hang out any of his portfolio on repo.

In large banks, the practice of RPing the government portfolio is almost universal. As noted in Chapter 5, such a bank views its government portfolio as a massive arbitrage rather than as a source of liquidity. Among smaller banks, practices with respect to the use of repo vary widely.

In a discussion of the use of the repo market by portfolio managers to borrow, a distinction should be made between portfolio managers who are using the market consciously to borrow and lever, and those who are, so to speak, coaxed into doing reverses. As noted in Chapter 9, when dealers want to short securities they will often cover their short by reversing in securities. If the security is not one that is readily available, the dealer will go to a broker of repo who knows what securities various banks, S&Ls, and other institutions have in their portfolios. The broker will attempt to get an institution that holds the needed securities to reverse them out by showing that institution an attractive arbitrage. Such a transaction looks like an ordinary repo but the initiative comes not from the institution that is borrowing but from the dealer who wants to cover a short. Many banks, S&Ls, and other institutions that would never use the repo market to borrow to meet a temporary cash need or to lever will reverse out securities that they intend to hold indefinitely, probably to maturity, to pick up basis points on an arbitrage.

Use of the T bill futures market

Portfolio managers who are free to use the T bill futures market are currently in the distinct minority, but for those who can, it offers an array of opportunities to lock in yields, arbitrage, hedge, and speculate. And a few portfolio managers use futures contracts extensively as one more tool of portfolio management. We discuss that in Chapter 14, which focuses on the bill futures market.

Shorting securities

It's unusual for the manager of a corporate portfolio to have authorization to sell securities short but not as rare as it used to be. The ability to short securities can be useful to a portfolio manager in a number of ways. For one thing, it permits him to arbitrage as dealers do—going long in an undervalued security and short in an overvalued security—as a speculation on a yield spread. A few corporate portfolio managers do this quite actively.

There are, as one portfolio manager noted, also tax reasons for shorting: "Say you have ballooned maturities in part of your portfolio out to 10 years. You were right on the market and have only 30 days to go to get a long-term capital gain. But you think the market might back up and you want to take some of the risk out of your position. To do so is easy—you short something similar. In the corporate tax environment, the tax on long-term capital gains is 30 percent, while the tax on ordinary income is 48 percent. With that sort of 18-point advantage, you have to be badly wrong on the short not to come out ahead shorting." For banks there is no incentive to short for tax purposes because their long-term capital gains are taxed as ordinary income.

Still another reason a corporate portfolio manager might want to short is because borrowing through a short seems less expensive than selling an attractive investment. Said one portfolio manager: "If we decided, yes, the market is in here [in a given maturity sector], then we would look for the cheapest thing [the instrument with most relative value] on a spread basis—CDs, BAs, or bills—and buy that. Even though bills might yield less than, say, Euro CDs, we might buy them because the spread on Euros into bills was too tight. We'd make the decision to buy or not and then buy the cheapest thing. When we made the decision to sell, we would sell the most expensive thing. But we could not short so we were sort of up against it at times when we had to sell. I had already bought the cheapest thing around, so generally I had to sell something cheap. It bothered me a lot not to be able to short when we needed cash, but perhaps it would have raised questions with stockholders."

The big shooters

We have drawn in this chapter and the last a distinction between dealers and portfolio managers that is perhaps too sharp. There are in the U.S. money market a number of huge liquidity portfolios taking positions that rival those taken by more than one dealer and a few of those are very actively managed. The people who run these portfolios utilize every tool of portfolio management that the dealers do—from creating future securities and figuring tails to shorting to do speculative arbitrages. Some also trade their positions as actively as a dealer. Said an individual who ran one such portfolio: "I sometimes bought securities today that I knew I would have to sell for cash the next day. I might even buy if I was bullish for the next few hours—I have bought securities on the day cash was needed and sold them later in the day if I thought the market would go up a couple of 32nds." The major differences between portfolios of this sort and a dealer operation are first that retail business is important to a dealer, and second that, whereas dealers are highly levered, a leverage ratio of 3 to 1 is highly unusual and probably top side for a liquidity portfolio.

Marking to market

In well-run short-term portfolios, it is common practice to mark the whole portfolio to market each day. The objective of running a portfolio is to maximize over time not interest accured, but *total financial return*— interest earned plus capital gains realized minus capital losses realized. A portfolio manager who has this objective will, if he buys a 2-year note with a 7 percent coupon and then finds that yields on the 2-year have risen to 8 percent, view his decision to have bought the 7 percent coupon as a serious mistake. Moreover, if he anticipates that rates will rise still further, he will sell out that security at a loss (convert his paper loss into a realized loss) and wait to recommit long-term until he thinks rates have stabilized.

The use of this tactic in portfolio management calls for a willingness to book capital losses, and that willingness is a hallmark of every good portfolio manager. Realizing losses is, however, difficult to do psychologically; it is something a trader must discipline himself to do. One advantage of marking a portfolio to market each day is that it helps get the focus of those who buy and sell for the portfolio off book value. As one portfolio manager noted: "If market value declines today and you book to market, tomorrow you start at that market value. And your gain or loss will be a function of whether tomorrow's price is better than today's." Said another: "If you mark to market, the past is gone. You've made a mistake, and the point now is not to make another one."

Tracking performance

Active management can substantially increase yield on a short-term portfolio. "You can as much as double yield on a short-term portfolio," said one practitioner of the art, "by arbitraging sectors and by changing maturities in response to interest rate forecasts."

In an institution where the short-term portfolio is actively managed, there are always people in top management who understand the credit market and who are therefore comfortable with creative management of the institution's portfolio. It is also the case that the focal point in management of the portfolio is on yield earned rather than on when money is needed. In other words, the portfolio manager's main concern in investing is with where relative value lies, not with when he needs cash; specifically he does not *fund to dates*—buy 3-month bills because he needs money 3 months hence.

Performance in every liquidity portfolio managed to maximize return is carefully tracked. A key element in this tracking is marking the portfolio to market so that the return-earned calculation incorporates not only realized, but also unrealized capital gains and losses.

Once performance is tracked, it is compared against a variety of yardsticks. A portfolio manager might, for example, compare his performance with what he could have achieved had he followed any one of several naive strategies: rolling overnight funds, rolling 3-month bills, or rolling 6-month bills. If the portfolio invests longer-term funds, the yardstick might be the yield on 2-year notes or on 3-year notes.

Another standard often used is the performance achieved by various money market funds, each of which runs in effect a large-liquidity portfolio.[10] Comparisons between the performances of two portfolios are, however, difficult to make. One has to ask about the differences in the

---

[10] A money market fund is a mutual fund that invests in money market instruments (see Chapter 21).

parameters: in maturity restrictions, in percentage restrictions, and in name restrictions. Also differences in the time flow of funds through two portfolios may affect their relative performances.

Still another approach used in evaluating performance achieved is to compare actual results with the optimal results that could have been achieved. In other words, to ask: How high was the return we earned compared with what we could have earned if our market judgments had always been correct?

Tracking performance and comparing it against various yardsticks are important not only because they give the portfolio manager a feel for how well he is doing, but also because they give management some standard against which to evaluate his performance. As one portfolio manager noted: "I'm a money market specialist working for an industrial concern so it's hard for management to evaluate what I do unless I give them some frame of reference."

In a few rare cases, the portfolio manager is not only judged, but also paid, according to how well he performs. That sort of arrangement is typically found only in a corporation or a bank that has a large short-term portfolio and has recognized that, to get professional management, it has to hire a street-oriented person who will never do anything but run money or work at a related job.

THE WAY IT'S DONE

We have discussed so far how a rather elite minority of portfolio managers who have wide latitude in what they may do and who possess the skill and judgment to make good use of that latitude manage their portfolios.[11]

Most liquidity portfolios—be they owned by corporations, banks, S&Ls, or other institutions—are managed without much sophistication; perhaps it would be more correct to say they are barely managed at all. The problem is often that top management has never focused on the question of what portfolio management is all about and how it should be done. In the case of corporations, management will often adopt the attitude: We're in the business of manufacturing, not investing. Having done that, they fail to apply to the management of their short-term portfolio the principles of management that they daily apply to the whole corporation. Banks and S&Ls that daily, in the course of their normal

---

[11] One observer in a position to know puts the number of really well-managed liquidity portfolios in corporate America at half a dozen. If people on the street (Wall Street, that is) were asked to compile their lists of those six corporations, no one would fail to mention Ford, which has portfolios universally viewed as being aggressively and astutely managed. Another portfolio that consistently gets kudos from the street is that of the World Bank.

business operations, assume carefully calculated credit risks are quite capable of simultaneously running their securities portfolios according to the guiding principle: buy Treasuries and mature them.

Restrictive guidelines

The failure of top management to be interested in and to have knowledge of what managing a liquidity portfolio involves almost invariably results in the establishment of extremely tight guidelines on what the portfolio manager may do, guidelines that reflect, as one portfolio manager noted, "the attempt of a bunch of guys who know nothing about securities to be prudent."

Tight guidelines make it impossible for a portfolio manager to use almost any of the strategies of portfolio management discussed earlier in this chapter. In particular, tight maturity guidelines can create a situation in which a portfolio manager has almost no leeway to raise yield by basing his investments on market judgments. For example, one giant U.S. corporation, which has volatile cash flows, will not permit its portfolio manager to extend further than 30 days; that still leaves him some room to make choices but none are going to be very remunerative because he is working at best with $8 basis points.[12] Not atypically, there is no one in his corporation who cares and no one who tracks his performance.

Another problem with tight guidelines is that they are sometimes written in terms of amounts rather than percentages. This can make a large portfolio difficult to manage and may also lead to a false sort of diversification. An extreme example of such guidelines is provided by a corporation that went so far as to limit the amount of T bills its portfolio could hold.

The accounting hang-up

The failure of top management to understand or interest itself in the management of the liquidity portfolio also results in what might be called the *accounting hang-up.* Specifically, it has created a situation in which the majority of portfolio managers, all of whom would describe themselves as *conservative,* believe that the correct way to manage a portfolio is to reduce their accounting risk to *zero.* In other words, they attempt to run the portfolio in such a way that they will *never* produce a book loss.

---

[12] The calculation:

$$0.0001 \times \frac{30}{360} \times \$1,000,000 = \$8.33$$

This obviously means that they can never take market risk of any sort: they can't do swaps that would produce a book loss regardless of how relative value shifts; when they need cash, they can't decide what to sell on the basis of relative value; they can't arbitrage; in fact, they are literally reduced to rolling overnight money and buying securities they intend to mature.

To appreciate fully how the decision never to take a loss restricts a portfolio manager, it is necessary to understand that when a portfolio acquires a discount security, such as bills or BAs, the accountant accrues each day interest income on that security at the discount rate at which it was purchased, so when the security is redeemed at maturity for full face value, all of the difference between the purchase price and the face value (i.e., the discount at purchase) will have been accrued as interest. This seems reasonable enough but it means, for example, that if a portfolio manager buys 6-month bills at 5.41 and resells them 3 months later at 5.61, that is, at a rate *above* that at which he bought the bills, *he will have incurred a capital loss even though in dollar terms he has earned money.* Table 10–2 spells out the mathematics of this. Note that

Table 10–2
Accounting treatment of $1 million of 6-month bills
bought at 5.41 and sold 3 months later at 5.61

Book value at purchase	$972,950
+ Interest accrued over 90 days	13,525
Book value at sale	$986,475
Price at sale	$985,975
– Book value at sale	986,475
Accounting capital gain (loss)	($ 500)
Price at sale	$985,975
Price at purchase	972,950
Actual gain	$ 13,025

by buying the 6-month bill at 5.41 and holding it for 90 days, the portfolio has earned $13,025 and the $500 capital loss occurs only because the accountant has accrued $13,525 of interest over the holding period.

The yields and maturities in this example were purposely chosen so that they are identical with the yields and maturities used in the example of riding the yield curve presented earlier in this chapter (see Table 10–1). Once these numbers are seen in the context of that example, it is clear that the unwillingness to take an accounting loss (to expose the portfolio to an accounting risk) rules out even the most basic investment strategy based on market judgment, namely, riding the yield curve. In this respect, note that in our example the portfolio manager who rode the yield curve stood to gain—if interest rates did not rise—an extra $1,000 of return, *and* he had a lot of protection against losing in terms of dollars earned but *not* against incurring an accounting loss.

Portfolio managers preoccupied with accounting losses and gains are encountered by dealers frequently. Said one: "It cracks me up when someone comes to me with BAs or bills and says, 'What's your bid?' and I say, '5.60,' and he says, 'I can't sell because I bought at 5.50 and I can't take a loss.' It makes no sense if he has held the instrument for awhile, but I do not question people any more. I figure they just don't understand the concept. Still it's crazy, if you have to generate cash, to say that you cannot sell the instrument it is best to sell because you cannot take a 10-basis-point loss." Said another dealer: "I talk to portfolio managers about this problem and encounter nothing but resistance. They do not care if they could earn more money, they are just not going to take a loss. It's an organizational but not a rational constraint."

The whole accounting problem applies not only to discount securities, but also to CDs and other interest-bearing securities, because the accountant accrues interest on them just as he does on discount securities; in addition, he amortizes over the time to maturity the premium on coupons purchased at a price above par and accretes the discount over the time to maturity on coupons purchased at a discount from par.

A negative sum game

The aversion to book losses and the failure to track performance that are characteristic of many institutions create a negative sum game for the portfolio manager. If he invests on the basis of market judgment, he ends up in a position where, if his judgment is wrong, the resulting losses—even if they are losses only by accounting standards—will be highly visible and criticized, whereas if his judgment is correct, the resulting gains will not be perceived by senior management.

The obvious response of the portfolio manager put in this position is to make no attempt to predict interest rates and to invest so as to avoid all market risk. If such a portfolio manager reaches for yield at all, he does so by buying P-2 paper or Euro CDs because they offer relatively high yields without ever asking whether they have *relative value*. Such portfolio managers think of themselves as sophisticated because they know a lot about many different markets, *but* when they need cash 3 months hence, they buy a 3-month instrument instead of making a conscious market decision.

Opportunity cost

The typical "conservative" portfolio manager thinks of himself as never having lost a penny or at least as not having lost very many, and his accountant will confirm that this is so. But in fact an institution with a portfolio run on the principle that it funds to dates and never takes a market risk incurs a large *opportunity cost,* namely, the earnings forgone because the responsibility to manage funds in the portfolio has been abnegated. An example is provided by the illustration of riding the yield curve given earlier in this chapter. The portfolio manager who rides the yield curve with a lot of basis points of protection built into his gamble does not have to be right more than half the time to noticeably increase yield. Thus, to refuse to do so in order to avoid the risk of an accounting loss implies a cost, one that is no less real because it is not perceived by most institutions.

There is also a more subtle aspect to opportunity cost. As one portfolio manager commented: "Most people you talk to will buy a 6-month bill and hold it to maturity and say that they are not taking any risk because they know what they are going to earn. That is farcical. They *are* taking a risk, one that is not measured by the accounting system but is measured in terms of opportunity cost. And the institution may in reality be affected by this risk. If rates rise sharply and the money invested could have been used elsewhere, there is a cost to having bought those securities. Either the institution has to finance them somehow or it may be forced into other business decisions that are suboptimal."

It is easy to find examples of common portfolio practices that can be pursued only at a considerable opportunity cost. One such practice is to say that if money is needed in 30 days, cash on hand should be invested in a 30-day instrument even though predictable cash flows will more than suffice to cover that need. Another is to invest a large amount of money in short-term instruments when it is clear that most of that money is not going to be needed in the short run or even in the long run. A corporation that pursues such a strategy, as some triple-A credits do, is paying a large premium year in and year out to ensure that it can survive even a severe credit crunch without mild discomfort.

With respect to the opportunity cost associated with the latter policy, one sales manager noted: "If stockholders realized what was going on in some corporations with cash holdings that are large relative to their total assets, what amount of money it is costing the company to not manage money, you might have some stockholder suits. I found one company that could go no longer than 90 days; they had a roughly $500 million portfolio; and the average life of their investments was about 60 days. They could never buy and sell, never swap. I figured that in 1976 the fact they could not extend to the 1-year area probably cost them 1½ to 2 percent in yield. On half a billion that could add significantly to the bottom line [$10 million if the increase in yield was 2 percent]. And there was *no* call for the funds."

It is sometimes suggested that the reason some large corporations do not manage their portfolios is that they have too much money; that is, it is not possible within the confines of the money market to actively manage $3 or $4 billion. Sums of that magnitude are, however, actively managed; the World Bank's $6 billion portfolio is a prime (and not unique) example.

As noted, there is an opportunity cost to not managing money. The counterpart is that it costs money to have someone manage a portfolio, consequently there is some level below which benign neglect—rolling commercial paper or investing surplus cash in a money market fund—is the preferable alternative. That cutoff point is hard to pinpoint; estimates put it anywhere from $10 to $30 million. Somewhere up from that, between $50 and $100 million, there are solid benefits to be reaped from having someone watch the market on a daily basis.

For the firm at the opposite pole, one with hundreds of millions to be managed in one or a number of portfolios, the optimal solution may be one that a few institutions in this position have adopted—namely, to hire a professional, give him wide guidelines, monitor his performance, and pay him on an incentive basis so that making market judgments is for him a positive sum game. A side benefit of doing so is that the same individual can be used, as is done in many corporations, to manage the parent's or its financing sub's commercial paper operations. Anyone who can manage a short-term portfolio well can manage a commercial paper operation equally well, since the latter is nothing but a *negative* portfolio.

Ignorance of opportunity cost and extreme risk aversion are not the only reasons why many large institutions have failed to opt for professional management of their portfolios. Another is that they would have to pay a professional money manager in toto what a senior executive earns. A third reason is that corporations, especially if they are headquartered in outlaying places, have difficulty attracting and holding street-oriented people.

For a large corporation that wants to aggressively manage its portfolio, the commonly practiced alternative tactic of having one fast-track rookie do the job for awhile and then train another to do it does not always work out. Said a portfolio manager who traveled that route: "Trading is an art form which I could not succeed in teaching my peers who had come through the system as I did. I would have done better to take on some kid hustling on the streets of Marrakech."

Part III

The markets

Chapter 11

The Federal funds market

SCENE: Late Wednesday afternoon on the Fed funds desk of a major New York bank.

"Where is that 150 million we bought?"

"The bank swears they sent it."

"Then why the hell hasn't the transfer gone through the San Francisco Fed?"

"The bank says their computer broke down. They had to deliver the transfer request by hand."

"Is that money coming or not? Call the New York Fed! Ask them if they'll keep the wire open or let us do an 'as of' tomorrow. Damn! This is enough to make an atheist out of a priest."[1]

---

[1] This actual situation resulted from something happening that was *never* supposed to happen. A wire transfer of Fed funds got lost in the Fed's computer network. The San Francisco Fed sent out the notice of the transfer of funds, but that message was not received by the New York Fed; it simply disappeared in the Fed's switching center at Culpepper, Virginia.

SETTLING WITH THE FED

Wednesday afternoon settlement with the Fed creates a great amount of tension for bankers, brokers, and the Fed. To understand why requires some knowledge of the rules by which banks settle.

All banks that are members of the Federal Reserve System are required to maintain reserves in the form of deposits at the Fed. Any vault cash banks hold also counts as reserves. The reserves that a bank must maintain during the current settlement week are based on the average daily deposits it held over a seven-day period two weeks earlier. The ratios used in calculating required reserves were given in Table 5–3. For reserve calculation purposes, the week begins on Thursday and ends on Wednesday. Thus, to a Fed funds trader, Friday is always "early" in the week.

In settling with the Fed, a bank starts with a certain *required* average daily level of reserves. It does not have to hit its required level everyday, but its average daily reserve balances over the week must equal this figure.

To make it easier for banks to settle, the Fed permits a bank to offset a deficiency (up to 2 percent of its required) in one reserve week with a surplus run in the previous week or with a surplus run in the following week.[2] The carry-over privilege is, however, limited to one week. A bank cannot go *red* (have a reserve deficiency) two weeks in a row; and if it goes *black* (runs a reserve surplus) two weeks in a row, the second week's surplus becomes excess reserves for which it gets no credit. Thus a bank's settlements with the Fed tend over time to follow a pattern, alternating red and black weeks.

The dollar total of the assets most large banks, with the exception of the B of A, choose to fund far exceeds their deposits. The reverse is true of most smaller banks. Thus, large banks have a chronic need to obtain funds to settle with the Fed, whereas smaller banks have a chronic need to invest excess funds to avoid running a surplus. The needs of both sorts of banks are well met in the Fed funds market. In this market, reserve-short banks buy Fed funds (funds on deposit at the Fed), and reserve-rich banks sell them. Since the open-market desk at the New York Fed works hard each settlement week to ensure that the quantity of reserves the banks need to settle is provided to them, all the banks do

---

[2] The 2 percent surplus or deficiency that a bank may carry forward equals 2 percent of the *total* reserves it must hold over the week, which in turn equals the bank's required reserves times seven; this is so because a bank's required refers to the *average* balance it must maintain over a seven-day period. Thus if a bank's required were, for example, $1 billion, it could carry forward a reserve surplus or deficit equal to:

$$\$1 \text{ billion} \times 7 \times 2\% = \$140 \text{ million}$$

manage—via the mechanism of the Fed funds market—to settle more or less within a whisker of where they meant to be each Wednesday.

THE FED WIRE

The operation of the Fed funds market and related activities requires tens of thousands of transfers of dollars daily among thousands of banks. This is possible in large part because of the Fed wire system. Under this system an individual bank's computer is linked by wire to the computer at its district Federal Reserve Bank, which in turn is linked to the Fed's central computer in Culpepper, Virginia; that computer switches inter-district messages between Federal Reserve district banks.

When a commercial bank wants to transfer funds (from its reserve account to that of another bank), it types out a computer message that goes directly to the Fed, and the required payment is automatically made. For example, if the B of A sold $20 million of Fed funds to Chase. it would send through its computer the appropriate message to the San Francisco Fed, which would debit B of A's account and relay the payment message via Culpepper to the New York Fed, which would credit Chase's account and notify Chase (Table 11–1).

Table 11–1
The B of A sells Chase $20 million of Fed funds

Bank of America		Chase	

Reserves
  −20 million
Fed funds sold
  +20 million
		Reserves
		  +20 million
			Fed funds
			  purchased
			  +20 million

San Francisco Fed		New York Fed	

	Reserves, B of A
	  −20 million
			Reserves, Chase
			  +20 million

The Fed wire began to assume its present form only a decade ago. Before that, even the big New York banks had to exchange checks to make payments to each other. Now they are linked by wire to the New York Fed and all interbank payments in New York, with the exception of Euro transactions (see Chapter 16), go over the Fed wire. The New York Fed was the first district bank to be linked by wire to member banks within its district. Until five or six years ago, the way the principal banks in St. Louis, which were across the street from the St. Louis Fed, com-municated with the Fed was to walk across the street and deliver a slip of paper. Now all the Federal Reserve District banks and most of their branches have extended access to the Fed wire to member banks having volumes of transactions justifying such access.

Banks use the Fed wire not only to handle their transactions in the Fed funds market, but also for other transactions. Each major bank has hundreds of correspondent banks that keep accounts with it, and it keeps accounts at other banks. Throughout the day monies are constantly being paid into and out of these accounts over the Fed wire in connection with securities transactions, collections, and so forth.

In addition, corporations and nonbank financial institutions are constantly requesting banks to make *wire transfers* of funds for them. For example, a large corporation might wire money from its account in a West Coast bank into its account at Citibank and then later in the day have those funds wired from that account to the account at Manny Hanny of a nonbank dealer from which they had bought governments. The money market, which is largely a cash-settlement market (payment is made on the day of a trade with "good"—*immediately available*—funds), generates a huge volume of traffic on the Fed wire.

The bank wire

In addition to being linked by the Fed wire, banks are also linked by *the bank wire*. This wire, which is a secure, closed-loop Telex system supported by a computer switch, is not a payments mechanism; it is an *advice medium* for about 220 member banks; the major traffic on it consists of messages advising the receiving banks of some action that has occurred. For example, Morgan gets an instruction from a corporate client to pay or transfer to the Continental Bank $5 million, perhaps in connection with the purchase of commercial paper. Morgan debits the account of the corporate client and credits the account of Continental at Morgan. At the same time, it sends a message over the bank wire to Continental saying that it is crediting their account for $5 million. Such transfers and wire advice continue throughout the day. Meanwhile Continental tracks these advices and at some point might wire back to Morgan: "You have credited our account six times for a total of $30 million today. Transfer $29 million to our account in Chicago at the Fed." By doing this Continental would get effective use of the funds in its account in New York. Or Continental might instruct Morgan to transfer through the Fed the funds in its account to some other New York bank to make a money market investment.

The gradual perfecting of the Fed wire has caused big changes in the way banks make payments. In particular the Fed wire has in recent years provided competition to the use of correspondent bank accounts. Banks have begun to conclude that there is no sense in running bank balances all over the country when they can have everyone exchange them through the Fed over the wire. Use of the Fed wire is fas. simpler because the bank has to track only one position rather than balances all over the country.

One difficulty posed by the increased use of the Fed wire is that banks get jammed up processing wires because wire activity severely peaks late in the afternoon, due in part to the many settlements that have to be made in connection with commercial paper transactions. Because of this traffic jam, every afternoon there are some payments that don't get made before the Fed wire shuts down.

The Fed wire has also provided competition to the bank wire. When a bank opts to make and receive all payments in Fed funds over the Fed wire, it has less need of the bank wire and traffic on this system is down.

Breakdowns

Because of the vast number of messages that pass daily over the Fed wire and the bank wire, it is essential, if the banking system is to continue to operate, that every bank's computer and the Fed's computer keep running. To prevent breakdowns, the Fed relies on redundancy and backup equipment. Still, on occasion, the Fed wire goes "down." When this occurs, it is held open longer than usual in the afternoon. Because the major banks could not tolerate a long breakdown in their computer operations, they have all designed their internal systems so that the maximum down time for a breakdown is no more than a few minutes.

Amusingly, the big New York banks, which had all supplied their computer systems with emergency generators years ago, woke up one day to ask: "What the hell would our computer centers, humming away in the midst of a blackout, be working on with the rest of the bank shut down in darkness?" So they supplied auxiliary power to all the major departments that provide inputs to their computer system: check collections, money transfer, and the trading room. Said the manager of one bank computer operation: "We have got that capacity and," reaching into his desk, "I keep a flashlight, too."

HISTORY OF THE MARKET

In 1921, some member banks were borrowing at the discount window, while others had surplus reserves for which they had trouble finding an outlet due to depressed market conditions. After informal discussions, the banks that were borrowing from the Fed began purchasing balances from the banks that had excess reserves, and the Fed funds market was born.

Trading in Fed funds continued throughout the 1920s but fell into

930s, when most banks had excess reserves for a
the early 1940s the banks purchased large amounts
of new government debt issued to finance the war,
he practice of settling their reserve positions by trad-
asury bills for cash settlement.

came clear that there was an easier way for the banks
to ~~soll~~ of selling bills among themselves, they began in the
early 1950s to sell one-day money among themselves.[3] And as they did,
the Fed funds market—dormant since the 1920s—was revived. Another
reason for the revival of the funds market was that, as interest rates
started to rise after the Treasury-Fed accord, everyone became more
conscious of the value of money left idle, and banks in particular began
to see the merit in keeping their excess funds fully invested. The revival
of the Fed funds market was particularly attractive for retail banks with a
customer base consisting largely of consumers. These banks needed an
outlet for their surplus funds, and they took up the practice of selling Fed
funds everyday to their large-city correspondents.

By 1960 these developments led to a situation where the big New
York and Chicago banks began to deliberately operate their basic
money positions so that they were always short, on the ground that they
needed room to buy all the Fed funds that were coming into them from
smaller correspondents. This was an attractive situation for the large
banks because Fed funds were the cheapest money around, and they
naturally asked: Why not use it for 10 percent of our overall needs?

In the late 1950s when the big banks sold to their correspondent
banks the "service" of buying up the latter's excess funds, they said, "Of
course if you ever need Fed funds, we will be happy to sell them to you."
This commitment came back to haunt them in 1963 when interest rates
started to take off in the aftermath of the Kennedy tax cut. By then the
smaller correspondent banks had developed an insight into the money
market; they began buying Treasury bills, which were then trading at a
higher yield than the discount rate, and financing them first with their
own surplus funds and then by purchasing Fed funds from the big banks.

At that time Fed funds had *never* traded higher than the discount rate.
The reason was that, since the banks bought Fed funds only to settle
their reserve positions and then only as an alternative to borrowing at the
discount window, any bank that was willing to pay more than the discount rate for Fed funds would naturally be subject to the accusation that
ior one reason or another it could not borrow at the window.

Gradually the situation became critical for the big banks because all

---

[3] This development was fostered by Garvin Bantel (now Garvin GuyButler), a firm that
once brokered call loans to brokers and was an important broker of listed bonds. Garvin is
now a major broker of several money market instruments, both domestic and Euro.

their correspondents were buying T bills at 4 percent, financing them with Fed funds purchased at 3½ percent (the level of the discount rate), and raking in the spread. This continued for more than a year, during which time the big banks became huge net sellers of Fed funds. To fund the sales, these banks were issuing CDs at rates higher than the rate at which they were selling Fed funds to their "valued" correspondents.

Something had to give. Finally, in 1964 Morgan decided that if any bank could get away with paying more than the discount rate for Fed funds, it could, and on October 4 of that year it bid 3⅝ for funds at a time when the discount rate was 3½ and funds were trading at 3½. The $500 million estimated to have been traded at this higher rate that day was a small sum by today's standards, but the gambit succeeded and began a new era in the funds market. Rapidly funds began to trade at a market rate that was determined by supply and demand and was affected by the discount rate only insofar as that rate influenced demand.

After funds began to trade at a market rate, the Fed funds market mushroomed and more and more banks got into it. Regional banks that at the inception of the market were selling funds to large banks began to operate their own regional markets. Before this development most trading in Fed funds was done in New York and Chicago, with perhaps a little in San Francisco. Small outlying banks with only a little money to sell were excluded from the market, because it made no sense for a bank with $100,000 of overnight money to sell to telephone New York when the rate it would get was 3 or 3½ percent.[4] However, when the regional banks began to buy Fed funds, it paid for a bank in Joplin, Missouri, to call St. Louis for $0.30 to sell even $50,000 of Fed funds. In the Fed funds market now, regional banks buy up funds from even tiny banks, use what they need, and resell the remainder in bulk amounts in the New York market. Thus, the Fed funds market resembles a river with tributaries; money is collected in many places and then flows through various channels into the New York market.

As the Fed funds market developed, some of the regional banks that entered it felt they were not in close enough contact with the market to call the last ¼ or ⅛; they adopted the practice of asking brokers to sell or buy money for them at whatever price the brokers thought was the best available. The amount of such *discretionary money* amounted at one time to a sizable sum. There is less of it around today because "most of the regionals," in the words of one broker, "like to believe they are a Chase or a Morgan. Also they are becoming more sophisticated."

In the days when Fed funds were first traded, "the market was," said one ex-trader from a large bank, "a travesty, a joke as far as being a real market. There were six or eight real decision makers in the entire

---

[4] At a 3½ percent rate, $100,000 of overnight Fed funds is worth $9.72.

market—a couple of brokers and the guys on the money desks of the top banks. When a top broker walked in on Thursday morning at the start of a new settlement week and said, 'Funds are $^{11}/_{16}$—$^{3}/_{4}$,' the market pretty much formed up around that. Few people would challenge that view because they knew a lot of banks had given that broker money to buy or sell at his discretion. On Broadway the *New York Times* drama critic can close a show. In every area you have opinion makers, and the Fed funds market was, and is, no exception."

Over time, the Fed funds market had evolved considerably. Initially Fed funds traded at quarters of a percent; then, as more participants entered the market and it became more competitive, funds began trading at eighths and then at sixteenths. Another break with the past is that, whereas the Fed used to let the funds rate fluctuate in a wide band, today it pegs that rate tightly. Commented one person at the Fed: "When we are in a period when our Fed funds target is not changing, money supply is growing at a steady rate, and we are at peace with the world, we are inclined to be more relaxed about the funds rate and to let it fluctuate within a ¼ band. But in a delicate situation where we want to give signals to the market—when they are misunderstanding our posture and we want to be sure they get the message—we might narrow that spread to $^{1}/_{16}$."

Because the Fed now pegs the funds rate so closely, the market feels more confident about where funds should trade than it once did. Also there are more people in the market forming opinions about where funds should trade. And there is more unanimity of opinion because these days *everyone* forms their opinions around an interpretation of Fed activity.

RUNNING A FED FUNDS DESK

The primary job of the manager of a bank's Fed funds desk is to ensure (1) that the bank settles with the Fed *and* (2) that in doing so it holds no more excess reserves than the amount, if any, that it can carry into the next week. This is a tricky job at a major bank because each day such a bank experiences huge, highly variable, and difficult-to-predict inflows and outflows of funds. These all influence the bank's balance at the Fed, so they have to be carefully monitored by the desk, which at the same time is buying or selling funds as necessary to develop the balance it wants for the day at the Fed.

The flows that affect a major bank's funds position come from various sources. Its correspondents sell it huge sums of money and sometimes they will ask to buy funds from it. Additional flows result from changes in correspondent bank deposit balances, changes in customer deposit balances (firms wiring money into and out of the bank), changes in the Treasury's balance in its tax and loan account, big loans coming on or going off the bank's books, purchases and sales made by the bank's portfolio and by the bank's dealer department, changes in the amount of CDs the bank has outstanding, changes in the level of RPs it does, flows from and to foreign branches, and—in the case of clearing banks— fluctuations in dealer loans.

Normally a bank's Fed funds desk starts the day with a sheet on which it projects the inflows and outflows that will affect its bank's reserve account at the Fed during the day. Some, such as flows generated by maturing RP and big loans going on or off its books, are known. The rest it estimates on the basis of past experience and any additional information available. The desk *heads out* (adds up and compares) all these figures to get its first estimate of what money it will need to buy or sell during the day. Then, as the day progresses and actual inflows and outflows occur, someone on the desk tracks these flows and their effect on the bank's balance at the Fed. This is boring and tedious work but must be done if the bank is to keep a handle on its position. As one Fed funds trader after another will note, the traders on the desk are only as good as their backup people. When one of the latter makes an error, the bank may inadvertently end up way black or way red, a situation that can create a problem on any day and a major bust on a Wednesday.

Here's one trader's scenario of the sort of difficulty that could crop up: "Say on Thursday we think we are $2 billion short and buy $2 billion, but actually we are only $1.5 billion short. We start Friday half a billion black on the accumulated. Now say the same thing happens again on Friday, so we end up going black again half a billion, only this time it's times three [because of the weekend]. That means we start Monday with a $2 billion accumulated black. Technically a bank is not supposed to go below 50 percent of its required; it's a technicality the Fed does not strictly enforce but they do remind you that you have gone below. Suppose that Monday to Wednesday we need only $600 million a day in our reserve account. If we respected the 50 percent rule, we would end up with $900 million of that $2 billion black we could not use up. Actually we would drain down our balance at the Fed as low as we dared and get rid of that money, but we prefer not to get in that position."[5]

At most major banks the Fed funds desk is managed very conservatively. The desk knows what average daily balance it must have to settle for the week, and it attempts each day to be within 10 percent of that figure. One reason is that, since Fed funds now trade in a narrow range—except when the Fed is moving the rate, there is not much profit to be earned by playing the rates, going long on a day when funds seem cheap and short on a day when they seem expensive.

Another reason banks are disinclined to play around on the Fed funds

---

[5] The 50 percent rule was established by the New York Fed for banks within its district. This rule was subsequently dropped, a fact of which not all banks are aware.

desk is that most of them are either big natural sellers or buyers of funds, and they work best—because of line problems—when operating from their natural stance. With the exception of B of A, most large banks are net buyers of funds. A bank will sell funds only to a bank to which it has extended a line and only up to the amount of that line. Thus, if a bank that is normally a net buyer of funds accumulates a big surplus position, it may have difficulty working off that surplus because it has insufficient lines to sell it.

Some state-chartered banks have an additional problem. The Comptroller of the Currency has ruled for national banks that funds purchases and sales are not to be treated as borrowings and loans for purposes of regulation. Thus, there is no legal limit on the amount of Fed funds a national bank may sell to another bank. In some states, however, sales of Fed funds are treated as a normal loan. In such states, a state-chartered bank can extend to another bank a line equal to only a small percentage of its capital.

A bank that cannot get rid of excess funds because of line problems can always sell these funds in the RP market, that is, provide dealers with secured loans. But in doing so it will typically get a lower rate than it would by selling funds, and it may end up selling off excess funds at a rate below that at which it purchased them from its correspondents.

Line problems can also constrain the amount by which even the largest and most well-thought-of banks can go red early in the week. When the Franklin and the Herstatt failed, banks were suddenly reminded of something they had almost forgotten—that the sale of Fed funds is an unsecured loan. In response, banks cut back on their lines for selling funds, and as a result banks do not have the leeway they once did to vary their daily purchases of Fed funds. Said one dealer: "If you think at the beginning of the week that the Fed is going to do a lot of adding and that funds are going to trend down, you might borrow a little less than you otherwise would have. But at a large borrowing bank you have such a big job to do that you cannot get far behind. You cannot borrow nothing on Thursday and hope to make it up the rest of the week. It cannot be done."

Conservative Fed funds traders, while they will not try to make money by dealing aggressively in funds, attempt to do what they can for the bank's profit and loss (P&L) statement in other ways. Said one typical of the breed: "We are not supposed to be a profit center. We do, however, usually make money if we sell funds or finance dealers loans. The dealer loans give us a better spread $3/16$ to $1/4$ over Fed funds, and it's a secured loan. But the real nature of our game is to buy cheaper than the effective funds rate. We make the bank money by saving it. A sixteenth is only $1.74 on $1 million but, with the amounts we borrow, sixteenths can mount up."

Dealing aggressively

While most Fed funds traders are conservative, and well advised to be so because that is what management wants, there are a few sharpshooters in the crowd. One trader of this genre, who was quite comfortable going above or below his daily required by 50 percent, commented: "I don't like to just pick up the phone and buy or sell. If I feel that there is strength in the market, I will wait to sell even if I have a lot to sell. Then in the early afternoon, there is the moment of truth. I have to make some sort of decision. You get a good sense of accomplishment when you wait and it turns out you were right. When it does not, you have to scramble. But that is part of the fun of doing it. The fun is to have a conviction and at times buy yourself long or sell yourself short."

Said a trader who liked to play even more: "Some guys act as if they settled every night. That is what you call a *day position*. I have a different philosophy. Say I need $100 million a day for seven days, that is, a $700 million cumulative. If I think rates are high one day, I might buy just $50 million and then pick up $150 million the day after if rates are more reasonable. Also I go where the money is cheapest. If it is cheaper to buy Euros, I buy Euros not Fed funds. If Euros are cheap, I will buy Euros and sell Fed funds.

"When I got this job they tended to think that you need $100 million a day. I said, OK, if I can get money cheap, I will buy $200 million and sell $100 million off at a profit and reduce my effective cost of funds. Not many people do that. I ask: How can a bank not leverage down their cost of funds by using this route? It takes extra work to buy and sell, but in the end you reduce your cost of money. Over the first quarter of this year, funds were stagnant at ⅝–¾. So, if I had just bought money all the time from our correspondents, as I should have, I would have had an effective cost on the $500 million to $1 billion I had to buy of 4⅝, that is, 4.63. My effective cost of money was 4.28, and I managed that in a market in which you have a ⅛ spread.

"A lot of banks look at the Fed funds guy as custodian of a checking account whose prime function is to make sure that the bank does not go OD at the Fed. The Fed funds market has not progressed as far as other markets have and it should. This is where the action is, where the basic position of your bank is settled.

"Too many people are stodgy. The way I look at it, Babe Ruth only hit .342, and he was a superstar. Ty Cobb, who had the best batting average ever, hit .367. So if you are right 75 percent of the time, you are going to make a lot of money. If you are gambling, you have to take the big loss to make the big win. Lots of guys say to me, 'I never took a big loss,' but they never made a big win either."

This quote illustrates well an attitude that is common on the street and characteristic of aggressive traders, dealers, and portfolio managers: there are plenty of gambles around in which you can count on being right more than half the time; if you are, you'll make money, so to not gamble is expensive and foolish.

Personnel and sophistication

Most of the traders on the funds desks of large banks have no special academic training for their job. They are people with a good memory, which a Fed funds trader requires, who started out in operations and just picked up trading. In a few banks the trading slot on the Fed funds desk is one that fast-track MBAs are passed through for a year.

At small banks the Fed funds desk is often run with much less sophistication than at large banks because the person who does the job is the treasurer of the bank and also has to handle governments, repos, and whatever. Sophistication, however, is not a function of only size. A trader at a bank that ranks 150th may be quite sophisticated, whereas one at a somewhat larger bank is merely an order clerk—when he has $10 million to sell, he calls the broker, gets a quote, hits the bid, writes a ticket, and thinks of himself as a trader.

Glamor

While a Fed funds trader may handle huge sums everyday, there is little glamor or recognition attached to the job, as is the case with most money market jobs. Said one trader who handles several billion dollars everyday: "I want out to dinner the other night with a fellow from Price Waterhouse. He said, 'What do you do?' I said, 'Trade overnight funds.' He said, 'Oh, how does your wife like your working nights?'"

Overnight money

The bulk of the money sold in the Fed funds market is overnight money. Much of this money is traded directly between the selling bank and the buying bank.

Because they depend heavily and persistently on purchases of Fed funds to cover their basic funding needs, most large banks go out of their way to cultivate smaller correspondents that find it convenient to sell their surplus funds on an ongoing basis to one or several large banks. A smaller bank could, of course, shop in the brokers market and try to pick up an extra $1/16$, but most don't because the amounts they sell are so small that the cost of trying would outweigh the potential gain. Overnight $1/16$ on $10 million is only $17, and that's before the phone bill is paid.

To cultivate correspondents that will sell funds to them, large banks stand ready to buy whatever sums these banks offer, whether they need all of these funds or not. If they get more funds than they need, they sell off the surplus in the brokers market. Also they will sell to their correspondents if the latter need funds, but that occurs infrequently. As a funding office of a large bank noted: "We do feel the need to sell to our correspondents but we would not have cultivated them unless we felt that they would be selling to us 99 percent of the time. On the occasional Wednesday when they need $100,000 or $10 million, OK. Then we would fill their need before we would fill our own."

When the Fed funds market was younger and less competitive and the smaller players were relatively unsophisticated, it was not uncommon for buying banks to pay their smaller correspondents a rate well below the New York rate. Today, however, most large banks pay correspondents that sell to them regularly some formula rate—the opening rate, the average rate for the day, or whatever. And, even though they know that they may well have to sell off some of the funds they purchase from correspondents, they do not try to arbitrage—buy low and sell high. A banker typical of this attitude said, "We will pay a bank in Cedar Rapids the same rate for $100,000 that we would pay the B of A selling us $100 million. We do that because we want the bank in Cedar Rapids to be coming back to us. Relative to other sources of funds, Fed funds are cheap and we try to cultivate this funding source."

A few big banks, however, still see a potential arbitrage, "trading profits," in selling off funds purchased from smaller banks and attempt to profit from it to reduce their effective cost of funds. Also a few tend to bid low to their correspondents. Said a trader typical of the latter attitude: "We have a good name in the market so I often underbid the market by a $1/16$. A guy with a few million to sell doesn't care. He's happy to get his money sold and get on with other banking business." The tendency to shave rates is particularly pronounced on Fridays because a Friday purchase is for three days.

One of the striking things about the Fed funds market is the wide access all banks have to it. A tiny bank with $50,000 of overnight money to sell won't be able to sell to one of the top money market banks because such a bank would not bother with such dribbles. But at a rate slightly off the market, it can sell its funds to a regional bank that is happy to take in small amounts either to fund its own position or to resell in larger blocks. The national market for CD money is open in real volume only to the top 25 banks or so in the country. But regional banks much smaller in size can and do buy large sums in the Fed funds market. The market is also open to foreign banks and foreign agency banks, which use it extensively.

There is some tendency in the Fed funds market for banks to expect banks they sell to be willing to sell to them, and a handful of banks will

Table 11–2
Federal funds transactions of money market banks ($ millions, except as noted)

Type	1978, week ending—							
	Jan. 4	Jan. 11	Jan. 18	Jan. 25	Feb. 1	Feb. 8	Feb. 15	Feb. 22
	Total, 46 banks							
Basic reserve position								
Excess reserves[1]	84	86	37	57	3	170	126	121
LESS:								
Borrowings at F.R. Banks	156	129	128	277	76	221	54	102
Net interbank Federal funds transactions	15,135	20,710	20,198	18,005	15,436	18,143	18,273	17,604
EQUALS: Net surplus, or deficit (—):								
Amount	−15,207	−20,754	−20,290	−18,225	−15,508	−18,193	−18,201	−17,584
Per cent of average required reserves	*94.4*	*132.5*	*115.9*	*114.0*	*98.3*	*115.2*	*114.0*	*113.4*
Interbank Federal funds transactions								
Gross transactions:								
Purchases	25,020	28,330	27,896	24,683	22,456	25,246	25,118	25,101
Sales	9,885	7,620	7,968	6,678	7,020	7,103	6,845	7,497
Two-way transactions[2]	6,092	5,221	5,511	5,575	5,351	5,671	5,990	6,078
Net transactions:								
Purchases of net buying banks	18,928	23,110	22,385	19,108	17,105	19,575	19,128	19,024
Sales of net selling banks	3,794	2,400	2,188	1,102	1,669	1,432	855	1,420
Related transactions with U.S. Govt. securities dealers								
Loans to dealers[3]	4,004	5,050	2,912	4,006	4,451	3,719	4,308	2,937
Borrowing from dealers[4]	1,693	1,462	1,776	2,340	2,462	2,091	1,946	2,474
Net loans	2,312	3,588	1,136	1,666	1,990	1,628	2,362	464
	8 banks in New York City							
Basic reserve position								
Excess reserves[1]	−46	94	21	30	52	23	4	45
LESS:								
Borrowings at F.R. Banks	101	27	.....	211	.....	14	36	.....
Net interbank Federal funds transactions	6,528	7,766	6,373	5,314	4,045	5,065	4,874	5,286
EQUALS: Net surplus, or deficit (—):								
Amount	−6,675	−7,699	−6,352	−5,496	−3,993	−5,056	−4,906	−5,241
Per cent of average required reserves	*109.4*	*129.8*	*93.1*	*92.6*	*67.3*	*83.2*	*80.6*	*85.4*

Interbank Federal funds transactions

Gross transactions:							
Purchases	7,291	8,342	7,297	6,246	5,032	6,432	6,121	6,665
Sales	763	576	924	932	988	1,367	1,247	1,379
Two-way transactions[2]	764	576	924	932	988	1,194	1,246	1,279
Net transactions:							
Purchases of net buying banks	6,527	7,766	6,373	5,314	4,045	5,238	4,874	5,386
Sales of net selling banks	.....	.....	.....	.....	.....	173	.....	100

Related transactions with U.S. Govt. securities

Loans to dealers[3]	2,718	2,902	1,747	2,200	2,250	2,283	1,941	1,580
Borrowing from dealers[4]	1,031	1,147	1,168	1,509	1,224	1,068	973	1,287
Net loans	1,687	1,755	579	691	1,026	1,215	968	294

5 banks in City of Chicago

Basic reserve position

Excess reserves[1]	91	−20	19	8	−1	20	17	7
LESS:							
Borrowings at F.R. Banks	.....	14	29	19	.....	.....	.....	.....
Net interbank Federal funds transactions	5,447	6,502	6,654	6,168	5,492	5,926	6,180	5,535
EQUALS: Net surplus, or deficit (−):							
Amount	−5,356	−6,536	−6,663	−6,179	−5,493	−5,906	−6,163	−5,528
Per cent of average required reserves	*339.2*	*441.5*	*387.7*	*399.2*	*361.6*	*379.4*	*387.7*	*373.8*

Interbank Federal funds transactions

Gross transactions:							
Purchases	6,539	7,492	7,928	7,256	6,714	7,063	7,056	6,931
Sales	1,092	991	1,274	1,088	1,222	1,138	876	1,396
Two-way transactions[2]	1,018	911	1,217	1,049	1,184	1,118	873	1,370
Net transactions:							
Purchases of net buying banks	5,522	6,582	6,710	6,206	5,530	5,946	6,183	5,561
Sales of net selling banks	74	80	57	39	38	20	3	26

Related transactions with U.S. Govt. securities

Loans to dealers[3]	180	387	201	206	341	253	283	242
Borrowing from dealers[4]	246	34	228	290	463	230	263	423
Net loans	−66	353	−28	−84	−122	23	20	−182

1 Based on reserve balances, including adjustments to include waivers of penalties for reserve deficiencies in accordance with changes in policy of the Board of Governors effective Nov. 19, 1975.
2 Derived from averages for individual banks for entire week. Figure for each bank indicates extent to which the bank's average purchases and sales are offsetting.
3 Federal funds loaned, net funds supplied to each dealer by clearing banks, repurchase agreements (purchases from dealers subject to resale), or other lending arrangements.

4 Federal funds borrowed, net funds acquired from each dealer by clearing banks, reverse repurchase agreements (sales of securities to dealers subject to repurchase), resale agreements, and borrowings secured by U.S. Govt. or other securities.

NOTE.—Weekly averages of daily figures. For description of series, see August 1964 BULLETIN, pp. 944–53. Back data for 46 banks appear in the Board's *Annual Statistical Digest, 1971–1975*, Table 3.

Source: *Federal Reserve Bulletin.*

sell funds to only banks with whom they have reciprocal lines. However, the need to "buy one's way in" is less pronounced in the Fed funds market than in the Euromarket, because banks in the Fed funds market tend to be one way most of the time—either consistent buyers or consistent sellers.

Some tiering exists in the Fed funds market, with poorer credits paying higher rates, but it is *much* less pronounced than in the CD market.

Volume

It is difficult to get a figure for the total volume of funds traded in the Fed funds market on the average day, and it is not clear that such a number would be meaningful because a lot of funds purchased are subsequently resold on the same day. Some idea of the dimensions of the market can, however, be gleaned from the statistics presented in Table 11–2. The top five lines in each section of the table show the extent to which a specific group of banks depends on net purchases of Fed funds and borrowings at the discount window to meet their reserve requirements. The figures are revealing. Week in and week out, the top 46 banks meet close to 100 percent (give or take a little) of their reserve requirements by buying Fed funds and borrowing at the discount window. The figures are slightly smaller for the top New York banks but they are much larger for the top Chicago banks, which daily borrow 300–400 percent of their required reserves almost exclusively in the Fed funds market.

The figures in the second part of the top section of this table, *Interbank Federal funds transactions,* show that the top 46 banks as a group buy a much larger quantity of Fed funds than they sell. On an average day, they buy well in excess of $20 billion of funds and sell less than $10 billion. Most of the banks in this group are net buyers of funds (gross *Purchases* minus *Two-way transactions* equal net *Purchases of net buying banks*). A few of these banks, however, are net sellers of funds (gross *Purchases* minus *Two-way transactions* equal net *Sales of net selling banks*). Note that not one of the top New York or Chicago banks is a net seller of funds.

The third section of Table 11–2, *Related transactions with U.S. government securities dealers,* shows that the top New York banks play a prominent role relative to other large banks in dealer financing (see *Loans to dealers* line). *Borrowing from dealers* is discussed in the next chapter.

THE BROKERS' MARKET

In addition to the huge volume of funds traded *directly* between big banks and their correspondents, there is also an equally large volume of overnight funds traded through *brokers*. Large banks lay off any excess funds they take in from their correspondents in the brokers market. Also, if their needs exceed the amounts they receive from their correspondents, they will buy funds through brokers. There are many regional banks, foreign banks, and foreign agency banks that also buy and sell funds through brokers. And those few funds desks manned by traders who *deal* in funds—buying and selling to pick up ⅛—add to the volume in the brokers market. Finally, there is the deposit-rich B of A, which everyday sells vast amounts of funds through brokers.

The major brokers in the market are Garvin GuyButler, Mabon Nugent & Co., George Palumbo & Co., and Maxcor. In addition to these, there are a number of minor brokers. Also, the Irving Trust runs a matching service for correspondents buying and selling Fed funds; this service is not precisely brokering and Irving does not charge for it.

The Fed funds rate is an add-on rate quoted on a 360-day-year basis. Thus if funds were trading at 5¾, a purchase of $50 million of overnight funds would cost the buyer

$$0.0575 \times \$50,000,000 \times \left(\frac{1}{360}\right) = \$7,986.11$$

In addition, he would pay brokerage costs equal to $0.50 per $1 million per day, which works out to slightly less than ¹/₅₀ of 1 percentage point. Brokerage is paid by both the buyer and the seller.

The volume going through the brokers varies from day to day. Thursday, which is the first day of the settlement week, is a slow day. After that things pick up. Friday transactions are particularly attractive to a broker because on them he earns a three-day commission; a Friday sale is unwound on Monday. On an active day, a top broker may handle more than $6 billion of overnight funds.

Function of the broker

The major function of the Fed funds brokers is communications. There are so many participants in the brokers market—all the top 300 banks plus a potpourri of foreign banks—that, in the absence of brokers, the banks would need a host of traders and telephones on their Fed funds desk to get their job done.

Each broker has a particular set of names that use him. There is, however, considerable overlap between the clients of the top brokers, since many banks use two or even three brokers on a regular basis. The brokers put in direct phone lines to any bank having a volume of trading through them that justifies the cost. They communicate with the rest over WATS lines. The phone bill for a broker is a huge expense; he is providing a communications network, and doing so is not cheap.

In addition to communications, brokers also provide the banks with anonymity. A top bank that has a big job to do values this because it fears that if it were a bid for or offer huge sums in its own name in the market, it might move the market.

The brokers market is really open to only those banks that buy and sell in volume. In Fed funds anything under $5 million is an odd lot. A small bank in Iowa that wants to buy $500,000 is better off going to its regional correspondent, since the New York brokers are not set up to handle trades of that size. Noted one broker: "We have a guy who sells through us $300,000 to $1 million everyday. He asks, 'What is the market?' We say, '$5/16-3/8$.' He says, 'What do I get for $1 million?' We have to say, '$1/8$.'"

Trading the sheet

A Fed funds brokering operation is not too impressive to look at: eight or ten people sitting around a desk, each constantly talking on one of a battery of direct phone lines facing him, and each constantly scribbling down bids and offers on a sheet of paper. That sheet, however bedraggled it may look, is a key part of the operation, since each person on the desk can, by glancing at it, see what banks are bidding and offering through the firm and what the amounts are.

Brokers will often describe what they do as *trading the sheet.* "We do not," said one broker, "trade in the sense of taking a position. But when someone acts in the market, how do we react? That is our trading decision. Thursday is difficult because it is a slow day. We end up with a sheet cluttered on both sides with bids and offers. If a name then comes in and says he wants to sell $20 million at the bid, we may have 25 names to choose from; ethically the best we can do is to decide who was there first. When the market is moving you do not have to worry about this because everyone will be satisfied. Wednesday is easy because it moves so fast."

Brokering is very much a team effort. Commented the head of one brokering operation: "This job takes concentration and coordination. To run an efficient shop, you cannot have two people on the phone saying the market is going down and three others saying it's going up. Avoiding that is hard because our thoughts on the market may change 20 times a day."

Many Fed funds brokers come out of the banks, and a number are ex-Fed funds traders. Such experience is valuable—an ex-trader knows how to quote the market and understands how to react to what the banks do.

Quoting the market

Broker: Hello. ¾ bid on 50. I am offered at 6 in two spots, 75 firm, 50 under reference.

Bank: I'll take 50.

Broker: OK, 50 done. Can I make it a C note?

Brokering occurs at a breakneck pace. The top New York banks do not want a lot of information, and a broker makes a fast quote to them. In a minimum of words he attempts to convey the tone of the market. He might, for example, quote the market: "$5/16$–$3/8$, last at $5/16$," or "$5/16$–$3/8$, quiet," or "Market last at $3/8$ looking like it might go to 7." Some regional banks want a slower quote and a little more information on market developments. Said one broker: "The worse even ask what the *handle* is."

In the Fed funds market, banks, in addition to putting *firm* bids and offers into the brokers, will also make *subject* bids and offerings. When a bank's bid or offer is subject or *under reference,* before the broker executes a trade for that bank, he has to go back and ask it if they will make their bid or offer firm. When the Fed goes into the market to do open-market operations, it creates uncertainty, and the brokers, in courtesy to their customers, treat all bids and offers as subject until they are renewed.

Part of the fun and the frustration of brokering funds is that the market is constantly changing throughout the day. Because of this, an important part of a broker's job is to get a line on the market, a feel for its tone and where it is moving. In doing so, he looks not only at his own market, but also at related markets. What is the rate on overnight repo? Where are Euros trading? The top Fed funds brokers also broker Euros and a variety of other instruments, so their people have constant and easy access to information on developments in related markets as they occur.

Fine tuning quotes

In the Fed funds market, whenever a buyer takes a seller's offering, the broker has to go back to the seller and tell him the name of the buyer and ask him if he will do the trade. The ethics of the game are such that the seller is supposed to do the trade unless he does not have a line to the buyer or his line to the buyer is filled. If the seller can do the trade, the broker than tells the buyer the seller's name, and the buyer and the seller clear the trade directly over the Fed wire. Brokerage bills are sent and paid at the end of the month.

Line problems and other subtleties make brokering more than just quoting two rates. A good broker knows what lines various banks have extended to other banks and how big they are. And he tries to guess during the day how much of those lines have been used up. Said one broker: "I know the B of A's lines better than they do. It's not that they tell me, but if they keep selling some guy x million day after day, I know pretty quickly what their line to him is."

"Because of line problems," commented the same broker, "the quote to each bank is individualized." Line problems become especially acute on Wednesdays when the banks settle and trading is active. "The quote will be one thing to Manny if they have been in the market all day long buying up everything in sight, and another story to Chase if they have been selling all day. A broker is foolish if he says, '5¼–⅜,' when there is nothing on the offer side good to the guy on the phone who wants to buy. We may have an offering but we say none. Or I can say, 'I am 5¼–⅜, but my offer is not good to you. I will work for you at that price.'"

Lines are particularly a problem for small regional banks, agency banks, and foreign banks that don't have the line coverage of big domestic banks and that consequently have to pay up to get money on occasion.

Another factor that individualizes the market is size. If a prime New York bank comes in and wants to buy $300 million, the broker is naturally tempted to do the whole trade with the B of A in one fast shot. Also, buyers occasionally want to buy in block size and won't mess around with nickels and dimes ($5 and $10 million pieces). This makes it difficult to sell for banks that for one reason or another have small lines to other banks.

Part of being a good broker is the ability to be a good salesman—to anticipate a customer's needs and to nudge him subtly into a trade. One broker noted: "This is a pattern market in the sense that many names do not change in their posture in the market very much. They are constantly one way or the other. You often know with a good customer what he is going to do and when he is going to do it. A good broker will anticipate what the bank is going to do without letting the bank know and without being pushy. The minute you see a borrowing bank's line ring, you get your people on the phones with the accounts that are going to be selling. So when the bank says, 'I will take 200.' you have the offers all lined up and can say, 'Sold 25,' 'Sold 50,' and so on."

The same broker went on to observe that "when you have a big buyer on the phone, you try to get a round number out of him. If he asks me how much I might be able to bring down [get for him] and I say 350, my next question might be: 'Do you want 450?' This is a volume market; we can put through a single trade for $450 million a lot easier than we can do five $1 million trades."

Knowing what a bank might want to do is also important because some big banks fear that showing all they want to do might distort the market. So a bank that is looking for $1 billion might bid for only $100 million. When a broker sells money to such a bank, he always tries to keep the trade going by asking: "Can I work some more for you?"

The Garban and Telerate screens both show constantly updated quotes on Fed funds so that buyers and sellers can use them to track what the market is doing.[6] However, a given broker's quotes may at any moment differ from those on the screen because the market moves so fast. Also, each broker has a somewhat different clientele so that quotes coming out of different brokers may vary slightly.

Not all trades in the Fed funds market are made at the going market rate. A few regional banks pay their smaller correspondents $1/16$ or $1/8$ less, while others will offer a small bank an extra $1/4$ to pick up other business with them.

The banks

It costs a bank money to buy and sell through a broker, but using a broker saves the bank time and cuts its phone bill. Said one trader: "When I have funds to sell, it is easier for me to go into the brokers and hit 10 or 15 bids than for me to call individual banks." Also there is the human factor. The same trader continued: "If I sell through the broker and then the rates fall, I feel, well, that bank was in there bidding at that rate. If I go in and sell direct and then the rate falls off, often the guy who sold will feel I knew something he did not. And the next time I call he bids below the market."

Most large banks use several brokers. One reason is that the more brokers a bank uses, the more exposure it gets. Another is that a bank with a big job to do may be able to operate faster by using several brokers.

A third reason some sharp traders use two brokers is that now and then the quotes at two major brokers will differ long enough to allow a profitable arbitrage. Said one trader: "The last time the Fed did reverses, Garvin was at $3/16$, Mabon at $1/8$. I bought through Mabon, sold through Garvin, and picked up $1/16$ on every buck I passed through."

Finally, there is the embarrassment factor. One dealing trader commented: "If on a Wednesday I buy funds at 6 through Mabon and now want to sell at 5, I will go to another broker. I made a mistake and it's embarrassing. The guy at Garvin says, 'Hey, you are going to sell before the bottom falls out.' He does not know I took in the money at 6."

The banks will also use the brokers to play games with each other and with the Fed. The Fed is constantly calling not only the money desks of the major banks but brokers of funds as well to check on tone and rates in the funds market. If a bank has a lot to buy and funds are firm, it may

---

[6] Garban brokers governments and agencies. See page 345.

buy a little at a high rate to see if it can't get the Fed to come into the market to do repo. Or, if it is very black, it may sell at low rates to get the Fed to do reverses. Also, banks sometimes try to influence where funds are trading by posting high bids when they want to sell and vice versa.

The opening

In the early morning the chatter in a broker's office is likely to run:

"Work for you? OK, I show you out."
"¼–⅜, the bid at 5 is junk. Japanese at 6. No opening yet."
"Light opening at ⁵/₁₆, a regional name. I am at ¼–⅜."

Calling an opening is a touchy affair for a major broker because a lot of big banks pay their correspondents the opening rate. Years ago the big New York banks tried on occasion to distort this rate. One broker said: "They were paying correspondents the opening rate at Mabon or Garvin. So to ensure they were not getting ripped off, they used to come into the market and hit the bids, and they had an official opening. That was a distortion since the market opened on the bid side. We stopped that because we thought it was unethical. They might sell $100 million at that price when they had $500 million that they were committed to buy at that price. We told the banks that if they satisfied every bidder on our sheet, we would call an opening. If not, we would not. That stopped that."

Sometimes the major brokers open ⅛ apart because one opens on the bid side of the market, the other on the offered side.

WEDNESDAY CLOSE

The most exciting and volatile time in the Fed funds market is Wednesday afternoon when the banks settle.

The Federal Reserve Act divides the country into 12 districts (Figure 11–1). Most of the time district lines do not mean much because Fed policy is set nationally in Washington. Wednesday afternoon, however, is an exception because the district lines determine the schedule according to which the Fed wire shuts down and when and how the moment of truth—did we settle?—is reached by banks in different areas.

The district banks and their branches in the eastern part of the country (roughly the first six districts plus Detroit) close down the wire for interdistrict transfers at 3:00 P.M. Eastern time and at 4:00 P.M. (4:30 P.M. on Wednesdays) for intradistrict transfer. In the Midwest, widely defined, the Fed wire closes down at 3:00 P.M. local time for interdistrict transfers and a half hour later for intradistrict transfers. The schedule is roughly the same in the Far West, district 12, but an hour later.

Because of the timing schedule, funds are actively traded on a nationwide basis through the New York brokers until 3:00 P.M. New York

Figure 11–1
The Federal Reserve System (boundaries of Federal Reserve Districts and their branch territories)

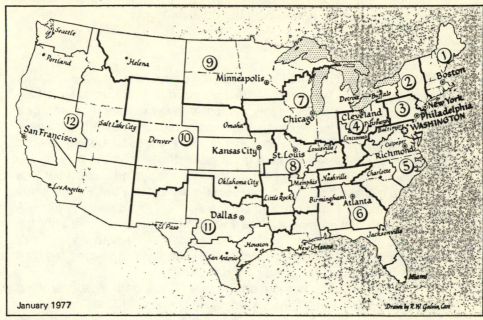

January 1977

Drawn by R. W. Galvin, Cart.

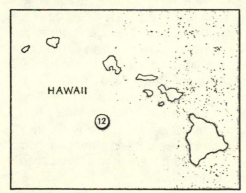

HAWAII

ALASKA

LEGEND

— Boundaries of Federal Reserve Districts

— Boundaries of Federal Reserve Branch Territories

⭐ Board of Governors of the Federal Reserve System

Source: *Federal Reserve Bulletin.*

⊙ Federal Reserve Bank Cities

• Federal Reserve Branch Cities

· Federal Reserve Bank Facility

time. After that, trading, especially on a Wednesday, may still be active in New York but it is confined to New Yorkers trading with other New Yorkers. Once New York shuts down, trading throughout the rest of the nation sputters on for a time but little brokering occurs in New York.

Extensions and as ofs

Often banks will ask the Fed to extend the time for which the Fed wire is held open because they need extra time due to a computer breakdown, the absence of some key person in the wire transfer room, or a transaction that has gotten lost in the system (recall the opening scene in this chapter). Usually the Fed will grant a short extension, and—if it grants it for one bank—it has to grant it for all banks in the district.

On Wednesday the loss of a transaction in the system, a mistake by a bank, or a mistake by a broker can set off a panic on a bank's Fed funds desk: they thought they had settled and suddenly find they have not. A bank in this position may ask the Fed to hold the wire open until the mistake is righted or may ask the Fed to permit them to do an *as of* transaction, that is, to do a transaction the next day and be credited for it as if the transfer had occurred on the previous day.

In the scenario that introduced this chapter, a bank was searching wildly for $150 million that had been lost in the system. The Fed is tough about doing "as of" transactions in such situations because, as someone at the Fed noted: "The way things work out is that if a West Coast bank is supposed to have sent Chase money and Chase did not get it, through no fault of either bank [something went wrong with the wire system or a computer], and if we then credit Chase as if the transfer had been made, there will be no offsetting debit for the West Coast bank; it will be a one-sided adjustment, and we end up giving money away free. The reason is that the West Coast bank will argue that they knew they had sent the money, and when they saw their balance [at the Fed], they assumed that this money had already been taken out and managed their balance accordingly. So to take the money from them now would cause them to end up short through no fault of their own.[7]

"When people reported things by hand, there was no such thing as 'as of' adjustments. The advent of computers gave rise to them—obliged us to give money away free because of mistakes that lie with the technology. The same thing occurs when governments and agencies [securities] are transferred over the Fed wire."

---

[7] Because of the huge volume of transfers being made into and out of a major bank's account at the Fed, it is not uncommon for such a bank to reconcile its balance at the Fed—which it can track throughout the day—with transfers into and out of that account after both it and the Fed have closed. Thus, a bank could make the honest mistake of assuming that its closing balance reflected an outward transfer that had not gone through.

A slightly different situation in which a bank might ask for an "as of" transfer is if it had made a mistake in tracking its own balance or if a mistake had been made by a broker. Here is an example of the latter. Late one Wednesday afternoon a broker commented: "We are in trouble. We thought a bank was willing to give up ⅛ to sell. He says he was not. They misunderstood me and I misunderstood them. Now we have a bank that is short $25 million. He is in District 4. If we cannot cover him now, we will try to find someone—our best bet is the B of A—outside the district and arrange an 'as of' sale.

"The Fed can be a son of a bitch about this sort of thing. This is an ethical business, so it is sad that when an honest mistake is made, they do not give much leeway. But if they are not strict about cutoff times, abuses occur—a bank seeing that the rate is higher in New York than in its own district transfers money into the New York district after the wire is strictly speaking shut down.

"For a small bank in Tulsa, losing $5 million is like Chase losing $250 million. The Fed thinks of the small banks as less sophisticated so it is more likely to let them do an 'as of' to cover a mistake than they are to let a New York bank do so."

On a bank's desk

Settling on a Wednesday is tricky for a bank's funds desk. It knows what target it wants to hit for the day but it doesn't know exactly what transfers are going to occur into and out of the bank's reserve account, *and* such transfers keep occurring right up to the end of the day. Said one trader on a Wednesday morning: "A big corporate just wired in $400 million. I don't pay attention to that—try to offset it. I know they will take it out. If they don't, we are going to have to call the Fed and try to do an 'as of' tomorrow, and if the Fed won't let us, then we'll get no use of that money, and it's a major bust."[8]

A bank can offset large and unanticipated inflows or outflows of funds right up to the moment the Fed wire closes by selling or buying additional Fed funds. However, the Fed funds rate sometimes gets out of hand on Wednesday afternoon when either bids or offers may be scarce.

A bank that finds itself unexpectedly in the red can, in addition to buying funds, go to the discount window. But if it is way red, it may have a collateral problem, that is, need to borrow more than the amount of collateral it has at the Fed. In that case, it either has to scurry to find funds or, if worse comes to worse, ask for an unsecured advance at the window. In the short run the Fed has to grant such an advance, but

---

[8] As a matter of practice, the Fed seeks to never do an "as of" transaction unless the Fed itself was at fault.

asking for it is a black mark against a bank, and the Fed will expect that bank to be more careful and conservative in the future.

The fact that a bank can run 2 percent short or long on its reserve balance and carry that over into the next reserve week gives it some leeway in settling. How much depends on whether it settled on the nose during the previous week. If, for example, it was red in the previous week, then in the current week it has to settle on the nose or run an excess.

Sometimes on a Wednesday, many banks end up with reserves imbalances in the same direction—they are all red or all black. This occurs because the Fed has misestimated the reserves available to the banks, and there are either too many or two few in the aggregate. When this occurs, the funds rate will start to move, and the Fed—taking its signal from the market—will come in, doing reverses if the banks are all black or repos if the banks are all red. The Fed, however, can't initiate open-market operations much later than 2:00 P.M. because the wire out of New York closes down at 3:00 P.M.

Late on a Wednesday, when the Fed can no longer act, the Fed funds rate can go anywhere and sometimes does. On Wednesday funds have traded as low as 1 percent and as high as 30 percent. (The bank that paid 30 percent on a Wednesday afternoon when funds were tight had a country-bank philosophy: We won't go to the window.)

Part of the reason the market becomes so volatile is that late on Wednesday volume can get so *thin* that a $10 million purchase will move the market up ½. A bank may also have to pay high rates late in the day because, while there are still funds offered in the market, they are not being offered by banks with lines open to it.

That the funds rate sometimes falls so low on Wednesdays is due to the way the carry-over provision operates. Suppose a few banks, the B of A included, end up late Wednesday way black due to bad numbers. As they pump out money, the funds rate will start to fall; this ought to attract buyers because banks can carry a reserve surplus from the current week forward into the following week, and sometimes the banks will bid for the surplus funds to carry them forward. It may, however, happen that most of the big banks were black the week before. If so, then if they go black again, they will get no credit for the current week's surplus. A bank in this position will bid for additional funds only if the rate is very low and only if it can buy more money than the black it is erasing. For example, if a bank were $80 million black in the previous week and planned to be $80 million short in the current week, it would pay it to decrease that short only if it bought more than $80 million and only if it bought that money very cheaply.

If a bank in such a position bids for funds, it will probably put in an *all or none* (AON) bid. An AON bid does not mean that the money all has to

Table 11-3
Reserves and borrowings of member banks ($ millions)

| | Weekly averages of daily figures for weeks ending — | | | | | | | | | |
| | 1977 | | | | | | | | | |
	Oct. 26	Nov. 2	Nov. 9	Nov. 16	Nov. 23	Nov. 30	Dec. 7	Dec. 14	Dec. 21p	Dec. 28p
All member banks										
Reserves:										
24 At F.R. Banks	27,026	26,929	26,301	26,963	27,541	26,779	26,368	26,374	27,646	27,431
25 Currency and coin	8,406	8,983	9,182	9,191	8,249	9,094	9,254	9,837	8,925	9,357
26 Total held[1]	35,502	35,987	35,557	36,221	35,856	35,938	35,687	36,275	36,630	36,846
27 Required	35,300	35,716	35,396	35,804	35,867	35,500	35,672	35,962	36,429	36,558
28 Excess[1]	202	265	155	417	−11	438	15	313	201	288
Borrowings at F.R. Banks:[2]										
29 Total	1,444	1,113	887	534	879	1,079	583	509	528	686
30 Seasonal	116	103	87	83	85	75	65	56	53	53
Large banks in New York City										
31 Reserves held	5,757	6,220	6,260	6,335	6,280	5,956	5,969	6,219	6,384	6,132
32 Required	5,777	6,175	6,214	6,314	6,322	5,848	6,087	6,182	6,401	6,269
33 Excess	−20	45	46	21	−42	108	−118	37	−17	−137
34 Borrowings[2]	200			60	252	252	37	93	50	32
Large banks in Chicago										
35 Reserves held	1,657	1,669	1,611	1,675	1,575	1,587	1,618	1,646	1,533	1,533
36 Required	1,643	1,648	1,624	1,638	1,594	1,570	1,620	1,631	1,574	1,593
37 Excess	14	21	−13	37	−19	17	−2	15	−41	−60
38 Borrowings[2]	15	17	14	13	33	31	9	8	27	73
Other large banks										
39 Reserves held	13,670	13,668	13,459	13,823	13,578	13,788	13,578	13,957	13,835	13,970
40 Required	13,582	13,601	13,478	13,689	13,602	13,638	13,609	13,840	13,985	14,080
41 Excess	88	67	−19	134	−24	150	−31	117	−150	−110
42 Borrowings[2]	586	631	560	168	298	386	287	211	232	293
All other banks										
43 Reserves held	14,418	14,424	14,221	14,388	14,423	14,607	14,522	14,453	14,502	14,653
44 Required	14,298	14,292	14,080	14,163	14,349	14,444	14,356	14,309	14,469	14,616
45 Excess	120	132	141	225	74	163	166	144	33	37
46 Borrowings[2]	643	465	313	293	296	410	250	197	219	288

[1] Adjusted to include waivers of penalties for reserve deficiencies in accordance with Board policy, effective Nov. 19, 1975, of permitting transitional relief on a graduated basis over a 24-month period when a nonmember bank merges into an existing member bank, or when a nonmember bank joins the Federal Reserve System. For weeks for which figures are preliminary, figures by class of bank do not add to total because adjusted data by class are not available. [2] Based on closing figures.

Source: *Federal Reserve Bulletin.*

come from the same source, only that it has to equal in total the amount bid for and be offered at the rate bid.

Weekly pattern in excess reserves

Because banks can carry forward reserve deficiencies and excesses in limited amounts, one would expect a pattern in banks' excess reserves, namely, that if they were *positive* one week, they would be *negative* the next. The figures in Table 11–3 show that precisely such a pattern exists in the excess reserves run by *large* banks in New York, Chicago, and elsewhere. However, for the banking system as a whole, excess reserves are consistently positive. The reason is that there are many smaller banks in the system that consistently run excess reserves either because they don't find it worthwhile to sell off the last penny of their surplus reserves or because they do not ever want to end up at the discount window and so manage their funds positions very conservatively.

THE FUTURES MARKET

So far we have been talking about the market for overnight funds for *immediate* delivery. Currently there is a lot of trading in overnight funds for *future* delivery (a sale on Friday for delivery on Monday), mostly in connection with Euro arbitrages.

The rather casual beginning of the futures market was described by one broker as follows: "Years ago the trader at a major New York bank said one day that he thought funds were going to be x and he would pay for tomorrow's money such and such a rate. I disagreed. So I called a couple of accounts of a speculative nature and they said, 'OK, we will sell funds at that rate for tomorrow.' That was the start of the futures market. People began to do it on a Wednesday if they had a feeling about where the market was going. Back then, $200 or $300 million was a big day in futures. Then people with fast pencils discovered that Euros could be arbitraged against Fed funds, and the futures market took off."

As explained in Chapter 17, domestic and foreign (and foreign agency) banks engage during the week in several mutually profitable arbitrage games. One calls for a foreign bank to sell Euros on Friday to a domestic bank and cover by delivering Fed funds on Monday. The other calls for a domestic bank to sell Euros on Thursday to a foreign bank and cover by delivering Fed funds on Friday. In each case, the sale of the Euros is made one or several days before the Fed funds are to be delivered.

A bank that sells Euros one day and in doing so locks itself into delivering Fed funds on a later date would expose itself to a *rate risk* if it did not buy the Fed funds forward. Most banks are unwilling to assume that risk.

So a huge market has developed in forward Monday funds, and as much as $1 billion of such funds may be traded through a single broker. The market for forward Friday funds is also active, but not quite as large.

The foreign banks that arbitrage Euros against Fed funds—Canadian agency banks are very active in the game—all buy and sell Fed funds in large amounts, much as domestic banks do. They extend lines to domestic banks, and domestic banks extend lines to them. The only wrinkle is that a foreign bank does not have a deposit account at the Fed, so the way it deals in Fed funds is to have funds wired into and out of its account at its clearing bank which is typically one of the top New York banks.

Agency banks and branches of foreign banks do not enjoy the same full market in Fed funds that domestic banks do. One reason is that some regional banks don't feel comfortable selling funds to foreign names. Also, some regional banks do not understand the arbitrages that go on between Euros and Fed funds and consequently the rationale for forward transactions in Fed funds.

Other banks are quite willing to extend lines to foreign banks, partly because these banks are sellers of overnight Fed funds and at times of term Fed funds and because these banks maintain deposit accounts with them. Sales of Fed funds to foreign names are also attractive because these banks have to pay up $1/8$ or $1/16$ to buy Monday funds forward. On a Friday, "Monday Feds" might be quoted to a prime agency name at $5^1/2$–$9/16$, whereas Monday Feds are going to trade in fact at $5^7/16$–$3/8$.

The foreign banks that play the arbitrage game normally have fair-sized lines at their clearing banks. They will pick up all the nickels and dimes they can from those regional banks that are willing to sell to them and then borrow whatever else they need from their clearing bank. In the funds market, as in others, Japanese names are the most difficult, and the Japanese consequently often have to pay the highest rates.

TERM FED FUNDS

Most transactions in the Fed funds market are for overnight (over the weekend in the case of Friday sales) funds. There is, however, also a market for what are called *term Fed funds*. On term transactions the funds are normally sold for a period of time, such as 30 days, 60 days, or 90 days, but longer-term transactions also occur; one Japanese bank bought term funds for an 18-month period. The market for term Fed funds is quietly building but it is still only a fraction of the size of the overnight market. A major broker might have a couple billion dollars of term funds outstanding.

The main advantage to a domestic bank of buying term funds is cost. A bank that wants to get some longer-term money on its books has a choice between CDs and term Fed funds. From the point of view of cost, term Fed funds have the attraction of being classified as a borrowing, not a deposit, so a bank buying term Fed funds incurs no reserve requirement and does not have to pay FDIC insurance. For example, in the 90-day area, this would mean that if term Fed funds were trading at anything less than a ⅛ spread above 90-day CD money, term Fed funds would be cheaper to the buying bank than CD money. Another advantage of term Fed funds is that they can be bought for a maturity of less than 30 days, which CD money cannot.

On a bank's statement, money that a bank has bought in the CD market shows up as "time deposits," whereas money a bank has purchased in the term Fed funds market shows up as "other borrowings." Banks like to have a lot of deposits to preserve the aesthetics of their balance sheet, so they limit the amount of term Fed funds they will buy even when there is a rate advantage to doing so. This is particularly true over the year-end statement date.

Some of the money sold in the term Fed funds market is sold by small domestic banks that might alternatively have invested in CDs issued by large banks. A small bank selling term Fed funds loses the liquidity it would have if it purchased a CD, but it gains a little extra return. Normally term Fed funds trade at a rate such that the cost saving to the buying bank (no reserves and no FDIC premium as on CDs) is split down the middle between the selling bank and the buying bank.

Many smaller banks that are consistent sellers of overnight Fed funds are not active sellers of term funds. One reason is that for a small bank, *selling* Fed funds everyday is its liquidity.[9] Even small banks have to settle with the Fed and their money positions change from day to day. They might have $300,000 available to sell one day, $350,000 the next day, and only $100,000 the day after that. If such a bank sold term Fed funds, it would be acquiring a fixed-rate term asset that it could not liquidate. Sales of day-to-day money, in contrast, give it great flexibility.

In 1970 the Fed ruled that Fed funds purchased by banks from agencies of the U.S. government, savings and loan associations, mutual savings banks, and agencies and branches of foreign banks operating in the United States were, like purchases of Fed funds from commercial banks, not subject to reserve requirements. Commercial banks at that time had already been buying Fed funds from some of these institutions, so the Fed's action simply made official what the banks had assumed to be Fed policy.

For a savings and loan association, a sale of term Fed funds with a maturity of no longer than 6 months is a qualifying asset for purposes of meeting short-term liquidity requirements. Because the rate on term Fed

---

[9] Note the contrast between small banks and large banks. For the large bank, the ability to *buy* overnight money is its major source of liquidity.

funds is quite attractive relative to other short-term rates, S&Ls have become major sellers of term funds to the banks. Some of these sales are made directly to the banks and others through the Federal Home Loan Bank system, which collects small amounts of overnight and term funds from individual S&Ls and resells them in round-lot amounts in the New York market. The FHLB also invests funds from its own liquidity portfolios by selling term funds.

Canadian agency and some other foreign banks are also substantial sellers of term Fed funds. At times they obtain the funds by *arbitraging* the CD and the term Fed funds market. They obtain funds by selling CDs on which they incur no reserve cost and pay no FDIC insurance and then resell those funds in the term Fed funds market.

Corporations can also get into the term Fed funds market indirectly. They do so by making a time deposit with a foreign or agency bank; this deposit, because it is booked offshore, is technically a Eurodollar deposit; the buying bank takes a markup and resells the funds in the term Fed funds market.

Because brokerage on Fed funds is paid on a per-day basis, sales of term Fed funds are attractive to a broker. Brokers thus constantly attempt to point out to participants in the market how they can profit either by buying or by selling term Fed funds. In particular, the brokers are active in getting agency, foreign, and other banks to engage in all sorts of arbitrages: Euros against term Fed funds, CDs against term Fed funds, and so forth. A broker that shows an agency bank an opportunity to arbitrage between the CD market and the term Fed funds market earns not only brokerage on term Fed funds placed through it, but also an 05 on the CDs sold through it.

The repo market

The market for Fed funds is one in which *immediately available* funds are lent on an unsecured basis. A market closely related to the Fed funds market is the *repo* market, in which immediately available funds are lent on a *secured* basis. We turn to the repo market in the next chapter.

Chapter 12

Repos and reverses

THE SALE-REPURCHASE MARKET is really several markets in one.[1] First, there is the vast *repo* market, in which dealers and large banks finance *on an ongoing basis* their holdings of securities by selling these securities under an agreement to repurchase. Second, there is the *reverse* market, in which portfolio managers who run standard hold-to-maturity portfolios of governments and agencies *occasionally* borrow money against securities they know they will never sell. They do so in order to arbitrage; for example, they borrow 90-day repo money at one rate and invest that money in 90-day Euro CDs that pay a higher rate. Such transactions are commonly referred to as *reverses* because the transaction is the reverse of a repo agreement. Finally, there is the *specific issues* market, in which dealers and a handful of other portfolio managers enter into repurchase agreements to obtain securities to cover a short.

To this should be added that one huge player in the sale-repurchase market, the Fed, does repos and reverses not to borrow money or securities but to adjust bank reserves.

---

[1] Much has already been said in this book about repos, reverses, and their uses. This chapter builds on and amplifies this earlier discussion.

Note that any transaction in the market we are talking about, whether it is called a *repo* or a *reverse,* takes the same form: on the day the transaction is initiated, securities are sold against money; and on the day the transaction is unwound, these flows are reversed—the money and the securities are returned to their original holders.

NATURE OF A REPO TRANSACTION

To people who come upon repos and reverses for the first time, they are the most confusing of all money market transactions. So a short description of how these transactions are done is in order. In any repo or reverse transaction, there is first a sale of securities and subsequently a repurchase. The essence of the transaction, however, is most typically that the buyer of the securities is making a secured loan to the seller— the securities sold serving in effect as *collateral* for that loan.

Pricing

An RP agreement can be set up various ways. The normal practice is for pricing to be *flat,* that is, on coupon securities the coupon interest that accrues over the life of the transaction is ignored.[2] Figure 12–1 presents confirmations from the borrower, a bank, on a term repo priced flat. Note that the purchase price (*principal amount*) on the sale confirmation is the same price that appears on the repurchase confirmation. The agreed-upon repo rate is 10 percent (the specimen dates from 1974), so the repurchase confirmation shows that the amount due to the lender at the time of repurchase is the principal sum plus $54,444.45 of accrued interest.

The repo rate is a straight add-on interest rate calculated on a 360-day-year basis. So interest due is figured as follows:

$$\text{Interest due} = \left(\begin{array}{c}\text{Principal}\\\text{amount}\end{array}\right) \times \left(\begin{array}{c}\text{Repo}\\\text{rate}\end{array}\right) \times \left(\frac{\text{Days repo is outstanding}}{360}\right)$$

Applying this formula to the example presented in Figure 12–1, we get

$$\$9,800,000 \times 0.10 \times \frac{20}{360} = \$54,444.45$$

which is the amount of interest that appears on the repurchase confirmation.

---

[2] Coupon securities are, except when the issuer is in default, sold in *outright* purchases at the quoted dollar price *plus* accrued interest. When a bond is in default and no interest payments are being made, it trades *flat,* that is, unpaid interest is not billed to the buyer but is his if the issuer later resumes interest payments. Given this use of the term *flat,* it was natural for participants in the repo market to describe repo transactions on which accrued interest is ignored in the pricing as being *priced flat.*

Figure 12–1
Confirmations on a term repo agreement

A. Sale confirmation

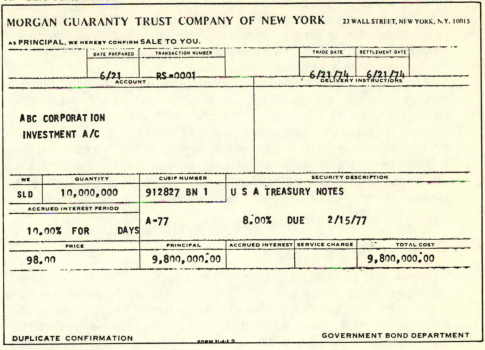

MORGAN GUARANTY TRUST COMPANY OF NEW YORK 23 WALL STREET, NEW YORK, N.Y. 10015

AS **PRINCIPAL**, WE HEREBY CONFIRM SALE TO YOU.

DATE PREPARED	TRANSACTION NUMBER		TRADE DATE	SETTLEMENT DATE
6/21	RS-0001		6/21/74	6/21/74

ACCOUNT

DELIVERY INSTRUCTIONS

ABC CORPORATION
INVESTMENT A/C

WE	QUANTITY	CUSIP NUMBER	SECURITY DESCRIPTION		
SLD	10,000,000	912827 BN 1	U S A TREASURY NOTES		

ACCRUED INTEREST PERIOD

10.00% FOR   DAYS

A-77   8.00% DUE   2/15/77

PRICE	PRINCIPAL	ACCRUED INTEREST	SERVICE CHARGE	TOTAL COST
98.00	9,800,000.00			9,800,000.00

DUPLICATE CONFIRMATION   FORM 51-4-1 D   GOVERNMENT BOND DEPARTMENT

B. Repurchase confirmation

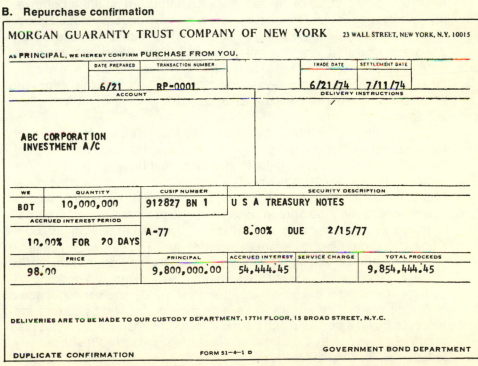

MORGAN GUARANTY TRUST COMPANY OF NEW YORK 23 WALL STREET, NEW YORK, N.Y. 10015

AS **PRINCIPAL**, WE HEREBY CONFIRM PURCHASE FROM YOU.

DATE PREPARED	TRANSACTION NUMBER		TRADE DATE	SETTLEMENT DATE
6/21	RP-0001		6/21/74	7/11/74

ACCOUNT

DELIVERY INSTRUCTIONS

ABC CORPORATION
INVESTMENT A/C

WE	QUANTITY	CUSIP NUMBER	SECURITY DESCRIPTION		
BOT	10,000,000	912827 BN 1	U S A TREASURY NOTES		

ACCRUED INTEREST PERIOD

10.00% FOR 20 DAYS

A-77   8.00% DUE   2/15/77

PRICE	PRINCIPAL	ACCRUED INTEREST	SERVICE CHARGE	TOTAL PROCEEDS
98.00	9,800,000.00	54,444.45		9,854,444.45

DELIVERIES ARE TO BE MADE TO OUR CUSTODY DEPARTMENT, 17TH FLOOR, 15 BROAD STREET, N.Y.C.

DUPLICATE CONFIRMATION   FORM 51-4-1 D   GOVERNMENT BOND DEPARTMENT

While flat pricing is common on repo agreements, such agreements may also be set up in other ways. The second alternative is that the repurchase price is set higher than the sale price, with the difference between the two equaling the interest due to the lender over the life of the transaction at the agreed-upon repo rate.

There is a third alternative to flat pricing that is sometimes used on coupon securities, but never for discount securities. Under it, the securities being RPed are priced at a dollar price plus accrued coupon interest, and the repurchase price is set at a different dollar price plus accrued coupon interest. In this case, the dollar prices on the sale and the repurchase are adjusted so that the net difference between the purchase price plus accrued coupon interest and the sale price plus accrued coupon interest equals the amount of interest due to the lender at the agreed repo rate.

CREDIT RISK AND MARGIN

If on a repo transaction, the amount lent were set precisely equal to the market value of the securities being purchased (accrued coupon interest being included in market value), the lender would receive collateral with a market value equal to 100 percent of the loan extended. He would, however, still be exposed to risk. Interest rates might rise, forcing down the market value of the securities he had taken in; if the borrower then went bankrupt and the repurchase were consequently not effected, the lender would be left holding securities with a market value less than the amount he had lent. Assuming the securities RPed has not been trading above par, the lender could make himself whole by maturing these securities, but if he needed the money he had lent, that might be impossible or it might be expensive because it forced him into other suboptimal decisions.

The borrower in a repo transaction also incurs a risk. Interest rates might fall during the life of the agreement, forcing up the market value of the securities he had sold. If the lender then went belly up, the borrower would be left holding an amount of money smaller than the market value of the securities he had sold. So, by retaining the money lent to him instead of effecting the agreed-upon repurchase, he would incur a loss

In every repo transaction, no matter how the collateral is priced, both the lender and the borrower are exposed to risk. The lender can seek to protect himself by asking for *margin,* that is, by lending less than 100 percent of the market value of the securities he takes in, but in doing so he *increases* risk for the borrower. Alternatively the borrower might seek to reduce his risk by asking for *reverse margin,* that is, by asking the lender to buy his securities at a price above their market value, but that would increase risk for the borrower. No strategy exists to simultaneously reduce risk for both the borrower and the lender.

Margin in practice

Participants in the repo market are very conscious these days of the risk to which repo transactions expose them. These risks were brought home to all by the failure, discussed later in this chapter, of Financial Corporation, which had big positions outstanding in both repo and reverse when it failed in 1974. Everyone who borrows or lends in the repo market seeks first and foremost to protect themselves by following the old street adage: Deal only with those you know.

Lenders usually seek additional protection by asking for margin, which is provided in several ways. First, when securities are RPed, they are generally priced *below* their market value. The amount of the *haircut* (difference between actual market value measured at the *bid* side of the market and value used in the RP agreement) is typically set at ¼ of a point on transactions of short maturity. Thus if a coupon for which the bid was "par 8" were RPed, the investor would lend only par.[3] If alternatively the securities RPed were 6-month discount paper (bills) quoted at 5 percent and therefore trading at a dollar price of 97¾, they would be priced at 97½ or maybe ⅝ in a repo agreement.

Pricing on an RP agreement depends both on the length of the transaction and on the current maturity of the securities RPed. An investor in a 6-month RP collateralized by long bonds might want 1½ points, 2 points, or even more margin.[4] Sometimes on term repo transactions, dealers demand the right to reprice; more about that later.

On coupon securities, the lender also gets a second sort of margin. The reason is that, in the pricing of securities RPed, except in rare instances, no account is taken of interest already accrued at the time the transaction is undertaken. As one dealer commented: "If I have coupons on which $350,000 of accrued interest is due in five days, they are still priced at the bid side of the market less ¼. Doing so is less time-consuming than figuring the accrued interest, adding it to the securities' dollar price, and then deducting ¼, but from a dollar and cents points of view, this practice makes no sense at all."

Note the lack of symmetry here. On discount securities, as opposed to coupons, there is no accrued interest, and consequently on discount securities no extra margin arises because accrued interest is ignored in pricing securities for RP.

Normally the current maturity of securities RPed is longer—often much longer—than the life of the repo agreement. Thus the rate of interest on an RP is typically less than the yield on the security RPed, and this difference generates a third sort of margin. To illustrate, consider an investor who takes in a 9 percent coupon and gets 4.5 percent on his

[3] A bid of par 8 means the bid is 100 8/32.

[4] Not all long bonds are acceptable as collateral on an RP transaction. Normally only securities with a current maturity of 10 years or less are used.

money. Over the life of the repo, this yield differential will generate for the investor—unless or until a coupon date occurs—extra margin at a rate equal to 4.5 percent of the par value of the securities RPed.[5] Extra margin is also generated in a similar but slightly different way on discount securities; their market value will rise over the life of the repo agreement at a rate equal to the discount at which they are selling.

GROWTH OF THE MARKET

Dealers first began to use the RP market to finance their positions shortly after World War II. Later, as large banks began to practice active liability management, they joined the dealers in the RP market, using it to finance not only their dealer positions but also their government portfolios. In the last few years the market, which was initially small, has grown dramatically. One reason is that in 1969 the Fed amended Regulation D to make clear that RPs done by banks against governments and agencies (banks were already doing them) were borrowings exempt from reserve requirements. The same amendment also specified that RPs done by banks against other instruments—CDs, BAs, and loans in particular—were subject to reserve requirements; the amendment thus killed the use by banks of the RP market to finance such instruments.

A second factor contributing to the rapid growth of the RP market was the Treasury's decision in 1974 to shift the bulk of its deposits from TT&L accounts at commercial banks to accounts at the Fed. This shift freed billions of dollars worth of governments and agencies that the banks had been holding as collateral against Treasury deposits for use as collateral in the RP market.

Acceptance by investors of repo as a money market instrument has grown in step with the increased use of the market by borrowers. The historical highs to which the Fed pushed interest rates on several occasions beginning in the late 1960s made corporate treasurers acutely aware of the opportunity cost of holding idle balances. In response they became big investors in RP, which offered them a medium for investing highly variable amounts of money on a day-to-day basis. By the mid-1970s most corporations, including many that a few years earlier did not know what RP was, had amended their bylaws to permit them to invest in RP.

State and local governments and their agencies have in recent years also become huge investors in RP. Such government bodies are frequently required by law to hold their excess cash in bank deposits or to invest it in governments and agencies. Also, they are typically not per-

---

[5] If a coupon date occurs during a repo, the coupon payment goes to the security seller, i.e., to the borrower.

mitted to take a capital loss on their investments, which means that they cannot invest in a security that they are not sure they will be able to hold to maturity. RP collateralized by governments and agencies offers state and local governments—whose regulations permit them to use it instead of outright purchases of governments—a way to invest tax receipts and proceeds of note and bond issues in *any* amount for *any* period of time. The volume of money going into the repo market from state and local governments can be huge. If New York State sells $3 billion of bonds, all

Figure 12–2
Sources of financing used by U.S. government securities dealers
($ billions)*

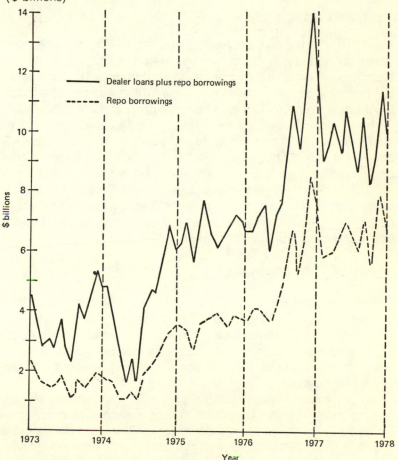

* The securities financed are primarily governments and agencies but also include some BAs, CDs, and other money market instruments.
Source: *Federal Reserve Bulletin.*

that money is immediately invested in the repo market and stays there until it is needed.

It is difficult to pinpoint the precise size of the repo market because borrowings by banks in the repo market are lumped with purchases of Fed funds for reporting purposes, and RP borrowings of other institutions (government securities dealers excepted) are not tracked by the Fed. An idea of the rate of growth of the RP market can, however, be gleaned from the figures the Fed does collect on the RP borrowings [technically borrowings from corporations and nonbank institutions] of U.S. dealers in government securities. These figures, which are plotted in Figure 12–2, show how rapidly RP financing by the dealers has grown and also how its growth has outstripped that of dealer loans from banks.

RP and market decisions

The RP market gives investors who are willing to base their investments on market judgments tremendous flexibility with respect to where along the yield curve they want to commit their funds. If the answer is at the very base of the yield curve, they can roll overnight repo indefinitely.

At times doing so can be very attractive. In 1974, when yields were high and looking as if they might go higher, Fed funds and repo traded in the range of 11–13 percent while short bills were yielding only 7–9 percent. Thus at that time a portfolio manager who owned short bills could, by selling his bills and investing in the same instrument under repo, have picked up 200–300 basis points in yield. Later in 1974, as it became clear that rates had started to decline, it was more attractive for the portfolio manager to own securities outright because doing so offered an opportunity for capital appreciation.

THE OVERNIGHT REPO RATE

The overnight RP rate, as Figure 12–3 shows, normally lies slightly below the Fed funds rate. There are two reasons. First, an RP transaction is in essence a secured loan, whereas the sale of Fed funds is an unsecured loan. Second, many investors—corporations, state and local governments, and others—who can invest in RP cannot sell, directly at least, Fed funds.

An institution that can't sell Fed funds could invest short term by buying securities due to mature in a few months or even a few days. Doing so, however, is usually unattractive. The yield on the 3-month bill typically hovers around the repo rate and on still shorter bills yield goes through (below) the repo rate. One reason is that many investors, including some state and local government bodies, can't invest in repos; they have to own the securities outright. A second reason for the thin supply of

Figure 12–3
The overnight RP rate tracks the overnight Fed funds rate closely

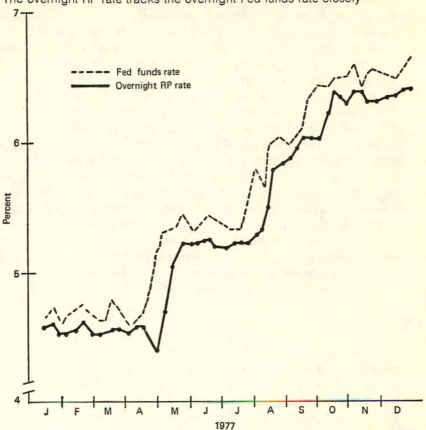

short bills is that they are often used by dealers as collateral for short positions (holding short bills for collateral exposes a dealer to no significant price risk). A third reason short bills are in thin supply is that many of them are held by investors who intend to roll them at maturity and who never consider the alternative of selling out early to pick up additional basis points. "There are," as one portfolio manager noted, "a lot of distortions in market rates because of the severe legal or self-imposed restrictions under which many portfolios are run."

The spread between the Fed funds rate and the repo rate can be anything from a full point to just a few basis points. How wide it is depends in part on the supply of collateral available. At times when the Fed is doing a lot of adding—for example, too offset a shift in Treasury balances—the supply of collateral on the street will dry up, and the spread between the repo rate and the funds rate will widen. At other times when the Treasury has just sold a large amount of new debt that has not yet been fully distributed, dealers will have a lot of collateral, and the spread between the Fed funds rate and the repo rate will narrow.

Most of the borrowing done in the repo market is collateralized by governments and agencies. Dealers, however, will also repo CDs, BAs, and sometimes even commercial paper. The spread between the RP rate on governments and that on other securities can be negligible if there is a shortage of collateral on the street, but normally this spread is 5 to 10 basis points, and it can get as wide as 15 basis points.

There are brokers in the RP market but they do not broker "stock" RP, that is, the RP normally done by dealers and banks to finance their positions and portfolios. Banks and dealers have a customer base with which they can do such transactions directly and efficiently. Also they view RP as a part of their customer line—one more thing they can show customers. So there is no room in this market for brokers.

No forward market exists in either overnight repo or term repo. However, a dealer or a bank will occasionally negotiate an RP deal ahead of time with, for example, a government body that knows that tax money will be coming in on some future date.

OPEN REPO

Under an *open* repo or *continuing contract,* a lender will agree to provide a dealer with some amount of funds for some period of time. The agreement can, however, be terminated by either side at any time. Also the dealer typically reserves the *right of substitution;* that is, he can take back securities he needs—because he has sold or wants to sell them—and give the lender other collateral in their place.

The rate paid on an open repo, which often varies from day to day, is normally set slightly above the rate on a straight overnight repo. The reason is that a dealer incurs smaller clearing costs when he does an open repo than when he does a series of overnight repos; and he is thus willing to pay up for money obtained through an open repo agreement.

TERM REPO

Dealers enter into term repo agreements to speculate—to create (as noted in Chapter 9) future securities they view as attractive.[6] Some large banks also use term RP to finance the longer governments in their portfolios in order to keep their "book" from being too short. Other large banks, however, rely strictly on overnight RP to finance their portfolios.

---

[6] See pages 226–29.

Said one banker typical of the latter group: "We do mostly overnight RP and feel comfortable with that because the demand placed on us for collateral is far greater than the supply of collateral we have. We could repo our government portfolio two or three times over everyday." Note this comment was made during a period of monetary ease.

In the repo market, as in other markets, the yield curve normally slopes upward, but at the very short end of the market, the curve frequently inverts; in particular the overnight rate is often a few basis points higher than the rate on 1- or 2-week repo. The reason is that short-period repo competes with commercial paper for investors' dollars, while the overnight repo rate relates to the frequently higher dealer loan rate that in turn keys off the Fed funds rate. Precisely what relationships exist among repo rates of differing maturities depend on the availability of financing to dealers and on the amount of collateral they have to finance.

In recent years there has been an extraordinary increase in the amount of funding to dates—tax dates, oil payment dates, etc.—that corporations do, and corporations as a result have become big lenders in the term repo market. The oil companies in particular have to accumulate huge dollar sums to pay the OPEC nations; these funds have to be stockpiled somewhere, and a lot of them are put into term repo. Public bodies are another big source of money in the term repo market.

Many investors, including municipalities and some financial institutions, cannot take a capital loss because of legal or self-imposed restrictions, but they can take an interest loss. Suppose such an investor has money that he thinks will be available for 6 months but that might be needed sooner. He can't invest in 6-month bills because, if he did, he might incur an accounting loss if he sold them.[7] He can, however, take the same or similar securities in on a 6-month reverse repo, that is, invest in 6-month term repo. The reason is that, if 3 months later the investor finds that he needs his money and the bill market is in the "chutes" (prices are down), he can repo out the collateral he has taken in. In doing so he may incur a *loss of interest* because the rate on the repo he does to borrow is higher than the rate on the term repo in which he invested (i.e., he may have negative carry on his offsetting repo transactions) *but* he won't incur a capital loss. Often municipalities can repo out securities they have obtained on a reverse repo but not securities they own outright. So a number of municipalities invest in term repo to get the protection and flexibility described in the example above.

THE REVERSE MARKET

Many smaller banks that won't trade their portfolios will occasionally reverse out securities for various reasons: because repo money is

---

[7] See pages 271–73.

cheaper than buying Fed funds, because—in the case of term repo—they expect the funds rate to rise and they need cash, or because they see an attractive opportunity to arbitrage.

S&Ls are also active in the reverse market. Most S&Ls do not trade their portfolios and anticipate holding most if not all the securities they own to maturity. They will put securities out on repo, but only when they are shown an opportunity to reinvest their funds at a higher yield in some other instrument—term Fed funds, BAs, or whatever. S&Ls came into the repo market in a big way after they were officially permitted in 1970 to sell term Fed funds. This gave them a new attractive opportunity for arbitrage because term Fed funds yield more than bank CDs. The big West Coast S&Ls are most active in the arbitrage game. They have large portfolios and big lines to New York banks. So if the rates are there, they will do trades in size.

When the yield curve is flat, banks and S&Ls may reverse out securities as part of an arbitrage for as little as a $^3/_{16}$ spread, but when the yield curve is steep they are likely to demand ½. Reverse agreements may or may not permit substitution. Typically they are done for a period of time ranging from 1 to 6 months.

For a bank or S&L that has securities a dealer wants, an alternative to reversing out these securities would be to do a straight loan—give the dealer the securities, take in other securities as collateral, and pick up a ½ percent borrowing fee. This second alternative is less attractive if the institution wants cash, which it well may if it anticipates a rise in interest rates and therefore wants to buy longer-term money.

Most states and municipalities are strict investors of cash. They will do repos but not reverses. There are some municipalities that will lend out securities in their portfolios, but the majority either do not have the right to do so or do not understand the transaction.

Risk and liquidity

There is no liquidity in a term RP; it is not an asset that can be sold, and the underlying agreement cannot be broken. Thus one might argue, as some have, that banks and S&Ls that put securities in their liquidity portfolios out on term RP are impinging on their liquidity. In all probability, however, they are in fact not. The reason is that most of the time they are reversing out securities that they would in almost no circumstance consider selling. Also, if worse comes to worse, they can raise cash by selling or RPing the asset they have acquired as the other leg of the arbitrage.

The one real risk in this game is that an unsophisticated portfolio manager might buy long bonds as a basis for arbitraging and not realize how great a price risk he was assuming when he did so. As one dealer noted: "Buying the 8's of '86 at a book yield of 7½ and RPing them at 4½ can look attractive to a small investor when the idea is presented to him. But should interest rates rise, he may get burned on this strategy because he loses more money selling these bonds than he has earned arbitraging against them." Note that risk arises here because the securities are purchased for the purpose of arbitraging rather than as a long-term investment.

Brokering of reverses

Reverses are often proposed to an institution by a broker who, because his firm brokers a range of money market instruments, is in a good position to point out attractive arbitrage opportunities—to provide "one-stop shopping." A broker of RP is a salesman as opposed to someone who is just fast on the phone; he has to convince the customer to take in money and then to put it out elsewhere.

"We do not," commented one broker, "just go in and say: "Hi. 30, 60, 90 days at 30, 45, and 55. Do you want to do $25 million?' We have to show people a reason to do a reverse. To be a good reverse broker you have to know as many alternative uses as possible for money, to have a working knowledge of and a feel for more areas than in any other money market job.

"You do not just walk in and do a trade with a guy, and you do not take no for an answer. There is some rate at which a trade will go. To put together a trade on which you make money takes time and work. You have to know what your customer can do in terms of investments and what the lender is going to demand in terms of margin. Every trade that is agreed upon with respect to amount and rate is done subject to *pricing*.[8] Different accounts demand different amounts of margin. Sometimes we can't get a trade off because the two sides are half a point away on the pricing. If we get in a bind on pricing, we just start all over again."

In the brokers market for RP and in the market in general, trades are agreed upon for round-lot sums, for example, $10 million. Then the precise amount of the loan is calculated, taking into account pricing and the way the agreement is set up. Thus on a $10 million trade, the dollars lent might be more or less than $10 million.

Reverses to maturity

As noted in Chapter 5, some portfolio managers are loath to sell high-coupon securities that are trading at a premium and recommit their

---

[8] *Pricing* refers here to the value that will be assigned to the securities reversed out. Margin is created for the lender in a reverse transaction by pricing the securities below market value.

funds to another instrument, because if they sell these securities, they will reduce the interest income they are booking. The repo market gives such portfolio managers a way to get around this predicament.

One dealer gave an illustration: "Say a bank owns the 7 7/8's of '78, which have 9 months to run. If the portfolio manager sells them, he won't be able to get a comparable coupon, so he refuses to sell. What he can do, however, is to put these securities out on repo until maturity, book the interest income on them, and use the cash he has generated to invest is some other attractive instrument. That's a common transaction now. A couple of years ago no one had heard of it."

Size

The reverse market is only a fraction of the size of the repo market but it is expanding rapidly. This trend is, moreover, likely to continue because most smaller banks and S&Ls are still quite unsophisticated in their use of the reverse market; consequently there are a lot of untapped resources in this market.

THE SPECIFIC ISSUES MARKET

Dealers go short for various reasons: as a speculation, to hedge a long position in a similar security, or to reduce their position so that they can make a big bid in a coming Treasury auction. The theory behind going into an auction short is that the new issue will, until it is distributed, yield more than outstanding issues; that, however, doesn't always occur when the Treasury is paying down its debt as it sometimes does, particularly on a seasonal basis. Whatever his motivation may be, a dealer who shorts a given issue has to obtain those securities somehow in order to make delivery. Normally the way he does so is by reversing them in rather than borrowing them.[9] Some widely placed issues, such as the 8's of '86, are easy to find. Others he has to hunt up on his own or with the help of a firm that brokers reverses.

The borrowers

The market for reverses to cover shorts is often referred to as the *specific issues* market because dealers shop in it for particular issues. Typically a dealer won't find another dealer who has the specific issue he needs and who also wants to finance it for some period. So dealers are only a minor supplier of collateral to the specific issues market. There is also a second reason for this. Said one dealer: "I deal in specific

---

[9] The economics of reversing in securities were discussed on pages 224–25.

issues only for myself. I will give them to some of my dealer friends but only because they will do the same for me. I try not to support the market for specific issues because I know that, if I give a guy $50 million year bills, he is shorting them and that is going to drive the market down. So all I am doing is hurting myself. If I can get an issue that is likely to be shorted in the future, I will hold it for myself."

The major suppliers of securities to (borrowers of money in) the specific issues and the general reverse market are banks. This accounts for the fact that the top banks in the country and in particular the top New York and Chicago banks all borrow, as Table 11-2 (pages 292–93) shows, substantial sums from the dealers. (The relevant entry in the table is the next to last line in each section, *Borrowing from dealers*.) Because banks reverse out so many securities to dealers, their net loans to dealers are much smaller than their total dealer loans.

S&Ls and certain other financial institutions are also large suppliers of collateral in the specific issues market. So too are a few municipalities and a few corporate portfolios. Reverses are, as noted, not well understood except by those who do them, so it is not surprising that one corporate portfolio manager commented: "I reverse out securities to dealers but I *never* refer to it around the company as 'lending out' our valuable securities."

Reverses in the specific issues market usually have a term ranging from one week to one month. Activity in this market is greatest during a bear market because dealers increase their short positions in a declining market.

The reverse rate

When a dealer lends out money as part of a transaction in which he is reversing in securities to cover a short, the rate he gets on his money is likely to be significantly *lower* than the going rate for financing general collateral in the RP market. "The rate on a reverse depends," as one dealer noted, "on the availability of the securities taken in. In today's market, the RP rate available to an investor willing to take in any type of collateral is 5¼. If I reversed in the year bill to cover a short, I might get only 4.60 on my money. If alternatively I shorted something in more plentiful supply, I might get 5 percent. There are no standard relationships. It is entirely a question of demand and supply."

The brokers

Dealers who want to reverse in a specific issue will often turn to a broker of RP. The brokers make it their business to know where various special issues are and at what rates they can be reversed in. The brokers are efficient in this area and can often get bonds for a dealer at as good a rate as he would if he could in fact find the bonds. An RP broker acts in effect as a commission salesman for the dealers; if he finds bonds, he earns a commission or a spread; if he does not, he is paid nothing for his trouble.

The brokers try not to take bonds from one dealer and give them to another. The dealers talk to each other and could arrange trades of this sort themselves. As a rule, the brokers will try to pull specific issues out of regional banks, S&Ls, and other smaller portfolios. In doing so, they are using their own special knowledge and thus providing a real service to the dealers.

Some brokers of RP will, when they have arranged a trade, give up names to the institutions on both sides of the trade, charge both sides a commission, and leave it to them to clear the trade.

Other brokers act as a principal in transactions they broker, taking securities in on one side and lending out money on the other. In doing so, a broker is acting as a credit intermediary and he incurs risk on both sides of the transaction. Brokers who act as principals in RP and reverse trades are, like all participants in the repo market, extremely careful to deal only with institutions whose credit they know to be unimpeachable.

When a broker acts as a principal in a reverse transaction, he works for whatever spread he can get; normally it ranges from an 01 to $1/8$, with the average being $1/16$. If, however, the broker finds a firm that wants to RP stock collateral and another that wants to borrow the same collateral as a special, he might be able to earn $1/4$.

DEALER BOOKS IN RP

In recent years a number of major dealers in government securities have begun to *run books* in repo and reverse; they take in collateral on one side, hang it out on the other side, and seek to earn a profit by charging a lending rate slightly higher than the rate at which they borrow. Part of the impetus for this development came from the failure of Financial Corporation, which made investors extremely wary of engaging in a repo transaction with a firm whose name and credit they did not know well. Firms that had difficulties borrowing directly from retail in their own name began to borrow from the dealers.

Minor dealers supply some collateral to the dealers who run books in repo. Banks are another big source. Said one dealer: "The banks who supply the collateral are not the New York City banks. It is the super-liquid regional banks like the Wilmington Trust, Seattle First, the U.S. National Bank of Oregon. Such banks have large portfolios for their size. They do not trade these portfolios actively; instead they make longer-term investments which seem to suit at the time they make them. If the securities later go under or above water, it does not really matter to them because they are running a standard, old-fashioned government portfolio and they are going to hold onto these securities forever. If they have some 8's of '86, they will have them until 1986 with 90 degree probability. If the liability manager at such a bank sees an opportunity to sell 90-day Euros at 6½ percent, he will come into the market and ask a dealer, 'What will you lend me against $20 million 8's of '86?' Frequently such banks are able to borrow locally at below-market rates but only in small amounts. When they want big money they have to come to the street. I might offer a lend to him at 5⅜. If he took the money, he would probably also use the offices of my firm to sell his Euros."

Aggressive corporate portfolio managers, S&L managers, and others also supply collateral to the dealers. Note that the collateral offered here is *stock* collateral. The dealer takes it in, not because he wants to short particular issues, but because he can refinance that collateral at a profitable spread.

Profit on a matched book

If a dealer repos out securities for the same time period that he reverses them in (for example, hangs out on repo for 30 days any collateral he reverses in for 30 days), he is said to run a *matched book.* Spreads on such transactions are narrow, but money can be made because volume is large. "A Fed funds broker," commented one dealer, "gets 50¢ a million per trade but he has no clearing costs. A dealer making a book in RP gets more but incurs clearing costs. Still if he can make a net nickel [5 basis points] on a matched sale book, that amounts to $1.40 per million per day, which is $1,400 per billion per day, and all you need to run such a book is a kid from Queens who can add."

On a matched book, a dealer incurs no rate risk. He incurs a credit risk on both sides of the transaction, but he can control this by being extremely careful about whom he deals with. Also, dealers in RP often try to get extra protection by asking for a bigger *haircut* (more margin) on securities they take in than they give on securities they put out. "On a billion dollar book," commented one observer, "a dealer should generate an extra $35 million from the difference in haircuts if he is dealing with pros. If it is amateur hour, he would probably get an extra $60 or $70 million of cheap money." Besides reducing risk, that extra money can generate additional profits if the dealer uses it to carry some high-coupon bonds that he would have held anyway.

Profits and risks on a mismatched book

Most dealers who deal seriously in RP *mismatch* their book. They seek to profit by *lending long and borrowing short.* Running a mismatched book in RP offers its own special risks and rewards. To understand them, one must visualize precisely what it means for a dealer to run a book in RP. Part A of Table 12–1 shows the flows that occur when a dealer reverses in securities on one side and RPs them on the other.

Table 12–1
Running a book in RP

A. Reversing in securities and RPing these securities creates a new asset and a new liability on a dealer's book

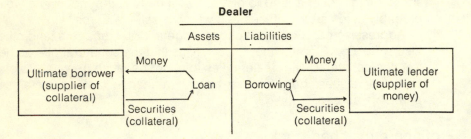

B. The dealer's book in RP

Dealer

Assets	Liabilities
Collateralized *loans* of varying maturities	Collateralized *borrowings* of varying maturities

The essence of a repo transaction is *not* that securities are being sold, it is that secured *loans* and *borrowings* are being made. Thus the securities "sold" should be thought of simply as *collateral.* Once they are thought of that way, it becomes clear that when a dealer takes in securities, he is making a *loan* that is an *asset* to him, and when he RPs these securities, he is creating a *borrowing* that is a *liability* to him. Thus a dealer's book in RP consists of a collection of collateralized loans and borrowings (Table 12–1, part B).

In effect, in running a book in RP, a dealer is acting as a *financial intermediary,* and in particular like a bank. He is taking in collateralized "deposits" on one side and lending out the money on the other. A dealer's book in RP is, moreover, much like a bank's Eurodollar book. All of the assets and liabilities that compose this book are *fixed in rate* and *fixed in term*. Thus to the extent that a dealer mismatches his book, he incurs exactly the same *rate risk* that a Euro banker does when he mismatches his book.

A dealer has *no* liquidity in his RP book. He can't sell loans he makes or otherwise liquidate them before maturity. Thus if he borrows short and lends long (e.g., finances a 30-day loan with overnight money), he incurs a *liquidity risk*. To fund his assets, he depends, like a bank, on his ability to continually buy large and highly variable amounts of money.

With that background in mind, it is interesting to hear a dealer who runs a mismatched book describe how he operates: "Suppose I reverse in the 8's of '86 at par for 90 days at 5⅜. I have assumed a risk. I am now long in 90-day reverse. It is like being long in 90-day bills that you cannot sell—but the yield is higher. I might blow it out [finance the reverse] overnight for a couple of days. Or I might instantly stick it out for 30 to 60 days because I can play the yield curve. Suppose there is a major discrepancy between 90 and 60 days, and I can finance that reverse at 5⅛ for 60 days. Then I have a piece of paper coming back at me in 60 days that I can value. I look at the tail and see I will own 1-month paper [60 days hence] at 5⅞. That seems like a reasonable gamble so, bang, I do it."[10]

Because the pricing of securities RPed depends on their market value and thus on interest rates, a firm running a speculative book in reverse incurs not only a rate risk and a liquidity risk but also the risk that its position will for some period of time eat up its capital. The same dealer continued: "I have built my tail. If my projection that interest rates are going to fall is correct, I benefit in two ways. First, my 30-day piece of paper comes back at me at 5⅞, and I can bang it out for the last 30 days at 4⅜. Look at the money I have made! Additionally the 8's of '86 are now worth more money. Consequently I can borrow [over the last 30 days], say, 103 against them instead of par, which never hurts when you are borrowing at the low end of the yield curve.

"The flip side of that is that there is no more stinko position in a bear market than a reverse position. Say interest rates rise. The 1-month paper I have created comes back at me at 5⅞ but I have to finance it at 6, so I lose money. Moreover, I can now borrow less money, maybe 3 points less. So hundreds of thousands of dollars of my working cash go bye-bye for 30 days. That hurts no matter who you are. You are losing in two directions at the same time. You lose on the trade, and you are out working cash. To run an unmatched book in speculative reverse, you have to be a well-capitalized firm or you will run into massive problems."

Repricing

To minimize the risk that a position in reverse will eat up capital during a bear market, many dealers running books in RP reserve the right to *reprice*. Said one such dealer: "In the reverse market there is an

---

[10] Recall the discussion on pages 226–29 of figuring the tail. That calculation is no different for reverses than it is for bills or other money market assets that are financed for some period.

informal right to reprice the instrument. If I were to take in $5 million of securities for 6 months and all of a sudden the market dropped 4 points, I would be out $200,000 of my capital. In that case I have the right to call the customer [the borrower] and say it is time to reprice. There is no set time period on repricing. It can be done during any part of the life of the instrument. It is an informal but understood part of the agreement, one that reduces risk for us.

"We ask for the right to reprice because in my opinion we are paid to forecast short-term interest rates, not what a 10-year government is going to be worth 5 or 6 months from now. Maybe I would feel differently if I were a government bond trader but I am not, and I will not do business with a guy who will not let me reprice. Another reason for repricing is credit risk. Say I am lending a guy 105 on an issue that is worth 101— what if he goes out of business?" While the right to reprice is reserved informally by some dealers, others make it a formal part of an RP agreement.

Note that a dealer reserving the right to reprice does not make a long-term RP borrowing unattractive to the borrower. Suppose a bank borrows 6-month money because it expects interest rates to rise and they do; then, because of repricing, the bank won't get full value for its collateral over the last part of the agreement, *but* it will still be getting cheap money.

The interdealer market

There is currently an *interdealer* market between six or seven firms in stock-collateral RP and reverse. This market serves a purpose similar in many respects to that of the interbank market in Eurodollar deposits for banks running Eurodollar books. In it a dealer can lay off or pick up money in different maturities.

The interdealer market in RP trades actively out to 6 months. The basic run is for 1, 2, 3, and 6 months, but if the market is very active, all 6 months will be quoted. There is usually a *nickel* spread (5 basis points) between the bid and the offer.

The market is extremely informal. A dealer might call another and say, "What are you doing in 90 days?" Answer: "I'm at 32–27." At that point, "I own them" or "You own them" suffices to signify that the trade is done.

The interdealer market trades in minimum blocks of $5 million, but a dealer can work up that amount or he can specify that his bid or offer is for less. If the collateral is an off-the-run bond, that is generally specified; on inactive issues, the bid will be somewhat back from the market.

Margin is subject to negotiation. One trader said: "You get to know what the different dealers' margin requirements are. These come into play somewhat in the quotes you give a dealer when he asks for a run. I am generally flexible about haircut requirements when I trade with other dealers. I am, however, less flexible when I deal with the few large corporations involved in the reverse market; and the amount of margin I demand from them is substantially more than what I demand from another dealer."

A forecast of rising interest rates will increase market activity because it brings additional collateral into the market. The appearance of attractive arbitrage opportunities does the same thing.

Some trades of RP and reverse between dealers are brokered. This most typically occurs between dealers who do not normally talk to and quote runs to each other.

Financial corporation

People on the street are today very conscious of the risks involved in repo and reverse transactions because of the sobering experience to which Eldin Miller, who headed Financial Corporation of Kansas City, treated them in 1975.

"Eldin," said a dealer who knew him well, "was a guy who had made a fortune in trucking. He came to New York looking like a church deacon. He didn't drink, he didn't smoke, and his personality was such that people tended to trust him."

Eldin rapidly built up a huge portfolio—it eventually totaled $1.8 billion—of governments financed almost solely in the RP market. He bought first bills and later coupons. So long as interest rates were falling or flat, there was a profitable arbitrage in this operation; Eldin was borrowing short, investing long, and raking in positive carry. Eventually, however, interest rates moved against him, and the carry on his position turned negative. This caused a cash drain, which Eldin met by RPing out discount securities at full face value. He was able to do this because, as one dealer notes, "Eldin ran into some real dummies who said OK he has 100 million of T bills, the dollar price on them is 96, but we will lend him par because it is too difficult to write funny number tickets."

As interest rates continued to go against him and he continued to experience a cash drain, Eldin—who learned street games fast—started reversing in securities and then shorting them. Since it is normal on a reverse to ignore accrued interest in pricing, Eldin was able to generate cash equal to roughly the amount of the accrued interest every time he reversed in a coupon and shorted it.

Even that ploy, however, did not suffice to meet Financial Corp.'s cash needs, and eventually the firm failed. The people who had lent the firm money had collateral but its market value was often less than the amount of the loan. Meanwhile the people who had borrowed money from the firm had that money but it was often a smaller amount than the market value (accrued interest included) of the securities they had reversed out to Financial Corp.

Many of those—whom Eldin reminded, by his dealings with them, that the prudent deal with only those they know and trust—were large, respectable, and normally astute institutions. That Eldin could fool them made him the object of some admiration among street traders. Said one: "The guy in Kansas had class. There are people who have embezzled $5 or $10 million. He did $1.8 billion!"

One of the disturbing questions raised by the failure of Financial Corp., which left in its wake suits that will take the courts years to settle, is who owns and owes what if one side on an RP transaction fails. Said one dealer in RP: "My position is that, if I have your bonds and you do not pay me back, it is my prerogative to sell those bonds and sue you for any difference. The distinction between RP and a collateralized loan is that in an RP transaction I own those bonds, whereas on a collateralized loan there are release agreements and certain legalities I have to go through before I can handle the underlying collateral as if I owned it. However, this is an issue on which there is at this point little legal precedent and thus no definitive answer. The whole question needs clarification."

THE USE BY THE FED OF THE RP AND REVERSE MARKETS

The Fed, as noted, uses repos and reverses extensively to effect short-term changes in the level of bank reserves. The Fed used *RP* for this purpose as early as 1917, but it did not begin to use this tool regularly until after World War II. The Fed first used *reverses* to drain bank reserves in 1966; the occasion was a sudden large increase in float caused by an interruption in airline service.

Prior to 1972, when the Fed did RPs, it offered the dealers a fixed rate, usually equal to the discount rate. In 1972 it changed this practice and switched to asking the dealers for competitive bids when it wanted to do repo and reverses just as it does when it wants to buy or sell securities.

Not long after this change, the Fed also permitted dealers to show customer money to it when it was doing reverses and customer collateral to it when it was doing repo. Many dealers' customers are, however, unaware that this possibility exists. One commercial paper issuer observed: "Sometimes on a Wednesday commercial paper issuers post attractive rates to get money, then rates start to sag in the money market, collateral dries up, and all of a sudden they get hit with money. In this sort of situation—the market falling apart—the Fed will generally come in and do repurchase agreements. A paper issuer with excess funds can at that point call a primary dealer and ask them to show, say, $20 million for him into the Fed. I do it, but I don't see many others doing it."

When it wants to add reserves for some period of time, the Fed will often do term repo with the dealers, that is, give them money for several days or as long as a week. The Fed used to permit dealers who did term repo with it to break the agreement or any portion of it. "That," as one dealer commented, "made a 6-day repo something you never wanted to miss. It was fantastic in terms of moving around your RP portfolio. If the market got better, you could break the RP. If you sold something, you could take the securities you had at the Fed and use them to substitute with an RP customer. The Fed meanwhile was going crazy with the cancelations, and they finally switched to fixed RPs to cut down their bookkeeping." The Fed has never permitted substitutions on repos it does with dealers.

Treasuries and agencies

Most of the collateral underlying the various repo and reverse transactions described in this chapter is governments and agencies. In Chapter 13 we turn to the markets in which these securities are bought and sold outright.

Chapter 13

Government and federal agency securities

THE GOVERNMENT MARKET, which used to be stuffy and humdrum, has evolved over the last decade into the most active, exciting, and innovative sector of the money market. The reasons are several. In 1961, Congress amended the tax law so that bank capital gains, which had been taxed at the capital gains rate, were taxed as ordinary income. "Overnight that change," one dealer noted, "converted 6,000 stodgy old bankers into portfolio managers who were supposed to make a profit." At about the same time, tightening and easing by the Fed began to create wide swings in interest rates. "Back in the old days," noted the same dealer, "bonds had no sex appeal. They were not going to change much in price so you bought them, clipped the coupon, and matured them. Then suddenly, because of big fluctuations in interest rates, it became possible for portfolio managers and dealers to make money positioning and trading governments."

The huge growth of the federal debt also contributed to the evolution of the government market by creating more supply and attracting more players into the market. So, too, did the freedom in which the government market operates. Ironically, the government market, unlike all other securities markets, except the municipal market, is not regulated by the SEC. Thus, it is a market in which the street, which likes to innovate, has had a free hand to do so, and it has done so repeatedly. In recent years, the development of the reverse market and the specific issues market has made transactions by dealers and portfolio managers that were unheard of a few years ago now commonplace. The government market is one of the few markets in which it is possible to run large short positions—to make money on a negative attitude—and growth of the reverse market has made shorting simpler, cheaper, and more attractive. Introduction of trading in T bill futures has also opened up a host of new strategies for both investing and speculating in governments.

A final stimulus to the development of the government market was the decision by the SEC to force stock exchange firms to negotiate commission rates. That change effectively cut stock house commissions by 75 percent, so they began looking for something new to do. They searched just at the time big money was being made by dealers in governments, and many decided to open government bond dealerships. A few lost large amounts of money, but a number prospered and stayed.

BILLS, NOTES, AND BONDS

Bills

The Treasury currently issues bills in 3-month, 6-month, and 1-year maturities. Bills are issued in denominations of $10,000, $15,000, $50,000, $100,000, $500,000, and $1 million. A round lot in the inter-dealer market is $5 million, and a retail customer who buys bills from a dealer will get a quote somewhat off the market unless he bids for size. Trades in the bill market are normally done for cash settlement.

Bills used to be issued by the Treasury in the form of bearer certificates. The Treasury and the Fed then made it possible to hold bills in *book-entry* form (described below), and since 1977 the Treasury has offered bills only in book-entry form.[1]

Notes

The Treasury currently auctions 2- and 4-year notes on a regular cycle. It began a regular cycle in the 5-year note but interrupted it in 1977. Other note issues with maturities ranging out to 10 years are also periodically offered by the Treasury during quarterly refundings. Notes are available in registered, bearer, and book-entry form.

When the Treasury wants to encourage individuals to invest in a new note issue, it sets the minimum denomination at $1,000. At other times it

[1] When the Treasury moved to book-entry bills, it made a limited exception for those institutional investors who were required by law or regulation to hold definitive securities. It offered to issue bill certificates in a $100,000 denomination to such investors through December 1978.

sets it at $5,000. Notes are also available in $10,000, $100,000, and $1 million denominations. Interdealer quotes in notes are understood to be good, unless otherwise specified, for $500,000 to $1 million depending on current maturity, and money market investors typically trade notes in size. The note market is a wholesale market, except for sales to individuals and small portfolio managers who typically buy to hold to maturity. Trades in the note market are done for both regular and cash settlement.

Bonds

Because Congress has granted the Treasury only minor exemptions from the 4.25 percent lid it imposes on the rate the Treasury may pay on bonds, the Treasury relies relatively little these days on the sale of new bond issues to fund the federal debt. It does, however, typically offer some bonds at quarterly refunding dates, often by reopening an old issue. Also, because of past bonds sales, there are a large number of government bonds outstanding.

Treasury bonds are issued in bearer, registered, and book-entry form. They come in denominations of $1,000, $5,000, $10,000, $100,000, and $1 million. Interdealer trades in bonds are usually for $500,000 or more, and the bond market, like the note market, is largely a wholesale market in which institutions buy and sell. Trades in bonds are normally done for regular settlement.

Treasury notes are not callable, but about half of the government bond issues outstanding are callable. Generally the call date is 5 years before maturity. On old low-coupon issues, the call provision is of small importance, but some new high-coupon issues might conceivably be called someday. On dealers' quote sheets, an 8.5 percent Treasury bond maturing in May 1999 and callable in 1994 would appear as

8½ B May 15, 99/94

In Treasury listings of outstanding issues, the same bond is denoted as

8½% 1994–99

Flower bonds. A number of old *low-coupon* government bonds that currently sell at substantial *discounts* carry a special feature. They are acceptable at par in payment of federal estate taxes when owned by the decedent at the time of death. In 1977, the capital gain realized at the time of the holder's death was made taxable. Currently, flower bonds maturing on the following dates are available: February 1980, April 1980, November 1980, June 1983, May 1985, February 1990, August 1992, February 1993, May 1994, February 1995, and November 1998. Some of the issues are callable and all are available in minimum denominations of $500.

Attraction to investors

Treasury securities offer the investor a number of attractive features. They expose him to zero credit risk and, while they yield less than other market instruments except for municipals, they are the most liquid instruments traded in the money market. Governments owe their liquidity to the fact that most individual issues are extremely large, and governments are thus not discrete heterogeneous instruments, like BAs or CDs. In early 1978, individual bill issues outstanding ranged from $3 billion to over $6 billion; the smallest note issue was $1.6 billion, but most note issues were much larger and several were in the $8 to $9 billion range. Bond issues are not that large, but their size is still substantial, $1.5 to $3 billion on recent issues.

Another advantage of Treasuries is that interest income earned on them is *not* subject to state and local taxation. Also, interest earned by holding a T bill to maturity can be treated for tax purposes as having all been earned in the year the bill matures.

A final attraction of governments is the wide array of these securities available. In early 1978, the Treasury had outstanding 40 different bill issues ranging in current maturity from a few days to a year, 75 note issues, and 28 bond issues. The current maturities of these note and bond issues ranged from a few days to almost 30 years.

Table 13–1
Public debt of the U.S. Treasury, October 1977 ($ billions)

Type and holder		
Federal Reserve banks	$ 94.6	
Commercial banks	100.5	
Mutual savings banks	6.0	
S&Ls	2.2	
Insurance companies	14.7	
Other corporations	23.8	
State and local governments	54.5	
Individuals	24.4	
Foreign	78.9	
U.S. government securities dealers	3.9	
Other (including federal agencies)	43.9	
Marketable treasury debt		$447.4
U.S. government agencies and trust funds	$136.9	
Individuals (savings bonds)	76.0	
Foreign (special issues)	21.1	
Other	14.9	
Nonmarketable treasury debt		$248.9
Total public debt		$696.3

Source: *Federal Reserve Bulletin.*

Ownership

Table 13–1 shows how ownership of the government debt is split between different classes of investors. The top part of the table, which refers to *marketable* Treasury debt, is of most interest for present purposes. It shows that commercial banks are the biggest single investors in marketable governments. They are closely followed by the Fed. State and local governments are also sizable investors. Among domestic investors, the next most important holders of governments are individuals and corporations.

One key entry in Table 13–1 is the close to $80 billion of governments held by foreign central banks. As this figure suggests, foreigners are at times important investors in Treasury debt. Whether they are in or out of the market can affect the rates at which the Treasury is able to sell new issues.

BOOK ENTRY SECURITIES

In 1976, the Treasury announced that it would move over time to a system under which virtually the entire marketable federal debt would be represented by *book-entry* securities instead of engraved pieces of paper. *Under the book-entry system, banks that are members of the Federal Reserve hold securities at the Fed in accounts on which record keeping is computerized.* All marketable governments may be held in book-entry form, and over 80 percent of the Treasury's marketable debt is now held in this form.

A bank typically has several different book-entry accounts at the Fed: for example, it may have one account for securities in which it has an interest—securities in its dealer position, securities in its investment portfolio, and securities it has taken in on repo; a second account for securities it is safekeeping for corporate and other investors; and a third account for securities it holds for dealers for whom it acts as a clearing bank.

The Fed's computer tracks the amounts and types of securities every bank has in each of its accounts. Each bank's own computer tracks for the investors and dealers for whom it holds securities what issues and amounts of these issues each such institution has placed with it.

In New York, the major banks are linked by wire to the Fed, and all securities transfers among them are made by *wire*. If Bankers Trust were, for example, to sell bills to Citibank, it would make delivery by sending a wire message to the Fed, whose computer would debit Bankers' account *for x* bills and credit Citi's account for the same number. Simultaneously, the Fed's computer would automatically transfer money equal to the purchase price of the bills out of Citi's reserve account at the Fed into Bankers' reserve account.

Approximately 80 percent of all wire traffic in governments occurs in New York and the equipment used there for making such transfers, while already sophisticated, is currently being upgraded. In other Federal Reserve districts, the technology used varies depending on what is cost justified by the local volume of wire traffic.

The movement to book-entry securities and wire transfers was precipitated in 1970 by the refusal of several major insurance underwriters to underwrite government securities held by dealers. Treasury notes and bonds (but not bills) could be registered, but in fact dealers and most major investors held them, as well as bills, in bearer form. So there was a huge volume of valuable bearer paper being stored and constantly moved about on the street, thus inviting theft.

Faced with an insurance crisis, the dealers began to hold their securities in accounts at the major banks. At the same time, the Fed initiated a system that made it possible for banks to wire during each business day securities between each other. At the end of the day, however, the banks had to show up at the Fed and take physical delivery on any issues on which they had been *net* receivers over the day and to make physical delivery of issues on which they had made *net* deliveries over the day. This procedure eliminated much messenger traffic in governments, but hundreds of millions worth of them still had to be carried between the banks and the New York Fed at the end of the day to effect net settlements. The introduction of book-entry securities eliminated these end-of-day movements.

The Treasury's decision to gradually move to a system in which all new marketable debt will be issued in book-entry form means that those state and local governments, pension funds, and other investors required by their bylaws or by law to take physical delivery of securities purchased will have to effect changes such that they can take delivery in book-entry form or else cease to invest in governments.

At the time the Treasury decided to move to book-entry securities, it offered to operate minimum-service book-entry accounts for individuals and institutional investors who did not want to deal through a commercial bank. The demand for this service has been negligible.

The Treasury does not charge for this service, but a Treasury account has certain disadvantages since it is designed primarily for investors who wish to hold their securities to maturity. A deposit for the full face amount of securities applied for must accompany tenders submitted for Treasury book-entry accounts. Securities held in a Treasury account cannot be used as collateral and cannot be sold without first being transferred to a member bank book-entry account. Transfers cannot be made until 10 business days after the date of issue nor later than 30 days before the maturity date. The Treasury must be notified to reinvest a maturing security at least 10 days before maturity. At maturity, the Treasury mails a check to the investor redeeming a security.[2]

Now that literally billions of dollars of governments are stored in the Fed's computers, the Fed faces a classic records protection problem. It undoubtedly has considerable backup to make its system fail-safe. Such backup can be provided in various ways, for example, by writing records out to disks or tapes and storing them in off-site locations.

The book-entry system for governments was designed by the Treasury in haste and under pressure, but it has worked efficiently and has been accepted with enthusiasm by dealers, banks, and most investors.

To move to book entry, the Treasury set up an enabling regulation that had the effect of law and, to the extent that it conflicted with portions of the uniform commercial code in regard to transfers and pledges, had the effect of overriding that law.

Since the Treasury moved to book entry, all federal agencies still issuing securities to the public have come up with their own versions of the Treasury's enabling regulation. And today most agency securities, with the exception of discount paper, can be held in book-entry form and are eligible for wire transfer.

Physical movements of CDs, BAs, commercial paper, and other bearer paper still occur between banks. Eliminating such movements by creating a book-entry system for these securities would, however, be difficult because they are so heterogeneous; each day commercial paper issuers and banks writing CDs create in effect tens of thousands of new instruments, some of which have very short lives. To put all of them on a book-entry system would be extremely complex.

RECOGNIZED DEALERS

Any firm can commence dealing in governments and federal agency securities. The Fed, however, will deal directly with only *recognized* or *primary dealers*.

In recognizing a dealer, the Fed looks for capital, character in management, and capacity in terms of trained personnel. Specifically before the Fed will do business with a firm, it wants to ensure the following: (1) that the firm has adequate capital relative to the position it assumes; (2) that the firm is doing a reasonable volume (at least 1 percent of market activity) and that it is willing to make markets at all times; and (3) that top management in the firm understands the government market—particularly the risks involved—and is making a long-term commitment to the market.

---

[2] Margaret Bedford, "Recent Developments in Treasury Financing Techniques," *Monthly Review,* Federal Reserve Bank of Kansas, July–August 1977, p. 15.

When a firm expresses an interest to the Fed in becoming a primary dealer, the Fed first asks it to report its trading volume and positions on an informal basis. If the firm appears to meet the Fed's criteria, the Fed then puts it on its regular reporting list. If, after a time as a *reporting dealer,* the firm still appears to meet the Fed's criteria, the Fed recognizes that dealer and does business with it.

The Fed welcomes the entry of new primary dealers into the government market for two reasons. First, such entry increases competition in the government market. Second, the more dealers there are, the greater is the dealer community's capacity to distribute the Treasury's burgeoning debt.

While the Fed expects a primary dealer to make markets at all times, it recognizes and accepts the fact that some shops tend to specialize at either the long or the short end of market.

The big profits primary dealers make in good years (there are big losses in bad years) and the decline in brokerage income on stock trades are two reasons many firms have in recent years set up dealerships in governments. Another is that firms that specialize in corporate bonds have felt it was important to get into the government market so they could have firsthand knowledge of developments there and so they could use governments as a tool in marketing new corporate bonds—sell corporates, for example, by swapping customers out of governments.

Setting up a dealership in governments is a time-consuming, difficult, and costly proposition. Trained personnel, which is in scarce supply on the street, must be hired and then welded into a team that works. Firms entering the government market normally expect to lose millions before they create an organization capable of producing profits.

AUCTION PROCEDURES

Bills

Bills with 3-month and 6-month maturities are offered by the Treasury each week. The new 3-month bill is always a reopening of an old 6-month bill. Except when holidays interfere, the size of the new bill issue to be offered is announced on Tuesday, the securities are auctioned the following Monday, and they are paid for and issued on the next Thursday. The Treasury also offers a new year bill every 4 weeks. It is announced on a Thursday or Friday, auctioned the following Wednesday or Thursday, and paid for and issued on the Tuesday after the auction.[3]

---

[3] For a description of how the auction works, see pages 153–54.

Banks and recognized dealers may submit tenders at the auction for the accounts of their customers as well as for their own account. Other bidders may submit tenders for only their own accounts. The Treasury accepts tenders from commercial banks, trust companies, and securities dealers without deposits; payment for securities purchased by these institutions must be made in immediately available funds on settlement day. All other bidders must submit the full face amount of the book-entry bills for which they apply; the Treasury remits to such bidders the difference between the face value of the bills they purchase and the purchase price they pay.

Any institution bidding for bills may pay for them with maturing bills, that is, by what is called *rolling bills*. In this case the Fed pays to the bidder on settlement day the difference between the value of its maturing bills and the price at which it has purchased new bills.

Competitive bidders in the auction submit tenders stating the quantity of bills they are bidding on and the price they bid. A subscriber may enter several bids, stating the quantity of bills he is offering to buy at each price. The price bid is based on 100 and is stated to three decimal places. An investor who, for example, bids 98.485 is offering to pay $98.485 per $100 of face value on whatever quantity of bills he bids for.

During the time between the day on which bills are auctioned and the day on which they are issued, the new bill issue, which has been sold but not yet delivered, is traded among investors and dealers on a *when-issued* basis. Securities traded on this basis are denoted *wi* on dealers' quote sheets.

Notes and bonds

The Treasury presently offers a mix of coupon issues at each of its regular quarterly refundings; these occur in February, May, August, and November. In recent years the quarterly refunding has usually included three issues: a 3- to 4-year note, a 7- to 10-year note, and a long-term bond. These issues are generally sold on consecutive days, with the security of longest maturity being sold last. In addition to its refundings, the Treasury also offers a 2-year note every month, a 4-year note in the third month of each quarter,and typically a 5-year note in the first month of each quarter.

In note and bond auctions, the normal practice (see Figure 13–1) is for investors to bid yields to two decimal places.[4] As in the case of bills, banks and recognized dealers may submit bids for notes and bonds for the accounts of their customers as well as for their own account. Bids from commercial banks, trust companies, and securities dealers do not

---

[4] See Chapter 7.

Figure 13–1
Tender form for a Treasury note issue

Do Not Combine Tenders for Coupon and Registered Notes on the Same Form.

TENDER FOR TREASURY NOTES OF SERIES L-1980

DATED AND BEARING INTEREST FROM FEBRUARY 28, 1978   DUE FEBRUARY 29, 1980

TO FEDERAL RESERVE BANK OF CHICAGO
FISCAL AGENT OF THE UNITED STATES
Box 834   Box 1059
CHICAGO, ILL. 60690   DETROIT, MICH. 48231

SUBSCRIBERS REF. NO. _____ DATE _____

Pursuant to the provisions of the Treasury Department Offering Circular, the undersigned offers to purchase the securities described above in the amount and at the price specified below, or any lesser amount that may be allotted. Payment will be made as indicated.

Separate Forms must be used if both Competitive and Noncompetitive Tenders are submitted. Amounts must be in multiples of $5,000

COMPETITIVE TENDER   DO NOT USE   **NONCOMPETITIVE TENDER**

PAR AMOUNT
must be in $5,000 multiples

$ _____ TO YIELD _____ %

(Yield must be expressed with not more than two decimal places, for example, 7.11%)

PAR AMOUNT
must be in $5,000 multiples

$ _____

At the Average Price of Accepted Competitive Bids.

(Not to exceed $1,000,000 for one bidder through all sources.)

➤ TENDERS MAY NOT BE ENTERED BY TELEPHONE. TENDERS BY WIRE, IF RECEIVED BEFORE THE CLOSING HOUR, ARE ACCEPTABLE. ◄

NAMES OF BIDDERS MUST APPEAR ON REVERSE SIDE

Payment due February 28, 1978 will be made as follows:

☐ CHARGE OUR RESERVE ACCOUNT
(Member banks only)

ABA No. _____

☐ BY DRAFT - See press release for details in regard to this type of payment. All checks must be made payable to the Federal Reserve Bank of Chicago and drawn on a bank within the 7th Federal Reserve District. (Checks by endorsement will not be accepted). Immediately upon receipt, all checks will be processed for collection.

☐ BY SURRENDER OF CURRENTLY MATURING OR MATURED TREASURY SECURITIES $ _____

(Note: Treasury Tax and Loan payment not permitted.)

Pieces	DENOMINATIONS FOR COUPON NOTES	AMOUNT	SERIAL NUMBERS
(a)	$ 5,000		
(a)	$ 10,000		
(a)	100,000		
(a)	1,000,000		
	BOOK – ENTRY		Indicate under delivery instructions the purpose of book-entry deposit.
	TOTAL		

DELIVERY INSTRUCTIONS – (Unless otherwise instructed ship allotted securities by registered mail to the undersigned pursuant to current postal regulations) No changes in delivery instruction will be accepted.

FOR BANKS ONLY
Deposit Under Book-Entry:

	F.R.B. CHICAGO	F.R.B. DETROIT
00 In our Investment Account (member banks own securities only)	$ _____	$ _____
02 As collateral-Treasury Tax and Loan Account	$ _____	$ _____
05 In our General Account (member banks for account of their customers)	$ _____	$ _____
Other (must be authorized)·· Please specify	$ _____	$ _____

SPECIAL DELIVERY INSTRUCTIONS: _____

PRIVACY ACT STATEMENT

The individually identifiable information required on this form is necessary to permit the tender to be processed and the securities to be issued. If registered securities are requested the regulations governing United States Securities (Department Circular No. 300) and the offering circular require submission of social security numbers; the numbers and other information are used in inscribing the securities and establishing and servicing the ownership and interest records. The transaction will not be completed unless all required data is furnished.

We hereby certify that we have not made and will not make any agreements for the sale or purchase of any securities of this issue prior to 12:30 p.m. CST, Thursday, February 16, 1978.
* We further certify that we have received tenders from customers in the amounts set forth opposite their names on the list which is made a part of this tender, and that we have received and are holding for the Treasury, or that we guarantee payment to the Treasury, of the deposits stipulated in the official offering circular.
* We further certify that tenders received by us, if any, from other commercial banks or primary dealers for their own account, and for the account of their customers, have been entered with us under the same conditions, agreements, and certifications set forth in this form.
* ADDITIONAL CERTIFICATION BY COMMERCIAL BANK OR PRIMARY DEALER.

DO NOT USE
Ref. No. _____
Delivery Instructions Checked By _____
Delivery Authorized by New Issues Div. _____
Payer _____ Prover _____
New Sec. Shipped On _____
Issue Treasurer's Check for $ _____

PLEASE TYPE OR PRINT

Name of Bank or other subscriber _____   Phone No. _____

Street Address _____

City and State _____   (Zip Code)

ABA No. (6 digit) _____   Signature _____   Title _____
FOR BANKS ONLY

Form 2233

(Any erasures or changes in amount or price must be authorized opposite change by signer of the form.)

[Left margin, vertical text:] Closing time for receipt of tenders: 12:30 P.M. Central Standard Time, Thursday, February 16, 1978. NONCOMPETITIVE TENDERS POSTMARKED WEDNESDAY, FEBRUARY 15, 1978 WILL BE DEEMED TO BE TIMELY.

have to be accompanied by a deposit. Other bidders must accompany their bids with a deposit, normally 5 percent, and must pay the remaining amount due with a check that will clear on or before settlement day or with immediately available funds on settlement day. Notes and bonds bid for in an auction may also be paid for with maturing securities.

During the one- to two-week period between the time a new Treasury note or bond issue is auctioned and the time the securities sold are actually issued, securities that have been auctioned but not yet issued trade actively on a *when-issued* basis.

Secondary market

Very little trading in outstanding notes and bonds occurs on organized stock exchanges. The New York Stock Exchange lists a few issues and the American Exchange (AMEX) offers odd-lot trading in a few others, but neither exchange moves much volume.[5] The real secondary market for bills, notes, and bonds is the dealer-made market, in which huge quantities of bills, notes, and bonds are constantly traded under highly competitive conditions at very small margins. Before we turn to that market, let's look at the brokers.

THE BROKERS

Dealers in government securities actively trade with retail and with each other. In dealing with each other, dealers often go through brokers. Currently, brokered trades represent about 70 percent of all interdealer trades and about 30 percent of total market trades.

The most important reason brokers are used in the government market is ease of communication. There are now over 35 primary dealers in governments and agencies, and their number keeps increasing. Thus, no government trader can keep in touch directly with all his counterparts. Another reason that brokers are needed is that different shops split responsibility for different issues in different ways. Thus, a trader who covers 2- to 4-year notes at one shop might have to call two different traders at another shop to get quotes in his area.

Currently, there are five brokers who service only dealers in governments and agencies. The two largest are Garban and Fundamental Brokers, Incorporated (FBI). Garban and FBI quote rates on a screen, the others quote over the phone.

---

[5] The recently established AMEX trading in odd lots of governments is primarily for the convenience of brokers. If the broker uses a dealer to execute a small buy or sell order, the dealer's fee eats up most of the commission that the broker charges the investor. In contrast, on bond trades executed on an exchange by a member firm, transaction costs to the broker are minimal.

A large dealer is likely to have one or two bill traders, two or three traders of Treasury coupons, and a couple of agency traders. Smaller shops have fewer. Currently, there are about 170 traders in governments and agencies among the primary dealers and almost as many brokers to serve them.

The brokers staff for peak periods because they have to service dealers adequately then in order to get business from them when things are slow. Staffing is the reason most brokers won't take bids or offers from retail. They could not service retail without hiring extra people, which in their view would be uneconomical.

Garban displays bids and offers placed with it on two screens, one for bills and agencies and the other for Treasury coupons. Each screen shows 40 issues. When a new bid or offering comes in, the broker receiving it types it into the computer, and the new quote appears on the Garban screen in all of the dealers' trading rooms within five seconds. A quote is good for two minutes. After that, "old" automatically appears on the screen and the broker goes back to the trader to see if he wants to renew his bid or offer.

The Garban screen also shows the size of bids and offers. Currently, $1 million is the minimum size that appears on the Garban screen, but trades of less than $1 million are also brokered by Garban and the other firms.

When brokers talk to traders, they do not give advice. Brokers have inside information on what large dealers are doing, so it would be unethical for them to express opinions on what the market is likely to do.

If a trader has a bid in the market, he gets the right of first refusal on any new offering. Thus, for example, if a trader had a bid in at 6 and someone else came in with a $1 million offering at 7, a Garban broker would call the bidder and say, "6–7, a million. Your bid." The trader could then say, "I bought them," or just, "OK," the latter indicating that he has no interest. The bidder has 30 seconds to pick up his phone and take the new offering; after that, it is fair game for anyone. During the first 30 seconds a quote is on the Garban screen, it blinks to show that it is new.

Whenever a trade is effected through Garban, their screen flashes "hit" or "tak" (for taken) so that the market can see what trades are done and the prices at which they are done.

Brokers do not give up names on trades done through them. The trades are cleared through the broker's clearing bank. If, for example, Salomon Brothers sold securities to Morgan through Garban, Sali would deliver these securities to Marine Midland, which clears for Garban, and Garban would redeliver to Morgan.

Brokerage on bills generally works out to $25 per $1 million. The brokers adjust the brokerage rate charged in terms of basis points to get to this figure—they work for ¼ of an 01 on the year bill and for ½ of an 01 on the 6-month bill. Recently, brokers reduced the fee charged on the 3-month bill to ¼ of an 01, which is $12.50 per $1 million.

On coupon issues, the brokerage rate is $1/128$, which equals $78.12 per $1 million. The rate on coupons used to be $1/64$, but competition and increased volume in the brokers market brought it down. Brokerage is paid only by the side initiating a trade, so *locked markets,* markets in which the bid and offer are identical, can and do occur in governments. Sometimes, when there is little interest in the market—no one wants to do anything—a locked market will persist for hours.

Brokerage on short coupons is so high that dealers prefer to trade them directly. This is a problem for both brokers and traders. The Treasury's decision to issue short notes on a regular schedule is creating a huge volume of outstanding short coupons. For these securities to be as actively traded as they might be, brokerage on short coupons will have to be reduced—something brokers are currently contemplating.

Brokers have to be careful about the rates they quote on the phone or put on the screen because they have to stand up to those quotes. Said one, "If we put a wrong number on the screen, most traders are good about it and tell us. But there are other traders who like to hang us. When their buttons light, you almost know that there is something wrong on the screen."

The Garban screen has been in operation for about 4 years. "A lot of guys did not like the screen at the beginning," said one broker. "The Salis, Morgans, and Merrills were used to getting preferential treatment—first call from the brokers." The screen endured, however, and it has contributed to the changing way business is done in the government market. The screen gave the traders one more way to play trading games. Also, as one trader noted, "a lot of this market is psychology, and when those CRTs start blinking hit, hit, hit, it has a tremendous impact."

THE GOVERNMENT MARKET

So far in this chapter we have concentrated on providing background information. Let's now turn to the government market and how it is made by dealers and investors.

Bidding in the auction

The cast of bidders in a typical Treasury auction is varied. The Fed holds a huge portfolio of bills, some portion of which matures each week. The Fed replaces some or all of its maturing bills by *rolling* them in the auction; it never bids for bills in the auction to increase the size of its portfolio. To add to its portfolio, the Fed buys bills in the secondary market from dealers.[6]

Retail is also a big factor in Treasury auctions. Before 1974, bill auctions were much smaller than they are today. At that time, it was common for investors to pay a dealer an 01 to make a competitive bid for them. This practice ensured the customer that he would obtain bills in the auction and at a fair price. Now Treasury auctions are so large, information on the price at which a new issue will be sold is so widely distributed, and the sophistication of retail customers is so much greater than it used to be that large portfolio managers feel either that they can price their own bids or that they can buy whatever they need in the secondary market at little or no spread over the price at which they could buy in the auction. Thus, fewer retail customers now pay dealers to bid for them, and those who do typically pay less than they used to—½ or ¼ of an 01.

The dealers are a third big factor in any auction. There are some dealers, Sali and Merrill, that can be counted on to almost always make big bids in an auction because of the huge size of their retail base. Then there are others that will sometimes bid for sizable amounts in an auction and other times bid for little or none at all.

Before the auction there is a buzz of auction talk among the dealers. Dealers know the size of the issues the Treasury is offering, and they try to assess the retail interest in these issues and what amounts other dealers are likely to bid for. That is the sort of information a trader requires to hone his bid down to the last decimal point.

Much of the talk between dealers before the auction focuses on what are going to be the *top* and the *tail* in the auction; in a bill auction the top is the highest price (lowest yield) bid in the auction and the tail is the lowest bid (highest yield) accepted in the auction. Dealers bidding on bills all want to hit the tail, which takes skill. On an auction day, one dealer noted: "Today I do not want to buy much. I am just trying to bid for where I think the tail will be. I am bidding for practice, to see if my market reading is accurate. You have to keep in touch because, when you really want to buy, you need to have the confidence."

The final moment of decision for a dealer comes at about 1:25 Eastern time. Then time runs out. He has to pick a price, grab a phone, and call a runner stationed near the Fed; the latter has a tender form all made out except for the bid prices, which he inks in at the last moment.

Once the Fed receives all the bids—the cutoff time is 1:30—it deter-

---

[6] To prevent the Fed from becoming a money-printing machine for the Treasury, the Fed has long been forbidden to buy—except on a rollover basis—other than small amounts of new Treasury debt directly from the Treasury. This prohibition has, under current institutional arrangements, *no* effect whatsoever on the size of the Fed's portfolio or on the amount of bank reserves it creates.

mines what bids it will accept and announces the results of the auction at 6:00 in the evening.

Table 13–2 shows the results of a bill auction held on February 26, 1978. Note that on the 3-month (13-week) bill, the top and the tail were separated by only 0.007 in price and by only 0.028 percent in yield. The difference between the top and the tail in auctions of Treasury notes and bonds is also usually quite small.

Table 13–2
Results of a weekly bill auction held February 26, 1978

	13-Week	26-Week
Applications	$4,694,685,000	$6,522,670,000
Accepted bids	$2,302,360,000	$3,500,570,000
Accepted at low price	64%	80%
Accepted noncompetitively	$ 386,900,000	$ 182,770,000
Average price	98.375 (6.429%)	96.608 (6.709%)
High price (rate)	98.381 (6.405%)	96.617 (6.692%)
Low price (rate)	98.374 (6.433%)	96.606 (6.713%)
Coupon equivalent	6.63%	7.04%

Supply in Treasury auctions varies from week to week and from month to month. At times when the Treasury is paying down the debt seasonally or extending the maturity of the debt, it will sell fewer bills than the amount maturing. At other times, it will increase the size of the regular weekly bill auctions. Supply offered also varies from one note auction to another.

Dealers act in part as distributors of the Treasury debt. How much distribution is required on a new issue depends on the relationship between the supply offered and demand by retail. When the Treasury is adding, it is likely that the new issue will sell at a fractionally higher yield than surrounding issues until it is distributed, and dealers consequently have a profit incentive to bid aggressively in the auction. When the reverse is true—the Treasury is, for example, reducing the size of a bill issue—there is both less need for the dealers to act as distributors and less profit incentive for them to bid aggressively in the auction.

THE BILL MARKET

Dealers not only distribute bill issues but also make a secondary market in bills by trading with each other and with retail.

Runs

Runs in the brokers' market and between dealers are for *current* issues, that is, those most recently auctioned. In 3-month and 6-month bills, an issue stays current for a week. During that period, the new issue is distributed to people who don't have it but want it and vice versa. After that activity in this issue dies down, a new issue is auctioned and becomes current, and action again picks up.

Bills are quoted in 01s. Thus, a trader's market in a given bill might be 6.10 offered and 6.12 bid. In the interdealer market, traders often redefine their bids and offers to half an 01 by using pluses; a bid of 12+ means that the trader is bidding 12½ basis points. The *handle,* 6 in the above illustration, is never quoted.

A broker's run in the bill market might be: "3-month 50–49, 2 by 5. 6-month at this juncture 70 locked, 10 million up. On the year bill 96–95, 10 by 1." When a broker quotes the size of the market as "2 by 5," he means that $2 million is bid and $5 million offered. When size is "10 million *up*," that means both the bid and the offer are good for $10 million. Sometimes dealers will make their bids and offers on an all-or-none basis. If the dealer bids for $5 million AON, no one can hit that bid for less than $5 million. Sometimes there will be a bid on an issue but no offer. In that case, the broker would quote the market, for example, as "70 bid without." On occasion, the market will go bidless or offerless for small periods of time, but eventually someone comes in to fill the gap.

The real market

Bids in the brokers market may or may not reflect the *real market,* that is, the bid and offered prices at which size could be done. One trader commented: "I think in part of the real market as the market away from the brokers. If I were to go to a retail account who owns bills I want, what would I have to pay to buy them on a swap, what would it cost me to get them from him to me?

"At times, quotes in the brokers market are distortions of the market because they are created to be misleading. Suppose I want to buy a particular bill, say, 100 million. I know that everyone is looking at the brokers market. So what do I do? I make a one-man market. I make them 85 locked, 5 up on both sides. Now I go around and call the dealers and ask them for a market in that bill and they will make it 85–83 or 86–84. I will buy them at 83 or 84 and then I will take my market out [of the brokers screen] after I have bought what I needed. Then, if I want, I can put another market in, and that becomes the market. These are the games played by traders. If you want to buy or sell, you try to distort what you really want to do. Depending on the market, this can be done at times with some success.

"Of course, when I put a locked bid with the brokers I have to stand up to both sides. It might not work. I might lock the market and get myself immediately lifted. If I wanted to buy, that would ruin that act; and now I would have to buy another 5 million. You cannot lock too far from the real market. But remember, we are talking about distorting the market an 01 or half an 01. That pays because I am trading big volume.

"If a dealer does not know if the market on the broker's screen is the real market, he has to spend some money to find out—to buy or sell to find out how real the bid or offered side is in terms of size. If he spends 10 million on bills and they are reoffered, then he knows that there is a genuine seller there. If he buys 5 and that is all he can buy, then maybe that is not the real market. Maybe the market is just holding up because the bid is stronger than the offer."

Trading wi and wi wi

Bills have long been traded on a when-issued basis between the auction and settlement dates. More recently, a new custom of trading bills wi after they are announced but before they are auctioned has developed. Traders refer to this as trading *wi wi*.

In bills, wi and wi wi trading is very active both between dealers and between dealers and retail. For a trader who wants to short the market, selling bills trading wi is more attractive than shorting an outstanding issue, because on a wi sale delivery does not have to be made immediately and a wi sale is thus simpler and cheaper than an ordinary short sale. For a dealer who wants to trade 3-month bills, buying them wi is at times the only way he can do so without incurring a negative carry. As one dealer noted: "The current yield structure encourages wi wi trading. Say Fed funds are 5.40, the RP rate on governments at 5.20, and the 3-month bill is yielding 5 percent on a discount basis, that is, a 5.10 bonded out yield. You can't carry that bill positively. But a lot of people like to trade it so they will trade it in the wi market because buying wi is not a negative carry."

Trading on a wi wi basis serves a useful purpose. The same dealer continued: "A lot of regional firms are trading the wi wi market very actively. Before the advent of such trading the recognized dealers with brokers wires were able to engineer auctions a lot easier than they can now because people outside the New York dealer community were not exactly sure where the market was. So, if three guys got together, they could—in the talk before the auction—push it an 01 or an 02, and buy most of the auction. Now, with all this wi trading, the regionals know where the market is because the bill has been trading wi three or four days before the auction.

"Also, a lot of times people who do not like the market will build up a short going into the auction, so half the issue is really taken care of before 1:30. That really stabilizes the market when you bring in a new issue."

Weekly cycle

There tends to be something of a weekly cycle in the way the bill currently being auctioned trades. "On Monday," one trader noted, "you have the auction. Then Tuesday, right after the auction, you generally do not see too much price improvement unless it was a very aggressive auction or some extraordinary event affects the market; on Tuesday, the market performs sloppily because you have people who can sell the issue whether they have it or not. On Wednesday, there is a day to go, and people who are short start to think—shall I take my short in or not; and the market tends to behave a little better. Then Thursday you have demand. The shorters have to cover or borrow, which is expensive. Also, the previous bill matures and people who have not rolled over in the auction have to put their money to work, so they go and invest in the new bills. This is the busiest day. Then Friday it tails off a bit."

Trading games

As noted, a trader may *paint a one-man picture* in the brokers market to distort other dealers' perception of where the market is. There are also other games traders play. Whenever the Fed comes into the market, the brokers treat bids and offers as under reference until they check them. "I have a guy at Chemical," said one broker, "who tells me when the Fed is in the market. Also the guy at Merrill tells me indirectly because he cancels all his bids and offers when the Fed is in the market. Sometimes he will cancel everything and nothing is going on. He is just creating an effect—having a lot of offers go off the screen at the same time. He is probably at the same time hitting any bids he can find at the other brokers."

The same broker described another strategy: "The traders at two top New York banks used to be good friends. They did a lot of volume through us just to show it on the screen. They paid the commission in order to influence the market. They might do as much as 50 million. It was most advantageous for them to trade on our screen because that way the message they were trying to send got around to everyone right away."

Quotes to retail and protocols

When a good trader gives quotes to retail he will not simply *bracket* the brokers market—quote a bid slightly above that in the brokers market and an offer slightly below that in the brokers market. He will quote on the basis of his own perception as to where the real market is.[7] Also, his quotes will be influenced by the size he wants to do or retail wants to do.

---

[7] Recall the discussion of trading on pages 239–40.

One dealer commented: "Say I wanted to buy size in an issue. The bid in the brokers market is 20–18, 10 by 5. I might bid 17 to retail for 50 million. That's an 01 less than the offered rate in the brokers market, but there I can buy only 5, not 50."

If a retail customer has a lot he wants to buy or sell and he wants to get the job done properly, there are certain protocols he should follow. Say he is a big seller; he should be reasonably open with a single dealer and get that dealer to work for him—to try to retail what he is selling piece by piece to people who might be buyers. Sometimes a big seller will hit every bid around for $10 or $20 million, the market gets swamped, and the dealers all end up competing with each other to unload these securities. A customer who sells that way gets a reputation and won't get the same treatment from dealers the next time.

The dealer is also expected to be fair with retail. Said one: "A professional dealer won't move the market on a customer who tells him he's a big buyer or seller." Another dealer commented: "Say I want to sell 100 million of an issue; the World Bank comes in and wants to sell to me and the market is 84–3; I will make him 86–5. He will know right away I am not his person. He will know I am trying to sell. I will be open with him—tell him I am not in a position to help him because I too have a position to unwind."

The protocol of openness does not apply between dealers. If a dealer is trying to sell in size, he will attempt to hide that from other dealers—to try, for example, to play the games described above in order to distort the market and cloak his true intent.

The 90-day bill rate

The Fed directly pegs a single interest rate, the Fed funds rate. In doing so, however, it strongly influences the level and pattern of other short-term interest rates. The 90-day bill rate is coupled to the Fed funds rate and other rates key off it, as the Fed funds rate changes, the whole structure of short-term interest rates changes.

Usually the 90-day bill trades, as Figure 13–2 shows, at or around the Fed funds rate. The reason is that the two rates are coupled by arbitrage. As one dealer noted: "If 90-day bills yield considerably more than the Fed funds rate, carry becomes positive, and firms like ourselves will buy 90-day bills and finance them. That puts some upside limit on the 90-day bill rate." When, in contrast, 90-day bills trade below the Fed funds rate—for example, because the Treasury is paying down in the bill area—at some point dealers' carry on 90-day bills becomes negative and dealers cease to position them; that in turn diminishes demand for the 90-day bill and sets some limit on how far through the Fed funds rate 90-day bills can trade.

Figure 13–2
The 90-day bill rate usually hovers near the Fed funds rate

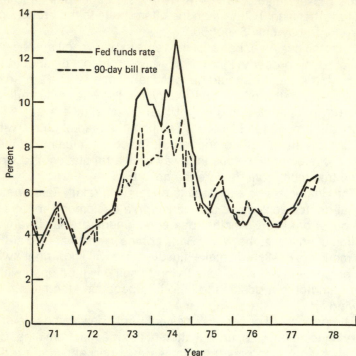

Changes in the 90-day bill rate are quickly transmitted to governments of other maturities. The same dealer continued: "The 6-month bill is a creature of the 90-day bill and technicals [prevailing supply and demand conditions]. At some spread of the 3-month bill to the 6-month bill, all the computers on the street tracking yield spreads and doing standard deviations [measuring statistically how unusual a given yield spread is in terms of historical experience] will tell dealers and investors to buy the 6-month bill and sell the 3-month bill. Using the 6-month bill becomes an extended part of using the 90-day bill because any trade always implies a future trade. For example, to buy a 90-day bill and roll it, instead of buying the 6-month bill, implies an outlook as to what the 90-day bill rate will be 90 days from now. We know all of that. It is almost too academic. We have it down to shorthand—we talk spreads."

Rates in other sectors of the money market key off rates in the government market. BAs, for example, carry some small credit risk and are less liquid than bills. Thus, BAs have to trade at some spread to bills. That spread is, however, not written in stone. If the supply of BAs increases, the spread will widen; and if the supply of BAs decreases, BAs may trade almost on top of bills.

Supply in different sectors of the money market and the search by dealers and investors for *relative value* establish the pattern of rates prevailing in the money market. That pattern changes constantly, but by and large it is always a rational, explainable response to underlying fundamentals: Fed policy, the supply and types of securities issued by the Treasury, the state of loan demand at the banks, the demand for BA financing, and so forth.

The reason that the Fed funds rate is coupled most directly with the 90-day bill rate and that changes in the Fed funds rate first have an impact on the 90-day bill rate is that the 90-day bill is the shortest bill that is auctioned weekly and has liquidity. It is thus the shortest issue in which dealers can react to what the Fed is doing or what they anticipate the Fed will do by going short or long in size.

The linkage—"ripple effect"—between the 90-day bill and other short-term rates has, however, become quicker than it used to be. The reason is the increase in sophistication at all levels—dealers, banks, and portfolio managers. With everyone's computer tracking yields spreads, the lags that used to occur between changes in the 90-day bill rate and other rates have almost disappeared, and short-term rates now move almost simultaneously in response to major developments such as a change in the funds rate.

Short bills

The market for *short bills* (under 90 days) is a thin market that behaves differently from the rest of the bill market. Supply is *fixed* in this part of the market, and there is a lot of demand from institutions that fund to dates and that can hold only Treasuries. Consequently, short bills typically trade through the overnight repo rate, as noted in Chapter 12.

Dealers trade short bills largely as a customer service; it is not a major money maker for them. If a dealer positions short bills, his carry is negative. Also, a dealer has to trade short bills at a *wide* spread just to cover his clearing costs. One dealer commented: "On longer bills, I generally quote a 2-basis-point spread to retail and I can operate at a tighter spread in the dealer and broker community. On very short bills—bills maturing within a week or two—I do not want to do trades on that basis because a couple of basis points would not cover my clearing costs." Writing a ticket is likely to cost a dealer $40, a 2-week basis point is worth less than $4; so a dealer has to pick up more than 10 basis points on both sides of a $1 million trade in 2-week bills just to cover his cost of doing the trade.

One of the reasons that CDs trade at higher yields than governments is that they are less liquid. In the 30-day area, however, CDs are often more liquid than bills. In CDs, the 30-day market is one of the best markets, and large size can normally be traded on an 05 spread. The contrast between the CD and the bill markets is due in part to the fact that a dealer's carry on a 30-day CD is not automatically negative.

In a dealership, the job of trading short bills is often given to a trainee. The market for short bills is quite stable so he can't lose much money, and trading these bills gives him an opportunity to learn the lingua franca and other fundamentals of bill trading before he goes on to trade longer bills, which is where the action is.

Due bills

A *due bill* is an IOU issued by a dealer that says the dealer owes the customer and will deliver certain securities to him at his earliest convenience. Dealers in governments had at one time, for specific short bill issues, more due bills outstanding than the Treasury had bills outstanding in these issues. Issuing due bills was in effect an attractive way for the dealers to borrow on the Treasury's credit.

Today the Fed frowns on the use of due bills; it requires that due bills outstanding for more than three days be collateralized, and the use of due bills has much diminished. Now dealers typically issue due bills as a convenience to their customers. One dealer commented: "Say we have a customer who wants to invest in a bill maturing in a few days. We can't get the bill because no one is offering it at a reasonable price, so we sell the customer a rate. Say we can repo at 4.50 and the best rate we can get the bill at is 4. We might offer the customer 4.25 on a due bill. This is a substitute from our point of view for repo financing. We do it to accommodate customers and are lucky to cover costs."

Another dealer observed: "We generally tend to 'paper bills' [give out due bills] on securities that we can't buy now and know we will be able to repurchase prior to maturity. Say a guy wants a 1-month bill I can't buy and I know he is going to sell that same bill in two weeks. I give him a due bill and then buy it back from him. This helps the customer because he gets interest income on his money and he is not forced to accept additional risk by buying something beyond the maturity range he wants."

Sometimes a dealer who gets failed to will give a due bill to a customer who he knows will take one and thus earn money on the fail.

TREASURY NOTES

The activities of a note trader closely resemble in some respects those of a bill trader but differ sharply in other respects because notes trade differently from bills. In the note market yields are quoted in 32nds, but quotes can be refined to 64ths through the use of *pluses;* an 8+ bid, for example, means that the bid is eight and one-half 32nds, which is $^{17}/_{64}$.

On dealers' runs for notes with less than a year to run, the normal spread between the bid and asked is $^1/_{32}$. On notes in the 1- to 2-year area, the spread widens to $^1/_{16}$, and on notes beyond one year, it is typically $^1/_8$, except on new issues that are very actively traded. Quotes on notes are normally good for $1 million but much larger trades and some smaller trades are also done.

As maturity increases in the note market, the number of active dealers decreases. In the two-year and beyond area, there are only about a dozen dealers who actively quote markets to other dealers. The rest basically refuse to make a market.

Notes are traded during the morning for both cash and regular settlement. After 12:00 or 12:30, however, trading is only for regular settlement. The reason is that on trades done after this time, it is difficult for a dealer to get tickets processed quickly enough to make timely delivery. On dealer-to-dealer and dealer-to-broker trades, there is a 2:30 cutoff for delivery. That cutoff gives the dealers half an hour, until 3:00, to redeliver securities to their customers. At 3:00 P.M., the Fed wire goes down for deliveries out of the New York district.

Wi trading

Notes are traded wi from the time an issue is auctioned until the settlement date. There is no wi wi trading in notes because the Treasury forbids it. The Treasury feels that it would be speculative and leave room for investors to be injured. Some dealers feel the same way; in their view, the government market is the last bastion of unregulated markets, and they want to keep it that way because they believe regulation generally hurts markets. It is, however, not clear that wi wi trading in the 2- and 4-year notes, which are auctioned on a regular cycle, would be detrimental to the market. Wi wi trading has, as noted, probably had a beneficial effect on bill auctions.

Current issues

In the note market, an issue is current from the time it is auctioned until it is replaced by another issue. Thus, the new 2-year note is current for a month, and new 4-year note for a quarter. A current issue trades much more actively than other issues until it becomes distributed or is replaced by a new issue. Although notes range in original maturity from 2 to 10 years, there are at any time only five or six current issues that are relatively new and actively traded at narrow spreads. Moreover, before the Treasury undertook its program of regularization of debt issuance, there were even fewer.

Many investors roll notes in order to stay in the current issue, just as they roll 3- or 6-month bills. Sometimes they will even give up coupon just to stay in a note that is active enough so that they can get a bid on $5 or $10 million in a market that is quiet or going down. Staying in the current bill allows the investor to increase yield by moving out on the yield curve while still maintaining liquidity. Dealers, too, like to position in current issues. As one noted: "When I go long or short, I like to stay as current as possible because that is where most people have buying and selling interest."

In longer notes, the market will sometimes go for months without a new issue, something that would be unimaginable in the bill market. When this occurs, trading volume in the market tapers off. Where and when the Treasury chooses to issue.its new debt also affect the yield curve. A trader of long notes commented: "We are going 6 months with no auction of a 3-year note. That will drive down the yield on the 3-year note relative to yields on other issues around it."

Short coupons

Coupons with a current maturity of a year or less are not actively traded. Part of the reason is that brokerage on bills is much less than that on coupons. Also, the bill market naturally tends to be active because there are so many bill auctions. Still, since the 2-year note cycle is so big, the point is being reached where there are more coupons due within a year than bills outstanding. Thus, the market for short coupons should be more active, and brokers realize that if they cut their fees in that area, which they are moving to do, volume would grow.

Another reason short coupons trade inactively is that it is difficult for government dealers to staff all their major chairs, so they put rookie trainees on short coupons—often in a bank, it's someone who has graduated from the Fed funds desk.

Seasoning and trading

Not all issues trade strictly on the yield curve. One of the reasons is the varying reception that different issues receive in the auction.

"It takes time," one dealer noted, "for an issue to get well distributed, *seasoned*. How long depends on how well the auction went. Some auctions are sloppy and some are good. If in an auction, retail steps up and takes half or three quarters of an issue and they never intend to reoffer these securities so they are put away right off the bat, the float cleans up in a hurry. In other auctions, you have the opposite; the dealer fraternity by and large buys up the issue, it does not have anyone to sell them to, and it takes forever to get rid of them. That causes anomalies in the yield curve. You will see in the 2-year note area situations where the current 24-month note is at 5.70, the 20-month note at 5.70, and the 19-month note at 5.60. Why the 10 basis point jump over one month and no jump over the next four? It is because there are dog issues out that never get as seasoned as the issues surrounding them."

How actively an issue trades over its life also depends on the reception it receives in the auction and on the volume in which it was offered to the market. One trader observed: "The 8's of '86 are a very popular 10-year note. When that issue originally came out, it was widely distributed in both individual and street hands. It is in ample supply, and it has been actively traded.

"If there is a lot of interest in an issue when it comes out, if it is large in size, and if it is widely distributed, it will continue to be actively traded. Profits can be taken, the issue becomes popular, and people buy and sell it. What counts is that there is sufficient size in trading hands—not necessarily dealers, but investors who are willing to trade. It is also important that traders be able to borrow the issue. If they can't, no one will short the issue, and it won't be actively traded. It is easy to borrow the 8's of '86, and for that reason it is easier for a dealer to make a market in them than in some obscure issue."

Trading notes

A note trader is responsible for a wide range of notes, even 30 or 40 in a big dealership. This is more than any one person can actively follow. So the typical trader concentrates on a few issues in his area. "Once you know the issues you follow closely," commented one trader, "there are relationships. In the 2-year area, if you know where the Junes are, you know where surrounding issues should be. Even if you do not trade the Julys for a week and you have a trade a day in the Junes, you know, if you are worth your salt, where the Julys should be."

Prices are much more volatile in the coupon market than in the bill market because maturities are longer. For this reason dealers take smaller positions in coupons than in bills, and the coupon positions they assume become smaller the longer the current maturity of the securities positioned. One dealer commented: "If our bill trader is sitting there with 100 million in bills, that might be equivalent in terms of risk exposure to a 50 million position in 2-year notes and—in a normal market—to a 10 million exposure in long bonds."

Because a trader in governments is responsible for only a limited maturity spectrum, he is not in a position to arbitrage one sector of the market against another. That is a function typically carried on in a dealership in a separate arbitrage account. However, he can and does attempt to arbitrage temporary anomalies along the yield curve in the sector he trades. "If I see a blip in the yield curve—the Julys are out of line with the Augusts—I will short the overpriced issue and buy the other," noted one trader. "Generally, the payoff on this sort of thing is $1/32$ or $1/16$."

Technicals

A coupon trader has to be concerned about more than the Fed funds rate. He also has to consider any factors that might affect the yield curve, and he has to follow closely the technicals—factors affecting supply and demand—in his market.

Bill traders can and do short particular issues but, as Table 13–3 shows, net as a group they always have a substantial *long* position in bills. The same is not true for coupon traders. At times, the dealer community will go net *short* in coupons, particularly in the 1- to 5-year area. When dealers short an area, they eventually have to buy securities from retail to cover that short.

Dealers establish short positions in anticipation of a decline in coupon prices or as part of an arbitrage, for example, by shorting the 2-year note and buying the 7-year note, which is a *bull market arbitrage.*

Whatever the reason for the short, a lack of securities on the street and a need to cover short positions can cause a *technical rally* in coupons. "Things in my part of the market," commented a trader of intermediate coupons, "can be technically bone dry in a way that never occurs in the bill market. The day before Carter killed the $50 tax rebate [April 1977] dealers were net short in my area 46 million. Carter's announcement [which caused a market rally] made the shorters uncomfortable; they wanted to cover and go long, but there were no notes around. So, we had a technical rally, and the securities were dug out of customers."

One of the technicals a note trader has to constantly consider is what the arbitragers might be doing in his area of the market. Commented one note trader: "Whenever something important—an economic or political development—that affects the market occurs, I have to think as much about what the arbitragers are going to do as about where the market in general is going. If I think our arbitrage guy is sitting there getting ready to buy 3-year notes and sell 7-year notes, I sure don't want to be short in the 3-year note even if I think that the market is going down."

Brokers

Traders of government notes and bonds use the brokers fully as much as bill traders do and for the same reasons. In the government market, as in other markets, one of the most important features of the brokers market is that whenever something occurs to cause a break in market activity, it serves as the arena in which trading is reestablished. It is part of the

Table 13-3
Positions of U.S. government securities dealers (par value; averages of daily figures, in $ millions)*

Item	1974	1975	1976	1977		1978	1977, week ending Wednesday			1978, week ending Wednesday		
				Nov.	Dec.	Jan.	Dec. 14	Dec. 21	Dec. 28	Jan. 4	Jan. 11	Jan. 18
U.S. government securities	**2,580**	**5,884**	**7,592**	**4,351**	**5,114**	**4,373**	**5,534**	**5,178**	**5,436**	**5,671**	**6,009**	**3,385**
Bills	1,932	4,297	6,290	3,784	4,312	4,052	5,090	4,923	4,062	4,431	5,639	3,613
Other within 1 year	-6	265	188	120	210	91	179	169	296	191	147	76
1-5 years	265	886	515	-135	377	120	93	-27	845	595	2	-389
5-10 years	302	300	402	383	66	-117	35	13	68	50	-96	-146
Over 10 years	88	136	198	199	147	227	137	100	167	405	315	230
Federal agency securities	**1,212**	**943**	**729**	**914**	**788**	**504**	**1,003**	**759**	**486**	**571**	**524**	**387**

* Net amounts (in terms of par values) of securities owned by nonbank dealer firms and dealer departments of commercial banks on a commitment, that is, trade-date basis, including any such securities that have been sold under agreements to repurchase. The maturities of some repurchase agreements are sufficiently long, however, to suggest that the securities involved are not available for trading purposes. Securities owned, and hence dealer positions, do not include securities purchased under agreements to resell.

Note: Averages for positions are based on number of trading days in the period; those for financing, on the number of calendar days in the period.
Source: *Federal Reserve Bulletin.*

protocol of the dealer fraternity that whenever something big—such as a move by the Fed—has an impact on the market and causes uncertainty as to where issues should trade, dealers do *not* call each other and ask for runs. They do, however, look to the brokers market for bids and offers, and generally someone is doing something there. Gradually, as a few trades are done through the brokers, more bids and offers are put into the brokers, and a semblance of order in trading is reestablished.

Games

Traders play the same trading games in the brokers market and elsewhere that bill traders do. "Trading is much like a poker game," said one note trader. "You try to bluff, to sound like a buyer when you are really a seller. You tell the guy you are in great shape for the market to go down when you are, in fact, long and hope he will buy some of your securities. When my boss says, 'Let's get down in position,' the first thing I will do is put a bid in the brokers. The only way to get down is to find some help [create some buyers]. Sometimes my bid will be low and sometimes it will be good; if I get hit, I have a bigger job to do.

"I have the ability to use two brokers at a time. Say the market is 10+ 11+; I have notes offered at 10+ and can't sell them. I will go out and buy them at 11+. Say I started with 30 million I bought at 9. By buying 5 million from another broker at a higher price than where I am willing to sell, I might lose $1/32$ on that 5 million but I now am much more likely to be able to get the other 30 million I own off and make $2^1/2$ or $1^1/2$ 32nds on them."

BONDS

Treasury long bonds extend in maturity past the year 2000 and are not part of the stock in trade of the money market.

Long bonds are much more volatile in price than short instruments, and the risks in positioning them are commensurately greater. As a result, traders of long governments will typically hedge the bulk of their positions. If a trader buys $1 million of long bonds from a customer and cannot immediately resell them, he will short a similar active issue and then wait and unwind the position when he can.

The number of players in long governments is much smaller than the number in short governments. It is not typical for one trader of bonds to call another for a run; and a lot of interdealer trading is done through brokers. Bond traders, like other traders, often phony up pictures in the brokers market.

In positioning, a trader of government bonds watches, in addition to developments in his own market, what is happening in the corporate sector, since a lot of bond portfolios invest in both governments and corporate bonds. A big new issue of Bell Telephone bonds will tend to depress the prices of governments in that maturity range as underwriters distribute the new Bells in part by swapping customers out of governments.

A trader in governments picks up money in several ways. He knows when certain institutions will swap from one issue to another—what spread it takes—and when that spread appears, he will get the customer to do the swap, picking up a small profit on the trades. Government bond traders are also active arbitragers. Some of the arbitrages they do are based on yield spreads, others on dollar price spreads.

DAILY TRADING VOLUME

Trading in the government market has expanded tremendously in recent years both because the government's marketable debt has grown so rapidly (see Figure 7–1) and because that debt is more actively traded than it used to be. Table 13–4 shows just how much trading in governments has expanded over the last decade and also where it is centered. By far the bulk of the action is in bills, but notes with 1- to 5-year maturities are also actively traded.

MERRY-GO-ROUND

The people trained to trade governments and agencies are all in the United States and mostly in New York. There are—assuming five traders to a shop—roughly 170 of them. The rapid expansion in the number of primary dealers in governments has placed a tremendous premium on good traders, and there is a constant flow of people from one shop to another as dealers buy good people away from each other.

Firms don't actively recruit people to be trained as traders. They end up taking someone who was working in the back office or whatever and putting him to work trading short coupons or some other area of the market where it is safe to let a rookie try his hand. Thus, it is not surprising that the head of one trading operation commented: "Staffing in some areas of the government market is horrible. A lot of traders are there simply because they grew up in the geographic area of New York. They are traders when their real natural destiny was to be a house painter."

FEDERAL AGENCY SECURITIES

The major federal agencies still issuing securities to the market have, as Table 13–5 shows, a wide range of coupon securities outstanding. Most agency issues are much smaller than comparable Treasury issues.

Table 13–4
U.S. government securities dealers transactions (par value; averages of daily figures, in $ millions)

Item	1969	1970	1971	1972	1973	1974	1975	1976	1977
U.S. government securities	**2,434**	**2,513**	**2,700**	**2,930**	**3,439**	**3,579**	**6,027**	**10,449**	**10,838**
By maturity									
Bills	2,078	2,032	1,988	2,259	2,643	2,550	3,889	6,676	6,746
Other within 1 year*	—	—	—	—	—	250	223	210	237
1–5 years	231	311	431	422	471	465	1,414	2,317	2,318
5–10 years	87	136	240	189	243	256	363	1,019	1,148
Over 10 years	39	34	41	63	83	58	138	229	388
By type of customer:									
U.S. government securities dealers†	946	977	940	726	665	652	885	1,360	1,267
U.S. government securities brokers†				411	795	965	1,750	3,407	3,709
Commercial banks	880	929	963	998	1,092	998	1,451	2,426	2,295
All others‡	511	510	664	796	886	964	1,941	3,257	3,567
Federal agency securities	**361**	**463**	**636**	**527**	**743**	**965**	**1,043**	**1,548**	**693**

* Not given in earlier *Federal Reserve Bulletins*.

† Combined in the *Federal Reserve Bulletin* until 1972.

‡ **Includes**—among others—all other dealers and brokers in commodities and securities, foreign banking agencies, and the Federal Reserve System.

Note.—Averages for transactions are based on number of trading days in the period. Transactions are market purchases and sales of U.S. government securities dealers reporting to the Federal Reserve Bank of New York. The figures exclude allotments of, and exchanges for, new U.S. government securities, redemptions of call or matured securities, or purchases or sales of securities under repurchase (resale), reverse repurchase (resale), or similar contracts.

Source: *Federal Reserve Bulletin*.

Table 13–5
Major federal agency securities (as of April 1978)

Agency	Security	Minimum denomination ($)	Bearer (B) and/or registered (R)‖	Original maturity	Number of issues outstanding	Volume of securities outstanding ($ billions)
Federal Home Loan Bank†	Bonds	10,000‡	B	1–20 years	38	21.3
Federal Land Bank†	Bonds	1,000	B, R§	2–15 years	45	20.4
Federal Intermediate Credit Bank†	Debentures	5,000	B	9 months–4½ years	16	10.3
Bank for Cooperatives†	Debentures	5,000	B	6 months–5 years	10	4.7
Federal National Mortgage Association†	Debentures	10,000	B	2–25 years	4	1.1
Government National Mortgage Association*	Participation certificates	5,000–10,000	B, R	10–20 years	19	2.5
Government National Mortgage Association*	Pass-through securities	25,000	R	12-year expected life	21,758 pools	55.0
Federal Home Loan Mortgage Corporation	Guaranteed mortgage certificates	100,000	R	10-year expected life	7	1.5
Federal Home Loan Mortgage Corporation	Mortgage participation certificates	100,000	R	12-year expected life	71 pools	5.5

* Backed by the full faith and credit of the U.S. government.
† Interest income exempted from state and local taxation.
‡ Smaller denominations available on some issues.
§ Bearer only on bonds with an original maturity of less than 5 years.
‖ These agencies are moving, except on pass-throughs, to book-entry securities.

The Treasury has a few bond issues outstanding that are less than $1 billion in size, but most of its coupon issues are in the $2 to $3 billion range and a few are as large as $8 or $9 billion. In agencies, in contrast, the size of outstanding issues typically runs from $300 million up to but not above $1 billion.

Distribution

Federal agencies sell new coupon issues to the market through selling groups. The practices of the Federal Home Loan Bank system in this respect are typical. The FHLB goes to the market on a regular basis every 3 months but will go more often when its need for funds is especially high. The FHLB announces the size of a new issue to be offered on a Monday. At that time the members of its selling group—about 140 dealers—begin to distribute the issue by determining (*circling* in street jargon) customer interest in it. Small regional banks and other investors that are not rate conscious will often put in a market order for the new issue, that is, agree to buy it before it is priced. Other buyers will make a subject bid for the new paper—agree to buy some amount of the issue if the coupon is set, for example, at 7.05 or better.

Dealers are each allocated a specific share of the total issue to be sold. They attempt to presell that share and, if they are more successful in doing so than other dealers, the FHLB increases their allocation.

On the day after a new issue is announced, the FHLB starts to think about pricing. It makes its own reading on the market, talks to people at the Treasury, and talks to 30 or 40 representative dealers about how well their presales of the issue are going and precisely where they feel the coupon should be set. The FHLB seeks to price the issue so that it will trade close to par. It announces its decision on pricing on Tuesday and the new issue begins to trade wi on Wednesday.

Dealers in a selling group get a fee, which ranges depending on the maturity of the issue from $0.50 to $3 per $1,000 on whatever securities they sell. Their function is to get the securities into the hands of a wide range of investors, not to position the new issue. However, in a sale characterized by poor retail demand, the major dealers would if necessary underwrite—buy for their own position—the new issue to get it sold.

The dealers who participate in the selling group are, of course, also market makers, and in that capacity they assume long and short positions in agencies. Sometimes after the sale of a new issue, dealers who like the issue will go back into the market as buyers and position it. This is not difficult to do. If an issue goes immediately to a premium of a few 32nds, some buyers will sell out and take their profit. This creates a floating supply, which the dealers must in effect distribute. How long distribution takes depends on the initial reception an issue gets in the market. If it is poor, the securities may overhang the market for a long period.

Agency securities trade wi for a week or two after they are priced and sold. The wi period used to be much longer because of the time required to print the actual certificates. Now, however, virtually all new agency issues are sold in book-entry form.

The secondary market

The secondary market in agency securities, like the secondary market in governments, is made by dealers trading with retail and with each other. There are, however, significant differences between the two markets. These result in large part from the fact that agency issues are smaller than Treasury issues and are traded less actively, as Table 13–4 shows.

Several primary dealers in governments are in the market every day trading agencies, but many others are sometimes players who will position when they like a spot in the agency market and otherwise ignore it.

Dealer's positions in agencies are much smaller than those in governments (see Table 13–3). Also in agencies, as in government notes and bonds, dealers sometimes assume net short positions, so the technical condition of the agency market, like that of the government note market, can become bone dry in particular sectors.

Interdealer quotes in agencies are good for only $500,000, and a lot of trades of that size are done. A $5 million trade is a big trade in the agency market except on a new or short-term issue. A $10 million trade is a rarity.

Spreads are wider in agencies than in governments, and agencies are consequently less liquid. An agency run includes the two newest FHLB issues, the two newest Federal Land Bank issues, the most recent Federal Intermediate Credit Bank issue, and the most recent Bank for Cooperatives issue. For on-the-run agency issues, the typical spread is $1/32$ for a 1-year maturity, $1/32$ to $2/32$nds for a 2- to 3-year maturity, and as much as $4/32$nds for a 10-year bond. As issues get seasoned, these spreads widen. One reason is that currently many of the investors in agencies are trust accounts, state and local governments, and commercial banks that mature the securities they buy and rarely do swaps.

Agency traders use brokers just as traders of governments do, but not as extensively. The market in off-the-run agencies is so thin that when a dealer wants to buy or sell such an issue, he will often be quite open about his position with other dealers to see if they can help him find securities he wants to buy or a buyer for securities he wants to sell. Said one dealer: "Look at my position. I have 940,000 of this issue, I am short 90,000 of that one, and I need 290,000 of this other issue. I am not going to go into the brokers market to clean up all that. I will go to other dealers and talk to them, to Sali and Merrill. They will help me, and I help them."

Currently there are outstanding a number of note and bond issues that were sold prior to 1974 by federal agencies, such as the Export-Import Bank and the Tennessee Valley Authority, which now borrow solely from the Federal Financing Bank. These issues are by and large put away and trade very inactively.

AGENCY DISCOUNT NOTES

In addition to selling coupon securities, the FHLB, the farm credit agencies, and Fannie Mae all borrow short term by issuing non-interest-bearing discount notes, which resemble Treasury bills.

These notes are sold through dealers who get an 05 for their effort. An agency selling notes will decide what rate to offer on its notes after conferring with dealers in its selling group about market conditions. Some post rates all the time but post competitive rates only when they want to sell. Agencies invest any excess funds they raise through the sale of discount notes in RP. That's a negative carry for them so they are careful not to raise more short-term money than they need.

Agencies use funds raised through the sale of discount notes to provide bridge financing to a date when they intend to issue longer-term securities. They also issue discount notes when money is tight and they need to borrow but do not want to borrow long term at high rates. The FHLB, for example, experiences a substantial demand for loans from S&Ls when money is tight, but this demand tapers off rapidly as interest rates fall. Thus, for the FHLB to borrow long term at high rates, as it did in 1974, it must lock up for a long period of time expensive money that neither it nor member S&Ls will later want.

Outstanding agency discount paper is not traded as actively as bills are and it is somewhat less liquid than bills. When the agencies are writing a lot of new paper, the dealers will bid for old paper to get customers to swap into new paper, and activity in the secondary market for such paper picks up. At other times when the agencies are not writing, activity drys up. A dealer will always give retail a bid on old paper, but getting an offer out of him may be more difficult, because in order to supply old paper, he has to go out to an account that has the paper and try to bid it away.

Agency discount notes trade at a spread over bills. This spread, which can be anything from 5 to 100 basis points, tends to rise whenever the agencies write a lot of paper and when money tightens.

BROKERING TO RETAIL

Brokers of money market instruments typically service only dealers. There is, however, one exception—Cantor Fitzgerald. This firm, which brokers governments and agencies, has over 300 clients, including most of the recognized dealers in governments, several dealers just entering the government market, and a large number of big retail accounts. All bids and offers made through Cantor Fitzgerald are displayed on three pages of the Telerate system.

When a trade is done through Cantor Fitzgerald, names are never given up. Securities sold are delivered to Cantor's clearing bank, which redelivers them to the buyer. In effect, Cantor acts as principal on both sides of the transaction, and for this reason it checks with extreme care the financial condition of a retail customer before it will do business with him.

Brokerage on trades made through Cantor Fitzgerald is paid by the side that initiates the transaction. The firm charges the same brokerage rates that other brokers do, except that on trades of long coupons it charges $1/64$ if the trade is for less than $5 million.

Because there are so many primary dealers that use Cantor Fitzgerald, the bids and offers it quotes can never be far from the inside market. Also, as one would expect, dealers are busy painting pictures on Cantor's screen just as they do on the Garban and FBI screens. And to the extent that Cantor's retail clients are less sophisticated than traders at the primary dealers, traders may play such games with slightly more success in Cantor's market than elsewhere.

Chapter 14

The Treasury bill futures market

FORWARD TRANSACTIONS ARE COMMON in many areas of economic activity including the markets for commodities. *In a forward transaction a seller agrees to deliver goods to a buyer at some future date at some fixed price.* For example, a farmer growing onions might, before the harvest, sell some portion of his crop to a buyer at a fixed price for delivery at harvest. For the farmer, this transaction reduces risk. To grow onions, the farmer incurs various costs; by selling his onions forward, he guarantees the revenue he will receive for his onions at harvest, and he thus locks in a profit on his operations. That profit may be more or less than what he would have earned if he had waited to sell his crop at harvest for whatever price was then prevailing in the *cash market* (market for immediate delivery) for onions.

Forward transactions are common in the money market. As noted in Chapter 11, there is a forward market in Monday Fed funds. Also, Euro time deposits are often sold for future delivery. And, as noted in Chapter 16, there is an active market in forward foreign exchange, for example, in German marks to be delivered against dollars at some agreed-upon exchange rate at some future date. The objective of many money market participants who operate in forward markets is to reduce risk. For example, a foreign bank engaging in weekend arbitrage (described in

Chapter 17) sells clearing house funds on Friday and, in order to cover that sale, has to deliver Fed funds on Monday. By buying the Fed funds forward, the foreign bank locks in the profit it earns on the transaction.

A *futures contract,* like a forward contract, specifies that the seller of the contract will deliver whatever item the contract is for to the buyer at some future date at some fixed price. Futures contracts differ, however, from forward contracts in several respects. First, *futures contracts are standardized agreements made and traded on exchanges that are chartered, designated, and licensed to serve as a trading arena in specific futures contracts.* Second, whereas forward contracts are normally custom tailored contracts made with the intent that delivery shall be made, *delivery is rarely made in connection with futures contracts.* Instead, a buyer of a futures contract will typically close out his position before the contract matures by making an offsetting sale of the same contract, a seller by making an offsetting purchase.

The reason delivery is not made is that people enter into futures contracts not to buy or sell commodities but either (1) *to offset risk on a long or short position in a commodity, that is, to hedge that position by taking an equal and offsetting position in futures,* or (2) *to speculate on a change in the price of the commodity or a change in price spreads.* The hedger attempts to put himself in a position where any losses he incurs on his cash position in the commodity (e.g., he is long and the price in the cash market drops) will be offset by an equal gain on his futures position. As shown in the examples presented below, he can accomplish this by establishing a position in futures and later closing it out. The speculator, who neither owns nor desires to own the underlying commodity, can also realize whatever gain or loss he makes on his speculation simply by closing out the position he has established in futures.

For a hedger a transaction in the futures market is a temporary substitute for a transaction in the cash or spot market. The hedger transacts in futures because at the moment he wants to trade the futures market offers greater liquidity than the spot market. For example a grain company which contracts to sell wheat forward to Turkey incurs a price risk which it could cover by immediately buying grain from farmers. The spot market in wheat may, however, be thin and illiquid at the time the forward sale is made; if so, the grain company would have to offer farmers a high premium to get them to sell, and the cheapest and most efficient way for the company to cover its price risk would be to go into the more liquid futures market and buy futures contracts. Later, as grain became available in the spot market, the grain merchant would piece out its purchase of grain, buying 10,000 bushels here, 20,000 bushels there, and simultaneously selling off a comparable amount of futures contracts.

BILL FUTURES

In January 1976 the *International Monetary Market* (IMM), which is now part of the Chicago Mercantile Exchange (CME), opened trading in futures contracts for 3-month Treasury bills. The trading of futures contracts for financial instruments was not new. In October 1975 the Chicago Board of Trade opened trading in futures contracts for Ginnie Mae pass-throughs, and prior to that the IMM had initiated trading in futures contracts for major foreign currencies. Still, introduction of the T bill futures contract was an important innovation for the money market because trading in Ginnie Mae pass-throughs and foreign exchange lies at the fringe of what could strictly be called money market activities.

In contrast, the T bill market is a key sector of the money market, and every money market participant could as part of their normal investing or borrowing activities find potential uses for sales or purchases of bill futures contracts.

The initial reception of the T bill futures contract by the street was marked by uncertainty and coolness. The dealers looking at the new market all groped for the "right numbers"; they asked what the relationship between spot and futures prices should be and how they could profit from trading in the new market. Many investors were confused about the nature of the contract and uncertain as to how they might or should use it. Also some felt that a contract traded by "commodities speculators" next to the pork belly pit was somehow suspect.

Nevertheless, the volume of contracts traded in the T bill futures market rose (see Figure 14–1) rapidly and dramatically; in fact, the market in T bill futures came to be used more widely and more rapidly than any futures market ever had been. Part of the reason was that dealers in governments quickly became active participants in the new market, following a pattern well established in other futures markets where dealers who position the commodity traded are big buyers and sellers of futures contracts.

At the beginning of 1978, daily volume in the bill futures market averaged $1 to $2 billion; in contrast, the volume of bills traded daily in the cash market by all recognized and reporting dealers in governments averaged $3 to $5 billion. This comparison is impressive for a futures market that is so new.

THE CONTRACT

The basic contract traded on the IMM is for $1 million of 90-day Treasury bills. Currently a contract matures once each quarter—in the third weeks of March, June, September, and December. There are eight

Figure 14–1
The monthly volume of T bill futures contracts traded on the IMM has expanded
dramatically since inception of the contract

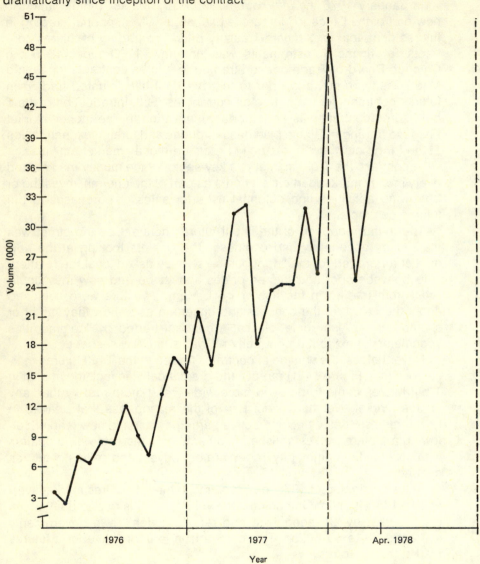

Source: International Monetary Market.

contracts outstanding, so when a new contract starts to trade, the furthest delivery date stretches 24 months into the future.

Price quotes

Bills trade and are quoted in the *cash market* on a yield basis. Because of this, the bid is always higher than the offer. Also, when yield rises, price falls, and vice versa. All this seems reasonable to a person accustomed to trading money market instruments, but it is confusing to an individual who is used to trading in either commodities or stocks. The IMM therefore decided not to quote bill contracts directly in terms of yield. Instead it developed an *index* system in which a bill is quoted at a "price" equal to 100.00 minus yield; a bill yield of 6.50 would thus be quoted on the IMM at 93.50. Note that in this system, when yield goes down, the index price goes up; and the trader with a long position in futures profits. This conforms to the relationship that prevails in other commodity futures markets, where long positions profit when prices rise and short positions profit when prices fall.

Price fluctuations

Price fluctuations on the IMM are in multiples of an 01, one basis point. Because the contract is for delivery of 90-day bills, each 01 is worth $25.

The maximum price fluctuation permitted in any one day is 50 basis points above or below the preceding day's settling price.[1] However, if on two successive days in any contract month, a contract closes at the normal daily limit in the same direction (not necessarily the same contract month on both days), an expanded daily price limit goes into effect. Specifically, on the third day the daily price limit on all contract months goes to 150 percent of the normal daily limit. If on that day any contract month closes at its expanded daily price limit and in the same direction as the preceding daily limit price change, the expanded daily price limit goes to 200 percent of the normal daily price limit and remains there as long as any contract month closes at this expanded daily price limit.

Clearing function of the IMM

Whenever a trade occurs on the IMM, there must be a buyer and an offsetting seller. Each trader's contractual obligation is, however, not to his counterpart in the trade but to the IMM. The IMM stands between the

---

[1] The *settling price* is the average of the highest and lowest prices at which trades occur during the last minute of trading.

principals in a trade; it is the opposite side of every trade effected on the exchange, even though it never itself assumes any net position long or short in bill futures. The IMM's purpose in acting as what might be called a supervisory *clearing house* is to guarantee the fiscal integrity of every trade made on the exchange.

Margin

An important part of the IMM's job in this respect is to oversee the enforcement of margin requirements and the monetary transfers they require. When a trader buys a contract on the IMM, he does not pay for it immediately, and if he sells a contract, he does not receive payment immediately. Both the buyer and the seller do, however, have to put up *margin.* Currently the minimum margin required by the IMM is $1,000 per contract. (A brokerage house through which an individual trader deals may require more.)

When a trader assumes a long or short position, he will incur gains and losses each day thereafter, as price fluctuates. The amount of each day's gain (loss) is added to (subtracted from) his margin account at the end of the day. For example, if a trader bought a contract at 99.50 and the settling price at the end of the day on that contract were 99.45, he would have incurred a loss equal to $125 (5 basis points times $25), and that money would be subtracted by his broker from his margin account. Some other trader would necessarily have made an equal and offsetting gain, and money equal to the amount of that gain would be added to his margin account. This adding and subtracting is done through the IMM, which collects money from brokers whose clients have incurred losses and transfers it to brokers whose clients have earned profits. Because margin balances are adjusted through the IMM at the end of each business day, a trader starts each day having realized through additions to or deductions from his margin account the net gain or loss he has made on his position since he established it. The IMM margin system converts on a daily basis what would be *paper* gains and losses into *realized* gains and losses.

If the balance in a trader's margin account falls below $700, the current *maintenance margin* limit, he must immediately deposit additional funds in this account to bring it back to $1,000. If he fails to do so, his broker is required to immediately close out his position. If, alternatively, a trader has earned profits and his margin account has therefore risen above $1,000, he may withdraw the additional funds.

The IMM's requirements with respect to the maintenance of margin guarantee that no trader's losses on a given day are likely to be significantly larger than the amount in his margin account and thus make it improbable that any investor would end up in a position of being unable to honor a contract he had made either by liquidating his position through an offsetting trade or by making or taking delivery of securities.

If a trader takes offsetting long and short positions in the two contracts closest to maturity, he is required to put up only $400 of margin and the minimum margin he must maintain is $200. On offsetting long and short positions in contracts farther out on the maturity spectrum, the trader must maintain margin equal to any loss he has incurred on that position. If there is none, he need not put up any margin.

Collateral in the form of securities may be used as margin so that the effective cost of putting up margin can be reduced to close to zero.

End of trading

Trading in a T bill futures contract terminates in the third week of the delivery month on the second business day following the weekly auction of 3-month bills. This would normally be a Wednesday. Settlement of futures contracts outstanding at the time trading is terminated is made on the following day, Thursday. This is also the day on which settlement is made on the 3-month cash bill just auctioned. Thus, there is always a new 3-month bill available for delivery on the day outstanding futures contracts are settled.

Buyers of futures contracts do not normally take delivery, but it can be done.[2] The buyer who wants to take delivery instructs the IMM that he wants delivery to be made at a particular Chicago bank. The IMM then instructs the seller's bank to make delivery there, and delivery is affected against payment in Fed funds.

Commissions

There used to be a minimum commission on a purchase or sale of T bill futures of $60. This was phased out with the switch to negotiated commissions, and the rates charged now vary from one brokerage house to another. Currently commissions charged are still quite high on small trades, but on large trades brokerage houses have been advertising rates that are only a small fraction of the old $60 rate. The commission charged is always a *roundturn* commission; that is, there is no additional charge when a trader makes an offsetting purchase or sale to close out his position. Thus a trader saves no commission charge by making or taking delivery of securities.

---

[2] During 1977 the total open interest (contracts outstanding) in all T bill futures contracts fluctuated from a single-day low of 2,348 to a single-day high of 17,444. Over the year 321,703 contracts were traded but delivery was made on only 471 contracts.

Regulation

Currently futures trading in bills and other financial instruments is regulated by the *Commodity Futures Trading Commission* (CFTC), which first authorized trading in T bill futures in November 1975. At that time the SEC, which regulates trading in most securities and in securities options, argued that contracts for the future delivery of securities were securities and that it should therefore have jurisdiction over the futures market in Treasury bills and other financial instruments. The CFTC countered that regulation of trading in such contracts fell within its purview because the law creating the CFTC gave it exclusive jurisdiction over trading in contracts for future delivery.

The dispute between the two agencies resurfaced in 1978 when the SEC recommended to Congress that it should take over the CFTC's authority to regulate futures trading in securities. The SEC's concern over futures trading in securities was heightened by the difficulties that arose in the dealer-made, off-the-board forward market for Ginnie Mae pass-throughs, when a small dealer, Winters, whose operations had been irregular, failed.

How the market is made

The market in cash bills, as noted in Chapter 13, is made by dealers in geographically disperse institutions who keep in contact through direct phone lines and through the brokers, and who are required to quote bid and asked prices to each other and to retail.

In the bill futures market, in contrast, all trades are made during regular trading hours in the bill pit on the floor of the CME in Chicago; the futures market is thus a single central market. Traders in the bill pit make their bids and offers known by crying them out. In the pit, all that is heard is the highest bid and the lowest offer. Anyone with a lower bid or higher offer remains silent until the market moves to his level. The face-to-face market in the bill pit is akin to the composite market that all the dealers in cash bills would make if they were in the same physical place.

There are three types of traders in the bill pit. First, there are employees of brokerage houses who execute trades for retail customers and for the brokerage house's own account. Many of these brokers also trade for their own accounts; a broker who does this is required to execute customer business before dealing for his own account. The second type of trader in the pit is the "deck holder." Deck holders sell a service to brokers; they handle limit orders (e.g., a customer orders to buy at 20 when the market is at 22) and stop-loss orders (a customer orders to sell if price falls to a certain level). A deck holder files all orders given to him by brokers according to price and then, as the market moves, executes those orders he can. Finally, there are private persons (locals) in the pit who trade for their own account on an outright speculative basis or more often on a spread basis; an individual who wants to trade bill futures on the CME floor can do so by buying a seat on the exchange.

A retail customer or dealer who calls another dealer in cash bills and gets a quote 64–65 can say to the dealer, "You sold bills at 64." He can't do that in the futures market. He can call a broker on the floor and get information on the price at which the last trade occurred and on what bids and offers currently are. But if he asks the broker to execute an order at the current bid or asked price, he can't be sure that the broker will be able to. In a fast market, the five yards from the broker's phone to the pit can be a long way, and the market may have moved by the time the broker gets there. Thus a retail customer has to deal in a slightly different way with a broker in the futures market than he does with a dealer in the cash market if he wants to get orders in size executed.

On the other hand, the retail customer has the advantage in the futures market that there is no distinction between the inside market and the market to retail. There is just a single centralized market with one price and his access to that market is as good as that of a large dealer. Few dealers in governments have become clearing members of the IMM, and those that have not, execute their orders through brokers just as retail customers do.

LOCKING IN A FUTURE LENDING RATE

The IMM has put out a lot of literature describing how the T bill futures market can be used: (1) by investors who know they will have short-term money to invest in the future, to lock in a future lending rate, and (2) by institutions that know they will have to borrow short term in the future, to lock in a borrowing rate. The purpose of this barrage of literature on hedging opportunities has been both to promote use of the market and to encourage the view that it is an arena in which conservative institutions can hedge real risks rather than a pit in which speculators engage in "manipulation and other abusive practices in securities trading," the potential—real or imagined—for which has been a publicly stated concern of the SEC.

The IMM calls locking in a lending rate a *long hedge*. To illustrate what's involved, suppose that an investor's cash flow projections tell him that he will have a large sum of cash to invest short term in the future; that is, he is going to be *long* in investable cash. He can simply wait to invest that cash until he gets it and take whatever rate is prevailing then, or as soon as his projections tell him how much cash he is going to have, he can lock in a lending rate by buying T bill futures contracts.

Table 14–1
A long hedge in T bill futures for bills with a $10 million face value

Step 1 (Thursday, third week of June):   Purchase ten September bill contracts at 5.50.

Put up security deposit.
Pay roundturn commission.

Step 2 (Wednesday, third week of September):   Sell ten futures contracts, buy cash bills.

Outcome 1:   Cash 91-day bill trading at 5.20.
Sell September contracts at 5.20.

Delivery value at sale	$9,870,000
−Delivery value at purchase	9,862,500
Profit on futures transaction	$ 7,500

Buy 91-day bills at 5.20.

Purchase price	$9,868,555
−Profit on futures transaction	7,500
Effective price of 91-day bills	$9,861,055

Calculate effective discount at which bills are purchased.

Face value	$10,000,000
−Effective purchase price	9,861,055
Discount at purchase............................	138,945

Calculate effective discount rate d at which bills are purchased.

$$d = \frac{D \times 360}{F \times 91} = \frac{\$138,945 \times 360}{\$10,000,000 \times 91}$$

$$= 0.055$$
$$= 5.50\%$$

Outcome 2:   Cash 91-day bill trading at 5.80.
Sell September contracts at 5.80.

Delivery value at sale	$9,855,000
−Delivery value at purchase	9,862,500
Loss on futures transaction	−$ 7,500

Buy 91-day bills at 5.80.

Purchase price....................................	$9,853,389
+Loss on futures transaction	7,500
Effective price of 91-day bills......................	$9,860,889

Calculate effective discount at which bills are purchased.

Face value.......................................	$10,000,000
−Effective purchase price.........................	9,860,889
Discount at purchase	$ 139,111

Calculate effective discount rate d at which bills are purchased.

$$d = \frac{D \times 360}{F \times 91} = \frac{\$139,111 \times 360}{\$10,000,000 \times 91}$$

$$= 0.055$$
$$= 5.50\%$$

Table 14–1 illustrates how this works. We assume that our invest
knows in June that he will have $10 million of 3-month money to invest i
September, and we assume additionally that when September arrives,
he intends to invest that money in bills. In June, the September bill
contract is trading at 5.50. If our investor buys 10 of these contracts, he
will earn 5.50 on the money he invests in September regardless of the
rate at which the cash 3-month bill is then trading.

One way he could get the 5.50 rate would be to take delivery in
September of the bills he purchased at 5.50. But, to see the nature of the
hedge, let's assume he does not do this. Instead, when his cash comes
in, he closes out his futures position and buys cash bills.

The first thing to note is that, as the September contract approaches
maturity, it must trade at a yield close to and eventually equal to the rate
at which the 3-month cash bill is trading. The reason is that if any divergence existed between these two rates as trading terminated in the
contract, there would be a potential for a profitable arbitrage. For example, if a few days before the September bill contract matured, it was
trading at a significantly higher yield than the cash bill, traders would
buy the contract, sell cash bills wi or wi wi, then take delivery in Chicago
to cover their short position in the cash bill, and make a profit on the
transaction.[3]

In Outcome 1 in Table 14–1, we assume that as the September contract is maturing, the 91-day cash bill is trading at 5.20 and the futures
contract is consequently also trading at 5.20. At this time our investor
sells his September contracts and buys the cash 3-month bill. He purchases his futures contracts at 5.50 and sells them at 5.20, a lower rate.
Since the delivery value of the contracts is higher the lower the yield at
which they trade, our investor makes, as Table 14–1 shows, a $7,500 profit
on his futures transaction.

When his profit on the futures transaction is deducted from the price at
which he buys cash bills, he ends up paying an effective price for his
cash bills that is $7,500 less than the actual price he pays. And this
lower effective price implies that the yield he will earn on his investment
is not 5.20, the rate at which he buys cash bills, but 5.50, the rate at
which he bought bill futures (see Table 14–1).

Because the prevailing yield at which the cash 3-month bill was trading in September was lower than the rate at which our investor bought
bill futures contracts in June, he made money by engaging in a long
hedge; that is, he earned a higher yield than he would have if he had not
hedged.

---

[3] In practice a maturing bill futures contract will trade during the last few days of its
life at a yield 1 to 3 basis points higher than the deliverable cash bill. The difference reflects the extra commission and other transactions costs that an investor would incur if
he bought bill futures and took delivery instead of purchasing new 3-month bills in the
cash market.

There is, however, a counterpart to this. As Outcome 2 in Table 14–1 shows, if in September the cash 3-month bill were trading at 5.80, our investor would have lost so many dollars on his hedge that he would in effect earn only 5.50 on the money he invested then.

Calculating in basis points

It is instructive to work out a hedge example in dollars and cents. However, it is quicker to follow what is going on in terms of basis points earned and lost. In our example, the investor buys September contracts at 5.50 and, according to Outcome 1, sells them at 5.20. On this transaction he earns on each contract for $1 million of bills 30 90-day basis points. By buying the 3-month bill at 5.20 and maturing it, he earns 520 90-day basis points per $1 million of bills purchased. So *net* he is going to earn 550 90-day basis points per $1 million of bills purchased, a yield of 5.50 over 90 days.

Actually the basis points earned on the cash bill are 91-day basis points and those earned on the futures contract are 90-day basis points. This difference, however, which is reflected in the numbers in Table 14–1, affects yield earned only in the third decimal point and then only in a minor way. So it can be ignored and we shall do so henceforth.

Perfect and imperfect hedges

The example we have just worked through was a *perfect hedge,* because our investor bought a futures contract for precisely the instrument and precisely the maturity of the instrument he intended to buy. In practice, a lot of hedges are *imperfect.* For example, our investor might have intended to buy cash bills at the beginning of September. If that were the case, the rate he would earn when he invested would be 5.50 *minus* the spread, if any, at which the futures contract was then trading to the cash bill. Specifically, if he bought the September contract at 5.50 and then invested at the beginning of September when the cash bill was trading at 5.20 and the futures contract at 5.25, he would earn only 25 basis points on his futures contract, so his yield on the money he invested would be only 5.45.

The hedge might also be imperfect because the investor intended to buy some other instrument, say, BAs, instead of bills. Suppose, for example, that when he bought his futures contract, 3-month BAs were trading at a 30-basis-point spread to bills. By buying bill futures contracts at 5.50, he does not lock up a 5.80 rate on his future investment in BAs. What rate he gets will depend on what happens to the spread at which BAs trade to bills; it might widen or narrow.

When an investor sets up an imperfect hedge, he insulates to a large

degree his position from general movements in the level of interest r
and thus avoids price level speculation. At the same time, however,
establishes what is in effect a speculation on the *basis,* that is, on th.
spread at which the futures contract trades relative to the cash instrument he is hedging; this speculation exposes the hedger to some risk of
loss or gain due to possible variations in the basis. Thus the successful
hedger needs a good feel for what the basis he is speculating on ought
to be at a given point in time and for how and in response to what factors
that basis might vary over time. Speculation on the basis has long been
the heart of hedging activity in grains and other commodities; it is an art
that investors and dealers in bills have had to learn.

LOCKING IN A BORROWING RATE

The T bill futures market can also be used to lock in a future borrowing
rate. This is done by *selling* bill futures contracts.

To illustrate such a *short* hedge, suppose that a dealer buys 6-month
bills at 6.70 and finances them for 3 months in the term RP market at a
rate of 6.50. By doing so, he creates 3-month bills that he will own 3
months hence at an effective rate of 6.90.[4] When he receives those bills,
he will either refinance or sell them. Whatever he does, whether he
profits or not on his overall transaction will depend on what happens to
money market rates over the 3 months he finances the 6-month bill he
has purchased. Rates might rise so steeply that he could only sell his
future bills at a loss or finance them at a negative carry.

To hedge against this possibility, our investor might sell T bill futures
maturing in 3 months. Assume he could do so at the rate of 6.70. Then he
would lock in a 20-basis-point profit ($500) on each $1 million of
6-month bills he purchased, financed, and hedged. Table 14–2 illustrates this for two possible outcomes.

Imperfect hedges

The sale of bill futures to hedge the financing cost or sale price of a
"tail" is not always a perfect hedge. There might be a gap between the
maturities of the future security being hedged and that of the futures
contract. Also, the future security financed might be a future CD or a
future BA. If so, the profit on the hedged transaction would depend on
what happened to the spread at which that instrument was trading to
bills. In the case of CDs in particular, if the banks started to write, the
spread might widen so far and so rapidly that an apparently locked-in
profit would turn into a loss.

---

[4] See the discussion of figuring the tail on pages 226–29.

Table 14–2
Hedging a 3-month T bill "tail" purchased at an
effective rate of 6.90

Outcome 1: 3-month bill trading at 6.50 3 months hence.

Gain on sale of future bill created	40 basis points
−Loss on sale and subsequent purchase of futures contract	20 basis points
Net profit on the transaction	20 basis points

Outcome 2: 3-month bill trading at 7.10 3 months hence.

Gain on sale and subsequent purchase of futures contract	40 basis points
−Loss on sale of future bill created	20 basis points
Net profit on the transaction	20 basis points

Another example of how the sale of T bill futures contracts could be used to hedge an anticipated borrowing cost would be the sale of bill futures contracts by a firm that anticipated borrowing in the BA market in the future. Again, the hedge would be imperfect, but it still might be useful.

In an imperfect short hedge, as in an imperfect long hedge, the hedger is speculating on the basis, and to place his bet well he needs to have a feel for the basis. The kind of trouble a careless hedger can get into was described by one dealer: "The trader at a big position house just stuck it in the ringer. After Carter announced that he was dropping the tax rebate program, the market rallied substantially, and this trader took on a major position in CDs. Time began to prove that this was going to be a stinko position as it became apparent that the Fed was going to tighten. This guy realized he had a big problem. Where do you sell CDs when the market is going down? Retail won't touch the stuff, and in the dealer market it is just a progression of bang, bang, bang—which dealer can call another fastest and hit their bid for 5 million. So your CDs become a hot potato for a while. This guy was watching this occur, he was trying to unload a $300 million position five at a time which doesn't work. So he said the hell with it and blew out bill futures, a theoretical hedge. What he failed to realize was that what was happening in the CD market had already been anticipated in the bill futures market. Consequently, his CDs continued to decline in price while his shorts in the bill futures market went against him because that market had already dropped 75 basis points in two days and was coming back from this overreaction. The trader finally dropped half a million on his CD position and another quarter of a mil. on his theoretical hedge."

SPECULATION

While a lot of the literature on T bill futures points up how they can be used to hedge, bill futures are also an attractive medium for speculating on changes in interest rate levels. This is important because a futures market cannot function effectively if it does not attract speculators willing to assume the risks that hedgers are attempting to shed.

If an individual felt strongly that interest rates were going to fall, he could speculate on that by buying cash bills, but financing a position of any size would take a lot of cash. The Fed imposes no margin requirements on purchases of governments, so an individual might be able to buy $1 million of bills by putting down as little as 10 percent of the purchase price in cash. He would, however, have to finance the other 90 percent at a borrowing rate of 1 percent or so above prime, so the carry on his position would be a sizable negative number, and the speculation would therefore be unappealing.

A purchase of bill futures would, however, be an attractive way for an individual to speculate on a fall in interest rates. All he would have to put down would be the roundturn commission plus a margin deposit.

A dealer is in a much better position than an individual to speculate on a fall in interest rates by buying cash bills because he can finance a long position in bills at the RP rate; and unless he buys very short bills, which would not be a logical way to speculate, his carry would be positive. Nevertheless, bill futures are an attractive speculative tool for dealers. There is some limit on how far a dealer can lever his position, and by buying bill futures instead of cash bills, he can speculate on a fall in interest rates without further levering his position.

To speculate in the cash market on a rise in interest rates, one has to go short. This is unattractive much of the time even for dealers because maintaining a short position in bills costs money. The normal way a dealer would obtain bills to make delivery on a short would be to reverse them in. The offset to the bills coming in is that the dealer lends money to the supplier or the securities at a rate equal to the repo rate or perhaps at an even lower rate if many dealers are trying to short these securities and there is thus a wide demand for them. Since the repo rate is normally below the bill rate, the dealer's carry on his position will be negative, which lessens his potential profit even if he is right and interest rates do fall.

Selling bill futures, as opposed to shorting cash bills, is a cheap way to speculate on a rise in interest rates. The only real cost the speculator incurs is the roundturn commission on the sale.

.ATIONSHIP OF FUTURE TO CASH RATES

Rates in the bill futures market ought to bear a definite relationship to rates in the cash market because there are various ways the two markets can be arbitraged.

To illustrate, assume the 3-month cash bill is trading at 6.40 and the 6-month cash bill at 6.60. Assume also that the bill futures contract maturing 3 months hence is trading at the same rate at which the 6-month cash bill is trading, namely, 6.60. These two rates are in fact often close.

Our assumed rate relationship creates an attractive arbitrage opportunity for anyone with short-term money to invest. Many of the investors who buy the 3-month bill do so because, to avoid price risk, they do not want to extend in maturity further than 3 months. To buy the 3-month bill instead of the 6-month bill, however, costs them 20 basis points, which works out to $500 per $1 million of bills over 90 days. This is a loss that the investor does not have to incur if the rate relationships that we have assumed prevail. The investor can lock in for 90 days the 6.60 rate offered on the 6-month bill by buying the 6-month bill and selling bill futures contracts maturing 3 months hence at 6.60. If he does this, then regardless of where the 3-month bill is trading 3 months hence, his loss (or gain) on the sale of the cash bill will be precisely offset by his gain (or loss) on the futures contract (see Table 14–3). So he has reduced to zero the price risk of holding the 6-month bill for 3 months.

Table 14–3
Locking in a rate for 3 months by hedging in the T bill futures market

Step 1: Buy $1 million of 6-month cash bills at 6.60.
Sell a bill futures contract maturing in 3 months at 6.60.

Step 2: Three months later sell the cash bills and liquidate the futures position by buying a bill futures contract.

Outcome 1: The 3-month bill is trading at 6.70.

Gain on sale and subsequent purchase of futures contract	10 basis points
−Loss on sale of cash bill	10 basis points
Net gain or loss on hedged position..............	0 basis points

Outcome 2: The 3-month bill is trading at 6.50.

Gain on sale of cash bill	10 basis points
−Loss on sale and subsequent purchase of futures contract	10 basis points
Net gain or loss on hedged position.............	0 basis points

Yield on hedged investment: 660 90-day basis points.

With respect to this example, it is interesting to note that with 3-month bill trading at 6.40 and the 6-month bill at 6.60, assuming hedged position in the 6-month bill will yield the investor a higher retur than buying and maturing the 3-month bill as long as the bill futures contract maturing in 3 months trades anywhere below 6.80. For example, if it were trading at 6.70, the investor's net return on a hedged investment in the 6-month bill would be the 6.60 rate yielded by that bill minus a locked-in loss of 10 basis points on his hedge in the futures market (he buys at 6.60 in the cash market and sells at 6.70 in the futures market); this works out to a net rate of 6.50, which is 10 basis points more than he could earn by investing in the 3-month bill.

As noted at the end of Chapter 8, the structure of rates in the cash market provides an implicit prediction of future rates. Specifically if the 6-month bill is trading at 6.60 and the 3-month bill at 6.40, this implies that the 3-month bill 3 months hence will yield 6.80. Thus what we have concluded is that, as long as the futures contract due to mature in 3 months is trading at a rate below the rate predicted in the cash market for the 3-month bill 3 months hence, it will pay the investor with 3-month money to buy the 6-month bill instead of the 3-month bill and hedge by selling bill futures contracts.

Suppose that the bill futures contract maturing 3 months hence was in fact trading at 6.80 and that the rates on the cash 3- and 6-month bills were 6.40 and 6.60, respectively. This would eliminate any possibility for an investor to increase his yield on 3-month money by buying the 6-month bill and selling bill futures. However, it would open the door for another sort of arbitrage, namely, buying bill futures contracts maturing in 3 months and shorting the 6-month cash bill. Three months hence the rates on the maturing futures contract and the cash 6-month bill, which will then have become a cash 3-month bill, must be identical. So the arbitrage would—ignoring transactions costs—lock in a 20-basis-point profit. Moreover, the potential for such an arbitrage would continue to exist so long as the futures contract maturing in 3 months was trading above the rate on the 6-month bill.

All this seems puzzling at first. To eliminate the opportunity for investors to arbitrage the cash and the futures markets, the rate on futures contracts has to be driven to a high level, but to eliminate the potential for the opposite sort of arbitrage, shorting the cash bill and buying the futures contract, the futures rate has to be driven to a much lower level. Where under these circumstances is equilibrium in the rate structure going to be?

The answer is simple. If all investors were willing to arbitrage the cash and the futures markets to increase yield and if the opposite sort of arbitrage were costless, the only tenable equilibrium structure of rates would be a flat yield curve—the 3-month cash bill, the 6-month cash bill, and the futures contract maturing in 3 months all yielding the same rate. With that rate structure, all opportunities for arbitrage between the cash and futures markets would be eliminated, and the two markets would achieve equilibrium.

Arbitrage in practice

In practice arbitrage obviously does not lead to a flat yield curve, and there are good reasons. First, the bill futures market is currently little understood by many investors and even less well understood by those who set the parameters by which portfolio managers operate. Thus it is the *exceptional* rather than the typical investor who both could and would seize on the opportunity described above to lock in a higher rate over 3 months by buying the 6-month bill and selling bill futures.

Second, shorting bills is expensive because the carry on the position is negative, so the spread between the rate on the bill futures contract maturing in 3 months and the rate on the 6-month bill would have to be wide in order to make the second sort of arbitrage we described, shorting cash bills and buying bill futures, profitable.

Thus, institutional constraints create a situation in which the arbitrages that theory suggests ought to flatten the yield curve actually come nowhere near doing so.

Rate structure and opportunities

So far we have concentrated for purposes of illustration on the relationship between the rates on the 3-month cash bill, the 6-month cash bill, and the futures contract maturing in 3 months. Because there are currently eight bill futures contracts outstanding, the range of opportunities for the investor to arbitrage the cash and the futures markets is much wider than our examples suggested. As Table 14–4 shows, for the investor willing to use the bill futures market, there are two ways to lock in a rate on 3-month money, three ways to lock in a rate on 6-month money, and four ways to lock in a rate on 9-month money. Clearly the investor who intends to invest for any of these periods should calculate and compare the rates offered him by each possible investment strategy and invest in the way that will yield the highest rate.

Note that one of the strategies outlined in Table 14–4 is to create what the street refers to as a *synthetic* security. An investor who has money to invest for 9 months does not have to buy the 9-month cash bill. He could alternatively buy the 3-month cash bill and two bill futures contracts, one maturing 3 months hence and the other maturing 6 months hence. Often the yield offered by a synthetic bill created by buying a short bill and a *strip* of bill futures contracts is higher than that available on the

Table 14–4
Possible strategies for investing money in bills over varying time periods

A. To invest money for 3 months:
    1. Buy the 3-month bill and mature it.
    1. Buy the 6-month bill and sell a futures contract maturing in 3 months.
B. To invest money for 6 months:
    1. Buy the 6-month bill and mature it.
    2. Buy the 9-month bill and sell a futures contract maturing in 6 months.
    3. Buy the 3-month bill and a futures contract maturing in 3 months.*
C. To invest money for 9 months:
    1. Buy the 9-month bill and mature it.
    2. Buy the 1-year bill and sell a bill futures contract maturing in 9 months.
    3. Buy the 6-month bill and a bill futures contract maturing in 6 months.*
    4. Buy the 3-month bill and two bill futures contracts, one maturing in 3 months and one maturing in 6 months.*

* Note: The yield on a synthetic bill created by buying a short cash bill and a strip of futures contracts is slightly greater than that on a cash bill of comparable maturity because, if the investor can fully reinvest the proceeds of maturing bills, he gets some compounding of the interest he earns.

cash security of comparable maturity. The same is true of synthetic coupons (government notes) created by buying a short cash bill and a strip of bill futures contracts. Note that in comparing the yield on a synthetic coupon with the yield at which the cash coupon of equivalent maturity is trading, the yield on the synthetic coupon, which is figured on a discount basis, must be converted to a bond equivalent basis to make it comparable to the rate quoted on the coupon.

How long the bill futures market will continue to offer imaginative investors returns above what they could lock up by investing in cash governments is difficult to say. Presumably at some point a few large investors will start taking advantage of any such opportunities offered by the market. The State of California, which invests huge amounts of pension fund money, has asked for permission from the state legislature to use the bill futures market, and other large investors are likely to follow its lead.

Accounting hang-up

Unfamiliarity with the bill futures market and restrictive investment parameters are not the only reasons many investors have eschewed use of this market. Another is the accounting hang-up we encountered in Chapter 10.[5] An investor, who—instead of buying the 3-month cash bill at 6.40 and maturing it—bought the 6-month bill at 6.60 and hedged it by

---

[5] See pages 271–73.

selling at 6.70 bill futures contracts maturing in 3 months, would earn an extra 10 basis points per $1 million of securities purchased. Thus in terms of dollars earned, the portfolio manager would have an incentive for engaging in this transaction. However, conventional accounting procedures give him a disincentive for doing so. The reason is that interest on the 6-month bill purchased would be accrued at the 6.60 rate; and when the portfolio manager unwound his position at the end of 3 months, regardless of how he did it, the accountant would show him as having taken net a capital loss (10 basis points on a *net* basis) on one or both legs of the transaction. Many portfolio managers refuse to ever take a capital loss and for this reason will not engage in a transaction that would result in one being taken even though the transaction locked in a higher dollar return.

Arbitraging a synthetic bill against a cash bill

In futures markets for commodities, people seek to hedge both natural long and short positions. A grain elevator operator, for example, ends up long in grain as part of his normal business operation, which is to buy grain, store it for some time, and then sell it. On the other hand, a flour miller who contracts to deliver flour at a fixed price at some future date assumes an implicit short position in wheat. To reduce the risk created by potential changes in the price of wheat, the elevator operator sells contracts for the future delivery of wheat, and the flour miller buys them.

It has often been observed that in the typical commodity market there are more participants with a natural long position than those with a natural short position, and for that reason the commodity must sell for future delivery at some discount to the cash price in order to entice speculators to go long in futures. This phenomenon, which is common, is known as *normal backwardation.*

With respect to the bill futures market, it is often argued that potential borrowers have more of an incentive to hedge their borrowing costs than potential investors have to lock up a future lending rate. Thus synthetic bills or coupons ought to yield slightly more than cash governments of the same maturity. This relationship in fact prevails most of the time and will probably continue to do so until a significant number of investors begin to regularly and actively consider the purchase of synthetic governments as a substitute for the purchase of cash governments.

The current tendency for synthetic securities created by buying a short bill and a strip of bill futures to yield more than a cash government of the same maturity creates the opportunity for a speculative arbitrage on that yield spread, one in which some dealers and investors engage. To illustrate, suppose that the cash year bill is trading at 6.65 and that yields in the cash and futures markets are such that a synthetic year bill

yields slightly less, 6.45 (Table 14-5). This is not a typical spread relatio
ship, but at times a synthetic security will trade through the equivaler.
cash security. An arbitrager seeing this relationship might, for example,
buy the cash year bill, repo it for 3 months, and sell a strip of three futures
contracts corresponding in maturity to the 9-month "tail" he is creating.
Suppose that 3 months later that spread went from the now 9-month cash
bill yielding 20 basis points more than the synthetic 9-month bill to its
yielding 20 basis points less. Then the arbitrager could close out his
position, having earned positive carry on his 3-month repo plus 40 270-
day basis points, a tidy profit on an operation that he could execute
without putting up anything but margin.

Table 14–5
Yield on a synthetic year bill

Yield on a cash 3-month bill	6.20
Yield on a bill futures contract maturing in 3 months	6.35
Yield on a bill futures contract maturing in 6 months	6.60
Yield on a bill futures contract maturing in 9 months	6.65
	4⟌25.80
Yield on a synthetic year bill	6.45

If, on the other hand, the synthetic bill were trading at an abnormally
high spread to the cash year bill, the arbitrage could be worked the other
way—by shorting the cash bill and buying a strip. Normally this arbitrage
does not work out as well as the one just described because of the cost of
shorting.

A synthetic 2-year note created by use of a longer strip of bill futures
can also be arbitraged against a cash note just as a synthetic bill can be
arbitraged against a cash bill. If, when rates were adjusted to an equivalent basis, the cash bill were yielding too much relative to the strip, the
arbitrager could short the strip and buy the cash bill. Or, alternatively, if
one contract in the strip seemed especially cheap, he could sell a number
of those contracts against the cash bill, making in effect a double speculation on the basis.

SPREADING

Another sort of speculation done on yield spreads in the T bill futures
market is *spreading* of the type actively done in other futures markets;
that is, the trader goes long one contract and short a neighboring contract on the expectation that as time passes, the spread between the two
contracts will either narrow or widen. Note that the spreader, like the
arbitrager in the preceding example, is protected from the risk of loss

due to a change in the overall level of prices or yields, because he is long in one contract and short in another.

Normally the yield curve is steep at its base and then gradually flattens. Suppose, for the purpose of illustration, that in the futures market, the yield curve has the shape pictured in Figure 14–2. The yield spread

Figure 14–2
Yields on bill futures contracts maturing in 3 to 15 months

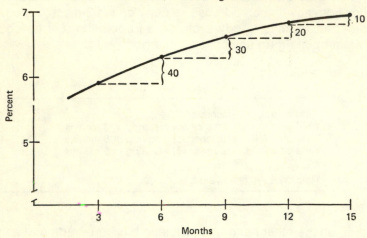

between the two contracts nearest maturity is 40 basis points; there are 30 basis points between the second and third contracts, 20 basis points between the third and fourth contracts, and 10 basis points between the fourth and fifth contracts. The spreader assumes that as time passes and the more distant contracts approach maturity, spreads between them will widen. Given this expectation he might, for example, short the contract maturing in 12 months and buy the contract maturing in 9 months. If over the next 6 months the spread between these two contracts widened from 20 to 40 basis points, he would be able to close out his position at a 20-basis-point profit.

Note that he earns a profit because, if the spread widens, the price of the futures contract in which he is long will rise in value relative to that in which he is short. Whether yields rise or fall over the holding period is immaterial to whether he profits or not. All that counts is that the spread widens, and his only risk of loss is thus that the yield curve will flatten so dramatically that the spread between the contracts in which he is long and short narrows rather than widens.

Traders who put on spreads are an important and permanent component of the bill futures pit. A spreader who sees selling in the March contract but knows that there is a bid in the Junes will buy the Marches, sell the Junes, wait until the pressure is off the Marches, and then turn the position around. Spreaders account for at least 60 percent of trading volume in the longer contracts. In carrying out operations of the above sort, spreaders perform an important market function—providing liquidity to the longer contracts.

OFF-THE-BOARD MARKET

The T bill futures market on the IMM operates in a fashion that seems awkward and different compared with what a money market person is accustomed to. A trader of cash bills is used to calling another and asking, "What's your market?" But he can't do that in the bill futures market. There isn't a market in the sense that one trader will make a market to another. There is a public outcry of orders. Someone on the CME floor in Chicago can tell a New York trader where the last trade occurred, that there are some buyers at 12, and that there may be some sellers at 14, but he can't give any indication of size. Another peculiarity of the IMM market to a money market trader is the way rates are quoted on the basis of a price index instead of yield. Dealers also view the margin requirements of the IMM as a bookkeeping nuisance. And, because of the way margin is adjusted daily to reflect gains and losses, tickets have to be rewritten whenever a position in bill futures is closed out, which is another large nuisance.

Several New York dealers have started to make an off-the-board market in T bill futures that operates in the way in which dealers and big investors are accustomed to deal with each other. In this market there are no margin requirements, prices are quoted on a yield basis, delivery times are the same as in the cash market, delivery tickets do not have to be changed on the delivery date, and paper profits are not paid out until the settlement date of the trade but also customers do not have to come up with money to cover paper losses before the settlement date.

The markets made by dealers trading T bill futures off the board are naturally closely dovetailed to what is going on in the Chicago market. However, these firms will make markets in bills that aren't traded on the exchange as well as in those that are.

As in RP, a dealer running a book in T bill futures can run a matched or an unmatched book. The natural inclination of a dealer is to run an unmatched book and incur some carefully controlled risks.

The major customers of firms making off-the-board markets in T bill futures are S&Ls, corporations, some state and local governments, some bank trust departments, a few national banks, and a lot of state banks. The Comptroller of the Currency has ruled that national banks may enter into futures contracts only to hedge. This ruling is a guideline that some large banks ignore, but most view it as sharply limiting the sort of transactions in which they may engage in bill futures.

To a commodities person it is not at all surprising that dealers in governments have begun to make an off-the-board *forward* market in bills. Dealers in grain have, for example, traditionally made forward sales of grain and then hedged their position in the futures market.

The forward contracts offered by dealers in governments differ from the futures contracts traded on the IMM in that the forward contract is a tailored contract while the futures contract is homogeneous. To the buyer of a forward contract, the custom-tailored nature of the contract may be a distinct advantage because he lacks either the expertise or financial resources to establish a position in futures. Also statutory regulations may prevent the buyer from entering into futures contracts but not from entering into forward contracts. The disadvantage of the forward contract is that it lacks the liquidity of a futures contract.

COMMERCIAL PAPER FUTURES MARKET

In addition to the market for bill futures, there is also a market in commercial paper futures that was opened in 1977 on the Chicago Board of Trade. The basic contract in this market is for $1 million of 90-day A-1 or P-1 commercial paper, and the contract is quoted in the same way as the bill futures contract. The daily price limit in the commercial paper futures contract is 25 basis points above or below the previous day's settlement price; this limit increases to 38 basis points when variable price limits go into effect.

The market for commercial paper futures was designed to give issuers of commercial paper a way to lock in future borrowing rates—to engage in the sort of hedge illustrated in Table 14–2.

Despite the fact that over $64 billion of commercial paper is currently outstanding, the market in commercial paper futures attracted little volume in the first months after it opened. There are several reasons. First, the market offers issuers of commercial paper a hedge that is imperfect at best since most commercial paper is issued with an original maturity of 30 days and under and the contract is for 90-day commercial paper. To remedy this defect, the Chicago Board of Trade sought, in the spring of 1978, permission to trade a new futures contract in 30-day commercial paper.

A second and more serious problem with the commercial paper futures market is that it is not clear what, if anything, could be gained by an issuer of commercial paper consistently hedging his borrowing costs in this market—something that current market volume would not permit any large issuer to do. For an issuer to hedge consistently would simply be to lock in period after period yesterday's forecast of tomorrow's lending rate, which would, if rates in the futures market were an unbiased forecaster of future spot rates, neither raise nor lower an issuer's borrowing costs over the long run but rather redistribute them so that they would be higher in some periods and lower in others than they would have been had he not hedged.

Actually rates in the futures market seem if anything to display an upward bias as a predictor of future interest rates. To the extent that this is the case, the paper issuer who hedged consistently would simply increase his long-run costs of borrowing. The same, of course, can also be said of the grain elevator operator who consistently hedges his position in cash grain. To the extent that normal backwardation operates in the grain futures market, an elevator operator who always hedges his position in cash grain by selling futures contracts will over time lose money on his hedges. Thus one might argue that he would be better off not hedging; instead he should simply take whatever gains or losses he incurs due to fluctuations in the cash price of grain and earn over the long run the industry average return on his storage operation. There are, however, two problems with this. First, the elevator operator may not have the capital to survive even one sharp fall in the price of cash grain. Second, by hedging his position, he is able to borrow much larger sums from banks to finance his inventory than he would if he did not hedge. Thus *because he hedges,* the grain elevator operator is able to engage in and to profit from his normal storage operation on a larger scale than he would if he did not hedge. For him the cost of hedging is a normal and unavoidable business expense, the incurring of which permits him to do more business and earn more profit.

The same cannot be said for a commercial paper issuer. In no way would consistent hedging of his borrowing costs permit him to enlarge the scale of his operations and thereby earn larger normal business profits. As noted in Chapter 19, for a commercial paper issuer the equivalent of the hedging cost that a grain elevator operator must incur is the cost of bank lines. A paper issuer may or may not think that he needs extensive line coverage, but to sell his paper he has to have it; so for him the cost of bank lines is a business expense that he must incur to operate on his desired scale.

All this is not to say that a commercial paper futures market in which real volume could be traded might not be useful to issuers. An issuer who expected rates to rise might well choose to lock in a future borrowing rate by selling commercial paper futures contracts. Note, however, that since he has to be in the market borrowing on a daily basis, such sales would differ subtly from the hedge in which a grain elevator operator engages. In effect, if the commercial paper issuer sold futures contracts occasionally, he would be taking a view of where he thought interest rates were going, and this would be somewhat akin to speculation in the futures market.

For any issuer who had the ability to forecast interest rates correctly more than half the time, such activity—call it speculation or hedging—might well be profitable. In fact, however, few issuers have used the commercial paper futures market. One reason is that commercial paper issuers are a very conservative group; second, they are not really money market people in the sense that, say, the New York dealers and some sophisticated portfolio managers are. Commercial paper issuers post the rates necessary to buy whatever money they need, but most don't have and don't really need to have the sort of sharp pencil that is part and parcel of a true money market trader.

Another reason for the slow growth of the commercial paper futures market is the fact that dealers in commercial paper act very much like brokers, while dealers in governments are true market makers who assume large positions long and short. Thus, where government dealers had an incentive to get into the bill futures market and quickly became active there, the same has not been true of dealers in commercial paper.

A final reason for the slow growth of the commercial paper futures market is the regulations under which some potential users of the market operate. The yield on bank CDs of a given tenor tracks more closely that on commercial paper than that on bills, the spread between yields on commercial paper and CDs, and that on bills tending to widen as money tightens. Thus, if a bank wanted to hedge the cost of future CD money, the most logical tack would be for it to establish a *cross hedge* by buying commercial paper futures. Explaining such a hedge to a bank regulator would, however, be difficult, and no bank has attempted to hedge in this way.

OTHER FUTURES MARKETS

There are two other financial futures contracts traded on the Chicago Board of Trade, one in Ginnie Mae modified pass-throughs with a principal balance of $100,000 and a stated interest rate of 8 percent, and a second in U.S. Treasury bonds with a face value at maturity of $100,000 and a coupon rate of 8 percent. Both contracts are quoted on a percentage of par; the minimum price fluctuation is $1/32$, which equals $31.25 per contract. Normal daily price limits are $24/32$ above or below the previous day's settlement price. This increases to $36/32$ when variable price limits go into effect.

Both contracts can be used to hedge and to speculate in much the same way that bill futures contracts are used. However, the contracts are for securities with a maturity that puts them well outside the range of what would normally be considered the money market. Ginnie Mae pass-throughs have an average expected life of 12 years, and deliverable grade bonds in the bond futures market must have a life to maturity or call of at least 15 years.

Trading in both Ginnie Mae futures and Treasury bond futures has grown rapidly and is currently very active. The Ginnie Mae contract in particular is used by mortgage bankers who put together pools of FHA and VA mortgages to back new issues of Ginnie Mae pass-throughs. Promoters of the Ginnie Mae futures market argue that it could also be used by S&Ls which make commitments to lend mortgage money in the future at a fixed rate. However, such commitments are not legally binding on the borrower, and a borrower may fail to take down a commitment, especially if rates fall. Thus, an S&L which used the market would be hedging an *option,* and such a hedge could, instead of preventing losses, actually exacerbate them.

Promoters of the market in government bond futures have argued that prudent portfolio managers investing in long bonds should use this market to hedge. Such a hedge, however, is likely to seem superfluous to the many portfolio managers who take the attitude; if we buy it, we will mature it. Also, as one banker noted, for a bank that actively manages its portfolio on the basis of its view on where rates are going, to hedge the position it established would be akin to trying to become "a little bit pregnant."

DEALER PROFITS

Dealers in governments often claim that the major source of the profits they make is not on picking up the spread between the bid prices at which they buy and the asked prices at which they sell, i.e., on their principal market making activities, but rather on the speculative positions they assume. This raises an interesting question: if it is in fact true that dealers make most of their money speculating, why haven't some of them cut back on the expensive facilities they maintain to trade with each other and with retailers and moved the bulk of their activities to the futures markets?

For a firm that wants to speculate, futures markets are, it can be argued, a more efficient trading mechanism than cash markets. A futures market offers a credit guarantee, a homogeneous commodity, minimum transaction costs, and a great potential for leverage; it also offers a cheap, clean way to go short.

The fact that government dealers remain very active in the cash market suggests that over the long run they in fact make much of their profits, perhaps more than they perceive, by creating efficient markets, by arbitraging, and by distributing Treasury debt.

Chapter 15

Certificates of deposit:
Domestic and Euro

OF THE PRINCIPAL SECTORS of the money market, the certificate of deposit market is the youngest, the first domestic negotiable CDs backed with a dealer commitment to make a secondary market in them having been issued in 1961. Since that time CDs have grown to become a major money market instrument, and money market banks have come to rely so heavily on the sale of CDs as a source of funding that it is impossible to imagine how they could manage their liability positions without them.

DOMESTIC CDS

Major U.S. banks get some large time deposits from domestic individuals, partnerships, and smaller corporations and from overseas customers who do not want the headache of safekeeping a CD even though the selling bank would do it for them. The total of such deposits is, however, limited relative to the banks' need for longer-term deposits. To fill the resulting gap, the banks turn to the one sector of the money market where they can buy longer-term funds in volume, the CD market.

A certificate of deposit is a negotiable instrument evidencing a time deposit made with a bank at a fixed rate of interest for a fixed period

399

(Figure 15–1). CDs bear interest and CD rates are quoted on an interest-bearing rather than a discount basis. Normally interest on a CD, which is calculated for actual days on a 360-day-year basis, is paid at maturity. However, on CDs issued with a maturity beyond one year, interest is paid semiannually. CDs trade in the secondary market most often for regular settlement, but cash trades can also be made.

Figure 15–1
A specimen CD

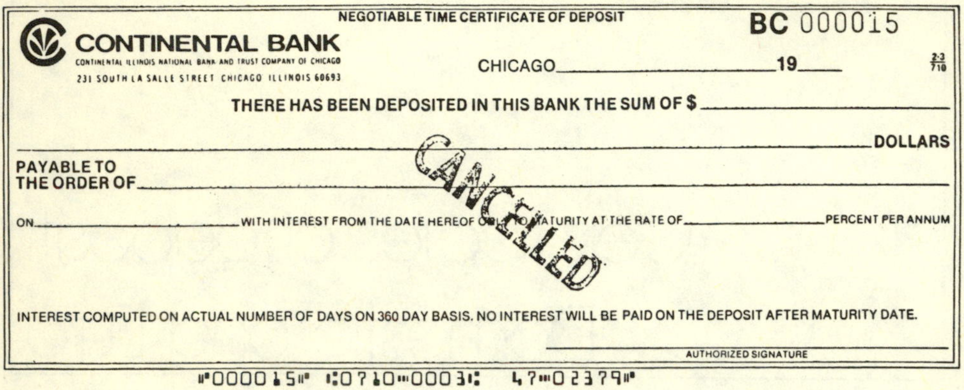
NEGOTIABLE TIME CERTIFICATE OF DEPOSIT
BC 000015
CONTINENTAL BANK
CONTINENTAL ILLINOIS NATIONAL BANK AND TRUST COMPANY OF CHICAGO
231 SOUTH LA SALLE STREET CHICAGO ILLINOIS 60693
CHICAGO ______ 19 ____
THERE HAS BEEN DEPOSITED IN THIS BANK THE SUM OF $ ______
______ DOLLARS
PAYABLE TO THE ORDER OF ______
ON ______ WITH INTEREST FROM THE DATE HEREOF ONLY TO MATURITY AT THE RATE OF ______ PERCENT PER ANNUM
CANCELLED
INTEREST COMPUTED ON ACTUAL NUMBER OF DAYS ON 360 DAY BASIS. NO INTEREST WILL BE PAID ON THE DEPOSIT AFTER MATURITY DATE.
AUTHORIZED SIGNATURE

CDs are normally issued in $1 million pieces. Smaller pieces, while technically negotiable, have poor marketability and trade at a concession to the market. Most CDs, regardless of where the issuer is located, are payable in New York. Thus, there is no need to ship the security out of New York to be presented to the issuing bank for payment at maturity.

CDs were introduced in 1961 by the New York banks in an attempt to tap the national market for deposits, and their example was soon followed by banks elsewhere. Since that time the volume of CDs outstanding has, as Figure 15–2 shows, risen dramatically albeit in a sharply fluctuating pattern.

When first issued, CDs were subject to a rate lid under Regulation Q. In 1969 this lid became a binding constraint as money market rates pushed through the Reg Q ceiling. The result was that money moved from domestic time deposits into Euro deposits, and U.S. banks lost $14 billion of CD money. In response they promptly borrowed the $14 billion back from the Euromarket; and the Fed's ill-conceived attempt to limit bank lending by cutting off the banks' access to bought money failed. Since 1973 the Fed has imposed no lid on the rate that banks can pay on time deposits of $100,000 or more. While the Fed could reimpose a rate lid on large-denomination time deposits, the unproductive outcome of its last sortie in this direction suggests that it is unlikely to do so.

Figure 15–2
Domestic CDs outstanding

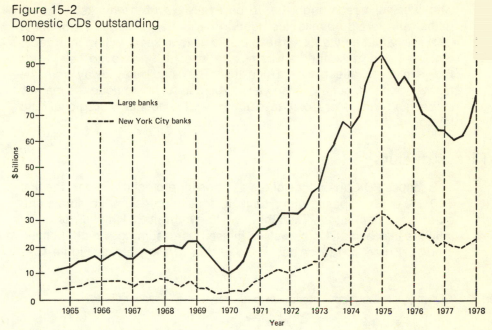

Source: *Federal Reserve Bulletin.*

Volume

Since the removal of Reg Q on CDs, changes in the volume of outstanding CDs have occurred largely in response to variations in the level of loan demand experienced by banks. This is to be expected since banks view CD money as a marginal source of funds to be drawn upon when an increase in loans has to be funded. In this respect, one particularly desirable characteristic of the CD market is its tremendous elasticity. CDs outstanding can and do fluctuate by tens of billions of dollars in response to changes in the banks' needs for CD money.

In addition to the cyclical ups and downs in the amounts of CDs outstanding, there are also seasonal changes. While any bank analyst worth his salt views CD money as bought money, banks still try to pick up "deposits" through the sale of CDs around statement dates. Because this quarterly phenomenon is particularly accentuated in December and because bank loans tend to run off in January, CD rates posted by banks often drop noticeably at the beginning of the year as banks withdraw from the market.

Another factor influencing the volume of CDs outstanding is the need that issuing banks feel to have a continuing presence in the market. As a funding officer of one large bank said: "It would be unthinkable for us, whatever our needs might be, to be totally out of the market." For regional and foreign banks, the need to be in the market on an ongoing basis is particularly acute. These banks have to keep selling in order to establish and maintain their names on investors' approved lists. Such banks must in effect walk a fine line. They can't stay away from the market too long, but they also have to be careful not to flood the market, since many investors can take only small amounts of regional and foreign names.

Risk and return

Because FDIC insurance offers a depositor protection on only the first $40,000 of his deposits with a bank, it is meaningless for corporate and other large depositors. Thus the investor who puts $1 million or many millions into bank CDs perceives himself as assuming a real, if small, credit risk. For this reason one would expect CDs to yield, as Figure 15–3

Figure 15–3
CD rates track but consistently exceed the yield on Treasury bills

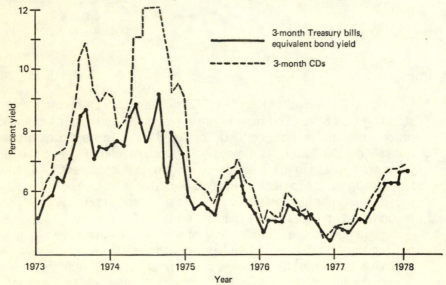

Source: *Federal Reserve Bulletin.*

shows they do, more than T bills of the same maturity. Another reason for the greater yield on CDs is that they are less liquid than bills.

Spreads between yields on bills and CDs widen when money tightens for several reasons. First, there is the familiar, if not particularly rational, tendency of investors to back away, when money market rates rise, from risks they willingly assume when rates are low in order to raise return on their investments. Second, the condition of the banking system appears to worsen when the nation's financial system is under strain; thus, the risks associated in the eyes of many investors with holding bank CDs tend to be positively correlated with the rate yielded by such instruments. Finally tight money tends, as suggested below to adversely affect the liquidity of CDs.

The major investors in bank CDs are corporations. CDs are also bought by state and local governments and by other financial institutions. Generally banks do not invest actively in CDs other than when they position them as a part of their dealer operation. The exception might be if rates were expected to drop sharply. There are two factors that discourage a bank from buying another bank's CDs. One is that a bank's holdings of CDs are not deductible from its reservable deposits, as are its demand deposits with other banks. Second, a bank incurs a reserve requirement if it RPs CDs except with another bank. In this respect it should also be noted that a bank may not invest in or buy back one of its own CDs. The Fed would view this as violating the condition that legally permitted the bank to issue the instrument, namely the receipt of a fixed-maturity time deposit.

Because CDs expose the holder to a credit risk, large investors in CDs seek to assess the creditworthiness of different banks. On the basis of such assessments, each investor establishes a list of banks whose CDs it is willing to buy and sets limits, *undisclosed lines* in street jargon, on the amounts it will deposit with individual banks on its approved list. The analysis investors put into deciding which banks they will invest with and in what amounts ranges from casual to elaborate. An average-sized S&L might check out the credit of a bank whose CD it was thinking of buying by asking its own bank whether it would sell Fed funds to the issuing bank. If the answer was yes, it would buy the CD. Such analysis, while unsophisticated, is cheap and quick. At the other extreme are investors who pour over the reams of detailed information on the financial condition of individual banks that is provided in publications put out by Sheshunoff & Co.; Keefe, Bruyette & Woods, Inc.; the Chase Manhattan Bank; and A. G. Becker. Not surprisingly the sale of such publications has risen dramatically since the Franklin National Bank got into trouble in 1974.

While many investors worry seriously about the possibility that a major bank issuing CDs might fail, other investors, including some of the most sophisticated, completely discount that possibility. In the words of one investor typical of this latter group: "Money market banks are agents of the central bank. The Fed knows it and they know it, and the Fed is not going to let one of them fail so long as they play ball. A bank that doesn't may end up closing or being merged with another bank, but depositors are not going to lose money. I do not worry about problems at the Chase versus those at the Morgan because the truth is that the Chase has no more chance of failing than the Morgan. Moreover, if either were to fail, conditions would be such that other worries would preempt my concern over lost CD dollars."

To such an investor the main reason for tracking the problems of individual banks closely is that other investors' reactions to these problems create market premiums and discounts, which in turn create opportunities and risks for all investors. The same individual went on to say: "If bad news comes out about the Chase, I know that the market is going to overreact. So I check with the dealers on the spreads at which Chase CDs are trading. If liquidity is still there, I dump my Citis and buy Chase CDs. Experience has proved me right."

Tiering

Prior to 1974 tiering in the CD market was modest, and CDs of all the top banks traded at roughly the same level. Then problems emerged at the Franklin and elsewhere in the banking industry, and things changed.

Investors began to look more closely at the condition of individual banks issuing CDs, and tiering became pronounced. It's difficult to generalize about tiering in top names other than to say that it appears to have become a permanent phenomenon. Who has to pay up changes over time as investors' perception of the financial strengths and weaknesses of individual banks changes. For example, when New York City appeared to be on the verge of bankruptcy, the top New York banks, all of which had substantial holdings of New York City securities, had to pay higher rates than top Chicago banks to issue CDs. Several years later the situation had reversed. The size of the spreads that exist between CDs issued by top banks is highly variable. They widen as money tightens; also whether money is easy or tight, the spreads are greater the longer the maturity of the securities compared.

The year 1974 was particularly hard on regional banks. At that time many CD investors reacted to the troubled state of the banking industry by paring regional banks from their lists of acceptable names. As a result some regional banks were forced out of the New York market and others had to pay high rates. As money eased, the situation reversed somewhat. Customers began looking at a wider range of names and found that some regional banks were strong credits compared with some of their big New York sisters. Gradually more regional names became acceptable to investors in the national market, and spreads narrowed between the rates at which prime regional names could issue CDs and those at which the nation's top banks could write. However, no matter how good they may be as credits, regional banks will never be able to sell their paper at the same rates top banks do, because they have so little paper outstanding that it does not trade as actively in the secondary market as the paper of large banks and it is thus less liquid.

Small banks often sell limited amounts of CDs to local customers at the rates posted by top banks. They can do so because local firms tend to place their liquidity with local banks. Access to the New York market is, however, closed to a small bank. As one investor noted: "A guy from Springfield can tell me he's better than Morgan and maybe he's right. But how could I resell his CD without my making the same case to the market? I can't, so I would not buy his CD."

Maturities

Most CDs issued in the U.S. market are in the 1- to 3-month area. There is a market in 6-month money, buy beyond that no issuing is done in real size. There are several reasons for the short maturities in the CD market. One is that many of the investors in CDs are corporations funding tax and dividend dates that are at most 90 days in the future. These investors need liquidity, and many prefer to obtain it by buying short-term securities that they can hold to maturity rather than by buying longer-term instruments whose liquidity is inherent in their marketability.

A second reason for the thin market in CDs with a maturity at issue of 6 months or longer is that, in normal times when the yield curve is upward sloping, it's cheaper for banks to buy longer-term money by rolling 3-month CDs. As one banker noted: "Six-month money is high-cost money. So you have to believe that the Fed is going to move dramatically to justify buying it on rate considerations alone. If you buy it at all, it's likely to be to improve—at an acknowledged cost—your liquidity." That statement is a bit strong. As noted on page 89, the low reserve requirement on long-term CDs does in fact encourage banks at times to buy 6-month money in volume.

The market for CDs with a maturity of 6 months or longer is referred to as a *professional investors market.* There are some trading accounts and speculative players who will buy these CDs, but most are sold initially to dealers. A dealer who buys such CDs often finances them for some period with term RP, thereby creating a future security with some built-in yield (recall Chapter 9's discussion of figuring the tail).[1] For a dealer to profit from this strategy, that is, to be able to sell out the future security he is creating at a profit, interest rates over the holding period have to fall, remain stable, or at least not rise sharply. This raises an interesting point. The dealer and the banker are both attempting to make sophisticated predictions as to where interest rates are going. If the dealer is

---

[1] See pages 226–29.

right in believing that he can make money positioning longer-term paper, then the banker is wrong in thinking that he can reduce funding costs by issuing it. A bank funding officer put this succinctly: "When dealers ask me why we don't do more business with them, my answer is that, if they are making money, I'm doing a lousy job. For us to do business, one of us has to make a bad mistake."

The Fed has often expressed concern over the short average maturity of bank CDs outstanding. To induce banks to issue longer-term CDs, the Fed first raised Reg Q ceilings on CDs of longer maturity and then cut reserve requirements on them.[2] However, when money tightens and interest rates rise—precisely the time when the Fed would like to see the banks buying some longer-term money, the average maturity of CDs outstanding actually falls noticeably. During such times the banks would like to issue longer-term CDs, but as a practical matter investors refuse to buy them. When money rates rise toward a peak, investors want to keep their options open. They will give banks money for only a month to ensure that they will be in a position to extend into longer maturities when rates peak. Investors, of course, are happy to buy longer-term CDs when rates are falling, but that's precisely the time when banks have no incentive to issue them.

THE NEW ISSUE MARKET

Most banks issuing CDs prefer to place as many of them as possible directly with customers. One reason for this is the feeling that the less visible borrowing a bank does through brokers and dealers, the better its credit will appear. A second reason is the fear that CDs issued through dealers may end up back on the street at just the time when the banks want to borrow additional funds, thereby creating a situation in which a bank has to compete with itself to write new CDs.

Despite their predilection for writing direct to customers, banks do issue a lot of CDs through dealers. As one funding officer whose attitude is typical noted: "All things being equal, we would rather place the deposit ourselves. But if a dealer is willing to take our CDs at a competitive rate and it fits our needs, we sell to them."

Every morning the major dealers call the banks to find out what CD *scale* (rates at different maturities) they are posting. If a dealer has an interest from a customer in a particular area of the market, he shows the bank a bid for a specific amount and maturity. Since the customer wants his instrument at par, if the bank accepts the bid, it issues the CD at par and pays a commission to the dealer by check.

Alternatively a dealer might be looking for CDs to position because he

---

[2] The Fed presently imposes no rate ceiling on CDs with denominations of $100,000 or more, but reserve requirements are still lower on longer-term CDs (see Table 5–3).

knows where he could sell them or because he thinks rates are going down. In that case he might call a bank and say, "We can use some 180-day CDs and our bid is 5.50." Should the bank reply, "Sorry we're at 5.45," the dealer might respond, "Too low," or "Oh, what the hell, we'll take them."

The initiative might also come from the bank's side. In CDs the floating supply is smaller than that in bills, and a CD dealer can at times move the market by ¼ with as little as a $25 million deal. For that reason a bank with a big program, say, raising $100 million, might come to a dealer and ask, "What do you think we can get it at?" or "Do you have any interest?" The dealer would spend five minutes calling customers to survey their needs, and even if retail interest was thin, he might, depending on his view of the market, bid on and position the securities with just a few presales.

A bank with a big program might also call a dealer and say, "We want you to know that we're writing in 180 days, our rate is 5.5, and we'll give you an 05 on what you sell." In that case the bank in effect hires a large sales force for a day for a small commission. The pressure on dealers to help banks either by positioning their paper or by providing them with a sales force becomes particularly acute when money is tight and banks need to write large amounts of paper to fund burgeoning loan demand.

Another advantage to a bank in using a dealer is that, when a bank writes a big program on its own, talk about what it's doing gets around. An investor who knows that a bank is writing big amounts at, say, 5.5 is likely to reason, "If the bank has that sort of appetite, I ought to demand ⅝." And pretty soon the bank finds it has to start stepping up its offering rate by 05s. If, in contrast, the bank operates through a dealer, it is often able to get in and out of the market at a single price.

Foreign bank branch CDs

Foreign bank branches issue CDs in the United States for various purposes. One is to fund loans made in the United States, and another is to take advantage of opportunities for arbitrage. If CD rates are right, a foreign bank may be able to take domestic CD money and place it at a positive spread in the term fed funds market or the Euromarket. In such activities, the foreign bank has the advantage over a domestic bank in that it does not have to maintain reserves at the Fed against the CD money it buys.

While dealers can be helpful to U.S. banks in writing CDs, particularly second-tier banks, they are a necessity to U.S. branches of foreign banks. A foreign bank branch trying to sell CDs in the U.S. market faces several problems. To many investors its name is not well known. Second, even investors who have heard of a particular foreign bank often fail to perceive that, say, Barclays or Crédit Lyonnais is a giant on the world banking scene just as is Citi or Chase. Third, many sophisticated investors feel that they don't know enough about French, Japanese, or other foreign accounting practices to read intelligently the financial statements of foreign banks.

In issuing CDs in the U.S. market, a foreign bank branch starts with a few U.S. commercial customers who, because they have dealt with that bank abroad, know it and are willing to buy its CDs. To sell beyond this limited customer base, a foreign bank branch has to turn to a dealer, who for an 05 will push that bank's paper by acquainting other investors with its name and credit. The resulting education takes time, so a foreign bank branch normally starts out having to pay substantially more than domestic issuers, a condition that gradually diminishes as its name grows in acceptability.

An alternative some foreign banks, including a few Japanese banks, have used is to post a low rate with dealers and then pay up to retail customers. One danger in this approach is that once customers get accustomed to earning a premium, they will expect to continue to get it. Another is that a bank that pays a large premium to the street may cheapen its name, which takes time and effort to reverse.

The typical buyer of a CD issued by a foreign bank is a *yield buyer*. To get that yield, he incurs what he perceives as some extra risk. In addition he accepts limited liquidity. Since most foreign banks issuing CDs in the U.S. market work through an exclusive dealer, the primary if not the only place where the holder of such a CD can get a bid on it is from the selling dealer. The latter may—given the state of the market—offer the CD holder a good bid, but still that holder is not in the comforting position of being able to shop on the street for bids as he would be if he held a Citi or a Morgan CD. Also, because of their limited supply, spreads between bid and ask quotes on foreign bank branch CDs are greater than those on top-grade U.S. paper.

We've said something about the tiering in the U.S. market between different U.S. names. If we look at the overall picture, the tiering becomes more complex. Many investors prefer a foreign bank CD issued out of New York to one issued out of London because they feel the latter exposes them to sovereign risk. Thus tiering in the overall CD market is roughly as follows. The lowest rates are paid by the top 25 U.S. banks on CDs issued in the U.S. market. The next lowest rates are paid on CDs issued by very top U.S. names in London. These are followed by CDs issued by good foreign names in New York. Finally, at the top of the yield scale are CDs issued by good continental names in London.

Shills and backdooring

Domestic banks have a sort of love-hate feeling for dealers. They realize that dealers can be useful to them in writing and that dealers make their paper salable by creating a secondary market for it. However, the banks don't like to pay the dealers an 05, and they don't want the dealers holding paper that could be dumped at an unpropitious moment on the street. Because of this ambivalent attitude, the banks and the dealers have at times played interesting games with each other.

A few banks absolutely refuse to sell to or through dealers. The dealers, not to be outwitted in their search for inventory, respond by finding corporations that are willing to act as "shills" for them. These corporations go to a bank, take down a big block of CDs on which they are sometimes offered a rate concession by the bank, and then turn around and sell this paper to the dealer for an 02, a practice known as *backdooring*.

The hoaxed bank often finds out. As one funding officer noted: "The dealers like nothing better than to call and say, 'Hey, we just got 50 million of your CDs at 5.60. You could have sold them to us direct and saved the hassle.' Still, when we started to use the dealers, I was amazed at how many of our 'customers' had been fronting for dealers."

Sometimes when banks have big programs to do, they practice price discrimination. They sell to big corporations through the bid side of the CD market to entice them into taking down a couple hundred million dollars of new CDs. Then, when they think these securities are put away at retail and will not come back to haunt them on the street, they offer the dealers maybe the last $50 million of the program at the true bid side of the market, after they have offered many big customers the dealers might call the same securities at a better rate.

The idea, of course, is not to ruffle the market, but the strategy frequently fails. The customers who buy the new CDs hit the dealers' bids with old CDs and the market backs up, which is exactly what the banks are trying to avoid. Meanwhile the corporations buying the new CDs and kicking out old ones take out a "nickel" or a "dime" (5 or 10 basis points) on the transaction.

As one ex-corporate money runner noted: "I never thought this practice did the banks any long-run good, and I never encouraged it. But if a bank offered me the opportunity to earn money, I was *not* there to turn it down. If they said they did not want the new CDs flogged on the street for a week, I would honor that. I would not backdoor the securities for an 02, but I would kick out some old CDs. In came some new Citis and out went some old Citis or Morgans or what have you. It was just a transfer on which I could take out 1/8 on the banks."

Practices of this sort are now less prevalent than in the past. The dealers are careful to monitor what is going on "away." Also, many banks realize that the dealers are more useful to them than they had thought and that the kind of aftertaste the market has for a bank's CDs depends partly on how fairly the bank treats investors and dealers when it issues.

Today many banks believe that it is not in their interest to offer similar institutions CDs of the same maturity at different rates or to sell a dealer a block of CDs and then raise rates five minutes later, leaving the dealer "hanging there" with paper at a loss. As one CD writer noted: "When I do a big block with a dealer and think that's it for awhile, I tell him. Naturally top management may suddenly change strategy and start selling again, but at least the dealer knows I tried to be honest. Dealers like this and regard banks who operate this way as 'professionals.' "

DEALER OPERATIONS

There are currently about 25 dealers in CDs, about 10 of whom are banks. Many dealers are relatively new at the game, being stock firms that entered the money market after negotiated commissions cut their brokerage income. There is a lot of variability in size and importance among dealers, and the key ones are the firms that were there originally: Salomon Brothers, Goldman Sachs, Discount Corp., A. G. Becker, First Boston, and Lehman Brothers.

A bank incurs a reserve cost, which a nonbank dealer does not, if it finances its CD position with RP money, as nonbank dealers typically do; but a bank can buy Fed funds which nonbank dealers cannot. A bank dealership has the advantage that its CD trader knows at least what his own bank plans in terms of writing CDs. One benefit to a bank of dealing in CDs is that the bank's CD trader, who is in constant contact with the market, can provide the banks' funding officers with useful, up-to-the-minute information on rates.

Part of a dealer's job is distribution, getting new CDs that banks want to write out into investors' hands for an 05. Since many sales of this sort are generated by inducing investors to swap out of old CDs into new ones, such sales often create the basis for an additional string of transactions.

A second and more important part of the dealers' job is creating a secondary market for CDs. Dealers do this by standing ready at all times to quote bids and offers both to retail and to other dealers. Because of the diversity of names and maturities in the CD market, dealers cannot short CDs, but in their role as market makers they do position them, sometimes in very large amounts.

Because bank CDs vary with respect to both credit risk and liquidity, depending on who the issuer is, CD dealers, like investors, establish lists of banks whose CDs they will buy and limits on the amounts they will position of each of these names. As might be expected, there is a certain amount of specialization among dealers. Some, for example, have made an effort to develop a market in foreign bank CDs, whereas others shy away from non-U.S. names. Also some dealers are stronger in regional names than others. All deal actively in major names.

The inside market

Dealers operate in two markets, the *retail market* in which they do business with customers and the *inside market* in which they trade with each other.

Because CD dealers have become so numerous and because they vary so in size and character, a given dealer will typically not deal actively with all of the other dealers in the market. Instead rings or cliques of traders who trust, talk with, and deal with each other develop, just as they do in the bill market.

In the interdealer market the normal round-lot trade is $5 million, but blocks of $2 and $3 million trade easily. Because CDs vary so much with respect to maturity and name, dealer runs in the CD market are quite different from runs in the bill market. Maturities from a month out to a year are quoted, but specific dates are not mentioned. Instead a dealer will give bid and asked prices for, say, "late Novembers" and "early Decembers." A dealer is not expected to necessarily have inventory or to show what inventory he has in every maturity. Thus in a given maturity he might bid "5.40 without," meaning that he has no offering. The accepted spread between bid and asked prices on a dealer run is 10 basis points, but in practice good names of short maturity may be quoted at an 03 spread. Also a dealer who is out to do something will narrow that down and "make a 1 spread."

When a dealer bids on, say, a $5 million offering from another dealer, he would naturally like to know if there's another big block behind that offering or if $5 million is it. That is exactly the sort of information the other dealer will not divulge, especially if he is a big seller.

When bids and offers are made in the dealer market, it's understood that they are good for the top "trading names"—Morgan, Manny Hanny, Citi, and Bankers—plus the B of A. If an offering a Chase, a Chemical, or a Chicago name, that has to be specified.[3] Normally there is not much of a dealer-to-dealer market in regional and foreign names. To sell that sort of paper, a dealer has to look to retail.

The brokers

In January 1976 one firm started brokering dealer trades in CDs, and since then another firm has entered the business. Brokers are actively used by CD traders for the same reasons they are used by traders in governments—they provide anonymity and speedy communication with

---

[3] Tiering in the CD market is constantly changing as the market's perception of the credit risks associated with different bank CDs and the amounts of CDs different banks write change. The remarks here and later in the chapter reflect the conditions that prevailed in mid-1977.

other dealers. Also a dealer may be able to do a large volume in the brokers market, which would be difficult to do direct. In the dealer-to-dealer market a $10 million trade is considered big, except between the largest shops, but sales of $50 million blocks have been done in one shot through a broker with a number of bids on his pad.

When a dealer puts a bid or an offering into a broker, he is expected to let it stand for two or three minutes. During that time the broker pounds his phone board, getting the information out to other dealers. The "pictures" quoted by brokers are in the actively traded areas, 3 to 6 months, and usually there is a two-way market. In CDs, as in bills, dealers play trading games, and the bid and ask quotes given by a broker in a particular maturity may be a "one-man picture." Whether they are or not is something the broker is not supposed to divulge.

Because of tiering in the CD market, a broker's run is often sprinkled with names. A Bank of America CD trades slightly better than top New York names, so a broker's picture in a given maturity might be: "Early Decembers 62-60, B of A's offered at 57. We have some Chase offered at 63 and there is a 65 bid for Chemicals."

Normally bids and offers are for $5 million blocks. If they are for more, the broker will specify by saying that the market is, for example, "10 by 5." In the CD market brokerage equal to an 01 is paid by the dealer that initiates a trade. Because brokerage is paid by only one side in each transaction, *locked markets* can occur. CD trades made between dealers, whether direct or through a broker, are cleared through one of the New York clearing banks.

Financing

Dealer inventories in CDs, with the exception of those held by bank dealers, are normally financed in the RP market. A dealer who wants to hold CDs available for immediate sale to customers will do overnight or very short-term RPs. If, alternatively, he wants to hold CDs for some time as a speculation, he will probably do term RPs for 30, 60, or even 90 days.

Since there is some credit risk attached to CDs as opposed to governments, the rate on RPs backed with CDs is often slightly greater than that on RPs collateralized with governments. How much a dealer has to pay up to RP nongovernment paper depends in part on market conditions and on the kind of paper he's financing—spreads are wider the tighter money is and the poorer the credit of the issuer. Cost also depends on how clever the dealer is. As one noted: "RP financing is an art. There's tiering in the RP market, but a dealer who knows his retail outlets—who they are and what they will take in terms of names and maturities—can finance CDs and BAs with RP money at or only slightly above the RP rate on governments."

In the RP market transactions from overnight out to 30 days are easy to do. RPs for 60 or 90 days are tougher because so many investors want liquidity. To get around this difficulty, some dealers permit customers to put an RP back to them at the bid side of the RP market. That gives the investor the opportunity to enjoy both liquidity and the higher yield of a longer-term RP.

When a dealer finances CDs in the RP market, he encounters a problem that he does not find when he finances discount securities such as T bills or BAs, namely, that financing CDs eats up dealer capital. CDs bear interest and the normal practice in the RP market is for a loan against such instruments to be made for only face value, *not* for face value plus accrued interest. Thus the dealer who buys a CD has to put up his own capital to finance any accrued interest. The problem of capital attrition becomes even more acute if the CD happens to be selling at a premium. Because accrued interest on a CD cannot be financed in the RP market, dealers are loath to take in old paper, especially if it carries a high coupon. For that reason a dealer offering "stale dated paper" in the interdealer market is expected to specify that it is such.

Dealer philosophy and position

Some of the profits a CD dealer earns arise from the 05s he picks up distributing new paper and from the chain of swaps that such distribution frequently sets off. In many areas of the money market, day trading is another important source of profit. This tends not to be so in CD trading because the CD market does not have liquidity in size.

To win big, a CD trader has to position. The extent to which shops active in the CD market are willing to position and the fashion in which they do so vary considerably. In some shops the primary focus is on keeping retail happy, and most of the inventory on the dealer's shelf is for sale, the occasional exception being when the dealer really likes the market and decides to gamble big. At the other extreme are *spectail* shops, that is, shops that specialize in speculation but also do some business with retail.

Since a trader can't short CDs, the only position he can take is a long one. As noted, a firm that assumes a speculative long position in CDs often does so by buying longer-term CDs and putting them out on term RP. This is the riskiest form such speculation can take but also the one that pays off most when the dealer is right.

In evaluating the merits of going long, a CD trader, like any other money market trader, watches the Fed's moves as well as every other indicator that might tell him something about future trends in interest rates. The main threats to the trader are (1) that interest rates in general might rise, (2) that short-term interest rates alone might rise due to a shift in the yield curve, and (3) that yields on CDs might rise relative to yields on other short-term instruments. With respect to this final risk, every CD trader constantly bears in mind that "any clown with a pencil [bank liability manager] can create as many CDs as he wants to"; thus predicting future spreads between CDs and bills is extremely difficult. Another special factor the CD trader faces is that liquidity is poorer in the CD market than in the bill market. Thus an ill-conceived long position in CDs will be harder and more costly to liquidate than one in bills.

Whatever his appetite for positioning may be, every dealer takes his relations with retail seriously. He earns from retail when he helps banks distribute. Also, retail is the only place he can unload regional and foreign bank CDs that end up in his position. And in bad markets retail may be the only place he can sell even the best-quality CDs he has in inventory. Finally, to every dealer retail is of crucial importance because a dealer looks to his retail customers as a source of RP money for financing his position.

LIQUIDITY

Since different dealers handle different names, an investor cannot count on getting a bid from every dealer on paper he holds unless it's top-name paper. He can, however, be sure that a dealer who has sold him paper will always make him a bid on that paper.

How far back a dealer's bid to retail will be from his offering rate depends both on the name on the paper and on market conditions. In a stable market the dealer might bid back an 02 to an 05 for major-name paper, whereas in foreign and other more difficult names, he might bid back 10 basis points or even 1/8. Naturally when the market is backing up, dealers' bids get more defensive, especially for regional and foreign names.

While liquidity in the CD market, measured in terms of spreads between bid and asked prices, is good in reasonably stable markets, it is also true that the CD market reacts more violently to an upward nudge in interest rates than does, say, the bill market. There are several reasons. First, when interest rates start rising, there is concern on the part of both dealers and investors that the banks will respond by writing more CDs; the specter of rising interest rates, which makes dealers and investors want to get out of CDs, gives the banks an equally rational incentive for creating more of them. Thus as money tightens, supply becomes much more uncertain in the CD market than in the bill market, and as a result the CD market tends to back up faster.

Another difference between the CD and the bill markets is that in the bill market there are many investors that are required by law, charter, or management-set parameters to limit their investments to governments or to governments and RP collateralized by governments. To the extent that these investors have funds to invest, they provide automatic support for the bill market. No such institutionally created support exists in the CD market.

During credit crunches prior to 1974, the problem of liquidity in the CD market was particularly acute. Dealers permitted themselves to get trapped with large positions and in self-defense simply ceased to bid. Once that occurred, the secondary market disappeared by definition; CDs did not trade, and they had to be bought as an investment.

While the CD market was not without its problems in 1974, it did give a better account of itself. Dealers had learned how to react to rising rates; they did not permit themselves to get trapped with big positions, and CDs continued to trade during the crunch.

Term CDs

The improvement that has occurred in the behavior of the short-term CD market during crunches bodes well for the future of the market for term CDs, that is, CDs with maturities ranging from 2 to 5 years. There is no way that banks can sell CDs in any maturity range without a viable secondary market because investors demand liquidity, which can be provided only through active market making and positioning by dealers. Positioning CDs eats up capital, and the capital attrition becomes increasingly large the longer the maturity of the CDs involved. Thus dealers were slow to make a market in term CDs.

In the fall of 1976, however, dealers started to take a serious look at this market—to work for spreads and to establish lines in bank names. They also retailed fair-sized term issues for Citibank and for Chase. These issues were anything but successful, partly because of pricing and market conditions, and dealers were left holding at a loss big positions in a thin market. Thus for a time it looked as if the term CD market might die at birth, but in retrospect it was probably only going through the same birth pangs that the original CD market did. The market for term CDs did come back, and over time it seems likely to grow and develop as more dealers make a commitment to it.

To provide the investor in term CDs with some liquidity in the absence of an active dealer market in such securities, the Morgan Bank came up with an interesting innovation, the *roly poly CD.* Under the terms of this hybrid, the depositor agrees to leave a deposit with the bank for some fixed period, say, 5 years. In exchange he receives, not a certificate with a 5-year maturity, but a succession of 6-month CDs, each carrying the 5-year rate offered at issue. The investor can sell these 6-month CDs as he receives them, but at the end of each 6-month period he is required to renew his deposit for another 6 months. The advantage to the investor is that he can always get funds on a short-term basis if he needs them by selling his current CD; moreover, since that instrument carries a rate well up on the yield curve, he has a chance of being able to sell it for a profit some of the time.

Savings and loan association CDs

Savings and loan associations, like banks, are permitted to issue large-denomination negotiable CDs free from any rate lid. A few do so through New York dealers, but the volume outstanding is small and likely to remain so. In the market for bank CDs, only paper issued by relatively large banks is traded actively enough to have real liquidity and thus to be attractive to investors in the national market. Since the country's largest S&Ls are small compared with even a respectable-sized regional bank, it's hard to envision how a large and active market for S&L paper could develop.

EURODOLLAR CDs

Eurodollar CDs were first issued in the London market in 1966 by Citibank. The new instrument was quickly and readily accepted by the market and, as Figure 15–4 shows, the volume outstanding rose rapidly. At the beginning of 1978, there were $22.9 billion of Eurodollar CDs outstanding. While this figure seems impressive, it is small compared with the approximately $70 billion of CDs outstanding in the domestic market. Part of the reason for the contrast lies in the smaller size of the Euromarket. A more important factor, however, is the differing roles that CDs play in the two markets. Selling CDs is *the* major way a domestic banker obtains longer-term funds, but for a Euro banker the CD market is merely an adjunct to the much more important interbank deposit market.

Characteristics

A Euro CD, like a domestic CD, is a negotiable instrument evidencing a time deposit made with a bank at a fixed rate for a fixed period (Figure 15–5). Euro CDs bear interest and Euro CD rates are quoted on an interest-bearing basis. Interest, which is calculated for actual days on a 360-day-year basis, is paid at maturity on Euro CDs with a maturity of 1 year or less and annually on those with a maturity of more than 1 year.

All Euro CDs are currently denominated in dollars. There is demand on the part of investors for CDs denominated in German marks and Swiss francs, but the German and Swiss central banks have requested that the Bank of England not permit the issuance in London of CDs denominated in their currencies. Their objective in doing so has been to discourage

Figure 15–4
Eurodollar CDs outstanding (U.S. $ billions)

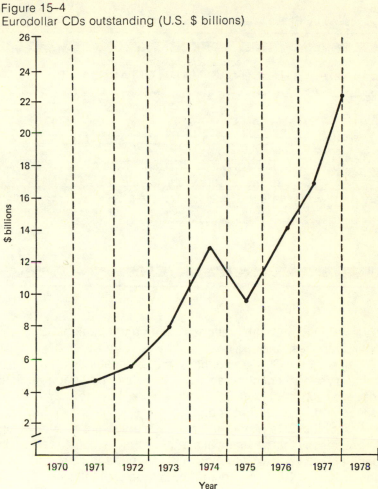

Source: Bank of England.

any innovation that in their view might create additional opportunities for speculation in their currency or encourage the use of their currency as a reserve currency. The Bundesbank has also discouraged the issuance of Euromark CDs outside of London.

For all intents and purposes the market in Euro CDs is a London market. Eurodollar CDs are issued in centers outside London, but their numbers are small and the liquidity and marketability of non-London CDs are limited. The major issuers of Eurodollar CDs in the London market are the branches of top U.S. banks. Eurodollar CDs are, however, also issued in London by the British clearing banks, the British overseas

Figure 15–5
A Euro CD issued by Chase in London

banks, Canadian bank branches, continental bank branches, Japanese bank branches, and regional U.S. bank branches.[1]

Sales of Euro CDs are normally made for settlement two days forward, although settlement on a same-day basis can be arranged. Settlement is made by payment of funds in New York, but the actual securities are issued and safekept in London.

Eurodollar CDs issued in London are subject to British regulations. These specify that payment at maturity must be authorized by the issuing bank in London, but actual payment is made in New York for value the same day the CD is presented in London for payment.

One problem both for banks issuing Euro CDs and for investors in these instruments is that, because of the difference in time zones between New York and London, it is impossible to synchronize—as is normally done in money market transactions—delivery of and payment on Euro CDs. To cope with this difficulty and to minimize the physical movement of securities, the First National Bank of Chicago has set up in London a *CD Clearing Centre,* which assures participants payment and delivery on any transaction they make with another member of the Centre.

Euro CDs, like domestic CDs, are normally issued in $1 million

---

[1] Deposit taking and short-term lending in the domestic sterling market are dominated in Great Britain by a few large institutions that are referred to as *clearing banks* because they are members of the London Clearing House. The British *overseas banks,* which have branches around the globe, are a relic of the British Empire, whose specific financial needs they developed to serve.

pieces. Euro CDs of $500,000 trade, however, at less of a concession to the market than do domestic CDs of similar size. Because most Euro loans are rolled every 3 or 6 months, the bulk of Euro CDs issued are in the 3- to 6-month maturity range. However, Euro CDs with maturities as long as 5 years are common; the proceeds of such term CDs are used to match fund assets of similar maturity.

Rates

The Fed has ruled that Euro CDs issued by foreign branches of U.S. banks are exempt from Reg Q because they are liabilities of the branch. Thus U.S. bank branches in London have always been free to pay the going market rate for CD money, a situation that led in 1969 to substantial gaps between the rates paid on CDs in New York and London. Today, with Reg Q in abeyance on all large-denomination CDs, rates on Euro CDs track domestic CD rates quite closely, as Figure 15–6 shows. Normally Euro rates are higher than U.S. rates, with the spread between the

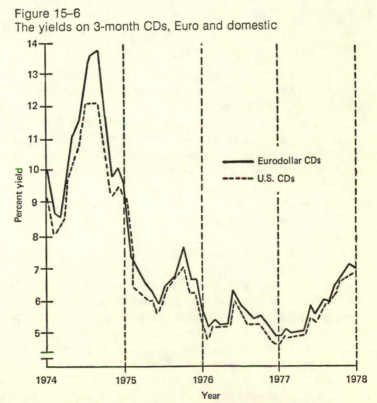

Figure 15–6
The yields on 3-month CDs, Euro and domestic

Source: *An Analytic Record of Yields and Spreads*, Salomon Brothers.

two being wider the tighter money is and the longer the maturity of the securities compared.

The gap between yields on domestic and Euro CDs is due to two factors. First, Euro CDs are less liquid than domestic CDs, for which investors demand a rate premium. Second, many U.S. investors view Eurodollar CDs as a riskier investment than domestic CDs either because they are worried about the loans that the London branches of U.S. banks have granted to places like Zaire or because they are concerned about the possibility that the British might act against the Euro operations of London banks. In this respect it should be noted that any Eurodollar CD issued by the London branch of a U.S. bank is a direct obligation of that bank, and *the credit is thus that of the parent.* Therefore an investor who is worried about, say, Chase London's loans to Zaire is not going to expose himself to any less risk if he buys a Chase New York CD in preference to a Chase London CD. So far as sovereign risk is concerned, it is true that some sticky legal questions would arise should the British stop payment on Eurodollar CDs issued in London. However, as noted in Chapter 6, the probability of their doing so is close to, if not zero.

The investors

Knowledgeable people in the London market estimate that as much as 50 percent of all Euro CDs are *lock-up CDs.* As noted in Chapter 6, a lock-up CD is really a Euro time deposit masquerading as a CD. Lock-up CDs are issued with the understanding that they will not be traded, and typically they are safekept by the issuing bank. Usually they carry yields close to the rate paid on time deposits of similar maturity. Lock-up CDs are bought primarily by foreign banks and bank branches in London and on the Continent; some, however, are purchased by U.S. bank branches in London. The motivation of the buyer is always to improve the cosmetics of his dollar book by giving his dollar assets the appearance of greater liquidity.

Another big chunk of money invested in Euro CDs comes from banks in the expatriate money belt of Switzerland: Geneva, Lausanne, and Lugarno. The money invested is customer money, and the Euro CDs acquired are almost never traded because the customers for whom Swiss banks invest are interested in avoiding taxes and obtaining safety, not in earning 16ths or 8ths through trading. Sometimes, of course, such a customer needs cash; if he does, the Swiss bank simply lends to him against his CD rather than selling the instrument.

A large fraction of the remaining Eurodollar CDs issued are sold to investors in the United States, often by U.S. dealers active in the London market. Some large and sophisticated U.S. corporate portfolio managers invest actively in Euro CDs and will readily swap back and forth between Eurodollar CDs and domestic CDs in response to changes in yield spreads. In general, however, sellers of Euro CDs experienced, until recently when attitudes began to change, only limited success with U.S. corporate portfolio managers. Many of the latter are either unfamiliar with the instrument or concerned about sovereign risk. Also, even the portfolio manager who views Euro CDs as an attractive investment vehicle may end up asking himself: Is explaining the instrument and the risk to the board worth an extra 30 basis points? Many of the Euro CDs placed in the United States are sold to smaller banks that view the instrument as giving them the opportunity to earn extra yield while still maintaining reasonable liquidity.

Tiering

In the London market a wide range of names is accepted both in the new issue and in the secondary market. However, few CDs other than those issued by top U.S. names are sold in the United States because that is all U.S. investors are currently willing to buy.[5] The narrow range of names acceptable in the U.S. market is a source of amazement to some British participants in the Euro CD market. As the head of a British discount house observed: "If you try to trade with a New York dealer, his idea of top American is seven names. God knows how he does a business. It is inconceivable to me that you can claim to be a market maker and trade only half a dozen names. There must be different levels at which and different volumes in which different names will trade."

And in London just these conditions prevail. Banks with better names can write more paper and pay less to issue than banks with lesser names; moreover the tiering between different names, which first became pronounced in 1974, is quite complex. At the top of the pile paying the lowest rates are the six largest U.S. banks. Tier two contains the next six U.S. banks. They are followed by the next ten U.S. names plus the British clearers and top Canadian banks. Top continental names fall below that tier. Finally at the bottom of the pile paying the most are merchant banks, Japanese banks, and some other lesser names.

One interesting feature of tiering among top U.S. names in London is that it is largely on the basis of size; when bad earnings caused Chase to pay up in New York, its need to do so was less pronounced in London. The Euro CD market is, however, much more susceptible to temporary indigestion due to large volumes than is the domestic CD market. Therefore rate tiering may reflect concern over a bank's issuing habits.

---

[5] The exception that proves the rule: West Coast banks will buy Japanese paper because they know the credits.

The new issue and secondary markets

Banks issuing Euro CDs in London prefer to sell directly to investors for exactly the same reasons they prefer to do so in issuing domestic CDs. However, they also issue through dealers and brokers.

The presence in London of U.S. dealers such as Salomon Brothers, Goldman Sachs, Lehman Brothers, First Boston, Merrill Lynch, and A. G. Becker is a relatively recent development. Becker, the first to arrive, came in 1972. Before that, the banks relied on *brokers* and the *discount houses* for any help they needed in selling CDs.[6]

The firms that took up brokering Euro CDs were London houses that were already actively brokering Euro time deposits, foreign exchange, and sterling deposits. These brokers are not permitted to talk to corporate retail, so primarily they brokered CDs between issuing and buying banks. Brokerage, paid by both sides, was initially $1/32$, but as volume increased, the banks beat down the rate first to $1/40$ and then to $1/50$. Discount houses, which do buy from and sell to retail, participated in the market in two ways. They bought CDs for position and to sell to retail. In the early days of the market, the discount houses received a *placing fee* (equal to brokerage due from the seller) on every CD they bought regardless of whether they held it or sold it to a customer.

With the arrival of the U.S. dealers in London, things changed. The dealers, who bought CDs initially through the brokers, eventually managed to go around them and deal directly with the banks. In doing so, moreover, they operated as they did back in the United States, taking a selling commission when it was the bank that wanted the dealer to work for it and buying on a net basis when it was the dealer that wanted to position the bank's CDs. This practice spelled an end to the placing fee the discount houses had been receiving.

Today the discount houses have largely retreated from the distribution of CDs to retail. Some, however, do supply Euro CDs to New York dealers that have no London office. The U.S. dealers that come to London enjoy several commanding advantages over the discount houses in trading and distributing CDs. First, the discount houses do not have and cannot get the retail outlets in the United States that the U.S. dealers have; this is important because only a handful of U.K. corporations are allowed to buy dollar CDs. Geography also puts the discount houses at a disadvantage with respect to market feel and information. As one discount house official put it: "We are operating in what is basically one facet of the New

---

[6] The *discount houses,* an institution peculiar to Britain, use call and overnight money obtained largely from banks to invest in and to trade short-dated governments, local authority bonds, U.K. Treasury bills, and commercial bills. In effect these institutions hold and invest a large portion of the British banking system's reserves.

York market. But we are 3,000 miles away, so we can't expose ourselves to the risks we would if we were sitting in New York."

Today the activities of the discount houses in the Euro CD market are confined largely to holding such CDs for carry profits. The houses buy CDs, finance them with short-dated funds at a positive spread, and stand prepared to run down their CD books smartly if that positive carry disappears. Discount houses still do some trading in CDs, but by U.S. standards they are not active traders.

The brokers are still present in the Euro CD market, but since the arrival of the U.S. dealers, their relative importance has diminished. Some of the brokers are in a better position than the discount houses to compete directly with the U.S. dealers for retail business in the United States. The reason is that they have opened New York offices or acquired New York partners that are in contact with domestic banks and other domestic retail as brokers of or dealers in Euro time deposits, Fed funds, and other money market instruments; this puts them in a position to sell Euro CDs directly to U.S. retail. Often such sales are part of a more complex transaction. For example, the New York arm of a London brokerage house might propose to a U.S. bank that it reverse out governments wanted by a dealer and invest the proceeds at a positive spread in Euro CDs brokered out of London.

The techniques used in brokering Euro CDs are much like those used in brokering Euro time deposits, which we describe in the next chapter. The broker quotes both bid and asked prices, and in doing so he is always careful to specify what category of paper he is talking about, for example, top American, Canadian, British clearer, regional American, or top continental. A bank that wants to write CDs will sometimes call a broker to get a feel for the support price in a given tenor. If the bank likes the level, it may ask the broker to sell what he can at that level or it may ask him to do some fixed amount. A broker who quotes bids and offers as firm is supposed to *substantiate* these quotes, for example, provide a would-be seller with a buyer at the bid price he has quoted unless line problems arise, that is, unless the buyer can't take the name the seller is offering. The brokers' primary customers are banks, the discount houses, and the U.S. dealers; the bank customers include some London banks that run a dealer operation in other banks' Euro CDs.

The U.S. dealers operate in the Euro CD market much as they do in the domestic CD market. If a bank that wants to write comes to a dealer, the dealer will take an 02, which equals the brokerage ($1/_{50}$) that the selling bank would have to pay if it sold through a broker. A dealer does not get brokerage from the customer to whom he sells the CD, but he does have profit opportunities that a broker, who never positions, does not; namely, he can profit from positive carry and from favorable movements in the market.

The dealers all regularly call the major issuing banks to give them runs. Generally their bids are good for $5 million, and they buy at a net price if their bid is hit. A few banks, when they want to do a sizable piece, will be quite open with a dealer they trust. They might, for example, ask the dealer, "If I wanted to do 50 million, what kind of a job could you do for me?" At that point the dealer would call New York to see how much and at what levels his firm could generate retail demand by bidding on securities in customers' portfolios, swapping, for example, customers out of bills into Euro CDs for a yield pickup. Then the dealer would call back the bank, giving it his firm's assessment of the market and a bid on the CDs the bank wanted to write. If word gets around that a large bank is writing a lot of CDs, this will move the market. Thus a bank will talk to a dealer in confidence about what it wants to do only if it is sure this confidence will not be betrayed.

For a bank that wants to write a lot of paper, dealers tend to be a more attractive outlet than brokers. The brokers, who can't position, sell mostly to other banks. They can place $2 million here and $5 or $10 million there, but unless a broker has a lot of bids on his pad, he won't be able to do a $25 or $50 million piece other than in bits and dribbles, a process that gives the market time to learn what the issuing bank is doing and to react to it. In contrast, a U.S. dealer, who is sourcing the huge domestic market, can and will bid on and buy in a single shot large blocks of new CDs. An additional advantage to an issuing bank of using a U.S. dealer is that securities sold to such a firm tend to move out of the London market into the U.S. market, which gets them out of the way of any additional CDs this bank might later want to write.

Any dealer who sells a Euro CD to retail will always bid at market for that CD if the customer later wants to sell it. In addition, the dealers and discount houses trade CDs among themselves. There is thus an active secondary market in Euro CDs. In this market the normal spread between bid and asked prices is 10 basis points, but it may narrow to 5 in active markets. The dealers trade with each other not only directly but also through the brokers, who offer them both information on where the market is and anonymity.

In the U.S. market CD brokers survive to the extent that they serve the CD dealers. In the Euro CD market, in contrast, the brokers and dealers are in part competitors since both deal directly with the banks and both compete directly for U.S. retail business. In a stable market brokers have some advantage over dealers because the total 04 they take from the buyer and seller is only a third of the $1/8$ spread that normally prevails between dealers' bid and asked quotes in the secondary market. On the other hand, if interest rates are falling and the banks are not writing, the dealers who have inventory are where the market is, for buyers at least. Also, if rates are rising, a customer who wants to sell may find that his best market is with the dealer from whom he bought, since that dealer will feel obligated to make him a reasonable bid.

Liquidity

While there is an active secondary market in Euro CDs, their liquidity—measured in terms of spreads between bid and asked quotes and volume that can be done at these quotes—is significantly less than that of domestic CDs. The reason is that the volume of Euro CDs outstanding is relatively small, and much of it is lock-up paper. In the Euro CD market, liquidity also depends on name. A seller will get a better quote on top-name paper that is traded among the dealers and can be sold through the brokers than on lesser-name paper that can be resold only to retail.

Communications

The Euro CD market is very much a two-continent market, with active trading in both London and New York. That such a market can exist is a tribute to modern communications techniques. Dealers show markets into Europe and the United States on a Reuters system much like the domestic Telerate system. To communicate across the Atlantic they use open telephone lines and dedicated Telex machines.

CDs versus time deposits

Most lending by banks in the Euromarket to other banks is currently done through the placing of time deposits rather than the purchase of CDs. For the lending bank, time deposits have two disadvantages: they are illiquid and they tie up the lines that each bank sets up to limit its exposure by country and by bank. Because of these disadvantages, some market participants feel that CD purchases will eventually displace deposit placements in the interbank market. If this were to happen, however, the discount at which banks can currently buy money in the Euro CD market would be eliminated, a development the banks are not yet prepared to accept.

Chapter 16

The Euro time deposit market

Broker: I'm $^7/_8$–$^3/_4$ in the one month. Do you do anything?
Dealer: I'll support you at $^7/_8$, and I'm in there for size.

Such is the chatter that fills the phone lines over which Euro time deposits are traded.

ROUND THE GLOBE MARKET

The market for Eurocurrency deposits follows the sun around the globe. On a working day it starts, due to the position of the international date line down the middle of the Pacific, at 9:00 A.M. local time in Singapore. Singapore is the major but not the only Southeast Asian center for trading in Eurocurrencies. Hong Kong is also an important center and some trading occurs in Kuala Lumpur. The banks that are active in the Singapore market, mostly foreign banks and in particular the big U.S. banks, do some trading there that is "a natural" against business in Southeast Asia, i.e., funding loans to finance and accepting deposits generated by economic activity in that area. Such activity, while growing, is still small compared with that in Europe and the United States, so much less natural business is done in Singapore than in London or New York.

427

A lot of the trading by banks in Singapore involves position taking against what will happen later in the day. In such trading, Singapore owes its importance to its strategic position geographically. It is instrumental in starting off each trading day because it is the first center in which the banks can react in volume to anything that might have happened after the New York close—a late economic announcement in the United States or an international incident such as war in the Middle East.

After the Euromarket opens in Southeast Asia, the next important centers to enter the market are those in the Middle East, Bahrain in particular. Here again natural activity is limited. Arab money is placed in the Euromarket largely through banks in Paris, London, and elsewhere in Europe; and Bahrain's importance is primarily as a booking center.

London and other European centers, which are the next to open, do so early in order to be able to catch the Singapore close. Singapore tends to be a net taker of funds, and as a result the London market often opens on the firm side due to buying interest from Singapore.

Because of the huge volume of natural activity in Eurocurrencies in London and other European centers, the New York market tends to lean on these markets. It opens early—some New York banks have traders at their desks as early as 5:00 A.M.—and it normally closes at noon as London closes. If, however, something important happens after noon New York time, the New York market works during the afternoon.

From the time New York closes until Singapore opens, the Euromarket goes through its "dark hours." Some trading occurs in San Francisco, the Philippines, and other centers, but the volume is so small that the banks cannot really react in size to any major development until Singapore opens.

THE BROKERS

The major banks in the London market post rates at which they are willing to take Eurodollar deposits of different maturities, and they do pick up a certain amount of money directly, particularly from banks on the continent. Much interbank trading in Euros is, however, done through brokers. Brokers are really a necessity in the Euromarket because the participants in this market are so numerous and are scattered all over the globe.

The brokering of Eurocurrency deposits is dominated by several British firms that have offices in London and other Euro centers. Most of these firms also broker foreign exchange, Euro CDs, and sterling, and each is a substantial operation. The London office of such a firm might, for example, employ as many as 100 brokers. It would have direct phone lines to all the major participants in the London market, an open phone line to New York, and phones and Telexes linking it to participants in other centers. In effect each brokerage firm is selling to its client banks a vast, fast-operating information network, which no bank could duplicate with its own resources.

In this respect it's interesting to note that the British, perceiving the importance of good communications to London as a financial center, have created excellent and relatively cheap phone and Telex facilities to link London with the rest of the world. Domestic communications are another matter. As one market participant noted: "I can always get Singapore or New York in seconds on the phone or the Telex, but if my house caught fire, it might burn down before I could get through to the local fire department."

Brokering Euros, like Fed funds, is a rapid-fire, bang bang, game. It requires total concentration on the part of the broker and an ability to simultaneously listen to the phone with the right ear and keep track with the left of any changes in quotes other brokers in the room shout out. Brokering requires thinking but only of the quickest sort. "The thing that comes closest to it in the United Kingdom is," said the director of a big brokerage outfit, "a British turf accountant [bookie] calling rates across the wire."

In London and many other centers as well, most of the Euro brokers and bank dealers as well turn out to be British and more specifically to be cockneys. For some reason the east end of London, an ordinary working-class area of London, seems, like similar areas in many big cities, to breed the sort of person that brokering and dealing require— one who is quick-witted and has a sense of humor that keeps him from going balmy at the end of a day of pressure. Perhaps another reason for the ubiquitous presence of the cockneys in the market (there's even a cockney dealer in the trading room of the Moscow Narodny Bank's London branch) is the fact that it takes one cockney to understand what another one is saying.

Brokering in the Euro time deposit market is an extremely professional operation. As noted in our discussion of a bank's Euro activities, one of the advantages to a bank of using a broker is anonymity. A large bank in particular can bid for large amounts of funds in this market without pushing up the price, something it could not do if it went direct.

To preserve anonymity it is a cardinal rule among brokers that they never give up the name of a bank bidding for or offering funds until one bank actually initiates a transaction. At that point the broker tells the lender the borrower's name so that the lender can check that his line to the borrower is not full. If it is not, the ethics of the game are that the lender must sell the funds he has offered to the bidding bank, in particular he is not to go around the broker and sell directly to the bidding bank.

Because Euro brokers have a reputation (one not shared by some continental brokers of foreign exchange) for not "blowing around" information on who is bidding and offering in their market, some large banks are willing to be quite open with their broker about what they want to do. A bank dealer, for example, might say to a broker, "In the sixes I want to do a really lumpy piece. What's that market really like? If I took 500 million, would it move against me?" Since a broker monitors the market minute by minute, that's a question to which he can give an informed reply. Thus in the eyes of a lot of bankers and brokers, an open relationship should exist between a good bank and a good broker. Yet that opinion is not universally shared. Many banks never tell their broker what they really want to do.

As we've said, a big part of the broker's job is to provide the banks with an information network. This is a vital service to the banks, and no large bank would start dealing in the morning without first calling the brokers to get a feel for levels and tone in the market. A good broker does more, however, than just quote prices. He works to narrow spreads and create trades by persistence, cajolery, pleading, humor, and any ploy he can come up with.

If, for example, the 1-month were quoted at $4^7/8$ to $^3/4$, the broker might call a bank and say, "Can you close that price for me?" If the bank dealer answered, "I'll pay 13," the market would be at $^7/8–^{13}/_{16}$, and the broker would start calling around to find a bank that would offer below $^7/8$. Suppose he found an offer at $^{27}/_{32}$. Now the bid and the offer would be only $^1/_{32}$ apart. At that point the broker and his colleagues, each of whom might have direct phone lines to a dozen banks, would start "banging around the board" (punching those direct phone line buttons) saying, "Anything in the one's? Nice close price." Eventually some bank would probably bite, and a trade would have been created and done.

Not every brokerage firm covers every bank. The typical brokerage firm may have 30 to 50 big banks that are very important customers and two or three times as many smaller customers that, even though they may deal only a few times a week, are useful because they give the market dealing ability and depth. As one broker noted: "Sometimes when the market seems stuck, a small- or medium-size bank will come up with a bit of natural to do. The resulting trade will set a mood for the market again, and suddenly we have a chain reaction of trades. If we had just a few big banks as customers, we might at times, particularly when the market is moving, be unable to get anything done because the customers would all be facing in the same direction, all be bidders or sellers. The beauty of having so many banks in the market is that their presence guarantees diversity of position and opinion, a condition that ensures a market will function and trade."

When a bank puts a bid or an offer into a broker, it is understood that the quote is good until a trade is made or the bank calls back to say, "I'm off." The broker for his part can be held to any price he quotes as firm provided that a line problem does not tie up a trade. If, for example, Chase London offered to sell 6-month money at the bid rate quoted by a broker, and the bidding bank then told the broker he was off and had forgotten to call, the broker would be committed to *substantiate* his bid by finding Chase a buyer at that price or by selling Chase's money at a lower rate and paying a *difference* equal to the dollar amount Chase would lose by selling at that rate. Because activity in the Euromarket is hectic, mistakes of this sort do occur and they can be expensive; on $5 million for 6 months, even $1/_{16}$ of 1 percent works out to $1,562.50. Since brokers operate on thin margins, a broker wouldn't be around long if he got "stuffed" often; so good brokers take a lot of care to avoid this sort of situation.

Whenever some important news hits the market—Citi raises its prime or whatever—the banks call the brokers to shout "Off, Off!" on their bids and offers, and a broker will quote rates on an "I suggest," "I think," or "I call" basis, which means that a bank can't hold him to these quotes. A sharp break in market activity puts a broker back in the position in which he started the day, with a blank pad. To get trading started again, he has to call around to the bank dealers to find out where they anticipate money will now trade, and then try to find some banks that will substantiate these new levels by making even small bids and offers that are firm.

QUOTES AND MATURITIES

In the market for overnight Federal funds, money is normally traded for immediate delivery. In the Euromarket, in contrast, the delivery date, or *value date* as it is called, is two days hence unless otherwise specified. Thus a spot transaction consummated on, say, a Tuesday would result in funds being delivered on Thursday. The Euromarket, however, also deals in overnight funds for immediate delivery and for delivery the next day. The former sort of transaction is referred to as a deal in *overnight* funds, the latter as a *tom next* (for tomorrow next) transaction in London and as a *rollover* in the United States.

Eurodollar deposits are quoted in the interbank market in a wide range of maturities: overnight, tom next, spot, the week, 1 to 6 months, and 1 to 5 years.

It's possible to carry out Eurodollar transactions in Federal funds (delivery in Fed funds and repayment in Fed funds), but the normal procedure is for payments and receipts of Euros to be made in clearing house funds. The mechanics of and the rationale for clearing Euro transactions through the New York Clearing House are described below. The important thing to note at this point is that clearing house funds differ from Fed funds in that they turn into immediately available funds, that is, Fed funds, only on the day after the delivery or value date. The distinction that exists in the Eurodollar market between the value date and the day on which good funds are available to the recipient creates, as described in Chapter 17, the basis for some very actively pursued technical arbitrages between Fed funds and short-dated Euros.

As a result of such arbitrages, the value to a U.S. bank of a Eurodollar deposit purchased is influenced by whether the deposit starts on a Friday, which makes it less valuable, or ends on a Friday, which makes it more valuable. Moreover, because of this distinction in value, there are special quotes for Thursday/Friday Euros and for weekend Euros. Also there is a distinction in quotes for the *fixed dates* (one month to one year) between those for *neutral periods,* those which have neither a Friday start nor a Friday finish, and those which do. This in turn means that there may be more than one quote for a given fixed date. For example, on a day when the 1-month period starting 2 days hence has a Friday start or a Friday finish, there will be a quote for the spot 1-month and another for the neutral 1-month; the latter period will be more whose start end are both within a day or two of the start and end of the spot 1-month.

For the neophyte in the Euromarket, getting from neutral quotes to spot quotes takes a little calculation. Not so for Euro dealers and brokers, who can move from one to the other in lightning speed. Once a good broker knows the "straight run" (the rates quoted for neutral dates), he can calculate in his head rates for periods off the run and in particular for nonneutral fixed dates.

Euros are quoted in 32nds, and spreads between the bid and the asked can range anywhere from $1/32$ in short-dated funds to $1/4$ or more in the longer dates. London quotes the rates "tops and bottoms," that is, the offered rate and then the bid rate. New York does the reverse for reasons now shrouded in history.

Euro brokers work for very small commissions, which are paid by both sides in a transaction and are calculated as a certain percentage per day of the amount traded. In London, brokerage is 0.020 percent on an annual basis; in New York, 0.0225 percent. The New York rate, which is higher, works out to $0.625 per $1 million per day, which means that brokers have to do many hundreds of millions of dollars of business a day to survive. Brokerage is higher in New York than in London because the New York market is less active than the London market. Presumably as activity increases in New York, brokerage there will fall to the London rate.

On occasion in the Euromarket, one encounters a situation in which the bid and asked rates are identical—what a Euro broker would call an *either-way market.* Since brokerage is paid by both the buyer and the seller in the Euromarket, an either-way market can occur only when the market in a given tenor gets "hung up on lines." For example, suppose Dresdner were offering $5 million of 1-month money through a broker and that Toronto Dominion decided to take this money. The broker would call

Dresdner and say, "OK, we will pay at your price," Dresdner would then ask, "Who is it?" and the broker would say, "Toronto Dominion." At that point Dresdner might say, "Done for 5," or "I'm full on that name," or "All I can do for him is two." In either of the last two cases, Dresdner would still have dollars to sell, Toronto Dominion would still have dollars to buy, and the two might end up quoting identical bid and offer rates.

The minimum size in which brokers of Eurodollars will deal is $1 million, but most trades are larger. In the market for overnight and short-dated funds, trades of $10, $20, $50, and even $100 million are common. In the fixed dates, trades of $20 million are considered good size with the average being more like $4 or $5 million.

Normally activity in the Euromarket is heaviest in the 6-month and under maturity range, since most of the assets Euro bankers are funding are either short in tenor or roll every 3 to 6 months. When borrowers anticipate that rates might rise and the yield curve is not too steep, activity will be centered in the 6-month area because borrowers will opt for a 6-month roll. If, alternatively, rates are expected to drop or remain stable, activity will be relatively strong in the 3-month area. Trades of very long-dated funds, up to 5 years, do occur in the interbank market, but normally they are not done through brokers because brokerage is high on a substantial trade of such long-dated funds.

Naturally brokers prefer trades in the longer dates to those in the shorter dates. But they try to give all their customers, including heavy traders in overnight funds, good service on the theory that if they support a bank in the short dates, they will occasionally get in on the gravy train when the bank trades longer-dated funds in the brokers market.

Eurodollar deposits are not a homogeneous commodity. They differ with respect not only to maturity but also to the credit risk associated with the name of the buying bank. Thus there is a tiering of quotes according not only to maturity but also to which bank is buying. In particular, for any maturity it is understood that bids in the brokers market are those of top-name banks, unless otherwise specified. Much of the time top British, Canadian, French, and German banks can buy funds at the same rates at which the top U.S. banks do, but on occasion they may have to pay an extra $1/16$ or so. Banks outside this elite group will consistently have to pay up, the amount being a function of their name and market conditions. Also branches of even the best-regarded banks, if they are located in centers to which the market attaches greater sovereign risk than it does to London, may have to pay a $1/16$ or so more than their London sister does.

As we've said, brokers never divulge the names of the banks that have placed bids and offers with them, but to cope with the problems posed by lines, names, and locations, they sprinkle their runs with bits of information that can be helpful to the bank to whom they are quoting the run.

For example, a broker might note that the bid in a given tenor was by a "prime name out of Hong Kong" or that the offer in some other tenor was from a "rather difficult lender," that is, one with lines to a limited number of banks.

To be as informative as possible, the brokers also throw in with their regular quotes some hints as to what is being done or could be done in the market. For example, a broker might note, "The threes are 6 $3/16$–$5/16$ but may come at $1/4$," or "Wednesday/Thursday funds are bid $7/16$ out of London and Bahrain and come OK at $1/2$." The variations are endless, but the point is that a good broker does more than just quote rates. He tries to give his client banks at a rapid-fire pace all the useful information he can.

CLEARING THROUGH CHIPS

In Chapter 6, in order to keep things simple we ignored the fact that Eurodollar transactions clear not over the Fed wire but through the New York Clearing House. Because this distinction creates the possibility for technical arbitrages between Fed funds and Euros, it has to be explored.

The New York Clearing House, which is one of the oldest and most prominent clearing houses in the country, was set up to provide a mechanism for clearing both customer checks and bank official checks. Since the institution of the Fed wire, the bulk of the funds New York banks exchange among themselves now go over that wire, but the Clearing House has assumed an important new function, *clearing Eurodollar payments* between domestic and foreign banks.

Almost every Euro transaction creates the need for an interbank payment. In the old days New York banks made such payments by issuing official checks, which were cleared through the New York Clearing House. A big New York bank might both issue and receive 1,500 or more official checks a day. Thus the clearing process was tedious, expensive, and involved a huge amount of paper work. Despite the enormity of the job to be done, checks received by the Clearing House were normally *cleared* on the same day so that *settlement* in Fed funds could be made between the banks on a timely basis the next day. Sometimes, however, checks got lost and clearing them could take three or even four days.

To reduce the unnecessary float such delays caused, the Fed strongly urged the New York Clearing House banks to set up a computerized communications network to handle interbank money transfers. This system, *CHIPS,* an acronym for *Clearing House Interbank Payments System,* went on-line with live transactions in April 1970. Participants in the CHIPS system include all ten New York Clearing House banks and about 60 other New York banking institutions that are associate members; the ranks of the latter include foreign bank branches, foreign agency banks, and Edge Act corporations set up by domestic banks.

Every participant in the CHIPS system has a terminal computer linked by leased telephone lines to the central CHIPS computer, through which it can directly send to and receive from CHIPS payments messages. The central CHIPS computer immediately processes all such messages. Then, at the end of the day, it produces item-by-item detailed reports of payments made to and received by each participating bank. Also, by netting debits and credits, it figures each participating bank's net position vis à vis every other participating bank and the system as a whole. On the first business day following clearing, the ten Clearing House banks settle with each other in Federal funds through adjustments in their reserve accounts. Associate members of CHIPS settle through adjustments in the balances they hold with designated Clearing House banks. The CHIPS system as it now operates is so efficient that it clears $50+ billion of payments per day without any of the delays and difficulties that used to occur under the old manual system.

SWIFT

Until recently it was common for banks to use Telex and other common carrier systems to transmit among each other payments instructions for international transactions that were eventually cleared through CHIPS. In 1973 the leading international banks began planning a *private* bank communications network called SWIFT, an acronym for Society for Worldwide Interbank Financial Telecommunications. SWIFT, a computerized message switch, is owned by the 450 banks—located in Europe, the United Kingdom, the United States, and Canada—that currently subscribe to the system. SWIFT first went live on a limited basis in Europe in 1977. It was then extended to North America, and expansion to the Far East was planned.

The major advantage of SWIFT is that it has a strict format requirement for messages. This makes it possible for subscribing banks to construct a computerized interface that will key messages transmitted via SWIFT directly into the CHIPS system. This change eliminates clerical processing of Telex messages and thus streamlines for subscribing banks the making and receiving of payments through CHIPS.

The clearing process in T-accounts

In Table 6–1, we worked through an example in which a Euro deposit was made and cleared. Had the transaction been made in Federal funds, as a few Euro transactions are, the table would have been complete and the deposit-accepting bank would in fact have received Fed funds on the day of the deposit.

Almost all Euro transactions are, however, cleared through CHIPS, and a bank accepting a Euro deposit therefore gets not Fed funds, but

Table 16–1
A Euro deposit is made and cleared through CHIPS

Day 1: Euro deposit made

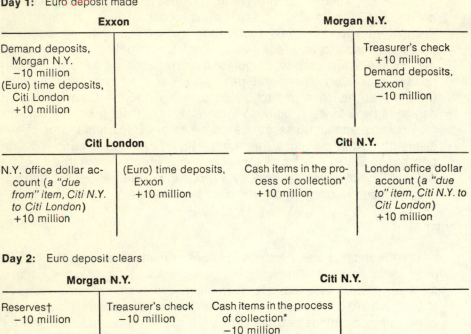

Exxon		Morgan N.Y.	

Demand deposits,
  Morgan N.Y.
  −10 million
(Euro) time deposits,
  Citi London
  +10 million
			Treasurer's check
			  +10 million
			Demand deposits,
			  Exxon
			  −10 million

Citi London		Citi N.Y.	

N.Y. office dollar ac-
  count (*a "due
  from" item, Citi N.Y.
  to Citi London*)
  +10 million
	(Euro) time deposits,
	  Exxon
	  +10 million
		Cash items in the pro-
		  cess of collection*
		  +10 million
			London office dollar
			  account (*a "due
			  to" item, Citi N.Y. to
			  Citi London*)
			  +10 million

Day 2: Euro deposit clears

Morgan N.Y.		Citi N.Y.	

Reserves†
  −10 million
	Treasurer's check
	  −10 million
		Cash items in the process
		  of collection*
		  −10 million
		Reserves†
		  +10 million	

New York Fed	

	Reserves,† Morgan N.Y.
	  −10 million
	Reserves,† Citi N.Y.
	  +10 million

* In this situation *cash items in the process of collection* are clearing house funds.
† Reserves are Federal funds.

clearing house funds on the day the deposit is received, that is, it gets a credit at the New York Clearing House. Clearing house funds become good funds on the first business day after clearing, when banks settle in Fed funds the debits created by clearing.

Just how this process affects the balance sheet entries that result from a Euro deposit is illustrated in Table 16–1. This table assumes, as did Table 6–1, that Exxon exchanges a demand deposit at Morgan New York for a Euro deposit at Citi London. When on day 1 of the clearing process Morgan receives Exxon's request to transfer funds from its account at Morgan to an account at Citi London, Morgan debits Exxon's account and issues a $10 million *Treasurer's check* through CHIPS to Citibank. This check is entered as a reservable deposit on Morgan's balance sheet so long as it is outstanding. Citi London receives, as before, the Exxon deposit and simultaneously gets a $10 million credit to its dollar account with head office. On the balance sheet of Citi New York, this rise in liabilities is offset by a $10 million increase in "cash items in the process of collection," an increase that represents the credit Citi receives at the New York Clearing House as a result of the payment Morgan has made to it through CHIPS. On day 2 of the clearing process, which is the next business day, Morgan and Citi settle (see the second half of Table 16–1) in Fed funds.

SWAPS—THE MECHANICS

A substantial part of the total Eurocurrency market represents, as we've said, deposits of nondollar currencies. Euro deposits denominated in currencies other than the dollar are actively traded in the interbank market in the same way that dollars are. The only significant difference is that the volume of trading in them is much smaller than the volume of trading in dollars.

Some of the trading in Eurocurrency deposits is generated by swaps, which, as noted in Chapter 6, are extensively used by banks to match assets and liabilities in their Euro books by currency and to create deposits in a desired currency as cheaply as possible. Not surprisingly the movement from fixed to floating exchange rates in recent years has changed somewhat the environment in which swaps occur. Due to the increased volume of hedging, forward markets have improved and bid–asked spreads in the foreign exchange market have, if anything, diminished. These developments favor the use of swaps. However, floating rates have also created a situation in which adjustments are made much more rapidly. If a rate gets out of line, creating a possibility for profitable arbitrage, someone will hit it quickly and put it back in line. Thus the opportunities available to a bank to cut funding costs by using swaps to create currency deposits are more evanescent than they used to be and where they are varies tremendously.

In Chapter 6 we described how a swap (*switch* to the British) operates in intuitive terms, but we did not derive a formula for calculating the all-in interest cost of funds generated through a swap. The easiest way to do that is by working through an example.

Swap: Dollars into DM

Suppose a bank that has committed itself to lend 6-month Euro DM is now faced with the task of funding this loan. It could take in the funds *natural,* that is, take a 6-month DM deposit, or it could take 6-month dollars and swap them into DM. To determine which approach is cheaper, the bank dealer has to calculate the *all-in* rate of interest the bank would have to pay on DM obtained through a swap and compare that with the interest cost on a natural DM deposit.

The all-in interest cost on a currency deposit obtained by swapping another currency into that currency is, as noted in Chapter 6, the interest cost on the original deposit *minus* the gain (*plus* the loss) on the swap calculated as an annualized percentage rate. A swap is a sell-now-buy-back-later transaction, for example, like shorting Ford stock in February and covering in June. On swap transactions the percentage rate of gain or loss is calculated as:

$$\frac{\text{Selling price} - \text{Buying price}}{\text{Selling price}}$$

Since in the swap at hand (dollars into DM) the bank is going to sell dollars spot and buy them back forward, the percentage rate of gain or loss on the swap can be expressed as follows:

$$\frac{\left(\begin{array}{l}\text{Selling price of \$s} \\ \text{in the spot market}\end{array}\right) - \left(\begin{array}{l}\text{Buying price of \$s} \\ \text{in the forward market}\end{array}\right)}{\left(\begin{array}{l}\text{Selling price of \$s} \\ \text{in the spot market}\end{array}\right)}$$

The rate given by this expression is the percentage rate of gain (loss) on the swap over the life of the swap. If the swap is for a period less than a year, as in our example, this figure will understate the annualized rate of gain or loss. To see why, note that if it were possible to earn a 2 percent gain on a 6-month swap, then repeating that swap twice during the year would result in a total gain of 4 percent over the year. To calculate the *annualized* rate of gain (loss) on a swap that extends less than a year, we have to divide the expression for the actual percentage gain (loss) on the swap by the fraction of the year that the swap is outstanding.

Let

$$t = \text{Days the swap is outstanding}$$

Then with rates quoted on a 360-day-year basis,

$$\begin{array}{l}\text{Annualized \% gain (loss)} \\ \text{on a swap of \$s into DM}\end{array} = \frac{\text{Selling price of \$s} - \text{Buying price of \$s}}{\text{Selling price of \$s}} \div \frac{t}{360}$$

If the spot rate for DM is quoted in the United States as 0.4375, that means it takes \$0.4375 to buy a deutsche mark.[1] Since the spot rate

---

[1] When a foreign currency is quoted in terms of the amount of local currency required to buy a unit of foreign currency, this is called a *direct quote.* In our example,

for DM is expressed in units of dollars per DM, it is the buying price of DM. To get the selling price of dollars, which we need to calculate the cost of the swap in our example, we have to invert the spot rate. For example, with the spot rate at 0.4375, the selling price of dollars is

$$\frac{1}{\$0.4375/DM} = 2.2857 \text{ DM/\$}$$

Let

$S = $ *Spot rate* for DM quoted in U.S. terms
$F = $ *Forward rate* for DM quoted in U.S. terms

Then in a swap of dollars for DM,

$$\text{The selling price of \$s} = \frac{1}{S}$$

$$\text{The buying price of \$s} = \frac{1}{F}$$

Substituting these values into the formula derived above, we get

$$\begin{array}{c} \text{Annualized \% gain (loss)} \\ \text{on a swap of \$s into DM} \end{array} = \frac{\frac{1}{S} - \frac{1}{F}}{\frac{1}{S}} \div \frac{t}{360}$$

$$= \left(1 - \frac{S}{F}\right)\left(\frac{360}{t}\right)$$

Above we said that the all-in interest cost of DM obtained through a swap equals the interest paid on the dollars borrowed *minus* the annualized rate of gain on the swap. Let

$i_{DM} = $ The all-in interest cost of the DM generated through a swap out of dollars
$r_\$ = $ The interest rate paid on the dollars swapped into DM

---

the rate 0.4375 is the U.S. direct quote for DM. The German direct quote for the dollar would be inverse of this rate, i.e.,

$$\text{German direct quote for \$s} = \frac{1}{0.4375 \text{ \$/DM}} = 2.2857 \text{ DM/\$}$$

In most countries, foreign exchange rates are quoted the direct way. The United Kingdom is, however, an exception. There rates are quoted the *indirect* way, which means that a British foreign exchange trader would, for example, quote the exchange rate between dollars and pounds in terms of the number of dollars required to buy one pound sterling. Note that this corresponds to the U.S. direct quote on pounds.

Then in symbols[2]

$$i_{DM} = r_\$ - \left(1 - \frac{S}{F}\right)\left(\frac{360}{t}\right) = r_\$ + \left(\frac{S}{F} - 1\right)\left(\frac{360}{t}\right)$$

To illustrate how this formula is used, let's work through a numerical example in which 6-month dollars are swapped into 6-month DM. Assume that the spot rate is 0.4375, the forward rate is 0.4455 (the forward mark is at a premium), the interest cost of 6-month Euro-dollars is 7.625 percent, and the bid-asked quotes on 6-month Euro DM are 4–4⅛ percent. Plugging the first three of these numbers (they are all quotes that prevailed one noon in the market) into our formula for i_{DM}, we get:

$$\begin{aligned}i_{DM} &= 0.07625 + \left(\frac{0.4375}{0.4455} - 1\right)\left(\frac{360}{180}\right) \\ &= 0.07625 - 0.03592 \\ &= 0.04033 \\ &= 4.033\%\end{aligned}$$

In following this calculation, note that because the forward DM was selling at a premium, the swap results in a gain. The annualized cost of the swap is thus negative and adding it to $r_\$$ reduces i_{DM} below $r_\$$, so far below $r_\$$ that borrowing expensive dollars and swapping them into DM turns out to be less expensive than buying 6-month DM at the offered rate of 4⅛ percent. Often in actively traded currencies the cost of a Eurocurrency deposit obtained through a swap lies in the mid-range of bid and offer quotes in the interbank market for deposits of that currency in that tenor.

Swap: DM into dollars

Swaps, of course, are done not only out of dollars into a foreign currency but also out of foreign currencies into dollars. Had, for example, the swap been DM into dollars, then we would have been interested in the all-in interest cost of the dollars obtained through the swap. That rate can be calculated as follows. Let

$i_\$$ = The all-in interest cost of the dollars generated through a swap out of DM

r_{DM} = The interest rate paid on the DM swapped into dollars

---

[2] This formula does not take into account the impact of hedging interest which is earned in DM and paid out in dollars.

Then

$$i_\$ = r_{\mathrm{DM}} + \left(\frac{F}{S} - 1\right)\left(\frac{360}{t}\right)$$

In this discussion of swaps we have consistently assumed that the mark was the foreign currency involved in the swap. The formulas we have derived are, however, naturally valid for a swap between dollars and any other Eurocurrency.

Arbitrage

Arbitrage strictly defined involves buying at a low price in one market and selling simultaneously at a higher price in a second market. Swaps in the Eurocurrency deposit market are nothing but a form of arbitrage, one that is so widely practiced that it creates, except under unusual conditions, a very consistent relationship in each maturity range between (1) the interest differential at which deposits of a given currency trade relative to Eurodollar deposits and (2) the premium or discount at which that currency trades relative to the dollar in the forward market for foreign exchange.[3]

While it is true that a dollar is a dollar, there are, as noted in Chapters 5 and 6, subtle differences to U.S. banks between Eurodollars and domestic dollars because of reserve requirements and other institutional factors. Thus, to some degree the Eurodollar market is separate from the domestic money market, a situation which creates the possibility for arbitrages between the two. The next chapter describes these arbitrages and the effect they have on the relationship between U.S. and Euro rates.

---

[3] The difference between the spot and forward rates at which a currency trades ($S - F$) is called the *swap rate.* Whenever short-term interest rates are lower on deposits of a nondollar Eurocurrency than they are on Eurodollar deposits, the swap rate on that currency quoted in U.S. terms will be *negative,* i.e., that currency will trade at a forward premium. Moreover, because of the activities of arbitragers—institutions seeking to borrow at one rate and lend at a higher one—the size of the premium will be such that the cost of borrowing that currency and swapping it into dollars will be equal or very nearly equal to the cost of borrowing dollars. Note that in our example of swapping dollars into DM, the interest rate on 6-month DM was lower than that on 6-month dollars, and the swap rate was accordingly negative

$$0.4375 - 0.4455 = -0.0080$$

Because the swap rate is the difference between the spot rate and a specific forward rate, its size depends on the tenor of the swap transaction.

Whenever short-term interest rates are higher on deposits of a nondollar Eurocurrency than they are on Eurodollar deposits, the arbitrage will work the opposite way, making the all-in cost of borrowing dollars and swapping them into that Eurocurrency approximately equal to the cost of borrowing that currency directly.

Chapter 17

Arbitrages between the U.S. market and the Euromarket

FIGURES 17–1 to 17–3, which plot U.S. and Euro rates in different maturity ranges, show that with the exception of overnight funds, Euro rates tend to be higher than U.S. rates most of the time.

The explanation is simple. At any one time there is a certain worldwide supply of dollars available to banks. A portion of these dollars are held by foreign institutions and other foreign investors, some of which prefer to deposit their dollars outside the United States. The majority, however, are held by U.S. investors. Many of the latter feel that placing dollars in the Euromarket exposes them to a significant sovereign risk, and they can therefore be induced to do so only if they are offered a premium rate on Euro deposits.

U.S. banks operating in both markets could attempt to get around the higher cost of Eurodollars by taking deposits in the domestic market and using them to fund their Euro operations, and at times they do. However, the full cost of the deposits they purchase in the domestic market exceeds the nominal interest rate they pay because of FDIC insurance and reserve costs. Thus, nominal Euro rates have to rise above domestic rates before the all-in cost of Euro deposits exceeds that of domestic deposits to U.S. banks. Foreign banks do not incur FDIC and reserve costs on funds they source in the U.S. money market, but they do have to

Figure 17–1
Overnight rates, Euros and Fed funds

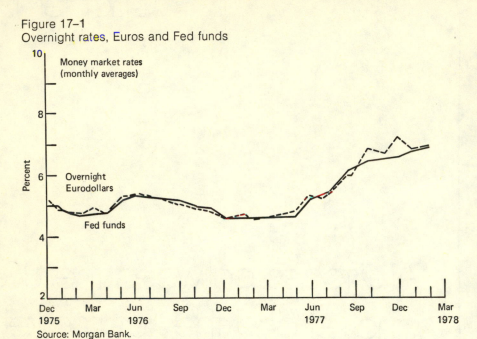

Source: Morgan Bank.

pay up in the U.S. market; also their ability to buy funds in this market is limited.

A second interesting feature shown in Figures 17–1 to 17–3 is the startling way in which U.S. and Eurodollar rates in differing maturity ranges track each other over time. Spreads widen and narrow and sometimes rates cross, but the main trends up and down are the same in both markets. There's no doubt that this consistency in rates is the work of arbitrage, but that still leaves open the question of where the major impetus for rate changes typically comes from. Are changes in U.S. rates pushing Euro rates up and down, or vice versa? A British Eurobanker succinctly answered that question: "The U.S. money market is the dog, the Euromarket the tail. Rarely does the tail wag the dog."

The truth of this statement has created a whole new set of Fed watchers—bankers in London, Paris, Singapore, and other Euro centers. Much as some of these bankers, especially foreign ones, would like to think of the Euromarket as an international market that responds largely to developments external to the U.S. economy, experience has taught them that whenever the Fed moves, its actions immediately affect the Euromarket. Consequently to be successful, Euro bankers have to understand the workings of the U.S. money market and follow closely developments there.

Figure 17–2
Yields on 3-month CDs, Euro and U.S.

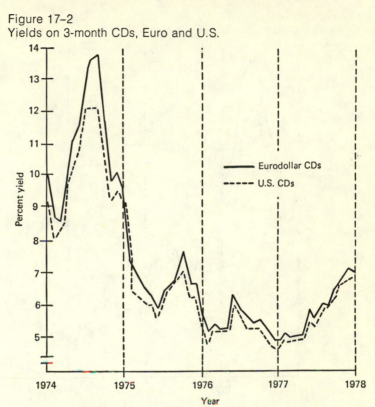

Source: *An Analytic Record of Yields and Spreads*, Salomon Brothers.

Two sorts of arbitrages link U.S. and Euro rates, *technical* and *transitory*. Technical arbitrages are most important at the short end of the market, and opportunities for them occur because of the way Euro transactions affect, due to institutional arrangements, the reservable deposits of U.S. banks buying and selling Eurodollars.

Transitory arbitrages, in contrast, are money flows that occur in response to temporary discrepancies that arise between U.S. and Euro rates because rates in the two markets are being affected by differing supply and demand pressures. Much transitory arbitrage is carried on by banks that actively borrow and lend funds in both markets. An example of such *intrabank arbitrage* would be a bank that responded to a relatively high rate on 6-month Euros by buying money of that tenor in the U.S. market and lending it in the Euromarket. Another group whose activities tend to pull together U.S. and Euro rates are investors who shift from domestic to Euro CDs and back in response to changing yield spreads. Finally, there is a small but growing number of borrowers who shift between the domestic and the Euromarkets in response to changes

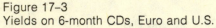

Figure 17–3
Yields on 6-month CDs, Euro and U.S.

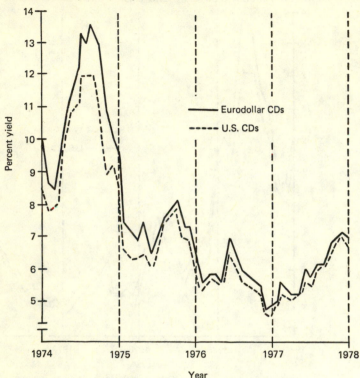

Year

Source: *An Analytic Record of Yields and Spreads,* Salomon Brothers.

in the relationship between lending rates in the two markets. Their activities too hold rates together.

RESERVE EFFECTS OF EURO TRANSACTIONS

When a domestic bank arbitrages between the domestic and the Euromarkets, it is always concerned with all-in cost and total return. An important element in the calculation of both is the effect that Euro lendings and borrowings have on the reserves that a domestic bank must maintain with the Fed.

As noted in Chapter 15, during 1969 U.S. money market rates rose above the Reg Q ceiling on the rate that U.S. banks could pay on large-denomination CDs. As a result money flowed out of the U.S. market into the Euromarket, and U.S. banks were forced to buy back that money from the Euromarket to fund their domestic operations. To thwart the backflow of funds from the Euromarket to the U.S. market, the Fed imposed under *Regulations D* and *M* a requirement that member banks hold reserves against Eurodollars borrowed by head office either from their own foreign branches or from foreign banks. Currently, Regs D and M, which have been subject to considerable change over time, require U.S. banks to hold reserves equal to 4 percent of their *net borrowings* from the Euromarket calculated over a 28-day averaging period.

A bank's Euro lendings and borrowings affect the reserves it must keep with the Fed not only because of Regs D and M, but also because of their impact on the bank's reservable domestic deposits as calculated by the Fed. To see this as well as the effect of Regs D and M, let's work through a simple example in which we assume that a New York bank borrows *overnight* Euros on Monday and repays them on Tuesday. Once the principles involved are understood, the time period of the taking or placing can be extended to any *neutral* period, that is, any period that does not start or finish on a Friday or the day before a holiday.

In Table 17-1 we assume that on Monday Chase New York borrows $20 million from the Euromarket, that is, buys a dollar deposit from an offshore bank or branch. This results in it receiving a $20 million credit in CHIPS, which shows up on the asset side of Chase's balance sheet as a $20 million increase in "cash items in the process of collection." On

Table 17-1
An overnight Euro borrowing (neutral basis)

Day 1: Monday

Chase N.Y.

Cash items in the process of collection +20 million	Euro borrowing +20 million

Day 2: Tuesday

Chase N.Y.

Fed funds +20 million Cash items in the process of collection −20 million	Euro borrowing −20 million Treasurer's check +20 million

Day 3: Wednesday

Chase N.Y.

Fed funds −20 million	Treasurer's check −20 million

Tuesday this CHIPS credit is settled in Fed funds, which causes Chase's holdings of Fed funds to rise by $20 million while cash items in the process of collection decrease by $20 million. On Tuesday Chase also repays its Euro borrowing (which goes off its books) by issuing a $20 million Treasurer's check to the lending bank through CHIPS. This results in Chase having a debit with CHIPS, which it settles on Wednesday in Fed funds; when it does so, the Treasurer's check goes off Chase's books, and Chase loses $20 million of Fed funds.

The effect of Chase's Euro borrowing on the reserves that it must hold against domestic deposits is zero on a net basis but not on a day-to-day basis. When a bank calculates its required reserves, the Fed permits it to subtract uncollected items from the domestic demand deposits it has received, the premise being that a bank should not be required to hold reserves on deposits against which it has not yet received good funds. These uncollected items show up on a bank's balance sheet as cash items in the process of collection. A bank, on the other hand, is required to hold reserves against any Treasurer's checks it issues so long as funds have not been collected against them, that is, as long as they are on the bank's books. Thus the effect of Chase's overnight Euro borrowing is to reduce its reservable demand deposits by $20 million on Monday and to increase them by a similar amount on Tuesday. There is no effect on Wednesday.

Currently large banks are required to hold reserves equal to 16¼ percent against demand deposits. Also, as noted in Chapter 11, a bank's current week's deposits determine the reserves it must hold two weeks later. Thus Chase's Euro borrowing, by reducing reservable deposits on Monday and thereby reducing for one day Chase's required reserves, gives Chase the use during a subsequent reserve period of an extra $3.25 million of Fed funds for one day. (The calculation is: 16¼% × $20 million = $3.25 million.) However, since the Treasurer's check Chase issues is reservable, on Tuesday exactly the opposite occurs; Chase loses for one day during a subsequent reserve period the use of $3.25 million of Fed funds.

So far as the reserves that Chase must hold against its Euro borrowing are concerned, they may range from 0 to 4 percent. What they are depends, because they are calculated on a net basis, on how much Chase lends into the Euromarket. Generally money market banks have so much flexibility that they can offset their borrowings (takings) from the Euromarket with lendings (placements) there, so net under Regs M and D they incur no required reserves on such borrowings.

To show how a neutral Euro placement (a deposit sale) affects a domestic bank's required reserves, we have to work through the effects on the bank's balance sheet of such a placement. Table 17–2 does that. There we assume that Chase New York lends on Tuesday $20 million of

Table 17–2
An overnight Euro lending (neutral basis)
Day 1: Tuesday

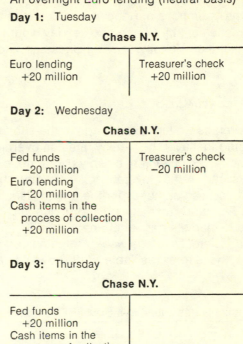

Chase N.Y.	

Euro lending
  +20 million
	Treasurer's check
	  +20 million

Day 2: Wednesday

Chase N.Y.	

Fed funds
  −20 million
Euro lending
  −20 million
Cash items in the
  process of collection
  +20 million
	Treasurer's check
	  −20 million

Day 3: Thursday

Chase N.Y.	

Fed funds
  +20 million
Cash items in the
  process of collection
  −20 million	

overnight (Tuesday/Wednesday) funds to an offshore bank or branch. To pay out the loan proceeds, Chase issues a Treasurer's check through CHIPS. On Wednesday, this check clears and Chase loses $20 million of Fed funds. On the same day the foreign bank repays its borrowing from Chase by issuing to Chase a check through CHIPS. This payment causes the $20 million Euro loan to go off Chase's books, and it adds $20 million of cash items in the process of collection to Chase's assets. Thursday, the final day of the transaction, the foreign bank's check to Chase is settled and Chase trades one asset, cash items in the process of collection, for another, Fed funds.

The effect of this transaction, like that of the Euro borrowing we worked through in Table 17–1, on the reserves that Chase must hold against domestic deposits is zero on a net basis but not on a day-to-day basis. The reason is that the Treasurer's check that Chase issues on Tuesday adds $20 million to its reservable demand deposits for that day, while the $20 million increase that occurs on Wednesday in

Chase's cash items in the process of collection reduces for that day its reservable demand deposits by a like amount.

So far as the operations of Regs M and D are concerned, note that a $20 million placement by Chase on Tuesday would precisely offset the $20 million taking on Monday, leaving Chase with no reserve liability on that borrowing.

TECHNICAL ARBITRAGES

With that preface we turn to arbitrage at the short end of the market. It is not surprising that average weekly rates on overnight Eurodollars and Fed funds track each other very closely over time, since U.S. banks and foreign banks can in their overall dollar funding operations substitute purchases of one sort of money for the other. Also, banks can arbitrage the Euro and Fed funds markets, buying in one and selling in the other if rates in the two markets get out of line.

However consistent *average weekly* rates on Fed funds and overnight Euros may be, these rates (as Table 17–3 shows) display on a day-to-day

Table 17–3
U.S. and Euro overnight rates during a week when Fed funds were trading at 5⅜ percent

	Mon/Tues	Tues/Wed	Wed/Thurs	Thurs/Fri	Fri/Mon	Average rate for the week*
Fed funds	5³/₈	5³/₈	5³/₈	5³/₈	5³/₈	5.375
Overnight Eurodollars	5³/₈	5³/₈	5³/₈	15¹/₂	2³/₁₆	5.527

* To determine the average rate on overnight Eurodollars, the sum of the five weekday rates must be divided by 7 because, as shown in Table 17–5, a purchase of Thurs/Fri Euros provides the buyer with good funds (Fed funds) for three days.

basis some startling discrepancies, which moreover follow a consistent weekly pattern. Normally overnight Euros sold on Thursday (Thursday/Friday Euros) trade at slightly less than three times the prevailing Fed funds rate, while Friday/Monday Euros trade at slightly more than one third of the Fed funds rate. These discrepancies in rates, which seem surprising at first glance, are the result of easily explained technical arbitrages that are regularly carried out each week by U.S. and foreign banks.

Weekend arbitrage

To see what's going on, let's start with *weekend arbitrage.* We suppose (see Table 17–4) that Chase New York takes on Friday for repayment

Table 17–4
Weekend arbitrage
Friday:

Chase N.Y.

Cash items in the process of collection +10 million	Due to Bank of Montreal (a Euro borrowing) +10 million

Bank of Montreal

Due from Chase N.Y. +10 million	Clearing House overdraft +100 million

Saturday/Sunday: No change

Monday:

Chase N.Y.

Cash items in process of collection −10 million Fed funds +10 million	Due to Bank of Montreal −10 million Treasurer's check +10 million

Bank of Montreal

Due from Chase N.Y. −10 million Credit at the Clearing House +10 million	Clearing House overdraft −10 million Fed funds purchased +10 million

Tuesday:

Chase N.Y.

Fed funds −10 million	Treasurer's check −10 million

Bank of Montreal

Credit at the Clearing House −10 million	Fed funds purchased −10 million

on Monday a $10 million deposit of Eurodollars from the Bank of Montreal through the latter's New York agency. The transaction is cleared through CHIPS in the normal way. Thus on Friday Chase New York experiences a $10 million increase in cash items on the process of collection, while the Bank of Montreal goes into a $10 million overdraft at the Clearing House. Since the markets are closed on Saturday and Sunday, these balance sheet changes persist over the weekend.

On Monday the Bank of Montreal uses $10 million of Fed funds it has purchased to cover its overdraft at the Clearing House. Chase meanwhile, through the normal settlement procedure, receives that $10 million of Fed funds and experiences simultaneously a $10 million decrease in cash items in the process of collection. On the same day, Chase New York issues a Treasurer's check to repay its borrowing from the Bank of Montreal. Clearing that check gives the Bank of Montreal a $10 million credit with CHIPS.

On Tuesday, the final day of the transaction, Chase settles through CHIPS with the Bank of Montreal by giving that bank $10 million of Fed funds, which it in turn uses to repay the $10 million of Fed funds it borrowed ("purchased") on Monday.

There's one final detail to be added to this scenario. When the Bank of Montreal placed weekend Euros, it assumed a short position in Monday Fed funds. Moreover, since Euros are normally traded for delivery two days hence, the Bank of Montreal might well have assumed this short position as early as the preceding Wednesday. To cover its short in Monday Fed funds, the Bank of Montreal could have simply waited until Monday and then bought Fed funds. But doing so would have exposed it to a rate risk, since the cost of Fed funds might have risen between the date on which it sold weekend Euros and the following Monday. To protect against this risk, the bank would probably have done what most banks selling weekend Euros do, namely, buy at the same time that they are placing weekend Euros, *forward* Fed funds for delivery on Monday. Such activity, which is substantial, constitutes almost the only forward sales that occur in the Fed funds market.

From a review of the various balance sheet changes recorded in Table 17–4, it is clear that by buying Friday Euros for Monday repayment the Chase has in effect borrowed Euros for three days in order to obtain Fed funds for one day. Thus, offhand one would expect the rate on Friday/Monday Euros to be one third of the prevailing Fed funds rate, but typically it is noticeably higher. Also, because forward Fed funds usually command a slight premium (¼ or ⅛), the rate at which the foreign bank selling weekend Euros covers its Monday short in Fed funds, while less than the effective rate at which it is selling those funds, is likely to exceed the prevailing Fed funds rate.

These observations raise the question of why weekend arbitrage occurs at all. As a result of the whole operation, Chase seems to be buying indirectly on Friday for Monday delivery Fed funds that it could buy more cheaply if it simply waited until Monday to make the purchase. The answer lies in the way the transaction effects the reserves Chase must maintain against *domestic* demand deposits. The $10 million increase in cash items in the process of collection that Chase experiences as a result of its Euro borrowing on Friday, Saturday, and Sunday reduces by a like amount Chase's reservable demand deposits for these three days. The $10 million Treasurer's check that Chase issues on Monday increases its reservable deposits on that day by $10 million. Thus net the transaction reduces Chase's reservable deposits by $10 million for two days.

This means that when Chase borrows $10 million of Euros over the weekend, it gets not only $10 million of Fed funds for one day, Monday, but also the use of an extra $3.25 million of Fed funds in a subsequent reserve period. (The calculation is: $16\frac{1}{4}\% \times \$10$ million $\times 2$ days $= \$3.25$ million.) In effect Chase is getting $1.33 of Fed funds for every $1 of Euros it borrows, and its effective borrowing rate thus equals the nominal rate on the Euro borrowing divided by a factor of 1.33. The Chase therefore can afford to pay a nominal rate for Fed funds that is higher than the prevailing Fed funds rate and still have an effective cost below that prevailing rate.

This can be illustrated with a simple example. Suppose that Fed funds are trading (as shown in Table 17–3) at 5⅜ percent, weekend Euros are trading at $2^3/_{16}$ percent, and forward Fed funds for Monday delivery are at $5^9/_{16}$ percent. If a foreign bank lends weekend Euros, it will earn the weekend rate of $2^3/_{16}$ percent for three days and it will incur a cost of $5^9/_{16}$ percent for one day on the Fed funds it borrows. Thus its profit rate (on an annualized basis) will be

$$3 \times 2^3/_{16}\% - 5^9/_{16}\% = 6^9/_{16}\% - 5^9/_{16}\% = 1\%$$

The Chase for its part in paying a nominal rate of $6^9/_{16}$ percent for Monday Fed funds, but its effective cost is

$$\frac{2^3/_{16}\% \times 3}{1.33} = 4.934\%$$

which is less than the assumed 5.375 percent prevailing Fed funds rate.[1]

---

[1] This calculation is an approximate one often used in banks. A more precise calculation for the assumed $10 million transaction is:

$$\text{effective cost} = \frac{\text{net interest paid}}{\$10 \text{ million}} \times 360$$

$$= \frac{\left(\$10 \text{ million} \times \frac{3}{360} \times 2^3/_{16}\%\right) - \left(\$1,625,000 \times \frac{2}{360} \times 5^3/_8\%\right)}{\$10 \text{ million}} \times 360$$

$$= \frac{\$1,337.67}{\$10 \text{ million}} \times 360 = 0.04816 = 4.816\%$$

In making the above calculation, we ignored the possibility that Chase might incur a reserve requirement as high as 4 percent on its Euro borrowing. Any such reserve liability would, of course, increase Chase's effective cost of funds but, as noted above, normally banks have sufficient flexibility to hold their net Euro borrowings to zero over each averaging period.

Some regional banks that are not members of CHIPS sell weekend funds to domestic banks on the same basis that foreign banks do, for settlement in Fed funds on Monday. They do this by asking a New York that is a member of CHIPS and at which they have an account to issue a Treasurer's check on their behalf to the bank to which they have sold funds. Issuance of this check, which is cleared through CHIPS, puts the regional bank in technical overdraft with its New York correspondent bank. To cover this overdraft, the regional bank buys Monday Fed funds, which it delivers to the New York bank. The regional bank profits from this transaction in exactly the way a foreign bank selling weekend Euros does. The transaction would, however, cost the regional bank's New York correspondent reserves if the Treasurer's check that bank issues on behalf of the regional bank were reservable. The Fed, however, has ruled that such checks are not reservable, so permitting a regional bank to engage in such arbitrage costs a New York Clearing House bank nothing.

Thursday/Friday arbitrage

As Table 17–3 shows, if a bank sells overnight Euros on Thursday, it gets an extremely high rate. To see why, we have to work through the mechanics of such a sale. In Table 17–5 we assume that Chase New York places $10 million of funds in the Euromarket on Thursday through its Nassau branch. The resulting time deposit is booked at Chase Nassau but it is Chase New York that issues a Treasurer's check to pay out the funds lent. As a result Chase Nassau's deposit balance with Chase New York decreases by $10 million.

On Friday this Treasurer's check is settled through CHIPS and Chase New York has to pay out $10 million in Fed funds, which it purchases to cover the transaction. At the same time, the borrower repays Chase Nassau by issuing a check to Chase through CHIPS. This causes a $10 million increase in Chase New York's cash items in the process of collection. Repayment of the borrowing also causes a $10 million increase in Chase Nassau's account with Chase New York.

These balance sheet changes bring Chase Nassau back to where it started. Chase New York, however, as a result of the Euro placement on Thursday will have on its balance sheet over the weekend an extra $10 million of cash items in the process of collection offset by an extra $10 million of Fed funds purchased. On Monday the payment made by the

Table 17–5
Thursday/Friday arbitrage

Thursday:

Chase N.Y.

	Nassau office dollar account −10 million Treasurer's check +10 million

Chase Nassau

Euro time deposits +10 million N.Y. office dollar account −10 million	

Friday:

Chase N.Y.

Cash items in the process of collection +10 million	Treasurer's check −10 million Fed funds purchased +10 million Nassau office dollar account +10 million

Chase Nassau

Euro time deposits −10 million N.Y. office dollar account +10 million	

Saturday/Sunday: No change

Monday:

Chase N.Y.

Cash items in the process of collection −10 million	Fed funds purchased −10 million

borrowing bank to Chase Nassau through CHIPS is settled in Fed funds and both these items go off to Chase New York's books.

A careful examination of Table 17–5 shows that Chase, by placing overnight Euros on Thursday, has in effect given up Fed funds for three days: Friday, Saturday, and Sunday. Thus one would expect the rate on Thursday/Friday Euros to be three times the Fed funds rate. In practice, however, it is typically something less because a domestic bank making such a loan has an effective borrowing rate that's lower than the nominal rate it pays. The reason is that, as a result of the sale of Thursday/Friday funds, the bank's reservable deposits on Thursday rise by $10 million but fall by a like amount on the following three days. Thus net the bank saves reserves on $10 million for two days. This in turn means that the bank gets the use (counting reserve dollars saved in a subsequent reserve period) of $3.33 of Fed funds for every $3 of Fed funds it has to purchase. (Note a Friday purchase of Fed funds lasts 3 days.) The bank's effective cost of funds is thus the nominal rate it pays divided by a factor of 1.1215, and it can therefore profitably sell Thursday/Friday Euros at a rate less than three times the Fed funds rate.[2]

We can illustrate this with the rates in Table 17–3. Specifically we assume that Fed funds trade at $5\frac{3}{8}$ percent and that Thursday/Friday Euros trade at $15\frac{1}{2}$ percent, a rate well below three times the prevailing Fed funds rate. To a domestic bank engaging in this arbitrage, the cost of funds would be the nominal rate paid for Fed funds times three divided by a factor of 1.1215. Thus the profit rate—lending rate minus effective borrowing rate—on the transaction works out to:

$$15\frac{1}{2}\% - \frac{5\frac{3}{8}\% \times 3}{1.1215} = 15.5\% - 14.378\% = 1.122\%$$

For a domestic bank, profit is not the only incentive for engaging in Thursday/Friday arbitrage. By doing this arbitrage, a domestic bank also builds up a Euro lending base against which it can borrow Eurodollars reserve free.

Nonneutral dates in general

The examples presented in Tables 17–1 to 17–5 show that the all-in cost to a domestic bank of a Euro borrowing as well as the all-in return on a Euro placement depend on two things: (1) the net effect, if any, of the transaction on the bank's reservable deposits, and (2) the duration of the transaction in Euros compared with its duration in Fed funds.

---

[2] Because of the reserve saving, it is–assuming no change in the Fed rate–as if the bank *net* had to purchase not $30 million of Fed funds over the weekend, but only $26,750,000. Therefore the nominal Fed funds rate must be divided by the factor

$$\frac{\$30,000,000}{\$26,750,000} = 1.1215$$

Any Euro transaction, such as the sale by a domestic bank of Monday/Tuesday Euros, that has no net effect on the bank's reservable deposits and results in a Fed funds transaction that matches in duration the underlying Euro transaction, is referred to as a *neutral* transaction. Our examples demonstrate that Euro transactions with either a Friday start or a Friday finish are *nonneutral*. Holidays, like weekends, can create nonneutral dates, and at times they also compound the effect on rates of a Friday start or a Friday finish by lengthening the weekend.

A nonneutral start or finish will, as we've shown, dramatically affect the rate on a transaction in overnight Euros. It will also affect rates quoted for longer dates, but the longer the period quoted, the less the effect. For example, if weekend Euros were trading at roughly 3 percent below the rate on neutral overnight Euros, then 1-month Euros with a Friday start might trade ¼ below neutral 1-month Euros, 2-month Euros with a Friday start ⅛ below neutral 2-month Euros, and 3-month Euros with a Friday start $1/16$ below neutral 3-month Euros.

In nonneutral transactions there is a benefit to a domestic bank in the form of a reserve saving. Usually this benefit is split between the borrower and the lender, with both getting slightly better effective rates than they otherwise would have. How it is split depends largely on supply and demand. It is, however, also influenced at times by the fact that some bank dealers have a *price on book mentality.* Such a dealer might, for example, be willing to place 1-month Euros in a period with a Friday finish at a lower effective rate than he would if he were lending for a neutral period, because on the period with the Friday finish he gets a relatively high nominal rate. Price on book mentality also works the other way. A bank dealer might be willing to pay up slightly to borrow during a period with a Friday start in order to lower his nominal borrowing cost. Price on book mentality tends to be most pronounced when the markets are very active.

The Fed's hide

When domestic and foreign banks engage in technical arbitrage, both profit. For this to occur, dollars must be taken out of someone's hide; and they are, the hide being that of the Fed. Thursday/Friday and Friday/Monday arbitrages work to the profit of banks on both ends of the transaction because they artificially reduce the reservable demand deposits of participating domestic banks, which in turn permits these banks during a subsequent reserve period to hold fewer dollars on deposit at the Fed at no interest.

The Fed perceives quite clearly its position in the arbitrage game, and it considered at one point calling a halt to the whole game by requiring that Eurodollar transactions be cleared and settled on the day they are made. In effect the Fed proposed that clearing house funds be eliminated and that the money market move to a one-funds market. Nothing ever came of this proposal for several reasons. First, the money market simply does not lend itself to the creation of a one-funds market. While many money market trades are made on a *cash* basis (settled in Fed funds on the same day they are made), many others are made on a *regular* basis (settled in Fed funds the day after they are made), and the value date on foreign exchange transactions is two days after the trade. A second difficulty with same-day settlement in Euros is that it would create an operational nightmare, given the differing time zones in which Euros are traded; it would in particular require that the Fed be open almost round the clock.

Money supply

One important and often neglected aspect of technical arbitrage between Eurodollars and Fed funds is that weekend arbitrage substantially reduces U.S. money supply figures. In calculating M1 (domestic demand deposits plus currency in circulation), the Fed subtracts cash items in the process of collection from total demand deposits. When cash items in the process of collection arise due to lags in the Fed's check clearing operations, this procedure prevents double counting of deposits. When, however, the offsetting transaction is a Euro borrowing, as it is in weekend arbitrage (see Table 17–4), subtracting out cash items in the process of collection artificially reduces the U.S. money supply. This reduction occurs, moreover, on three days: Friday, Saturday, and Sunday. One day of this three-day effect is offset by the issuance on Monday of the Treasurer's check, which is included in M1.

The Fed publishes no estimates of the volume of weekend arbitrage but it is certainly substantial, and it must exert a significant effect on domestic money supply figures. Since the Fed is primarily concerned not with absolute size of the money supply, but rather with growth and variations in its size over time, the impact of weekend arbitrage on money supply figures may be of little importance. Whether or not it is depends largely on how steady the volume of such arbitrage is. Any sharp fluctuations in the volume of weekend arbitrage would distort week-to-week money supply figures and could conceivably influence Fed policy.

As noted, it's easy to talk in theory about measuring the money supply, but it is difficult in practice to come up with a number that has a clearly defined meaning and can be measured with precision.[3] The impact of weekend arbitrage on the money supply is just one more example of the problems that beset the measurement of money.

---

[3] See pages 21–22 and 212–13.

ARBITRAGES IN THE LONGER DATES

Supply and demand pressures in the U.S. and Euromarkets are constantly changing, and rates in both markets constantly adjust up and down in response. They do not, however, adjust independently, because there are strong forces pulling these rates together. Many investors will readily switch back and forth between Euro and domestic CDs depending on rate spreads and where they perceive greater relative value to be. Borrowers too are becoming increasingly sophisticated, seeking to borrow in the market in which all-in lending rates are least. Finally, the big banks are ever alert to any opportunities for profitable arbitrage created by rate discrepancies between the two markets.

Still, as Figures 17–2 and 17–3 show, in the longer dates Euro rates are almost always higher than comparable domestic rates. There are several reasons, some obvious and some not so obvious, why these rate discrepancies are not arbitraged out.

First, the fact that for a U.S. bank the all-in cost of domestic CD money exceeds the nominal rate paid permits some fairly large rate discrepancies to persist. As one U.S. banker noted: "Today 6-month Euros are at 6⅛. I could buy 6-month money in New York at 5¾, but the all-in cost would be 6.03. That sort of arbitrage [buy at 6.03 and sell at 6.18] is probably not worth the bookkeeping. But if the domestic all-in rate fell to 5.70, I might do the arbitrage in size."

The "might" arises because of a second problem a bank faces in such arbitrage—whether it can use the money. The same banker went on to say: "It's pretty tough to just go out and buy domestic money and relend it in the Euromarket because you've got to have the credit lines to sell it. Chances are that you are already using your lines to the fullest, so you can't just say—hey, let's do 2 billion."

The "2 billion" was clearly hyperbole because a third and crucial problem U.S. banks face when they arbitrage the domestic and Euromarkets in the longer dates is the limit that market depth imposes on the size in which such arbitrages can be done. The U.S. and Euromarkets differ sharply in structure. In the Euromarket it's easy for a bank to borrow 6-month, 1-year, or longer-maturity money in size. In the United States, in contrast, it's difficult for a bank to do so; the domestic CD market has great depth in the 3-month area but beyond that it becomes increasingly thin. The sharpness of the contrast between the two markets is illustrated by one banker's remarks: "Currently domestic 6-month CDs are 6⅞. If we took the view that rates were going to rise steeply, we might well take 6-month Euros to fund our domestic book because, whereas we could do only 50 million at the domestic 6-month rate, we could do 250 million at the Euro 6-month rate."

The thinness of the U.S. market in longer-term funds means that wher

Euro rates in the longer dates rise to a substantial premium above U.S. rates, it is difficult for U.S. banks to arbitrage that rate differential in size. This is not, however, to say that such arbitrage doesn't occur. If, for example, a bunching of 6-month rollovers in the Euromarket causes the spread between domestic and Euro 6-month rates to widen, banks will pull money out of the domestic market and place it in the Euromarket. But because of the thinness of the domestic market in 6-month money, the volume of such arbitrage may be insufficient to arbitrage out the rate differential.

Any arbitrage that calls for a bank to lend term funds into the Euromarket will also permit that bank to pull back Euros in some other tenor reserve free. Usually the funds pulled back are short dated, so a bank considering such an arbitrage will be concerned with the relationship between U.S. and Euro rates not only in longer dates, but also at the short end of the market.

A final factor that probably bears some responsibility for discrepancies between long U.S. and Euro rates is the difference in bank lending practices between the domestic and Euromarkets. A domestic banker uses the bulk of the funds he buys to finance floating-rate loans, and he can therefore continually roll relatively short-term liabilities without experiencing any real interest rate exposure. The Euro banker in contrast has to finance fixed-rate assets, many of which have a 6-month life; thus he must constantly take a view on interest rates, asking whether he should or should not borrow long money. That is something the domestic banker rarely does. In effect lending practices can at times create in the Euromarket a demand for long money and a willingness to pay up for it that do not exist in the same degree in the U.S. market because a domestic banker in borrowing long is more likely to be assuming than cutting interest rate exposure.

Chapter 18

Bankers' acceptances

BANKERS' ACCEPTANCES OR BILLS OF EXCHANGE, as they are also called, are an extremely old financial instrument. As far back as the 12th century, early forms of this instrument were being used to finance international trade. For the two centuries prior to the creation of the Fed, the pound sterling was the predominant currency in which world trade was denominated and financed, and a market in sterling bankers' acceptances flourished in London.

When the Federal Reserve System was created in 1913, it was felt that a domestic bankers' acceptance market patterned after the London market should be developed to enhance the role of New York as a center of international trade and finance, to promote domestic foreign trade, and to improve the competitive position of domestic banks. Thus the founders of the Fed empowered national banks to accept time drafts, which these banks had previously not been permitted to do. They also took other actions to support the growth of this infant market, including permitting the Federal Reserve to rediscount and purchase eligible acceptances.

By the late 1920s a domestic market in bankers' acceptances had, with the Fed's help, become well established and more than $1.7 billion of acceptances were outstanding. Then due first to the Depression and

461

then to World War II, acceptances outstanding declined sharply. In May 1945 they totaled only $104 million. After the war, as international trade revived, acceptance financing again became popular; and by the end of 1973, the total volume outstanding was $8.9 billion. Since that time this volume has, as Figure 18–1 shows, increased dramatically.

Figure 18–1
In recent years the volume of BAs outstanding has expanded at an extremely rapid pace. Note that the big growth of BAs other than those used to finance U.S. exports and imports reflects in large part the financing of foreign oil imports in the U.S. money market. These figures do not include finance bills.

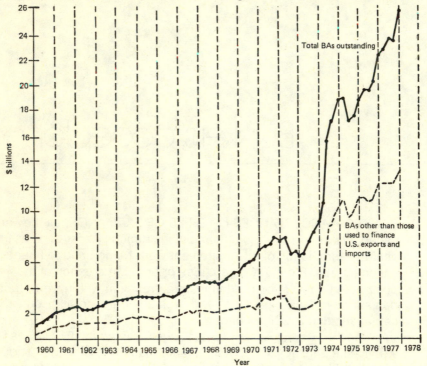

Source: *Federal Reserve Bulletin.*

THE INSTRUMENT

A bankers' acceptance is a time draft, that is, an order to pay a specified amount of money to the acceptance holder on a specified date. BAs are drawn on and accepted by a bank that, by accepting the draft, assumes responsibility to make payment on the draft at maturity.

Creation

Under current Fed regulations BAs may be created by accepting banks to finance foreign trade, the domestic shipment of goods, domestic or foreign storage of readily marketable staples, and the provision of dollar exchange credits to banks in certain countries.

In Chapter 3 we gave one example of how a BA might be created. A U.S. importer wants to buy shoes from a foreign seller and pay for them several months later. To obtain the necessary financing, he has his own bank write a letter of credit for the amount of the sale, which it sends to the foreign exporter. When the shoes are exported, the foreign firm, using this letter of credit, draws a time draft on the importer's U.S. bank and discounts the draft at a local bank, thereby obtaining immediate payment for its goods. The exporter's bank in turn sends the time draft along with proper shipping documents to the importer's U.S. bank. This bank accepts the draft—at which point it becomes an irrevocable obligation of the accepting bank—and pays out the proceeds of the draft to the exporter's bank. The accepting bank may then hold the accepted draft as an investment or it may sell it in the open market. When the draft matures, the drawer is responsible for paying the accepting bank the face amount of the draft.

If a U.S. firm exports goods using BA financing, the process is the reverse. For example, a Japanese firm that wanted to purchase U.S. goods on credit might arrange for a letter of credit from a New York bank, under which this bank would agree to accept dollar drafts drawn by a U.S. exporter to cover specified shipments to the Japanese importer.

While the drawing of BAs is frequently preauthorized by a letter of credit, in many instances BAs also arise out of contractual arrangements that are less formal than a letter of credit and are later supported by appropriate documentation. In effect BAs can be created in a myriad of ways. Precisely how a given BA is created depends very much on who the participants in a transaction are and on the nature of that transaction.

Creating BAs requires a great deal of specialized knowledge on the part of the accepting bank. Consequently it is carried on only by a limited number of banks that have foreign departments staffed by personnel who are very knowledgeable about the market. In addition, a large proportion of BAs are originated by Edge Act corporations, which as noted in Chapter 5, are specialized subsidiaries set up by banks to engage in international banking. Currently the majority of all acceptances are, as Table 18–1 shows, originated in New York, San Francisco, and Chicago.

It used to be that the majority of bankers' acceptances were created to finance domestic exports and imports. This changed in 1974 when the

Table 18–1
Bankers' acceptances outstanding by
Federal Reserve district, January 31,
1978 ($ millions)

Boston	408
New York	14,236
Philadelphia	475
Cleveland	712
Richmond	312
Atlanta	276
Chicago	1,530
St. Louis	101
Minneapolis	114
Kansas City	60
Dallas	712
San Francisco	6,316
Total	25,252

Source: Federal Reserve Bank of New York.

price of oil increased dramatically. At that time the Japanese and others began to borrow in the domestic BA market to finance their imports of oil. As a result the BA market grew sharply. Also, as Table 18–2 shows, it changed in character. Currently roughly half of all BAs outstanding are created to finance the storage or shipment of goods between foreign countries; and most of these BAs represent financing of *third-country trade,* that is, transactions in which neither the exporter nor the importer is a U.S. firm.

Table 18–2
Bankers' acceptances outstanding according to the nature of
the transaction financed, January 31, 1978 ($ millions)

Imports	6,637.4
Exports	5,839.8
Goods stored in or shipped between foreign countries	11,550.1
Domestic shipments	56.7
Domestic storage	1,167.2
Dollar exchange	0.5
Total	25,251.7

Source: Federal Reserve Bank of New York.

The prominence of third-country financing in the U.S. acceptance market reflects the fact that the U.S. market is the only world financial center in which there is a wide market for dollar-denominated acceptances. This, however, may change, as there is talk in London of starting a market there in Eurodollar bankers' acceptances.

Characteristics

BAs are a discount instrument and yields on them are quoted on a bank discount basis. Most BAs are backed by documentation such as invoices, bills of lading, or independent terminal or warehouse receipts. This documentation is held by the accepting bank, so the instrument sold to investors is, as Figure 18–2 shows, a simply drawn note. This note

Figure 18–2
Specimen bankers' acceptance, Harris Bank

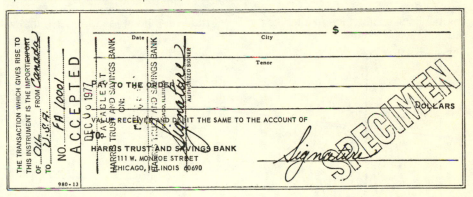

describes the nature of the transaction being financed and has been stamped "accepted" by the accepting bank. BAs are generally issued in bearer form. They may be drawn for varying maturities, but the largest volume of BAs traded in the market is in the 3-month area.

The amount of BA financing required by a borrower depends on the transaction he is financing; it may be a very large sum or it may be small. The BA market, however, trades in round lots—$100,000 or more typically $500,000. A bank asked to finance a multimillion-dollar transaction will generally divide the amount into several drafts, each for $500,000. Banks may also combine drafts for several smaller amounts into a single marketable draft. Odd-lot BAs for less than $100,000 are sometimes sold by banks to individuals, but only during periods of tight money when rates on such instruments become attractive to the small investor.

The risk to an investor of holding a BA is minimal. The instrument not only constitutes an irrevocable primary obligation of the accepting bank but is also typically a contingent obligation of the drawer, and it is an obligation of any other institutions that have endorsed the instrument. During the 65 years that BAs have been traded in the United States, no investor in BAs has ever suffered a loss of principal.

There are currently 14 primary dealers in BAs who make an ongoing market in this instrument, and a number of other firms deal in BAs on an occasional basis. The volume of trading in the secondary market for BAs is such that BAs are at least as liquid as CDs in terms of the spreads at which they trade.

As Figure 18–3 shows, the BA rate closely tracks the bill rate. In the 3-month area, the traditional spread is 15 to 25 basis points, but when money is easy BAs may—depending on the supply in the market—trade just a few basis points above the bill rate.

Figure 18–3
The bankers' acceptance rate tracks the T bill rate, with the spread between the two widening when money is tight

Source: *Federal Reserve Bulletin.*

ELIGIBILITY REQUIREMENTS

A high official of the New York Fed recalls that when he first came to the bank, one of the initial questions he had to answer was: Are yak tails readily marketable? That's not what one would call common knowledge, but fortunately he was able to come up with a quick answer—yes, they are—because he had just read that yak tails were used in the United States to make high-quality Santa Claus beards. And why, one might wonder, did the New York Fed care about the marketability of yak tails? The answer is that it determined whether a particular BA was or was not eligible.

To understand how the BA market works, its potential benefits to borrowers and to banks, and how investors view BAs, one has to know something about eligibility requirements.

The initial Federal Reserve Act specified that BAs eligible for discount at or purchase by the Fed had to meet certain requirements. These, as noted in the second column of Table 18–3, are very involved. Generally their spirit is that for a BA to be eligible, it should finance a short-term (no longer than 6 months), self-liquidating commercial transaction of one of several specified types.

The implications of this set of criteria for eligibility have changed considerably over time. The initial intent and practice were that banks experiencing a temporary need for funds would sell to the Fed, that is, rediscount at the discount window, BAs and other eligible paper. Later open-market operations replaced the discount window as the Fed's primary tool for creating bank reserves, and the Fed's view as to what was an appropriate use of the discount window changed. As a result, no bank would today ask the Fed to rediscount a BA to maturity in order to raise funds, because doing so would violate the spirit in which loans are currently made available at the discount window.

The key importance today of the eligibility requirements stated in the original Federal Reserve Act (see the third column of Table 18–3) is that only acceptances that are deemed eligible according to these requirements can be sold by member banks without incurring a *reserve requirement.*

Currently banks can and do create large numbers of ineligible acceptances. If they sell such acceptances in the market, they incur a reserve requirement. The resulting reserve cost is passed on by the bank to the borrower. Thus a borrower who requires ineligible as opposed to eligible BA financing pays a higher rate.

Eligibility for purchase

In the early 1970s the Fed was active in the BA market in four ways: it bought BAs for its own portfolio and did RP with BA dealers as part of its normal open-market operations, in addition it lent to banks at the discount window against BAs as collateral, and it bought—adding its own guarantee to them—BAs in the open market for the account of foreign central banks.

Table 18–3
Prime bankers' acceptances eligibility and reservability

Type of bankers' acceptance	Eligible for		Reserves required‡
	Purchase*	Discount†	
Export-import, including shipments between foreign countries			
Tenor—6 months or less	Yes	Yes§	No
6 to 9 months	Yes	No	Yes
Domestic shipment, with documents conveying title attached at the time of acceptance			
Tenor—6 months or less	Yes	Yes§	No
6 to 9 months	Yes	No	Yes
Domestic shipment, without documents conveying title			
Tenor—6 months or less	Yes	No	Yes
6 to 9 months	Yes	No	Yes
Shipment within foreign countries			
Tenor—any maturity	No	No	Yes
Foreign storage, readily marketable staples secured by warehouse receipt			
Tenor—6 months or less	No	Yes§	No
6 to 9 months	No	No	Yes
Domestic storage, readily marketable staples secured by warehouse receipt			
Tenor—6 months or less	Yes	Yes§	No
6 to 9 months	Yes	No	Yes
Domestic storage, any goods in the United States under contract of sale or going into channels of trade and secured throughout its life by warehouse receipt			
Tenor—6 months or less	Yes	No	Yes
6 to 9 months	Yes	No	Yes
Dollar exchange, required by usages of trade, only in approved countries			
Tenor—3 months or less	No	Yes	No
3 to 9 months	No	No	Yes
Finance or working capital, not related to any specific transaction			
Tenor—any maturity	No	No	Yes

* Authorizations announced by the Federal Open Market Committee on April 1, 1974.
† In accordance with Regulation A of the Federal Reserve Act.
‡ In accordance with Regulation D of the Federal Reserve Act.
§ Providing that the maturity of nonagricultural bills at the time of discount is not more than 90 days.
Note: Tenor refers to the full length of time of the acceptance from date of inception to maturity.
Source: Ralph T. Helfrich, "Trading in Bankers' Acceptances: A View from the Acceptance Desk of the Federal Reserve Bank of New York," *Monthly Review*, Federal Reserve Bank of New York, February 1976, p. 54.

Buying BAs for its own portfolio on its own initiative was nothing new for the Fed. It did this continually from the inception of the BA market to encourage the market's growth. By 1974 a considerable change had occurred in the composition of the BAs that were being created by the banks. At this time the Fed decided to modernize its rules relative to what BAs it could purchase as part of its open-market operations; responsibility for setting eligibility requirements for purchase was passed from the Board of Governors to the Federal Open Market Committee. The new eligibility requirements relative to purchases issued by the FOMC are summarized in the first column of Table 18–3. One major change was that BAs with a maturity of up to 9 months became eligible for purchase even though they were not eligible for discount, provided they met other eligibility requirements.

At this time, when the FOMC desk bought BAs, it did not usually ask dealers to specify in advance the names of the banks that had created the acceptances the dealer was offering; and the Fed did not attempt to distinguish gradations of quality among different banks' paper. Instead it asked the dealers only that they offer it *prime* paper. The Fed's main criterion for determining that a bank's paper was prime was that it be traded in reasonable volume and with reasonable frequency in the secondary market, in other words, that the paper be acceptable to the market.

In the market's view, however, there were and still are quality gradations in paper, and tiering exists in the rates paid by different institutions. To avoid acquiring undue amounts of paper considered by the market to be less attractive, the Fed instructed dealers to offer and deliver to it a reasonable mix of acceptances created by prime banks. If the Fed's holdings of any one bank's paper became unduly large, it would temporarily refuse to accept that name until its holding was reduced to an acceptable percentage.

The Federal Reserve Bank of New York has for years purchased for foreign correspondents (mainly other central banks) government securities, agency securities, and bankers' acceptances.

Prior to November 8, 1974, the Federal Reserve guaranteed the acceptances it purchased for its foreign correspondents. The policy of guaranteeing acceptances held by foreign correspondents was developed in the process of working out reciprocal correspondent relationships with other central banks during the early years of the Federal Reserve System. Such guarantees were at that time considered useful in encouraging the development of the bankers' acceptance market. In part, due to the favorable rate spread between acceptances and Treasury bills, foreign correspondent holdings of bankers' acceptances guaranteed by the Federal Reserve increased rapidly during 1974 to a level of about $2 billion. Against this background, officials of the Federal Reserve concluded that there was no longer justification for extending a guarantee favoring a particular private market instrument or a particular group of investors.[1]

As a result of the Fed's decision to stop guaranteeing BAs, the number of foreign banks buying these instruments dropped by about two-thirds, and the holdings of the remaining foreign customers fell to about $300 million in 1975. To cushion the effect on the BA market of the large drop in foreign purchases, the Fed temporarily increased its own purchases of BAs by roughly the amount that foreign bank purchases of them had declined.

Then gradually the Fed let its own BA holdings drop. Finally, in March 1977, when the Fed was buying for its own portfolio only an insignificant amount of BAs—$1 or $2 million on a daily basis—it determined that the BA market was mature enough to no longer need federal support, and it stopped buying BAs for its own portfolio.

Eligibility requirements with respect to purchases still have significance, however. BAs that are eligible for purchase are eligible for RP, and the Fed continues to do RP with BA dealers (it never does reverses with them).

The ability to do RP with BA dealers gives the Fed one more useful way to make temporary injections of reserves into the banking system. It also gives the Fed's BA staff a chance to spot check the acceptances RPed by the dealers to the Fed in order to determine that eligibility requirements are being met. It is market practice for a bank that issues paper ineligible for discount to stamp "ineligible" on that paper.

Currently banks may use as collateral for loans at the discount window any BAs that are eligible for purchase by the Fed, and any other paper that meets the general eligibility standards established by the window.

DOLLAR EXCHANGE ACCEPTANCES

Most bankers' acceptances are based on specific merchandise trade or storage transactions. *Dollar exchange acceptances* are an exception. They are time drafts drawn by foreign banks—usually central banks—on U.S. banks that accept these drafts. Specified countries, mostly in Latin America, have issued dollar exchange bills to obtain dollars to satisfy temporary, and often seasonal, needs. A one-crop country might, for example, issue dollar exchange bills to pay for imports of seed and other raw materials needed during the growing season of a crop whose sale at maturity would produce dollars.

---

[1] Ralph T. Helfrich, "Trading in Bankers' Acceptances: A View from the Acceptance Desk of the Federal Reserve Bank of New York," *Monthly Review,* Federal Reserve Bank of New York, February 1976, p. 53.

Dollar exchange bills have never been a large item in the BA market. Outstanding amounts have ranged between $50 and $200 million. Presumably the countries that issue them have the perhaps cheaper alternative of borrowing in the Euromarket.

FINANCE BILLS

It has been the Fed's traditional view that BAs are to be used to finance only a specified set of self-liquidating commercial transactions. They are not to be used to provide working capital. Precisely how a line can be drawn between the two is something that calls on occasion for bankers to apply the wisdom of Solomon. Grain stored in an elevator may be financed by a BA since it is going to be sold, therefore the elevator operator's investment in inventory is self-liquidating. But if cotton is stored at a mill, funds used to finance it are considered to be working capital even if the cotton is still owned by a broker rather than by the mill. One of many gray areas would be the financing of tobacco, where the storage process included curing, a form of manipulation of the commodity stored. For bankers, a real problem in this area is that they are working with regulations that are subject to interpretation, often after the fact.

During the late 1960s when the Fed tightened money severely on several occasions and made it difficult for the banks to meet loan demand, the banks conceived the idea of selling *working capital* BAs; that is, they would issue normal commercial loans in the form of BAs—also called *finance bills*—and sell them in the open market. This technique permitted the banks to continue to make loans at a time when their reserve position was so tight that they could not otherwise have done so.

By mid-1973 the amount of working capital BAs outstanding had reached a record $1.5 billion. At that point the Fed imposed reserve requirements on the sale of such acceptances; this action caused a rapid and sharp contraction in their use.

Noted one banker of the Fed's ruling: "It was a dictatorial act of fiat. There is no way that the sale of such BAs should be considered reservable deposits. They are sales of assets."

The Fed's ruling raises an interesting issue. If banks were permitted to sell working capital BAs free from reserve requirements, their loan portfolios would have some liquidity. Also, during a monetary crunch, it would permit the banks to go on lending no matter how much the Fed tightened, since at some rate it is always possible for banks to sell BAs to the market. Permitting the banks to operate this way would, of course, eventually drive open-market interest rates high enough so that it would become economically infeasible for certain corporations to borrow; thus the effect of the Fed's tightening would in time be felt because gradually some firms would be rationed by *price* out of the loan market.

Rationing loan demand by price would presumably cause loans to flow to those firms that could use borrowed funds most productively. But the Fed, although it would not say so publicly, feels that it would be politically infeasible to permit interest rates to rise to market-clearing levels. Therefore it prefers to maintain a system in which it can periodically induce crunches that force the banks to curtail lending. During such crunches the major commercial paper issuers are in no way inhibited from borrowing, since they can always sell their paper no matter how tight money gets. Thus the effect of the current system is to place the major burden of a credit crunch on firms that for one reason or another do not have access to the commercial paper market and must therefore rely on bank credit. The justice of such a system as well as its economic rationality seem questionable at best.

BANK PRICING AND SALE

When a bank creates an acceptance, it prices it as follows. First, it checks the rate at which paper of the maturity it is creating and carrying its name is trading in the dealer market, that is, the rate at which it could sell the acceptance in the market. To this rate it adds on any reserve cost it would incur in selling the acceptance. Reserve requirements on ineligible acceptances and finance bills are frequently altered by the Fed and have ranged from 2.5 to 8 percent. They also depend on the tenor of the instrument created.

To the sum of these two costs, the bank adds on a commission for its services. The standard acceptance fee used to be 1.5 percent, and this figure is still often quoted as a standard. However, in practice the acceptance fee charged by a bank may range anywhere from 50 basis points to 2 percentage points. It tends to be less for prime customers than for less prime customers. Also, when money is easy and loan demand is slack, many banks will cut their acceptance fee—sometimes by quoting a low all-in rate—to compete for additional BA business.

The acceptance fee charged is also a function of the amount borrowed. On odd-lot acceptances, certainly on those less than $100,000, a bank will charge an extra 10 or 20 basis points because such acceptances can only be sold at a concession to the market.

Selling versus holding

Once a bank creates a BA, it can either hold the instrument as part of its loan portfolio, that is, as an investment, or sell it to the market. Bank attitudes on this point vary considerably. When the Fed is tightening and banks are short on reserves, they will normally choose to sell out BAs in order to be able to fund more straight loans.

When money is easy, there is more variability in bank behavior. Some banks make it a practice to consistently sell a large proportion of the BAs they create to correspondents and foreign customers who demand them as a means of accommodating these customers and improving their relationship with them. For other banks, the decision about whether to sell BAs is strictly an investment decision.

Noted one such banker: "We will hold BAs if we think that rates are coming down and will sell them if we think that rates are going up. However, our decision on BAs is usually weighted toward selling them out rather quickly, because if you have a profit in them and you sell them out fast, you get the profit for sure and right away for the whole maturity of the BA. If you wait, you are speculating on what will happen to the cost of funding. BAs are a relatively low-yield instrument and your spreads are rather narrow. So it does not take much of a rise in interest rates to take you from a profitable to an unprofitable position in BAs. Also the cost of funding BAs is not as low for a bank as for a dealer because a bank incurs a reserve requirement when it RPs acceptances unless it does the RP with another bank. Because of this, the cheapest way for us to fund BAs is usually with Fed funds."

Another banker made the same point more succinctly: "Whenever we position BAs, it is a rate decision. I tell our trader, any time we think it is a good idea to buy 90-day money, he had better not build up any assets— just sell the BAs we create out to the market."

A funding officer at still another large bank took a somewhat different point of view. He said: "We turn out BAs whether money is easy or tight. We can make short-term investments in bills, and we think we can manage a bill portfolio in a way to maximize return better than we can manage a BA portfolio. We notice we differ from other banks in this respect but we have tested our policy and think it permits us to make more money."

Finally, it should be noted that some banks will build up their BA holdings when loan demand is slack in order to show a stronger loan position on their balance sheet. BAs held as an investment are recorded on a bank's balance sheet as loans.

BORROWING VIA THE BA ROUTE

A firm with a financing need will attempt to borrow in the cheapest way possible. A domestic firm that uses BA financing could alternatively use a straight bank loan. The advantage of the BA financing is that it is cheaper, and the decision to use BA financing is therefore typically a rate decision.

To illustrate the cost calculation, suppose that the discount rate on 6-month acceptances is 5.40 and that the estimated average floating prime over the next 6 months is 7.00. Assuming an acceptance commission of 1.50, the cost of the acceptance loan on a simple interest basis would be 7.15, as Table 18–4 shows. That is more than the prime rate, but when the cost of compensating balances—which must be maintained against a loan but not a BA borrowing—is taken into account, the total cost to the borrower is, in our example, less if he uses BA financing than a straight loan.

Table 18–4
Comparing the cost of BA financing with that of a bank loan

Acceptance		Bank loan	
Discount rate for a 6-month acceptance	5.40%	Estimated average floating "prime" rate	7.00%
Acceptance commission	1.50%	Implicit cost of holding 20% compensating balances†	1.75%
Total cost to borrower on a bank discount basis	6.90%	Total cost to borrower on a simple interest basis	8.75%
Total cost to borrower on a simple interest basis*	7.15%		

* Recall the formula on page 40. Because the prime rate is quoted on a 360-day-year basis, the appropriate conversion formula here is:

$$r = \frac{d \times 360}{360 - d \times t}$$

† If a borrower has to hold 20 percent of the amount borrowed as compensating balances, he must borrow a sum equal to 125 percent of the amount he actually needs, and consequently the effective loan rate he pays is 125 percent of the nominal loan rate. Note: 125 percent of 7 percent is 8.75 percent.

The commercial paper market is the cheapest source of short-term financing available to firms. Borrowing via the BA route is a way for a firm that does not have direct access to the open market—because it cannot sell commercial paper—to obtain indirect access to this market; the access is more expensive because the firm must pay the accepting bank a fee for opening the door for it to this market.

Many domestic firms that use the BA market are financing commodity imports and exports, frequently huge amounts. These firms have tremendous financing needs. Also due to the extreme variability of commodity prices, their financing needs are equally variable and also unpredictable. Because of this, such firms, in addition to trying to minimize their borrowing costs, feel the need to maintain as many sources of financing open to them as possible. Thus some top firms finance part of their needs in the commercial paper market, part in the BA market, and part with bank loans.

Bank loans become an attractive alternative to BA financing when the borrower is not sure how long he will need financing. The reason is that if a borrower repays a BA early (as Fed regulations require him to do if the underlying transaction is terminated early), no proportion of the bank commission on the BA is repaid to him. He does get a prorated rebate on the discount fee, but minus ¼ or so.

The Japanese are such large users of the domestic BA market in part because they have very limited access to the commercial paper market. Many Japanese BAs are created by U.S. banks, but the U.S. branches of Japanese banks have also begun to create acceptances in their own name. U.S. branches of banks from other countries have also entered the acceptance business.

THE DEALER MARKET

In recent years, as the volume of BAs outstanding has soared, there has been a large increase in the number of firms that deal in BAs.

The Fed buys for foreign accounts and does RP with firms that it recognizes as dealers in BAs. Its criteria for recognizing BA dealers are similar to those for recognizing dealers in governments. To become a recognized dealer in BAs, a firm must be in the market on a daily basis, trade in significant volume, maintain a portfolio of satisfactory size, be reputable and financially sound, and have competent management and staff. In 1970 there were only half a dozen recognized BA dealers; today there are 14.

The recognized dealers include most of the major money market dealers, some firms that specialize in BAs, and several banks. In addition to these, there are several other bank and nonbank dealers that trade BAs on a less active basis.

All of the BA dealers will make markets in the paper of major banks. Some, in addition, specialize in making a market in the paper of a selected group of regional banks.

Most of the BA dealers rely heavily on RP financing that they obtain from corporations and state and local governments. For odd pieces and regional names that are hard to RP, they use dealer loans for financing. When money is easy, BAs can be RPed at rates equal to or only slightly above the rates at which governments can be RPed. When money tightens, the spread widens.

THE NEW ISSUE MARKET

At the beginning of the decade, when the BA market was small—$7 billion of outstandings—the dealers did not position much, and activity in the market was light. At that time it was a tradition, respected by all the dealers, that the spread between their bid to the banks and their offer to retail was ¼. Thus, if the banks were creating BAs at 5, the dealers would automatically resell them to retail at 4¾. With all the dealers posting and bidding the same rates to the banks, which dealers got what was a function strictly of their relationships with particular banks. To break this pattern, Merrill and Sali in 1970 began quoting competitive rates; and once they did, all the other dealers followed.

Now BAs are issued to the market much as CDs are. The dealers call the banks with bids, and issuing banks call the dealers asking for bids. When some major banks want to sell, they will shop all the dealers; others use a selected few whose style they like.

In BAs, as in CDs, the banks prefer to sell, to the extent possible, their BAs directly to retail to keep the floating supply of their paper on the street at a minimum. As one dealer noted: "Banks still bow down to the idol of retail. I see it all the time. I will call a bank and bid him a 5.35, and he will say, 'I have nothing.' Then two minutes later a retail customer will call and offer us, at ⅜, 25 million of that bank's BAs which he has just bought at 40. Here I am buying the same 25 million I wanted from one of the bank's 'retail' customers at 2½ basis points less than I bid the bank. Banks that sell cheaper to retail than to dealers are not optimizing. Banks recognize this and now write to dealers more than they used to."

In bidding for paper from the banks and reselling it to retail, the dealers try to take out an 05, but in competitive markets for top names they often work for as little as an 03 or an 02.

Some dealers won't take less than a $5 million block from a bank, but others will take smaller amounts, recognizing that for the sake of relationships, they have to help the banks get rid of their smaller blocks.

Regional names

Prior to 1974 the Fed supported the market for regional bankers' acceptances by buying such paper for the account of foreign buyers and adding its guarantee to it. When the Fed stopped this practice, some of the regional banks took a beating. The year 1974 was characterized by tight money and well-publicized difficulties in the banking industry. Investors then became very credit conscious. Prior to that time most big investors would buy the paper of any $1 billion bank. But in 1974 some investors began to revise their criteria and decided that size was equal to quality. With a number of them saying they would take only the top 10 or 15 banks' paper, the regionals were forced to pay up, and tiering developed. Later the acceptability of regional bank BAs, like that of regional bank CDs, improved; and today there is a good market for regional bank BAs.

Currently the New York BA market is open to at least the top 100 banks in the country. However, the regionals are in a different position from the top banks. To develop a market in New York for their paper, and in particular to get it classified as *prime* by the New York Fed (which now means eligible for repo with the Fed), such a bank has to find two or three dealers who will bid on and make a market in their paper. No dealers make markets in all banks' BAs, and different dealers specialize in different regional names. To sell regional names, a dealer has to look to retail, since the interdealer market in BAs, as in CDs, is largely in top-name paper.

Foreign banks are in much the same position as regional banks. They have to develop a relationship with several dealers who will promote their names and establish a market in their BAs. Japanese and other foreign banks that have done this have gotten on the Fed's list of prime names.

Three-name paper

A certain amount of what is known as *three-name paper* has traded in the BA market, although such paper is less common now than it used to be. Some investors, often foreign, would ask a bank to purchase an acceptance of another bank, endorse it, and sell it to them. The demand for such three-name paper came from several sources—some investors who were incredibly conservative and others who simply wanted a particular bank's paper but could not find it in the market.

Tiering

Since 1974 tiering has been a continuing phenomenon in the BA market. It is difficult to generalize about the structure of this tiering because it changes depending on supply conditions and on how tight money is. Generally the top seven to ten banks sell their paper at the lowest rates. Then there is another tier that extends out to perhaps the 25th bank. Weaker banks in both tiers pay up, especially when money is tight. Somewhere around perhaps the 40th largest bank tiering fades, and banks beyond that size all pay pretty much the same rates.

Japanese paper trades at varying spreads off the New York market. The size of the spread is a function of what quantity of paper these banks are supplying to the market and of how tight money is.

Most banks give their Edge Act subs names such as Bank X International, so that the name of the parent bank is obvious to the investor. Currently there is a tendency for Edge Act BAs to trade at 1/8 or so above the rate at which the parent bank's BAs trade. This spread tends, however, to be less for the Edge Acts of top banks that issue very large amounts of paper to the market.

To narrow the spread between the rates at which parent bank and Edge Act BAs trade, many banks are currently stamping the paper accepted by their Edge Act subs as "accepted" by the parent, thereby creating a sort of hybrid variety of three-name paper.

Many investors know that there is a distinction between eligible and ineligible BAs, and they want only eligible paper. This makes little sense, since from their point of view this distinction is of no importance. Said one dealer: "Many investors seem to think that the Fed will act as some sort of lender of last resort on eligible BAs. They simply don't understand what eligibility is all about."

THE SECONDARY MARKET

In BAs dealers make bids and offers to each other much as they do in CDs. Quotes might be for early Junes or late Septembers, and names are often specified, as in CDs, because there is tiering in the market. Spreads between bids and offers run from an 02 to 05.

A dealer's bid or offer to another is understood to be good for $5 million. If a dealer hits another dealer's bid or takes his offer and then wants to do more business, he will ask the other dealer: "Where are you now?" and the other dealer, having just done a trade, is free to adjust his quotes.

There is no obligation, as in the government market, for one BA dealer to make a run to another recognized dealer, and many dealers actively trade with only a few other dealers on a direct basis. In 1977 a broker entered the BA market, and a lot of interdealer trading in BAs is now done through this broker. The broker takes an 01 on all trades done through him.

INVESTORS IN BAs

BAs have many attractive characteristics to investors. Risk is minimal; also, the instrument is quite liquid. Any of the dealers will give retail a bid on top-name paper, usually no more than an 05 off the inside market. In regional BAs, as in regional CDs, an investor can always get a bid from the dealer from whom he bought the paper but that may be the only dealer to give a bid. Thus liquidity, in the sense of being able to shop around for bids, is less for regional paper than for top-name paper. How attractive the return on BAs is relative to that on bills, which are definitely more liquid, varies, as Figure 18–3 shows. At times the spread of BAs to bills can be very attractive, so BAs possess real relative value.

One advantage of the BA market over the CD market is that rates do not tend to back up quite so fast as they sometimes do in the CD market. As one dealer noted: "In BAs there is some sort of governor on the total supply that can come out. If banks put out 100 million of December BAs, you can be sure that that will be it. But you can buy 100 million of December CDs at 9:00 a.m. and then at 10:00 a.m. have another four banks in there selling a billion more CDs at a higher price."

As the size of the BA market has expanded, so too have the number and variety of investors in the market. Corporations, bank trust departments, savings banks, and foreign banks have been in the market for a long time. One banker noted: "The Swiss investment banks are heavy buyers of acceptances from us and from the dealers, mostly for their customers. They like the instrument: it yields more than T bills, it's marketable, and it's short in tenor; also they have told us they think it's a safer investment than CDs because there is a goods transaction underlying it."

In 1974 the amount of BAs outstanding jumped from $9 to $18 billion in one fell swoop. With oil imports being financed in the BA market, it is now not uncommon to get $25 or $50 million blocks. This has attracted a lot of new investors to the market. Municipalities, which like the safety of the instrument, and federal agencies have been the biggest new entrants to the market over the last few years. Also, banks are becoming more aggressive buyers of other banks' BAs. As one dealer noted: "You can find even small banks taking down big—250 million—positions in BAs and playing them against the funds rate. They get a better rate that way than by selling Fed funds."

There seems at this point considerable potential for further growth in the BA market. Japanese banks have been aggressive borrowers in the market, and it seems likely that other foreign banks will also become more active.

Chapter 19

Commercial paper

COMMERCIAL PAPER is an unsecured promissory note with a fixed maturity. In other words, the issuer of commercial paper promises to pay the buyer some fixed amount on some future date but pledges no assets, only his liquidity and established earning power, to guarantee that he will make good on that promise. Public offerings of commercial paper are exempt from SEC registration and prospectus requirements so long as the issuer uses the proceeds to finance current transactions and the maturity of the paper sold is no longer than 270 days.

Commercial paper is typically issued in bearer form (see Figure 19–1), but it can also be issued in registered form. Rates on commercial paper, like those on bills, are quoted on a bank discount basis. It used to be that all commercial paper was issued as discount notes, but it is now becoming increasingly common for paper to be issued in interest-bearing form; the main reason for the switch is that it makes transactions and initial calculations simpler for everyone.[1]

---

[1] All commercial paper rates are quoted on a discount basis. When paper is sold on an interest bearing basis, the issuer converts the rate paid from a discount basis to an equivalent simple interest rate so that the investor gets the same effective rate of return regardless of whether he buys paper on a discount or interest-bearing basis.

Figure 19–1
A commercial paper specimen, Haverty Furniture Companies

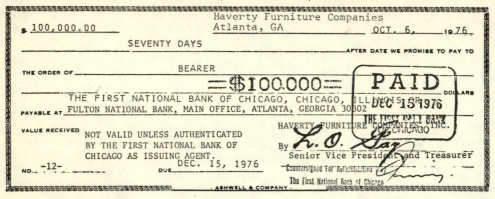

The commercial paper market is almost solely a wholesale market. A few issuers will sell paper in amounts as small as $25,000 and $50,000 to individuals and small firms, but in most cases $100,000 is the minimum denomination in which paper is issued, and multimillion-dollar sales are common.

The major investors in commercial paper are large institutions—insurance companies, nonfinancial business firms, bank trust departments, and state pension funds. Banks, which once were large buyers of commercial paper, do not now buy much paper for their own accounts. S&Ls are permitted to buy commercial paper but do not do so because it is not eligible to be counted as part of their liquidity reserves.

ISSUERS OF PAPER

The large open market for commercial paper in the United States is a unique feature of the U.S. money market. Its origins trace back to the early 19th century when firms in need of working capital began using the sale of open-market paper as a substitute for bank loans. Their need to do so resulted largely from the unit banking system adopted in the United States. Elsewhere, it was common for banks to operate branches nationwide, which meant that seasonal demands for credit in one part of the country, perhaps due to the movement of a crop to market, could be met by a transfer of surplus funds from other areas. In the United States, where banks were restricted to a single state and more often to a single location, this was difficult. Thus, firms in credit-scarce, high-interest-rate areas started raising funds by selling commercial paper in New York City and other distant financial centers.

For the first 100 years or so, borrowers in the commercial paper market were all nonfinancial business firms: textile mills, wholesale jobbers, railroads, and tobacco companies, to name a few. Most of their paper was placed for a small fee by dealers, and the principal buyers of paper were banks. Then in the 1920s the character of the market began to change. The introduction of autos and other consumer durables vastly increased consumers' demands for short-term credit, and that in turn led to the creation and rapid growth of consumer finance companies.

One of the first large consumer finance companies was the General Motors Acceptance Corporation (GMAC), which financed consumer purchases of General Motors autos. To obtain funds, GMAC (*Gee Mack* in street argot) began borrowing in the paper market, a practice that other finance companies followed. Another innovation by GMAC was to short-circuit paper dealers and place paper directly with investors, which made sense because GMAC borrowed such large amounts that it could save money by setting up in-house facilities to distribute its paper.

Despite the advent of finance company paper, the paper market shrank during the 1920s, stagnated during the 1930s, and then slumped again during World War II, with the result that by 1945 paper was a relatively unimportant instrument. Since then the volume of commercial paper outstanding has grown steadily and rapidly. One reason is the continuing growth that has occurred since World War II in the sale of consumer durables and consumers' increasing propensity to finance their purchases with credit.

A second factor contributing to the growth of the commercial paper market was the Fed's decision to pursue tight money with a vengeance on a number of occasions starting in the mid-1960s. In 1966 and again in 1969, firms that were accustomed to meeting their short-term borrowing needs at their banks, found bank loans increasingly difficult to obtain. The reason was that on both occasions money market rates rose above the rates that banks were permitted under Regulation Q to pay on CDs, and consequently the banks had difficulty funding new loans. Once firms that had previously borrowed at banks short term were introduced to the commercial paper market, they found that most of the time it paid them to borrow there because money obtained in the open market was cheaper than bank financing, except in periods when the prime rate was being held down by political pressure.

As Figure 19-2 shows, from the end of 1968 to the beginning of 1978, the amount of commercial paper outstanding increased from $22 billion to $65 billion—an increase of almost 200 percent.

Today nonfinancial firms—everything from public utilities to manufacturers to retailers—still issue paper, and their paper, which is referred to as *industrial paper,* accounts for about 24 percent of all paper outstanding (Table 19-1). Such paper is issued, as in the past, to meet seasonal needs for funds and also as a means of interim financing, that is, to

Figure 19–2
Commercial paper outstanding has risen dramatically

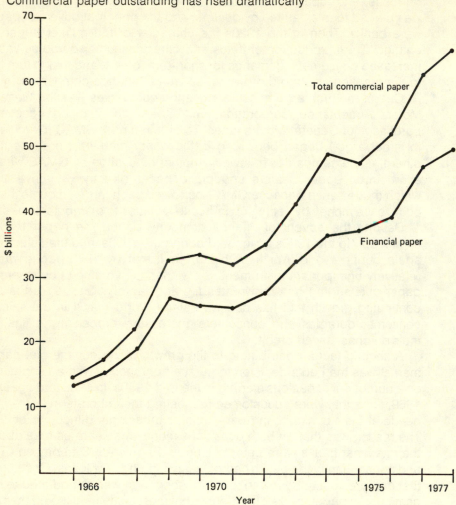

Financial paper includes paper issued by finance companies, bank holding companies, and other financial institutions.
Source: *Federal Reserve Bulletin.*

obtain funds to start investment projects that are later permanently funded through the sale of long-term bonds. In contrast to industrial borrowers, finance companies have a continuing need for short-term funds throughout the year; they are now the principal borrowers in the commercial paper market, accounting for 62 percent of all paper sold.

In the recent years of tight money, bank holding companies have also joined finance companies as borrowers in the commercial paper market. Many banks are owned by a holding company—an arrangement offering

Table 19–1
Commercial paper outstanding at the beginning
of 1978 ($ millions)

All issuers	64,571
Financial companies*	
Dealer-placed paper†	
Total	8,899
Bank-related	2,132
Directly placed paper‡	
Total	40,231
Bank-related	7,003
Nonfinancial companies§	15,443

* Institutions engaged primarily in activities such as, but not limited to, commercial, savings, and mortgage banking; sales, personal, and mortgage financing; factoring, finance leasing, and other business lending; insurance underwriting; and other investment activities.

† Includes all financial company paper sold by dealers in the open market.

‡ As reported by financial companies that place their paper directly with investors.

§ Includes public utilities and firms engaged primarily in activities such as communications, construction, manufacturing, mining, wholesale and retail trade, transportation, and services.

Source: *Federal Reserve Bulletin.*

the advantage that the holding company can engage in activities in which the bank itself is not permitted to engage. Initially bank holding companies borrowed in the commercial paper market partly to fund bank operations, which they did by purchasing a portion of the bank's loan portfolio. In August 1970 the Fed ruled that funds channeled to a member bank that were raised through the sale of commercial paper by the bank's holding company or any of its affiliates or subsidiaries were subject to a reserve requirement. This ruling eliminated the sale of bank holding company paper for such purposes. Today bank holding companies, which are, as Table 19–1 shows, still active issuers of commercial paper, use the proceeds obtained from the sale of paper to fund their activities in leasing, real estate, credit cards, and other nonbank lines.

BANK LINES

While commercial paper may have an initial maturity as long as 270 days, the average maturity of paper issued has declined sharply over time, and today it is less than 30 days. There are good reasons for this short average maturity. By issuing the bulk of their paper in the under-30-days maturity range, paper issuers are able to pay low rates because they are borrowing at the base of the yield curve; in addition, they escape competition from banks that cannot write CDs with an initial maturity of less than 30 days.

Because of the short average maturity of commercial paper outstanding, issuers must currently pay off each month billions of dollars of maturing paper. An individual issuer is sometimes able to pay off maturing paper on a seasonal basis with funds generated from his operations, and sometimes he pays it off with funds generated by the sale of new long-term debt. But by far the bulk of all maturing commercial paper is paid off by *rolling* that paper; that is, the issuer sells new paper to get funds to pay off maturing paper.

This situation creates a risk for both the issuer and the investor in paper, namely, that an adverse turn in events—say, the failure of a big issuer—might make it inordinately expensive or even impossible for the issuer to sell new paper to pay off maturing paper. To obviate this risk, all issuers back their outstanding paper with *bank lines of credit*.

An issuer who did not pay the insurance premium, which the cost of bank lines really is, might at some point find himself in a position where difficulties in marketing new paper forced him to sell off assets at fire sale prices or to cut back on the volume of his business. Issuers' concern over this eventuality has a basis in fact. When the Penn Central went bankrupt with $82 million in commercial paper outstanding, this created difficulties for all issuers, and in particular for those whose financial condition was not robust. Very tight money, as in 1974, also creates difficulties for issuers who do not have a top credit rating.

A second reason commercial paper issuers pay to acquire bank lines, whether they think they need substantial amounts of them or not, is that investors demand that paper be backed by bank lines before they will buy it.

Amount of lines

Most issuers attempt to maintain 100 percent line backing for their paper or a figure close to that. There is, however, a lot of variability among issuers and even for individual issuers over time.

An issuer who has a big seasonal need to borrow, say, at Christmas, will allow his percentage of line backing to fall temporarily during such a period. Also an issuer who pays down the amount of commercial paper he has outstanding because he had funded some of his debt with a new long-term issue may go *overlined* for a period, that is, have line backing in excess of 100 percent. Banks that grant a firm a line do not like to have that firm terminate the line after 1 month and ask to have it extended again 6 months later; so going overlined at times is a price issuers pay to maintain good relations with their banks.

The biggest single issuer of commercial paper, the General Motors Acceptance Corporation, has less than 60 percent line backing for its paper because it borrows so much that it would have difficulty getting 100 percent line backing, even if it used every bank in the country. Also, some of the other huge top-grade issuers have line backing well below 100 percent.

How much line backing is really needed by an issuer as insurance is very much a function of its position. The top issuers have had to pay up at times for money but they never experienced real difficulty in selling their paper even during the Penn Central crisis or during periods when money was extremely tight.

Types and cost of lines

There is considerable variability in the types and costs of lines that commercial paper issuers used to back their paper. Issuers have some standard line agreements; under them if the issuer activates a line, his borrowing automatically turns into a 90-day note. Issuers also have a lot of *swing* lines, on which the issuer can borrow one day and repay the next if he chooses. Swing lines are attractive to issuers because occasionally issuers experience very temporary needs for cash; for example, on a given day an issuer may not sell as much paper as anticipated but may be able on the next day to cover this deficiency.

It used to be normal practice for issuers to pay for lines with compensating balances; and the standard formula was a 10 percent balance against the unused portion of the line and 20 percent balance against any monies taken down under the line. Those figures, while still standard, are more honored in the breach than in the observance. What an issuer pays a bank for a line is very much a matter of negotiation. The strongest issuers pay much smaller compensating balances than the standard figures. Also banks sometimes permit double counting; that is, they will permit balances to be counted as compensation both for normal activity in the issuer's bank account (check writing, wire transfers, etc.) and as payment for a credit line.

In recent years it has become increasingly common for issuers to pay a fee instead of balances for lines, or a fee plus reduced balances. Banks initially resisted the trend toward fee lines but have gradually given in on that point. For an issuer to pay on a straight fee line of ⅜ or ¾ percent fee is cheaper, except when money is very easy, than for him to hold compensating balances with his bank. Foreign banks entering the United States have encouraged the trend toward fee lines by offering U.S. companies cheap fee lines as a sort of loss leader—to obtain some business and justify their existence here. The cost of fee lines varies over time, being greatest when money is tight.

A number of commercial paper issuers back some small portion of their outstanding paper with *revolving lines of credit.* Under a revolver, the bank customer pays a commitment fee of ¼ percent on top of the normal compensation he pays the bank for the line. In exchange for that extra commitment fee, the bank guarantees that it will honor the line for some number of years. The major advantage this sort of line offers the customer is that it guarantees that no matter how tight money gets or what happens to his position, he can borrow from the bank. As sort of icing on the cake, the issuer obtains the additional advantage that, because he can turn any borrowing under the line into a term loan, he can treat commercial paper backed with a revolver as long-term debt for statement purposes.[2]

Most firms that have taken out revolvers did not have the strongest credit rating possible and wanted to ensure that money would be available to them from their banks under any circumstances. One such issuer noted: "In the latest period of market tightness, the commercial paper market had problems. There was the failure of W. T. Grant and the difficulties of the REITs [real estate investment trusts], and the banking community itself was experiencing shock waves.[3] Because of all that, there were questions within and without the banking industry as to how good bank lines were, particularly annual credit lines. Some companies attempted to activate credit lines without success. They got either a direct refusal or a refusal on the basis that a material adverse change had occurred in their condition. So being an A company [A bond rating] in a market dominated by AA and AAA companies, we felt it was prudent to strengthen ourselves in the minds of investors and one way to do this was to put together a multiyear credit, which we did."

Testing lines

A number of issuers make it a practice to test their lines of credit; that is, they will borrow on a rotating basis, whether they need to or not, small

---

[2] Some multiyear credit lines do give the lender a chance to take a second look at a company before permitting them to take down any funds under their line. If a multiyear line agreement contains a "no change in material circumstances" clause, borrowing under it may not be treated as long-term debt.

[3] REITs invest in a diversified portfolio of equity holdings in real estate and in mortgage loans (the latter include construction loans, site development loans, and long-term first and second mortgages). REITs got their start in 1961 when Congress exempted them from paying the federal corporate income tax on income distributed to shareholders, provided that at least 90 percent of total net income earned was so distributed.

REITs, like mutual funds, obtain equity capital by selling shares, but the similarity ends there. In contrast to stock and bond mutual funds, REITs have borrowed heavily directly from banks and by selling commercial paper and debentures.

During the tight money period of 1969–70 when traditional mortgage lenders were hard put to meet borrowers' demands for money, REIT growth became spectacular and REITs became the hot new investment vehicle. Then in 1974, soaring borrowing costs, bloated construction costs due to spiraling inflation, overbuilding, and a number of other ills hit the REITs. Lenders, particularly banks who had sponsored some large REITs, made every effort to help the REITs avoid bankruptcy. Nevertheless, some—including an industry giant, First Mortgage Investors Trust (FMI)—failed and defaults occurred on their securities.

amounts from each of the banks that have granted them lines. One motivation for doing such testing even when money is easy is to build goodwill with banks that are glad at such times to get a new loan on their books.

Other issuers never test their lines. One such issuer observed: "Testing lines is expensive and time-consuming. Also it does not mean much because you really can't test lines against the set of circumstances that might cause you to really want to use them. We don't borrow against our lines when money is easy to build our banking relationships; and the counterpart to that is that, when money is tight and banks don't want loans, we stay out of the banks even though there would be a cost advantage in borrowing from them."

A few issuers of commercial paper have used Eurodollar revolving lines of credit to back some portion of their outstanding paper. The REITs in particular established a number of such lines in London with the understanding that they would never be used, but when the REITs fell upon hard times some of these lines were used. A few U.S. utility companies also have used Euro lines to back their commercial paper.

RISK AND RATINGS

Since the early 1930s the default record on commercial paper has been excellent. In the case of dealer paper, one reason is that, after the 1920s, the many little borrowers that had populated the paper market were replaced by a much smaller number of large, well-established firms. This gave dealers, who were naturally extremely careful about whose paper they handled, the opportunity to examine much more thoroughly the financial condition of each issuer with whom they dealt.

Since 1965 the number of firms at any one moment issuing significant quantities of paper to a wide market has increased from 450 to 700, the number being smaller when money was tight and greater during periods of monetary ease. Of these many firms, whose ranks are constantly changing, only five have failed over the last decade. Three of these five were small domestic finance companies that got caught by tight money; in each case the losses to paper buyers were small, $2–$4 million. The fourth firm that failed was a Canadian finance company that had sold paper in the U.S. market; losses there totaled $35 million. The fifth failure, one that shook the market, was that of the Penn Central which, at the time it went under, had $82 million of paper outstanding.

One favorable result of the Penn Central's failure is that rating of paper became more widespread and rating standards were tightened. Today a large proportion of dealer and direct paper is rated by one or more of three companies: Standard & Poor's, Moody's, and Fitch.

Paper issuers willingly pay the rating services to examine them and rate their paper, since a good rating makes it easier and cheaper for them to borrow in the paper market. The rating companies, despite the fact that they receive their income from issuers, basically have the interests of the investor at heart for one simple reason: the value of their ratings to investors and thereby their ability to sell rating services to issuers depend on their accuracy. The worth to an issuer of a top rating is the track record of borrowers who have held that rating.

Each rating company sets its own rating standards, but the approaches are similar. Every rating is based on an evaluation of the borrowing company's management and on a detailed study of its earnings record and balance sheet. Just what a rating company looks for depends in part on the borrower's line of business; the optimal balance sheet for a publishing company would look quite different from that of a finance company. Nonetheless, one can say in general that the criteria for a top rating are strong management, a good position in a well-established industry, an upward trend in earnings, adequate liquidity, and the ability to borrow to meet both anticipated and unexpected cash needs.

Since companies seeking a paper rating are rarely in imminent danger of insolvency, the principal focus in rating paper is on *liquidity*—can the borrower come up with cash to pay off its maturing paper? Here what the rating company looks for is ability to borrow elsewhere than in the paper market and especially the ability to borrow short-term from banks. Today for a company to get a paper rating, its paper must be backed by bank lines of credit.

Different rating firms grade borrowers according to different classifications. Standard & Poor's, for example, rates companies from A for highest quality to D for lowest. Also it subdivides A-rated companies into three groups according to relative strength, A-1 down to A-3. Fitch rates firms F-1 (highest grade) to F-4 (lowest grade). Moody's uses P-1, P-2, and P-3, with P-1 being their highest rating.

What factors separate differently rated borrowers? The answer is suggested by the following summary of the requirements a company must meet to qualify for Standard & Poor's ratings.

A rating
1. Liquidity ratios are adequate to meet cash requirements.
2. Long-term senior debt rating is A or better; in some instances BBB credits may be allowed if other factors outweigh the BBB.
3. The issuer has access to at least two additional channels of borrowing.
4. Basic earnings and cash flow have an upward trend, with allowances made for unusual circumstances.
5. Typically, the issuer's industry is well established and the issuer should have a strong position within its industry.
6. The reliability and quality of management are unquestioned.

B rating
   1.   Liquidity ratios are good but not necessarily as high as in the A category.
   2.   Long-term senior debt rating is no less than BB.
C rating
   1.   There would be wide swings in liquidity ratios from year to year.
   2.   Long-term senior debt rating would not be of investment quality.
D rating
   Every indication is that the company will shortly be in default.[4]

Standard & Poor's has phrased the meanings of its ratings in less formal terms as follows:

"A-1" to us means a company that is overwhelming—a Sears, a Shell Oil, a Union Carbide, GMAC, or an IAC. . . An "A-2" is a very good credit and basically has no weaknesses. It has a good operating record and is a long-time company, however, it just isn't overwhelming. . . An "A-3" to us and our department of professional skeptics is a good credit, but generally has one weakness which can range from a company that is growing too fast and constantly needs money to a company that has temporary earnings problems. . . Our "B" rating . . . is reserved for companies who are relatively young or old and are mediocre to fair credit risks and should use the commercial paper market only during periods of relative easy money. Our "C" rating is reserved for companies who are in serious financial difficulties.[5]

From the above quotes it is clear that a company has to be in top financial shape to get any sort of A rating from Standard & Poor's and the same is true of a P (for prime) rating from Moody's. Commercial paper investors are, however, a very conservative lot—disinclined to take any sort of extra risk to earn an extra ⅛—and a large number of them will buy only A-1 and P-1 paper. Paper rated A-3 and P-3 is not salable except to a very limited class of investors. These include some insurance companies that, because they hold large bond portfolios, spend a great deal of time tracking on an ongoing basis the earnings and conditions of a wide range of firms.

RATES AND TIERING

In the early 1960s when the commercial paper market was smaller, all issuers paid pretty much the same rates to borrow there. Then after the Penn Central's failure and periods of extremely tight money, investors became very credit conscious; they wanted top names, and rate tiering

---

[4] See "Corporate Bonds, Commercial Paper, and S&P's Ratings," a talk given by Brenton W. Harries, President, Standard & Poor's Corporation, on May 6, 1971, in Philadelphia, Pennsylvania.

[5] Speech by Brenton W. Harries, President of Standard & Poor's.

developed in the market. That tiering today is a function not only of issuers' commercial paper ratings but also of their long-term bond ratings. The market makes a distinction between A-1 issuers with a triple-A bond rating and those with only a double-A bond rating. Part of the reason is the desire of many investors to buy only unimpeachable credits. Also looking up an issuer's bond rating is quick way for an investor to check for himself the credit of an issuer with whom he is unfamiliar.

Commercial paper, as Figure 19–3 shows, yields slightly more than Treasury bills of comparable maturity, the spread being greatest when money is tight. There are two reasons for this. First, paper exposes the investor to some small credit risk. Second and perhaps more important, paper is much less liquid than bills because there is not, as noted below, a very active secondary market in commercial paper.

Figure 19–3
Commercial paper consistently yields a somewhat higher rate than Treasury bills of the same maturity

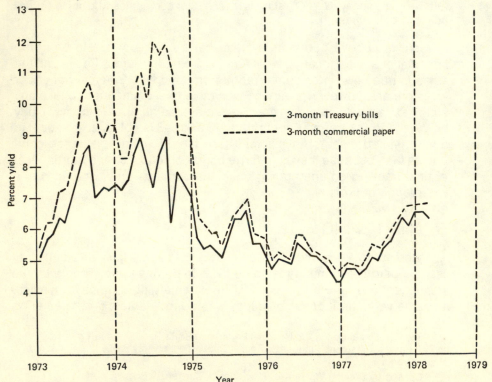

Source: *Federal Reserve Bulletin* and Salomon Brothers, *An Analytic Record of Yields and Yield Spreads.*

DEALER PAPER

As Figure 19–4 shows, a large proportion of commercial paper has been and continues to be issued through dealers. Most of the paper placed through dealers is industrial paper, but some of it is issued by smaller finance companies and bank holding companies.

Figure 19–4
Percentage of commercial paper issued through dealers

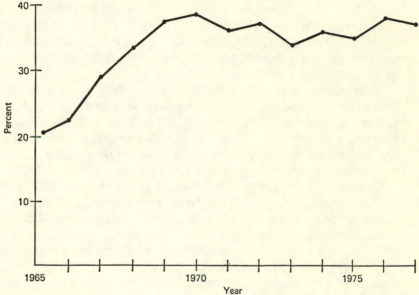

The two largest dealers in commercial paper are Goldman Sachs and A. G. Becker. Lehman Brothers, Salomon Brothers, First Boston Corporation, and Merrill Lynch are also important, and in addition there are a number of fringe dealers.

Issuers who sell through dealers inform the dealer how much they want to sell each day and in what maturities. Each dealer has a sizable sales force, which in turn contacts retail customers daily to tell them what names are available in what maturities and at what rates.

The standard fee dealers charge issuers of commercial paper who sell through them is ⅛ of one percent, which works out to be $3.47 per $1 million per day. In exchange for this fee, the dealer assumes a number of responsibilities vis à vis both issuers and investors. First, every dealer carefully checks out the credit of each firm that sells paper through him. The dealer has a fiduciary responsibility to do this. In addition, he wants to ensure that he does not throw his own name into question in the eyes of either issuers or investors by selling the paper of an issuer who goes bankrupt. A second responsibility of the dealer is to introduce the name of a new issuer to investors. This he does by having his sales force constantly show the name to investors and explain to them who the issuer is and what his credit is.

Some sophisticated issuers will themselves set the scale of rates to be offered on their paper in different maturities ranges. And, if they do not want money badly, they may post rates slightly off the market in an attempt to pick up some cheap money.

Most issuers, however, rely on the dealer to determine what rates should be posted on their paper. The dealers are all in competition with each other for issuers, and for this reason they all try to post the lowest rates at which it is possible to sell whatever quantity of paper an issuer who sells through them wants sold.

If an issuer gives a dealer the right to determine what rates will be offered on his paper, the dealer in turn assumes an obligation to position at these rates any of that issuer's paper that is not sold. Normally a dealer finances paper thus acquired through dealer loans. Such financing is expensive and the carry is therefore likely to be negative, so dealers tend to view positioning paper as unattractive.

Of course on longer-term, higher-rate paper, the dealer's carry might well be positive, especially if he financed in the RP market. Some dealers, however, are loath to position paper to earn carry profits or to speculate; they believe they should reserve their capacity to borrow for financing the paper—in amounts that cannot be predicted—that they might have to position as an obligation to their issuers. Also some dealers take the view that, if positioning longer-term paper that an issuer of theirs wants to sell seems to be an attractive speculation because they expect rates to be stable or falling, it is their responsibility to advise the issuer that he would be better off issuing shorter-term paper.

Dealers don't like to sell very short-dated paper because their transactions costs can easily be greater than the fee they earn selling such paper. But to avoid positioning paper, they will on occasion even sell 1-day paper. Also at times they will, if necessary, *break rates* to get paper sold, that is, offer higher rates than those they have posted.

On some dates, such as a tax date, it is more difficult and thus more expensive to sell paper. To help a customer who needs to borrow a lot of money on such a date, a dealer may suggest that the issuer borrow a day or two early to get a lower rate and then put the money back to the dealer under a repo agreement. If the issuer has a good name, it is often possible for him to get on such a *bridge repo* the same rate at which he borrowed so that borrowing for an extra few days costs him nothing and borrowing early thus saves him money.

Because they are assuming various and sometimes costly responsibilities to issuers, dealers attempt to get an exclusive relationship with each issuer who uses them. Such relationships are common, but some issuers do use more than one dealer. This is true in particular of the utilities, which are accustomed to issuing bonds through competitive bidding.

Secondary market

Every dealer who sells commercial paper stands ready to buy back paper sold through them at the going market rate for paper of that grade and current maturity plus ⅛ or so. Also, if an investor wants paper of an issuer who is not selling on a particular day, a dealer will attempt to find an investor who holds that issuer's paper and swap him out of it to generate supply.

Thus there is some secondary trading in commercial paper, and the amount of such trading is increasing over time. However, commercial paper is nowhere near as liquid as, for example, Treasury bills. An investor who holds commercial paper cannot really count on getting a bid on it from more than one dealer, and an ⅛ bid above the market is a fairly wide spread.

The failure for an active secondary market to develop in commercial paper is due to several factors. Commercial paper outstanding is even more heterogeneous in character than bank CDs outstanding and thus more difficult to trade actively in the secondary market. Also many buyers of commercial paper are hold-to-maturity investors, so there are minimal demands made on dealers to take back paper. One major dealer estimated that their "buy backs" run to only 1 to 1½ percent of the paper placed through them.

Opportunities for growth

While the commercial paper market is primarily a domestic market, there are a few foreign companies that borrow large sums in it. One is Electricité de France, the nationalized French electric company, which issues commercial paper through Goldman Sachs to finance oil imports and pays with dollars.

Most of the Fortune 500 either are cash-rich firms, such as IBM, or are already issuing commercial paper through dealers or direct. Thus the richest potential source of growth for the dealers would be to introduce more foreign borrowers to the U.S. commercial paper market—to sell, for example, commercial paper issued by multinational corporations such as Imperial Chemical Industries and British Petroleum, firms that could profit by taking advantage of the lower borrowing rates prevailing in the U.S. market. Some such companies have already borrowed long-term in the U.S. market, but one thing that holds many back is the high cost of converting their accounting data to the U.S. format.

Picking a dealer

In selecting a dealer, issuers look for one who will get them the lowest borrowing rates possible and who also stands ready to position their paper. Most seem to feel that there is relatively little difference among the major dealers.

Some issuers prefer to deal with the firm that acts as their investment banker. Others prefer to split their business. One advantage to issuers of selling commercial paper is that doing so acquaints a wide range of investors with their name and credit, something that helps when they go to the market to sell long-term bonds.

DIRECT ISSUE PAPER

About 60 percent of all commercial paper outstanding is placed directly by the issuer with investors. Firms issuing their paper direct—there are less than 80 that do—are mostly large finance companies and bank holding companies. Some of these finance companies, such as GMAC, Sears Roebuck Acceptance Corporation, and Ford Motor Credit, are captive finance companies that borrow primarily to finance the credit sales of the parent industrial company. Others, such as Household Finance, Beneficial Finance, and Associates Corporation of North America, are independent finance companies.

The major incentive for an issuer to go direct is that, by doing so, he escapes the dealer's 1/8 commission. For a firm with $100 million of commercial paper outstanding, this would amount to a saving of $125,000 a year. However, the direct issuer has to set up its own sales organization. A firm with a top credit rating can sell a huge amount of commercial paper through a small sales force—three to six people. Thus for such a firm, it pays to go direct when the average amount of paper it has outstanding climbs to somewhere between $150 and $200 million. A few issuers who are big borrowers in the paper market continue to use a dealer either because they anticipate selling long-term debt to reduce their short-term borrowing or because the amount of paper they have outstanding goes through sharp seasonal variations.

Direct issuers determine each day how much they need to borrow, what maturities they want, and what rates they will post. They then communicate their offerings to investors in three ways. All of the big directs post their rates on Telerate. In addition, their sales representatives call various investors. As one such representative noted: "There are a large number of A-1, P-1 issuers who are posting the same rates. So the sales representative's job is partly to develop personal relationships that will distinguish his firm in investors' eyes from the crowd."

The third way that the top direct issuers sell their paper is by posting their rates on bank money desks. Banks are forbidden by the Glass-Steagall Act from acting as dealers in commercial paper, but they can and do post rates for issuers and arrange sales of their paper to investors. The banks do this partly to service clients who use them to invest surplus funds. By posting paper rates, the banks can offer such investors a full menu of money market instruments. Also, direct issuers typically purchase large backup lines from banks that post their paper rates.

The rates that a direct issuer has to pay are a function of its name, credit rating, and use of the market. A firm that is not a prime borrower and uses the market extensively will have to pay up.

Once a direct issuer posts rates, he carefully monitors sales throughout the day by his own sales force and on bank money desks. When money market conditions are volatile, an issuer may change his posted rates several times a day in order to ensure that he gets whatever amount he set out to borrow. Also if he achieves that goal early in the day, he will typically lower his rates to make his paper unattractive to investors and thereby stem any further inflow of funds.

Most issuers will break rates for a large investor if they want money. Some, when they are just entering the market, will also consistently offer selected large investors rates slightly above their posted rates. The prevalence of rate breaking tends to increase when money is tight and to decrease when it is easy.

An issuer who fails to borrow as much as he had intended to can always fall back on his bank lines. In addition, when money is easy and the demand for bank loans is slack, some banks will position short-term paper at a rate equal to the Fed funds rate plus a small markup; this is a way of giving the issuer a cut-rate loan.

Prepayments

The big direct issuers of commercial paper will all prepay on paper they have issued if the investor needs money before the paper he has purchased matures. Some issuers do this at no penalty. Others will give the investor on a prepayment the rate that he would have gotten on the day he purchased his paper if he had bought paper for the period he actually held it. The no-penalty system would seem to invite abuse—to encourage investors to buy, whenever the yield curve is upward sloping, paper of a longer maturity than that for which they intend to invest in order to get a higher rate. Issuers, however, figure that game out quickly and don't let an investor get away with it for long.

One reason issuers are so willing to prepay is that most do not want investors to sell their paper to a dealer, for fear that the dealer's later resale of that paper might interfere with their own sales. Still a few of the largest issuers, GMAC in particular, will occasionally sell longer-term paper to dealers who position it for carry profits and as a speculation.

MASTER NOTES

Bank trust departments have many small sums to invest short term. To provide them with a convenient way to do so, the major direct issuers of commercial paper offer bank trust departments what are called *master notes*. A master note is a variable-rate demand note on which the issuer typically pays the rate he is posting for 180-day money, that rate plus ¼, or some similar formula rate.

A bank trust department with whom an issuer has opened a master note invests monies from various trust accounts in it. Then each day the bank advises the issuer what change, if any, has occurred in the total amount invested in the note. From a trust department's point of view, a master note provides such a convenient way for investing small sums to any date that it typically keeps the balance in any note issued to it close to the limit imposed by the issuer on the size of the note; daily variations in the size of a large master note—say, one for $15 million—might be no more than $100,000.

For the issuer, master notes provide a dependable source of funds and reduce bookkeeping costs. Money obtained through a master note is, however, expensive for the issuer because a long-term rate is paid, and most issuers limit the amount of master notes they will issue to some percentage—typically well below half—of the total commercial paper they have outstanding.

A and B notes

Because bank trust departments keep master notes filled up most of the time, some direct issuers said to them: Look, you have a master note for *x* million, and most of the time you have it 90 percent full. Let's call the top half of that note an *A note;* you can take money out of it on demand. The bottom half of the note we will call a *B note;* on that part you have to give us a 13-month notice to withdraw funds.

The advantage to the issuer of this arrangement, which is now common among direct issuers, is that the issuer gets cheap money that he can record on his balance sheet as *long-term* debt. From the trust department's point of view, the arrangement provides a high rate on what is really short-term money, because different monies are constantly being shifted into and out of the overall note.

Issuers of B notes argue that such debt is not commercial paper, but rather a private placement. Still such debt is recorded in money market statistics as commercial paper. A few issuers who do not offer B notes fear that by doing so they would be making an offering that, due to its term and the lack of a prospectus, would not comply with SEC regulations.

Because of the attraction of B notes to the issuer, many issuers who offer master notes to bank trust departments will not issue an A note unless they also get a B note.

Direct issuers could easily sell master notes to insurance companies and to money market funds, but they have not done so because they can get all the master note money they want from bank trust departments.

Laying off money

It is difficult for the big direct issuers to borrow on a given day precisely the quantity of money they need. Typically they borrow slightly more; and at times, if they are not quick in cutting rates, they may be hit with a lot of unwanted funds because rates elsewhere in the market are falling.

Direct issuers all run a short-term portfolio to lay off excess funds. Their investments include a wide range of money market instruments and are made with varying degrees of sophistication.

Because they can borrow short-term at very low rates, the big directs with prime names could arbitrage—buy short-term money in the commercial paper market and lay it off at a positive spread elsewhere. That, however, is not done out of a concern for the aesthetics of the balance sheet. One individual responsible for investing excess funds raised by a large direct issuer observed: "We would not take on money to lay it off at a profit. But as a matter of policy we stood on a posted rate, and sometimes we got hosed with excess money. Then we'd lay that off. I wanted to look at it differently: we can raise money at 4 and lay it off at 5, let's make a million. But management wanted the ratios of the credit company to conform to what people analyzing the company's credit wanted. Maybe they were overly conservative, but we never borrowed as an arbitrage."

Shelf paper

A number of the big direct issuers are now offering medium-term notes in the 2- to 5-year area. There are two possible approaches to selling such notes. One is for the issuer to go to a dealer who is a pro and have him sell a single large issue. The other approach is for the issuer to sell himself what is called *shelf paper*. The issuer registers a note issue with the SEC and then posts a scale of rates each day on notes of varying maturities; that scale is simply an extension of the yield curve of rates he is offering on short-term commercial paper. Money pulled in by selling notes this way is cheaper than money obtained by making a single large note placement through a dealer. Another advantage to an issuer of offering shelf paper is that it makes him more interesting to investors; he is no longer just a source of commercial paper—he can now offer the investor instruments that range in maturity from 1 day to 5 years. Some direct issuers anticipate a big expansion of borrowing in the intermediate-note area.

PRIVATELY PLACED PAPER

Commercial paper, to be exempt from registration with the SEC, is supposed to be used to finance short-term commercial operations. Paper can, however, also be used to finance long-term assets if it is sold through a restricted offering, that is, offered directly by the issuer or through a dealer to only a limited number of investors. Such private placements of paper are not uncommon. They have been used, for example, by oil companies to finance the Alaskan pipeline during its construction, by bank holding companies to partially finance their leasing operations, and by others to finance the acquisition of various long-term assets.

The SEC has also begun to allow firms to issue, through restricted offering programs, commercial paper with an initial maturity of more than 270 days. The issuer of such paper must make full disclosure to prospective investors of what the paper proceeds are to be used for. He must also give a list (up to 100 names are permitted) of the investors from whom funds will be solicited to the SEC, which must approve of this list. Long-term paper offered on a restricted basis has been used by utilities to fund construction payments.

DOCUMENTED DISCOUNT NOTES

Some smaller or less well-known firms have borrowed in the commercial paper market by issuing *documented discount notes*. This paper is backed by normal bank lines plus a letter of credit from a bank stating that the bank will pay off the paper at maturity if the borrower does not. Such paper is also referred to as *LOC* (letter of credit) *paper*.

Obtaining a letter of credit to back its paper may permit an issuer to get a P-1 rating on LOC paper, whereas on its own paper it would get only a P-3 rating. Documented discount notes, which represent only a very small fraction of total commercial paper outstanding (current outstandings are about $800 million), have been issued by a variety of companies, including firms that sell nuclear fuel or energy derived from it, leasing companies, REITs, mortgage companies, and the U.S. subsidiaries of several Japanese trading companies.

CANADIAN PAPER

Many of the big domestic finance companies also have extensive operations in Canada that they finance in part with commercial paper. Also there are some U.S. industrial firms operating in Canada that issue commercial paper.

When interest rates are significantly higher in Canada than in the United States, much Canadian paper is sold in the States. The investors who buy such paper do not want to expose themselves to a foreign exchange risk by holding on an unhedged basis commercial paper denominated in Canadian dollars. So investors in such paper hedge, typically in one of two ways. A few large investors will arrange their own hedge: buy Canadian dollars spot, invest in Canadian dollar paper, and sell the proceeds forward.[6] The other approach is for issuers or dealers to hedge large amounts of Canadian paper and sell it to investors for U.S. dollars. Such paper is referred to as *dollar pay* paper.

When Canadian rates are higher than U.S. rates, covered interest arbitrage forces the Canadian dollar to a discount in the forward market so that the U.S. investor loses on his swap. As a result, rates on hedged Canadian paper typically exceed by only a very small margin rates offered on U.S. paper.

EUROPAPER

Beginning in the mid-1960s, when exports of capital from the United States were restricted by taxes and other measures, several corporations began to issue dollar-denominated commercial paper through U.S. dealers in London. The market for Europaper, which offered investors an opportunity to diversify out of Eurodollar time deposits, started small but showed signs of promise. Then, when it had grown to about $100 million in outstandings, the United States eliminated the Interest Equalization Tax. This change made it cheaper for corporations to borrow in the United States, and the market in Europaper dried up. Since Euro rates are unlikely to ever be less than domestic rates, the market in Europaper will probably never be revived, unless the United States again imposes restraints on the outflow of capital.

---

[6] Recall the discussion of swaps and hedges in Chapter 16.

Chapter 20

Municipal notes

THE TERM *MUNICIPAL SECURITIES* is used in blanket fashion by the street to denote all debt securities issued by state and local governments and their agencies. The latter includes school districts, housing authorities, sewer districts, municipal-owned utilities, and authorities running toll roads, bridges, and other transportation facilities.

Municipal securities are issued for various purposes. Short-term notes are typically sold in anticipation of the receipt of other funds, such as taxes or proceeds from a bond issue. Their sale permits the issuer to cover seasonal and other temporary imbalances between expenditure outflows and tax inflows. In contrast, the sale of long-term bonds is the main way that state and local governments finance the construction of schools, housing, pollution-control facilities, roads, bridges, and other capital projects. Bond issues are also used to fund long-term budget deficits arising from current operations.

In recent years the total amount of municipal securities outstanding has grown at a rapid pace, much more rapidly in fact than the Treasury's outstanding debt. The latter, however, is still larger; at the beginning of 1978, there were $465 billion marketable Treasury issues outstanding and approximately $275 billion of municipals. The bulk of outstanding municipals, over 95 percent, is accounted for by long-term bonds. The remainder represents short-term borrowings via the sale of tax, bond, and revenue anticipation notes.

Municipal securities are lumped into two broad categories: general obligation securities and revenue securities. In the case of *general obligation securities* (GOs), payment of principal and interest is secured by the issuer's pledge of its full faith, credit, and taxing power. Usually this means that the securities are backed by all of the issuer's resources plus its pledge to levy taxes without limits on rate or amount. In some states and localities such a pledge can be made only on a qualified basis because the issuer's taxing power is limited to some maximum rate. In that case the issuer's GOs constitute what are called *limited-tax securities*.

Revenue securities are those on which interest and principal payments are made solely from revenues derived from tolls, user charges, or rents paid by those who use the facilities financed with the proceeds of the security issue. An example would be bonds used to finance construction of a toll bridge and secured by revenues generated by this facility.

TYPES OF MUNI NOTES

In a discussion of the money market, the focus with respect to the municipal market must be on the note market. Investors who buy municipal bonds frequently hold them to maturity, and for this reason these securities are not actively traded as they approach maturity.

Municipal notes fall into four categories: tax, bond, and revenue anticipation notes, plus a special class of federally backed notes called *project notes*.

Tax anticipation notes. *TANs* are issued by municipalities to finance their current operations in anticipation of future tax receipts. Usually they are general obligation securities of the issuer.

Revenue anticipation notes. *RANs* are offered periodically for much the same purpose except that the revenues anticipated are other than general tax receipts. RANs, like TANs, are usually GO securities.

Bond anticipation notes. *BANs* are sold to obtain interim financing for projects that will eventually be funded long-term through the sale of bonds. Normally, payment on BANs is made from the proceeds of the anticipated bond issue. BANs are also usually GOs.

Project notes. PNs are issued through bimonthly auctions by the U.S. Department of Housing and Urban Development (HUD) on behalf of local authorities. The funds obtained are used by these authorities to finance federally sponsored programs for urban renewal, neighborhood development, and low-cost housing. Payment on PNs is made by rolling these securities or by issuing bonds, whose proceeds are used to provide long-term funding. PNs are backed by the full faith and credit of the federal government. The basis for this backing is that HUD enters into an agreement with PN issuers guaranteeing unconditionally that the federal government will, if necessary, lend the issuer an amount sufficient to pay principal and interest on its notes.

CHARACTERISTICS

Municipal notes are issued with maturities ranging anywhere from a month to a year. There are so-called municipal notes with maturities at issue as long as 3 years, but they are not technically speaking true muni notes.

Most municipal notes are issued in *bearer* form (Figure 20–1). For securities of such short duration, registration would not be worth the trouble involved and as a practical matter does not occur.

The minimum denominations in which municipal notes are issued range from $5,000 to $5 million. The choice depends on whether the market for the issuer's securities is likely to be composed of partly individuals, only institutions, or only very large institutions. Thus part of a dealer's job is to advise an issuer as to where the market for his securities is and what minimum denomination he should set. When New York City began experiencing difficulty selling its notes, dealers suggested that the city cut the minimum denomination on its notes so they would appeal to a new class of investors, individuals. That was good advice from dealer to client, but in retrospect it looked like a conspiracy to defraud the little guy. As a result dealers now shy away from suggesting that a borrower with a credit problem issue in small pieces.

Most municipal notes are *interest bearing* but they may also be issued in *discount* form. The reason for the declining popularity of discount issues is the public's lack of sophistication. If a municipality authorized to borrow $400 million gets $395 million by selling discount notes, the public will think that the municipality has not exhausted its borrowing authorization, which can pose problems if the municipality needs to borrow more money. At times discount notes can be sold at a lower interest rate than interest-bearing notes, but usually the difference is very small. Interest on municipal notes that bear interest is normally paid at maturity. Discount notes are redeemed at face value at maturity.

Measured in terms of participating issuers, the muni note market is extremely broad, with something like 18,000 communities financing in it. The CD market, in contrast, is open in volume to perhaps 25 banks. A community's access to the muni note market depends on its credit, rather than on its size or the size of its issues. Most municipalities are not New York Cities that borrow tomorrow what they spent yesterday; and those that are not have easy access to the municipal market.

Figure 20–1
A municipal note

No EA- 567

UNITED STATES OF AMERICA
STATE OF ILLINOIS
COUNTY OF COOK

**BOARD OF EDUCATION OF
THE CITY OF CHICAGO**

$25,000

5¼%
**EDUCATIONAL FUND NOTE,
SERIES OF JANUARY, 1978**

DATED JANUARY 15, 1978

PRINCIPAL DUE
APRIL 9 1979

INTEREST PAYABLE
AT MATURITY

PRINCIPAL AND INTEREST PAYABLE AT THE
**OFFICE OF THE CITY TREASURER
OF THE CITY OF CHICAGO**
EX-OFFICIO SCHOOL TREASURER
OF THE BOARD OF EDUCATION OF THE
CITY OF CHICAGO
IN THE CITY OF CHICAGO, ILLINOIS
OR AT THE
**OFFICE OF THE FISCAL AGENT
OF THE CITY OF CHICAGO**
IN THE CITY OF NEW YORK, NEW YORK
AT THE OPTION OF THE HOLDER

The amounts and types of short-term borrowing that a municipality can engage in are controlled by state law. California sets the rules for how Los Angeles County can borrow, and New York State law enfranchised New York City to accumulate a huge volume of short-term debt. Some states' laws on local borrowing are more liberal than others, and in the case of New York State, hindsight suggests that the state's control was too liberal.

Taxation

The most important advantage of municipal securities to the investor is that interest income on them is exempt from federal income taxes and usually from state and local taxes within the state in which they are issued. Interest income on municipal securities issued within territories of the United States and securities issued by certain local housing and urban renewal agencies operating under HUD are exempt not only from federal taxes but also from state taxes in *all* states. The federal tax exemption has a constitutional foundation; the courts have ruled that the constitution bars the federal government from imposing on the states without their consent any taxes that would interfere with the latter's governmental functions. Whether federal taxation of interest paid on municipal securities would in fact constitute such interference is unclear. The issue has never been tested in the courts because in every revenue act passed since the original one in 1913, Congress has excluded income on municipal securities from taxable income. As noted, the states reciprocate by exempting income on federal securities from state taxation. Thus, state and federal taxation of interest income on each other's securities is characterized by *reciprocal immunity*.

To compare yield on a municipal security with that on a taxable security, an investor has to compute the *equivalent taxable yield* on the municipal security; that is, the *taxable* return that would leave the investor with an *after-tax* return equal to the return paid on the municipal security. For example, for a corporation taxed at a 50 percent marginal rate, the equivalent taxable yield on a new muni note offered at 3 percent would be 6 percent.

The exemption from federal taxation granted on income from municipal securities applies only to interest income paid by the issuer either directly or indirectly in the case of discount notes. If, due to the rise in interest rates, a municipal security trades below its issue price, the buyer of this security will receive not only tax-free interest income, but also a taxable capital gain. Because of this, equivalent taxable yield on a municipal is lower, relative to the yield to maturity at which the municipal is quoted, if that security is selling at a discount than if it is selling at par. In contrast, a taxable bond selling at a discount yields more after-tax income than one that sells at par and offers the same yield to maturity.

Table 20–1 shows the relationship between yield on a tax-exempt municipal and equivalent taxable yield for investors in selected federal tax brackets. The figures in the table are based on the assumption that the securities are trading at par; also no account is taken of possible state taxes. As the figures show, the value of the tax exemption granted on income from municipal securities is greater, the higher the investor's

Table 20–1
Equivalent taxable yields for selected marginal tax rates

Municipal coupon (percent)	Investor's federal tax bracket (marginal tax rate)			
	15%	25%	50%	70%
4.0	4.71	5.33	8.00	13.33
4.5	5.29	6.00	9.00	15.00
5.0	5.88	6.67	10.00	16.67
5.5	6.47	7.33	11.00	18.33
6.0	7.05	8.00	12.00	20.00
6.5	7.64	8.67	13.00	21.67
7.0	8.23	9.33	14.00	23.33
7.5	8.82	10.00	15.00	25.00
8.0	9.41	10.67	16.00	26.67
8.5	10.00	11.33	17.00	28.33
9.0	10.59	12.00	18.00	30.00
9.5	11.18	12.67	19.00	31.67
10.0	11.76	13.33	20.00	33.33
10.5	12.35	14.00	21.00	35.00
11.0*	12.94	15.33	22.00	36.67

* One issue of Big Mac (Municipal Assistance Corporation for the City of New York) offered this coupon. As indicated by both foresight and hindsight, it was a risky issue.

tax bracket. For example, the equivalent taxable yield on a municipal security paying 5 percent is only 5.88 percent for an investor whose marginal tax rate is 15 percent, but it is 16.67 percent for an investor whose marginal tax rate is 70 percent. Thus the muni market attracts highly taxed investors.

An interesting feature of the muni market is that individual issues tend to have *regional* markets in which they sell best. One reason is the state and local taxation of income. A municipal security issued by New York City offers a much higher equivalent taxable yield to an investor who lives in that city and has to pay high city and state income taxes than it would to an out-of-state investor. A second factor that creates regional markets for municipal securities is the taxes on intangibles that many states levy. Normally this tax is not applied to local issues. Thus to a resident of a state such as Ohio, which has a low tax on income but a high tax on wealth, ownership of local municipal securities offers a double-barreled tax advantage.

Tax reform. Because interest income on municipals is tax exempt, an individual with a lot of capital can earn a huge tax-free income by investing in municipals, and many wealthy individuals do just that. Periodically, this practice leads to calls for tax reform in general, and in particular for ending the tax exemption on municipal securities. These calls are countered by considerable pressure from state and local governments to maintain the present system, which permits municipal issuers to borrow more cheaply than they otherwise could. Nevertheless, change may come.

The current system of reciprocal tax immunity amounts to an expensive and inefficient federal subsidy of state and local borrowing. It has been estimated that every $1 saved in borrowing costs by municipal issuers costs the federal government $2 to $3 in lost tax revenue. Another disadvantage of the current system is that it *narrows* the market for municipals, because only investors taxed at high marginal rates—and that leaves out many institutional investors—have any incentive to invest in municipals. To make matters worse, the rapid post–World War II growth in municipal issues has required that investors in progressively lower marginal tax brackets be drawn into the municipal market. As a result the differential between taxable and nontaxable rates has tended to narrow, and the value to municipal issuers of the federal tax exemption has diminished correspondingly. Recent high inflation rates have, however, tended to offset this trend by pushing investors into constantly higher marginal tax brackets.

A possible alternative to the present system would be for Congress to end the federal tax exemption for municipal securities and provide a federal subsidy for municipal issues, perhaps coupled with a federal corporation to insure municipal issues for a fee. Proposals of this sort have often been made but never acted upon.

Credit risk

Municipal securities, unlike governments, expose the investor to a credit risk. Consequently for a municipal issue to sell in the national market, it must be rated, like commercial paper. The major rating services providing this service are Moody's and Standard & Poor's. Some smaller firms also rate issues within individual states. Many municipal issues are rated by both Moody's and Standard & Poor's; the Moody's rating, however, is considered stronger and carries more weight with investors. For corporate securities the reverse is true, with the Standard & Poor's rating being the weightier.

As in the case of commercial paper ratings, the rating services' first allegiance is to the investor, even though the issuer pays for the rating. The reason is that only ratings from a service with a good track record increase an issue's marketability and consequently are of value to the issuer.

In establishing a rating, the rating services' major concern is whether the borrower will be able to make promised payments of interest and principal. The first thing the rating services look at is the pledge behind the issue, which may be a general obligation pledge, a limited tax pledge, a revenue pledge, or a mix of these. In the case of GO issues, a crucial factor is the relationship between the issuer's total debt burden and its tax base. In the case of municipal bonds, projections into the future necessarily play a major role in any rating; the rating service has to ask how the community issuing the security is likely to fare over time: Is it growing? Does it have a diversified economy? Is local government well managed? In the case of revenue bonds, the main focus is on whether the facility being financed—be it a toll bridge or a college dorm—is providing a service that the public will purchase in sufficient quantity to permit the issuer to pay off its debt.

Whatever form a particular municipal issue takes, much information and analysis go into rating it. All this is summarized in a shorthand way by assigning to the issue one of a limited number of possible ratings. The bond ratings given by the national rating services and their interpretations are listed in Table 20–2.

Table 20–2
Ratings given by Moody's and Standard & Poor's on municipal bonds

Rating interpretation	Moody's*	Standard & Poor's†
Best-quality grade	Aaa	AAA
High-quality grade	Aa	AA
Upper medium grade	A	A
Medium grade	Baa	BBB
Speculative grade	Ba	BB
Low grade	B	B
Poor grade to default	Caa	CCC
Highly speculative default	Ca	CC
Lowest-rated grade	C	C

* Bonds of the highest quality within a grade are designated by A-1 and Baa-1.
† For rating categories AA to BB, a plus sign is added to show high relative standing, a minus sign to show low relative standing.

Short-term municipal *notes* are rated separately by Moody as follows:

Notes and other short-term loans that are rated **MIG 1** are judged to be of the best quality, carrying the least degree of short-term risk.

Notes and other short-term loans that are rated **MIG 2** are judged to be of high quality, bearing little risk that all terms as to time and amounts will be met.

Notes and other short-term loans that are rated **MIG 3** are judged to be of favorable quality, with all security elements accounted for but lacking the undeniable strength of the preceding grades.

Notes and other short-term loans that are rated **MIG 4** are judged to be of adequate quality, carrying specifiable risk but generally protected into investment status.[1]

---

[1] Moody's Investors Service, Inc., *Moody's Bond Record.*

The ratings assigned to municipal securities by the rating services are taken by investors as an important indication of quality and risk, and affect the yield at which they trade. Direct comparisons are, however, difficult to make because the yield on a muni note is affected by so many things—what type of note it is (TAN, BAN, or RAN), how much paper the issuer has in the market, and whether the paper is "double tax exempt," that is, offers an extra tax exemption from high state and local taxes to local investors.

A rating is not a once-and-for-all affair. Ratings on individual issues are constantly upgraded or downgraded in light of changes in the position of the issuer. Sometimes, instead of changing the rating of a given issue, the rating services will withdraw their rating altogether, as they did in the case of several New York issues. Generally, what this means is that circumstances surrounding the issue have become so uncertain that a meaningful rating cannot be given. It may also reflect the rating services' belief that the adverse factors creating the uncertainty may be temporary.

Municipal bond insurance.   To increase the marketability of their issues, in recent years several municipal issuers have had payment on new bond issues insured for a fee by one of several consortia of insurance companies, MGIC, MBIA, and AMBAC. From the issuer's point of view, whether such insurance is worth the premium paid depends on how much the insurance reduces the coupon that the issuer must offer investors. Apparently the reduction is significant because the number of insured new issues has increased dramatically since New York's difficulties were first publicized.

Up to this point there has been no insurance of muni note issues. As a matter of policy the insurers do not touch notes, presumably because their fee is so large that on a short-term issue the cost would be prohibitive.

Investors

The distribution of outstanding municipal securities among investor groups differs sharply from that of federal and federal agency securities. Since the single most important advantage of municipals to the investor is the federal tax exemption, the groups that hold these securities are those to whom this exemption is worth most.

Commercial banks, whose interest income is not shielded from federal taxation, hold close to 50 percent of total outstanding municipals. Individuals hold another 25 percent. Most of the remainder is held by casualty insurance companies and other nonbank financial institutions that pay a high tax rate on any interest income they receive. Life insurance companies and pension funds, to which the exemption is of small importance because of the low rates at which their income on invest-ments is taxed, hold very few municipals.

Whether municipals are attractive to nonfinancial corporations de-pends on the amount and type of borrowing they do. The Internal Reve-nue Service (IRS) Code prohibits, except for specifically exempted in-stitutions such as banks, the expensing of interest on funds borrowed for the purchase or for the continuance of carry of tax-exempt securities. The precise meaning of this prohibition is a gray area because the IRS has issued few definitive rulings despite the multitude of requests it has received from investors for such rulings.

Borrowing money to directly fund holdings of municipal securities and expensing the interest paid on the borrowing is clearly a prohibited arbitrage. Many corporations take the view, however, that if they have borrowed money long term to, for example, fund plant construction and don't spend all of the money right away, expensing the interest on the bond issue and simultaneously investing the surplus funds in tax exempts is OK.

Also, some corporations with debt outstanding will invest in muni notes funds that they have earmarked for a specific purpose such as funding dividends. The view here is that holding munis is permissible because the investment bridges a gap between an inflow of funds and a specific outflow that must be met. Despite these practices, some hard-nosed corporate lawyers advise a firm against buying munis if it has any debt outstanding.

In this respect it should also be noted that there is also an IRS guideline that states that a corporation's holdings of municipal securities should not exceed 2 percent of its total assets. Investors are careful to comply with this ruling.

The major investors in the muni note market are by and large the same as those that are important in the muni market overall—commercial banks, cash-rich corporations such as the drug companies, and wealthy individuals. The one exception is the casualty insurance companies, which are not important investors in notes.

In several respects, the muni note market differs significantly from other sectors of the money market. First, it is more of an investors' market; that is, people who buy notes generally have a bona fide need for tax-free income, and they need it to the maturity date. Moreover, on the maturity date they will probably roll their old notes into new "tax frees." That is not to say that investors who expect interest rates to rise won't sell muni notes, but generally they don't play the yield curve game or other-wise trade these securities. In the muni note business most sales are to investors who hold to maturity.

A second distinctive feature of the muni note market is that individuals become a *huge* factor in this market when rates are attractive. The moment good credits start paying tax-free rates that exceed rates on passbook savings accounts at a bank or S&L, the public moves funds in volume into the note market.

Yield

The yield on any particular muni note issue depends on the credit of the issuer, the maturity of the issue, the general level of interest rates, and the value of the tax exemption to investors.

Given that the tax rate on profits is 48.5 percent, it seems reasonable to assume that the average marginal tax rate of investors in the municipal market is around 50 percent. If so, then when taxable Bell (AT&T) bonds trade at 8 percent, a good muni credit ought to be able to borrow long term at 4 percent. In actual practice, however, muni bonds have never traded at their full taxable equivalent; the good muni credit would probably have to pay 5 percent if Bells were yielding 8 percent. The reason is that Congress keeps discussing possible tax reform in the municipal area, reform that could leave an investor in municipal bonds holding low-yielding securities worth much less after reform than before.

Because muni notes have such short maturities, this uncertainty effect does not spill over into the muni note market. PNs, which are really backdoor Treasuries, trade much of the time at or very near half the yield on Treasury bills of equivalent maturity. In fact sometimes, when supply is limited and there are a lot of high-tax-bracket (60+ percent) investors in the market, they will even trade through this level.

Volume outstanding

As Figure 20–2 shows, the muni note market, which is currently a $14 billion a year market, grew steadily until 1975, after which it took a noticeable dip. Prior to 1974, the typical municipal officer in charge of debt issuance, usually a senior civil servant who had been around forever, operated on the principle that you don't sell long-term munis except when they yield around 3 percent. Also, in some states, the rate a municipality could pay on bonds was limited by law. Massachusetts, for example, would not permit municipalities to pay more than 2.5 percent on bonds. The upshot was that by 1974 a lot of municipal funding officers were rolling large quantities of notes, waiting for low rates that never came.

The dip that began in 1975 in municipal notes outstanding was in large part the result of New York City's well-publicized difficulties. These forced the city, which had been a huge issuer of notes, and some other poorer credits as well out of the note market. New York City's difficulties also caused banks and dealers to take a closer look at the note issues

Figure 20–2
Volume of municipal notes outstanding

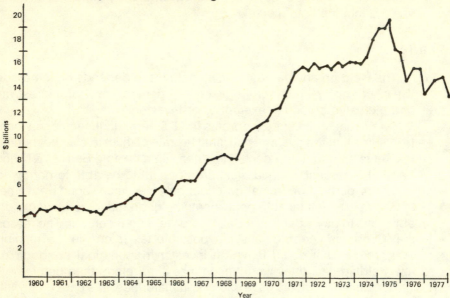

Source: Board of Governors of the Federal Reserve System.

they were underwriting. Before no one had been concerned about or even knew if the anticipated tax revenues of a municipality selling TANs would suffice to cover these securities. After New York's problems, however, the banks and dealers started to ask such questions and to say to municipalities: You can't continually roll notes you can't pay off; you have to fund such accumulated debt long term. As a result some municipalities were forced to refund note issues with long-term bonds at the worst possible moment. In effect the dealers, having turned cautious, saddled some communities that could have borrowed at 5 or 6 percent in normal times with 20-year problems in the form of bonds carrying a 9 or 10 percent coupon; on $10 million that works out to be an extra $400,000 of interest a year.

THE NEW ISSUES MARKET

State and local governments and the authorities they create run into short-term needs for cash that are totally separate from their long-term capital needs; and when they do, they borrow just like any other spending unit. Because state and municipal borrowers differ sharply in size and character, the fashion in which they issue notes varies widely, a situation that has no parallel elsewhere in the money market.

At one extreme is the situation where a town needs $50,000 to pay for a fire engine and the tax receipts are not coming in until later. It goes to its local bank and signs a $50,000 note, which the bank calls a TAN and sticks in its portfolio. Deals of this sort, which represent perhaps 99 percent of all muni note deals, are not made on a competitive basis. The rate on the note is not a market rate of interest but often something related to prime.

At the other extreme is a situation where the amount of money to be borrowed is huge, and the loan may not be in the strict sense a *bridge financing*—one that tides the borrower over until some identifiable receipt comes in. Often state or local governments are doing just what the federal government does: they have gotten themselves operating on a perpetual cash-deficit basis and they are always in arrears because future taxes are spent before they are collected.

At this end of the spectrum, one might, for example, find Los Angeles County going to the Bank of America to borrow, just as the small town in the example above went to its local bank to get money. Only Los Angeles County needs $350 million instead of $50,000. This is more exposure than the B of A wants with one borrower, so—and this is where the analogy between the little borrower paying for a fire engine and the big borrower breaks down—the big borrower's bank says, "OK, we'll get you the money, but we have to do a public offering."

On small-sized muni borrowings, it is not uncommon for the banker and the borrower to work out a sweetheart deal. The borrower sells the bank a note to finance a cash need that won't occur for 60 or 90 days. It then places the funds borrowed in a CD issued by the lending bank. If that bank has a high effective tax rate, there is an automatic arbitrage involved for both sides. The municipality earns a higher rate on the CD than it is paying on its note. Meanwhile the bank profits because the interest it pays to the municipality is a deductible expense, whereas the income it earns on the muni note is tax exempt.

Not all anticipatory borrowing by state and local governments involves an attempt to cash in on an arbitrage created by federal tax laws. A big borrower like New York State might, for example, borrow at a given point in time several billion dollars not due to be disbursed until a month or two later simply because the market looked attractive then. However, any municipal borrower that takes down short-term funds before it needs them, whatever its motivation may be, creates a profitable arbitrage because it can always invest the loan proceeds in RP or other money market instruments at a spread above its borrowing rate.[2]

---

[2] Prior to 1969 some municipalities issued *arbitrage bonds;* that is, they borrowed money specifically to reinvest it in higher-yielding taxable securities. The Tax Reform Act of 1969 ended the exemption from federal taxation of interest income on arbitrage bonds. The act, however, also stated that a municipal security would not be treated for tax purposes as an arbitrage bond simply because the proceeds of the issue were invested temporarily until needed in taxable securities.

Disclosure

Issuers of municipal bonds obtain their authority to issue such securities from the state constitution or statutes. In some cases this authority is limited, and a favorable vote by the electorate may be necessary before bonds can be issued and sold.

The legality of every municipal bond issue must be approved by an attorney. Typically such opinions are obtained from one of a number of recognized firms of bond attorneys who specialize in municipal law. The legal opinion on a bond issue is either printed on the back of the bond or attached to the security.

Municipal securities are specifically exempt from the registration requirements of the 1933 Federal Securities Act. The only exception is industrial development issues that do not qualify for tax exemption. However, every issuer of new municipal bonds must—in order to make their issue salable—prepare a detailed prospectus describing the issue and giving comprehensive data on which investors may judge the credit behind the issue.

In the muni note market, as opposed to the municipal bond market, disclosure on publicly issued securities used to be rather casual. The issuer would put together a one-page statement of condition, a balance sheet, and a flowchart (the municipal equivalent of a cash flow or income statement). This would be certified and possibly, but not necessarily, audited. And that was it.

In the wake of New York City's difficulties, however, pressure arose for change. Politicians in Washington thought investors in municipal securities deserved more information on the issuer's condition. Also, dealers experienced heightened concern over their liability if disclosure on securities they underwrote proved inadequate, so they refused to bid on note issues on which disclosure was incomplete. As a result issuers of muni notes have begun to provide quite detailed information on their condition, often by updating their latest bond prospectus.

Before dealers bid on a muni note issue or negotiate the sale of such an issue, they often do their own research on the quality of the issue. They look at the community selling the notes: at its tax collections and tax base, at who lives there, and at the profitability of local industry. Research of this sort protects the dealer. It also gives him a selling point when he approaches retail. Additionally it may permit a dealer to expand his business by finding borrowers with good credit who through no fault of their own find access to the public market difficult. This happened to some New York communities when the difficulties of New York City and New York State cast a pall over all municipal securities issued within the state.

An interesting question with respect to disclosure is why, as New York City slipped deeper and deeper into trouble, Moody's did not react faster in downgrading the city's securities and why the banks that were under-writing the city's issues did not sense trouble sooner.[3] The view of one person close to the scene is that, when the rating services and the bankers looked at the city's statement of condition, they simply could not believe that things were as bad as the numbers indicated. In their guts they thought there must be a mistake somewhere, that the city must have revenues or something it was not disclosing. No one could really believe that city officials thought that ever-increasing borrowing was a way to balance the city's budget. Unfortunately, the numbers were not lying and the unthinkable was not only thinkable, but fact.

Sale of a public issue

Municipal notes issued through a public offering are sold by dealers who also make a secondary market in these securities. There are about ten firms, seven banks and three nonbank dealers, that have made a strong commitment to the muni note market and participate in it on a steady basis. There are another ten note dealers that are sometimes players.

About 90 percent of all publicly offered muni note issues are sold to dealers through competitive bidding. In the muni note market, even though it is a sector of the money market, the overriding philosophy is that of investment banking—developing a constituency that follows the securities being bid on and getting these securities sold. Thus a muni note dealer, in bidding on and positioning securities, is more interested in what the muni note market is likely to do than in market rates in general. He wants, for example, to know how many highly taxable investors are currently in the market.

Large issuers of muni notes will normally advertise upcoming issues in *The Daily Bond Buyer* or elsewhere in order to get as many bids as possible. Smaller issuers, in contrast, may send notices of sale to only four or five friends. As one dealer noted: "You have to hustle to find out what's there. It's not like a T bill auction where the whole world is invited."

How dealers bid on an issue depends on the size of the issue. On a big issue, say, $400 million or more, the dealers will form syndicates and there may be no more than two bids. In contrast, on a $10 to $20 million issue, individual dealers feel they can handle that size alone, and there may be 10 or 15 bids.

The smaller an issue, the more difficult it is for a professional note dealer to know whether he is going to be able to buy the notes in a truly competitive situation. For one thing, there is always the possibility that a

---

[3] In the spring of 1975 New York City's notes were rated MIG 1 by Moody's even after the market would no longer accept new issues of its debt securities.

bank will step in and make a particularly attractive offer because the issue fits its investment needs. Also a local bank may put in a low bid because of a prearranged arbitrage. As one dealer noted: "At times we will bid for 20 or 30 million for a good West Coast credit. We perceive the market for a double-A county credit to be 3.25, so we bid 3.40 to offer at 3.25. Then we find that some local bank has bid 2.98. We ask what the hell is he doing, since PNs in that maturity are trading at 3.15. Then we find out that the county needs the money for only 3 weeks out of a 30-week borrowing period, which leaves 27 weeks for the bank and the county to work an arbitrage based on their effective tax rates."

When dealers form a selling syndicate to bid on and distribute an issue, they usually work on an undivided account basis. Some syndicate members might take $30 million, others less. Each assumes responsibility for the profit or loss on its share. In addition, even if a member sells its share, it is responsible, along with the other syndicate members, for any balance of the issue that remains unsold. In the muni note market, the emphasis is on distribution, getting the securities in and shoving them out. Thus, a dealer will be open with other dealers about his position, and if he has been successful in buying a big issue, he may offer a selling concession to other dealers to get them to work on distributing these securities.

What sort of spread dealers try for when they bid on a new issue depends on the credit of the issuer. On top credits the dealer may work for only an 05 or an 04, while on a lesser credit he might want ⅜ of a point or more. If a dealer offers other dealers a selling concession, this will normally run one third to half of his gross spread.

A note dealer bidding on a new issue cannot strictly speaking presell, but he will solicit interest and take orders, many of which fall through because he misses the deal. In the muni note market the whole distribution of a $100 million issue might be to only five customers. Thus syndicates of the size required in the muni bond market are not needed.

When-issued trading

There is normally a one-week gap between the time notes are awarded to the successful bidder and the time they are issued. The exception is PN notes, on which there is a one-month delay. During that time the new issue is traded on a *when-issued* basis.

Dealer financing

From a tax point of view, a bank's assets and liabilities are treated as being totally commingled. Thus a bank dealer can carry muni notes tax exempt, and so long as the bank has taxable income, financing its position in muni notes will yield the bank a positive carry under all money market conditions.

A nonbank dealer, in contrast, has to acquire specific liabilities to finance tax-free notes, and when it does, it loses under current tax laws the benefit of the tax exemption on the coupon. Thus nonbank dealers can finance tax-exempt notes only at a negative spread. To get around this problem, nonbank dealers have two options. One is simply to sell their position to a bank for purposes of carry. Under such an arrangement, the nonbank dealer sells his securities to a bank at par and then buys them back from the bank, again at par, as he sells them. A second alternative is for a nonbank dealer to open a joint account on a trading basis with a bank. Under this sort of agreement the bank carries the securities and gets the benefit of the positive carry. The bank also assumes underwriting responsibility, and the bank and the nonbank dealer split the underwriting profit or loss.

THE SECONDARY MARKET

There is an active secondary market in muni notes, but it differs in flavor and character from secondary markets in other money market instruments.

Every dealer in muni notes will make a market to customers in anything they have sold him, and dealers do some secondary trading to satisfy customer needs. Investors, however, do not work their muni note portfolios as hard as they do their taxable portfolios; they buy tax exempts for yield and taxables for trading purposes. One deterrent to trading muni notes is tax considerations. An investor who, when interest rates decline, sells off munis at a gain and replaces them with a lower coupon in effect trades a future stream of tax-exempt income for a current taxable gain, which amounts to giving income to the IRS. Dealers generate a certain amount of secondary market trading by investors in the course of distributing new issues; they track their customers' holdings and might, to get a new 9-month state note sold, encourage customers to swap out of an old 8-month note for some pickup in yield.

The inside or interdealer market in muni notes is active when dealers are long in securities. The job of the muni note dealer is distribution, and he is successful to the extent that he pushes one issue after another out to retail. It is when such distribution fails on one or several issues and a lot of securities are backed up on the street that trading between dealers really comes alive, with every dealer trying to get back his bid.

Muni note dealers do not usually quote runs to each other except occasionally in a few actively traded issues. They deal with each other more on a "can do" basis. A dealer will call another to ask for a bid on a particular issue, and the other dealer will tell him what side of the market he's on. In muni notes dealers are not, as in governments, secretive about their positions. They usually advertise them in the hope that other dealers will work on them.

In the interdealer market, quotes are always good for $1 million but trades as large as $200 million are done, and $50 million trades are common. Spreads are narrow and may approach those in the bill market when big blocks of high-quality paper trade.

A dealer in muni notes *cannot* short an outstanding issue because in doing so he would be creating new tax-free interest, something that only states and municipalities are permitted to do. A dealer can short municipal issues while they are trading on a "when, as, and if issued" basis, but that is risky. The issues are so distinctive and discrete that the substitution and swapping capabilities that are present in corporates and governments do not exist. If the dealer can't find the actual securities to cover his short, he faces a huge legal problem. Because of this disincentive, almost no one shorts munis even during when-issued trading.

The fact that muni dealers do not go short means that the dealers are always either a little long or a lot long in the market. Thus the muni note market never achieves the kind of bullish technical position that sometimes occurs in governments—there are a lot of shorts around and a dealer can just feed securities into the market.

Price volatility

Interest income on municipal securities is tax exempt, but capital gains and losses on such securities are treated for tax purposes in the same way as on taxable securities. Because of this asymmetry in tax treatment, when interest rates move, municipals are more volatile in price than are taxables.

To see why, suppose that PNs with a 6-month maturity are issued at 4 percent and 6-month bills at 8 percent. Later interest rates rise, and the bills issued at 8 percent fall sufficiently in price to yield 9 percent. The PNs issued at 4 percent also fall in price and as they do, investors in them acquire taxable capital gains. This means, assuming that investors' average marginal tax rate is 50 percent, that the PNs have to rise on a *percentage basis* twice as fast in yield as (fall faster in price than) the bills in order to continue to offer investors an equivalent taxable yield equal to half the yield on the bills.[4] Specifically, if Treasuries went to 9 percent, the PNs in our example would have to trade at 5 percent; that would give investors an after-tax yield equal to the 4 percent coupon plus 50 percent of the 1 percent return that accrues in the form of a

---

[4] In our example the yield on Treasuries goes from 8 to 9 percent, a 12.5 percent increase in yield. The PNs rise in yield from 4 to 5 percent, a 25 percent increase in yield.

capital gain—a total after-tax rate of 4.5 percent, which equals just half the 9 percent rate at which taxable Treasuries are trading. Should interest rates now reverse the trend and start to fall, the muni notes would rise in price faster than the taxable bills, again for tax reasons.

A leading indicator

In a bull market developments in the muni market can at times be a precursor of things to happen. As conditions ease and money starts piling up at the banks, banks often react by buying notes before bills. On occasion this has caused the note market to take off while the bill market just sat there, and notes ended up trading on a tax-equivalent basis through bills. In a bear market, in contrast, because notes have a reputation for being less liquid than bills, investors often sell their notes first. Thus the note market may lead the bill market down.

Money market funds, an attractive alternative for the small portfolio manager

A MUTUAL FUND is a device through which investors pool funds to invest in a diversified portfolio of securities. The investor who puts money into a mutual fund gets shares in return and becomes in effect a part owner of the fund. Professional guidance is provided by an outside management company, which charges the fund a fixed fee equal to some small percentage of the fund's total assets. The majority of mutual funds, including those best known to investors, invest almost exclusively in common stocks. Some of these funds have growth and long-term capital gains as their primary objective; others seek high and consistent dividend income. There are also mutual funds that invest in bonds in order to obtain a high and consistent yield at minimum risk.

When money market rates soared above time deposit rates, the stage was set for the birth of a new breed of mutual funds—funds that were able to offer investors high return plus high liquidity by investing in high-yield, short-term debt securities. Mutual funds of this sort are known as *money market funds*. They first appeared in 1974 and there are now over 40 of them.

RAISON D'ÊTRE

Money market funds were initially designed to meet the needs of the small investor, for whom investing in money market securities is awkward for several reasons. Minimum denominations are high. Buying securities and rolling them over involves more work than some people care to bother with, and having a bank or broker take over that job involves high transaction costs. Also for some instruments, yields on small denominations are lower than those on large denominations. Finally, the investor with limited funds can't reduce risk by diversifying, that is, by buying a mix of different money market securities.

None of these difficulties exists for the money market funds that pool the resources of many investors. Because these funds handle large sums of money, high minimum denominations pose no problem. Transaction costs in terms of both money and time spent per dollar invested are minuscule. Finally, money market funds are in a position to buy a wide range of securities, thereby reducing risk.

THE WAY THEY WORK

Forgetting technicalities and legal niceties, a money market fund very much resembles a special bank (one that would be illegal in the United States[1]). This special bank accepts demand deposits only, pays daily interest on these deposits, invests all its deposits in money market instruments, holds no reserves, and keeps only a very small profit margin for itself. For the investor, the only significant differences between banking at such a special institution and putting money into a money market fund are that (1) deposits in a money market fund are *not* insured as bank deposits are, and (2) there are minimum-denomination requirements to meet on initial deposits and on certain types of withdrawals.

Investing in a fund

Money market funds do not accept deposits; they sell shares— typically $1 buys one share, but at some funds the share size is larger. All funds calculate interest daily on outstanding shares and credit interest to the investor's account periodically, usually at the end of the month. Interest credited to an investor's account buys him more shares. Normally money market funds do not issue share certificates. Instead, they send out periodic statements showing deposits, withdrawals, and interest credited to the investor's account.

---

[1] It would be illegal, not because it wouldn't be sound, but because U.S. banks are not permitted to pay interest on demand deposits, and all banks that are members of the Federal Reserve System are required to hold reserves at the Fed.

Initially some money market funds were load funds; that is, some of the money invested went to pay a commission to the broker who sold the fund. Today, however, no-load funds are the rule, which makes sense since money market funds are used by many investors much as a checking account—a place to hold temporary liquidity; and deposits and withdrawals are therefore frequent.

Withdrawing funds

Withdrawals can be made from money market funds anytime on demand and without penalty. Typically withdrawals can be made by requesting a fund to send the investor a check or to wire out funds from his account at the fund to an account at a commercial bank. A third method of withdrawing funds is by writing a check. Most money market funds have set up an arrangement with a commercial bank under which the investor is supplied with checks and can make withdrawals and execute payments simply by drawing a check against that bank. Generally the check has to be for some minimum amount—$500 or $1,000. When the check is presented to the bank against which it is drawn, that bank covers it by redeeming the required number of shares in the investor's fund account. (With this sort of fund, "shares" resemble very closely interest-bearing demand deposits.)

Where the money goes

Since money invested in a money market fund is available to the investor on demand, a money market fund must be prepared for large and unpredictable withdrawals (redemptions of shares for cash). To do so, all funds hold a portfolio of highly liquid money market instruments. In early 1978 the average current maturity of securities in the portfolios of the seven largest funds ran from 42 to 106 days (Table 21–1).

Generally funds can meet the cash requirements generated by redemptions through the inflow of funds from new investors plus payments on maturing securities. However, if these sources of funds prove inadequate, the fund can generate additional cash by selling off assets in its portfolio. Since funds hold large amounts of very short-maturity securities, the risk of capital loss on such sales due to adverse movements in market price is small.

Money market funds seek to offer the investor not only liquidity and high return, but also *safety of principal*. Thus the typical fund is restricted, as noted in its prospectus, from the following: investing in stocks, convertible securities, and real estate; buying on the margin; effecting short sales; trading in commodities; acting as an underwriter of securities; and placing more than a small percentage of total assets in the securities of any one issuer.

Table 21-1
Money market fund statistics, January 30, 1978

Assets ($ mil)	Fund	Net Yield (%'s) Week Ending 5/17	30-day ave. current	30-day ave. mo ago	Average Maturity (days)	U.S. Treas	U.S. Other	Repo's	C.D.'s	Banker's Accept	Comm'l Paper	Euro C.D.'s	Other
	MARK-TO-MARKET FUNDS												
$ 8.1	American General	6.3	5.4	5.6	101	31	–	–	–	–	69	–	–
22.8	American Liquid Trust	6.4	6.3	6.6	26	–	–	7	–	93	–	–	–
32.0	Anchor Daily Income	6.2	5.8	5.8	90	–	–	18	69	–	13	–	–
68.9	Capital Preservation	5.8	5.7	5.6	22	100	–	–	–	–	–	–	–
15.0	Cash Mgmt Trust	6.3	6.3	5.4	109	11	5	–	55	20	–	–	9
118.6	Cash Reserve Mgmt	6.7	6.2	6.1	24	–	2	4	23	44	16	11p	–
31.3	Centennial Cash Mgt Trust [k]	6.3	6.3	6.2	21	–	–	5	27	39	29	–	–
19.8	Columbia Daily Income	5.1	4.9	6.5	126	–	–	17	15	35	31	–	2
3.7	Current Interest	6.0	6.5	6.8	48	–	–	2	34	12	51	–	1
705.2	Dreyfus Liquid Assets	6.6	6.5	5.3	96	–	–	9	78	3	10	–	–
62.4	Dreyfus Money Market [k]	6.5	6.3	6.2	105	3	–	9	74	9	14	–	–
8.2	Eaton & Howard Cash	6.5	6.4	6.4	42	–	–	–	67	–	33	–	–
117.0	FedFund	6.0	6.1	6.0	66	87	13	–	–	–	–	–	–
47.8	Federated Money Mkt [k]	7.5	7.5	7.4	183 L	2	4	1	63	9	–	–	21
586.1	Fidelity Daily Income	n/a	5.8	4.9	50	–	–	14	64	–	22	–	–
6.5	Financial Daily Income [h]	7.2	5.9	6.0	25	3	–	–	–	–	90	–	7c
12.7	First Multi Daily Inc	6.3	6.4	6.3	n/a	–	–	–	100	–	–	–	–
3.3	Franklin Resources Liq	6.7	5.3	6.2	70	53	9	–	34	–	4	–	–
36.0	Gradison Cash Reserves	6.1	6.1	6.0	59	–	–	15	36	49	–	–	–
11.9	Holding Trust	7.3	7.2	6.7	64	–	–	6	65	9	10	–	10g
143.6	Intercapital Liquid Asset [k]	6.2	6.3	6.2	41	–	–	2	42	–	56	–	–
74.8	Kemper Money Market	n/a	5.5	5.5	95	–	–	–	54	–	46	–	–
52.3	Liquid Capital Income	6.1	6.0	5.9	20	–	–	2	8	–	19	–	71a
14.6	Mass Cash Mgmt Trust [k]	6.2	6.4	6.5	30	–	3	–	4	48	44	–	1
816.9	Mer Lynch Ready Assets	n/a	5.8	6.1	88	15	–	1	63	9	12	–	–
24.1	Midwest Income	6.4	6.3	6.1	19 S	6	–	64	32	9	–	–	–

Assets	Fund		Yield			Days								
70.2	MoneyMart Assets		6.0	5.9	6.0	62	-	-	10	54	16	3	17p	-
69.5	Oppenheimer Monetary		6.3	6.4	6.2	26	-	-	6	29	-	65	-	-
11.4	Putnam Daily Div Trust	k	6.1	5.1	5.7	94	3	-	-	47	26	23	-	1
310.0	Reserve		6.6	5.9	6.2	46	-	-	10	25	1	34	64p	2
49.9	Rowe Price Prime Res		6.5	6.4	5.0	53	-	-	-	14	14	34	36p	-
240.7	Scudder Mged Reserves		6.4	6.3	4.6	72	2	2	-	43	2	48	-	2
45.5	SteinRoe Cash Reserves		6.4	6.4	7.0	83	14	-	5	55	3	23	-	-
553.8	TempFund		6.7	6.7	6.6	62	6	-	45	-	48	-	-	1
20.0	Trinwall		5.9	5.4	5.7	106	10	44	30	1	-	-	-	9
15.9	Union Cash Mgt		6.4	6.4	6.3	28	17	-	-	12	-	71	-	-
21.0	Whitehall Money Mkt		6.6	6.5	5.5	90	8	1	52	14	20	-	-	5c
4,448.2														
	Average Yield		6.37	6.12	6.02									
	-- 5 largest funds		6.50	6.14	5.81									

STRAIGHT LINE ACCRUAL FUNDS

Assets	Fund		Yield			Days								
71.5	Daily Income		6.5	6.4	6.2	60	-	-	32	63	-	4	-	1
349.1	Federated Master Trust	k	7.0	7.0	6.9	69	-	-	-	-	-	100	-	-
49.6	Fund/Govt Investors		6.3	6.2	6.1	73	-	12	11	11	4	62	-	-
395.1	Institutional Liquid		6.7	6.7	6.6	88	-	-	11	89	-	-	-	-
108.5	Money Market Mgmt		6.2	6.1	6.1	59	-	-	32	28	8	32	-	-
38.3	Scudder Cash Inv Trust		5.9	5.8	5.8	33	31	-	6	-	-	-	-	-
560.0	Trust/US Govt Secs		6.4	6.4	6.3	75	7	87	-	-	-	-	-	-
37.1	White Weld Govt		6.6	6.3	6.2	51	7	93	-	-	-	-	-	-
169.1	White Weld Money Mkt		6.5	6.5	6.4	45	9	-	-	31	18	42	-	-
1,778.3														
	Average Yield		6.46	6.38	6.28									
	-- 5 largest funds		6.56	6.54	6.45									
$6,229.8	Total Assets - All Funds													
	Average Yield - All Funds		6.39	6.20	6.07									
	Average Maturity (wtd by assets)		70	71	74									

Source: *Donoghue's Money Fund Report*, published weekly by William E. Donoghue, Holliston, Mass. 01746; copyrighted material reproduced with permission of the author.

The bailiwick of the money market funds is the money market. As a group, they place almost all the funds invested with them in short-term governments and agencies, negotiable CDs, bankers' acceptances, RPs, and commercial paper. There are, however, differences in practice. A few conservative funds stick to governments and agencies. The more aggressive hold a wider range of money market instruments, including some Euro CDs (see Table 21–1).

Mark-to-market and straight-line-accrual funds

Most money market funds mark their portfolios to market daily to reflect any appreciation or depreciation that has occurred in the value of their assets due to fluctuations in interest rates. Some funds reflect such appreciation or depreciation in the value of their assets through minor changes in their share values. Others reflect it by including changes in asset values in the interest return they credit to shareholders' accounts.

A few money market funds make it a practice to hold money market instruments they have acquired to maturity. They do not mark their portfolios to market daily, and the interest credited each day to the investors in such funds equals the average yield on all securities in the fund's portfolio. A few individuals on the street and at the SEC have voiced concern that such straight-line-accrual funds could operate like a Ponzi scheme—Ponzi, in honor of Charles Ponzi, a Boston swindler who ran a con game in which early investors were paid off with funds supplied by later investors, leaving nothing for the last investors getting out.

How does Charles Ponzi enter the picture with respect to straight-line-accrual funds? Suppose short-term interest rates were to rise sharply; then the market value of the securities in the fund's portfolio would be temporarily depressed. Suppose also that a large number of investors simultaneously redeemed their fund shares for cash. It is conceivable that such a fund would be forced to sell off some of its securities at a loss, and that the actual *market* value of the securities backing its remaining outstanding shares would fall below its fixed share value. In that case, if redemptions continued, the fund would run out of money before all shares were redeemed.

This eventuality, while theoretically possible, has a small probability in practice. For it to happen, interest rates would have to rise very sharply *and* rapidly; and *all* the money invested in the fund would have to be *hot* (very sensitive to interest rates), an improbable constellation of conditions.

Nevertheless, the SEC, after considering the question for two years, ruled that it would not allow amortized cost valuation for debt instruments with a current maturity of more than 60 days because such valuation does not reflect the "fair value of the underlying portfolio."

The SEC's ruling was challenged by a number of funds, in particular, funds serving clients such as bank trust departments and local government bodies that were unwilling or unable to invest funds in an instrument to which even a small market risk attached. In response to this challenge, the SEC exempted from its ruling 13 funds which agreed to limit their sales to institutions and to require an initial minimum investment of $50,000. The exempted funds also agreed to limit the average maturity of their portfolios to no more than 120 days, to buy no securities with a current maturity of more than one year, and to severely restrict turnover in their portfolios.

GROWTH OVER TIME

The fear of the SEC and others who worry about the valuation of money market funds on a straight-line accrual basis is that much of the money invested in such funds is *hot* money that may rapidly disappear if short-term interest rates fall below the deposit rates offered by savings institutions.

In this respect Figures 21-1 and 21-2 are revealing. Between late 1975 and early 1978, the yields paid by money market funds fluctuated up and down through a 300 basis point range and twice fell for months well below the maximum rate (5 percent) that banks may pay on savings accounts. During the same period, the total amount of money invested in money market funds (Figure 21-2) changed little. The total assets held by these funds dipped slightly when fund yields slipped below the rate paid on bank savings accounts, but it grew rapidly in early 1978 when money market rates took off. The moral is clear: It is high rates that initially attract investors to money market funds. However, once investors put their money in these funds, they are impressed by the convenience and services offered, and consequently they leave their money with the funds even when fund yields become comparatively unattractive. Money invested in money market funds is *hotter* on the way *in* than on the way *out*.

USEFULNESS TO THE PORTFOLIO MANAGER

Although money market funds were initially designed to offer individual investors a way to invest indirectly in money market securities, they can also be extremely useful to a corporation or other institution running a small short-term portfolio because the small portfolio manager labors under several disadvantages.

Figure 21-1
Yields paid by money market funds (monthly average)

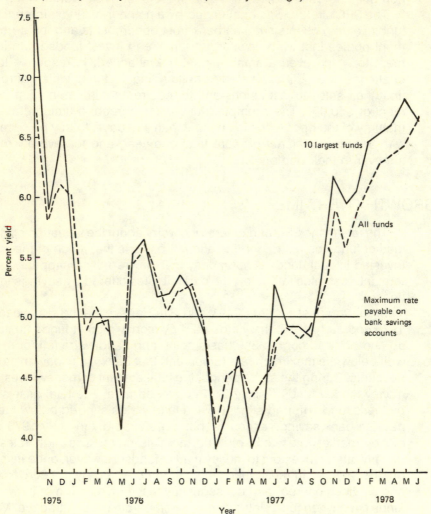

Source: *Donoghue's Money Fund Report*, published weekly by William E. Donoghue.

First, since minimum denominations are high in many sectors of the money market (the marketability of a negotiable CD suffers if its face value is less than $1 million), it is difficult for a person managing $10 million or less to diversify adequately; he has only limited ability to reduce credit risk by holding a mix of names and to reduce market risk by investing in different types and maturities of instruments.

Also, the net yield earned on a small portfolio is reduced much more by transactions costs than is the net yield earned on a large portfolio. If a bank imposes a $25 fee on an overnight repo, that fee will, on a

Figure 21–2
Money invested in money market funds and business savings accounts at commercial banks

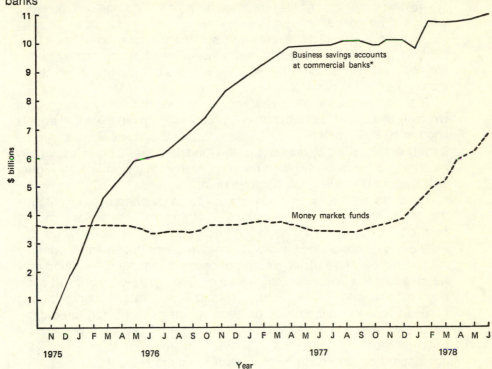

* The business savings for months other than those which are end-of-quarter call dates are estimated by the Federal Reserve Board.

Sources: *Donoghue's Money Fund Report,* published weekly by William E. Donoghue; and the Federal Reserve Board.

$250,000 repo, reduce a gross yield of 5 percent to 2.8 percent. Moreover, if the portfolio manager must, in addition, pay a fee to wire his money into and out of the borrowing bank, his net yield will be still lower.

Another problem for the small portfolio manager is that he will inevitably end up buying and selling securities at rates that are less favorable than those which big investors can obtain by bargaining with and shopping the dealers. The problem is particularly acute for the portfolio manager who directs his investments to regional banks rather than to the national money market. An example is provided by an Ohio bank which, at a time when top Chicago banks were paying 4.6 percent for 1-month CD money, was offering local corporations 4 percent for 1-month money and 4.2 percent if they ran their money through a Euro time deposit in the Caribbean.

Still another problem with a small portfolio is that it typically suffers from unprofessional management. The reason is that the gains to be earned by managing a small portfolio—for example, by following the market and making the sort of maturity choices described in Chapter 10—are so small in absolute terms that hiring a skilled portfolio manager would not be cost effective.

Because it is difficult to manage small short-term balances effectively, it would make sense for many institutions holding money of this sort to invest it in a money market fund instead of investing it directly in money market instruments.

The money market fund charges, of course, for its expenses, that typically amount to ½ of one percent, plus a management fee that equals another 50 basis points or so. These charges are, however, likely to be largely or fully offset by the fact that the fund, because it is professionally managing a big pool of short-term funds, can earn a significantly higher *gross* return than the small portfolio manager can.

There are also additional advantages to be gleaned by an institution that uses a money fund. Because history suggests that outflows of money from such a fund will be largely offset by inflows, a money fund can extend further out on the yield curve with less risk than a small portfolio manager could. As a result, a corporation investing in a money fund may be able to get a 90-day or longer rate on 30-day, 15-day, or even overnight money, with minimal market risk.[2] This aspect of a money fund is particularly important to a corporation which has difficulty predicting cash flows and which, if it did not invest in a money fund, would consequently feel constrained to roll overnight repo, or to invest in very short-dated commercial paper in order to minimize market risk.

An institution investing in a money fund may also find that its balances with the fund can be used in part as an interest-bearing substitute for checking account balances it formerly maintained. Most money funds will permit investors to write large checks directly against a zero-balance checking account maintained at a bank associated with the fund. An institution that writes checks against a money fund saves an amount equal to the charges the bank would have imposed for clearing these checks. In addition, it continues automatically to earn interest on its balance with the fund until the checks it has written clear, which often takes several days.[3] Taking advantage of float can significantly increase

[2] While the highest and lowest yields posted by money funds typically vary at any point by a wide range (150 to 200 basis points) due to differences in their portfolios and accounting policies, the average yield offered by the funds has approximated over time fairly closely the yield on the 90-day bill.

[3] One fund, Capital Preservation, offers investors the opportunity to write checks against accounts in any one of four locations: Boston, San Francisco, Great Falls, and Miami. These locations—selected on the basis of an extensive survey of the time actual checks took to clear—offer the investor the possibility to extend float to the maximum achievable by writing, for example, checks against a West Coast bank to pay East Coast bills.

the yield earned on balances invested short term in a money fund. This is particularly true if the money withdrawn from the fund by writing checks is wired into the fund, so that float operates on only one end of the transaction, the one that increases yield to the investor. Still another advantage of writing checks against a money fund is that a firm which does so need not track daily when these checks clear as it would have to if it wrote checks against a bank account that it was attempting to keep at the minimum level its bank required to compensate for services provided.

Low usage by business firms

Despite the fact that a firm with small short-term balances to manage could often do better using a money fund that invests directly in money market instruments, business usage of money funds is still small. It is estimated that currently only slightly over a $1 billion of the money invested in money funds comes from corporations.

There are several reasons for this low usage. First, many corporations think of mutual funds as a vehicle for individuals who can't invest efficiently, which supposedly a corporate treasurer can do. Second, there is the ego problem. The person who is in the best position to perceive the benefits of switching to a money fund is the portfolio manager, who, if he advises such a switch, will eliminate part or all of his own job. Finally, there is the familiar friend, unmeasured opportunity cost. The typical small firm doesn't track the return it earns on its portfolio and then ask: What cost if any did we incur in terms of foregone earnings by doing it ourselves instead of using a money fund?

Money fund yields: A yardstick

In Chapter 10 we stressed the importance of consistently monitoring the yield earned on a portfolio, and of comparing that yield with some yardstick. For a small portfolio manager, the natural yardstick is the yield offered by money funds, because such funds have the same investment objectives he has: preservation of capital, high liquidity, and high return, in that order.

To make the yield comparison, the portfolio manager should first determine what *net* yield he is earning on the funds he invests, when all transactions costs and all internal costs—part or all of his own salary, clerical costs, and an appropriate amount of overhead—are subtracted from the gross dollars earned on the portfolio. This net yield should then be compared with the net yield offered by money funds.

Also, the opportunity for a firm with an account at a money fund to use that account as a partial substitute for holding demand deposit balances should be taken into account. Money funds offer the business firm a chance to get paid for *having* a checking account instead of *paying* for it; and this opportunity to increase return should be taken into account in the profitability calculation.

However hard it may be on the corporate ego, the firm that finds it can do better with a money fund than by investing on its own should adopt the philosophy: If you can't beat them, join them.

IMPORTANCE IN THE MARKET

While money market funds have grown rapidly from zero outstandings in 1974 to a current level of over $5 billion, they still play a relatively small role in the money market. There are, in fact, several corporate and other institutional short-term portfolios that alone exceed in size the total assets of all money market funds.

Money funds have, however, a tremendous potential for growth. The number of corporations and other business firms who use money funds is undoubtedly far below the number who could do so profitably. One indication is the $10 billion (Figure 21–2) which is currently invested in business savings accounts at banks. These accounts, which are insured by the FDIC only on the first $40,000 invested, have a number of disadvantages compared to money funds: They may not exceed $150,000 in size; they may not under Reg Q pay more than 5 percent;[4] and they do not offer the investor the check writing privileges money funds do. In view of this, it would seem that money funds could attract most of the money invested in business savings accounts if they made the right case to business investors. In addition, money funds ought to be able to attract a lot of business funds that are currently tied up in demand deposits or invested directly in the money market.

Bank trust departments, which are the source of about 50 percent of the money invested in money funds, are another class of investors that money funds are likely to be able to tap for increasing quantities of money. A bank trust department is not permitted to commingle agency and trust monies in a master note or in an in-house short-term money fund. It may, however, invest these differing sorts of money in a single outside money fund because that fund will maintain separate accounts for each investor. A side benefit of this is that a money fund provides a bank trust department with free subaccounting services, something it does not get with a master note.

Individuals comprise a third important class of investors in money funds. These investors have barely begun to realize the potential bene-

---

[4] The maximum rate that S&Ls and other nonbank savings institutions may pay on business savings accounts is 5¼ percent.

fits available to them by maximizing to the fullest extent possible their use of such funds, both as a vehicle for investing savings and temporary surplus funds at low risk, and as a partial substitute for checking account balances. NOW accounts already provide some competition in this area but, given the regulations on the terms under which they may be offered and the service charges banks are likely to impose on them, money funds will probably retain a competitive edge in bidding for the funds of depositors who maintain large balances at banks and who occasionally write large checks, something that just about every homeowner with a mortgage does.

Appendix

by John Friel

Yield calculations
for the portfolio manager

THIS APPENDIX explains what is meant by *yield* and *total return*, two terms that are often misunderstood and misused. *Yield* can best be described as the expected rate of return on a security at the time of purchase. In calculating yield, the first assumption is that the security is held to maturity. The second and less obvious assumption is that all cash flows from the investment—coupon payments and principal payments, if any—are reinvested to the time of the security's maturity at a rate equal to the expected yield.

This second assumption is often ignored, yet it is crucial when a security has a high coupon or a long term to maturity. For example, a 9 percent 20-year corporate bond purchased at par would yield 9 percent at purchase. However, the *total* (actual) *return* over the life of the investment would be substantially less than 9 percent if the coupon payments were reinvested in securities yielding only 6 percent. Total return expresses the total dollars earned as a percentage of the amount invested in the security over the holding period. Yield is at best an expectation of the return to be earned. Whether that expectation is fulfilled depends on how closely actual reinvestment rates meet the assumptions in the yield calculation.

The concept of total return is important to the active portfolio m ager. Many securities in an actively managed portfolio will not be held to maturity. Instead, the manager will continually adjust the types and maturities of the securities he holds as market conditions change.

The discussion of *riding the yield curve* in Chapter 10 illustrates this type of management. The portfolio manager described there desired an investment for a short period, 90 days. A 6-month bankers' acceptance was a better investment than a 3-month acceptance because the yield differential between the two instruments was so large that market rates could have risen almost a full percentage point in 3 months, and the 6-month security would still have provided the same total dollar return as the shorter security. The example dramatized an important fact of portfolio management: any choice of investment implies a forecast of interest rates. Recognition of this is important. In the example, choice of the shorter-maturity BA implies a strong belief that rates could rise 1 percent or more in 3 months.

Often discussed among portfolio managers, but rarely written about, is the distinction between *market valuation* and *accounting valuation*. Using the latter valuation, buying the 6-month BA might cause the manager to take a capital *loss*. If the 6-month security were ultimately sold for a 50-basis-point loss (well within the 100-basis-point break-even range), many observers of the accounting data would note that loss and mentally penalize the portfolio manager for his actions. Yet, the objective of a corporation is profitability, and the manager's choice under these circumstances would contribute more to the bottom line than choosing the shorter security to avoid a possible loss. A good manager may purchase a security, expecting to take an accounting loss, because he expects this investment to return more dollars than the best alternative investment. This is the essence of the distinction between total return and the accounting preoccupation with capital gains and losses.

YIELD CALCULATIONS

The remainder of this appendix is devoted to formulas helpful to the portfolio manager. Before proceeding, one caveat is in order: There is no such thing as *the* yield calculation. All yield calculations are based on certain assumptions, and these are not uniform across various types of securities. For example, the yield on federal agency issues is computed assuming a 360-day year with 30-day months, whereas the yield on governments is calculated assuming a 365-day year.

Many investors are surprised to discover that the *yield* on overnight repurchase agreements is higher than the nominal RP rate. This is so because of daily compounding and because of the 360-day-year rate basis used in calculating interest on such agreements. The problem of comparability is especially important for the active shorter-term portfolio manager.

The pension fund manager also cannot ignore the mathematics of yield calculations. For him the comparability problem is not as great as the problem of cash flow reinvestment. Two 20-year bonds, one with a 3.5 percent coupon and the other with an 8 percent coupon, will produce vastly different dollar returns over that period.

This appendix addresses these problems by providing a uniform way of valuing expected returns on various types of securities. The methodology chosen is to calculate a daily average compounded rate for each security. One of several possible methods for annualizing these daily rates is described below. The method used is unimportant as long as it is consistently applied. What is important is that all investments be reduced to a single standard for comparison.

Accrued interest calculations

Different conventions are used for calculating interest on each type of coupon security. It is helpful to review them before proceeding to yield calculations.

Government notes and bonds. These securities accrue interest on an actual day basis, assuming a 365-day year (or 366 days in a leap year).

$$\text{Accrued interest} \atop \text{(\% of par)} = \frac{\text{Coupon rate}}{2} \times \frac{\text{Actual days since last coupon or issue}}{\text{Actual days in total coupon period}}$$

Example. Accrued interest as of 3/2/78 for the 7⅝% note due on 8/15/78. The last coupon date is 2/15/78.

$$\text{Accrued interest} = \frac{7.625}{2} \times \frac{2/15/78 \text{ to } 3/2/78}{2/15/78 \text{ to } 8/15/78}$$

$$= \frac{7.625}{2} \times \frac{15}{181} = 0.31595304\% \text{ of par}$$

Occasionally, government notes and bonds are issued with an irregular first coupon period. If the first coupon period is short, accrued interest is calculated as follows:

$$\text{Accrued interest} = \frac{\text{Coupon rate}}{2} \times \frac{\text{Actual days from issue to settlement}}{\text{Actual days from assumed normal last coupon to first payment date}}$$

Example. Accrued interest for settlement on 6/7/78, for a 7% note due on 10/31/80, with an issue date of 5/20/78. For the maturity of 10/31, the normal coupon dates would be 4/30 and 10/31.

$$\text{Accrued interest} = \frac{7.00}{2} \times \frac{5/20/78 \text{ to } 6/7/78}{4/30/78 \text{ to } 10/31/78}$$

$$= \frac{7.00}{2} \times \frac{18}{184} = 0.3423913\% \text{ of par}$$

Also, note that the coupon amount actually paid on the first coupon date (10/31/78) will be a fraction of the normal payment.

$$\frac{\text{Short first}}{\text{coupon payment}} = \frac{7.00}{2} \times \frac{5/20/78 \text{ to } 10/31/78}{4/30/78 \text{ to } 10/31/78}$$

$$= \frac{7.00}{2} \times \frac{164}{184} = 3.11956522\% \text{ of par}$$

The more common form of irregular first coupon is the *long* first coupon. In this case a partial first coupon is deferred until the next full coupon payment. The amount of coupon paid will equal the normal payment plus a fractional payment for the beginning period.

Example. Accrued interest for settlement on 9/10/75, for the 8¼% note due on 8/31/77, and issued on 8/29/75, with a long first coupon.

$$\frac{\text{Accrued}}{\text{interest}} = \frac{\text{Coupon rate}}{2} \times \left(\frac{\text{Days from issue to end of partial period or settlement}}{\text{Total days in first period}} + \frac{\text{Days from beginning of second period to settlement}}{\text{Total days in second period}} \right)$$

$$= \frac{8.25}{2} \times \left(\frac{8/29/75 \text{ to } 8/31/75}{2/28/75 \text{ to } 8/31/75} + \frac{8/31/75 \text{ to } 9/10/75}{8/31/75 \text{ to } 2/29/76} \right)^*$$

$$= \frac{8.25}{2} \times \left(\frac{2}{184} + \frac{10}{182} \right) = 0.271485\% \text{ of par}$$

* Because 1976 is a leap year, the normal coupon period is 8/31/75 to 2/29/76.

Once the first coupon payment is made, all subsequent accrued interest calculations are based on normal coupon periods.

Federal agency notes and bonds. Accrued interest for most agency securities is determined using an assumed 30-day month and 360-day year. The following rules are useful in determining the number of days of accrued interest:

1. Determine the total number of days from the last coupon to the settlement date.
2. One day is subtracted for each first of the month occurring within the period when the first follows a 31st.

3. When the first of March is included within the period, two days are added to the total (except in a leap year when only one day is added).

Example. Accrued interest for settlement on 6/3/78, of a Federal Home Loan Bank bond at 7⅜% due 8/25/80. The coupon payment dates are 2/25 and 8/25.

1. Actual days from 2/25/78 to 6/3/78 = 98.
2. Subtract 2 days for 4/1 and 6/1 since both follow a 31st.
3. Add 2 days since 3/1 falls within the period.

$$\text{Accrued interest} = 7.375 \times \frac{(98 - 2 + 2)}{360} = 2.007638\% \text{ of par}$$

Example. Accrued interest for settlement on 9/7/78 for a FHLB bond at 8¼% due 11/25/90.

1. Actual days from 5/25/78 to 9/7/78 = 105.
2. Subtract 3 days for 6/1, 8/1, and 9/1.

$$\text{Accrued interest} = 8.25 \times \frac{(105 - 3)}{360} = 2.3375\% \text{ of par}$$

ANNUALIZATION

To make yields on different securities comparable, a daily average rate of return must be calculated for each. Also these daily rates must be annualized. The method we suggest is to annualize the daily yields by compounding them over a 365-day year. This is done as follows:

$$\begin{matrix}\text{Equivalent} \\ \text{compounded} \\ \text{annual} \\ \text{yield} \\ \text{(decimal)*}\end{matrix} = \left(1 + \begin{matrix}\text{Daily} \\ \text{yield} \\ \text{(decimal)}\end{matrix}\right)^{365} - 1$$

* In this equation yield is expressed as a decimal rather than as a percentage, e.g., as .075 as opposed to 7.5%.

Note this is *not* the only way to annualize daily yields. It is, however, necessary that all daily yields be annualized in the same way so that differences in daily yields are correctly reflected in annualized yields. For example, daily yields could be annualized by multiplying them by 365 to get a measure of annualized return on a simple interest basis.

Annualizing daily yield by compounding is, however, preferable, since it is more consistent with the basic calculation of the daily yields.

It is also more appropriate for short-term securities, such as repurchase agreements, on which daily compounding is feasible.

U.S. TREASURY BILLS

Treasury bills are purchased at a price less than par, as are bankers' acceptances and other discount securities. These securities are all quoted on a discount rate basis. The dollar price and yield at purchase are calculated as follows:

$$\text{Dollar price} \atop \text{(\% of par)} = 100 - \left(\frac{\text{Discount} \atop \text{rate} \times \text{Days to} \atop \text{maturity}}{360} \right)$$

$$\text{Daily average} \atop \text{yield at purchase} = \left(\frac{100}{\text{Dollar purchase} \atop \text{price}} \right)^{\left(\frac{1}{\text{Days to} \atop \text{maturity}} \right)} - 1$$

The *total rate of return* for a discount security sold *prior* to maturity is determined using the same calculation.

$$\text{Total rate of return} \atop \text{(daily average)} = \left(\frac{\text{Dollar sale price}}{\text{Dollar purchase} \atop \text{price}} \right)^{\left(\frac{1}{\text{Number of} \atop \text{days held}} \right)} - 1$$

Example. A 6-month Treasury bill maturing in 182 days is purchased at 6.65%. The bill is sold 91 days later at a discount of 6.45%.

$$\text{Daily average} \atop \text{yield at purchase} = \left(\frac{100}{96.63806} \right)^{\left(\frac{1}{182} \right)} - 1 = 0.018792\%$$

Annualizing this, we get:

$$(1.00018792)^{365} - 1 = 7.098\%$$

However, the total rate of return earned on holding this security for 91 days is somewhat higher.

$$\text{Total rate of return} \atop \text{(daily average)} = \left(\frac{98.36959}{96.63806} \right)^{\left(\frac{1}{91} \right)} - 1 = 0.019517\%$$

which annualized is:

$$\text{Equivalent} \atop \text{compounded} \atop \text{annual} \atop \text{yield} = (1.00019517)^{365} - 1 = 7.383\%$$

NEGOTIABLE CERTIFICATES OF DEPOSIT

CDs are quoted according to the rate of interest they pay. The following formula is used to calculate the total dollar purchase or sale amount (principal plus accrued interest):

$$
\begin{array}{l}
\text{Sale or} \\
\text{purchase price} \\
\text{(dollars)}
\end{array}
=
\left(
\dfrac{360 + \dfrac{\text{Coupon}}{\text{(decimal)}} \times \dfrac{\text{Days from issue}}{\text{to maturity}}}
{360 + \dfrac{\text{Sale or}}{\substack{\text{purchase} \\ \text{rate (decimal)}}} \times \dfrac{\text{Days from}}{\substack{\text{purchase to} \\ \text{maturity}}}}
\right)
\times
\begin{array}{l}
\text{Par} \\
\text{amount}
\end{array}
$$

CDs with maturities of less than a year pay interest at maturity. The yield calculation is as follows:

$$
\begin{array}{l}
\text{Daily average} \\
\text{yield at purchase}
\end{array}
=
\left(
\dfrac{\text{Proceeds at maturity}}{\substack{\text{Purchase price} \\ \text{(dollars)}}}
\right)^{\left(\frac{1}{\substack{\text{Days from purchase} \\ \text{to maturity}}}\right)}
- 1
$$

The total rate of return for a CD held for a period of N days is:

$$
\begin{array}{l}
\text{Daily average} \\
\text{rate of return}
\end{array}
=
\left(
\dfrac{\substack{\text{Dollar proceeds} \\ \text{from sale}}}{\substack{\text{Purchase price} \\ \text{(dollars)}}}
\right)^{\left(\frac{1}{N}\right)}
- 1
$$

These same calculations can be used for any security paying interest in a single payment at maturity. This would include term Fed funds, RPs, term notes, U.S. Treasury and agency securities with a current maturity of 6 months or less, Bank for Cooperatives 6-month notes, and Federal Intermediate Credit Bank 9-month notes. Fed funds and RPs are purchased at par and accrue interest for the actual number of days held. Treasury and agency securities are, as noted above, purchased at a price plus accrued interest.

Example. Determine the yield on a 9-month FICB issued on 3/1/78 with a 7% coupon if the security is purchased on 6/1/78 at par.

$$
\begin{array}{l}
\text{Daily average} \\
\text{yield at purchase}
\end{array}
=
\left(
\dfrac{\text{Proceeds at maturity}}{\substack{\text{Purchase price} \\ \text{(dollars)}}}
\right)^{\left(\frac{1}{\substack{\text{Days from purchase} \\ \text{to maturity}}}\right)}
- 1
$$

$$
=
\left(
\dfrac{100 + \dfrac{7}{360} \times 270}{100 + \dfrac{7}{360} \times 90}
\right)^{\left(\frac{1}{183}\right)}
- 1
$$

$$
= 0.018482\%
$$

Annualizing this, we get:

$$\begin{matrix} \text{Equivalent} \\ \text{compounded} \\ \text{annual} \\ \text{yield} \end{matrix} = (1.00018482)^{365} - 1 = 6.978\%$$

COUPON SECURITIES

This category includes all U.S. Treasury, agency, and corporate securities paying interest on a periodic basis. For example, a 3-year CD paying interest annually would fall in this category. Since all multiperiod yield calculations require an iterative solution, a computer or sophisticated calculator is necessary to do them. The yield formulations presented below are consistent with the daily average yield calculations used above for other securities.

Regular coupon payments

Let

P = Price of security (% of par)
A = Accrued interest (% of par)
N = Total number of coupons to be paid
D = Time between coupon payments; for semiannual coupons this is assumed to be 182.5 days
t = Days from current date to next coupon payment
C = Coupon payments (% of par), normally half the coupon rate
M = Principal proceeds at maturity, normally equal to 100
i = Daily average yield; this daily average rate can be annualized according to the convention previously described

Then

$$P + A = \left(\sum_{K=1}^{N} \frac{C}{(1 + i)^{(K-1)D+t}} \right) + \left(\frac{M}{(1 + i)^{(N-1)D+t}} \right)$$

The daily average rate of yield is calculated by solving this equation for i.

Irregular coupon payments

For securities issued with an irregular first coupon, the above formula needs to be modified only for the first coupon payment. Let

C^* = Irregular coupon payment expressed as a percentage of par

Then

$$P + A = \frac{C^*}{(1 + i)^t} + \left(\sum_{K=1}^{N-1} \frac{C}{(1 + i)^{KD+t}} \right) + \left(\frac{M}{(1 + i)^{(N-1)D+t}} \right)$$

Once the first irregular coupon has been paid, all subsequent yield calculations are based on the regular coupon formulation.

Note that these formulas for calculating yield on securities will often produce yields that differ from those shown on quote sheets. One reason is the use of a daily compounded rate rather than a semiannually compounded rate. A second reason is the different assumptions commonly used in calculating yields on Treasury and agency securities. This is seen in the example given above of a 9-month FICB security. The commonly used yield calculation for the FICB would be based on a 360-day year, and 180 days of interest would be assumed to be received over a 180-day period. However, the astute money manager realizes that he would in fact receive 180 days of interest over 183 days. His effective yield would thus be somewhat lower than that stated on the quote sheet, since on 3 days he would receive no interest.

The methodology presented here compensates for such differences in assumptions. Yield on each security is calculated so that it is directly comparable with yields on similar or dissimilar instruments.

TOTAL RETURN FOR A COUPON SECURITY

In the case of a bond, the fact that it is unlikely that all coupon cash flows will be reinvested at the same rate as the original yield at which the bond was purchased makes the standard yield calculation of little value for a longer-term portfolio. Determining a likely reinvestment rate for these flows results in an expected total rate of return that is more helpful to the manager in his decision making. The calculation of this expected rate of return is as follows. Let

r = Assumed coupon reinvestment rate on a daily compounded basis

If, for example, the reinvestment rate were 7%, the correct value for $(1 + r)$ would be:

$$(1.07)^{\left(\frac{1}{365} \right)} = 1.00018538$$

Then the equation given above for calculating i becomes

$$P + A = \frac{\left(\sum_{K=1}^{N} C(1 + r)^{(N-K)D} \right) + 100}{(1 + i)^{(N-1)D+t}}$$

Since $(1 + r)$ is known, this equation can be reduced to a deterministic form, eliminating the need for an iterative approach. The equation becomes:

$$(1 + i) = \left[\frac{\left(\sum_{K=1}^{N} C(1 + r)^{(N-K)D} \right) + 100}{P + A} \right]^{\left[\frac{1}{(N-1)D+t} \right]}$$

This equation can be easily resolved on most programmable calculators. It will provide the pension manager with a more realistic expected total rate of return, i, than does the standard calculation.

The remainder of the appendix provides a detailed discussion of the example of riding the yield curve given in Chapter 10. All calculations are made on a dollar basis for simplicity and clarity. This example demonstrates in a powerful way the value of the analytic approach proposed here to making portfolio decisions.

DETAILED EXAMPLE OF RIDING THE YIELD CURVE

Market setting in late April–early May, 1977.   The Federal Reserve was tightening. The Fed funds rate, which had been at 4⅞ in early April, was at 5¼ to 5⅜, and the general market expectation was that it would rise to 5½ and remain there in the near future.

Portfolio objective.   Pursue investments consistent with an investment time horizon of 90 days because of anticipated cash needs in 90 days. This objective implied investments of a relatively short maturity.

Many investment alternatives were available in this situation. For simplicity we focus on three:

1.   90-day fixed repurchase agreements available at 5.50 percent.
2.   90-day bankers' acceptances available at 5.40 percent.
3.   180-day bankers' acceptances available at 5.90 percent.

The calculations comparing these alternatives follow. All assume an equal dollar investment of $970,500. For the acceptances this implies odd par amounts, which would be unrealistic. However, for a multi-million-dollar portfolio, the particular par amounts in which various securities were available would pose no problem.

Break-even calculation for Alternatives 1 and 3

Alternative 1.   Invest $970,500 in 90-day RP at 5.50%.

Earnings on investment $= (0.055) \left(\frac{90}{360} \right) (\$970,500) = \$13,344$

Alternative 3.   Purchase 180-day acceptance at 5.90% and resell it 90 days later.

Sum invested	$970,500
This investment must return the same dollar amount as Alternative 1	13,344
Minimum market value of acceptance at sale	$983,844

Note that a 90-day acceptance with a purchase price of $983,844 would be selling at a discount of 6.462%.

Break-even calculation for Alternatives 2 and 3

Alternative 2.   Buy a 90-day acceptance and hold it to maturity.

Par amount purchased	$983,781
Sum invested	970,500
Earnings on investment	$ 13,281

Alternative 3.   Purchase 180-day acceptance at 5.90% and resell it 90 days later.

Sum invested	$970,500
This investment must return the same dollar amount as Alternative 2	13,281
Minimum market value of acceptance at sale	$983,781

Note that a 90-day acceptance with a purchase price of $983,781 would be selling at a discount of 6.487%.

Conclusion

Our analysis illustrates that if the 90-day BA rate rose over 100 basis points—from 5.40 to 6.46—over the next 90 days, the portfolio manager would still earn the same or slightly more by choosing the 180-day BA over an investment in either term RP or a 90-day BA. Thus if the manager predicted that interest rates were likely to rise but not that much, he should choose the 180-day BA over both 90-day RP and 90-day BAs.

Moreover, if his rate forecast proved to be pessimistic and interest rates actually fell over the investment period, he would have earned still more by buying the longer-term BA than he would have by making either of the two alternative investments.

Glossary

Common money market and bond market terms

Accretion (of a discount): In portfolio accounting, a straight-line accumulation of capital gains on discount bonds in anticipation of receipt of par at maturity.

Accrued interest: Interest due from issue or from the last coupon date to the present on an interest-bearing security. The buyer of the security pays the quoted dollar price plus accrued interest.

Active: A market in which there is much trading.

After-tax real rate of return: Money after-tax rate of return minus the inflation rate.

Agencies: Federal agency securities.

Agency bank: A form of organization commonly used by foreign banks to enter the U.S. market. An agency bank cannot accept deposits or extend loans in its own name; it acts as an agent for the parent bank.

Agent: A firm that executes orders for or otherwise acts on behalf of another (the principal) and is subject to its control and authority. The agent may receive a fee or commission.

All-in cost: Total costs, explicit and other. Example: The all-in cost to a bank of CD money is the explicit rate of interest it pays on that deposit *plus* the FDIC premium it must pay on the deposit *plus* the hidden cost it incurs because it must hold some portion of that deposit in a noninterest-bearing reserve account at the Fed.

All or none (AON): Requirement that none of an order be executed unless all of it can be executed at the specified price.

549

Amortize: In portfolio accounting. periodic charges made against interest income on premium bonds in anticipation of receipt of the call price at call or par at maturity.

Arbitrage: Strictly defined, buying something where it is cheap and selling it where it is dear; e.g., a bank buys 3-month CD money in the U.S. market and sells 3-month money at a higher rate in the Eurodollar market. In the money market, often refers: (1) to a situation in which a trader buys one security and sells a similar security in the expectation that the spread in yields between the two instruments will narrow or widen to his profit, (2) to a swap between two similar issues based on an anticipated change in yield spreads, and (3) to situations where a higher return (or lower cost) can be achieved in the money market for one currency by utilizing another currency and swapping it on a fully hedged basis through the foreign exchange market.

Asked: The price at which securities are offered.

Away: A trade, quote, or market that does not originate with the dealer in question, e.g., "the bid is 98—10 away (from me)."

Back up: (1) When yields rise and prices fall, the market is said to back up. (2) When an investor swaps out of one security into another of shorter current maturity (e.g., out of a 2-year note into an 18-month note), he is said to back up.

Bank discount rate: Yield basis on which short-term, non–interest-bearing money market securities are quoted. A rate quoted on a discount basis understates bond equivalent yield. That must be calculated when comparing return against coupon securities.

Bank line: Line of credit granted by a bank to a customer.

Bank wire: A computer message system linking major banks. It is used not for effecting payments, but as a mechanism to advise the receiving bank of some action that has occurred, e.g., the payment by a customer of funds into that bank's account.

Bankers' acceptance (BA): A draft or bill of exchange accepted by a bank or trust company. The accepting institution guarantees payment on the bill.

BANs: Bond anticipation notes are issued by states and municipalities to obtain interim financing for projects that will eventually be funded long term through the sale of a bond issue.

Basis: See **Basis price.**

Basis point: $1/100$ of 1 percent.

Basis price: Price expressed in terms of yield to maturity or annual rate of return.

Bear market: A declining market or a period of pessimism when declines in the market are anticipated. (A way to remember: "Bear down").

Bearer security: A security whose owner is not registered on the books of the issuer. A bearer security is payable to the holder.

Best-efforts basis: Securities dealers do not underwrite a new issue, but sell it on the basis of what can be sold. In the money market, usually refers to a firm order to buy or sell a given amount of securities or currency at whatever best price can be found over a given period of time; can also refer to a flexible amount (up to a limit) at a given rate.

Bid: The price offered for securities.

Block: A large amount of securities, normally much more than what constitutes a round lot in the market in question.

Book: A banker, especially a Euro banker, will refer to his bank's assets and liabilities as its "book." If the average maturity of the liabilities is less than that of the assets, the bank is running a **short** or **open** book.

Book-entry securities: The Treasury and the federal agencies are moving to a book-entry system in which securities are not represented by engraved pieces of paper but are maintained in computerized records at the Fed in the names of member banks, which in turn keep records of the securities they own as well as those they are holding for customers. In the case of other securities where a book-entry system has developed, engraved securities do exist somewhere in quite a few cases. These securities do not move from holder to holder but are usually kept in a central clearing house or by another agent.

Book value: The value at which a debt security is shown on the holder's balance sheet. Book value is often acquisition cost ± amortization/accretion, which may differ markedly from market value. It can be further defined as "tax book," "accreted book," or "amortized book" value.

Bridge financing: Interim financing of one sort or another.

British clearers: The large clearing banks that dominate deposit taking and short-term lending in the domestic sterling market in Great Britain.

Broker: A broker brings buyers and sellers together for a commission paid by the initiator of the transaction or by both sides; he does not position. In the money market, brokers are active in markets in which banks buy and sell money and in interdealer markets.

Bull market: A period of optimism when increases in market prices are anticipated. (A way to remember: "Bull ahead.")

Bullet loan: A bank term loan that calls for no amortization. The term is commonly used in the Euromarket.

Buy back: Another term for a repurchase agreement.

Calendar: List of new bond issues scheduled to come to market shortly.

Call money: Interest-bearing bank deposits that can be withdrawn on 24-hours notice. Many Euro deposits take the form of call money.

Callable bond: A bond that the issuer has the right to redeem prior to maturity by paying some specified call price.

Canadian agencies: Agency banks established by Canadian banks in the United States.

Carry: The interest cost of financing securities held. (See also **Negative carry** and **Positive carry.**)

Cash management bill: Very short-maturity bills that the Treasury occasionally sells because its cash balances are down and it needs money for a few days.

Cash market: Traditionally this term has been used to denote the market in which commodities were traded against cash for immediate delivery. Since the inception of futures markets for T bills and other debt securities, a distinction has been made between the cash markets in which these securities trade for immediate delivery and the futures markets in which they trade for future delivery.

Cash settlement: In the money market a transaction is said to be made for cash settlement if the securities purchased are delivered against payment in Fed funds on the same day the trade is made.

Certificate of deposit (CD): A time deposit with a specific maturity evidenced by a certificate. Large-denomination CDs are typically negotiable.

CHIPS: The New York Clearing House's computerized Clearing House Interbank Payments System. Most Euro transactions are cleared and settled through CHIPS rather than over the Fed wire.

Circle: Underwriters, actual or potential as the case may be, often seek out and "circle" retail interest in a new issue before final pricing. The customer circled has basically made a commitment to purchase the note or bond *or* to purchase it if it comes at an agreed-upon price. In the latter case, if the price is other than that stipulated, the customer supposedly has first offer at the actual price.

Clear: A trade is carried out by the seller delivering securities and the buyer delivering funds in proper form. A trade that does not clear is said to **fail.**

Clearing house funds: Payments made through the New York Clearing House's computerized Clearing House Interbank Payments System. Clearing house debits and credits are settled in Fed funds on the first business day after clearing.

Commercial paper: An unsecured promissory note with a fixed maturity of no more than 270 days. Commercial paper is normally sold at a discount from face value.

Competitive bid: (1) Bid tendered in a Treasury action by an investor for a specific amount of securities at a specific yield or price. (2) Issuers, municipal and public utilities, often sell new issues by asking for competitive bids from one or more syndicates.

Confirmation: A memorandum to the other side of a trade detailing all relevant data.

Consortium banks: A merchant banking subsidiary set up by several banks that may or may not be of the same nationality. Consortium banks are common in the Euromarket and are active in loan syndication.

Convertible bond: A bond containing a provision that permits conversion between the issuer's bonds and common stock at some fixed exchange ratio.

Corporate bond equivalent: See **Equivalent bond yield.**

Corporate taxable equivalent: Rate of return required on a par bond to produce the same after-tax yield to maturity that the premium or discount bond quoted would.

Country risk: See **Sovereign risk.**

Coupon: (1) The annual rate of interest that a bond's issuer promises to pay the bondholder on the bond's face value. (2) A certificate attached to a bond evidencing interest due on a payment date.

Cover: To eliminate a short position by buying the securities shorted.

Credit risk: The risk that an issuer of debt securities or a borrower may default on his obligations, or that payment may not be made upon sale of a negotiable instrument. (See **Overnight delivery risk.**)

CRTs: Abbreviation for the cathode ray tubes used to display market quotes.

Current coupon: A bond selling at or close to par, that is, a bond with a coupon close to the yields currently offered on new bonds of similar maturity and credit risk.

Current issue: In Treasury bills and notes, the most recently auctioned issue. Trading is more active in current issues than in off-the-run issues.

Current maturity: Current time to maturity on an outstanding note, bond, or other money market instrument; for example, a 5-year note 1 year after issue has a current maturity of 4 years.

Current yield: Coupon payments on a security as a percentage of the security's market price. In many instances the price should be *gross* of accrued interest, particularly on instruments where no coupon is left to be paid until maturity.

Cushion bonds: High-coupon bonds that sell at only a moderate premium because they are callable at a price below that at which a comparable noncallable bond would sell. Cushion bonds offer considerable downside protection in a falling market.

Day trading: Intraday trading in securities for profit as opposed to investing for profit.

Debenture: A bond secured only by the general credit of the issuer.

Debt leverage: The amplification in the return earned on equity funds when an investment is financed partly with borrowed money.

Debt securities: IOUs created through loan-type transactions—commercial paper, bank CDs, bills, bonds, and other instruments.

Default: Failure to make timely payment of interest or principal on a debt security or to otherwise comply with the provisions of a bond indenture.

Demand line of credit: A bank line of credit that enables a customer to borrow on a daily or on demand basis.

Direct paper: Commercial paper sold directly by the issuer to investors.

Direct placement: Selling a new issue not by offering it for sale publicly but by placing it with one or several institutional investors.

Discount basis: See **Bank discount rate.**

Dealer: A dealer, as opposed to a broker, acts as a principal in all transactions, buying and selling for his own account.

Dealer loan: Overnight, collateralized loan made to a dealer financing his position by a money market bank.

Discount bond: A bond selling below par.

Discount house: British institution that uses call and overnight money obtained from banks to invest in and trade money market instruments.

Discount paper: See **Discount securities.**

Discount rate: The rate of interest charged by the Fed to member banks that borrow at the discount window. The discount rate is an add-on rate.

Discount securities: Noninterest-bearing money market instruments that are issued at a discount and redeemed at maturity for full face value, e.g., U.S. Treasury bills.

Discount window: Facility provided by the Fed enabling member banks to borrow reserves against collateral in the form of governments or other acceptable paper.

Disintermediation: The investing of funds that would normally have been placed with a bank or other financial intermediary directly into debt securities issued by ultimate borrowers, e.g., into bills or bonds.

Distributed: After a Treasury auction, there will be many new issues in dealers' hands. As those securities are sold to retail, the issue is said to be distributed.

Diversification: Dividing investment funds among a variety of securities offering independent returns.

DM: Deutsche (German) marks.

Documented discount notes: Commercial paper backed by normal bank lines plus a letter of credit from a bank stating that it will pay off the paper at maturity if the borrower does not. Such paper is also referred to as **LOC** (letter of credit) **paper.**

Dollar bonds: Municipal revenue bonds for which quotes are given in dollar prices. Not to be confused with "U.S. Dollar" bonds, a common term of reference in the Eurobond market.

Dollar price of a bond: Percentage of face value at which a bond is quoted.

Don't know (DK, DKed): "Don't know the trade"—a street expression used whenever one party lacks knowledge of a trade or receives conflicting instructions from the other party (for example, with respect to payment).

Due bill: An instrument evidencing the obligation of a seller to deliver securities sold to the buyer. Occasionally used in the bill market.

Dutch auction: Auction in which the lowest price necessary to sell the entire offering becomes the price at which all securities offered are sold. This technique has been used in Treasury auctions.

Edge Act corporation: A subsidiary of a U.S. bank set up to carry out international banking business. Most such subs are located within the United States.

Either/or facility: An agreement permitting a bank customer to borrow either domestic dollars from the bank's head office or Eurodollars from one of its foreign branches.

Either-way market: In the interbank Eurodollar deposit market, an either-way market is one in which the bid and asked rates are identical.

Eligible bankers' acceptances: In the BA market an acceptance may be referred to as eligible because it is acceptable by the Fed as collateral at the discount window and/or because the accepting bank can sell it without incurring a reserve requirement.

Equivalent bond yield: Annual yield on a short-term, non–interest-bearing security calculated so as to be comparable to yields quoted on coupon securities.

Equivalent taxable yield: The yield on a taxable security that would leave the investor with the same after-tax return he would earn by holding a tax-exempt municipal; for example, for an investor taxed at a 50 percent marginal rate, equivalent taxable yield on a muni note issued at 3 percent would be 6 percent.

Euro CDs: CDs issued by a U.S. bank branch or foreign bank located outside the United States. Almost all Euro CDs are issued in London.

Euro lines: Lines of credit granted by banks (foreign or foreign branches of U.S. banks) for Eurocurrencies.

Eurobonds: Bonds issued in Europe outside the confines of any national capital market. A Eurobond may or may not be denominated in the currency of the issuer.

Eurocurrency deposits: Deposits made in a bank or bank branch that is not located in the country in whose currency the deposit is denominated. Dollars deposited in a London bank are Eurodollars, German marks deposited there are Euromarks.

Eurodollars: U.S. dollars deposited in a U.S. bank branch or a foreign bank located outside the United States.

Excess reserves: Balances held by a bank at the Fed in excess of those required.

Exchange rate: The price at which one currency trades for another.

Exempt securities: Instruments exempt from the registration requirements of the Securities Act of 1933 or the margin requirements of the Securities and Exchange Act of 1934. Such securities include governments, agencies, municipal securities, commercial paper, and private placements.

Extension swap: Extending maturity through a swap, e.g., selling a 2-year note and buying one with a slightly longer current maturity.

Fail: A trade is said to fail if on settlement date either the seller fails to deliver securities in proper form or the buyer fails to deliver funds in proper form.

Fed funds: See **Federal funds.**

Fed wire: A computer system linking member banks to the Fed, used for making interbank payments of Fed funds and for making deliveries of and payments for Treasury and agency securities.

Federal credit agencies: Agencies of the federal government set up to supply credit to various classes of institutions and individuals, e.g., S&Ls, small business firms, students, farmers, farm cooperatives, and exporters.

Federal Deposit Insurance Corporation (FDIC): A federal institution that insures bank deposits, currently up to $40,000 per deposit.

Federal Financing Bank: A federal institution that lends to a wide array of federal credit agencies funds it obtains by borrowing from the U.S. Treasury.

Federal funds: (1) Noninterest-bearing deposits held by member banks at the Federal Reserve. (2) Used to denote "immediately available" funds in the clearing sense.

Federal funds rate: The rate of interest at which Fed funds are traded. This rate is currently pegged by the Federal Reserve through open-market operations.

Federal Home Loan Banks (FHLB): The institutions that regulate and lend to savings and loan associations. The Federal Home Loan Banks play a role analogous to that played by the Federal Reserve Banks vis à vis member commercial banks.

Figuring the tail: Calculating the yield at which a future money market instrument (one available some period hence) is purchased when that future security is created by buying an existing instrument and financing the initial portion of its life with a term RP.

Firm: Refers to an order to buy or sell that can be executed without confirmation for some fixed period.

Fixed dates: In the Euromarket the standard periods for which Euros are traded (1 month out to a year) are referred to as the fixed dates.

Fixed-dollar security: A nonnegotiable debt security that can be redeemed at some fixed price or according to some schedule of fixed values (e.g., bank deposits and government savings bonds).

Fixed-rate loan: A loan on which the rate paid by the borrower is fixed for the life of the loan.

Flat trades: (1) A bond in default trades flat; that is, the price quoted covers both principal and unpaid, accrued interest. (2) Any security that trades without accrued interest or at a price which includes accrued interest is said to trade flat.

Float: The difference between the credits given by the Fed to banks' reserve accounts on checks being cleared through the Fed and the debits made to banks' reserve accounts on these same checks. Float is always positive, because in the clearing of a check, the credit sometimes precedes the debit. Float adds to the money supply.

Floating-rate note: A note that pays an interest rate tied to current money market rates. The holder may have the right to demand redemption at par on specified dates.

Floating supply: The amount of securities believed to be available for immediate purchase, that is, in the hands of dealers and investors wanting to sell.

Flower bonds: Government bonds that are acceptable at par in payment of federal estate taxes when owned by the decedent at the time of death.

Foreign bond: A bond issued by a nondomestic borrower in the domestic capital market.

Foreign exchange rate: The price at which one currency trades for another.

Foreign exchange risk: The risk that a long or short position in a foreign currency might, due to an adverse movement in the relevant exchange rate, have to be closed out at a loss. The long or short position may arise out of a financial or commercial transaction.

Forward Fed funds: Fed funds traded for future delivery.

Forward forward contract: In Eurocurrencies, a contract under which a deposit of fixed maturity is agreed to at a fixed price for future delivery.

Forward market: A market in which participants agree to trade some commodity, security, or foreign exchange at a fixed price at some future date.

Forward rate: The rate at which forward transactions in some specific maturity are being made, e.g., the dollar price at which DM can be bought for delivery 3 months hence.

Free reserves: Excess reserves minus member bank borrowings at the Fed.

Full-coupon bond: A bond with a coupon equal to the going market rate and consequently selling at or near par.

Futures market: A market in which contracts for future delivery of a commodity or a security are bought and sold.

General obligation bonds: Municipal securities secured by the issuer's pledge of its full faith, credit, and taxing power.

Give up: The loss in yield that occurs when a block of bonds is swapped for another block of lower-coupon bonds. Can also be referred to as "after tax give up" when the implications of the profit (loss) on taxes are considered.

Glass-Steagall Act: A 1933 act in which Congress forbade commercial banks to own, underwrite, or deal in corporate stock and corporate bonds.

Go-around: When the Fed offers to buy securities, to sell securities, to do repo, or to do reverses, it solicits competitive bids or offers, as the case may be, from all primary dealers. This procedure is known as a go-around.

Good delivery: A delivery in which everything—endorsement, any necessary attached legal papers, etc.—is in order.

Governments: Negotiable U.S. Treasury securities.

Gross spread: The difference between the price that the issuer receives for its securities and the price that investors pay for them. This spread equals the selling concession plus the management and underwriting fees.

Haircut: Margin in an RP transaction, that is, the difference between the actual market value measured at the bid side of the market and the value used in an RP agreement.

Handle: The whole-dollar price of a bid or offer is referred to as the *handle*. For example, if a security is quoted 101–10 bid and 101–11 offered, 101 is the handle. Traders are assumed to know the handle, so a trader would quote that market to another by saying he was at 10–11. (The 10 and 11 refer to 32nds.)

Hedge: To reduce risk, (1) by taking a position in futures equal and opposite to an existing or anticipated cash position or (2) by shorting a security similar to one in which a long position has been established.

Hit: A dealer who agrees to sell at the bid price quoted by another dealer is said to *hit* that bid.

In the box: This means that a dealer has a wire receipt for securities indicating that effective delivery on them has been made. This jargon is a holdover from the time when Treasuries took the form of physical securities and were stored in a rack.

Indenture of a bond: A legal statement spelling out the obligations of the bond issuer and the rights of the bondholder.

Investment banker: A firm that engages in the origination, underwriting, and distribution of new issues.

Joint account: An agreement between two or more firms to share risk and financing responsibility in purchasing or underwriting securities.

Junk bonds: High-risk bonds that have low ratings or are actually in default.

Leverage: See **Debt leverage.**

Leveraged lease: The lessor provides only a minor portion of the cost of the leased equipment, borrowing the rest from another lender.

LIBOR: The London Interbank Offered Rate on Eurodollar deposits traded between banks. There is a different LIBOR rate for each deposit maturity. Different banks may quote slightly different LIBOR rates because they use different reference banks.

Lifting a leg: Closing out one side of a long-short arbitrage before the other is closed.

Line of credit: An arrangement by which a bank agrees to lend to the line holder during some specified period any amount up to the full amount of the line.

Liquidity: A liquid asset is one that can be converted easily and rapidly into cash without a substantial loss of value. In the money market, a security is said to be liquid if the spread between bid and asked prices is narrow and reasonable size can be done at those quotes.

Liquidity diversification: Investing in a variety of maturities to reduce the price risk to which holding long bonds exposes the investor.

Liquidity risk: In banking, risk that monies needed to fund assets may not be available in sufficient quantities at some future date. Implies an imbalance in committed maturities of assets and liabilities.

Lock-up CDs: CDs that are issued with the tacit understanding that the buyer will not trade the certificate. Quite often the issuing bank will insist that the certificate be safekept by it to ensure that the understanding is honored by the buyer.

Locked market: A market is said to be locked if the bid price equals the asked price. This can occur, for example, if the market is brokered and brokerage is paid by one side only, the initiator of the transaction.

Long: (1) Owning a debt security, stock, or other asset. (2) Owning more than one has contracted to deliver.

Long bonds: Bonds with a long current maturity.

Long coupons: (1) Bonds or notes with a long current maturity. (2) A bond on which one of the coupon periods, usually the first, is longer than the others or than standard.

M1: Money supply measured as the amount of demand deposits plus currency in circulation.

M2: M1 plus small-denomination savings and time deposits at commercial banks.

M3: M2 plus deposits at nonbank savings institutions.

M4: M2 plus large-denomination CDs.

M5: M3 plus large-denomination CDs.

Make a market: A dealer is said to make a market when he quotes bid and offered prices at which he stands ready to buy and sell.

Margin: In an RP or a reverse repurchase transaction, the amount by which the market value of the securities collateralizing the transaction exceeds the amount lent.

Marginal tax rate: The tax rate that would have to be paid on any additional dollars of taxable income earned.

Market value: The price at which a security is trading and could presumably be purchased or sold.

Marketability: A negotiable security is said to have good marketability if there is an active secondary market in which it can easily be resold.

Match fund: A bank is said to match fund a loan or other asset when it does so by buying (taking) a deposit of the same maturity. The term is commonly used in the Euromarket.

Matched book: If the distribution of the maturities of a bank's liabilities equals that of its assets, it is said to be running a *matched book*. The term is commonly used in the Euromarket.

Merchant bank: A British term for a bank that specializes not in lending out its own funds, but in providing various financial services such as accepting bills arising out of trade, underwriting new issues, and providing advice on acquisitions, mergers, foreign exchange, portfolio management, etc.

Money market: The market in which short-term debt instruments (bills, commercial paper, bankers' acceptances, etc.) are issued and traded.

Money market (center) bank: A bank that is one of the nation's largest and consequently plays an active and important role in every sector of the money market.

Money market fund: Mutual fund that invests solely in money market instruments.

Money rate of return: Annual money return as a percentage of asset value.

Mortgage bond: Bond secured by a lien on property, equipment, or other real assets.

Multicurrency clause: Such a clause on a Euro loan permits the borrower to switch from one currency to another on a rollover date.

Municipal (muni) notes: Short-term notes issued by municipalities in anticipation of tax receipts, proceeds from a bond issue, or other revenues.

Municipals: Securities issued by state and local governments and their agencies.

Naked position: A long or short position that is not hedged.

Negative carry: The net cost incurred when the cost of carry exceeds the yield on the securities being financed.

Negotiable certificate of deposit: A large-denomination (generally $1 million) CD that can be sold but cannot be cashed in before maturity.

Negotiated sale: Situation in which the terms of an offering are determined by negotiation between the issuer and the underwriter rather than through competitive bidding by underwriting groups.

Neutral period: In the Euromarket, a period over which Eurodollars are sold is said to be *neutral* if it does not start or end on either a Friday or the day before a holiday.

New issues market: The market in which a new issue of securities is first sold to investors.

New money: In a Treasury refunding, the amount by which the par value of the securities offered exceeds that of those maturing.

Noncompetitive bid: In a Treasury auction, bidding for a specific amount of securities at the price, whatever it may turn out to be, equal to the average price of the accepted competitive bids.

Note: Coupon issues with a relatively short original maturity are often called *notes*. Muni notes, however, have maturities ranging from a month to a year and pay interest only at maturity. Treasury notes are coupon securities that have an original maturity of up to 10 years.

Odd lot: Less than a round lot.

Off-the-run issue: In Treasuries and agencies, an issue that is not included in dealer or broker runs. In bills and notes normally only current issues are quoted.

Offer: Price asked by a seller of securities.

One-man picture: The picture quoted by a broker is said to be a one-man picture if both the bid and the asked prices come from the same source.

One-sided (one-way) market: A market in which only one side, the bid or the asked, is quoted or firm.

Open book: See **Unmatched book.**

Open repo: A repo with no definite term. The agreement is made on a day-to-day basis and either the borrower or the lender may choose to terminate. The rate paid is higher than on overnight repo and is subject to adjustment if rates move.

Opportunity cost: The cost of pursuing one course of action measured in terms of the forgone return offered by the most attractive alternative.

Option: (1) **Call option:** A contract sold for a price that gives the holder the right to buy from the writer of the option over a specified period a specified amount of securities at a specified price. (2) **Put option:** A contract sold for a price that gives the holder the right to sell to the writer of the contract over a period a specified amount of securities at a specified price.

Original maturity: Maturity at issue. For example, a 5-year note has an original maturity at issue of 5 years; one year later it has a current maturity of 4 years.

Over-the-counter (OTC) market: Market created by dealer trading as opposed to the auction market prevailing on organized exchanges.

Overnight delivery risk: A risk brought about because differences in time zones between settlement centers require that payment or delivery on one side of a transaction be made without knowing until the next day whether funds have been received in account on the other side. Particularly apparent where delivery takes place in Europe for payment in dollars in New York.

Paper: Money market instruments, commercial paper and other.

Paper gain (loss): Unrealized capital gain (loss) on securities held in portfolio, based on a comparison of current market price to original cost.

Par: (1) Price of 100 percent. (2) The principal amount at which the issuer of a debt security contracts to redeem that security at maturity, *face value.*

Par bond: A bond selling at par.

Pass-through: A mortgage-backed security on which payments of interest and principal on the underlying mortgages are passed through by an agent to the security holder.

Paydown: In a Treasury refunding, the amount by which the par value of the securities maturing exceeds that of those sold.

Pay-up: (1) The loss of cash resulting from a swap into higher-price bonds. (2) The need (or willingness) of a bank or other borrower to pay a higher rate in order to get funds.

Pickup: The gain in yield that occurs when a block of bonds is swapped for another block of higher-coupon bonds.

Picture: The bid and asked prices quoted by a broker for a given security.

Placement: A bank depositing Eurodollars with (selling Eurodollars to) another bank is often said to be making a placement.

Plus: Dealers in governments normally quote bids and offers in 32nds. To quote a bid or offer in 64ths, they use pluses; for example, a dealer who bids 4+ is bidding the handle plus $4/_{32} + 1/_{64}$, which equals the handle plus $9/_{64}$.

PNs: Project notes are issued by municipalities to finance federally sponsored programs in urban renewal and housing. They are guaranteed by the U.S. Department of Housing and Urban Development.

Point: (1) 100 basis points = 1 percent. (2) One percent of the face value of a note or bond. (3) In the foreign exchange market, refers to the lowest level at which the currency is priced. Example: "One point" is the difference between a sterling price of $1.8080 and $1.8081.

Portfolio: Collection of securities held by an investor.

Position: (1) To go long or short in a security. (2) The amount of securities owned (long position) or owed (short position).

Positive carry: The net gain earned when the cost of carry is less than the yield on the securities being financed.

Premium: (1) The amount by which the price at which an issue is trading exceeds the issue's par value. (2) The amount that must be paid in excess of par to call or refund an issue before maturity. (3) In money market parlance, the fact that a particular bank's CDs trade at a rate higher than others of its class, or that a bank has to pay up to acquire funds.

Premium bond: Bond selling above par.

Prepayment: A payment made ahead of the scheduled payment date.

Presold issue: An issue that is sold out before the coupon announcement.

Price risk: The risk that a debt security's price may change due to a rise or fall in the going level of interest rates.

Prime rate: The rate at which banks will lend to their best (prime) customers. The all in cost of a bank loan to a prime credit equals the prime rate plus the cost of holding compensating balances.

Principal: (1) The face amount or par value of a debt security. (2) One who acts as a dealer buying and selling for his own account.

Private placement: An issue that is offered to a single or a few investors as opposed to being publicly offered. Private placements do not have to be registered with the SEC.

Prospectus: A detailed statement prepared by an issuer and filed with the SEC prior to the sale of a new issue. The prospectus gives detailed information on the issue and on the issuer's condition and prospects.

Put: See **Option.**

RANs: Revenue anticipation notes are issued by states and municipalities to finance current expenditures in anticipation of the future receipt of nontax revenues.

Rate risk: In banking, the risk that profits may decline or losses occur because a rise in interest rates forces up the cost of funding fixed-rate loans or other fixed-rate assets.

Ratings: An evaluation given by Moody's, Standard & Poor's, Fitch, or other rating services of a security's creditworthiness.

Real market: The bid and offer prices at which a dealer could do size. Quotes in the brokers market may reflect not the real market, but pictures painted by dealers playing trading games.

Red herring: A preliminary prospectus containing all the information required by the Securities and Exchange Commission except the offering price and coupon of a new issue.

Refunding: Redemption of securities with funds raised through the sale of a new issue.

Registered bond: A bond whose owner is registered with the issuer.

Regular way settlement: In the money and bond markets, the regular basis on which some security trades are settled is that delivery of the securities purchased is made against payment in Fed funds on the day following the transaction.

Regulation D: Fed regulation currently requiring member banks to hold reserves equal to 4 percent of their net borrowings over a 28-day averaging period from foreign offices of other banks.

Regulation M: Fed regulation currently requiring member banks to hold reserves equal to 4 percent of their net borrowings from their foreign branches over a 28-day averaging period. Reg M also requires member banks to hold reserves equal to 1 percent of all Eurodollars lent by their foreign branches to domestic corporations for domestic purposes.

Regulation Q: Fed regulation imposing lids on the rates that banks may pay on savings and time deposits. Currently time deposits with a denomination of $100,000 or more are exempt from Reg Q.

Reinvestment rate: (1) The rate at which an investor assumes interest payments made on a debt security can be reinvested over the life of that security. (2) Also refers fo the rate at which funds from a maturity or sale of a security can be reinvested. Often used in comparison to "give up" yield.

Relative value: The attractiveness—measured in terms of risk, liquidity, and return—of one instrument relative to another, or for a given instrument, of one maturity relative to another.

Reopen an issue: The Treasury, when it wants to sell additional securities, will occasionally sell more of an existing issue (reopen it) rather than offer a new issue.

Repo: See **Repurchase agreement.**

Repurchase agreement (RP or repo): A holder of securities sells these securities to an investor with an agreement to repurchase them at a fixed price on a fixed date. The security "buyer" in effect lends the "seller" money for the period of the agreement, and the terms of the agreement are structured to compensate him for this. Dealers use RP extensively to finance their positions. Exception: When the Fed is said to be doing RP, it is lending money, that is increasing bank reserves.

Reserve requirements: The percentages of different types of deposits that member banks are required to hold on deposit at the Fed.

Retail: Individual and institutional customers as opposed to dealers and brokers.

Revenue bond: A municipal bond secured by revenue from tolls, user charges, or rents derived from the facility financed.

Reverse: See **Reverse repurchase agreement.**

Reverse repurchase agreement: Most typically a repurchase agreement initiated by the lender of funds. Reverses are used by dealers to borrow securities they have shorted. Exception: When the Fed is said to be doing reverses, it is borrowing money, that is, absorbing reserves.

Revolver: See **Revolving line of credit.**

Revolving line of credit: A bank line of credit on which the customer pays a commitment fee and can take down and repay funds according to his needs. Normally the line involves a firm commitment from the bank for a period of several years.

Risk: Degree of uncertainty of return on an asset.

Roll over: Reinvest funds received from a maturing security in a new issue of the same or a similar security.

Rollover: Most term loans in the Euromarket are made on a rollover basis, which means that the loan is periodically repriced at an agreed spread over the appropriate, currently prevailing LIBOR rate.

Round lot: In the money market, round lot refers to the minimum amount for which dealers' quotes are good. This may range from $100,000 to $5 million, depending on the size and liquidity of the issue traded.

RP: See **Repurchase agreement.**

Run: A run consists of a series of bid and asked quotes for different securities or maturities. Dealers give to and ask for runs from each other.

S&L: See **Savings and loan association.**

Safekeep: For a fee banks will safekeep (i.e., hold in their vault, clip coupons on, and present for payment at maturity) bonds and money market instruments.

Sale repurchase agreement: See **Repurchase agreement.**

Savings and loan association: National- or state-chartered institution that accepts savings deposits and invests the bulk of the funds thus received in mortgages.

Savings deposit: Interest-bearing deposit at a savings institution that has no specific maturity.

Scale: A bank that offers to pay different rates of interest on CDs of varying maturities is said to "post a scale." Commercial paper issuers also post scales.

Seasoned issue: An issue that has been well distributed and trades well in the secondary market.

Secondary market: The market in which previously issued securities are traded.

Sector: Refers to a group of securities that are similar with respect to maturity, type, rating, and/or coupon.

Securities and Exchange Commission (SEC): Agency created by Congress to protect investors in securities transactions by administering various securities acts.

Serial bonds: A bond issue in which maturities are staggered over a number of years.

Settle: See **Clear.**

Settlement date: The date on which a trade is cleared by delivery of securities against funds. The settlement data may be the trade date or a later date.

Shop: In street jargon, a money market or bond dealership.

Shopping: Seeking to obtain the best bid or offer available by calling a number of dealers and/or brokers.

Short: A market participant assumes a short position by selling a security he does not own. The seller makes delivery by borrowing the security sold or reversing it in.

Short bonds: Bonds with a short current maturity.

Short book: See **Unmatched book.**

Short coupons: Bonds or notes with a short current maturity.

Short sale: The sale of securities not owned by the seller in the expectation that the price of these securities will fall or as part of an arbitrage. A short sale must eventually be covered by a purchase of the securities sold.

Sinking fund: Indentures on corporate issues often require that the issuer make annual payments to a sinking fund, the proceeds of which are used to retire randomly selected bonds in the issue.

Size: Large in size, as in "size offering" or "in there for size." What constitutes size varies with the sector of the market.

Skip-day settlement: The trade is settled one business day beyond what is normal.

Sovereign risk: The special risks, if any, that attach to a security (or deposit or loan) because the borrower's country of residence differs from that of the investor's. Also referred to as **country risk.**

Specific issues market: The market in which dealers reverse in securities they want to short.

Spectail: A dealer that does business with retail but concentrates more on acquiring and financing its own speculative position.

Spot market: Market for immediate as opposed to future delivery. In the spot market for foreign exchange, settlement is two business days ahead.

Spot rate: The price prevailing in the spot market.

Spread: (1) Difference between bid and asked prices on a security. (2) Difference between yields on or prices of two securities of differing sorts or differing maturities. (3) In underwriting, difference between price realized by the issuer and price paid by the investor.

Spreading: In the futures market, buying one futures contract and selling a nearby one to profit from an anticipated narrowing or widening of the spread over time.

Stop-out price: The lowest price (highest yield) accepted by the Treasury in an auction of a new issue.

Street: Brokers, dealers, and other knowledgeable members of the financial community; from Wall Street financial community.

Subject: Refers to a bid or offer that cannot be executed without confirmation from the customer.

Subordinated debenture: The claims of holders of this issue rank after those of holders of various other unsecured debts incurred by the issuer.

Swap: (1) In securities, selling one issue and buying another. (2) In foreign exchange, buying a currency spot and simultaneously selling it forward.

Swap rate: In the foreign exchange market, the difference between the spot and forward rates at which a currency is traded.

Swing line: See **Demand line of credit.**

Swissy: Market jargon for Swiss francs.

Switch: British English for a swap, that is, buying a currency spot and selling it forward.

Tail: (1) The difference between the average price in Treasury auctions and the stop-out price. (2) A *future* money market instrument (one available some period hence) created by buying an existing instrument and financing the initial portion of its life with term RP.

Take: (1) A dealer or customer who agrees to buy at another dealer's offered price is said to take that offer (2) Euro bankers speak of taking deposits rather than buying money.

Take-out: (1) A cash surplus generated by the sale of one block of securities and the purchase of another, e.g., selling a block of bonds at 99 and buying another block at 95. (2) A bid made to a seller of a security which is designed (and generally agreed) to take him out of the market.

Taking a view: A London expression for forming an opinion as to where interest rates are going and acting on it.

TANs: Tax anticipation notes issued by states or municipalities to finance current operations in anticipation of future tax receipts.

Tax anticipation bills (TABs): Special bills that the Treasury occasionally issues. They mature on corporate quarterly income tax dates and can be used at face value by corporations to pay their tax liabilities.

Technical condition of a market: Demand and supply factors affecting price, in particular the net position—long or short—of dealers.

Tenor: Maturity.

Term bonds: A bond issue in which all bonds mature at the same time.

Term Fed funds: Fed funds sold for a period of time longer than overnight.

Term loan: Loan extended by a bank for more than the normal 90-day period. A term loan might run 5 years or more.

Term RP (repo): RP borrowings for a period longer than overnight, may be 30, 60, or even 90 days.

Thin market: A market in which trading volume is low and in which consequently bid and asked quotes are wide and the liquidity of the instrument traded is low.

Tight market: A tight market, as opposed to a thin market, is one in which volume is large, trading is active and highly competitive, and spreads between bid and ask prices are narrow.

Time deposit: Interest-bearing deposit at a savings institution that has a specific maturity.

Tom next: In the interbank market in Eurodollar deposits and the foreign exchange market, the value (delivery) date on a Tom next transaction is the next business day. (Refers to "tomorrow next.")

Trade date: The date on which a transaction is initiated. The settlement date may be the trade date or a later date.

Trade on top of: Trade at a narrow or no spread in basis points to some other instrument.

Trading paper: CDs purchased by accounts that are likely to resell them. The term is commonly used in the Euromarket.

Treasurer's check: A check issued by a bank to make a payment. Treasurer's checks outstanding are counted as part of a bank's reservable deposits and as part of the money supply.

Treasury bill: A noninterest-bearing discount security issued by the U.S. Treasury to finance the national debt. Most bills are issued to mature in 3 months, 6 months, or 1 year.

TT&L account: Treasury tax and loan account at a bank.

Turnaround: Securities bought and sold for settlement on the same day.

Turnaround time: The time available or needed to effect a turnaround.

Two-sided market: A market in which both bid and asked prices, good for the standard unit of trading, are quoted.

Two-way market: Market in which both a bid and an asked price are quoted.

Underwriter: A dealer who purchases new issues from the issuer and distributes them to investors. Underwriting is one function of an investment banker.

Unmatched book: If the average maturity of a bank's liabilities is less than that of its assets, it is said to be running an unmatched book. The term is commonly used in the Euromarket. Equivalent expressions are **open book** and **short book.**

Value date: In the market for Eurodollar deposits and foreign exchange, value date refers to the delivery date of funds traded. Normally it is on spot transactions two days after a transaction is agreed upon and the future date in the case of a forward foreign exchange trade.

Variable-price security: A security, such as stocks or bonds, that sells as a fluctuating, market-determined price.

Variable-rate loan: Loan made at an interest rate that fluctuates with the prime.

Visible supply: New muni bond issues scheduled to come to market within the next 30 days.

When-issued trades: Typically there is a lag between the time a new bond is announced and sold and the time it is actually issued. During this interval, the security trades **wi,** "when, as, and if issued."

Wi: When, as, and if issued. See **When-issued trades.**

Wi wi: T bills trade on a wi basis between the day they are auctioned and the day settlement is made. Bills traded before they are auctioned are said to be traded wi wi.

Without: If 70 were bid in the market and there was no offer, the quote would be "70 bid without." The expression *without* indicates a one-way market.

Yankee bond: A foreign bond issued in the U.S. market, payable in dollars, and registered with the SEC.

Yield curve: A graph showing, for securities, that all expose the investor to the same credit risk, the relationship at a given point in time between yield and current maturity. Yield curves are typically drawn using yields on governments of various maturities.

Yield to maturity: The rate of return yielded by a debt security held to maturity when both interest payments and the investor's capital gain or loss on the security are taken into account.

Conversion Table
Discount Rate to Equivalent Bond Yield

Discount rate	Equivalent bond yields at varying maturities							
	1 mo.	2 mo.	3 mo.	4 mo.	5 mo.	6 mo.	9 mo.	1 yr.
4 %	4.07	4.08	4.10 '	4.11	4.12	4.14	4.15	4.18
4$^1/_8$	4.20	4.21	4.23	4.24	4.26	4.27	4.29	4.32
4$^1/_4$	4.32	4.34	4.36	4.37	4.39	4.40	4.42	4.45
4$^3/_8$	4.45	4.47	4.49	4.50	4.52	4.54	4.56	4.59
4$^1/_2$	4.58	4.60	4.61	4.63	4.65	4.67	4.69	4.73
4$^5/_8$	4.71	4.73	4.74	4.76	4.78	4.80	4.83	4.87
4$^3/_4$	4.84	4.85	4.87	4.89	4.91	4.93	4.95	5.00
4$^7/_8$	4.96	4.98	5.00	5.02	5.05	5.07	5.09	5.14
5	5.09	5.11	5.13	5.16	5.18	5.20	5.22	5.27
5$^1/_8$	5.22	5.24	5.26	5.29	5.31	5.33	5.36	5.41
5$^1/_4$	5.35	5.37	5.39	5.42	5.44	5.47	5.49	5.55
5$^3/_8$	5.47	5.50	5.52	5.55	5.57	5.61	5.63	5.69
5$^1/_2$	5.60	5.63	5.65	5.68	5.71	5.74	5.76	5.83
5$^5/_8$	5.73	5.76	5.79	5.81	5.84	5.87	5.90	5.97
5$^3/_4$	5.86	5.89	5.92	5.94	5.97	6.00	6.03	6.10
5$^7/_8$	5.99	6.02	6.05	6.08	6.11	6.14	6.17	6.24
6	6.11	6.15	6.18	6.21	6.24	6.27	6.31	6.38
6$^1/_8$	6.24	6.27	6.31	6.34	6.37	6.41	6.45	6.52
6$^1/_4$	6.37	6.40	6.44	6.47	6.51	6.54	6.58	6.66
6$^3/_8$	6.50	6.53	6.57	6.60	6.64	6.68	6.72	6.80
6$^1/_2$	6.63	6.66	6.70	6.74	6.77	6.81	6.85	6.94
6$^5/_8$	6.75	6.79	6.83	6.87	6.91	6.95	6.99	7.08
6$^3/_4$	6.88	6.92	6.96	7.00	7.04	7.08	7.13	7.22
6$^7/_8$	7.01	7.05	7.09	7.13	7.18	7.22	7.27	7.36